The
CALIFORNIA
CONDOR

A Saga of Natural History and Conservation

The
CALIFORNIA CONDOR

A Saga of Natural History and Conservation

NOEL SNYDER AND
HELEN SNYDER

Academic Press

San Diego San Francisco New York
Boston London Sydney Tokyo

Academic Press
A Harcourt Science and Technology Company
Harcourt Place, 32 Jamestown Road, London NW1 7BY, UK

http: //www.academicpress.com

Academic Press
A Harcourt Science and Technology Company
525 B Street, Suite 1900, San Diego, California 92101-4495, USA

http: //www.academicpress.com

ISBN: 0-12-654005-5

A catalogue record for this book is available from the British Library

Designed and Typeset by Peter Champion
Printed by Colourbooks, Glasgow

00 01 02 03 04 05 BP 9 8 7 6 5 4 3 2 1

Contents

About the Authors

For over thirty years, Noel and Helen Snyder have been immersed in field conservation studies of birds, but their careers have also included university teaching, writing, and music. Noel earned simultaneous Bachelor's degrees in music (majoring in cello) at the Curtis Institute of Music, and biology at Swarthmore College. He chose the life sciences as a professional career and went on to complete a Ph.D. in evolutionary biology at Cornell University. Helen completed her Bachelor's degree in biology at Oberlin College and was also pursuing graduate studies at Cornell when they joined forces in 1967.

The Snyders' field efforts have included behavioral and ecological studies of many raptor species, which have resulted in numerous scientific papers and a lively book on the raptors of North America, published by Voyageur Press in 1992. In 1972, they joined the Endangered Wildlife Research program of the U.S. Fish and Wildlife Service and the U.S. Forest Service to conduct research and conservation efforts for the critically endangered Puerto Rican Parrot. These studies were followed by research and conservation efforts for the Everglade Kite and the California Condor. For work on the Puerto Rican Parrot and California Condor, Noel received the William Brewster award of the American Ornithologist's Union, a Distinguished Achievement award from the Society for Conservation Biology, and the Conservation Medal of the Zoological Society of San Diego.

From the late 1980s to the present, the Snyders have been based in southern Arizona, where they have conducted research on Goshawks and Thick-billed Parrots. These activities have been varied with participation in research and conservation training programs focused on parrots in Jamaica, St. Lucia, and Mexico. They played a central role in recent successful efforts to ensure the protection of Cave Creek Canyon of the Chiricahua Mountains from mining development, and have spent considerable recent energies aiding campaigns to preserve important montane habitats in Mexico.

Photo Credits

Dedication

We dedicate this book to all those who have given their time and energies to help conserve the California Condor through the 20th century. We want especially to acknowledge the accomplishments of the many field and zoo biologists of the intensive program of the 1980s. Their extraordinary efforts laid the groundwork for successful conservation of the species, and although the process is not yet complete, the species would surely have been lost by now without the contributions of these people. Their long vigils observing events at remote and rugged nest sites, their steady nerves in the complex egg-pickups made to form a captive flock, their patience in tracking radio-tagged condors, their skill in hatching and rearing condors in captivity, and their diligence in many other aspects of the program, from trail construction to photo-censusing work to last-ditch attempts to save condors dying of lead poisoning, were key elements of a campaign that no participant will ever forget.

The condor program of the 1980s was a high-tension crash program, and the friendships formed during the struggles and conflicts inherent in such programs often prove to be long-lasting. Most of the people involved have now dispersed far and wide from condor affairs, but it is remarkable how many stay in contact and still look back upon those years as a profound experience. Despite the stress and fatigue, it was a privilege to participate in the program, and that participation was largely its own reward.

Here, however, we wish to express a personal tribute to those who worked the hardest. As in all wars, those on the front lines of the condor program were the ones who made the greatest contribution, not the generals in Washington and Sacramento, not the troop commanders back at base camp, and surely not the scribes who try to interpret events from afar. The number of people participating in the program of the 1980s, either as employees or as volunteeers, was large. Some will be mentioned in special contexts in the chapters that follow, and at the end we will attempt an acknowledgments section that we hope may give at least a partial indication of the magnitude and diversity of contributions that have been made.

The summit of Mt. Pinos, California (**above**) was once renowned as a traditional summer gathering point for California Condors. Our first sighting of the species (**below**) was an adult cruising so low over the crest we could hear the hiss of the wind passing through its wing feathers.

Prologue

Mt. Pinos, at nearly 9000 feet, is the highest peak in the rugged canyon-scarred region just northwest of Los Angeles. In mid-late summer its conifer-studded slopes give welcome relief from the monotonous heat of the lowlands, and it has long been a popular destination for hikers and campers from all over southern California. Perhaps the cool temperatures are also the reason why Mt. Pinos was once a favored summer assembly point for California Condors. Soaring majestically on wings spanning close to 10 feet, these huge vultures were a familiar sight near the summit, especially during the late morning and afternoon hours. The mountain served as an important loafing and roosting area for condors foraging in the foothills of the San Joaquin Valley a little farther to the north. To the south a complex landscape of cliffs and gorges comprised the major nesting region for the species.

With road access running right to the peak, Mt. Pinos was well known as one of the most accessible and reliable locations for condor-viewing. For many, the mountain was the only place they had ever encountered the species and was a favored site to take family and friends to see their first condors. The mountain was also the original site of the annual Condor Watch and Tequila Bust, an informal weekend gathering of miscellaneous condor enthusiasts that was inaugurated in the mid 1970s. While there was still an appreciable condor population left in the wild, the bust never failed to produce sightings of condors, along with other reliable California-style social benefits.

In late August of 1970 the Condor Watch and Tequila Bust had not yet been invented, but we had heard about the condors of Mt. Pinos. As a diversion we decided to visit the mountain, taking time out from our studies on the ecology and behavior of Goshawks, Cooper's Hawks and Sharp-shinned Hawks in Arizona. The field season was winding down, and the drive from our study area took only a full day, so why not? We knew little about the condor, and certainly had no premonition that we might someday be spending nearly every conscious moment in a desperate effort to preserve this mysterious giant bird, but we were intensely interested in endangered species, and there were few to rival the condor in notoriety, even then. Noel was teaching courses in conservation at the University of South Florida at the time, so it surely wouldn't hurt to strike up an acquaintance with the species.

It's hard to recollect now what our expectations might have been about the chances of seeing condors, but we well remember the long drive up the mountain and the pleasure of meeting two people at the top who were directly involved in efforts to study and save the species, John Borneman and Roland Clement of the National Audubon Society. John, the younger and more talkative of the two, had been recruited for condor field studies and conservation education efforts from a singing career with the Dapper Dons of Disneyland, and he obligingly filled us in on his five years of diverse and sometimes humorous experiences with the species. Roland, a more scholarly and reserved individual, was the National Audubon Society's Vice President for Science and had been the society's representative on the Condor Advisory Committee, the most important body then active in setting conservation priorities for the species. From John and Roland we quickly learned what was being done and what needed to be done for the species in the view of the organization that had been most committed to condor conservation over the years.

We did see condors, but not until late afternoon. John and Roland had gone, and when the first birds arrived we were essentially alone on the summit, patiently scanning the skies on the northwestern side of the peak. One adult in particular came sailing in so close overhead that we could easily see the clear white feather triangles on the underside of its wings and hear the surprisingly noisy hiss of the wind passing through its wing tips. We watched in amazement as this condor inspected us briefly, then banked and began to descend, circling down just below us and almost immediately landing on the broken top of a medium-sized fir only a few yards distant. The bird yawned as we moved in closer and paid us virtually no attention as it preened and rested, its naked head gleaming bright orange in the sunlight. It was an astonishingly imposing creature, even if its obvious lack of concern over our presence did not quite fit its press notices as a species of great wariness.

The condor stayed in the treetop for perhaps a half hour or more, allowing us to study some of its physical characteristics in detail. Especially notable were bizarrely puffed-out cheeks, a dark saddle of close-cropped feathers in front of the eyes, a shaggy neck ruff of long pointed dark feathers that could be raised and lowered at will, and a long hooked bill that was largely enveloped in fleshy tissue — strange features that contributed greatly to the bird's exotic aura.

Other features were less flamboyant, but no less distinctive. The bird's gray feet were large and strong, but were equipped with only relatively short claws quite unlike the talons of predatory raptors. They seemed better adapted for walking than for gripping a perch or killing prey. With its wings folded, the bird's feathers were almost uniformly black, save for a ragged white bar near the center of each wing. And although characteristic traces of white excrement clung to its legs, the condor looked clean and vigorous. Its relaxed and confident demeanor gave no indication that it might recognize that it was one of the last members of a highly endangered species.

For nearly a half hour the condor preened and rested atop a fir before launching once again into flight and disappearing to the west on a long glide.

As it shifted about on the perch, the condor was completely silent and unhurried, and we wondered how many times it might have rested on this same limb in earlier visits to the mountaintop. It gave the impression of being a very old bird, but there was no way to determine its age. Conceivably, it had seen more sunrises than we had, as condors in captivity are known to live for many decades. And in retrospect we now wonder if this bird might possibly have been one of the very individuals we were to study in great detail some years later when we ourselves joined the condor program. Idle speculations, perhaps, but here was a species with a life-span potentially rivalling that of the human species.

Eventually the condor opened its mammoth wings once more and sailed off to the west after a few ponderous flaps to power it through the air. More like an airplane than any normal bird in the steadiness of its flight, it glided rapidly on a long bee-line trajectory that took it around the corner of nearby Sawmill Mountain and abruptly out of sight. It had departed without a backward glance, apparently with important commitments elsewhere, but it left us in a state of wonderment that persists even today.

With this superb ending to our first day on Mt. Pinos we elected to stay for another. Our decision was rewarded by sightings of five individual condors soaring and perching in the area, though none closely approached the mountaintop. We did not know it at the time, but these five individuals, together with 22 more seen simultaneously in the Glennville region far to the northeast of Mt. Pinos, constituted one of the largest single day totals of that era seen outside of the annual October Condor Surveys (see Wilbur et al. 1972). In the late 1960s, the October Surveys were still yielding over 50 birds, but these individuals were spread out over a substantial U-shaped region that extended from far up the Coast Ranges, down and across through the Transverse Range, and back up the Tehachapis and Sierras on the east side of the San Joaquin Valley as far north as Sequoia National Park and beyond. With nests, roosts, and foraging areas dispersed throughout this range and with a breeding season that extended almost year-round, one could never expect to see the whole population simultaneously assembled at any one or even several locations.

None of the birds we saw on our two days on Mt. Pinos was a dark-headed or ring-necked immature, and we learned that there were concerns at the time that the ratios of younger birds to full adults observed in the most recent October Surveys were abnormally low, suggesting that reproduction might be depressed in the species. Interpreting these figures, however, posed many challenges, as there were other possible explanations for the low ratios, and in fact the accuracy of the low ratios was in some question. We would later find ourselves immersed in attempts to interpret these very data. But in 1970, concerns over age ratios were just emerging and were primarily the domain of the U.S. Fish and Wildlife Service, U.S. Forest Service, California Fish and Game, and Audubon Society biologists then working with condors.

Our focus lay elsewhere. We were just tourists, enjoying the deep blue skies and golden meadows of a beautiful mountaintop and the tremendously thrilling experience of seeing condors for the first time. Like others who had seen the California Condor up close in nature, we knew we had experienced one of the most awesome wildlife spectacles on the planet. We now clearly understood why the species had long been revered in the ceremonies of Indian tribes up and down the West Coast, and why it had become such an important national symbol of wildlife conservation. Famed as an improbable survivor from the continent's pre-history of dire wolves, sabre-toothed cats, and flesh-eating teratorns, it seemed an almost perfect embodiment of the spirit of timeless and unfathomable nature.

Surely the California Condor must not be allowed to disappear. The calls for efforts to save it had been sounded since the turn of the century. And long before the passage of the first federal Endangered Species Preservation Act in 1966, the condor had received concerted conservation attention, especially through creation of sanctuaries and education programs to end various forms of human harassment. Yet despite these measures, there had been no signs of a population recovery, and in fact the condor still appeared to be losing ground.

It would be another 10 years before we would see California Condors again, and under profoundly worsened circumstances for the species. By 1980, the total condor population had apparently dropped to fewer than 30 birds, and it had become clear that the species was in a rapid tailspin toward extinction. Now the emotions evoked by sightings of condors were strongly colored by the imminence of the species' prospective demise, and the need for an all-out effort to prevent this from occurring was obvious to nearly all.

By that time we had left the University of South Florida. We had joined the Endangered Wildlife Research Program of the U.S. Fish and Wildlife Service in 1972, becoming involved first in an even more desperate conservation program for the Puerto Rican Parrot. This bird was down to just 16 individuals in the wild, and we spent five years in a last-ditch campaign to reverse its inexorable and rapid decline (see Snyder et al. 1987b). Our primary emphasis was intensive research to determine the causes of the decline, especially through studies of reproduction and mortality rates and by identifying weak points in the species' demography. But we also developed a variety of conservation measures based on research results as they were obtained. As in most work with critically endangered species, research and conservation activities went hand in hand.

The parrot turned out to have a number of serious problems, but the most easily corrected was frequent destruction of its nests by another species of hole-nesting bird that had recently invaded the parrot's range – the Pearly-eyed Thrasher. By detailed experimental study of the nest-site preferences and tolerances of both the parrots and the thrashers, we were able to devise a means for preventing thrasher depredations by modifying the structure of parrot nests. The nest modifications led to a crucial increase in parrot reproduction and a slow recovery of the population.

Part of the effort to save the Puerto Rican Parrot involved the establishment of a captive flock to serve as a fail-safe population of last resort and a source of birds to bolster the wild population. In developing a captive program we became directly aware of the potential of captive breeding to help bail out severely stressed species, but also of the limitations of this technique. More importantly, our experiences in Puerto Rico led to a firm belief in the absolute necessity for intensive research to pinpoint the problems of threatened species so that effective remedies could be devised to sustain wild populations. As we shall see, these same issues would later become central in debates over strategies with the California Condor.

After leaving Puerto Rico, we worked for two years with the Florida Everglade Kite, another of the endangered birds being studied by the Endangered Wildlife Research Program. This had long been a favorite species of ours, and we had already done some research on its feeding behavior in the late 1960s. The Everglade Kite is a specialist predator of large freshwater snails, and we had been especially interested in its relationship with the giant Florida apple snail. In the late 1970s, however, our research focused on the demography of the species, especially studies of its reproductive characteristics that we carried out in collaboration with Steve Beissinger and Rod Chandler (Snyder et al. 1989).

The kite turned out to be a paradoxical bird; a species with extremely poor nesting success, yet with substantial production of young in good food years. This unusual combination of characteristics resulted largely from very long breeding seasons, which allowed multiple breeding attempts by individuals, overwhelming the poor success of most attempts.

The breeding potential of the species was further enhanced by a unique system of mate desertion, whereby one member of most pairs, either the male or the female, would abandon its mate, usually while they still had young in the nest. The deserter was then free to immediately begin a new nesting attempt with a new mate, while its old mate was stuck with several more weeks of parental care. Thus when food was abundant, most broods were fledged and carried to independence by single adults, and consistent deserters had a chance to produce three and conceivably even four broods in a year!

In drought years when food was scarce, on the other hand, relatively few kites attempted even one nest, and mate desertion did not occur. In fact, large areas of the Everglades went bone dry, and the kites were forced to flee to limited deep-water refugia where just surviving, let alone breeding, was difficult. Thus the species was highly variable in reproductive output from year to year, and our studies helped reveal why the kite population is so extremely sensitive to fluctuations in water levels.

Another issue we addressed during our years with the kites was the potential impact of a major new airport on the kite population. A new jetport proposed for a site near Miami would have resulted in commercial aircraft flying low over the most important nesting colony then known. Together with Paul Sykes, we expressed concerns to the Fish and Wildlife Service that this siting could pose a major threat to the species. The Service responded by insisting on a thorough evaluation of potential impacts. Direct tests of such impacts became possible with the cooperation of Eastern Airlines, which agreed to reprogram its pilot-training efforts in the region so that Boeing 727s might fly low over the very colony in question at the projected frequency and altitude of aircraft coming in to land at the proposed airport.

Surprisingly, the kites showed no detectable changes in behavior or ecology as a result of the low experimental overflights. They apparently adapted as easily as humans to the frequent approaches and teeth-rattling decibels of giant metal raptors close overhead, and our 10-day study gave no evidence that a new jetport would directly harm the species. The jetport has not been built to this day, but for reasons unrelated to potential disturbance effects on the kites.

The jetport study gave us a broadened understanding of the potential effects of disturbance that would later be useful in dealing with similar issues with the California Condor. It was also a striking example of how apparently major threats to endangered species can sometimes turn out to be minor threats on close examination, another lesson that would emerge repeatedly with the condor. The Everglade Kite was not a critically endangered species like the Puerto Rican Parrot or the California Condor, and it definitely was not a species that needed captive breeding for its conservation. Nevertheless, the techniques involved in its detailed study, including radio-telemetry and close observation of nests, were much the same as would prove valuable in condor studies.

We first became involved in California Condor conservation while working with the Everglade Kite. Noel was asked by the Fish and Wildlife Service to help evaluate a condor report that had been drafted in 1978 by a special panel of the American Ornithologists' Union and National Audubon Society. This report focused on the dire status of the species and the need for a crash program involving modern techniques such as radio-telemetry and captive breeding to elucidate the precise causes of endangerment and ensure survival of the species. Noel found the report to be valuable, especially because of its emphasis on intensified research and its recognition of the need for captive breeding. The report was endorsed by the Fish and Wildlife Service and proved tremendously important in generating a new intensive program for the condor.

Nevertheless, the report made little reference to earlier recommendations by Carl Koford, the first major researcher of the species. It was viewed by many of Koford's followers as an alien document that had turned its back on much of the wisdom gained by his extensive and admirable work in the 1930s and 1940s. The emerging rift between the traditional "hands-off" conservation philosophy of Koford and his followers and the more "activist" orientation of most concerned conservationists was not healed by this report, and as necessary and valuable as the report was, it did not lead to full consensus. A debate soon developed that progressed to open warfare between opposing points of view. This sort of political heat was not something that we had had to deal with in previous programs, and when we became involved in the condor program in 1980 we were quite unprepared for the political duels that would occupy a major part of our lives for the following six and a half years.

For a time, however, the AOU-Audubon Report caught Koford's followers by surprise, and its acceptance by the Fish and Wildlife Service allowed the National Audubon Society the leverage it needed to successfully lobby Congress for a new expanded condor program. The Audubon Society itself had only recently resolved its own internal conflicts over hands-off versus activist approaches to the condor. Its important role in creating the new program, largely through the efforts of Dick Plunkett and Gene Knoder, was a dramatic departure from earlier policies.

The new program was approved by Congress in 1979 and was set up with two organizations, the U.S. Fish and Wildlife Service and the National Audubon Society, sharing lead responsibilities in field research and conservation activities. Other agencies that joined in the new program included the U.S. Forest Service, whose lands included most nesting and roosting areas of the species, the Bureau of Land Management, which administered some additional lands in the condor range, and the California Department of Fish and Game, which administered state research and conservation efforts for wildlife. In addition, the Los

Angeles Zoo and the Zoological Society of San Diego (including both the San Diego Zoo and the San Diego Wild Animal Park) soon became crucially involved in captive breeding aspects of the program. All these agencies were coordinated by a reorganized Condor Recovery Team, an advisory body sponsored by the Fish and Wildlife Service and made up of appropriate representatives from the agencies and the academic community. However, final authority for policy matters in the program rested with the Fish and Wildlife Service itself and the California Fish and Game Commission.

Shortly after the new program was passed by Congress, Noel was asked by the Fish and Wildlife Service to lead the new expanded condor field program for that agency while John Ogden was asked to lead field efforts for the National Audubon Society. Exactly how these two agencies would relate to one another was not yet clear, but both John and Noel accepted their new roles with a naive confidence that they would be participating in a program where all parties would recognize the crisis at hand and find ways to make things work efficiently and amicably.

We moved to California in early 1980 eager to work on the conservation of a truly fascinating and impressive species, but with only minimal relevant experience to help us deal with the political aspects of condor affairs. We soon discovered that success in the biological sphere depended crucially on surmounting formidable opposition to new research and conservation initiatives, and our years in the program were in part an intense education in how to make biological imperatives politically feasible. In the process we gained a first-hand awareness of the many constraints and frustrations inherent in heavily-funded conservation programs for high-profile species.

In this book we hope to give the reader an appreciation of both the basic biology of the condor and the dynamics of condor conservation from a viewpoint mainly inside the conservation and research program. Many books, book chapters, and articles have already been written on the condor program of the 1980s, but virtually all have been by people who were not participants in the program, and most reflect orientations and biases that most of us who were actually involved find quite misleading or beside the point. Although no one view can hope to express the full truth of the history of condor conservation and research, because no one bears witness to all relevant occurrences, we have been dismayed by how far from reality most accounts have strayed, with events and motivations of involved personnel and agencies often thoroughly distorted. Our experience with how "condor history" has been written so far makes us wonder how much of the rest of history has been invented by journalists anxious to create interesting stories or push their own theories, rather than by real historians with a sincere objective of documenting what actually happened.

We believe that accuracy should be the overriding goal of this book. The real history, as we lived it, was intriguing enough without embellishment, although much of the story has never been told. What we will report here is reality as we knew it, presented as objectively as we are able. But it will not be the whole reality, partly because no one knows what that is and partly because the full story is so complex that considerations of space alone dictate the omission of some materials.

Part of the reality we will discuss involves events we would prefer to forget, especially our highly-publicized loss of a condor chick in a handling accident in mid 1980. This particular event, however, was of major importance to the program and influenced many other events of the following years. Understanding its significance is basic to understanding what happened through this period. Fortunately, though the impacts of this event were great, they did not completely incapacitate the conservation program, and it did recover in time.

The California Condor, despite its reputation as the very essence of wilderness, is a species that has interacted closely with humanity for many centuries. Any book portraying the species solely as a creature apart from our own species would miss much of the breadth of its existence. Yet it is a bird that has clearly not thrived in company with civilization over the long term. Finding out exactly why this has been so has been a complex detective story with many innocent parties unfairly accused and a primary villain surprising to many observers. The long process of discovering the causes of the condor's decline is the underlying story of this book, and the knowledge gained in the effort is a key foundation for the ultimate rescue of the species.

Much of the effort to determine causes of decline has been focused on gaining a comprehensive understanding of basic condor natural history. We will have much to report on this subject, especially many extraordinary experiences in studying wild nesting pairs. But we also feel a strong obligation to present enough of the important events in the history of condor conservation that the reader can begin to appreciate why so many bitter battles have always surrounded the species and just how much difficulty there can be in achieving lasting conservation of some endangered species. The problems are mostly not biological in nature, but are problems in how the human species grapples with conservation challenges. We are not terribly good at this, especially in the long term, and it is important to examine ways in which the process might be improved.

If all this sounds as though the condor story still lacks a proper Hollywood ending, we would like to reassure the reader that we actually feel quite upbeat about the future of the condor, and hope this basic message will not get lost in the discussions of faulty conservation strategies and episodes of conservation lunacy and sleaze. There is much to be learned about how conservation actually works by examining the example of the condor, and conservation does sometimes work, though often at the expense of tremendous commitments by involved people, and often in spite of formidable obstacles.

Part I of the book is a general review of the condor, its cultural importance to native American civilizations, and efforts to study and conserve it prior to 1980. In Part II, we move on to discuss the design and testing of new research and conservation thrusts for the 1980s. A more lengthy Part III presents a series of chapters on the results of the natural history and biological studies of the 1980s; what we learned about wild condors, and what the results obtained implied for conservation of the species. Part IV gives a detailed account of conservation activities for the species in the 1980s; how they evolved, and where they led. Part V considers more recent events, especially progress of the captive breeding program and of efforts to reestablish the species in the wild. Finally, Part VI examines the future and presents broad conclusions drawn from the condor conservation program, analyzing their relevance to endangered species conservation in general.

PART I
HISTORICAL AND
BACKGROUND MATTERS

Some Perspectives on Basic Condor Biology

Before launching into a detailed discussion of the biology and conservation of the California Condor, we need to present a basic description of just what sort of creature the species is. Here, we not only consider major characteristics of the condor itself but also place the condor in the context of scavenging birds in general, tracing broad aspects of their evolutionary history, considering some of their ecological adaptations, and touching on certain unique problems they face in their role as carrion consumers.

Renowned as a Pleistocene relict that has long outlived its proper place in the ages, the California Condor (*Gymnogyps californianus*) has sometimes been dismissed as a senescent species somehow irrelevant to the modern world (Miller 1942). One almost imagines the birds doddering along with canes and wheelchairs, barely able to cope with the daily needs of existence, and waiting pathetically for the end to come. Nevertheless real condors presumably know nothing of such dubious characterizations. They show obvious vigor, agility, and charisma, and have no apparent shortage of the same drives for self preservation as typify ourselves. The concepts of species senescence and terminal disintegration are difficult to fathom once one observes condors in life, and if condors are refugees from the Pleistocene, so too are we, and essentially all other species alive today.

At an average weight of about 8.5 kg (19 lbs), the California Condor is an impressively massive bird. However, it is not the heaviest bird now to be found in North America. Trumpeter Swans (*Cygnus buccinator*) and male Wild Turkeys (*Meleagris gallopavo*) often weigh more. Still, the condor's wingspan of 9 to 10 feet (2.9 m) exceeds that of any other living North American species, and it is the largest soaring bird in our avifauna, only slightly smaller than the Andean Condor (*Vultur gryphus*) of South America.

If we extend comparisons to extinct species, however, both California and Andean Condors are dwarfed by a number of gigantic birds, possibly also partly scavengers, that once roamed the Western Hemisphere. Most notable among these was *Argentavis magnificens*, an extraordinary creature from Argentina some 5–8 million years ago (Campbell and Tonni 1980, 1981, 1983; Campbell and Marcus 1990). *Argentavis* was the largest known flying bird of all time, with an estimated wingspan of approximately 23 feet (7 m) and a weight of approximately 75 kg (160–170 lbs). Another giant of the past was *Teratornis incredibilis*, with an estimated wingspan of 17–19 feet (5.5 m). This species was first described from a Nevada bone deposit, believed to be late Pleistocene in age (Howard 1952). Other fossils found more recently indicate that *Teratornis incredibilis* existed back to the early Pleistocene.

Even at the very end of the Pleistocene, some 10,000 years ago, species larger than *Gymnogyps californianus* still coursed the California skies. Remains of *Teratornis merriami*, a species with an estimated wingspan of 11–12 feet (3.5 m), and *Breagyps clarki*, a condor just slightly smaller, were both found in some numbers in the Rancho La Brea deposits of Los Angeles. Very possibly, both these now extinct species were still alive to be seen by the earliest human inhabitants of North America (Howard 1962, 1974).

The fossil history of the California Condor itself extends back into the Pleistocene to at least 40,000 years ago. The Pleistocene form of the California Condor was slightly larger than the contemporary, and was originally described as *Gymnogyps amplus*, a species separate from the California Condor (Fisher 1944, 1947). However, *amplus* was clearly very similar to and presumably directly ancestral to the California Condor of today, and is more appropriately classified as a temporal subspecies of the California Condor, *Gymnogyps californianus amplus,* than as a distinct species (Emslie 1988b).

Other species currently included in the genus *Gymnogyps* include a fossil condor from the Pleistocene of Peru, *Gymnogyps howardae* (Campbell 1979), and a species from Florida 1 to 1.5 million years ago that Emslie (1988b) christened *Gymnogyps kofordi*, appropriately honoring Carl Koford's enduring contributions to condor biology and conservation. Emslie suggested that *Gymnogyps kofordi* was sufficiently distinct that it clearly merited recognition as a separate species, but he also remarked that it may have been an ancestral species to both *amplus* and *californianus*.

Still another Pleistocene condor from Cuba, *Antillovultur varonai* (Arredondo 1971), is perhaps best classified as another species or subspecies of *Gymnogyps* (i.e., *Gymnogyps varonai* or *Gymnogyps californianus varonai*) rather than as belonging to a separate genus (Olson 1978, Emslie 1988b).

Living Relatives, Ancestral Relationships, and Comparisons between Old and New World Vultures

The California Condor, together with the Andean Condor, the King Vulture (*Sarcoramphus papa*), the Black Vulture (*Coragyps atratus*), and three species of the genus *Cathartes* – the Turkey Vulture (*Cathartes aura*), the Yellow-headed Vulture (*Cathartes burrovianus)*, and the

Greater Yellow-headed Vulture (*Cathartes melambrotus*) – comprise the living members of the avian family Vulturidae (Cathartidae), commonly known as the the New World vultures. Fossil vulturids also include six additional genera of condors, *Breagyps, Hadrogyps, Pleiogyps, Geronogyps, Aizenogyps*, and *Dryornis* (Emslie 1988a, 1998) and a variety of other smaller genera now extinct. The earliest of the condors, *Hadrogyps*, dates from the mid-Miocene of California, approximately 13–15 million years ago, whereas the earliest known vulturids, all relatively small species, date from the late Eocene or early Oligocene of France and Mongolia, approximately 37 million years ago (Olson 1985).

The very largest of ancient flying birds – *Argentavis* and *Teratornis* – were not technically condors or vulturids but belong to a closely related family, the Teratornithidae, which are sadly now all extinct (Miller 1909). Rea (1983) suggested that the teratorns were about equally related to the vulturids as to the storks and deserved to be retained as a distinct family. However, other workers (Brodkorb 1964, Emslie 1988b) have argued that the teratorns are sufficiently close to the vulturids that they should be considered a subfamily of the Vulturidae rather than a separate family. Whether the teratorns may have been scavengers, predator–scavengers or consistent predators has been discussed by Campbell and Tonni (1983), who favor an emphasis on predatory habits, based on jaw structure.

Of the living vulturids other than condors, only the Turkey Vulture occurs in the range occupied in recent times by the California Condor, although the condor's prehistoric range overlapped part of the range of the Black and King Vultures in the southeastern states, and fossil Black and King Vultures are known to have been contemporary with condors in the Rancho La Brea deposits of Los Angeles. Turkey and Black Vultures also occur farther south in Central and South America, and all the other living vulturids are residents of Central and/or South America.

The vulturids have long been classified as Falconiformes, an order that has traditionally also included more typical diurnal birds of prey such as falcons, hawks, eagles, Old World vultures, ospreys, and secretary birds (families Falconidae, Accipitridae, Pandionidae, and Sagittariidae). However, for some decades now, the placement of the New World vultures in the Falconiformes has been questioned by serious students of avian systematics, who have suggested that vulturids are actually more closely related to storks than to the typical diurnal birds of prey (Jollie 1953, Ligon 1967, Rea 1983, Olson 1985, Sibley and Alquist 1990). In its most recent discussion of avian relationships, the American Ornithologists' Union (1998) has at last reclassified the group with the storks (order Ciconiiformes) as closest relatives, although some continue to argue that the group is closer to accipitrids than to storks (Griffiths 1994). If the vulturids belong in the Ciconiiformes, then so also do the teratorns because of their acknowledged close relationship with the vulturids. Thus, most ornithologists of today believe that neither the New World vultures nor the teratorns are close relatives of the Old World vultures, whereas the latter are clearly allied with the typical diurnal birds of prey. The similarity of the Old and New World vultures appears to be a striking example of evolutionary convergence, not closely shared ancestry. Further, recent biochemical studies of Wink (1995) and Seibold and Helbig (1995) suggest that the Old World vultures themselves may be comprised of two separate lineages convergently adopting a scavenging way of life from distant accipitrid ancestors.

Regardless of who their closest relatives may truly be, the vulturids are a distinct group with a number of special anatomical and behavioral features. All are carrion feeders with feet adapted for walking, not seizing prey, and all have naked heads, presumably as an adaptation to reduce feather fouling when thrusting their heads into the juicy inner recesses of carcasses. Moreover, all are species without true syringeal vocalizations, although they are capable of a variety of wheezes, snorts, and hisses audible at close range. In addition, they all show thermoregulatory behavior known as urohydrosis, in which they drench their legs with their own excreta during hot weather. This cools first their legs then their entire bodies via cooled blood from the legs circulating throughout the body. Urohydrosis is very unusual in the bird world, being found elsewhere only in the storks and certain boobies, and is one of the principal behaviors linking the vulturids to the storks.

Another trait shared by all vulturids is the lack of typical nest-building behavior. All species in the group lay their eggs directly on the floors of sheltered locations such as caves or hollow tree stumps, and none gather sticks or other pieces of vegetation from outside of their nest chambers to create recognizable nest structures. The California Condor, nevertheless, does assemble small pieces of gravel and debris from within its nest chambers to form coarse, loose surfaces on which to rest its eggs.

Old World vultures, by contrast, do have true (although often rudimentary) syringeal vocalizations, do build nests of twigs and branches, and do not practice urohydrosis. Nevertheless, like the New World Vultures they are mostly carrion feeders, show a reduction of feathering of their heads, and have feet adapted for walking rather than seizing prey. Other apparently convergent similarities of Old and New World vultures include various aspects of reproductive biology, such as (1) near equal sharing between the sexes of incubation and brooding of young, (2) feeding of young by regurgitation, and (3) a usual absence of "courtship" feeding of females by males, all features that are unusual for typical diurnal birds of prey.

Curiously, the oldest fossil representatives of the New World vultures come from the Old World, while New World deposits in turn have yielded many fossil relatives of the Old World vultures (Olson 1985).

Together, the New and Old World vultures presently occupy parts of all continents except Australia and Antarctica, though they are missing from the more northerly regions of North America and Eurasia. Their current absence from latitudes above about 50 degrees north seems to be related to an avoidance of taiga and tundra habitats, where carrion food may be relatively scarce. However, the recent discovery of fossil California Condor bones in a Pleistocene taiga bog deposit in New York State indicates at least intermittent vulturid use of this habitat before the late Pleistocene megafauna extinctions (Steadman and Miller 1986).

Food scarcity does not provide a plausible explanation for the absence of vultures from Australia, where a great variety of marsupial mammals have occurred in abundance. Mundy et al. (1992) attributed this absence mainly to Australia's separation from the other continents prior to the evolution of either New World or Old World vultures, to the difficulties vultures have in crossing oceans, and to the general avoidance of forested habitats by Old World vultures. Old World vultures have not spread to any of the heavily forested islands of the East Indies and would face formidable sea crossings in reaching New Guinea and moving from New Guinea to Australia. Rising masses of heated air do not normally occur over water, making it difficult for large soaring birds such as vultures to maintain altitude over substantial distances. Although Eurasian Griffons (*Gyps fulvus*) are known to struggle, with much flapping, across the Strait of Gibraltar, a distance of roughly 8.5 miles (13.7 km), the only vulture species known to cross more substantial water gaps are the Turkey Vulture in the New World and the Egyptian Vulture (*Neophron percnopterus*) in the Old World, both of which are only moderate in size and have relatively low wing loading (mass per wing area). In the absence of vultures, Australia's carrion resources have become the domain of Wedge-tailed Eagles, kites, dingos, and hordes of meat-eating fly maggots.

The general avoidance of forested areas by Old World vultures has been explained by Houston (1984a, 1985, 1986) in several ways. First, none of the Old World vultures is known to locate food by odor, as do New World vultures of the genus *Cathartes*. Keen olfactory abilities of the *Cathartes* vultures allow them to sniff out carrion with remarkable efficiency in densely vegetated habitat (Owre and Northington 1961; Stager 1964; Houston 1986, 1988a, 1994; Graves 1992; and Gomez et al. 1994). In turn, other New World vultures, especially Black and King Vultures watch the foraging activities of *Cathartes* vultures and by following their lead are also able to exploit carrion supplies in forests, even though these other species apparently lack the capacities to find food by odor themselves (Houston 1984b, *but see also* Lemon 1991).

A second factor favoring exploitation of forest carrion by New World, but not Old World, vultures is an apparently greater abundance of carrion in New World tropical forests, mainly due to the existence of sloths in the New World but not in the Old World. Houston (1984a) estimated that New World tropical forests may offer densities of carrion that are several times as great as those in Old World tropical forests.

Finally, competition for carrion food supplies from blowflies is evidently much less intense in the New World than in the Old World, a factor that may greatly enhance the relative availability of food for vultures in New World forests. The comparatively poor carrion supplies in Old World forests may simply not have provided the Old World vultures any evolutionary incentive to develop an acute sense of smell. The only Old World vulture to inhabit tropical forest ecosystems is the aberrant Palm-nut Vulture (*Gypohierax angolensis*), a species that feeds primarily on vegetable materials, especially palm fruits, which are presumably much easier to locate visually in forested areas than is carrion.

Although the olfactory abilities of the *Cathartes* vultures would presumably allow them to find food in the dark, it is noteworthy that no species of vulture is known to practice nocturnal foraging. Mundy et al. (1992) noted two instances of unidentified vultures attending carcasses at night in Africa, but these seemingly could have been birds simply remaining at carcasses after sunset. The evident absence of nocturnal foraging is probably a reflection of commonly poor soaring conditions at night, difficulties in seeing carcasses in the dark, and risks of approaching carcasses that may be attended by difficult-to-detect mammalian predator–scavengers.

As Mundy et al. (1992) have pointed out, both the New and Old World vultures probably owe their adaptive radiations largely to the evolution of a variety of large grazing ungulates in the early Eocene epoch, some 50 million years ago. Ungulate carrion forms the major food supply for both groups overall, and neither could have plausibly evolved before the great blossoming of ungulates, which in turn followed the widespread development of grasslands worldwide.

Despite the relatively recent development of both vulture assemblages, both have experienced many speciations and extinctions during their short histories. Present-day vulturids are much less diverse than the vulturids of the Pleistocene, presumably mainly because of the massive Pleistocene extinctions of mammals in the New World. Old World vultures disappeared completely from the New World at about the same time. The Old World vultures of Africa, in contrast, are still largely dependent on a Pleistocene mammalian megafauna (although this too is now declining rapidly), and they comprise many more species, each with its own ecological specializations. Whereas the New World vultures presently include only two large species (the Andean and California Condors), one medium-sized species (the King Vulture), and four smaller species (the Black Vulture and three *Cathartes* vultures), the Old World vultures include a total of 15 species, 11 of which can be found in Africa alone. One African country, the Sudan, boasts a total of nine different vulture species, the greatest vulture diversity of any country in the world.

As discussed by Kruuk (1967), Houston (1975), König (1983), and Mundy et al. (1992), the Old World Vultures can be separated into a number of functional groups. One includes seven species of relatively social griffon and near-griffon vultures in the genera *Gyps* and *Pseudogyps* (often lumped into a single genus *Gyps*). These seven species are adapted to feed very rapidly on the inner tissues of large carcasses and normally consume the major portion of these carcasses. They form the core species dominating carcasses during the main feeding frenzy in the mid-stages of carcass exploitation, and normally prevent all others from feeding at this time. All species in this group are relatively uniform in color and morphology, being relatively large and basically brown in hue, and all possess exceptionally long, snake-like necks. Moreover, all are social in nesting habits. The five highly social *Gyps* vultures congregate in dense cliff colonies, whereas the two *Pseudogyps* species nest mainly in less concentrated, but still loosely social, groups in trees.

The other Old World vultures are a diverse assemblage of mostly solitary scavengers, that feed mainly on external parts of carcasses and that fulfill more specialized roles in carcass exploitation. Two species, the White-headed Vulture (*Trigonoceps occipitalis*) and the Hooded Vulture (*Necrosyrtes monachus*), are commonly the first species to land at carcasses, but are generally soon displaced by the more aggressive *Gyps* and *Pseudogyps* vultures, after which they get much of their food as scraps on the periphery of the main feeding frenzy.

A third relatively specialized species is the Lappet-faced Vulture (*Torgos tracheliotos*), which normally dominates carcasses at the very last stages of exploitation when the soft tissues have nearly all been consumed and all that is left is bones, skin, and other connective tissues. It is a very large species, has the largest bill of all vultures, and is normally considered the most formidable of all Old World vultures, but the Lappet-faced Vulture does not normally fight with *Gyps* and *Pseudogyps* vultures for access during the main phase of carcass exploitation. In fact it does not even normally land near a carcass until the main squabble is over (Mundy et al. 1992). Its reluctance to challenge *Gyps* and *Pseudogyps* vultures may be due to the difficulties and risks any species would have in displacing griffons in the midst of a feeding frenzy, when all heads are buried in the carcass and essentially no individuals are looking around at their surroundings. Lappet-faced Vultures normally take over carcasses only when griffons have mostly finished feeding and are standing around in the vicinity with their heads raised.

Lappet-faced Vultures are the only vultures capable of ripping apart the skin and other connective tissues of large carcasses, but this does not necessarily mean that they can support themselves on such tough materials. Mundy *et al.* (1992) questioned whether skin and connective tissue might provide an adequate food supply, and suggested that both the Lappet-faced Vulture and the White-headed Vulture might instead rely mainly on killing small vertebrates to sustain their needs. The remains of small vertebrates are frequent at nests of both species, and this suggests that they may not be primarily dependent on the scraps they may be able to glean from large vertebrate carcasses. Although direct observations of their killing prey are scarce (Kruuk 1967), this could be largely an observational artifact due to the difficulties of actually seeing such behavior.

Other solitary Old World Vultures have very specialized scavenging roles. Perhaps the most bizarre of all is the Bearded Vulture (*Gypaetus barbatus*), a species that subsists largely on a diet of large vertebrate bones which it breaks into manageable chunks by dropping them on rock anvils from the air (Terrasse et al. 1961, Houston and Copsey 1994; Brown 1989, 1990a,b,c; Brown and Plug 1990). Two other species, the Hooded Vulture and Egyptian Vulture (*Neophron percnopterus*), have in many regions developed commensal relationships with human settlements, feeding mainly on refuse and small carcasses which they can consume without major competition from griffon vultures (Mundy et al. 1992, Meretsky 1995). The Egyptian Vulture is also famous for its ability to eat the eggs of Ostriches (*Struthio camelus*). These it breaks apart by throwing rocks at them with its bill, one of the best-known examples of tool-using in birds (see Van Lawick-Goodall and Van Lawick 1966, Brooke 1979, and Thouless et al. 1987). The Hooded Vulture is renowned for an eagerness to take vertebrate feces as part of its diet, a tendency also found in other Old and New World vultures (including both Black and Turkey Vultures). Evidently, the dung of lions is especially attractive to African vultures, presumably because of its relatively high nutritional value (Houston 1988b).

The individual species in New and Old World vulture assemblages have not evolved in exactly parallel fashion. Although there are some conspicuous resemblances between certain Old and New World species pairs, most New World species lack close ecological and behavioral counterparts in the Old World and vice versa, despite the relatively similar ecological roles of vulture communities as a whole in both parts of the world. Thus, although the Black Vulture of the New World is closely similar to the Hooded and Egyptian Vultures of the Old World in overall size, bill shape, and tendency to adopt a commensal relationship with humans, this species commonly adopts an almost griffon-like role as a central player in frenzies at large carcasses (Stewart 1978, Coleman and Fraser 1987), including a willingness to crawl completely inside carcasses. Such behavior is not normally seen in Hooded and Egyptian Vultures. The *Cathartes* vultures have no obvious close counterparts among the Old World Vultures, either in foraging behavior or at carcasses. Similarly, no New World vulture shows any close resemblance to the bone-feeding Bearded Vulture and fruit-eating Palm-nut Vulture. In certain respects the two condors resemble the griffon vultures, especially in their frequent dominance of carcasses and their tendency to follow other species to food, but the condors have much shorter necks and thus cannot feed as easily on the innermost portions of large carcasses. At least in recent times, they have rarely been seen in feeding groups as large as those of griffon vultures, and they differ completely from the griffons in their tendency to nest solitarily in territories of considerable size.

Perhaps the Old World vulture that is most like the California Condor in its behavior, morphology, and ecology is the Lappet-faced Vulture. Closely similar in size and wingspan, these two species look alike in many ways. Both are basically black, have conspicuously red or orange heads, and have conspicuous white underwing triangles that apparently function as signals in aggressive interactions. Further, both nest singly in dispersed territories, taking enough time in each breeding attempt that they may often not breed every year. Moreover, both have very similar rates of nest success at about 40–50%, and both usually fly in pairs year-round, except during the incubation and early nestling periods. Principal differences center around the nature of their respective nest sites (cliff caves for the condor, and trees for the Lappet-faced Vulture) and in the presumed tendency of the Lappet-faced Vulture to take some living prey. In addition, the huge bill size of the Lappet-faced Vulture contrasts with the more modest bill of the California Condor, and may be an adaptation for feeding on the tough skin and connective tissue of large carcasses, which the condor normally avoids. One final similarity between these two species that is worth mentioning is the fact that nestling California Condors and Lappet-faced Vultures are both sometimes observed making mock prey-captures, stabbing out with one foot to pin some object to the ground (Snyder 1988, Mundy et al. 1992). This behavior has not been recorded for adult condors and suggests that the ancestry of the California Condor, like that of the Lappet-faced Vulture, might once have included species with more predatory behavior than is now seen in the Vulturidae.

Most New World vultures, like most Old World vultures, are basically nonmigratory. Nevertheless, one New World species, the Turkey Vulture, and one Old World species, the Egyptian Vulture, do make extensive seasonal movements. The annual migration of millions of Turkey Vultures from the United States and Canada funneling down through eastern Mexico to Central and South America each fall and returning in the spring is one of the most spectacular migrations known among all birds. No clear migratory movements are known for the California Condor, though it is possible that some seasonal movements might have been made by nonbreeders of now extinct populations. With reproductive cycles lasting more than a year, breeding condors would presumably be precluded from making seasonal migrations.

Habitat Needs and Prehistoric, Historic, and Recent Range of the California Condor

The fossil record suggests that the California Condor may once have occupied much of North America, with specimens from Florida, New York State, the Pacific Coast and south from Nevada, Arizona, New Mexico, and Texas into northern Mexico (Miller 1910, 1911, 1943, 1960; Miller and Howard 1938; Wetmore 1931a,b; Steadman and Miller 1986; Emslie 1987). Of special interest has been the finding of a Pleistocene boreal-bog deposit in New York State that contained condor bones associated with remains of typical plants and animals of the taiga, including spruce, mastodonts, and caribou (Steadman and Miller 1986). Evidence of the condor in such northerly habitat, along with California Condor fossils from Florida and diverse regions of the Southwest, makes a case for very wide habitat and climatic tolerances in the species. Wide habitat and climatic tolerances have also characterized the remnant historic population on the Pacific Coast.

In fact, the major generalizations that can be drawn regarding habitat needs for the species are that (1) condors undoubtedly can exist only in areas with adequate carrion food supplies, (2) as large soaring birds, condors need habitat with reasonably reliable winds or thermals, and (3) condors probably need foraging habitat that is sufficiently open that they can readily discover and safely access adequate amounts of carrion food. Nesting habitat requirements, as we will see in more detail in Chapter 11, may be a bit more specialized in the need for nest sites free from major threats of nest predators. Nevertheless, the nest sites

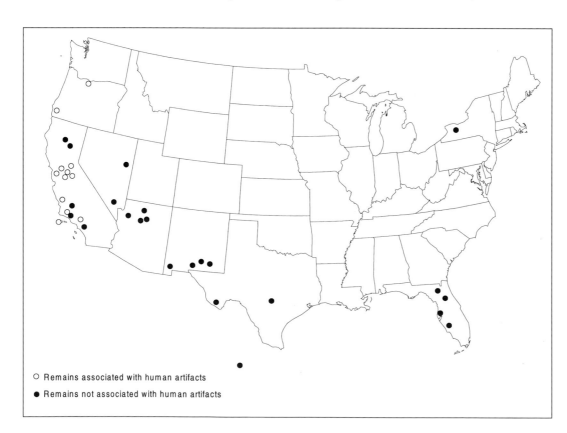

○ Remains associated with human artifacts

● Remains not associated with human artifacts

Prehistoric records of the California Condor in North America include bones (solid circles) from a variety of late Pleistocene sites across the continent and archeologic remains (open circles) in California and Oregon. Records illustrated here are from tabulations of Simons (1983) Wilbur (1978b), and Steadman and Miller (1986).

used by condors have been sufficiently diverse in their physical characteristics that it is doubtful that nesting might be limited by topographical or vegetational requirements in many regions (Snyder et al. 1986).

As with many animal species, the most important factor determining past distributions of the California Condor may have been food supplies. So far as is known, wild California Condors are exclusively carrion feeders, and although there has never been a truly unbiased, quantitative study of foods taken, either in the fossil record (Emslie 1988c) or in more modern times (Koford 1953, Miller et al. 1965, Wilbur 1978b, Collins et al. 2000), it is clear that the species tends to feed mainly on large vertebrate carcasses, mostly terrestrial mammals. By comparison with existing coastal populations of the Andean Condor that have been studied by Mike Wallace and Jerry McGahan, it is also likely that coastal populations of the California Condor once took substantial amounts of carrion from aquatic environments, including fish, marine mammals, and marine birds. Indeed, there are old records of California Condors feeding on dead whales and fish (Gambel 1846, Taylor 1859b, Lewis and Clark 1905, Kofoid 1923).

It is widely assumed that post-Pleistocene California Condors became limited to the West Coast and immediately adjacent regions because of the massive extinctions of New World megavertebrates that took place roughly 10,000 years ago (Koford 1953; Martin 1967, Emslie 1987, 1990). Clearly, these extinctions must have greatly altered food availability for the condor in many regions. Emslie (1987), for example, documented bone fragments of a variety of now-extinct mammals, including mammoths, camels, horses, and mountain goats, in Pleistocene condor nests in the Grand Canyon of Arizona.

Nevertheless, there have been a number of published sight records of California Condors in Arizona, Utah, Idaho, Montana, and Alberta within historic times, many of them reasonably close to the Grand Canyon (Fannin 1897, Lyon 1918, Schaeffer 1951, other references in Rea 1981, and Snyder and Rea 1998). Although no fossil condor materials have been found in the Grand Canyon (or elsewhere in the inland West) that date any more recently than about 10,000 years ago, and although many cave sites have by now been sampled in this region, we question that enough sampling of former nest caves has been done to completely rule out the existence of small numbers of condors persisting continuously in the region into recent times. Alternatively, Emslie (1987) has suggested that records of condors in the Grand Canyon region around the turn of the century may have represented a recent reinvasion from California, due perhaps to the widespread introduction of livestock into the region in the 1700s.

Koford (1953), as Swarth (1914) before him, was inclined to dismiss all the early Arizona and Utah sight records of condors as implausible, but good reasons for this view were not given by either author. Rejection of all records from this region amounts to doubting the capacities of a number of highly regarded early ornithologists (Coues, Mearns, Jacot, Henshaw). We see no reason to disregard their reports.

The Idaho record of Lyon (1918), also seems credible, in part because the behavioral details given ring so true. This report concerns two condors flushed from a sheep carcass near Boise, Idaho in 1879 and describes the birds being much larger than Turkey Buzzards, making hissing sounds, and running a long distance to get into flight. The Lyon report also states that condors (California Vultures) were not uncommon in the region prior to the start of efforts to control wolves with poisoned carcasses. Perhaps condor movements in this region followed the Columbia and Snake Rivers and were fueled to some extent by fish carrion from the salmon runs.

In connection with the Lyon report, it is relevant to note an 1827 report obtained by David Douglas of condors in the Idaho region (Douglas 1914). Etienne Lucien told Douglas that during the summer, condors "were seen in great numbers in the woody parts of the Columbia, from the ocean to the mountains of Lewis and Clark's River, four hundred miles in the interior." As Schaeffer (1951) pointed out, the region referred to here is presumably the drainage basin of the upper Snake River in present day Idaho, the locality of Lyon's report. But because Etienne Lucien was also the source of an erroneous account of condors laying clutches of two black eggs in twig nests lined with grass, most recent observers have discounted his geographical claims. Perhaps this is too hasty a dismissal of all he had to say.

Schaeffer (1951) recounted interviews with Blackfoot Indians strongly suggesting occasional presence of condors in their lands immediately adjacent to the Rocky Mountains in northern Montana and southern Alberta during the 19th century and possibly into the early 20th century. Schaeffer's engrossing article details a number of sightings by tribal elders of "omaxsapilau," a giant raptor clearly differentiated from the Golden Eagle ("pilau") and the Bald Eagle ("ksixkikini"). One of these accounts described this huge bird as being black and having a ruff and naked head, a description strongly suggesting a juvenile condor. Other accounts gave characteristics that generally give a good match to the condor, but with some small discrepancies here and there. Taken together, the reports are quite persuasive.

The Fannin (1897) report of two condors in Alberta does not give supporting details and has been questioned by some observers, although Fannin's earlier 1880 sighting of two condors in British Columbia has not been controversial. In view of the contemporary nearby reports detailed by Schaeffer (1951), we believe Fannin's sighting should not be treated too skeptically.

Thus, although the main historic range of the California Condor clearly extended along the West Coast from extreme southern British Columbia in Canada south through Washington, Oregon, and California to the Sierra San Pedro Martir of northern Baja California, Mexico (Koford 1953, Wilbur 1978b), there are enough credible historical records of condors considerably inland from the coast to suggest that the species also ranged farther east, although the birds may have been relatively rare in easterly locations.

Curiously, there is no good evidence, either historical or in the fossil record, to suggest that the California Condor ever systematically exploited carrion from the huge migratory herds of bison (*Bison bison*) that roamed the Great Plains into historical times (see discussion in Emslie 1987). By comparison, Houston (1974a, 1974c, 1976, 1978) described the adaptations of Rüppell's Griffon Vultures (*Gyps rueppellii*) that have allowed them to specialize on migratory herds of ungulates, especially wildebeest and zebra, in central Africa. Houston documented these large vultures (only slightly smaller than condors) flying as far as 150 km (93 miles) from nests to locate mammal herds during the breeding season. Nevertheless, he concluded that the use of such distant food supplies for breeding was just marginally possible for *Gyps rueppellii*, since the physical condition of adult vultures declined noticeably through the breeding season.

The apparent absence of any major dependence of condors on bison herds in the Great Plains might relate to the great distances traveled by many migratory bison herds (Hornaday 1889), which may have put them beyond any consistently practical foraging range for condors tied to fixed nest sites for long breeding seasons. Alternatively, the apparent general absence of condors from the region may have resulted simply because large regions of the Great Plains may not offer adequately safe nesting or roosting sites. The extent and severity of winter snow cover in the northern Great Plains could also have played a role. The only historical records we have uncovered of condors apparently associated with bison carcasses in the Great Plains region are those of Schaeffer (1951) immediately adjacent to the Rocky Mountains in Montana and Alberta, as discussed above.

The first (type) specimen taken of a California Condor for science was a bird collected in Monterey, California by Archibald Menzies of the Vancouver Expedition in 1792 (Shaw and Nodder 1797), although there were several earlier written accounts clearly referring to this species (see Grinnell 1932, Harris 1941). Condors were also described by the Lewis and

Range of the historic wild California Condor population in the 1940s based on records of Koford (1953) and Robinson (1940) and range of the species in the 1980s as determined from records in the modern program. Evidence suggested all individual condors in the 1980s may have been familiar with the entire range of the species as it then existed.

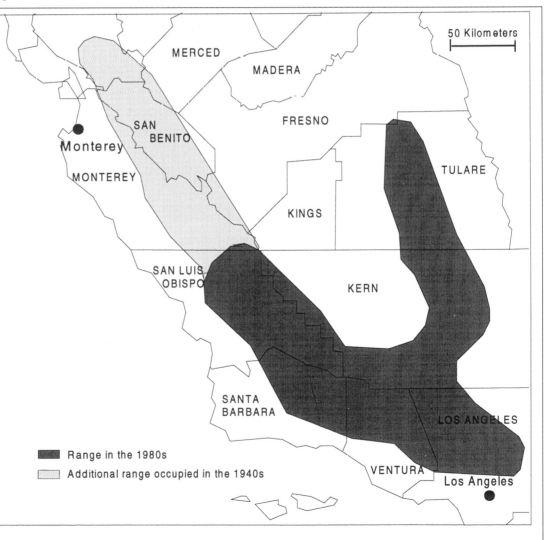

Clark expedition of 1805–1806 for a number of localities along the Columbia River between Oregon and Washington (Harris 1941), and although Koford (1953) argued that the condors seen in this region were most likely wanderers from California, Phillips (1968) and Wilbur (1973) suggest more plausibly that they may have been residents. The latter possibility could be confirmed by the discovery of former condor nests and eggshells in the region, something we venture to predict may not be too long in coming, given the rapidly increasing interest in avian paleontology in this country.

Koford (1953) and Wilbur (1978b) provided a thorough accounting of the progressive shrinkage of the range of the California Condor up to the early 1950s. By around 1850 the species was largely gone from Washington and Oregon (although apparently reliable sightings persisted as late as 1904 for southern Oregon – Finley 1908a). The last confirmed sightings for Baja California date from the 1930s, and by the 1940s the condor was known only from California itself. Here it persisted in a wishbone-shaped range surrounding the southern San Joaquin Valley that was delineated in considerable detail by Robinson (1940) and Koford (1953). The overall range continued to contract until the 1980s, although the numbers of condors were now declining much more swiftly than the size of their range.

The major change in distribution between 1950 and 1980 was the loss of the northwest portion of the range, extending from northern San Luis Obispo County through eastern Monterey and western Fresno Counties to San Benito and Santa Clara Counties (Koford 1953, Wilbur 1978b). Condors were reported in good numbers in this region up until the 1960s and nested just south of here until 1970, but there was no documented regular occupancy of this region during the 1980s. The final range of the species in the 1980s remained virtually stable until the last bird was trapped into captivity in 1987. For the last few years, at least, the range of each individual condor was roughly equivalent to the total range for the species (Meretsky and Snyder 1992).

Basic Vital Statistics

The California Condor, like most vulturids, but unlike the Andean Condor, displays no clear sexual differences in coloration or morphology, although it does show a variety of age-related coloration changes. At hatching, condor chicks have white down and usually naked yellow-orangish heads and necks. The white body down is replaced by a gray down within several weeks, and a short gray down begins to develop on the head and neck by about 50 days of age. Juvenile feathers begin to appear at about two months of age, and the skin color of the head changes from fleshy to slate gray at about 18 weeks, although some birds have fairly grayish head skin from hatching. In the fully developed juvenile plumage, the bill is black, the gray-black head and neck are largely covered with gray down, the iris is brown, and a feather ruff at the base of the neck is well developed. The body feathers are uniformly blackish, except that many have paler brownish margins at their ends. The tips of several of the greater secondary coverts are pale gray, forming a ragged bar near the center of the folded wing. The trailing edge of the extended wing has a scalloped edge, resulting from the somewhat pointed ends of the secondary flight feathers. The wing-lining triangles on the

Usual changes in head coloring and feathering with age, as illustrated by John Schmitt: A. first two years, B. third summer, C. fourth summer, D. fifth summer, and E. full adult. Full adult coloration and feathering is normally achieved at about 6 years, although some variability in rates is seen among individuals. In the wild, no breeding has been documented in individuals lacking full adult head coloration.

Plate 1

Male of the Sespe Sanctuary pair (SSM) on habitual cliff perch near his nest of 1983. His air sacs are fully inflated in display posture.

underside of the extended wings are basically white but are irregularly mottled with dark brown markings and usually a dark spot near the body.

The above colors remain pretty much the same through the next year of the bird's life, except that the scalloped appearance to the trailing edge of the wing disappears with wear and wing feather molt. In the third spring of the bird's life, the skin of the base of the neck starts to become pinkish and this color gradually extends onto the head as down begins to disappear from the head. This "ring-necked" condition generally continues through the bird's fourth spring and summer, becoming more conspicuous in this year, and then diminishing as orange head colors become more prominent. Through the ring-neck stage, the underwing triangles remain basically white mottled with dark markings, and the light bars across the upper surfaces of the wings formed by the greater secondary coverts remain pale gray.

During the bird's fifth and subadult year, a condor gradually achieves full adult coloration, with head color gradually becoming full orange except for a saddle of very short black feathers in front of the eyes. The bill color changes from black to ivory, the underwing triangles change from mottled to pure white, and the bars on the tops of the wings change from light gray to pure white. Occasionally birds retain one or two mottled underwing feathers for a year or two after otherwise full adult coloration is achieved (especially obvious in one bird, SSM, studied from 1981 through 1984). Similarly, John Schmitt has documented one captive individual that delayed development of fully white upperwing bars until 7 years of age. Thus the speed of developmental color changes varies among individuals. The iris color of full adults is brownish red, but the iris is surrounded by bright red sclera. Adults also have conspicuous reddish air sacs in the throat and breast regions which, like the more orangish sacs in the cheeks, can be inflated with air during sexual and aggressive display.

Molt of flight feathers is exceedingly slow and irregular in pattern, with birds replacing only about half their flight feathers each year. Correspondingly, most flight feathers molt only once every two years (Snyder et al. 1987a). For the longer primary feathers (the finger-like feathers at the wingtips) a single feather takes about four months to complete growth and is normally over 600 mm (24 inches) long when fully grown. The shafts of these wing feathers are large and hollow, and were once used as containers for gold dust by early prospectors (Anthony 1893, Scott 1936a, Harris 1941, Bidwell 1966).

With wing feathers growing so slowly and feathers being shed throughout the spring and summer months, California Condors are in some degree of flight feather molt for about 9 months of the year, and normally have a complete set of full-grown flight feathers only during the winter months. These are also the months when foraging is most difficult because of short day lengths and frequent lengthy periods of bad weather. Molt may be timed to maximize flight capacities during this relatively stressful period.

Male California Condors are usually larger than females, with an average male weight (crop empty) of about 19.4 lbs (8.8 kg) compared with 17.9 lbs (8.1 kg) in females (weights taken by Don Sterner from 28 captives at the San Diego Wild Animal Park). These figures fall short of the average weight of 20 lbs given by Koford (1953) and Snyder (1988), no doubt because some of the weights available earlier were of birds with crops variously distended with food. In its male size superiority, the California Condor is similar to the Andean Condor, but differs from other smaller vulturids and essentially all falconiformes, in

Condor breeding habitats are diverse: **top left**, view to the north near the base of a giant sequoia in the Sierra Nevada in which a condor pair nested in 1984; **top right**, caves in the inner gorge of the Grand Canyon of Arizona where condors nested during the late Pleistocene; **below left**, the Hole-in-the-wall cliffs of the Sespe Condor Sanctuary where condors congregated for roosting, bathing and nesting during the 1930s and 1940s; and **below right**, the headwaters of the Agua Blanca drainage where the last nesting of wild condors occurred in 1986.

which females average larger than males. The significance of large females in most of the latter species remains one of the more controversial aspects of their biology (Snyder and Wiley 1976), with no consensus as to what functions it may serve, despite numerous hypotheses. With clear male size superiority, the two condor species follow the pattern found in most birds, although sexual size differences in condors are not great. Large Old World Vultures follow the usual accipitrid pattern of females larger than males.

Both condor species, like other vulturids, nest in sheltered caves or hollows, often on steep slopes or cliffs, although it seems likely that the California Condors that were resident in Florida during the Pleistocene may have nested mainly in protected sites in hollow trees or thickets because of the unrelievedly flat terrain of nearly the entire state. The Turkey and Black Vultures that currently breed in Florida characteristically nest in dense palmetto thickets, although they commonly use cliff sites elsewhere. Some of the Andean Condor nest sites found by Mike Wallace in coastal Peru, where it is relatively flat, have been little more than partially shaded crannies tucked against boulders on modest slopes. The very first credible description of a California Condor nest was a hollow, apparently at the base, of a tall oak tree in the Santa Lucia Range near Monterey (Taylor 1859a).

No evidence exists for wild California Condors breeding in less than adult plumage, so the presumed normal age of first breeding cannot be earlier than six years. Further, although captives have occasionally laid eggs at five years, the earliest confirmed breeding of a known-age wild condor was at six years (REC in 1986). Once pairs form, they have not been observed to break up over the years, except when one adult has died. Pair members typically, but not always, forage together throughout the year, except during the incubation and early nestling periods when they alternate reciprocally in foraging and nest-tending duties. Males have not been seen to feed their mates during the early stages of breeding, and adults share incubation and brooding duties more or less equally.

Both condor species invariably lay one-egg clutches and have long incubation periods, long nestling periods, and long periods of dependency of juveniles on adults after fledging. In the California Condor, with incubation running 53 to 60 days, a nestling period averaging about 5–6 months, and period of full fledgling dependency of about another 5–6 months, the total length of a nesting cycle is more than a year. The only cases in which we have observed egg laying in a year following a successful breeding have involved early fledging in the first year followed by late egg laying in the next year (SS1 pair in 1981–82, SB pair in 1982–83). Egg laying does not normally occur in a year following a relatively late fledging, and thus the highest rate of nestling production is two young in three years, if fledglings survive to independence.

Nestlings and fledglings solicit food by stiffly beating their partly open wings and are fed by both parents. Transfer of food takes place entirely by regurgitation, normally bill to bill. For about the first two weeks, newly hatched chicks are brooded nearly continuously when they are not being fed. During the next two weeks brooding becomes more intermittent and is finally abandoned during the day at about 1 month of age. After this point both parent birds are off on the foraging grounds pretty much full time during the midday hours, except when they return periodically, either singly or together, to feed their chick. Brooding at night continues irregularly for another week or two. During the latter stages of the

Early stage condor nestlings have naked heads but have bodies covered with down that changes from white to gray between about three and six weeks of age. *Top*, a chick about 9 days old photographed by Carl Koford in 1941; *middle*, the same nestling photographed by Koford at about 29 days of age; and *bottom*, a 55 day old chick photographed by William Finley and Herman Bohlman in 1906.

nestling period chicks receive an average of about 1.2 feedings per day.

When the structure of the nest site permits, a chick may begin to wander outside the entrance as early as 6 weeks old. Chicks are clumsy and suffer frequent slips and falls at first, but seem highly curious about their environment, testing objects with their bills, flapping their wings, leaping about, rapidly turning while jumping, capturing objects under one foot or in the beak and then whirling around and carrying them away, and so on. Long before fledging they commonly wander about on slopes many meters from the nest cave, but return to the nest cave from time to time and are usually fed at the nest entrance. At this stage they are relatively vulnerable to predators such as Golden Eagles. Possibly as an adaptation to help adults locate their wandering chicks, late stage nestlings have a band of white down on the upper surfaces of the wings, which flashes conspicuously when the nestlings beat their wings in begging for food.

Fledging (i.e., the first flight) often occurs when the adults are away from the nest area, and fledging birds often appear to have no idea where they are going, ending their first

Late stage condor nestlings are nearly uniformly dark grey in feather coloration. **Above**, a chick approximately 16 weeks old photographed in its nest by Carl Koford in 1940. In July 1983 we discovered a lead bullet in the substrate of this same nest. The nest was adjacent to and in full view of an oil-drilling pad.
Below, Cachuma near her nest in the Sespe Sanctuary at about 18 weeks of age in November 1983. Late stage chicks freely wander the slopes near their nest caves, but are easily found by their parents because of white patches of down on the tops of their wings that flash as they beat their wings.

flights only when they crash into hillsides or brush. Sometimes several more days may pass before they again reach an open enough spot on foot to allow another flight attempt.

Fledglings generally stay in the immediate vicinity of the nest cave for several months. The earliest instance we have witnessed of them following their parents out to the foraging grounds took place slightly less than four and a half months after fledging. Full dependency of fledglings on adults lasts for about 5–6 months, and sightings of adults feeding juveniles in the late spring and summer months suggest that fledglings may remain partially dependent for perhaps another half year.

General Lifestyle

A reliance on large vertebrate carcasses for food carries a number of important consequences for the biology of large vultures in general, and the California Condor in particular. Such consequences have been particularly well explored in a fine series of papers on griffon vultures by David Houston (1974a,c, 1975, 1976, 1978, 1979, 1980b, 1987, 1989, 1990). Large carcasses tend to be thinly and often erratically distributed, requiring very strong powers of flight and effective searching strategies among birds attempting to exploit them. In studies of a number of species (e.g., Meretsky's 1995 study of Egyptian Vultures) it has been clear that skills in finding and competing for food are strongly related to an individual's age. The relatively slow process of gaining such skills probably underlies the slow development of sexual maturity in these birds, as the chances of breeding successfully may be low until they have gained considerable experience. Mundy et al. (1992), for example, documented ages of first breeding ranging from 3 to >6 years in the various species of African vultures.

The California Condor, like the Andean Condor and large Old World Vultures, is well-endowed physically for long-distance commuting (see Spaar 1997), and exhibits patterns of foraging that allow it to maximize its chances of finding food. Condors, like other large vultures, appear to have superb eyesight, and in soaring high above the landscape can watch the activities of other scavengers, including other condors, to find food efficiently. Condors are not usually the first species to find a carcass, but arrive relatively soon afterwards, presumably attracted mainly by the behavior of Common Ravens (*Corvus corax*), Turkey Vultures, Golden Eagles (*Aquila chrysaetos*), and occasionally Bald Eagles (*Haliaeetus leucocephalus*) assembling at the carcass. Often the first species to arrive is the Turkey Vulture, aided by its keen sense of smell. However, foraging Turkey Vultures are rare in substantial parts of the recent condor foraging range, especially the southern San Joaquin Valley foothills, and here the first species to find a carcass is often the Common Raven.

Unavoidably, condors and other species assembling at carcasses of large vertebrates often find themselves in a bewildering social environment of competition and potential predation risks from their own and other scavenging species, including both mammals and other birds. The complexity of this social environment apparently puts a premium on learning abilities in the species involved. Unlike pure predators, scavengers rarely have a food item to themselves, and they have to know how to evaluate a great variety of factors in making adaptive decisions in direct confrontations with other scavengers so they don't wind up dead, wounded, or

Typical foraging habitats for California Condors are foothill grasslands or open oak-savannah regions that allow unobstructed access to carrion foods: **top,** the Tejón Ranch in the Tehachapi Mountains overlooking the San Joaquin Valley from the southeast; **middle**, the former San Emigdio Ranch, now the Wind Wolves Preserve, overlooking the San Joaquin Valley from the south; and **bottom**, the Santiago Ranch overlooking the San Joaquin Valley from the southwest.

starving. Some animal trainers in our acquaintance claim that scavenging birds are remarkably quick at learning new tasks and are among the most intelligent of avian species. By comparison, purely predatory birds, much as we admire their skills in capturing prey, often seem much less inspired in their capacities for dealing with novel or complex social situations.

In their daily foraging patterns, California Condors generally rise late and retire early, commonly not taking to the air before mid morning and often returning to roost by mid afternoon. This abbreviated daily schedule appears to be largely controlled by the winds, as condors have great difficulty staying aloft without uplift from general air-mass movements or local thermal activity. Air movements are characteristically strongest during the middle hours of the day and often die to nothing overnight.

Foraging is also sometimes completely forestalled by inclement weather, an important factor during frontal systems in the winter and early spring, especially during El Niño years. During the El Niño winter and spring of 1983, good foraging weather only developed every three or four days and generally did not last for more than a day or two. During the summer and fall months, in contrast, the monotonously clear southern California weather allows efficient foraging on nearly every day.

Even with good weather, condors commonly have only 5 or 6 hours to spend foraging each day, especially during the short days of winter. Depending on where they roost, two or more of these hours may be consumed simply in commuting between roosts and foraging grounds. This does not leave much time for actual foraging, and during many days the birds apparently fail to find or consume food.

Before launching into their first flights of the day, condors usually preen and sun on their roost perches, often snag-topped bigcone Douglas firs (*Pseudotsuga macrocarpa*) in the southern part of their recent range. In sunning, the birds extend their wings fully and either face the sun or directly away from it, so that the sun shines directly on either the upper or lower surfaces of their flight feathers. Similar sunning behavior is typical of a fairly wide variety of large soaring birds, including storks and large Old World vultures, although its purpose is not fully understood. Potential functions include the drying of flight feathers from dew and rain, warming of the birds' bodies and appendages, and reduction of feather deformations caused by flight (Grier 1973, Houston 1980a, Clark and Ohmart 1985). Of these, the drying function may be the most important.

In flight, condors normally flap only during take-off and landing, and are close to the size limit for sustained flapping flight (see Pennycuick 1969). However, we have seen them flap for long distances in aggressively chasing eagles away from their nesting terrritories. In normal foraging flight, they circle and cruise above the terrain like gliders, often singly or in loose groups with other condors. Their height above ground varies, and the birds are obviously attracted to groups of cattle and other livestock, possibly because they sometimes contain moribund individuals. This tendency to closely inspect livestock concentrations may also explain why condors often come in close to inspect human gatherings. Sadly, this same tendency makes the birds relatively vulnerable to shooting.

Under optimal wind conditions, condors can attain some formidable speeds as they glide along ridge lines or other topographic features. Radio-tagged condors have sometimes been tracked by airplane at ground speeds of 70–95 kph (40–60 mph), and during the 1980s

The CV pair of condors sunning near their nest in 1983. Sunning condors orient their outstretched wings perpendicular to the rays of the sun, but may face either toward or away from the sun.

it was possible for an individual to cover nearly the entire range of the species in a single day's flight when conditions were favorable (Meretsky and Snyder 1992). However, ground speeds of foraging birds are commonly much lower than this, often on the order of 50 kph (30 mph), as the birds are obliged to circle and gain altitude periodically in their forward progression (see Spaar 1997).

In an apparent effort to increase their efficiency in locating unpredictable food sources, condors practice a mixed strategy in patrolling their foraging grounds. They will congregate and feed intensively in certain parts of their range when local abundances of food develop, as for example when local cattle disease outbreaks occur, but they also continue to cruise over other parts of their range, very likely to track food abundance on a wider scale. Perhaps because of the general advantages in such wide-scale monitoring, programs to feed the historic wild condor population at "carcass restaurants" never resulted in the birds becoming exclusively dependent on provided food (Wilbur et al. 1974, Wilbur 1978a, Snyder and Snyder 1989). Similar results have been noted in studies of Egyptian Vultures under various provisioning regimes (Meretsky 1995, Meretsky and Mannan 1999).

One of the consequences of an erratic food supply is that condors, like other vultures, must sometimes take foods that are relatively decayed or go without food, though it is clear that vultures in general prefer relatively fresh meat when it is available (Finley 1910, Houston 1986). For most animals rotten meat is a very risky diet because it is sometimes contaminated with toxic chemicals excreted by bacteria, most notably *Clostridium botulinum*. Most animals that eat such food are vulnerable to botulism, a flaccid paralysis of the voluntary muscles commonly leading to death by cardiac or respiratory failure.

Outbreaks of botulism sometimes cause tremendous mortality in wild bird populations, but it is perhaps not surprising that vultures have developed a near immunity to this threat. Experiments by Kalmbach (1939) indicated that Turkey Vultures are about 100,000 times as resistant to botulism as pigeons, and the same sort of resistance seems likely in condors. Despite their abilities to handle this sort of toxicity, vultures now face toxic threats from a great variety of chemicals that are relatively new in the environment and for which they have had little time to develop effective defenses. As we shall see in the chapters ahead, the California Condor is highly vulnerable to the lead contamination now occurring frequently in its diet.

As a generality, cases of vultures feeding on the carcasses of other vultures (cannibalism) appear to be very rare, as discussed by Clinton-Eitniear and McGehee (1994). And although Black and Turkey Vultures commonly feed on road-killed vertebrates, these do not normally include members of their own species, even though road-killed vultures are seen on occasion. In brief and casual experiments in the 1970s, placing carcasses of road-killed Turkey Vultures next to other vertebrate carcasses at feeding stations in Florida, we noted that the dead vultures seemed to strongly inhibit use of the sites by other vultures. Potentially, vultures can recognize dead members of their own species at a carcass as a strong signal of high risks in feeding, and deliberately avoid such carcasses.

California Condors are far from obliged to eat every day. Their soaring flight is sufficiently energy efficient and their crop storage capacities are large enough that they can survive on considerably less frequent meals. In observations of condor nests we have seen incubating birds go as long as 10 days without feeding, and data on lead-poisoned birds suggest that it may take more than a month for a full-grown bird to starve to death when fully deprived of food (see Chapter 12). Nevertheless, it appears that condors must obtain a full meal at least every two to three days on average to maintain body weight, judging from food consumption rates of captives and their measured crop storage capacities.

The actual food consumption rates of large vultures appear to vary greatly, due in large part to the erratic nature of their food supply, and Houston (1976, 1978) has suggested that this variability may be one of the underlying causes for their low clutch sizes and slow growth rates of chicks. Almost all large vultures lay single-egg clutches and take more than 100 days for nestlings to reach fledging age (data in Mundy et al. 1992). In comparison, large eagles mostly have clutches of two and nestling periods of about 70 to 90 days (Cramp and Simmons 1980). Presumably, it is a better strategy for large vultures to be conservative in clutch size and chick growth rates than for them to overcommit in reproductive investments and frequently come up short.

Such a strategy may be especially adaptive with respect to certain nutrients that are in chronic short supply for large vultures, particularly calcium. Diet of these species is biased heavily toward flesh from large mammalian carcasses and does not include the substantial amounts of bone that are available to large raptors that normally kill much smaller vertebrates. The soft tissues of large carcasses are low in calcium, and the bones of large carcasses are mostly too big for the vultures to swallow. Bone is the primary dietary source of calcium for skeletal development of vulture chicks, and thus the large vultures often find themselves in difficulty obtaining enough calcium for reproduction. To solve this problem, they often seek out bone (or other calcium sources, e.g., mollusc shells) additional to what they normally find in carcasses.

Problems in obtaining enough calcium for breeding have been especially acute and dramatic with the Cape Griffon Vulture (*Gyps coprotheres*) of South Africa. Here, as Noel and John Ogden had an opportunity to witness in 1980, and as will be discussed in more detail in Chapter 5, chicks were often under such extreme stress from low calcium in their diet that they suffered bone breakage while still in their nests. Peter Mundy and John Ledger, who were working intensively on the problem, concluded that it stemmed largely from the extirpation of bone-crushing scavengers, particularly hyenas, over wide regions (Mundy and Ledger 1976, 1977). The bone fragments left at carcass sites by these mammalian scavengers were believed to be the main source of dietary calcium for the vultures. In their absence the birds were having great difficulties finding enough bone for successful breeding.

Evidently, the California Condor has never suffered calcium deficiencies to the extent of those documented for the Cape Griffon Vulture, but we found considerable evidence during the 1980s to suggest that it too had difficulty in obtaining enough calcium for chick development. For one thing, we routinely observed nestling condors sifting through the floors of their nests with their bills and swallowing any bone material and other light-colored objects (including chunks of excrement) that they found. For another, adult condors were sometimes seen picking over vertebrate skeletons devoid of any fleshy materials in an apparent search for small bones. One pair of condors we frequently watched foraging on foot along a lakeshore was obviously attracted to light colored objects, including plastic cups and pieces

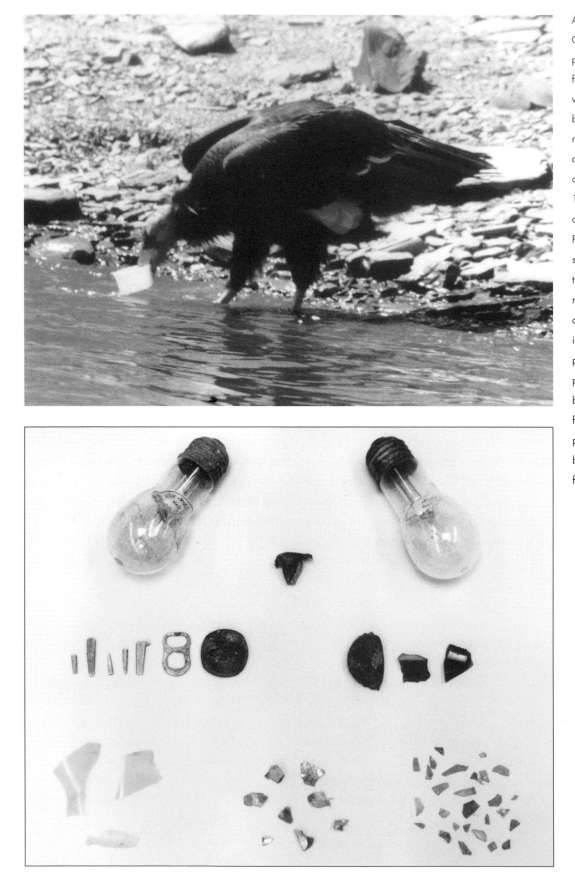

Artifact collection by California Condors presumably stems largely from the birds mistaking white or shiny objects for bone or shell material normally consumed as a dietary supplement. **Above**, one pair of condors of 1981–82 frequently "beach-combed" along the shores of Pyramid Lake and routinely sampled plastic objects with their bills. **Below**, man-made artifacts sifted from condor nests in the 1980s included small pieces of plastic, metal, and glass presumably brought in by the birds, as well as antique flashbulbs left by an early photographer and a lead bullet (between the flashbulbs).

of styrofoam. They repeatedly picked up such objects with their bills, then discarded them, possibly because of their soft textures. We also found instances of shiny pieces of metal, glass, and plastic in condor nest substrates, just as such objects were known from Cape Griffon Vulture nests. In both species the adults had probably mistaken these objects for bone and brought them in as part of the diet for their chicks. Clam and snail shells found in condor nests probably reflect similar efforts to obtain calcium.

Regardless, we recorded no cases of broken wings in nestling condors during the 1980s. One case was documented by Carl Koford in 1939 (Koford field notes), although it is possible this instance may have resulted all or in part from problems Koford experienced in chick handling, rather than from calcium deficiency.

Overall, we think it likely that the difficulties in obtaining calcium have been an important contributing cause to the very slow growth rates of condor chicks and the invariable clutch size of one egg for the species, as hypothesized by Houston (1978) for large griffon vultures in general. As we shall see in Chapter 10, the length of the nestling period, at 5–6 months, runs about a month longer in the California Condor than in the Cape Griffon Vulture, even though the two species are almost identical in size and weight and have identical incubation periods. Could the slower development of condor nestlings reflect even greater calcium supply problems for condors than for Cape Griffons during the evolutionary history of these species?

The very low reproductive rates and slow progress to maturity characteristic of the California Condor and other large vultures mean that all these species must maintain low mortality rates to persist. As a rule of thumb, such species cannot tolerate losses greater than about 10% annually (Houston 1974b). The large vultures all have potentially long lifespans, in some cases comparable to our own, but they cannot compensate for excess mortality by increasing their reproductive rates. Thus excessive mortality due to poisoning, shooting, and collisions with powerlines poses special difficulties for these birds, and their conservation can be assured only by minimizing such pressures.

California Condors in Prehistoric, Historic, and Modern Human Cultures

The California Condor had tremendous symbolic importance to early native American societies within its historic range. Likewise, the Andean Condor was a powerful cultural icon for indigenous peoples of western South America. This historic, and evidently prehistoric, reverence for condors should come as no surprise, as it surely stems from the same roots as our contemporary fascination with these two species. In their mastery of the skies, condors outstrip all of their fellow flying creatures. Their immense size and grandeur in flight inspire our imagination and dreams. Who amongst us has not yearned for condorlike abilities to sail through the air, silently surveying the forests and plains, moving long distances without a wingbeat, and landing at will on precipitous crags? Our own earthbound capacities are so meager by comparison, we cannot escape awestruck admiration and envy in encountering these species.

However, if any native American civilizations were ever contemporaneous with now-extinct juggernauts such as *Teratornis merriami* (with an estimated wingspan of 12 feet) and conceivably *Teratornis incredibilis* or *Argentavis magnificens* (with estimated wingspans of 18 and 23 feet, respectively), these much larger species would likely have enjoyed an even more revered status. Kroeber (1925) and Harris (1941) described and discussed ritual garments of northern California tribes that featured condor feathers spliced together to create artificial feathers of even greater size. This practice might plausibly have developed as an aftermath of the extinction of species larger than condors from the region.

The human species is generally believed to have arrived in the New World near the very end of the Pleistocene (roughly 12,000–12,500 years ago). Thus early North Americans almost surely interacted with *Teratornis merriami* (Howard and Miller 1939) Whether there might also have been human contact with living *Argentavis magnificens* or *Teratornis incredibilis* is much less clear. Too few fossils have been found of these latter species to allow any confident judgement as to how long they persisted toward the present. Had people been resident in the Western Hemisphere while they still existed, these birds would doubtless have been featured in the legends and artwork of numerous societies.

The enduring religious and cultural importance of California Condors to native civilizations is reflected in condor remains in middens, representations of condors in cave art, and traditional ceremonies utilizing the condor as focal elements. Much of the evidence for these connections has been summarized by Simons (1983) and Bates et al. (1993). Here we touch mainly on highlights from these reviews and on evidence for more recent symbolic and practical importance of the condor in human cultures.

Condor Names through the Ages

Native American peoples knew the California Condor by many different names. Wilbur (1983) lists some of these, *sul, wech, niniyot, mo'lok, moloku*. Others include *holhol, panes, almiyi,* and *huyawit* (Hudson and Underhay 1978). Dozens of additional names are given by Merriam (1979). Some of these have been used in recent years to christen individual California Condors hatched in captivity.

Many of the early Spanish-origin inhabitants of California called the condor *huitre* or *wietro*, evidently derived from the Spanish name for vulture, *buitre*, and this name was still in use by old-timers at Fort Tejón at the turn of the century (Grinnell 1905, Smith and Easton 1964). Koford (1953) still found vaqueros of Baja California using the name *buitre* in 1949.

Among Northern-European settlers, the California Condor was not known as such through much of the 19th century. Instead the species was usually called the Vulture, the California Vulture, or the Royal Vulture in early historical accounts. The shift to the name condor occurred in the 1850s, largely thanks to articles on the species published by A.S. Taylor, whose usage was an extension from the common name of the South American Andean Condor. The name condor appears to have come from *cuntur* or *kuntur*, a Quechua name for the South American bird. California Condor is surely a major esthetic improvement over California Vulture, and it is easy to appreciate why it became the preferred name (rather more rapidly for the public than for worthies of the American Ornithologists' Union, however). One wonders if the name California Vulture had endured to the present whether quite the same degree of mysticism and reverence for the bird, not to mention controversy over its conservation, might have developed in our own culture.

The name California itself may have had an origin in condor lore. White (1940) suggested that California could have originated, via *Californe*, in the ancient Persian name *Kari-farn*, a mythical mountain of paradise inhabited by amazons and griffins (the latter being creatures that were half eagle and half lion). In support of this possibility, White reproduced a passage from Garci Rodriguez de Montalvo's popular romance "Las Sergas de Esplandian" published about 1510, before the real California received its name:

> "Know, that on the right hand of the Indies there was an island called California,
> very close to Earthly Paradise, which was peopled with black women, without any

man among them, who lived almost in the manner of the Amazons ... In this island called California, because of the great ruggedness of the country and the innumerable wild beasts that lived in it, there were many griffins, such as were found in no other part of the world."

White argued that early Spanish explorers encountering condors in Baja California could well have been reminded of such tales of the land of griffins, and since Baja California was early thought to be an island, the name Califerne or California might have been readily adopted. Indeed, California is clearly illustrated as an island on many of the first maps of the New World (e.g., the maps of Henricus Hondius in 1630, and Pieter Goos 1666). Maps portraying California as an island were frequent until the middle of the 18th century in spite of the fact that reasonably correct depictions were also present as early as the late 16th century (e.g., the map of Abraham Ortelius of 1570).

Ritual Sacrifice and other Ceremonies

Among native American tribes, the most famous condor ceremonies involved ritual sacrifice. Sacrificial ceremonies were known throughout much of the West Coast range of the California Condor, and were also practiced within the range of the Andean Condor in western South America. Only verbal records exist for the ceremonies in California, but striking photographs of one such ceremony in Peru were obtained by Jerry and Libby McGahan in early 1970. Jerry McGahan's (1971) written account provides an instructive overview:

"A bizarre Peruvian event takes the lives of ten to fifteen condors a year in public executions held each February. Near the end of our fieldwork, Libby and I drove north into the mountains to the Callejón de Huaylas region to view these rites.

We had to hike seven miles to reach the village of Cashapampa, where an *arranque del cóndor* – 'pulling of the condor' – was to occur. We arrived a bit early, and met an American missionary who talked with us about the fiesta.

'The condor is trapped on the puna [tableland]' he said. 'Men waiting in a covered pit reach through a fist-size opening to grab the leg of any condor attracted to the bait. Comrades then rush up to complete the capture.'

While we talked, men finished an arch of poles. They tied fruits, presents and bottles of chicha to one end of a rope that ran through a pulley at the top of the arch. Later the condor would be suspended alive from the same rope, and blows rained on him....

A long file of horsemen had entered the arena, preceded by a band playing quenas and drums. Now the mounted villagers began to gallop through the arch, grabbing at the objects tied to the rope. An individual on foot jerked at the rope's opposite end, trying to snatch the prizes out of reach at the last moment. Shouts from the crowd greeted any successful grab.

'Here comes the condor!' Libby cried. Two men rode into the arena, each holding the condor by a wing. They tied his feet to the end of the rope where the objects had been. Then they released the bird. He tried to flap skyward.

Riders began circling through the arch again, this time flailing at the great bird with their fists. At first the condor's flapping, and tugs on the rope, kept all but a few from striking him. But as he became exhausted and the pace of circling increased, more and more blows fell true. Clouds of dust hid the mounting frenzy as rider after rider pummeled the spinning mass of feathers until the condor was dead.

A knot of horseman gathered beneath the arch. One of them pressed his mouth to the condor's gaping beak. With his teeth he ripped out the condor's tongue. Next year this man would have the honor of dispatching the team to catch another condor."

Andean Condors figure prominently in the culture of native Peruvians. **Above**, a flute or quena made from a wing bone of a condor. **Below**, an Andean Condor escorted into arena for sacrifice ceremony in 1970.

Andean Condor pummeled to its death in annual sacrifice ceremony witnessed by Jerry and Libby McGahan in Cashapampa, Peru in 1970.

The grisly ritual witnessed by the McGahans may well have represented a blending of ancient Inca and early Spanish traditions, but as Jerry McGahan noted, the ceremony's precise origin, evolution, and meaning had by then been erased by time. Perhaps the underlying significance of this and other condor sacrifices may have resided in some sort of perceived transfer of power from the bird sacrificed to those engaged in the ritual, symbolized by their taking of its life with their bare hands.

In California, similar traditions often involved condors taken as nestlings, rather than as free-flying birds. Prior to sacrifice, these birds were raised to fledging age in captivity. Often the ritual sacrifices were mourning ceremonies commemorating the death of revered leaders. One such was the renowned Panes festival of the Luisenos of the San Diego region. The Panes celebration was an annual event and took place in many separate villages. Harris (1941) offered a translation of an early 19th century account of this ceremony by Friar Geronimo Boscana of the Mission San Juan Capistrano:

"The most celebrated of all their feasts, and which was observed yearly, was the one they called the 'Panes,' signifying a bird feast. Particular adoration was observed by them for a bird resembling much in appearance the common buzzard, or vulture, but of larger dimensions [quite clearly a condor]. The day selected for the feast was made known to the public on the evening previous to its celebration, and preparations were made immediately for the erection of their Vanquech, into which, when completed, and on the opening of the festival, they carried the Panes in solemn procession, and placed it upon the altar erected for the purpose. Then, immediately, all the young, married and unmarried females, commenced running to and fro, with great rapidity; some in one direction and some in another, more like distracted than rational beings; continuing thus racing, as it were, whilst the elder class of both sexes remained silent spectators to the scene. The 'Puplem' painted as has been heretofore described, looked like so many devils, in the meantime dancing around their adored 'Panes.'

These ceremonies being concluded, they seized upon the bird, and carried him in procession to the principal Vanquech, or temple, all the assembly uniting in the grand display – the Puplem preceding the same, dancing and singing. Arriving there, they killed the bird without losing a particle of its blood. The skin was removed entire, as a relic, or for the purpose of making their festival garment, 'Paelt.' The carcass they interred within the temple in a hole prepared previously, around which all the old women stood collected, who, while weeping and moaning most bitterly, kept throwing upon it various kinds of seeds, or particles of food, and exclaiming at the same time 'Why did you run away? Would you not have been better with us? You would have made pinole as we do.' Other expressions equal in simplicity were made use of, and as the ceremony was concluding, the dancing commenced again, and continued for three days and nights, accompanied with all the brutalities to which they are subject.

The Indians state that said 'Panes' was once a female who ran off and retired to the mountains, when accidentally meeting with 'CHINIGCHINICH,' he changed her into a bird, and the belief is, that notwithstanding they sacrificed it every year, she became again animated, and returned to her home among the mountains. But the ridiculous fable does not end here; for they believed, as often as the bird was killed, it became multiplied; because every year all the Capitanes celebrated the same feast of Panes, and were firm in the opinion that the birds sacrificed were but one and the same female. They had no evidence, however, of where she lived, or where she originated, and neither were the names of her parents known. The commemoration of the festival was in compliance with the commands given by Chinigchinich."

The killing of the Panes without shedding a drop of blood was evidently achieved by suffocation or pressure on the heart and lungs. Each tribe obtained its sacrificial condors from nests considered to be tribal property. The sacrificial cycle began with the close observation of the nests to determine their stages of activity. When the young condors neared fledging, one was removed from its nest with appropriate ceremony. The bird was then brought back to the village where it would later be sacrificed and was raised with great care by the village chief. When the bird was fully grown, the chief scheduled the sacrificial ceremony.

Similar ceremonies were also well known for tribes farther north in California, such as the Miwok, and were apparently also practiced by the Chumash in the heart of the most recent range of the condor, although documentation is less conclusive for this region (Hudson and Underhay 1978). Many of the ceremonies in California used Golden Eagles instead of condors, perhaps in part when condors were unavailable. Choice of the species to be sacrificed on particular occasions was apparently also influenced by which celestial body was prominent at the time of the ceremony. Eagles seem to have been selected for rituals concerned with the Evening Star (Venus), whereas the condor was apparently associated with the planet Mars.

Not all condors taken for ceremonial purposes were captured as nestlings. Some, such as those killed for condor impersonation ceremonies by the Pomo, were trapped as older birds using meat baits, sharpened bone "hooks", and line (Loeb 1926). Others were killed with bows and arrows (Gifford 1926). Pit-trapping, as described by McGahan (1971) and Schaeffer (1951) appears to have been a common capture method for large birds of prey in North America as well as South America, and may also have been commonly used for California Condors. The techniques employed and the impacts on different age segments of wild California Condor populations evidently varied substantially, depending on tribal traditions.

Ritual killing of sacred animals was not a practice limited to the New World. Frazier (1935) pointed out parallels in the ritual killing of sacred rams in ancient Egypt and sacred serpents in West Africa. Thebans and other Egyptians who worshipped the god Ammon held an annual ceremony in which they killed a ram, skinned it and clothed the image of their god in the skin. They then mourned over the ram and buried it in a sacred tomb. The close similarity of this ceremony to the Panes ritual, and the general prevalence of sacrificial ceremonies in ancient cultures worldwide, lead one to suspect that the origins of the condor-sacrifice ceremonies are far older than the arrival of the first humans in the New World.

California Condors were also important to early tribes in a variety of rituals that did not

California Condors in cultures of native North Americans: ***top***, condor-feather (left) and eagle-feather (right) capes on mannikans of native Californians in the Peter the Great Museum of Anthropology and Ethnography, St. Petersburg, Russia; ***bottom left***, 4 cm high stone figurine, apparently based on a California Condor, in the Paquimé Museum, Casas Grandes, Chihuahua, Mexico; and ***bottom right***, Fred Magee, native Luiseno, holding a condor feather skirt some time before 1942.

specifically feature sacrifice. Live condors employed in some celebrations were not killed, but were freed at the end (Simons 1983). Similarly, McGahan (1971) reported that live Andean Condors were often set free after Peruvian ceremonies that pitted the condors against bulls in ritual combat. Many ceremonies involved dancers dressed in condor skins or condor feather bands. Shamans of Central Miwok tribes acquired their powers from condors, allowing them to suck supernatural poisons from their patients' bodies (Freeland and Broadbent 1960). In an obsidian initiation ceremony practiced in Humboldt County, condor feathers were pushed down the throats of young participants until only the ends of the quills projected from their mouths (Kroeber 1925). Among the Yokuts, the wings of condors were believed responsible for both solar and lunar eclipses, and some Yokut communities believed that the moon was actually eaten by a condor (Hudson and Underhay 1978).

One of the more curious beliefs concerning condors and other vultures was that "vulture stones" found in their nests had magical powers (Hudson and Blackburn 1986). By means of these stones it was possible to find "hidden things and things pretty far away, but not too far away." Vultures and condors were considered to be expert at finding lost objects. Among the Western Mono and Yokuts tribes, "money finders" wore full-length cloaks of condor feathers that reputedly enabled them to find lost valuables (Driver 1937).

Among the Chumash, condor feathers were used to make ceremonial poles which were mounted in piles of small stones in conspicuous locations, often in connection with the winter solstice (Hudson and Blackburn 1986). Condor feathers were also found in an arrow-making kit discovered in a cave in Castro Canyon of Santa Barbara County (Hudson and Blackburn 1982).

These practices, and many others (especially well documented in Kroeber 1925), clearly reflected a fundamentally sacred and magical, as well as utilitarian, significance of the California Condor to virtually all indigenous peoples sharing its range.

Condor Remains in West Coast Archeological Sites

Simons (1983) discussed the occurrence of California Condor remains associated with human artifacts in 13 archeological sites in California and Oregon. These sites ranged in age from approximately 10,000 years ago until early historic times, and the numbers of condors per site ranged from single individuals to as many as 63 at the Five Mile Rapids site in Oregon. In some cases the condors had evidently been deliberately buried by humans, perhaps as in the Panes ceremony described earlier.

California Condor artifacts found at several of the sites included whistles fashioned from long bones of the wing, sometimes incised with various geometric designs. A similar whistle (quena) made from an Andean Condor wing bone is illustrated by McGahan (1971). Wands made from condor humeri and partially covered with natural asphalt and shell beads have also been found. Other California Condor artifacts from archeological sites include decorative feather bands made from condor flight feathers laced together with plant fibers.

Rock Art

Above the entrance to Condor Cave in Santa Barbara County is a marvelous pictograph of a condor apparently taking off into flight. It is about 60 cm wide and is executed mostly in white, although the head is red. Located along the southern escarpment of the Hurricane Deck, Condor Cave was evidently once a winter solstice observatory of the Chumash (see Smith and Easton 1964, Hudson and Underhay 1978), but now stands silent and empty. Our single visit to the site was during a winter evening just after the solstice and left us with a powerful sadness as to the passage of time. Although condors were well known along Hurricane Deck earlier in the century, it had been many years since they were regularly seen in the vicinity. The Chumash of the region were also gone, although a few of their descendants still survived, mostly absorbed into nearby modern communities. Now, mere vestiges of their former dominant presences, both condors and Chumash had been all but swept away by the tumultuous changes of the past two centuries. We had been born too late to witness their age of glory.

Chumash pictograph of a California Condor at the entrance to Condor Cave, a winter solstice observatory in Santa Barbara County.

Condor-like pictographs have also been found in many other cave sites in the recent range of the species, although in most cases it is difficult to be sure if the stylized representations are truly of condors rather than of other raptor species or of humans dressed in feather regalia. A variety of these pictographs are reproduced in Grant (1965) and Hudson and Underhay (1978). The area around one of the pictograph caves along Alder Creek in Ventura County was still frequented by condors when we visited it in June of 1982. In fact, an immature condor sailed low over our heads when we approached the site, and on a steep slope overlooking the cave only a few hundred meters distant we discovered a condor nest cave that had probably been active not long before. Fred Sibley had also noted condors active in the area in early 1967, including a recently fledged youngster, but he was unable to locate the nest site from which the youngster had fledged. We strongly suspect that the site we found was this nest.

Controversy over Condor Cultural Associations in the Inland West

Claude Schaeffer (1951) detailed ethnographic evidence among the Blackfoots and nearby tribes in northwest Montana and southwest Alberta for bygone ritual practices with condors similar to those once practiced by the tribes of California. His interviews with a variety of colorful individuals, including Yellow Kidney, George Bull Child, Louis Bear Child, Rides at the Door, Chewing Black Bones, and Dog Takes a Gun, revealed practices of ritual sacrifice and fabrication of feather and bone whistle artifacts, and suggested a high regard for the species as a sacred bird invested with the power of the sun.

Is there any evidence for similar rituals among the native American societies farther south in the Inland West? Simons (1983) listed a variety of cave sites from Arizona, Nevada, New Mexico, and Texas that contain both condor remains and human artifacts from the late Pleistocene and more recently, and it has commonly been assumed that these cave deposits might indicate simultaneous presence of humans and condors in these regions (e.g., Kiff 1983). However, Simons argued that the condor remains in these caves were likely introduced by natural nonhuman processes, since the human artifacts and condor remains were not closely associated and none of the condor remains had been used to make artifacts. Emslie (1987, 1990) reinforced this view with carbon dating data indicating, at least in a number of cases, that the condor materials were substantially older than the human artifacts, with none of the former being more recent than about 9,500 years ago. Emslie (1987), McCusick (1976), Strand (1998), and others also record a complete absence of condor remains from relatively recent archeological deposits studied in the inland Southwest.

Thus, there has been considerable recent doubt that condors may have persisted long enough in the inland Southwest to have interacted directly with humans. However, the historical sightings of the species from western Arizona and Utah summarized in the preceding chapter provide some counter evidence. A couple of additional examples below also suggest the possibility of early human–condor connections in this region, but the evidence overall is much less convincing than for the West Coast and Blackfoot regions and suggests that condors were either much rarer or disappeared much earlier in most parts of the inland Southwest.

At about the time of the winter solstice, but also scheduled for the appearance of the full moon, the Zunis of northwestern New Mexico celebrate an annual Shalako ceremony. This joyous occasion, also practiced in modified form by some Hopis (Fewkes 1893–1894, Hough 1917), involves the entire community and features all-night dances by bizarre "mudheads" and other symbolic figures. The ceremony is open to the public and serves to bless all new buildings constructed during the year, although more basically it honors the sun at the birth of a new year. The central figures, who visit the new houses, are six Shalakos – four of them representing the cardinal compass directions, one representing the zenith overhead and one the nadir below.

When we travelled north to watch the ceremony in late 1988, we were surprised to discover that the Shalakos were almost identical effigies of a giant bird, standing perhaps 10 feet (3 m) tall and operated by Zunis concealed within. Largely clad in white garments and reminiscent of giant snowmen, the Shalakos had long wooden beaks that could be clapped loudly together by the operators within. They also had conspicuous dark neck-feather ruffs and crowning fans of Golden Eagle feathers, and were adorned with the feathers of Scarlet Macaws (*Ara macao*) and the skins of foxes and wild cats. Curiously, the Shalakos also possessed horns, possibly of bison or cattle, projecting from the sides of their heads, suggesting some sort of hybrid bird-mammal concept.

What were the Shalakos originally? Could they have been patterned in part on the California Condor, or perhaps even a giant teratorn? Their huge size, bird-like bills, and conspicuous black feather neck ruffs suggested some relationship to condors, but there were obviously many features from other sources as well. The overall white coloration of the effigies was a striking antithesis of the condor, but could this have been the color of one of the giant teratorns? No one we asked seemed to know the origins of the figures, and our subsequent examination of published accounts of the Shalako ceremony was not much more illuminating (e.g., Fewkes 1893–94, Bartlett 1905, Hough 1917, Bunzel 1932, Coze 1954, Gonzales 1966). These accounts were focused on descriptions of historical practices and bypassed the more difficult question of the origins of effigy features. Nevertheless, they did strongly suggest that such effigies and ceremonies tended to evolve over time, progressively obscuring their roots.

Despite the murky haze of the centuries, it is worth noting that one of the Shalakos, the one associated with the zenith, was known as Knife-wing or Kwatako, a giant eagle of somewhat indeterminate properties. It seems possible that Kwatako might bear some ancient relationship to the condor. The other Shalakos were associated with various contemporary mammals – bear, wolf, mountain lion, badger, and mole. And although no condor remains are known from Zuni or Hopi archeological deposits or other archeological deposits of the Southwest dating back to about 1,000 A.D. (e.g., Emslie 1987, Strand 1998, McCusick 1976), this does not preclude the persistence of legends from earlier times when ancestral peoples may have interacted directly with condors or teratorns, either in their present, or in earlier homelands. Thus, although the overall ethnographic and archeological evidence from the Hopis and Zunis gives no clear evidence for any recent condor associations, more distant relationships remain a possibility.

The Paquimé ruins in northwestern Chihuahua, Mexico – not far south of the New Mexico border – also lie outside the range in which early coexistence of condors and humans is well documented. Lying east of the Sierra Madre Occidental in the high temperate valley of the Rio Casas Grandes, these ruins represent an impressive monument to a civilization that reached its peak between 1250 and 1450 A.D. and that suddenly came to an end, perhaps at the hands of unknown invaders, disease, or some other catastrophe. At its height, the Paquimé society was technologically and culturally advanced, with a sophisticated system of aquaducts, exquisite pottery featuring wildlife motifs, and huge adobe buildings whose ruins can still be seen today.

Of great interest is the part of the ruins in which Scarlet Macaws were held in batteries of earthen cages. These birds were sacrificed in ritual ceremonies, and their feathers were traded throughout the Southwest (Di Peso 1974). As wild populations of Scarlet Macaws have never been found closer than about 800 miles (1300 km) from Paquimé, and are limited to tropical habitats, the macaws of Paquimé were presumably acquired from civilizations much farther south. The Scarlet Macaw is nevertheless a common decorative motif in the pottery of Paquimé, providing a good illustration of the caution with which such artifacts should be viewed as evidence for local occurrence of particular species in the wild.

In early 1998 we visited the Paquimé ruins with a particular interest in seeing the wildlife artifacts of the ruins and learning whether there was evidence that the inhabitants might have bred the Scarlet Macaws in captivity, as opposed to just housing them as a continuing source of feathers. On visiting the museum at the ruins, however, our attention was quickly diverted from macaws to another species. Among the excavated artifacts on display was a tiny black stone figurine that bore a striking resemblance to a California Condor. Was it in fact a California Condor? And if so, was it an indigenous artifact or something that had originated elsewhere?

From published records (Di Peso et al. 1974), we learned that the figurine came from the middle Paquimé period and was made of dacite, an indigenous material. However, Di Peso and his team identified the figurine as a macaw, perhaps in large part because of the many other art objects from the ruins that clearly represented macaws. But unlike a macaw, this figurine had a bill that extended forward from the head and a relatively short distance out from the bird's "face." The huge downward-projecting bill shape of a macaw was clearly absent, although it was accurately rendered in other macaw artifacts from the ruins, especially painted representations on pottery. The bill of the figurine appeared undamaged, suggesting that it was deliberately fashioned as it now appears and was not condorlike in shape just because of past breakage. If it was not actually based on a California Condor, why would this particular "macaw" figurine have been carved so like a California Condor, a condor with its cheeks inflated in typical display posture (see photo on page 16 for comparison). We know of no bird species other than the California Condor that might have provided a reasonable model for the figurine.

Nevertheless, the true identity of the figurine may be irresolvable, and we must admit that, despite its close resemblance to a California Condor, it is possible the effigy might be a relatively poor representation of a macaw. No other "condor" artifacts or remains are known from the Paquimé ruins or, for that matter, from other prehistoric sites in the whole region, so many may continue to favor the macaw interpretation. However, for us the resemblance to a condor remains striking and beyond mere accident. If so, the existence of the figurine could be an indication that condors were still to be found in the local region some 600–700 years ago. Alternatively, condors or their effigies could have been occasional items of trade in the region and have originated elsewhere, much like the macaws.

Aside from possible condor origins for the Zuni Shalakos and the Paquimé figurine we have found no other evidence of interactions of native tribes of the inland Southwest with condors, although there are many traditions celebrating vaguely described "thunderbirds" or "rocs" among native civilizations throughout the West (see Schaeffer 1951, Wilbur 1983). The evidence for specific condor–human relationships in the Southwest is thus much more equivocal than the evidence in West Coast localities and in the range of the Blackfoots farther north. However, available evidence does not rule out a remnant presence of condors in the inland Southwest during recent millennia. Observers who demand tangible specimens and numerous historical accounts or ethnographic references before allowing the possibility of such persistence perhaps expect too much of the stability of human traditions, the completeness of archeological deposits, and the literary propensities of early settlers. The absence of unambiguous paleontological or archeological evidence does not prove the absence of the species for periods and regions where it may have been relatively rare.

Impacts of Ritual Sacrifice and Other Early Cultural Practices on Condor Populations

How important the early condor-killing ceremonies may have been in depressing condor populations has been discussed by Simons (1983), who presented an optimistic view that the effects were probably minimal and that condor populations probably remained stable despite these practices. He argued that the numbers of condors taken for ceremonial purposes were relatively few and that native tribes might simultaneously have been benefitting condor populations by inadvertently providing them with supplemental food. Indeed, Timbrook et al. (1982) described regular vegetation-burning practices of the Chumash and other tribes that could have provided carcasses for condors. However, if prehistoric condor populations were not food-limited in the first place, these food benefits may have been of little significance in redressing the apparently relentless depredations on nestlings and older birds.

In contrast to Simons, McMillan (1968) argued that the impacts of early tribes on condors were likely substantial and that millennia of ceremonial sacrifices were an important factor leading to the extreme wariness of nesting condors. Although we do not agree that nesting condors are as wary as McMillan claimed, we do agree with his general view that the ceremonial practices may have had major impacts. Certainly the archeological and ethnographical evidence suggests that the ceremonial killing of condors was routine in numerous tribes. The account of Friar Boscana, for example, indicated the potential annual sacrifice of a condor in each native American village in the San Diego region.

Nevertheless, attempting any quantitative estimate of the total annual ceremonial take of condors in pre-European times is surely a questionable enterprise in view of the extremely fragmentary nature of the historical data available. Having said this, we still feel it is of value to make some rough calculations of what may be an upper limit of impacts, based on density of villages and a surely invalid assumption that all villages might have had an annual condor sacrifice ceremony. Hudson and Underhay (1978) suggested roughly 100 square miles (260 square km) per village for the Chumash region. If one assumes some generality to this figure and divides it into the rough known shared territory of condors and native Americans in California, just from San Francisco south to the Mexican border, one arrives at a potential annual take on the order of 700 condors. Although this is no doubt an unrealistically high estimate for a variety of reasons – especially because the ceremonies often involved eagles rather than condors and were known to be less frequent than annual in many regions – it nevertheless is a staggeringly high number that still remains impressively high even if divided by 10.

Consequently, even though some early historical accounts suggested substantial numbers of condors, we believe it is an open question how much larger these populations might have been in the absence of the ceremonial sacrifices and far from certain that condor populations were stable under such practices. The frequent taking of nestlings may have had less impact on condor populations than the taking of adults, but both sorts of predation were practiced. Even if limited to nestlings, regular and widespread sacrifices could have had a major effect in view of the low reproductive rate of the species.

The fragmentary history of the extirpation of a race of the King Vulture that once occurred in Florida, Louisiana and possibly other southeastern states provides further insight into the damage that may have resulted from the ceremonial practices. This vulture was described in vivid and meticulous detail in a fascinating account by William Bartram during his travels in Florida in 1775, and also by Du Pratz (1758) in his *Histoire de la Louisiane*, but was never again seen or recorded by naturalists. Bartram (1791) called this bird the Painted Vulture (*Vultur sacra*) and offered some additional information that suggests a plausible cause for its disappearance:

> "The Creeks or Muscogulges construct their royal standard of the tail feathers of this bird, which is called by a name signifying the eagle's tail: this they carry with them when they go to battle, but then it is painted with a zone of red within the brown tips; and in peaceable negotiations it is displayed new, clean, and white: this standard is held most sacred by them on all occasions, and is constructed and ornamented with great ingenuity. These birds seldom appear but when the deserts are set on fire (which happens almost every day throughout the year, in some part or other, by the Indians, for the purpose of rousing the game, as also by the lightening): when they are seen at a distance soaring on the wing, gathering from every quarter,

and gradually approaching the burnt plains, where they alight upon the ground yet smoking with hot embers: they gather up the roasted serpents, frogs, and lizards, filling their sacks [crops] with them: at this time a person may shoot them at pleasure, they not willing to quit the feast, and indeed seeming to brave all danger."

Du Pratz' (1758) description similarly emphasized the ornamental uses made of feathers of the King Vulture: "As it is rather rare, it is prized among the natives, who pay a high price for the wing quills as an adornment of the 'peace-pipe'."

Frequent torching of the landscape by the tribes of Florida may well have increased food supplies for King Vultures, much as vegetation burning may have provided food for condors in California. Burning the plains continues today for the annual sugarcane harvest in southcentral Florida and provides a bounteous supply of carrion for Turkey and Black Vultures (Snyder and Snyder 1991). Nevertheless, the use of King Vulture feathers for ornamental purposes could have provided the incentive for an unsustainable slaughter of the wild population, especially in view of Bartram's description of how easy the birds were to kill when they were gorging themselves on serpents. In any event, the food benefits provided by burning practices were evidently inadequate compensation for other detrimental influences, and the King Vulture soon disappeared completely from the region. What detrimental influences the species may have faced other than feather harvest are completely speculative. However, we know of no reason to rule out the possibility that it was the feather harvest alone that led to the species' demise.

The emerging viewpoint of paleontologists is not that early human societies were prudent in exploitation of wildlife resources, but that even without advanced technology they frequently drove vulnerable species to extinction (Martin 1967, Olson and James 1982, Diamond 1993, Steadman 1995). And although there are no rigorous data as to the effects of various ritual practices on condor populations, we believe that early use of condors for ritual purposes may have substantially depressed local condor populations, leading to continuous overall population declines long before the arrival of Europeans. Prior to such persecution, condors may once have been far more abundant than indicated by any of the historical records. Further, it seems possible that the declines in condor abundance indicated in the most recent Rancho La Brea deposits (Howard and Miller 1939) may conceivably have been caused mainly or in part by human activities. Could the decline and fall of *Teratornis merriami* and still other large raptors and vultures of La Brea have had a similar cause?

The Quill Trade Among Early Gold Prospectors

Another human activity that may have significantly reduced local California Condor populations during the 19th and early 20th centuries was the shooting of condors by early prospectors to obtain feather quills for gold-dust containers. The most famous account of this practice is that of Anthony (1893), who wrote,

"Every Indian and Mexican gold miner is provided with from one to six of the primary quills of this species for carrying gold dust, the open end being corked with a plug of soft wood and the primitive purse hung from the neck by a buckskin string. All of the dead birds that I saw in Lower California had been killed for their quills alone."

Another visitor to Lower California (Baja California) who gave testimony to this practice was Carroll Dewilton Scott (1936a), who wrote,

"Around our camp-fire the first night sat two persons who had killed three condors in four years. Phil Melling, aged thirteen, shot a young bird in 1932, in a pine tree twenty feet from him with a .22 rifle. The reason given was that the bird looked neither like a buzzard nor a condor and Phil wanted to have a close-up.... The other person was one Antonio, a cattleman of the mountain, who shot a condor in 1933 and another in 1932. He said the birds spread disease among the cattle, but he sold all the quills to prospectors. Multiply Antonio and Phil by two or three and the years by two or three and we have a good clue to the condor situation on the San Pedro Martir... Some of our informants told us it was a poor year to see condors because, on account of the excellent season, there were no dead animals.... Our conclusion was that every year was a bad year for condors in the Sierra San Pedro Martir."

Thus, the practice of shooting condors for their quills continued for a least a number of decades in the Sierra San Pedro Martir and could plausibly have been a major factor in the extirpation of the local condor population (which disappeared by the late 1930s). However, such quill collecting was not limited to this region. John Bidwell wrote in 1890 about life in California in the 1840s (Bidwell 1966), and here we find another description of the same practice:

"It is not generally known that in 1841 – the year I reached California – gold was discovered in what is now a part of Los Angeles County. The yield was not rich; indeed, it was so small that it made no stir. The discoverer was an old Canadian Frenchman by the name of Baptiste Ruelle, who had been a trapper with the Hudson Bay Company, and, as was not an infrequent case with those trappers, had drifted down into New Mexico, where he had worked in placer mines. The mines discovered by Ruelle in California attracted a few New Mexicans, by whom they were worked for several years … New Mexican miners invariably carried their gold (which was generally small, and small in quantity as well) in a large quill – that of a vulture [condor] or turkey buzzard. Sometimes these quills would hold three or four ounces, and, being translucent, they were graduated so as to see at any time the quantity in them. The gold was kept in by a stopper. Ruelle had such a quill, which appeared to have been carried for years."

Still another account was given by Koford (1953), who reported, "J.D. Reyes, resident of Cuyama Valley since 1887, told me that the quills of condors and other large birds were formerly used for carrying gold dust and that they were sold for a dollar each." In those early days a dollar was a substantial amount of money, and if this was the true value of a condor quill, it presumably put a substantial price on the head of any condor close enough to be shot by anyone aware of its value in trade.

In his paper on condor feathers, Loye Miller (1937) remarked, "The early gold miners of the western placers are reported to have used condor quills as containers for their gold dust. Because of lightness and unbreakable texture, they might have served very well. A quill of the dimension just recorded was filled with fine uniform grained sand which was then poured into a ten cubic centimeter graduate which it filled just to the top. Such a container, then, would seem to have a very appreciable capacity for so concentrated a form of wealth as gold dust."

An excellent illustration by John Ridgway of one of the condor gold quills is given in Harris (1941), but Harris was disinclined to believe that use of such quills was widespread, acknowledging only that "there may have been a lone forty-niner who once attracted some local attention by storing his stock of the precious dust in a necklace of condor quills…" Harris' skepticism is to some extent surprising, as he was familiar with the accounts of both Anthony (1893) and Scott (1936a). Nevertheless, he has been followed in his dismissive conclusions by most recent writers on condors. We disagree with his judgment on this subject, just as we differ with his dismissal of the potential impacts of early predator poisoning campaigns, usually involving strychnine, on condors (see following chapter). The available evidence on use of condor quills for gold-dust containers – four independent accounts in three widely separated regions in a period extending at least from the 1840s to the 1930s – is far more compelling than "perhaps a lone forty-niner" … and suggests that many condors may have been shot for their quills in the 19th and early 20th centuries. Conceivably, such shooting may have been much more important than museum collecting in the past woes of the species.

Other Detrimental Cultural Practices

Aside from the killing of condors for quills, and the collecting of condor specimens for museums, the early shooting of condors may have stemmed mostly from curiosity or from the thrill of firing at large wildlife targets. As Carroll Dewilton Scott (1936b) aptly remarked "men who dared not meet a grizzly could kill a condor and boast of it the rest of their lives." Similarly, curiosity appears to have been the major motivation for shooting Imperial Woodpeckers (*Campephilus imperialis*) in the Mexican Sierra Madre Occidental, and was likely the main cause of the extinction of this species (Lammertink et al. 1996). Because of the condor's diet of carrion and its frequent rank odor, it seems unlikely that many individuals were shot to be eaten, although we note a South American tradition of killing Andean Condors to obtain eyes, bones, hearts, and stomachs for medicinal uses (McGahan 1971). Likewise, rural African cultures often kill large vultures to obtain organs for "muti" –

magical purposes – see Mundy et al. (1992). It appears to have been recognized early that the California Condor was not a direct menace to livestock or children (although see Scott 1936a), and the species does not appear to have been persecuted to any significant extent for alleged threats to humanity. Harris' (1941) dismissal of the importance of the early use of condor feather quills as pipestems seems to rest on relatively firm ground. To our knowledge, only Douglas (1829) reported such a practice. Similarly Koford's (1953) skeptical remarks on the potential use of condor feathers for bee brushes seem appropriate for lack of corroborating evidence.

Modern Cultural Relationships

Although the days of ritual condor-sacrifice ceremonies and widespread shooting of condors to obtain quills for gold dust are now gone, California Condors still have a substantial cultural importance in modern societies. No review of the symbolic importance of the species would be at all balanced without some passing mention of modern manifestations. Condors still permeate our society as names and logos for numerous sports teams and businesses, especially those in the aviation industry. Other modern usages include motifs on ceramics and textiles, not to mention frequent guest appearances in Gary Larson cartoons. Although perhaps not as familiar to the general public as roadrunners, condors are widely recognized, perhaps in part because of the gusto with which they are assumed to consume dead cowboys and other unfortunates perishing in our trackless deserts. And although we are reluctant to admit publicly to perusing the supermarket literature, we can testify that condors also appear with gratifying regularity in noted journals such as Weekly World News as they attack jetliners and space shuttles, routinely carry off full-grown bartenders to unspeakable fates, and sometimes hybridize with bigfoots with horrible consequences. Condors obviously still fulfill a fundamental cultural need of contemporary society, and if they did not really exist, we surely would have to invent them.

Condor Research and Conservation in the Early-Mid 20th Century

To understand the development of intensive research and conservation efforts for the California Condor in the past two decades, it is essential to review the history of earlier efforts in these spheres. In Snyder and Snyder (1989) we gave a brief review of this history. What follows here is a more comprehensive presentation.

Condor research and conservation efforts before 1980 can be divided into a number of major eras, conveniently identified by the names of the principal individuals active with the species in various periods. Although there is some overlap among eras and there are some blank periods when little attention was paid to the species, the major eras we recognize are those of Finley, Robinson-Easton, Koford, Miller-McMillan, Sibley, and Wilbur. To use these particular names is not to deny the very significant roles of other important figures, for example John Borneman and Dick Smith in the 1960s and 1970s, but is to focus on the individuals most dominant in their times.

Perhaps more than any other North American bird, the condor has attracted conservation attention from a great variety of individuals and organizations. The seemingly endless debates and controversies over its plight are in part a product of this diversity.

The Finley Era

As was ably reviewed by Harris (1941), the early (18th and 19th century) history of the California Condor was characterized by many short accounts by early explorers, settlers, ornithologists, and egg collectors who were greatly impressed by their encounters with the giant bird. But although these early writers gave some valuable information on the distribution and habits of the species, they also helped to spread considerable misinformation,

The most famous pair of California Condors ever studied: the Eaton Canyon birds photographed on a snag near their nest in 1906 by William Finley and Herman Bohlman.

including occasional gross exaggerations of the species' size and fanciful assertions as to its breeding habits, for example, the tale of Etienne Lucien mentioned earlier that condors laid clutches of two black eggs in grass-lined nests in trees. No truly concerted studies of the condor were made until the work of William Finley just after the turn of the 20th century. Finley's efforts and conclusions were sufficiently insightful that we believe it is appropriate to begin our summary with the contributions of this remarkable gentleman.

William L. Finley was born in 1876 and spent much of his long life studying and popularizing the birds of the western states. His place in history has been secured primarily as a superb early bird photographer (Mathewson 1986), but his important role as a pioneer conservationist deserves far more recognition than it has received. Among other accomplishments, Finley was a major motivating force, in part through his friendship with Theodore Roosevelt, for the preservation of a number of extraordinary bird habitats, including the Three Arches seabird colonies of coastal Oregon, and the Klamath, Tule, and Malheur marshlands, which remain among the most productive wetland habitats left in North America. He published numerous articles on the birdlife of the western states and served to inspire a whole generation of naturalists and conservationists. As Roger Tory Peterson so aptly remarked, "Finley's contributions to environmental awareness can be equated to that of only one other naturalist who was on the scene in the West during these early years – John Muir." Muir's important conservation role, however, did not have direct relevance to the fate of the California Condor.

Together with his long-standing collaborator, Herman Bohlman, Finley carried out the first-ever detailed study of a nesting pair of California Condors in 1906 and his published articles on this study and the more than 250 photographs taken of these birds, some of which we reproduce here, endure as a monumental accomplishment (Finley 1906, 1908a, 1908b, 1908c, 1908d, 1909, 1910; Finley and Finley 1915, 1926). The pair under study was nesting in Eaton Canyon of the San Gabriel Mountains, which overlook Los Angeles from the north. Today, Eaton Canyon still looks much as it must have in 1906, thanks to its extremely rugged terrain, but the condors are gone, the last pair of the San Gabriels being seen and photographed in early 1980, and not in Eaton Canyon.

The Eaton Canyon pair existed at least as far back as 1895, and although its nest site was not found until 1906, the possibility that condors were nesting there became apparent in 1905 when a fledgling together with two adults was discovered by Philip Pinger, a geology student who was prospecting the canyon. Subsequent searches by J.B. Dixon and Joseph Grinnell confirmed condors in the area found by Pinger, but it was not until March of 1906 that an actual nest was discovered by Finley, together with Grinnell and Walter Taylor. In the confused jumble of rocks in the precipitous canyon, the exact site, behind a slab of rock leaning against a near vertical cliff face, was not revealed until Finley fired shots from a revolver to flush the incubating bird.

By great good fortune, one of the very first visits of Finley and Bohlman to the nest – on March 23 – occurred just as the chick was hatching, so on this and repeated visits they were able to gain an accurate record of the developmental stages of the chick by age. A hatching date of March 23 implies a probable laying date between January 22 and January 27, which to this day represents the earliest date of egg laying known for the species in the

Herman Bohlman (above) and William Finley (below) scale the steep slopes of Eaton Canyon in their landmark study of California Condors.

wild. The adults were extremely approachable at the nest, allowing photography without any need for concealment in a blind, and in his writings Finley described the species as a bird with a remarkably unsuspicious nature, a distinct contrast to the image later projected by Koford and the McMillan brothers of a species incredibly wary of man. Our own experience with nesting condors supports Finley on this score.

William Finley (**above**) with nestling and adult California Condors near their nest in Eaton Canyon in 1906. **Below**, General, the fledgling condor from the Eaton Canyon nest, sunning at Finley's home along the Willamette River in Oregon.

The nestling condor of 1906 was taken captive by Finley on July 5 and was reared successfully at Finley's home along the Willamette River in Oregon. Finley's bird "General" was later donated to the New York Zoological Park, and lived for eight years, after serving as a focus for several articles on condor maturation and behavior. Its untimely death was due to a rubber band inadvertently swallowed from its cage floor (Mathewson 1986).

Finley (1908a) later published a very useful review of what was then known about condors. In this publication, he emphasized the pessimistic conservation prospects of the species, which he attributed largely to poisoning and shooting activities. In his words:

"Formerly the California Condor was frequently seen about the mountainous regions of central and southern California. The birds were fearless and tame about their nesting places. There are many records of their being shot merely because they furnished good marks for irresponsible hunters who wandered thru these mountains.

The main cause which has been given for the decrease in condor numbers seems to be that when stock raising became common in California years ago, in order to secure pasture during the dry months, the rangers were compelled to drive their herds back into the more remote mountainous parts. Here they invaded the retreats of panthers, grizzlies, and coyotes. These preyed upon calves and sheep and created considerable damage. The quickest and best way of getting rid of these animals was by baiting the carcasses with poison. Since the condors came to feed on the poisoned animals, numbers of the big birds were undoubtedly killed in this way.

Almost any other bird might hold its own in the struggle for existence against these forces, but the condor is too slow in recuperating its numbers. Even under favorable circumstances, each pair of condors will raise but one offspring a year. Oftentimes a pair of condors are very irregular in nesting. One collector states that in a certain locality where a pair of the birds live, they have nested but three times in about twelve years. Under these conditions it is not surprising that the condor numbers are decreasing, and unless the needed protection is given, this bird will undoubtedly follow the Great Auk."

Dawson (1923), Scott (1936b), Robinson (1940), Harris (1941), Koford (1953), and Wilbur (1978b) were later inclined to dismiss the possibility that substantial numbers of condors might have been killed by early predator-poisoning campaigns. Their skepticism stemmed from the fact that almost all reports of such poisoning were based on hearsay, not rigorous first-hand scientific documentation. Nevertheless, we suggest that this hardly disproves the case, as one would not have expected to see much, if any, careful documentation of poisoning incidents during early times, least of all by those doing the poisoning. No one disputes that widespread poisoning of predators, especially with strychnine, occurred in the late 19th and early 20th centuries in California. And if such poisoning was common, it would be amazing if it were not killing large numbers of condors, especially judging from the widespread losses of vultures to strychnine poisoning (likewise targeted mainly against predatory mammals) that have been documented in recent times in Africa (Mundy et al. 1992).

It is pertinent to repeat an account by José Jesús López, the long-standing foreman of the Tejón Ranch, as recounted by Frank Latta in his Saga of El Rancho Tejón (1976). Although this account could also be dismissed as hearsay, the amount of detail offered leaves us with little doubt as to the devastating impact of early poisoning practices on condors, especially when read alongside the accounts of Taylor (1859b), Henshaw (1876), Streator (1888), Finley (1908a), Lyon (1918), and others:

"For a number of years before I arrived at the ranch [1874], Mr. Beale had employed Pete Miller to kill bears. This he did by shooting, trapping, and poisoning. In the mountains he hunted them, and also caught them in traps or deadfalls made of heavy timbers. When they killed sheep or cattle he put poison in the carcasses. Strychnine generally was used in such poisoning, but Miller used a special poison of his own. The nature of this poison he kept secret from everyone. It would kill everything; condors, buzzards, crows, ravens, foxes, coyotes, wolves, coons, wild cats, mountain lions, and bears. We even had dogs, valuable dogs, killed by this poison. Later I learned that Miller used cyanide of potassium. I was assured by everyone that before this poisoning was done, both wolves and condors were plentiful in the Tejón country."

Two relatively recent documented cases of apparent strychnine poisoning of condors (Miller et al. 1965; Borneman 1966) give further evidence of the susceptibility of the condor to this toxicant. Both these cases date from a time when use of strychnine had declined greatly from historical levels. But by this time, it is also fair to assume that reports of poisoning were much more likely to be published than earlier.

Thus, we believe that Finley was correct in identifying both poisoning and shooting as the probable major causes of historic decline of the condor, but in addition to the poisoning resulting from predator control that Finley recognized, we would add another sort of poisoning that may have been equally, if not more important – lead poisoning resulting from condors swallowing bullet fragments in carcasses. Lead poisoning of condors presumably did not just start in the 1980s when it was first documented, but had undoubtedly been going on since the arrival of European man in the condor's homeland, centuries earlier. And just as we feel one cannot dismiss a historical role for lead poisoning just because there was no early documentation of this stress, we feel that denying an important role of predator poisoning campaigns in the woes of the species because historical condor deaths to poisoning were documented only by hearsay, would be to misinterpret the situation badly. Hearsay is not always erroneous.

Unfortunately, although Finley spoke eloquently for the importance of addressing the threats to condors, his pleas did not lead to any concerted conservation actions for the species. Nevertheless, the killing or collecting of condors or their eggs was made illegal by the California Legislature and Fish and Game Commission in 1905. And although such protection was very difficult to enforce and did not address such threats as inadvertent poisoning, the frequency with which condors and their eggs were taken from the wild, declined steeply after 1910 (Wilbur 1978b). The last grizzly bear was exterminated from southern California in 1922, and wolves were gone by 1924 (Schoenherr 1992), so poisoning campaigns against these predators presumably declined greatly in urgency by early in the present century. However, once the bears and wolves were gone, coyotes and ground squirrels took their place as the intolerable enemies of ranchers and as targets for poisoning campaigns. Although strychnine was gradually replaced by other poisons, such as thallium and compound 1080, at least some of these other poisons also posed threats to condors.

Finley and his companions were not the only condor enthusiasts active at the turn of the century, and indeed this period represented a climax for the collection of condor eggs and skin specimens, not to mention live specimens for zoos (Wilbur 1978b). In the period between 1881 and 1910 a total of 111 birds and 49 eggs were known collected from the wild (well over half the total ever known taken), and in 1897–98 alone at least 20 birds and 7 eggs were secured. This take, insofar as birds were collected, must be considered one of the significant historical stresses on the species. The impact of egg removals was presumably much less because relatively few eggs were taken and the species was capable of replacement-clutching.

One of the more colorful early collectors was a chap named Whitaker, who homesteaded along the Piru Creek, a rugged gorge of Ventura County that was the scene of the first gold strike in California many decades earlier. Whitaker mainly made ends meet by tending orchards of apricots and oranges and caring for an apiary of hundreds of bee hives at the junction of the Piru with the Agua Blanca. But as a sideline, he also procured several live condor nestlings for exhibit at the National Zoo in Washington, one of which lived a full 45 years.

Whitaker collected young condors by lowering a fearless young Indian girl down to the nest caves on a long rope, as described in an article in Overland Monthly, entitled Capturing the Great American Condor (Whitaker 1918). Remarkably, in 1968 Fred Sibley and John Borneman discovered the remains of one of the ropes possibly used by Whitaker in his condor collecting efforts. Badly deteriorated by exposure to the elements, this rope was coiled in a small cave near the top of a cliff from which Whitaker had taken a nestling lower down in 1904. The mountain peak just to the east of this nest site still bears Whitaker's name.

This same cliff was one of the two condor nest cliffs that Whitaker showed Frank Chapman of the American Museum of Natural History in 1906. Scenery near the site was later reproduced in a condor nest diorama that still can be seen at the museum. This same site was also the one from which we very nearly lost fearless young Bay Roberts in 1982. Bay, one of the best rock climbers on the research team of the 1980s, was attacked by a swarm of wild bees, conceivably direct descendants of Whitaker's apiary, while preparing to sift the nest bottom for old condor eggshells. With no place to flee from the bees in the shallow nest cave, she had no choice but to climb back up her rope fully exposed to their attacks.

Chapman's expedition with Whitaker was described in his Camps and Cruises of an Ornithologist of 1908, an account that also detailed his attempts to bait in condors on Devil's Potrero high above the Agua Blanca. This remote grassy opening in the dense chaparral, not far from another of Whitaker's condor nests, was the former wilderness hideout of the notorious bandit, Tiburcio Vasquez. A generation earlier, Vasquz had achieved considerable local

Above, three pioneer ornithologists and egg collectors – left to right, Gordon McMillan (brother of Ian and Eben), William Leon Dawson, and Kelly Truesdale – at the start of their famous expedition of April 1911 to confirm that Truesdale's condor eggs were not fakes. **Bottom left**, Robert Easton, father of the Sisquoc Condor Sanctuary, in 1935. **Bottom right**, Cyril Robinson, U.S. Forest Service condor researcher and conservationist of the 1930s.

renown, robbing and terrorizing travelers venturing north through the mountains from Los Angeles. Vasquez enjoyed a Robin Hood-like reputation, sharing his booty with the needy, but unlike that more famous rogue, he was ultimately captured and hanged (Saunders 1924).

As a bait to induce condors to land on Devil's Potrero, Chapman used a burro "which chanced to die at this time," no doubt with a bullet hole in its cranium. The burro carcass worked splendidly in attracting Turkey Vultures, but the nearest any condor came to feeding was a bird that circled low over the bait and landed on a nearby tree. Unfortunately, Chapman was outside his blind at the time, and the bird caught sight of him and left before he could conceal himself.

Although Chapman's experiences with condors were as much recreation as science, there was no clear line separating the two endeavors in those days, and Chapman was only one of a number of early ornithologists making their way into the back country to see the giant vulture. Another with a special interest in the condor was William Leon Dawson, famed for his lavish Birds of California, published in 1923. Accounts both in that volume and in Man and the California Condor by Ian McMillan (1968) describe Dawson's 1911 journey to a condor nest in San Luis Obispo County with Kelly Truesdale, an eccentric early egg collector. Truesdale was the instigator of this journey, as he needed Dawson to confirm to John Thayer, an eastern egg collector, that the eggs he was offering for sale were really condor eggs, not fakes. McMillan's retelling of this and other trips of Truesdale surely ranks as one of the most delightful and vivid accounts of early egg collectors ever written. In his youth McMillan and his brothers often helped Truesdale in egg-collecting expeditions and he knew this extraordinary individual as a personal friend. This was the same Ian McMillan who would later become a major actor in condor controversies of the 1950s and 1960s, collaborating with his brother Eben and Alden Miller in a study of the species sponsored by the National Audubon Society and the National Geographic Society, and later becoming a curmudgeon-at-large regarding all matters relating to condors.

The Robinson–Easton Era

Other than the protection given the species by the state of California in 1905 and the conservation concern generated by William Finley, few developments of the early 20th century held much conservation benefit for the condor. Significant activities to aid the species were not initiated until decades later when Cyril Robinson, the Deputy Supervisor of the Los Padres National Forest, and Robert Easton, a local businessman, organized research and conservation efforts on its behalf (Ford 1986, Taylor 1986). During the mid-1930s Robinson carried out an ambitious survey of condors in the national forests of southern California and assembled an impressive amount of information on their distribution, numbers, and biology. Unfortunately, this work has received virtually no recognition, in part because none of it was ever published in established journals, and in part because it was shortly to be overshadowed by the work of Carl Koford.

Robinson and Easton were also the first people to recognize the importance of the Sespe and Sisquoc regions to condors, and with the support of the National Audubon

Society, they persuaded the Forest Service to establish a formal 485 ha condor sanctuary in the Sisquoc area in 1937 (see map in following chapter). The stimulus for the creation of the Sisquoc Sanctuary was the discovery of numerous condors using the area, especially near Sisquoc Falls, and an apparent threat to the area in the form of a proposed Forest Service fire road that would have run right through it and given the public easy access. At that time, the Forest Service was busily constructing fire control roads throughout the Los Padres Forest in an effort that can now be viewed as a more or less pointless campaign to stop fires in a habitat type that is largely maintained by and fully adapted to fire (Minnich 1983). In any event, Easton was able to deflect construction of a road through the Sisquoc by offering the Forest Service access for an alternative road through a private inholding that he owned along the Sierra Madre Ridge. Easton's son, another Robert Easton, was later to become a principal figure in successful efforts to create the San Rafael and Dick Smith Wilderness Areas which gave additional protection against development not just to the Sisquoc region itself, but to a vast region of National Forest Lands in Santa Barbara County.

Robinson's studies were summarized in a number of internal USFS reports (Robinson 1936a,b, 1939, 1940), and when Carl Koford began studies in 1939, he was able to use this information to great advantage. Of particular interest, Koford's renowned estimate of 60 condors in the wild, first given in his doctoral thesis of 1950, was preceded and may well have been influenced by Robinson's estimate of 60 condors in the Los Padres National Forest in 1934, an estimate that for some reason was neither acknowledged nor discussed by Koford.

Two other persons active at the same time, who were also of considerable importance to the history of condor studies, were J.R. Pemberton, a Los Angeles geologist and wildlife photographer, and Ed Harrison, a Los Angeles businessman and photographer. Although they never published more than brief accounts of the species, Pemberton and Harrison eagerly pursued its habits, often as field companions of Carl Koford, and took movies and still photographs of some remarkable scenes of nesting behavior and mass feedings at carcasses. Their photographic record of the condors of the 1930s and 1940s is on file at the Western Foundation of Vertebrate Zoology and represents a fascinating documentation of the condors of that era. Pemberton was also a major figure in creating momentum for the development of Koford's study and served as a partial patron of the study.

The Koford Era

Clearly the most pivotal individual ever to be involved in condor research and conservation was Carl Koford. His doctoral studies of the species stand as a tremendous achievement, and he probably accomplished as much as any one individual could have, given the general state of ecological knowledge at the time and the difficulties inherent in condor studies. Although we will offer criticisms of certain aspects of his work, these should not be interpreted as blindness to the awesome quality of his overall contributions. Hindsight is a tremendous advantage, and we recognize fully that Koford was working with many research handicaps that no longer exist. He worked remarkably hard and produced a doctoral thesis that was nothing less than a landmark study.

Carl Koford with condor nestling "Oscar" from his most intensively studied nest in 1939.

Originally trained as a mammologist, Koford received a fellowship to study condors arranged by John Baker of the National Audubon Society through Joseph Grinnell of the University of California at Berkeley. Koford was first a student of Grinnell and later of Alden Miller after Grinnell's death, and was an extremely devoted field researcher. His systematic studies began in 1939 and led to many important advances in our knowledge of the general biological characteristics of the condor. His field notes are models of objectivity and meticulous detail, and he applied himself with zeal to the task of understanding a species that has always been very difficult to study. Koford did not even have an automobile for his first year of study and had to hike formidable distances repeatedly, often in very difficult terrain. Considering the logistic challenges he faced, the fact that he was able to accomplish as much as he did was extraordinary. Nevertheless, many important questions were simply beyond the capacities of a solitary worker to resolve at that time, especially with the tools then available for research.

Over his four years of intensive research (1939–1941, 1946), Koford followed the reproductive biology of a number of condor pairs. The most intensively studied pair was one of 1939 that he watched at relatively close range on an irregular basis through most of the incubation, nestling, and postfledging periods. Other nests were studied primarily by periodic visits to the nest caves themselves.

Although Koford made no specific calculations of nesting success, he assumed roughly 50% success in population projections, and examination of his monograph and field notes does indicate indeed that about half the nests he found were successful from the egg stage (Snyder 1983). Causes of nesting failure were for the most part uncertain. Eggs broken by unknown agents were found in three (possibly four) nests. The chick in another nest suffered a broken wing, which evidently caused its death. This injury may have arisen from mishandling during banding, judging from Koford's notes, but might alternatively have been due to calcium problems (see Chapter 1). At one nest that Koford entered on a near-daily basis for a period of several weeks prior to hatching, the eggshell became damaged and the chick did not hatch. Koford attributed this failure to the activities of a nearby trail crew, although it could as well have resulted from his own frequent nest visits or may have been an entirely natural failure due, for example, to ravens.

At still another nest, studied mainly by Telford Work, Al Wool, and Harold Hill (while Koford was away on military duty in World War II in 1945) the chick died of unknown causes late in the nestling period. Koford later surmised that the nest might have been lost at least in part because of human disturbance (it was visited with some frequency), but he presented no direct evidence for this conclusion. The chick was discovered dead on a trip to the nest cave by Don Bleitz, Telford Work, a Collier's Magazine photographer, and a female professional model. Plans had been made to photograph the model interacting with the young condor for an article in Collier's (a scheme that even then must have broken some records for questionable taste). In any event, the chick had already been dead for some time and its carcass had evidently been partly eaten by terrestrial mammals, although this could have represented scavenging rather than predation (Bleitz 1946). And although arsenic was found in subsequent analysis of the dead chick, the contamination could well have occurred post mortem, as the carcass was stored in a museum case prior to analysis, and arsenic was then a common preservative used for museum skins. A plausible cause of death was never established.

Koford did not determine what fraction of the adult population was attempting to breed. This is as important a question as nesting success in understanding overall productivity, but in practical terms it was one of the questions that was simply beyond reach at the time. Koford lacked accurate information both on the size of the condor population and the total number of breeding pairs, and with the methods available at the time it might have taken 100 Carl Kofords to have obtained reasonable estimates of these quantities.

In addition to nesting studies, Koford made trips throughout the condor range, interviewing people familiar with the species and observing the birds feeding, roosting, and interacting with other scavengers. This effort, building on earlier work by Robinson, led to the first comprehensive picture of the condor's distribution and the first comprehensive identification of principal nesting areas, roosting areas, and flyways.

One of the more intriguing accounts detailed in Koford's notes that clearly revealed his skills in evaluating interview information was a 1939 visit with an egg collector named Badger, who knew of a condor nest in Santa Paula Canyon. Collecting condor eggs was by then strictly illegal, but Koford correctly surmised that Badger might still be raiding nests. This was ultimately confirmed many years later, after Badger's death and after his egg collection was acquired by the Western Foundation of Vertebrate Zoology. In fact, Badger had taken an egg from the Santa Paula nest in the same year he was interviewed by Koford, and when Koford and Ed Harrison checked the nest in the fall of that year, they found an extremely young chick, evidently hatched from a replacement egg (Harrison and Kiff 1980).

Koford's published conclusions about major threats to the condor (Koford 1953) were wide-ranging, but fell short of being definitive. About potential reproductive problems he said little, emphasizing only that the intrinsic rate of increase was very low (he had not documented replacement clutching and doubted the species could breed annually). And even though nesting success was reasonably good during his studies (despite high levels of disturbance at several nests), he discussed at length the potential detrimental effects of human disturbance on reproduction.

Although he had no information on mortality rates, Koford did provide an extensive list of known and suspected causes of death. But aside from emphasizing wanton shooting and past museum collecting, he was unable to identify which mortality factors might be most important and did not specifically address the question of whether mortality factors could have been the main cause of the species' endangerment. In view of the information he had available and the research techniques then available, he could hardly have drawn firm conclusions on these subjects.

Koford's remarks on the potential effects of 1080 poisoning were circumspect, in contrast to the later emphasis given this toxicant by the McMillan brothers. Although he had watched condors feeding on 1080-poisoned ground squirrels (*Spermophilus beecheyi*), he detected no signs that they suffered any ill effects as a result, although he did not consider this conclusive evidence that they were unaffected. To this day, there has not been a single well-documented case of a condor adversely affected by 1080.

His evaluation of the threat of strychnine poisoning resulting from predator control campaigns was to point out that reports of mass deaths of condors to this cause were only hearsay and to acknowledge only that "it is conceivable that occasionally a condor eats one of these baits."

Otherwise, in his remarks on conservation, Koford cautioned against further photography of the species and voiced his support for the establishment of sanctuaries to minimize disturbance to nests and roosts. The Sespe Sanctuary, established in 1947 in the Los Padres National Forest north of Fillmore, was a direct result of his studies. This magnificent region of sandstone cliffs and canyons was Koford's principal study area and encompassed many of the known condor nests.

Koford also warned against captive breeding, as he was extremely doubtful that captive-reared condors could be successfully reestablished in the wild. Similarly, he opposed artificial feeding programs, which he believed would run the risk of concentrating condors in areas where they could be wiped out by disasters and would lead to the birds losing the fear of humans they needed for survival.

Overall, Koford's conservation approach was to recommend reductions of nearly all conceivable threats to the species in the wild, coupled with an aversion to anything hinting of direct human management. However, he was unable to provide any quantitative assessment as to which threats might be most important. He was completely unaware of one of the most important threats, lead poisoning, and he did not acknowledge the probable major influence of past predator-poisoning efforts on survival of the species.

Koford's recommendations for condor conservation were to become the standard for several decades, and by the 1970s Koford himself had become a cult figure for wilderness enthusiasts, famed for his espousal of noninterventionist techniques in studying and conserving endangered species. In later years he pursued a variety of field research projects, perhaps most notably with vicuñas and mountain lions, but his place in history will surely always rest with his work on the California Condor, his first major field study.

In his 1953 monograph, Koford stated his belief that the condor population had been stable for about 30 years. Unfortunately, he did not back up this conclusion comprehensively, and we consider it likely incorrect. The range of the species was still contracting throughout this period (e.g., the population in Baja California evidently disappeared at this time), and flock counts in certain areas (e.g., Santa Barbara County) were showing major declines. Maximum flock counts in other areas, in particular the Sespe Sanctuary region of Ventura County, may have appeared to be increasing, but the better coverage resulting from Koford's own efforts, not real increases in condor numbers, could easily be the explanation for this trend.

Given the sorts of data he had available, Koford faced an essentially impossible task in attempting to accurately estimate the size of the condor population, but he was undoubtedly under tremendous pressure to do so. Possibly responding in part to Robinson's earlier estimate of 60 individuals in the Los Padres National Forest, Koford put forth his own well-known estimate of 60 condors, which then became dogma for decades, despite the fact that the underlying logic of this estimate was far from rigorous (Snyder and Johnson 1985a,b; Johnson 1985). Likewise, Robinson's population estimate had not been based on rigorous methodology (it was a summation of high counts in the Sespe and Sisquoc regions).

Koford was impressed that the largest single flock sightings obtained during his studies (maximum of 42 birds) were no larger than his largest simultaneous counts in several areas, and evidently because of this, he felt that the largest single counts could be relatively close to total population counts. Evidently, he arbitrarily added 50% to the highest counts to come to a total population estimate. However, the highest single and simultaneous counts could just as easily have been much smaller than the total population in view of the small number of sites covered in his few simultaneous counts and the vagaries of condor movements from day to day. Using such procedures to divine total numbers is more akin to wild guesswork than to reasonable inference.

Essentially all recent researchers tackling the condor numbers question (e.g., Sibley, Wilbur, and ourselves) have come to the conclusion that based on area by area comparisons of numbers of condors seen back through time, Koford's estimate fell well short of true numbers. In fact, to arrive at this estimate, he had to reject one particular single-day composite count by two members of the California Department of Fish and Game in 1942 that totalled some 122 birds. In our judgement, Koford very likely had been dealing with a population somewhere in the vicinity of 150 individuals, an estimate that closely matches an unofficial 150+ bird estimate offered by the Department during the early 1950s (McMillan 1953).

Koford's own recognition of the possibility that there might be more than 60 condors in the population was clear from statements in his doctoral dissertation (Koford 1950):

"If my estimate of 60 condors is in error it is too conservative. If there are 100 condors, so much the better for the survival of the species."

For whatever reasons, these qualifying remarks to his population estimate did not appear in his published monograph, leading followers to attach a significance to the 60-bird figure that simply was not warranted (e.g., McMillan 1985). The political ramifications of this omission were many and varied, and will be discussed more thoroughly below and in the chapters that follow.

Koford was responsible for one of the most important shifts in human perceptions of the condor. Whereas Finley had earlier popularized an image of nesting condors as extremely tolerant of humans, Koford's (1953) condor was an incredibly shy and sensitive creature, almost completely intolerant of the presence of man. This was a surprising development, especially because there are no indications from Koford's field notes that he held this view when conducting his research. Koford entered active nest caves with frequency and gave no indication that he thought this might be harmful for the birds. For example, he visited his nest No. 5 of 1941 a total of 14 times during the incubation period. One suspects that in entering this nest so many times he hoped to document the hatching of the egg and gain a better appreciation of length of the incubation period, but this is only speculation. The major puzzle is why he later came to project an image of the condor as a creature so wary of humans. Koford had not observed any nest desertions resulting from his own routine entries of nests. Yet he declared the condor to be likely to desert should a person so much as "expose himself" within a few hundred meters of an early-stage nest (see Koford 1953, 1979, McMillan 1981).

We can only speculate on what caused the shift in views, but one possibility is that Koford, late in his study, may have begun to have misgivings about the conduct of his early research, a feeling triggered perhaps by the failure of an egg to hatch at one nest of 1941, the possible breakage of a nestling's wing during handling in 1939, or the failure (to unknown causes) of a heavily visited nest of 1945. However, Koford still continued to enter nests freely as late as 1946, the last year of his intensive field studies, so we are inclined to doubt the validity of this interpretation.

Rather, we believe that the change was more directly related to the process of securing a Sespe Sanctuary in the late 1940s and early 1950s. The goal of establishing the sanctuary is clear in the correspondance between Koford and Alden Miller from the very start of Koford's studies in 1939, and appears to have been an overriding consideration. The Sespe Sanctuary was first established as a 14,000 ha preserve in the Los Padres National Forest in 1947, was later enlarged to 21,450 ha and partially withdrawn from mineral leasing in 1951, and was finally withdrawn entirely from mineral leasing in 1970. During this period, there was considerable discussion about the need for the sanctuary and the degree to which it should be closed to the public, with strong opposition coming from economic interests anxious to exploit mineral resources, especially oil, in the sanctuary area.

It seems quite clear in retrospect that advocates of the sanctuary found it advantageous to present an image of the condor that emphasized both its low numbers and its sensitivity to disturbance. It should not come as a tremendous surprise that relatively low estimates of condor numbers were put forth and that the species was packaged as an incredibly wary creature badly in need of a sanctuary. The goal of sanctuary establishment came to dominate all other goals.

In this process, the qualifications that Koford expressed regarding his estimate of condor numbers in his thesis were omitted from the published version, and the figure of 60 birds became established as a fact beyond question. Meanwhile, the image of the condor as a man-intolerant species struck a resonant chord in wilderness enthusiasts enthralled with a species of rarity and mystery. The species took on new attributes that some may have felt quite sincerely would help ensure its conservation and that at the same time may have fulfilled very fundamental twentieth century human needs for a species that might epitomize unknowable pristine nature, a species totally apart from modern humanity.

Perhaps the real condor did not quite fit this symbolic role, but it came close. Without a doubt, its enormous size and striking appearance were inspiring. Its nesting areas were certainly wild, remote, and spectacular, and its very name sounded a note of unfathomable power. Although its basic lack of wariness did not harmonize well with the overall image, this could be simply overlooked or misrepresented. The fact that the condor was heavily dependent on domestic livestock and hunter-killed wildlife for food in some of the most degraded grasslands of the region was not quite right either. But although these lands were not wilderness, they were certainly picturesque enough, and what apparently really counted was the fact that the ranches had been there long enough that no one remembered what the lands looked like before them. If not true wilderness, they were at least pastoral enough to evoke powerful emotions of nostalgia for a disappearing America that blended with the appeal of wilderness. Conservation of the condor, in the minds of many, became equivalent to trying to hold on to the past, not the distant past that no one remembered, but a more recent past that included herds of sheep and cattle and ranching as a way of life. Condor conservation became a crusade difficult for anyone depressed with the march of civilization to resist.

In this evolution of perceptions, it has often seemed to us that the primary goals of condor conservation became badly distorted. As some passionate condor aficianados have been fond of saying, the condor "is" habitat, and from the time of establishment of the Sespe Sanctuary to the more recent fights for a Sespe-Frazier Wilderness, and for a Hudson Ranch sanctuary, one cannot escape the impression that for many people involved, preserving habitat and preserving an image of the condor as a paragon of wilderness have been more important than saving the condor itself. These *are* important and attractive goals in their own right, but they have turned out to be ones that have often conflicted with preserving the condor as a viable biological species.

Donald D. McLean, an employee of the California Department of Fish and Game during the Koford era, touched on some of these disparities in a letter to Allan Phillips dated March 14, 1958, in which he primarily discussed his sighting of a group of 85 condors in the Antelope Valley north of Neenach in 1942, a sighting mentioned (and dismissed) by Koford (1953) with a terse "This is more than my estimate of the total population." Excerpts from McLean's letter follow:

"Perhaps when you are told to slant your findings to fit your sponsor, you have to do it or lose your funds?? Of course the whole condor study program was set up as a propaganda scheme to get the condor sanctuary.... Birds on P145 [McLean's sighting as mentioned in Koford's monograph] were feeding on a large dead steer that had died of anthrax or black-leg, one of a number that had died there. Some 25–30

condors were around the relatively fresh carcass. Most of the remainder were standing on the dry grass slopes of two small knolls just above the dead animal. Some were
circling low over the area and brought our attention to the spot. They were "counted", not estimated, not only by me but by my chief at the time [in the Department of
Fish and Game], J.S. Hunter … Joe was not able to see the group on one of the
knolls. I took 16mm movies of all I could get, but of course I could not get them all
in the picture at one time. Carl [Koford] could never seem to arrange to see these
films. So far as I know the picture is still in the possession of H.M. Bourland and is
incorporated [in] two 400-ft reels of condor film which we worked on together …

Now here is something I have rarely mentioned to anyone: about 2 hours and
80 air miles later, on the same day, we were travelling up the western side of the
Carrizo Plains in San Luis Obispo County and saw 37 condors feeding on and standing about several dead sheep. I don't say that some of the Antelope Valley condors
could not have beaten us up to the Carrizo Plains, but I doubt that well fed condors
would have crossed the Tehachapi Mountains and headed that far north to take on
another feed of sheep, with still plenty of beef available.

I can't be convinced by anyone that there are any less than 50 breeding pairs of
condors.… I know of a considerable number of nesting areas not mentioned in any
publications and I'm not about to reveal them, that is, the exact areas.

Carl spent by far the largest part of his time in the one area which had been
pre-chosen as the proposed condor sanctuary.

Nests in the Havila and Piute ranges south of Kernville and the eastern Tehachapis
east of Monolith, as well as those on the Hurricane Deck, east of Los Olivos in Santa
Barbara County and the Caliente Range on the west side of the Carrizo Plains in
San Luis Obispo County, have failed to make the printed page, of late, at least. I find
no mention of any nest in the Piru Gorge either, one of them can be walked to by a
lady in high heels, as it is in a round jug-necked hole on a smooth solid rock slope
of about 20 degree slope.

Condors are not about to become extinct, providing a good portion of them
nest elsewhere than in the 'sanctuary.' No sheep or cattle there."

Although we have not seen the McLean condor film, Fred Sibley was able to see it in early
1967 and has confirmed that it scans over many condors, although as McLean indicated, it is
not possible to count more than 25 or so in view at once. We agree with McLean's conclusion
that it would be unlikely for the sightings in the Antelope Valley and the Carrizo Plains to have
included the same individuals. The short time difference between these sightings would imply
a rate of travel exceeding normal condor flight speed over varied terrain. As to the accuracy of
other statements made by McLean in his letter, we do not know whether condors once nested in all the locations he mentioned, although condors definitely have nested in some of these
areas and most are reasonable possibilities. We have attempted to locate his site east of
Monolith, as did Fred Sibley, but without success, though we would stop short of saying that
condors never nested there. It is too easy to miss old condor nests. On other subjects, Mclean
(now deceased) has been a source of mixed reliability. According to Lloyd Kiff, his informa-

tion on old Peregrine (*Falco peregrinus*) nest sites has been relatively poor, whereas according to Fred Sibley, his information on old Pileated Woodpecker (*Dryocopus pileatus*) territories, as checked by G. Christman, has been impressively accurate.

Regardless of whether or not one accepts McLean's condor sighting of 1942, it appears likely that this record became the basis for the unofficial estimate of 150 or more condors left in the wild by the California Department of Fish and Game. This estimate accords well with our own independent estimate of the condor population at that time, and had relevance not only for discussions over the establishment of the Sespe Sanctuary, but also for a much more tempestuous controversy that arose during the same period and challenged the most fundamental assumptions of the Koford-Miller approach to condor conservation. The issue was captive breeding of condors and, more specifically, a permit granted by the California Fish and Game Commission to the San Diego Zoo for capture of two wild California Condors. We turn now to a discussion of this controversy as it had profound effects on the course of condor conservation for the next three decades.

The early request of the San Diego Zoo to begin captive breeding of condors is a classic example of the failure of an idea that was ahead of its time. Belle Benchley and K.C. Lint of the zoo had had great success during the 1940s breeding Andean Condors in captivity, including the routine laying of more than one egg per year by their breeding pair through deliberate replacement clutching. As a natural extension of this success Benchley approached the Department of Fish and Game in 1949 with a proposal to take a pair of California Condors, not just to breed them in captivity, but to serve also as a source of birds to release to the wild in an effort to bolster the wild population.

The Department of Fish and Game favored the idea of captive breeding, as it believed that taking of two birds posed no significant threat to a wild population it believed numbered about 150 birds. With the support of the Department, the California Fish and Game Commission readily approved the permit, although it expressly forbade releases of progeny to the wild, apparently fearful that this might introduce diseases from captivity into the wild population (an issue on which the Commission was as ahead of its time as was the San Diego Zoo in suggesting captive-breeding for reintroduction).

Then the mountains began to shake. Alden Miller, Carl Koford, John Baker of National Audubon Society, and Ian McMillan all protested the action in lockstep, publishing a number of articles denouncing it as possibly the difference between survival and decline of the wild population. Miller (1953) pointed out that trapping two adults could disrupt the reproduction of two pairs in the wild, or even more if more than two birds had to be trapped to get a male and female, and how this, paraphrasing Koford's calculations, might lead to failure of as much as 60% of the five pairs normally successful during any one year! As Miller summed up the situation:

> "The danger in trapping and removing adults lies then in tipping the balance in this precariously situated species. It is difficult to say, scientifically, which straw will break the camel's back, but cutting significantly into the annual reproduction of a threatened species seems distinctly dangerous. Even if the disruption from trapping were

not disastrous, several years would be required for the species to recover its former numbers after the adults were taken."

This dire warning took no note of the clear intentions of the San Diego Zoo to trap immatures if at all possible, and was of course the worst of all conceivable worst cases, based on calculations that today seem extraordinarily naive and conservative in their assessment of condor numbers and reproductive capacities. Like McLean, we believe that there were probably on the order of 40–50 pairs of condors active in the wild population in the late 1940s, producing roughly 20–25 fledglings each year. If so, the removal of two immatures or adults from this population could not reasonably have made any significant difference to the survival prospects of the species.

Nevertheless, we do not doubt that Miller and his allies had a rational cause for their protest. What they feared most of all, we believe, was that captive breeding would become a substitute for efforts to save the wild population, and might ultimately lead to opening the Sespe Sanctuary to development. Furthermore, we have little doubt that for some people the possibility of opening the sanctuary to oil exploration and hunting would indeed be an underlying motive for their supporting captive breeding, though it is clearly not the way the San Diego Zoo viewed the situation. It is really no surprise that the proposal of the zoo was greeted with deep suspicion and hostility. Zoos had no appreciable record of conservation success at that time, and such a role for zoos was then totally contrary to popular perceptions.

San Diego Zoo's early attempts to obtain wild condors for captive breeding failed largely because of bad luck. The trapper involved (L. W. Walker) tried a variety of techniques, including a pit trap, a walk-in trap, and noose carpets around carcasses. But although he caught numerous Turkey Vultures and Golden Eagles, and although condors came to some of his baits, they always managed to elude capture (Millard 1958). Meanwhile, Ian McMillan and other opponents went over the heads of the Department and Commission to successfully lobby the California Legislature to specifically prohibit any taking of wild condors after early 1954. Trapping efforts were stopped at this point, much to the relief of the opponents of captive breeding.

Ironically, nearly thirty years later, it fell to the San Diego Zoo, together with the Los Angeles Zoo, to initiate a full scale captive-breeding program with the condor in what proved to be the only hope for survival of the species.

The winners of the early battles to establish the Sespe Sanctuary and prevent captive breeding were emphatically the National Audubon Society, Miller, Koford, the McMillans, and their supporters. They also won a more subtle and ultimately much more important campaign. Through their efforts, the condor was enshrined as a species too sensitive to even approach safely, too sensitive to study closely, and too delicately balanced above extinction to allow any capture of individuals for any purpose. The condor had become untouchable.

Its image had also become unviewable. Sally Spofford, former manager of the Laboratory of Ornithology at Cornell University and Helen's former boss, once gave us a particularly revealing personal account of Alden Miller's zealously protective attitude toward the species:

"In 1962, the International Ornithological Congress met in Ithaca, N.Y. at Cornell University. Statler Hall was the headquarters, but most of the registrants spent time at the Laboratory of Ornithology at Sapsucker Woods.

The Lab, of course, had displays of all kinds, played recordings of bird songs, sponsored early morning breakfasts and field trips, and the staff kept busy answering questions and assisting the visitors.

One exhibit dreamed up by the late Dr. Arthur A. Allen was a series of four color enlargements of America's four rarest birds: the Ivory-billed Woodpecker, Trumpeter Swan, Whooping Crane, and California Condor. The pictures of the first three had been taken by Dr. Allen. Fred Truslow contributed a magnificent photograph of the condor. He had been privileged to spend some time in condor country, and that is a story in itself. He was closely supervised, and faced some opposition to his getting pictures, but a more cautious photographer in respect to avoiding disturbance to birds could rarely be found.

When Dr. Alden Miller came to the Lab the first day and saw the picture of the Condor he became, to put it mildly, very upset. He rushed to Dr. Allen's office and demanded that the picture be removed. He was of the school of thought that any form of publicity for the bird was harmful to it – that it would inspire others to invade the condor refuge, etc. etc. Doc was unable to persuade him otherwise.

However, instead of removing the picture – and the label stating that the exhibit showed *four* rare birds – Doc draped a piece of burlap over the offending photo, with no explanation. My desk, in the little front office, faced the exhibit – and I was rewarded with a wonderful show of human curiosity. Visitor after visitor stopped in front of the exhibit, cautiously looked in all directions, then lifted the burlap and peeked quickly. Fred Truslow found a good vantage point, sitting on the wastebasket by my desk (which he often referred to as a seat of learning), and relished the show immensely."

For those on the fringe of condor conservation efforts, with no real personal experience with the species, the perception of it being an extremely wary and sensitive creature has been a comfortable, even attractive idea, seemingly consonant with the rarity of the species. And to have researchers such as Koford, Miller, and the McMillans affirming this perception put it beyond question for many conservationists.

Nevertheless, wild condors have continued to have a contrary habit of flying in curiously from a distance to circle low over hikers' heads, sitting placidly for frame-filling portraits by wilderness photographers, accepting banana peels and peanut butter sandwiches from back-country explorers, and walking unconcernedly along the shores of a heavily-boated lake with waterskiers whizzing along only a few meters away (all are documented occurrences). The mental contortions required to square such observations with the image of a condor completely intolerant of man have sometimes been awesome.

Eben McMillan (1981) offered perhaps the most detailed reconciliation of these apparently contradictory concepts:

"You know, behaviorists, working with other animals, have established that there is what is known as a delayed response to disturbance. Photographers see this a lot. You go in to photograph a bird on a nest, and the bird will sit right there; you scare it off, and it'll come right back. You're ready to come back in two days and there's nothing there. This kind of thing happens again and again. The way the bird behaves when you're there is no indication at all of what the bird is going to do six, 24, or 48 hours later. Carl [Koford] brought this out in his paper on the condor. He told about things he had seen where the birds would respond to a disturbance, or a pressure, long after it happened. The birds might be roosting in a particular tree, and a guy would drive some cattle through or a birdwatcher would come up. And the birds would sit right there while the cattle went by underneath. Maybe the guy had seen them for a week coming to that roost, but the next day they didn't come back. Not only that, they never came back at all; they never came to use that tree again, as a roost. Carl was one of the early observers of this phenomenon, the delayed response."

The preceding argument was to become an enduring, yet unprovable, article of faith among program opponents in the 1980s. Perhaps the nesting birds that disappeared in McMillan's illustration were victims of nest predation caused by the photographer exposing the nest to view or leaving a scent trail to the nest, and perhaps his condors would never have come back to roost in that particular tree, disturbance or no disturbance. Did anyone, in fact, sit in view of the tree month after month to see whether condors ever came back? Although Koford did discuss the possibility of delayed responses in his monograph, he also documented numerous instances of condors returning to nests and roosts time and again, despite high levels of disturbance, in part from his own visits.

And strangely, the condor pair (SMM and SMA) we observed walking along the beach of a lake used heavily for recreation during the early 1980s did keep coming back week after week, month after month. Sometimes they walked within 5 m of us even though we were in full view. Often as they puttered through debris on the shore they did not even look up as speedboats roared by. We waited patiently for a sign of a delayed response in these birds.

Nevertheless, it would be inaccurate to imply that all condors have been as approachable as the lake pair. This pair, which had a nest site close by, evidently had become thoroughly habituated to people through frequent entry of people into their nesting territory. As in most bird species, different individual condors exhibit different tolerances for human approach and, as in many other species, juveniles tend to be especially confiding. We grant that some individuals may flush from a nest when a person is still many meters away. But as we learned during egg collection operations during the mid-1980s, such wariness is exceptional, and most incubating birds will not leave nests until intruders are very near. On one occasion Koford had to throw rocks at the cliff next to a nest to get an adult to appear at the entrance for Pemberton's photographic efforts. Such tolerance of disturbance is virtually unknown in most large raptor species.

Fred Sibley, in his 1967 field notes, made an interesting observation on the absence of long-term effects of human disturbance on a traditional condor roost in northern Kern County:

"A roosting locality on Breckenridge Mountain referred to in Koford's notes was watched for one day and two birds were seen. When Koford first found this roosting site in 1946 there was considerable human disturbance, and one would have expected the birds to have moved elsewhere. The morning I watched there was heavy traffic on a road 200 yards from the roost, moderate activity at the numerous summer homes 1/2–1 mile away, a chain saw going within 1/2 mile of the roost and one ear-splitting sonic boom which echoed and reechoed up and down the mountain. Despite all this activity the birds departed at a 'normal' time over an hour after the 'disturbance' activities had reached their plateau."

This roost continued to host condors until well into the 1980s.

In sum, although we grant that there is virtually no evidence of condors in the historic wild population ever coming voluntarily into settled areas, the species has been one of the most approachable large birds we have encountered in the wild. That said, we still believe there are some risks to nest entry and especially to handling of chicks, and we still support generous protected areas around nests and roosts. But the notion that condors will desert nests and roosts merely because someone walks nearby is clearly at odds with an immense body of observational evidence. There are far more wary birds in the wild than the condor, and as long as this species is not actually molested, it appears to handle the intrusions of our species without major upset. The alleged great wariness of the species is a myth.

How crucial then has the Sespe Sanctuary been for survival of the condor? This is not an easy question to answer, and we must admit we are basically very pleased that the sanctuary was established and strongly support its maintenance. But to be fair, we believe the fate of the species would have been about the same with or without the sanctuary. Most pairs in the 1980s, and almost surely in Koford's day as well, nested outside the sanctuary, and these nesting areas have been almost as well protected as those inside by their remote locations and the surrounding brushy terrain. It is difficult to argue that the sanctuary has greatly slowed the population decline when the principal problems of the species, as we shall see, have evidently been on the foraging grounds many kilometers away.

On the other hand, more condors might have been shot or otherwise molested in the sanctuary region if a sanctuary had not been established. More oil roads would probably have been built, making it easy for gunners and curiosity seekers to approach certain nests. The fact that we found a spent bullet in the nest litter of one sanctuary site close to an oil well (Snyder *et al.* 1986) was a clear indication that even though nesting condors might not greatly fear humanity, the risks of nesting in accessible areas can be substantial.

Regardless, the condor population continued to decline steadily in spite of creation of the Sespe Sanctuary. Had the sanctuary proven sufficient to stop the condor's decline, the Koford-Miller-McMillan victory of perspectives would not have been especially harmful. But the Sespe Sanctuary, and in fact the whole sanctuary approach, clearly proved inadequate. And now the image of the species that accompanied this approach became an oppressive curse to effective conservation, a curse that endured nearly 30 years, totally inhibiting much needed research at times and preventing even tentative experimental attempts at captive breeding. In the balance, we believe that the price paid for the sanctuary in terms of lost research and conservation opportunities and in terms of later research being focused too tightly on this piece of real estate, was excessive. We do not believe that the end justified the means.

The Miller–McMillan Era

Following Koford's study and the establishment of the Sespe Sanctuary, there was considerable hope that the species' conservation might be assured. The U.S. Forest Service (USFS) and National Audubon Society (NAS) sponsored a succession of patrolmen for the sanctuary who made efforts to monitor condor numbers and document nests, but the data collected were of very uneven quality. By the late 1950s and early 1960s, concerns arose that condor numbers were still declining, and in 1963 and 1964 the NAS and the National Geographic Society (NGS) sponsored a follow-up study to Koford's research. The field work in this study was carried out by two rancher friends of Carl Koford — Ian and Eben McMillan — while Alden Miller, Koford's former major professor at Berkeley, provided academic input by supervising the planning, data analysis, and write-up of results. Miller's role in this study was similar to his role in Koford's study. Although his participation in Koford's studies had been much less visible, he had been very closely involved in Koford's project, even to the extent of drafting some of Koford's progress reports and drafting revisions to Koford's thesis prior to its publication. In fact, there are more than a few observers who believe it was Alden Miller, rather than Carl Koford, who was the principal architect of the traditional philosophy of condor conservation that dominated the scene from the late 1930s into the 1970s.

The McMillan brothers were the most prominent figures active with condors in the middle historical period that we ever had a chance to meet. Both were deeply committed to condor conservation and were thoroughly distrustful of the government and the National Adubon Society, and perhaps especially government and Audubon biologists such as ourselves. Nevertheless, Eben in particular was a very friendly host the few times we met

Eben (left) and Ian McMillan (right) on the watch for condors over Cholame Flats in December 1964.

with him, and we will never forget the day in 1980 he joined an expedition including Noel, Jan Hamber, and John Ogden for a grueling hike to a condor nest cliff in San Luis Obispo County. Over 12 years earlier Fred Sibley had cut a trail through the chaparral to reach this cliff, and Eben knew of its approximate location, as he had accompanied Fred on one trip to the cliff. But 12 years is a long long time in the life cycle of chaparral vegetation, and the trail had become completely overgrown and was only occasionally discernible by weathered machete scars on stumps of old branches. Despite his advanced age, Eben led us steadily along the route, his hands bloodied by the rough interlaced branches, and we were deeply impressed by his strength, good humor, and optimism. Progress was so slow, we barely struggled out of the brush before dark, and if we had failed to do so, we would have been hard put to fight our way free as we had neglected to bring any flashlights. Eben endured it all without a murmur of complaint. Whatever his objections to the condor program of the 1980s, he did not let them interfere with his basic kindly instincts to be courteous and helpful to people in the program.

We met Eben's brother Ian only once – at a tense public debate over the condor program in late 1982 in Santa Barbara, where he rose dramatically to challenge the accuracy of reproductive statistics Noel was presenting. Though he did not identify himself as he launched into his confrontation, we knew immediately who he must be. Before this meeting Ian had voluntarily withdrawn from condor controversies for a number of years, so we did not know whether his reemergence might be a preview of clashes to follow. As it turned out, however, the condor program was about to enter the only period of relative peace it was to enjoy in all the years of our participation, and we never encountered Ian McMillan again.

The Miller–McMillan study of 1963–64 was run very differently from Koford's in a number of respects. Most importantly, no effort was made to find and study nests, a response to Koford's admonitions regarding the dangers of nest disturbance. Thus, there was no direct evaluation of the reproductive performance of the population. Instead, the fieldwork was largely limited to an evaluation of food availability, a collection of data on condor numbers and distribution, and an assembly of information on mortality threats to the species. For these tasks, Miller et al. relied heavily on interviews with ranchers, USFS employees, and other individuals knowledgeable about condors.

In their summary report Miller and the McMillans concluded that whereas there had been 60 condors in Koford's day, there were now only about 42 birds, and the decline was due to excessive mortality from shooting and poisoning, not to reproductive problems (Miller et al. 1965). They were confident that food was no problem.

The population estimate of 42 birds was based largely on comparisons of sizes of the largest flocks these researchers could document with the largest flocks documented by Koford and then factoring down Koford's population estimate accordingly. Thus, the accuracy of their estimate depended crucially on the accuracy of Koford's estimate. Unfortunately, like Koford, they came across one sighting made by someone with good credentials that was larger than their total population estimate. How they handled this count is worth considering in some detail.

The sighting in question was made by Bert Snedden, a rancher in the southern San Joaquin Valley foothills who had known condors all his life (some of his early sightings were recorded by C.S. Robinson). Snedden told the McMillans that in the fall of 1961 he and his sons had seen a total of 63 condors, in two simultaneous groups of 30 and 33 birds, circling over his ranch. But when this sighting appeared in Miller et al. (1965), the total given was only 33 birds, with no discussion of their modification of what Snedden had told them.

Eben McMillan's field notes provide some insight as to why Snedden's count was nearly halved in Miller et al. (1965). In his original analysis of 1963 Eben found Snedden to be a highly reliable observer and rated it 95% sure that Snedden's full count was accurate. Still, he speculated there was a 5% chance that the more distant of the two groups of birds seen just might have been a migrating flock of Swainson's Hawks (*Buteo swainsoni*), which vaguely resemble condors in color pattern underneath. By the time of Miller et al. (1965) this 5% chance had evidently evolved into near certainty, and one of Snedden's two groups of condors was no longer to be considered credible.

Bert Snedden was deeply offended by the way his sighting was treated by Miller et al. In late 1983 he told us that he recalled counting the 63 birds four times as they circled overhead and that they were all, without doubt, condors. We know of no compelling reasons to reject his count. Accepting half his count, while rejecting the other half without comment, anomalously rates him as both a reliable and unreliable observer simultaneously.

Our own evaluation of the Miller–McMillan population estimate, given in Snyder and Johnson (1985a,b) and Johnson (1985), is that since it was based primarily on comparisons of flock sizes between their study and Koford's study, it was probably subject to roughly the same error factor as Koford's estimate (about two to three), yielding an adjusted estimate somewhere between 80 and 120 condors for their study. However, if one estimates the magnitude of decline on the basis of the very largest condor flocks during the Koford and Miller–McMillan studies (the McLean count of 122 birds in 1942 and the Snedden count of 63 birds in 1961), one might alternatively conclude that the percent decline between the two periods could have been even larger than that computed by Miller and the McMillans. Thus, if there were really about 150 birds in the 1940s, the numbers in the early 1960s might have been only about 75–80 birds. All these extrapolations are of course based on an untestable assumption that the largest flocks seen might bear some sort of constant relationship with total population sizes. This assumption may not be a very good one.

Although the Miller–McMillan team devoted much of their paper to anecdotal and direct evidence of shooting threats to the condor, perhaps the most interesting aspect of their study was their discussion of the possible causes of death of three condors recovered in three different areas near Granite Station of Tulare County during the early 1960s. No broken bones were found in any of these birds, nor were there other signs that they had been shot. But in one case, when the head of the dead bird was placed in a dermestid beetle colony for cleanup, all the beetles promptly died. Their deaths suggested to Miller et al. that poisoning was also probably the cause of the condor's death, although no specific poisons were ever confirmed. This condor had hung in a barn for several years before Miller et al. obtained it, so it was quite dried out, although there was still some meat in the skull. However, unknown to Miller et al., but later learned by Fred Sibley from Ben Easley, an agent involved with ground squirrel control operations in the region, the condor carcass had evidently been deliberately sprayed with DDT to keep down the flies as it hung in the barn. This provides a plausible explanation for the death of the dermestids independent of what may have killed the condor, although it does not rule out the possibility that the condor died of poisoning.

The other two condors picked up dead or dying near Granite Station were also possibly poisoned, but no definite residues of poison were ever found in any of the birds. The McMillans nevertheless strongly suspected 1080 was responsible because the birds were found in areas treated with 1080 to kill ground squirrels. These dead condors became the foundation on which the McMillans based a continuous campaign against use of 1080.

However, if these condors were poisoned (which does not seem unlikely), the poison(s) involved may well have been something other than 1080. Lead poisoning, for example, was neither looked for nor ruled out, and as we now know from evidence of the 1980s, lead has been a very important toxin that has almost certainly been killing condors for centuries. The symptoms seen in one of the three birds prior to death − emaciation and lack of coordination − are typical of lead poisoning. Another possibility was strychnine poisoning, although strychnine is often sufficiently fast-acting that poisoned animals do not go far from the scene of poisoning and these condors were not found near poisoned carcasses.

Although we agree with Miller and the McMillans that the major cause of decline for the condor has been excessive mortality, their reasons for this conclusion are not convincing in the light of current knowledge. From sightings in the field, they believed there were at least 10 different immature condors in the wild during their study, and since their total population estimate was roughly 40 birds, they concluded that about 25% of the population was made up of immatures. They considered this fraction to be a healthy one, indicating the species was not having reproductive problems. Therefore, the causes of decline had to be mortality factors.

However, if (as we believe) the total condor population during the Miller-McMillan study was at least nearly twice as large, 10 immatures accounted for only about 12–13% of the population, which is hardly conclusive evidence for good reproduction. Nevertheless, there could well have been more than 10 immatures alive in the population at the time. The methods of observation used by Miller et al. were far too crude to rule out greater numbers of immatures, and in fact, the ratios of immatures to adults they saw in many flocks suggested, but did not prove, greater numbers. Thus it is very possible, although undemonstrated, that condors were reproducing normally at the time.

In summary, neither Miller et al. nor Koford had obtained the sort of data necessary to establish conclusively whether the decline of the condor was primarily due to reproductive problems or mortality problems, or to a combination of the two. Although many bits and pieces of information had been collected on various threats to the species, there was as yet no true understanding of what major forces were driving the decline.

The major advance achieved by the Miller–McMillan study over that of Koford was that Miller and the McMillans were convinced that the condor population was in rapid decline whereas Koford had believed it was essentially stable. Nevertheless, the conservation recommendations of the two studies were almost identical. Like Koford, Miller and the McMillans called for federal protection of the condor, increased education and law enforcement efforts to reduce shooting and molestation, increased protection from human disturbance for nesting and roosting areas, further study of the effects of poisons (especially 1080) on surrogate species, and a full-time condor warden to patrol areas of high condor activity. In addition they called for an end to coyote control using poisoned carcasses and recommended closure of some specific condor flyways to shooting, especially the Sierra Madre Ridge in Santa Barbara County and Pine Mountain in Ventura County. Furthermore, they called for the prohibition of low-flying aircraft over the Sespe Sanctuary. But we must emphasize that neither Koford nor Miller et al. recommended a cessation of all shooting in the range of the condor. Then, as now, such a step would have been politically explosive, and very likely counterproductive to condor conservation. Likewise they did not press for an immediate ban on use of 1080, probably for similar reasons.

Most of these recommendations were ultimately implemented. The condor was given federal protection under the Endangered Species Acts of 1966 and 1973; greatly increased education on the plight of the species did occur through publication of numerous magazine articles and books and through innumerable talks and discussions, especially those given by John Borneman of NAS; protection of the Sespe Sanctuary was enhanced by seasonal firearms bans in buffer areas and by closure of outlying nesting areas such as the Piru Gorge; while private inholdings in the Los Padres National Forest, such as the Green Cabins and Coldwater Canyon nesting areas, the Indian Creek area, and the Hi Mountain nesting area were purchased and given protection. In addition, the Percy Ranch adjacent to the Sespe Sanctuary was purchased and set up as the Hopper Mountain National Wildlife Refuge, and a large part of the condor nesting range in Santa Barbara County was set aside as the San Rafael and Dick Smith Wilderness Areas. Furthermore, a full-time condor warden (John Borneman) was appointed by the NAS in 1965; the Sierra Madre Ridge Road was kept closed to public vehicles; aircraft were banned from the Sespe Sanctuary region; and an intensive study of the field effects of 1080 poisoning of ground squirrels was conducted by the U.S. Fish and Wildlife Service in 1977 (but indicated no clear threats to raptors or vultures – see Hegdahl et al. 1979). In addition, coyote trapping by the Animal Damage Control (ADC) branch of the U.S. Fish and Wildlife Service became limited to scent-baited traps. Good summaries of many of these and other conservation actions are given in Wilbur (1978b) and Jurek (1983).

Despite the many protective steps taken, the decline of the species continued. Some still blamed bureaucracy for inaction, and many still continued to believe in the adequacy of the recommendations of Koford and Miller et al. In hindsight, the failure of these recommendations to reverse the decline is not surprising. For even if these recommendations had been implemented to everyone's complete satisfaction, even if the whole Los Padres National Forest had been sealed tight from human entry, even if not a single condor had been shot since the 1940s, and even if 1080 and strychnine poisoning had been completely stopped throughout the condor range, the chances were still very large that the decline of the species would have continued, possibly at virtually the same rate as actually occurred. Three out of four condors found dead in the 1980s were victims of lead poisoning, very possibly caused by entirely legal hunting of wildlife such as deer in areas far from the Los Padres Forest. The recommendations of Koford and Miller et al. did not address this threat. Nor did they address the threat from collisions with overhead wires, which is now known to be a substantial hazard to large vultures in general and has been a major mortality factor for recent releases of condors to the wild. Koford and Miller et al. drew reasonable conclusions from the information they had available, but their information was far too incomplete to allow development of an adequately successful conservation plan.

The proper response to this failure should have been, and ultimately was, a general recognition that much better data were needed on the causes of the condor's decline, but for some, further research was not only unnecessary but unacceptably dangerous, and the decline of the species was still to be attributed to a failure of bureaucracy to save enough habitat and to stop 1080 poisoning and wanton shooting of condors.

The Sibley Era

During the mid-1960s the viability of the Sespe Condor Sanctuary was threatened by proposed dams along Sespe Creek above Fillmore. The U.S. Fish and Wildlife Service (USFWS) responded by sending Fred Sibley to California to evaluate the potential impacts of the proposed dams on condors. Sibley, like Carl Koford, proved to be an extremely dedicated field researcher, and his four years of condor studies (1966–1969) were tremendously productive.

Nevertheless, Sibley's tenure in California was viewed with some suspicion by Koford and the McMillan brothers, and he soon found himself under bitter criticism for following a relatively independent approach to condor research. Koford's antagonism to USFWS efforts with condors may to some extent have been a turf response, but it may also have been prompted by a failure of the USFWS to favor his offer to conduct research with surrogate Turkey Vultures on the effects of toxic materials, especially compound 1080, that might be affecting California Condors. Koford submitted his proposal to the USFWS in 1967, and later to the NAS, but was not successful in obtaining funding. This rebuff could well have led Koford and the McMillans to question the motives and wisdom of both organizations, as they believed 1080 poisoning was potentially a major factor causing the endangerment of the species.

As one of the first field biologists of the newly created Endangered Wildlife Research Program of the USFWS, Sibley's approach to the Sespe dams issue was to determine whether anticipated disturbance from the dams might threaten the continued use of any condor nests. He launched a massive effort to find active and old condor nest sites, both in the path of the proposed project and elsewhere, and he closely studied their features, especially various human disturbance characteristics, that might determine whether sites were usable by condors. Each site found was carefully measured, mapped, and scored by a diverse set of criteria.

Assisting with Sibley's nest investigations and other condor research projects of the late 1960s were John Borneman and Dean Carrier. Borneman had been appointed condor warden for the NAS in 1965, following recommendations of Miller et al. that such a position be established. Carrier was the first U.S. Forest Service (USFS) condor biologist and began studies in 1968.

Four condor researchers of the 1960s and 1970s: **above**, Dick Smith (left) with Fred Sibley (center) and John Borneman (right) at the start of a pack trip to the Santa Barbara back country in 1967 – an expedition derailed by a late spring snowstorm; **bottom left**, Fred Sibley roping to an old condor nest below Hole-in-the-wall of the Sespe Condor Sanctuary; and **bottom right**, Jan Hamber, collaborator with Dick Smith in Santa Barbara County condor studies.

Sibley located a large number of condor nests. Most were old inactive sites that he found by following up on old accounts of egg collectors and records obtained by Koford, and by systematic rope work on cliffs. His field trips were often monumental tours of multiple sites in extremely difficult terrain, and his field notes revealed a dogged physical endurance that seemed superhuman when we later revisited many of the sites he had explored. As a rule of thumb, we learned to expect that at most we might be able to visit only about half the number of sites he covered in an equivalent length of time, and at a price of near total exhaustion.

The nest-investigation studies led to a thorough report on the likely impacts of the proposed Sespe dams on condor reproduction (Sibley 1969). Sibley found no active condor nests close to sources of disturbance, such as paved roads. Whether this was a result of human harassment or predation on condors nesting too close to disturbance, a result of responses of the birds to disturbance, or only a chance effect was unclear, but the prudent response to this information was to create safety zones around active and recently active sites. Since the proposed dams and associated developments fell within critical distances of a number of active and recently active condor nests, Sibley's report predicted significant effects on condors. But even before Sibley's report was published, the Sespe dams project was shelved because local residents failed to approve a bond issue necessary for the project to proceed.

Despite Sibley's success in researching the Sespe dams issue and the defeat of the proposed dams, Koford and the McMillans were not pleased. The fact that Sibley had entered many condor nests during his research was contrary to their recommendations, and for his transgressions Sibley soon found himself under vigorous attack, primarily by Ian McMillan. As Fred later described the situation to us in a letter,

> "Borneman has probably told you about the wonderful meal Ian invited us to. This was 6–8 months after I had arrived in California. It was to be a chance to meet on Ian's turf and out of the limelight to discuss some of the condor problems and get to know each other. When we arrived he showed us California Quail and more California Quail – his real passion – and told us of the many things he had learned about the birds [truly impressive] without a lot of chest thumping or exaggerations. Then we sat down to a marvelous steak dinner. After the blessing Ian said, 'Fred isn't IT TRUE!! YOU'VE !!! BEEN GOING INTO CONDOR NESTS!!!!!!' His wife then pitched in from the other side, 'TRUE. DON'T DENY IT!!! IAN IS RIGHT.' This continued from first one and then the other until John and I finished our meals and left.... He didn't seem to know how to approach an issue except by hurling accusations at the other side."

The attacks went fully public in 1970 with an article of Ian's that alleged that Fred's nest entries had caused the wild condor population to cease reproduction:

> "Although serious breakdowns have occurred in the administration of the Sespe Sanctuary, the closed area has functioned with dramatic effect as an indispensable wilderness home for the condors. In the years of intensive research which led to establishment of the refuge, Carl Koford, who carried out the study, found a maximum of four active nests in one year. In 1967, a total of six active condor nests were found in a new research project by the U.S. Fish and Wildlife Service. Five of these were in or near the Sespe Sanctuary.
>
> This could only indicate that after twenty years in operation the refuge was functioning most effectively in accord with its purpose. It is my considered opinion that without the special protection given this vital nesting retreat, the California Condor would now be extinct.
>
> It might seem from this, that a favorable and optimistic account of the condor program can be given. Instead, an alarming and perhaps disastrous development must be reported. The new condor research, which began in 1966, is part of the much publicized Federal Endangered Species Program. Its main operation, as confirmed in the discovery of six active nests in 1967, has obviously been to find and

examine condor nests. Another early result of the project was the delivery in the spring of 1967 of a strong, healthy young condor to a zoo in Los Angeles. This brings into focus an orientation toward artificial propagation that has quickly become the main aspect of the federal project....

With the annual search for active condor nests continuing unabated, opponents of this practice have hoped that the damage done to the condor population might be less than the previous [Koford's] research would indicate. But instead, the appeals and protests now appear to have greatly understated the potentialities of the new disturbance. Only a single occupied nest has been found in the two years following 1967 when the six active nests were examined. Since that year, no nestings have been known to occur in the Sespe Condor Sanctuary or nearby areas. The single nest that has been found to be occupied in 1968 and 1969 is remote from the Sespe Sanctuary by a distance of some 90 airline miles. Yet even as it became obvious that the research operations might be causing a general nesting failure, this single site has been repeatedly invaded during the nesting period."

Several comments should be offered on McMillans assertions. First, the captive condor delivered to the Los Angeles Zoo in 1967 had nothing to do with an "orientation toward artificial propagation in the federal project" and was hardly a healthy bird (see details below). Second, it is highly unlikely that Koford found more than a small fraction of the nests active in the Sespe Sanctuary during his study. His field notes reveal that he did relatively little searching for nests, and many of the sites he studied had in fact been found by others. Third, as detailed in Snyder (1983), six active condor nests were indeed found in 1967, but contrary to McMillan, another six nesting attempts were detected in 1968–1969 (with considerably reduced field survey effort in 1969). Furthermore, two of the latter nests were within the Sespe Sanctuary. Considering the uncertainties and difficulties in finding active condor nests, these data cannot be used as evidence for a dramatic decline in nesting activity, and even if there was a decline (as we suspect there probably was, in line with the overall decline of the population), it surely does not follow that it must have been caused by research activities.

In fact, Sibley's field notes make it clear that the great majority of active nests discovered during those years were not even approached until after young had fledged or after the nests had failed (Sibley deliberately avoided approaching known nests in the early stages of breeding). Adult birds were not even in attendance at the times of nest examination in almost all cases. How nest examinations in these cases could have caused cessation of breeding is beyond comprehension.

And of the five nests Sibley entered while they were active, only one subsequently failed, with no evidence that failure had anything to do with nest entry. Especially interesting is the fact that although Sibley entered the successive active nests of a pair in San Luis Obispo County once each year from 1967 through 1969, chicks fledged each year from this territory and the pair returned annually to nest again.

Surely, if Sibley's brief nest entries had caused cessation of breeding, we should have observed similar effects in the pairs from which we repeatedly took eggs or young from

1982 through 1986. Yet every one of these pairs continued to breed year after year (most in fact laid multiple eggs each year). There were absolutely no signs that our operations (which involved not only nest entries, but considerable disturbance from numerous nearby people and noisy helicopters) gave them any second thoughts about breeding again. In most cases courtship resumed within a couple days of an egg removal. True, the pairs moved from one nest site to another in successive breeding attempts, but this occurred whether or not we entered nests when they were active. During our years of study, the only factors that ever stopped any of the breeding pairs from egg laying were mortality of one or both adults or presence of a dependent fledgling from the previous year. Thus McMillan's claim that Sibley's activities stopped reproduction of the species has no plausible foundation.

Fred Sibley had already departed from the condor program by the time of McMillan's published accusations, and he made no formal response to the charges. Had Fred continued longer in the program, we doubt that the affair would or should have slowed him down perceptibly. Nevertheless, we strongly suspect that the near absence of any detailed studies of nesting condors that characterized the next 10 years of the program may have been stimulated in part by the reticence of administrators and researchers alike to deal with renewed vitriol of Ian McMillan.

Sibley was also a central figure during the early years of the annual October Survey, a giant simultaneous count of condors from strategic lookouts throughout the known range. The Survey was initiated in 1965, with Alden Miller acting as the original chairman of the organizing committee. However, Miller died of a heart attack at about the time of the first Survey, and its successful completion was overseen by Bob Mallette of the California Department of Fish and Game (CDFG) and John Borneman of the NAS (Mallette and Borneman 1966).

The October Survey continued each year through 1981, with the exception of 1979. Although procedures were originally designed to yield a standardized minimum estimate of population size, the counts turned out to be quite variable from one year to the next, presumably because of weather influences, changes in foraging patterns of birds, changes in numbers of observers and lookouts, and other factors (see discussion in Verner 1978, Wilbur 1978b). There were also some difficulties in determining whether birds seen at one lookout might be the same as ones seen at another lookout at a different time, and hard decisions had to be made in coming up with total numbers of birds seen, especially considering the fact that a single bird could cover a large fraction of the known range within a single day under optimal conditions (see Meretsky and Snyder 1992).

Nevertheless, despite the vagaries of the counts, they did serve to give some idea of minimum size and overall trends of the population. During the late 1960s, counts generally exceeded 50 individuals, though totals dropped to less than 20 individuals by the early 1980s. These counts, along with other population estimates from the 1950s through 1980s are illustrated in the graph below. Mainly on the basis of the survey, Sibley believed that the wild population consisted of about 60 individuals during the late 1960s. This estimate was identical to Koford's for the 1940s, but although this suggested at face value that the population was relatively stable, and led to assertions to this effect by some Department of Fish and Game

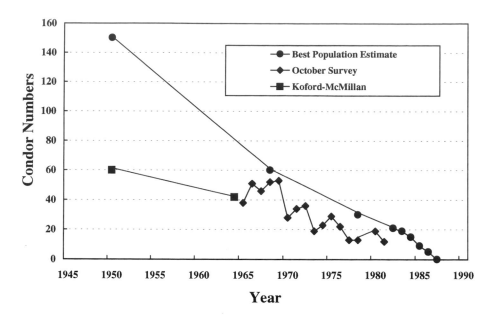

Population estimates of the historic wild California Condor population from 1950 through 1987. Best population estimates include estimate of Fred Sibley for 1968, Sandy Wilbur for 1978, and potentially error-free counts from photo census from 1982 to 1986. Estimate of 150 birds for 1950 was based on comparisons of flock sizes in the late 1960s with those during Koford's study and the probable existence of about 60 condors in 1968.

and Forest Service personnel, it was obvious that many fewer birds were then being seen in all parts of the range than in Koford's day. Sibley believed that Koford may even have had as many as 200 condors alive in the wild during his study, an estimate that we would not rule out, although we favor a somewhat more conservative rough estimate of 150 individuals.

Ian McMillan vigorously contested the validity of the October Survey when it yielded much higher counts for the late 1960s than the population estimate of 42 birds given in Miller et al. (1965) for the early 1960s. When the 1966 count totaled 51 individuals, McMillan wrote a strongly critical letter to the Department of Fish and Game, and in response the organizers of the survey invited him to attend the analysis sessions of the counts in 1967 and 1968. Some indication of the highly charged atmosphere of these meetings can be glimpsed from Fred Sibley's notes on the 1967 session:

"Ian McMillan, Dr. Carl Koford, Dr. Ken Stager, Dr. Peter Ames, and Clint Lostetter attended the Friday critique in addition to the survey evaluation subcommittee. After about an hour's presentation of methods and results Ian asked a few questions and made a few statements but could never really get started. At one point he stated that 21 birds seemed an unusually high number for a single station, Koford who had spent both days there said he felt that was a very reasonable estimate. Ian then attacked the total of 12 birds during a one hour period on the same station. John Borneman pointed out that Ben Glading and Roland Clement had had 13 condors in view at one time during this period (the two official observers were snowed under by photographers and visiting dignitaries and were unable to keep up with the flow of birds. They recorded only 7 birds at one time). At another point Ian stated that observers were probably misidentifying adult and juvenile birds due to poor training and lack of experience. To prove his point he cited three juveniles seen in one group at station 50B but not seen at station 50A less than a mile away. Ken Stager had identified the three birds and both he and Carl Koford, station 50A, confirmed that there were many times during the day when birds could be seen from one station and not from the other, although the two sets of observers could see each other.

The consensus was that the final total (46 birds) is a conservative estimate from the data and an even more conservative estimate of the total population. Koford in particular felt that birds were missed by observers and that the limited data submitted by the observers caused us to lump many sightings which were really of different birds. Most agreed that the greater the concentration of birds the greater the gap would be between the estimated number and the actual number. Finally, as in other years there were at least four birds seen by unofficial observers or on the periphery of the range the next day which were not included in our figure of 46. Koford even jokingly remarked that we had almost convinced him there were 100 birds."

In spite of the high degree of consensus among participants that the October Survey counts of the late 1960s indicated a minimum population of over 50 birds (official counts were 38, 51, 46, 52, and 53 birds for 1965 through 1969), McMillan continued to claim that the survey was greatly overestimating the population and that the 42-bird estimate of Miller et al. (1965) was still valid (McMillan 1970, 1971).

Our own judgment is that Sibley's population estimate of 60 birds for that time period was a good one, as one can arrive at roughly the same estimate by comparing area-specific flock sizes seen during his studies with flock sizes seen in more recent years when population size was finally known accurately. The October Survey was abandoned in 1982 when a comprehensive method of censusing condors through systematic photography of flying birds and identification of individuals was developed (Snyder and Johnson 1985a,b).

Sibley (1968) reported a nesting success rate of 45% for condors in the late 1960s, a rate closely resembling that of Koford. Although egg breakage was frequent in the 1960s and shells collected by Sibley averaged very thin (Kiff et al. 1979, Snyder 1983, Snyder et al. ms), the rate of egg breakage did not show any clear increase over that during Koford's pre-DDT study, and there were still many condor fledglings being recorded in the 1960s. These latter features, as we will discuss much more thoroughly in Chapter 11, did not suggest that the species was suffering from the classic DDT syndrome of reproductive collapse, a conclusion that was also voiced early by Ian McMillan (1968).

It was not yet possible to estimate what fraction of the adult population was attempting to breed. Despite Sibley's great success in locating nests, it is quite clear from more recent information that he could not reasonably have found all active pairs (a task far beyond the limited manpower available then). However, Sibley's efforts were sufficient to establish reasonably strong use of the Sespe Sanctuary by breeding pairs and frequent nesting by pairs outside the Sanctuary.

Population counts and productivity records were still too crude to permit calculations of overall mortality rates during the Sibley years. Only one dead condor was found during this period (a chick that apparently fell from its nest cave). However, one starving fledgling was recovered in Matilija Canyon in 1967 and may have been in difficulty because of its parents' reluctance to enter a summer homes area where it had wandered or perhaps because one or both parents had died.

Sibley and Borneman attempted to release the Matilija bird back to the wild after feeding it back to good health, but they were unsuccessful and almost lost the bird in the process. As a reasonable first step, the bird was tethered on a leash attached to a stake next to a deer carcass placed near its presumed nest site. Sibley and Borneman hoped its parents would return to feed it, and if that occurred, planned to follow with a full release of the unfettered bird. Unfortunately, although several condors did land next to the bird, they treated it aggressively, and in the ensuing confusion, the bird's stake broke free. The bird took to the air, disappearing over a nearby hill with its leash and stake trailing from one leg.

During the following four days, Sibley, Borneman, and others made exhaustive efforts to relocate the bird but never caught sight of it. Finally on the fifth day, John Lorenzana at last discovered it bloodhound style by smelling it and moving upwind to a dense patch of chaparral where it hung upside down, dangling from a branch with one foot entangled by the leash and stake. Because of the near fatal outcome of the release effort and the damage to the bird's foot from its entanglement, a decision was made at this point to keep the bird captive at the Los Angeles Zoo. For the next 15 years this bird, "Topatopa," was the only California Condor in captivity.

Sibley left the USFWS condor program prematurely in 1969, not because of condor issues, but largely because of his dissatisfaction with governmental response to the notorious oil spill off Santa Barbara, which occurred early in the year. Fred immediately began efforts to document effects of the spill on wildlife as part of his regional responsibilities. But he was soon ordered to abandon such research and not to make any public statements as to effects of the spill, even though the carnage of seabirds, marine mammals, and shellfish was obvious and devastating. Meanwhile the state of California put out a press release alleging no major negative effects of the spill. In effect, both the federal and state governments were in collusion with the oil industry in attempting to suppress information on the disaster. In dismay, Fred decided it was time to sever his connections with the USFWS.

His departure was a tragic loss for the program, although we cannot fault his reasons for leaving. At the time he left, Sibley had no strong views about the causes of condor decline, although he was concerned about the possibility that food shortages might be limiting reproductive effort, a concern that was tested on a large scale by his successor, Sanford Wilbur.

The Wilbur Era

A primary focus of Sanford Wilbur's research was an experimental attempt to increase condor reproduction in the Sespe Sanctuary by providing a good food supply nearby (Wilbur et al. 1974, Wilbur 1978a). The feeding effort was started in 1971 and continued right into the 1980s, pursued in the latter years by Mike Silbernagel of the Hopper Mountain National Wildlife Refuge. Carcasses of large vertebrates, primarily deer and goats, were provided once a week throughout the year from 1971 to 1973 and twice-weekly from 1974 to 1977. These carcasses received considerable, if irregular condor use over the years. Nevertheless, although use was heavy at times, it was never sustained for long, and overall the condor pop-

Sandy Wilbur, the second condor researcher for the U.S. Fish and Wildlife Service, at entrance to old condor nest in San Luis Obispo County in 1970.

ulation never became consistently dependent on the food provided. Nor was there any clear evidence for increased reproduction in the Sespe Sanctuary. Quite clearly, the condors had many other sources of food available to them and continued to forage mainly in other areas. Thus the feeding program gave no good evidence that the condors were food limited.

Perhaps the most unfortunate aspect of these results was not so much that the feeding program failed to achieve its stated goal, but that the results were later disregarded as the whole issue of feeding condors arose again in the crisis period of 1985, a topic we consider in detail in Chapter 14.

Wilbur also worked hard to get good estimates of the condor population size, and we believe his figures of 50–60 condors in 1968 and 25–35 condors in 1978 (Wilbur 1980) were excellent, although recent evidence shows that some of his assumptions were not entirely justified. By a close examination of records of condor sightings, Wilbur came to the conclusion that there were actually two populations of condors, a Sespe–Sierra population and a Coast Range population, with a boundary between the two running roughly along the Ventura–Santa Barbara County line. In his view these populations did not normally mix and thus could be considered separate entities in combining counts to arrive at total population estimates.

With the benefit of post-1981 abilities to identify individuals through photography, and later telemetry, we can now say that Wilbur was only partly right. Although adult condors nesting in the Sespe region essentially never crossed the county line to appear in nesting areas in Santa Barbara County, and vice versa, these same birds did mix freely on the foraging ground in the San Joaquin Valley foothills. Indeed every bird in the population, whether from the Sespe–Sierra region or the Coast Range (Santa Barbara) region was documented using virtually the entire foraging range – a giant J-shaped region bordering the southern San Joaquin Valley (Snyder and Johnson 1985a,b; Meretsky and Snyder 1992).

Nevertheless, Wilbur was quite justified in differentiating the Sespe Sanctuary birds from those counted in the nesting areas of Santa Barbara County (at least adults). Although there was only one condor population, adults from all nesting areas normally confined their movements to direct commutes to the nearest portions of the foraging range in the San Joaquin Valley foothills, and from thence moved up and down the foraging grounds, and finally straight back to the same nesting areas from which they originated (see map in Chapter 8). Thus, adults, unless they were unpaired individuals looking for mates, did not normally fly along the mountain ranges from one nesting area to another, parallel to the foraging range. In contrast, immatures wandered much more unpredictably throughout the entire range, including all the nesting areas. The mix of birds of all ages on the foraging grounds was quite thorough, though there was a tendency for adult birds to frequent parts of the foraging range closest to their nesting areas (Meretsky and Snyder 1992).

The important point to emphasize is that whereas Koford (1953) evidently assumed that any bird seen in the Sespe Sanctuary in Ventura County could be the same as any bird seen in the Sisquoc Sanctuary in Santa Barbara County the next day, we now know that movements between the sanctuaries were relatively rare and limited almost entirely to immatures when they did occur. Koford's failure to differentiate birds in the sanctuary regions explains, at least in part, why his population estimate was so low.

Overall, Wilbur (1978b) concluded that the main cause of the recent population decline was a breakdown in reproduction, not in nesting success but in the failure of many pairs to attempt breeding. However, a widespread failure of pairs to attempt breeding is difficult to prove unless one carefully monitors all nesting areas in the early breeding season, an enormous task. As we will discuss in much more detail in Chapter 11, Wilbur did not actually document any nonbreeding pairs, and in examining his field records we believe that his conclusion was primarily due to the fact that his research efforts were concentrated so heavily in the Sespe Sanctuary region, giving a low priority to comprehensive checking of known and potential nesting areas elsewhere. We know of no good evidence that condors were suffering from infrequent breeding efforts, either in Wilbur's time or in more recent years. The low numbers of breeding pairs found by Wilbur were evidently mainly an artifact of his limited search efforts.

One of the condor pairs that was followed during the 1970s was a pair in the back country of Santa Barbara County that became an obsession of an articulate and extraordinarily energetic newspaperman in the city of Santa Barbara, Dick Smith. Smith first found this pair while roaming the wilds near Big Pine Mountain in 1973, and he and his associate, Jan Hamber, also of Santa Barbara, made efforts to locate and study the pair through the rest of the 1970s as it moved among successive nest sites, fledging a number of young (Smith 1978). Smith's inspirational passion for wilderness led ultimately to the establishment of an official wilderness bearing his name in the region where this condor pair was active. After his death in 1977, Jan Hamber and her husband Hank continued studies of the birds and eventually joined the expanded program for condor research and conservation in 1980.

Two of Wilbur's important contributions were the publication of an extensive bibliography of condor references and a tabulation of all known records of mortality in the wild population (Appendices II and V of his 1978b monograph). Causes of death were unknown in a considerable fraction of the mortality records, but of those in which a cause had been identified (rightly or wrongly), shooting loomed as the most important problem, accounting for 64% of the losses (excluding mortality to egg collecting, museum collecting, and other purposeful collecting). This finding apparently supports the emphasis given to shooting by Koford (1953) and Miller et al. (1965). However, as we will discuss in Chapter 12, shooting is a factor that is likely to be substantially overrepresented in such a list, and its true importance relative to other sources of mortality may have been much less than Wilbur's figures suggest at face value.

In summary, despite the many years of very important and admirable research by Wilbur, Sibley, Miller et al., Koford, Robinson, and Finley, the causes of the condor's decline were still not well understood by 1980, not even to the extent that one could be confident whether primary difficulties lay in reproduction or mortality. In large measure, this unfortunate situation was not the fault of the researchers, but of the difficulties in resolving these questions because of the extremely wide-ranging habits of the species and great practical difficulties in assessing its demographic characteristics, especially with the manpower and tools then available for research. Researchers following Koford and Miller et al. found their hands tied by political restraints that placed certain powerful research methods "off limits," especially radio-telemetry and visual marking of birds for individual identification. The fear that such methods would in themselves endanger the species even led at times to the extreme point of view that even passive observation of nests from considerable distances was unacceptably risky. Yet without good answers to the question of what was causing the decline, there could be little hope of reversing the condor's dismal prospects. The conservation measures tried since the 1930s had clearly failed to arrest the approaching extinction of the species.

On the administrative side of condor affairs, the early 1970s saw the development of several formal conservation documents. The California Department of Fish and Game prepared an "Operational Management Plan for the California Condor" (Mallette 1970), which was followed in 1971 by a U.S. Forest Service "Habitat Management Plan for the California Condor" (Carrier 1971). Then in 1974, a Recovery Plan for the California Condor was developed by the Recovery Team under the leadership of Sanford Wilbur (U.S. Fish and Wildlife Service 1975). The Recovery Team itself was a successor to the old Condor Advisory Committee that was first established after Koford's study to provide recommendations to the Forest Service on condor matters, but through various reincarnations evolved into an advisory body to the USFWS after passage of the federal Endangered Species Acts. The California Condor Recovery Plan was the first such plan developed for any endangered species.

All the documents produced during the early 1970s were in essence elaborations of conservation recommendations developed in earlier decades, and for the most part they proposed traditional noninterventionist approaches. It was not until the mid-1970s that the inadequacy of existing measures became apparent to most observers. By this time, the worsening status of the species was becoming clear from declining totals of the October Survey, while the failure of the Sespe Sanctuary feeding program to result in any certain increase in reproduction was also apparent. The causes of the decline were still in dispute, and it was obvious that only a few years remained before the species would become extinct.

With the growing appreciation that traditional approaches were ineffective, the Recovery Team issued a Contingency Plan in 1976. This plan emphasized a crucial need for captive breeding to ensure survival of the species and was followed by a gloomy analysis of the status of the recovery effort by Jared Verner (1978) that forecast extinction unless more active approaches were taken in conservation.

Despite the generation of these documents and the consensus they represented for members of the Recovery Team and biologists close to the program, there was as yet insufficient political will to effect fundamental changes in the research and conservation program. The crucial step in effecting real change was the creation of a joint panel of nine scientists outside the program by the American Ornithologists' Union and the National Audubon Society in late 1977, a step urged by Sanford Wilbur, among others. This panel, chaired by Robert Ricklefs, met to review all relevant data on the biology and conservation of the species and issued a 1978 report urging a much more intensive program, including an emphasis on such approaches as captive breeding and radio-telemetry (Ricklefs 1978). The report was endorsed by the U.S. Fish and Wildlife Service, and by late 1979 the National Audubon Society, armed with the findings of the panel, had successfully lobbied Congress to establish a greatly expanded effort to conserve the species.

PART II
STRUGGLES TO LAUNCH A NEW PROGRAM

Battles in the Political Arena

The report of the AOU–Audubon Panel (Ricklefs et al. 1978) provided a logical framework for a new research and conservation effort for the condor. Widespread support for the report developed quickly, both within the ornithological and conservation communities and within the U.S. Fish and Wildlife Service. With active promotion by the Audubon Society, this support soon led to Congressional approval of a new expanded condor conservation program. Our personal involvement in the condor program began at this point, as the USFWS asked Noel to join John Ogden of the NAS in developing and implementing a new intensive field effort for the species.

However, Congressional approval and funding for a new program did not bypass normal permitting procedures of the U.S. Fish and Widlife Service and the California Fish and Game Commission. The first task faced by the combined Audubon–Fish and Wildlife Service Condor Research Center, created in 1980, was to generate comprehensive research and conservation plans and to gain state and federal approval for these plans. Until such approval was obtained, field activities of the program were limited largely to efforts to locate nesting pairs and study their biology from distant observation points.

The process of planning a new intensive program involved extensive informal and formal public meetings to encourage input from all interested parties. Shortly after our arrival in California we had our first of a number of meetings with members of several California-based organizations that saw a very different road to condor conservation than that recommended by the AOU–Audubon report. The organizations involved were Friends of the Earth, the Sierra Club, Scenic Shorelines, and the Golden Gate chapter of the Audubon Society. In addition, several private parties not generally attending the meetings held similar sentiments, especially the McMillan brothers and Steve Herman, who had been close compadres of Carl Koford.

Had he not just died in December 1979, Carl Koford himself would presumably have also been a member of this alliance. Before his death, he clearly expressed his sentiments in a personal interview later reproduced in Phillips and Nash (1981) and in an article entitled "California Condors, forever free?" published in 1979 by the Santa Monica Bay Audubon Society. In these presentations, he reiterated his opposition to virtually all intensive research and conservation activities with the condor, urging that "all nests should remain inviolate" and warning that the capture of adults for marking purposes could lead to pair break-ups and other detrimental effects. For Koford, the benefits of marking individuals were at best doubtful whereas the biological harm of such efforts to the wild population seemed "certain." He further expressed strong skepticism that captive condors could ever be reintroduced successfully to the wild. In his passionate remarks, it is not difficult to see the roots of a demonization of the program and its participants that became a major thrust of program opponents.

With the death of Koford, the principal spokesmen for those opposing the new program were David Brower of Friends of the Earth, who was renowned for his fervent efforts on behalf of wilderness preservation, and David Phillips, also of Friends of the Earth. For convenience we will refer to the alliance of opponents as the Friends of the Earth (FOE) alliance, although we acknowledge that not all participants in the alliance thought exactly alike on issues and some might not like this terminology. It is important to point out that the Sierra Club, in particular, had difficulty developing a consensus position on condors. Some members were enthusiastic supporters of the FOE viewpoint, while others were not and favored an orientation closer to our own.

Debates with Program Opponents

Our first meeting with the FOE alliance came too late to allow us to meet Carl Koford, but it offered a chance to meet another legendary individual – David Brower. Having just read John McPhee's "Encounters with the archdruid," a fascinating account of Brower's role in earlier conservation battles, we were expecting a charismatic and provocative figure, someone who would be a formidable advocate for condor conservation, even if his approach might not be entirely compatible with our own. But if we had been hoping for a lively and valuable discussion with Brower, possibly leading to real program improvements, it was not to be.

Brower and his colleagues were not troubled by doubts as to what was causing the condor's difficulties and appeared to be mostly interested in lecturing us on the virtues of habitat conservation and Carl Koford's "hands off" approach to condor studies. They were evidently unaware of just how "hands on" Koford's research activities had in fact been, and clearly had little interest in discussing the scientific uncertainties as to the causes of the condor decline and effective ways of resolving these uncertainties. The meeting was a thorough disappointment, although we gained a clear appreciation of just how zealous and humorless members of the alliance could be in opposing new approaches to condor research and conservation. Their god was a mythological Carl Koford, a man who had learned all there was to know about condors by patiently observing them from long distances. Alternative approaches were blasphemy.

During the meeting we became especially aware of the intense opposition of the FOE alliance to radio-telemetry and captive breeding. Like Koford, members of the alliance saw no need for telemetry and feared that capturing condors and attaching transmitters to them posed unacceptable risks. They argued that captive breeding would be a dead end for the conservation of the species, was not needed, and represented an obvious evasion of what they believed should be the major thrusts of efforts to save the species (see Brower 1990).

From the point of view of members of the FOE alliance, the road to success in condor conservation was to be found in carrying out the recommendations given in Koford (1953) and Miller et al. (1965), particularly as regards habitat protection, shooting threats, and threats of 1080 poisoning. They claimed that the failure of these recommendations thus far to reverse the species' decline was not due to imperfections in the recommendations, but to the fact that they had never been comprehensively implemented and given a chance to work. In addition, they were convinced that the creation of a Sespe-Frazier Wilderness Area, one of their principal goals, might be a key to saving the species. The condor "is" habitat, they maintained, and any program to conserve the species must be based heavily on habitat protection. The proposed wilderness, which historically had been used heavily by condors for breeding, would have incorporated the existing Sespe Condor Sanctuary, but would have also included substantial additional National Forest lands.

In fact, we saw no significant problems with the creation of a Sespe-Frazier Wilderness, but we failed to see how this would significantly improve the lot of the condor, and were unwilling to endorse the wilderness as the central solution to the woes of the species. In simple terms, if the Sespe-Frazier region was already of such a character as to be appropriate for wilderness designation – and it was – calling it by a new name would not change anything of significance for the condor. In itself, a Sespe-Frazier Wilderness could hardly be expected to reverse the steady and rapid decline of the species.

In our view, something had to change in a major way for there to be any expectation of recovery of the species. The crucial need was for intensive research to reveal where the major problems of the species might lie so there could be a chance of correcting them. Thus "saving" habitat, such as the Sespe-Frazier region, would not be enough. And if lack of enough suitable habitat was a major problem for the species, one would have to increase the amount of suitable habitat, not just preserve the status quo by creation of a wilderness area.

However, we saw no good evidence that habitat was a major immediate problem for the species. Our interpretation of the available data was that the causes of decline of the species were mostly unknown. We did not even know if the most important problems were ones affecting reproduction or were problems of excessive mortality, let alone what the specific problems might be. Further, we saw little chance of resolving these unknowns in the absence of radio-telemetry. From our experience studying other species, we knew that this technique could not only lead to rapid quantification of factors causing the population decline but also result in major improvements in censusing and characterizing habitat relationships of the wild population – subjects for which knowledge was still inadequate despite decades of study with less intensive methods. Trapping and radio-telemetry techniques had by then been tested with a number of vulture species without any significant safety problems or any signs of detrimental behavioral responses, so the risks of such activities appeared to be acceptably low. To shun radio-telemetry would be to accept the much larger risk of remaining in ignorance of the real causes of the species's decline.

One of our concerns, for example, was the possibility that lead poisoning from ammunition fragments in carcasses could be a major threat to the species. Part of condor diet was known to be animals, for example deer, that had been shot by hunters, and some of these carcasses were presumably contaminated with small lead bullet fragments. Two King Vultures and one Andean Condor were known to have died in captivity after the accidental ingestion of small pieces of lead (Locke et al. 1969, Decker 1979), so we were concerned that wild California Condors might also be susceptible to such poisoning. But the importance of this potential threat had not been evaluated, and it was hard to see how this could be accomplished in the absence of a means such as radio-telemetry that would allow us to recover dead condors for necropsy.

The FOE alliance clearly believed that enough was known about the problems of the condor that additional intensive research of this sort was not needed. For their response to the potential lead threat in particular, we refer the reader to a colorful 1983 Atlantic Monthly article by Kenneth Brower (David's son), in which our concerns about the potential lead poisoning of wild condors are casually dismissed by David Phillips with a misinformed remark that Topatopa, the long-standing captive condor at the Los Angeles Zoo, was more contaminated with lead than any wild condor had ever been. Our first confirmed case of a lead-poisoned wild condor was to occur only 6 months after the appearance of this article. The dead condor was located by radio-telemetry. Two additional condor deaths to lead poisoning were soon to follow. Topatopa is still alive today and has lead levels in his tissues that have been measured as only slightly elevated above background levels.

But we are jumping ahead in time here, and must return to a 1980 context. In particular, we want to address the possibility that the intense and politically effective opposition we were to experience in the early 1980s from the FOE alliance might have been significantly lessened had we been willing to endorse publicly a Sespe-Frazier Wilderness Area as a step likely to resurrect the condor. Although we were concerned that the endorsement of dubious solutions to the condor's woes might reduce the impetus toward effective solutions and might ultimately undermine our credibility as scientists, could compromising on this issue have allowed some productive lessening of conflict? This possibility needs to be raised, even though we are highly skeptical now, as we were then, that such a strategy might have significantly reduced the intense opposition of the FOE alliance to captive breeding and radio-telemetry. The alliance was arguing that a Sespe-Frazier Wilderness, together with the stopping of shooting and 1080 poisoning of condors, could be expected to all but guarantee survival of the species. With such an assertive stance, the alliance could hardly admit a pressing need for further research and captive breeding at the same time. In any event, from the point of view of the alliance, our failure to endorse a Sespe-Frazier Wilderness as a central solution for the condor probably was as clear evidence as could be summoned that we were consumed with the attractions of technological solutions to the point of rejecting other more benign and beneficial solutions.

For the record, we never spoke out against the establishment of a Sespe-Frazier Wilderness.

However, we did note that wilderness designation might perversely bring more people into the area than were currently using it (almost none at all were using it). Increased levels of human usage had been a common result of the establishment of other wilderness areas. Although we doubted that increased human traffic (within limits) would have made much difference to the condor, the alliance itself was deeply concerned about the effects of human traffic near condor nests.

Ironically, a front-page photo in a Sierra Club brochure published in early 1980 to promote the hiking attractions of the proposed wilderness area, illustrated a relatively accessible and scenic condor nest cliff that had been active in the late 1960s and would again be active in the mid 1980s. Two actual nest caves were clearly visible in the photo. Although the authors of the brochure were undoubtedly unaware that the photo illustrated a condor nest cliff, they were inadvertently encouraging human activity close to nesting condors, and this was a direct result of the campaign for the wilderness area.

The campaign to establish a wilderness was ultimately successful, but not until 1992. In its final boundaries, the Sespe Wilderness did not include Frazier Mountain, but it did include a large fraction of the Sespe and Piru watersheds, altogether some 88,910 hectares of mountainous terrain that still remain largely free of human impacts. The Sespe Wilderness, together with four other wilderness areas established at the same time (the Chumash Wilderness, the Matilija Wilderness, the Garcia Wilderness, and the Silver Peak Wilderness), together with three wild and scenic rivers created at the same time (the Sespe, Sisquoc, and the Big Sur), and together with other wilderness areas established earlier (the San Rafael Wilderness, the Dick Smith Wilderness, the Ventana Wilderness, and the Santa Lucia Wilderness), encompassed a very large fraction of the known condor nesting range of the 20th century, as can be appreciated from the map below and the map giving nest locations in Chapter 8. Nevertheless, by 1987 the lands included in all these existing and prospective

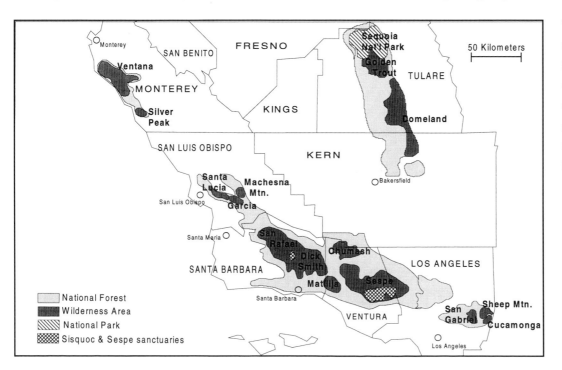

Wilderness areas now comprise a substantial fraction of the historic range of the California Condor in southern California, but all protect primarily condor nesting habitat, not foraging habitat.

wilderness areas were all to become empty of condors – for reasons that wilderness status of these areas offered no cure.

Our attempts to convince the FOE alliance that captive breeding was an essential conservation step were no more successful than our efforts to convince them that radio-telemetry was desperately needed. Our assessment of captive breeding was that it was a crucial back-up security measure to counter the possibility of failure of other conservation measures, and also represented a potential source of birds to bolster the remnant wild population. It seemed likely, judging from experience with other vulturids, that the condor would breed well in captivity and could be reintroduced to the wild. The wild population was now so small and declining so fast, it might easily be lost before its causes of decline could be determined. Further, there was a real chance that even if the major causes of decline could be quickly identified, they might not be correctable in the time left available. In that event all might be lost if a captive population were not in place. We were not suggesting that all remaining condors be taken captive, but the formation of a captive population with some of the remaining individuals now seemed an essential step. From genetic and husbandry standpoints, a captive flock should probably have been started much earlier than 1980, but in fact the deliberate taking of wild condors to form a captive flock would not be initiated until late 1982.

To some members of the FOE alliance, the concept of captive breeding condors was apparently so repugnant and divergent from their image of the condor as the essence of wilderness, that they proclaimed their preference for "death with dignity" for the species, should captive breeding be its only salvation. And although the alliance apparently fought captive breeding primarily because they saw it as a mechanism to avoid other solutions, and because of their esthetic objection to captive condors, it was also clear that they doubted that there were necessarily as few condors left as we believed. In retrospect, the estimate of about 25 birds we were using at the time, based mainly on work of Sandy Wilbur, was actually quite good, though possibly slightly low. We grant it was impossible then to give rigorous documentation for this estimate.

In sum, we felt that the position of the FOE alliance represented little more than a continuation of strategies that had failed to work for over 30 years. We disagreed with the assertion that the recommendations of Koford (1953) and Miller et al. (1965) had never really been tried. In fact they had nearly all been tried to the best of the abilities of involved agencies (see Wilbur 1978b, Jurek 1983, Snyder and Snyder 1989), and there was no reason to be confident that 100% implementation might be any more effective than less-than-100% implementation if some important causes of decline were not addressed in these recommendations.

With hindsight, we can state with considerable confidence that the condor would surely have been lost even had the recommendations of the FOE alliance been followed to a full and perfect extent, because they left one of the most important causes of decline, lead poisoning, unrecognized. Despite the convictions of the FOE alliance, the true causes of decline were still largely unknown at the time, and we faced a difficult prospect in convincing skeptics that new approaches to ferret out these causes were essential and needed quickly.

Our meetings and debates with the FOE alliance did not result in either side changing its position in any substantial way, and we became increasingly aware of how difficult it might be to get the new program launched at the state level. It was clear that the alliance was going to do everything in its power to block the new program, and it did not take long to find out that they were far more skilled than we were in using the local media to promote their goals. The issues were sufficiently complex that many observers found it very difficult to evaluate the relative merits of the opposing proposals. Further, we suffered a major disadvantage in not being native Californians and in being newcomers to the condor program. From a local perspective our credentials were not nearly as strong as those of Koford and the McMillan brothers, whose recommendations were based on considerable personal experience with the species. The best we were able to achieve in newspaper articles and television coverage was a noncommital 50-50 standoff with opponents. But in fact, our opponents had achieved much more than we had by creating widespread doubt that the new program was necessary and safe.

For the next few months we faced the same set of opponents at every formal public meeting on condors around the state. The debate became steadily more polarized into "hands on" versus "hands off" options, even though many of our proposals were traditionally hands off in nature. Radio-telemetry was characterized as "mutilative biology" and its benefits were ignored. Captive breeding was nothing less than a transformation of the species into "feathered pigs." We found ourselves painted as out-of-touch scientists "on the take" with federal monies and motivated primarily by desires to manipulate wildlife and publish papers. It was a disturbing experience to be so accused, and sadly we did a generally poor job of defending ourselves, not being accustomed to public attacks and character assassination.

The position of the FOE alliance vigorously opposing two of the main thrusts of the new program left little room for finding a common ground, and we proceeded ahead with the development of a permit proposal that included these new thrusts, despite the less than impressive media support we had garnered. We were as little inclined to compromise on focal issues as was the FOE alliance, and it would be up to the California Fish and Game Commission to decide which position made more sense.

The Permit Request

The 1980 permit application, as it was submitted to the California Fish and Game Commission, contained the following major elements: (1) a request to place radio tramsmitters on ten condors, (2) a request to trap one immature female into captivity – a potential mate for Topatopa, the long-standing single captive bird at the Los Angeles Zoo, (3) a request to take blood, feather, and fecal samples from trapped condors, in addition to examining them for parasites, measuring and weighing them, and sexing them by laparoscopy, and (4) a request for authorization to use cannon nets, clap nets, or walk-in traps for capturing condors.

The "mate for Topatopa" restriction was not much of a start toward captive breeding and was much less than we had hoped to see in the request. It represented a politically cautious, rather than biologically sensible, approach to an especially controversial aspect of the program. Topatopa was an obviously human-oriented condor, likely with very limited potentials for captive breeding. Further, it would take some luck and perhaps many months to succeed in capturing an immature female, delaying the establishment of a captive flock needlessly on the questionable assumption that the first female captured would actually pair with Topatopa.

As an alternative, we had tried to gain internal support for a request to initiate the taking of captives by multiple-clutching of wild pairs and artificial incubation of their eggs. By that time, it was well known that captive Andean Condors would readily lay replacement eggs, so it seemed likely that wild California Condors would do the same. The outstanding virtue of gaining captives through multiple clutching was that of all available techniques it would have the least impact on the wild population. However, others involved felt that since replacement-clutching had not yet been demonstrated conclusively for the species, and since Koford had asserted so strongly that it was unlikely, it would be too provocative, politically, to include such a proposal in our first permit request, especially because Sandy Wilbur had claimed that the wild population had in any event nearly ceased breeding.

We did not anticipate or encounter any difficulties in gaining approval for the permit proposal from the U.S. Fish and Wildlife Service. Approval at the state level was much more uncertain. Hearings on the proposal by the California Fish and Game Commission were scheduled for late May of 1980, which gave only a relatively short time to gain official support for the proposal. Noel and John Ogden immediately began efforts to meet with members of the Commission to explain the program and answer concerns. Shortly after starting this effort, however, we received word from the Washington office of the Fish and Wildife Service that we were not to approach members of the Commission, as this was a violation of protocol. This prohibition of contact with commissioners was hardly helpful to our cause, and in retrospect we suspect that the Washington officials might have been misled on this issue by officials in Sacramento who were anxious to control information flow to the Commission and ensure their own powers to influence Commission decisions without major competition from the condor program.

For nearly three years, however, we were under orders not to talk privately with commissioners unless they approached us. We assumed this policy was legitimate, and followed it. But when one commissioner later learned that we had not been discussing matters with them because of orders from Washington, his incredulous remark to Noel was, "Everyone else talks to us, why shouldn't you? We thought you were just ignoring us." Certainly the FOE alliance on the other side appeared to be sparing no efforts in lobbying the commissioners.

By way of further explanation here, it is important to emphasize that the Commission, not the Department of Fish and Game, had the final say in wildlife policy matters for the state of California, and in effect the Department worked for the Commission. This important point was often to be inexplicably forgotten by Fish and Wildlife Service administrators in Washington. As events proceeded in the years to follow, these officials often responded to demands from the head of the Department of Fish and Game as if the Department was in control in California. It was not. The key to achieving progress in condor affairs at the state level was to understand this simple truth.

Although the Department of Fish and Game was a signatory party to the new program, it was clear from the start that the Department felt its primary role was to serve as a "watchdog" over the program, rather than to stick its neck out and be a real participant in the program. Through the early years, especially in the efforts to obtain permits from the Commission, our major political hurdle was getting the Department to support needed actions. However, the head of the Department – Charles Fullerton – played a consistently inscrutable role in condor policies, so that we never knew what Department recommendations were going to be on any permit request until the hearings in front of the Commission. Employees working under Fullerton assured us that they knew no more than we did as to what Department policies would be. There was no real negotiation with the Department. We simply had to live with whatever policies Fullerton came up with, at least in the early 1980s, when the Commission simply enacted Department recommendations on condors as a matter of course.

Fortunately, this would all change in late 1982 when Commission members began to take a strong interest in the condor program, making efforts to discuss matters with us outside of the context of Commission meetings, and often responding more positively to input from the Condor Recovery Team and Condor Research Center than to input from the Department. After this point, the Department became much more cooperative, supportive, and involved in the program. Ultimately, the Commission would become the most progressive and important political force working for rational conservation of the species. It kept the program on track through the mid 1980s even when there was strong pressure from the Audubon Society and Fish and Wildlife Service to ignore recommendations of the Recovery Team and to move the program in questionable directions. These developments will be discussed in detail in later chapters.

In any event, once the gag order precluding direct approaches to commissioners came down from Washington in 1980, we were left with the permit request as a sole means of convincing commissioners of the need for the new program. Unfortunately the request was reminiscent of a phone directory in its bulk and took considerable work to comprehend. And although we would have an opportunity to make brief verbal arguments at the Commission hearing in May, there would be insufficient time to justify the new program fully. Although it seemed unlikely that the new program would be totally rejected by the Commission – after all, the Department of Fish and Game was an ostensible cooperator in the program – we were very concerned that enough restrictions might be enacted that the program would be hobbled right at the outset.

The Santa Barbara Hearing

The Commission hearing on the condor program permit was held on May 30, 1980 in Santa Barbara and attracted a capacity audience, including numerous opponents giving impassioned pleas for rejection of the request. The general atmosphere was tense and unpredictable, and although the commissioners tried hard to keep things civil and rational, there were continual outbursts reminiscent of a debate in the House of Commons. One rowdy opponent had to be forcibly ejected when it appeared he might totally disrupt proceedings. There were also moments of bizarre levity, such as the testimony of Roland Ross, an opponent of the program, who proceeded to demonstrate aspects of condor flight. Our own testimony, by comparison, was much too sober to provoke any surprise or delight in the congregation.

David Brower, who obviously wanted to be the last to speak during the public testimony, had to keep falling back to the end of the line as others took their places behind him. He had his wish, and once he had the floor, proceeded to deliver a soaring speech excoriating the program proposal and threatening legal action against the state should it grant the permit request. It was vintage Brower and provoked visible consternation among the commissioners, although it probably did little to advance the FOE agenda and may even have encouraged commissioners to take a position more favorable to the permit request.

Charles Fullerton, representing the Department, spoke after public testimony was completed. He supported certain aspects of the permit request but he opposed others, a pattern demonstrating Fish and Game independence from the program that we would see repeated invariably during the next few years (but with progressively less support for program recommendations).

In the end the Commission did grant a first state permit to the condor program. The terms of the permit – which were an enactment of Department recommendations – were reasonably liberal regarding radio-telemetry, allowing us to radio the 10 condors requested, but they did not authorize blood sampling and the use of cannon-netting in trapping condors. Initiation of captive breeding was limited to a "mate for Topatopa", as in our timid request. Events would later demonstrate that we would be faced with this absurd restriction through most of 1982.

However, the length of the delay in beginning establishment of a captive flock was not due only to permit restrictions. Instead it was largely our own fault, stemming from a blunder that was to lead to cancellation of state permission for virtually all intensive research and conservation activities through most of 1980, all of 1981, and most of 1982. This blunder was the accidental death of a condor chick in a handling mishap only a month after our first state permit had been issued. We turn now to this incident because it was a controlling event for such a long period in the program, and significantly delayed the initiation of crucially needed activities.

Loss of a Chick in Handling

Biologists working to preserve endangered species normally proceed on the basis that they are trying to minimize risks to populations rather than necessarily minimizing all risks to individuals in the populations. The process of preserving populations can sometimes entail some risks to individuals. Moreover, foregoing all risks to individuals can often mean that larger risks of remaining ignorant about causes of decline are taken. If, for example, there are important problems affecting chick development, such as parasites or diseases or problems with insufficient nourishment, it is usually impossible to detect such problems unless chicks are examined closely, measured, and weighed at periodic intervals. For this reason intensive conservation efforts with endangered birds usually involve studies of growth and development of chicks. These efforts entail some risks of accidents or stress reactions of chicks to handling, but for most species such risks turn out to be of near negligible magnitude. Alas, this did not prove to be the case for the condor, and a chick was lost to stress of handling at the very start of the new program.

Before becoming involved in the condor program, both John Ogden and we had handled and measured many hundreds of chicks of different species, mostly raptors, in various programs. We had not lost chicks in these programs and we did not anticipate unusual problems in handling condor chicks, as we knew that Carl Koford had handled a number of condor chicks back in the 1930s and 1940s. Chick-examination was something that we considered to be a relatively routine part of research activities, and with the existing uncertainties as to what the condor's major problems might be we assumed that it would be valuable to study growth and development of chicks.

Our first state and federal permits were broadly enough worded to allow such activities, and after confirming that this was so with officials in Washington and Sacramento, we proceeded ahead, although there were some who advised (wisely as it turned out) that we should not take such risks so early in the program. The risks of handling chicks turned out to be far greater than anticipated, and for the chick that was lost, we clearly did not take enough precautions to adequately minimize risks. This failure was in part a consequence of the ease with which we had handled a first condor chick two days earlier, a chick that accepted handling without struggling or detectable stress. Without question we should not have generalized from this experience and should have been much more cautious with the second chick than we were.

The second chick was considerably older than the first and behaved quite differently. It struggled in response to the handling, and was sufficiently stressed that it quite quickly succumbed. Actual handling of the second chick had been delegated to Bill Lehman, one of the biologists on the research team, when it turned out that the nest site could not be reached without rope work. And although Bill had participated in handling the first chick on the previous day, he had no assistance in handling the second chick and found it difficult to control. By the time Noel and John, in voice contact with Bill from the top of the cliff, learned of the problems, it was already too late.

Responsibility for the loss lay clearly with Noel and John, not with Bill Lehman, and necropsy of the chick the following day indicated no reasons other than stress for its death. There was little to be said except that sufficient precautions had not been taken – a mistake of stupendous proportions. Actual handling should not have been attempted by one person alone, a veterinarian should have been present, and when difficulties arose the handling should have been aborted. Our personal conclusion after the loss of the chick was that we now knew that the risks of chick handling were sufficiently great that the program should not for the foreseeable future even contemplate pursuing such activities, not that clearance to do so would be forthcoming in any event.

The consequences of loss of this chick, although serious enough in their impact on the tiny population of condors left, were devastating from a political standpoint. The permit from the state Fish and Game Commission was immediately revoked, leaving the program without clearance to conduct any intensive activities of any sort for an indefinite period. Committees were established on top of committees to investigate the incident, and there was no defense. The program suffered a massive loss of credibility and was thrown into a mode of despair and near impotence.

We had only ourselves to blame. Through failure to take enough precautions, we had handed the FOE alliance a near complete victory in the general public's perceptions of how condor conservation should be conducted. Their dire predictions of the consequences of intensive activities had been immediately confirmed. If there had been anyone in doubt as to whether condors were too sensitive to endure intensive conservation efforts, there was no longer. And if there had been any doubts that the people in charge of the program were callous and incompetent, these too were dispelled. It was only through time and steady progress with the "hands-off" efforts that we could pursue, that the program was able to return to intensive activities over two years later. By then it was almost too late.

Thus, despite the crisis situation faced by the California Condor in 1980, launching a new intensive program on its behalf was extraordinarily painful and slow, and we have to accept much of the blame for this. The loss of the chick was a nightmare that will never disappear completely, and once the program did return to an intensive mode, we lived in continuous dread of another similar occurrence. One more instance could easily have sounded a death-knell for both the conservation program and the species, and surely would have destroyed our own residual credibility in the field of conservation, even if we were to escape immediate lynching. In most respects, we would rather have been somewhere else during this period, but although Noel offered to resign from the program after the loss of the chick, the Fish and Wildlife Service encouraged him not to do so. We were now effectively trapped in the program, with no real alternative but to try to make a success of things in spite of our massive early setback. Fortunately, the chick death of 1980 would prove to be the last such incident to haunt the program.

CHAPTER FIVE

Africa and Peru

Our loss of a condor chick in a handling accident in mid 1980 and the immediate loss of state authorization to conduct radio-telemetry and captive-breeding greatly restricted potential activities of the newly launched conservation program. Nevertheless, we proceeded with what activities were still possible without state authorization. Our efforts to find and observe nesting pairs continued unaffected, and we continued as well with efforts to develop radio-telemetry technology and to evaluate sexing and trapping alternatives that we hoped might eventually gain state approval. Also in the fall of 1980, we spent a month participating in an Andean Condor project in the Sechura Peninsula of Peru, and Noel and John Ogden visited vulture projects in Namibia, South Africa, and Zimbabwe, primarily dealing with Lappet-faced Vultures (*Torgos tracheliotos*) and the Cape Griffon Vulture (*Gyps coprotheres*). The Andean Condor and the Lappet-faced Vulture were perhaps the closest counterpart species to the California Condor to be found in other parts of the world. Direct experience with these species and with the techniques being used to study them in the field promised to be especially valuable in developing a productive program in California.

The Peruvian project was under the leadership of Mike Wallace. Sponsored by the U.S. Fish and Wildlife Service, its primary focus was an effort to evaluate release methods of captive-reared Andean Condors to the wild, an important prerequisite for future release efforts with the California Condor. The project formed Mike's Ph.D. research at the University of Wisconsin and followed Master's degree research he had conducted in Florida examining release methods for captive-reared Black and Turkey Vultures. We had earlier gotten to know Mike when he was pursuing these Black and Turkey Vulture studies, as we were involved in nearby studies of Everglade Kites at the same time.

The various African studies were run primarily by Peter Mundy, John Ledger, Charles Clinning, and Angus Anthony of the Vulture Study Group. These projects dealt mainly with basic natural history investigations. However, considerable attention was also being given to problems that Cape Griffon Vultures were then experiencing with calcium deficiencies in their diet, electrocutions by power lines, and poisoning campaigns directed mainly against mammalian predator-scavengers.

Peru

Joining us in the Peruvian expedition were John Ogden, Gene Knoder, and Phil Ensley. John and Gene had collaborated earlier in considerable bird census work from small airplanes and were looking forward to aerial tracking of radioed condors. Phil was a veterinarian with the Zoological Society of San Diego. Much of what we wanted to accomplish in Peru centered around an evaluation of alternative methods for capturing, sexing, and handling condors, and Phil's experience in working with captive Andean Condors promised to aid these endeavors significantly.

The research site for the Andean Condor project was the uninhabited Sechura Peninsula, jutting like a thumb into the Pacific Ocean along the northwest coast of the country. For the most part, this peninsula is a desolate, low elevation region of sand dunes and gravel-cobbled pans, but its central core is a chain of naked rocky hills. Too low to be called mountains, these hills nevertheless offer dramatic vistas of the surrounding moonlike terrain and have scattered low cliffs that are marginally adequate as nest sites for vultures. Almost no roads penetrate the region, and at the time of our visit, terrestrial vegetation was extremely sparse. Trees were short and thorny, and were limited mainly to the larger washes. Large areas lacked any plant cover whatsoever. Apart from a few feral goats and burros, there were almost no mammals to be seen, and apart from vultures, there were very few birds.

The vultures, however, were common and included three species – Black and Turkey Vultures and Andean Condors. These were evidently feeding mainly on marine carrion washed ashore on the west and north sides of the peninsula. Due to upwelling, the waters just offshore were rich with nutrients and supported teeming populations of fish, cormorants, boobies, penguins, porpoises, and whales. Natural mortality of such creatures represented a bounteous food supply, and the beaches were strewn with bleached whale bones, dead fish, and dying seabirds, surely a vulturid vision of paradise.

The substantial carrion food supplies of the Sechura and the near absence of human settlements were two of the primary reasons why Mike Wallace had chosen the region as a study site. By the time of our arrival, Mike had already released a number of captive-bred Andean Condors in the vicinity, and he and several Peruvian and U.S. assistants were busy monitoring the ordeals of these birds as they learned how to soar and forage. Over the next several years, Mike's project was to prove a major success in assimilating captive-bred condors into the wild population and in testing various techniques that would later be used with the California Condor.

The obstacles in the way of this success were sometimes daunting. For example, war broke out briefly between Ecuador and Peru midway through the releases, and Mike and his assistants suddenly found themselves separated by enemy lines from some of the released birds.

Andean Condors still remain a reasonably common species in northwestern Peru. **Above**, an adult female in flight near nesting cliff in the foothills of the Andes. **Below**, an adult female on the Sechura Peninsula calmly takes control of a carcass found first by the Turkey and Black Vultures.

Getting food to the birds under such circumstances took a major commitment of stealth and courage. On another occasion, distant Peruvian villagers recovered the dead body of one of the project's radioed condors, and Mike was faced with major political problems in explaining away what was believed to be a "CIA spy condor." The challenges of conducting research in foreign lands sometimes include difficulties that no one can begin to anticipate.

Our major goal in visiting the project was to evaluate the effectiveness and safety of several means of trapping wild condors — in particular, walk-in traps and clap (or bow) nets, as well as the rocket net that Mike was already using. Walk-in traps function on the same principle as lobster pots, allowing a target species easy access into, but only a confusing exit from, a maze-like net enclosure. Clap nets function like the two halves of a clam shell, enveloping a target animal attracted to a centrally-located bait. Rocket nets shoot powered projectiles carrying a huge wide-mesh net over birds assembled at a carcass.

It was easy enough to build walk-in traps from locally-available materials, but we found on our arrival that, contrary to advance information, Mike did not have a bow- or clap-net. We were faced with finding the component parts for construction of such a net from local sources. Unfortunately, even after exhaustive searching in Piura, the largest city in northern Peru, we could not find some of the needed parts, in particular, any suitable springs, and we had to jury-rig several clap net designs, including one powered by multiple small springs.

Results of the trapping efforts clearly indicated that of the methods tested the only truly efficient means of trapping Andean Condors was the rocket net. And in the nearly vegetation-free deserts of the Sechura Peninsula, the fact that the rocket net was powered by massive flaming projectiles did not offer any conceivable hazard of starting fires. However, we concluded that rocket nets would be unacceptably dangerous in the grasslands of California, especially if a rocket were to break free from the net in a trapping effort.

The other trapping methods tested also had major drawbacks for trapping California Condors, but for different reasons. Andean Condors proved quite reluctant to enter a walk-in trap and had to adopt exactly the right position at a carcass for a clap net to work. In addition, Turkey Vultures tended strongly to foul up the working mechanisms of clap nets with earth and debris before condors arrived. These factors ruled out clap nets and walk-in traps as desirable methods for California Condors.

We left Peru convinced that none of the methods tested there offered a practical, safe, and efficient means of trapping condors in California. Instead, the cannon net that was being used by vulture researchers in Africa offered a much more promising solution. On our trip to Africa we had ample opportunity to see and evaluate the cannon net, as we will discuss below. The projectiles for a cannon net do not contain explosives and are simply cylinders of metal fired like bullets, so they pose relatively low risks of starting fires. Nevertheless, we would later learn that cannon nets were not completely free of fire hazards if any organic materials were left on the ground immediately in front of the cannons.

The efforts in Peru also included radio-tagging wild Andean Condors with a specially designed transmitter that mounted on the leading edge of the wing, the patagium. These radios were attached to numbered plastic tags so that birds could be identified visually as well as by their radio signals. The patagial mount proved to be an excellent attachment method that caused the birds no apparent difficulties. The radio-telemetry efforts with California Condors initiated two years later used similar transmitters, except that they were considerably lighter in weight, thanks to skillful engineering by Bill Cochran.

During the Peru expedition, we had an opportunity to track some of the condors tagged in the Sechura Peninsula all the way back to the Andes across nearly 100 miles (160 km) of flat desert. For this task, Gene Knoder had flown a small plane all the way to Peru from the U.S. It proved crucial in demonstrating that the condors of the Sechura Peninsula were not an isolated population, but a population in regular contact with condors from the Andes. Helen was aboard the plane tracking the very first birds into the Andes, and

Trapping efforts with Andean Condors on the Sechura Peninsula: *top*, rocket-net trapped condors at the carcass of a burro; *middle*, head of trapped male adult, illustrating distinctive comb structure and ***bottom***, Mike Wallace (left) and Willie Torres (right) transfer a condor to a sky kennel for transport to the field lab.

we soon followed up with a trip by truck to the rugged escarpment where the birds had been located from the air.

Here we spent a spectacular day with nine Andean Condors circling close around us at the top of the escarpment. One of them was a marked individual from the Sechura, an adult male who proved to be associated with a mate and a juvenile near a nest on an easily accessible cliff ledge. The escarpment was not in the high Andes but in cactus thornscrub habitat in the foothills of the Andes, and we were delighted to find King Vultures, and Black and Turkey Vultures also assembled here, as well as a resident Peregrine Falcon who repeatedly dived with tremendous vertical stoops on the condors sailing by. The capacities of radio-telemetry to lead us to these birds and nesting locations clearly demonstrated the values of this technique for studies of California Condors.

The Turkey Vultures of the Sechura Peninsula proved to be very different from Turkey Vultures in the U.S. Their scarlet heads were much more vivid than the more purplish heads of typical North American birds, but strangely, the scarlet color blanched to pale white whenever an individual took over possession of a carcass and began to feed. We had never seen such head color changes in Turkey Vultures in the U.S. And although there were a few potentially North American purple-heads, presumably wintering birds, among the scarlet-headed local birds, these purple-heads likewise did not show head-color changes around carcasses. The scarlet-headed birds were generally dominant over the purple-heads, and sometimes exhibited a transitional head coloration, half white and half red. With such conspicuous head coloration differences among the Turkey Vultures, it is worth considering that the populations involved might actually be distinct enough to merit classification as separate species and not just races of the same species. Although currently considered a race of the Turkey Vulture (*Cathartes aura jota*), the coastal South American population was originally described as a separate species (*Cathartes jota*).

During the Peru studies, we also had a chance to observe the abilities of Turkey Vultures to locate food by odor. Although it was clear that much of the natural food for vultures in the area was carrion washed up from the sea, the baits used in the vulture studies often included road-killed dogs and pigs, and sometimes burros and goats. We generally stock-piled carcasses to be used as vulture baits under big straw mats at the campsite. These carcasses were not visible from above but they were easily detected by the Turkey Vultures, who came right into camp following their noses upwind and landing aside the carcass depots. Probably because of their keen olfactory abilities, Turkey Vultures were the first avian species to arrive at all the carcass setups we prepared in Peru, though one carcass was found first by a diminutive Sechura fox. Black Vultures were not common in the area and arrived later if they arrived at all, presumably attracted by the Turkey Vultures already present. Similarly, Andean Condors did not come to all carcasses, but when they did arrive, they were always late-comers.

There were several locally nesting pairs of Andean Condors on the Sechura Peninsula, but many condors seen in the area had their home bases far away in the Andes. These latter birds commuted back and forth, apparently to take advantage of the marine food resources on the coast. None of the condor pairs located was actively breeding at the time of our visit, but Mike later discovered that reproduction was widespread during the tremendous surge in food supplies that was associated with the El Niño weather of 1983.

The behavior of Andean Condors captured with nets in Peru proved to vary with age, just as we later observed with California Condors. Adults were sufficiently docile and passive when held with their wings restrained that it was not necessary to restrain their heads during the attachment of radio transmitters or taking of blood samples. This passive behavior, however, changed instantly to vigorous and dangerous self defense if wing restraint was relaxed. In contrast, young birds struggled constantly and were capable of dangerous biting even with their wings restrained. The bill of the Andean Condor, like that of the California Condor, is razor sharp and capable of quickly slicing flesh to the bone, so juveniles had to be handled with great care. The relatively docile behavior we saw in wing-restrained adult Andean Condors was very similar to the behavior of adult Lappet-faced Vultures captured during our trip to southern Africa. The basic reasons for these behavioral similarities are unknown, but represent another aspect of the apparent convergence in characteristics of large Old and New World vultures.

Africa

The expedition to southern Africa got off to an uncertain start. When Noel and John arrived in Johannesburg they were met by Peter Mundy and Russel Friedman of the Vulture Study Group. Unfortunately, Peter had just discovered that he had allowed his government permit to conduct cannon-netting of vultures in South Africa to lapse. There was no way to remedy this oversight quickly, and it threatened to undermine the success of the entire expedition.

However, Peter suggested that there was really no problem, as it was only a day's drive to Zimbabwe where he had a trapping permit still in effect. In fact, the trapping would be better in Zimbabwe than in South Africa, as Angus Anthony had a thriving population of Lappet-faced Vultures under study in Zimbabwe, and there we would have our best chance for close observation of this species. In addition, the drive north would offer a chance to see quite a bit of South Africa. Even though the revolution that had just led to a new government in Zimbabwe (and a new name for what used to be Rhodesia), was only just over, this should not affect trapping efforts in the country.

Thus, the primary expedition destination became Gonarezhou National Park in the southern part of Zimbabwe, although our originial plans had not included a visit to this country When Noel and John reached the park with Peter and one of Peter's photographer friends, they were joined by park officials in another vehicle for the short trip to the prospective trapping site along the Lundi River. Gonarezhou was a spectacular location for all sorts of African wildlife, and it was easy to see the benefits of working in the area. The downside of working there, however, became evident only a short time later.

Though the revolution was over, the soldiers on Mugabe's winning side were still assembled in encampments, and one of these was located near the boundary of the park. Noel and John were unaware of the existence of the encampment until the trapping caravan unexpectedly encountered a flimsy log barricade across the road only a few kilometers from the vulture trapsite. The caravan was quickly surrounded by a band of heavily-armed soldiers, whose leader was obviously well lubricated with ethanol and apparently looking for something to relieve the tedium of postwar inaction.

The placing of a barricade across the road had not been officially authorized, and one of the park officials in the forward vehicle was incensed. Unfortunately, showing his anger was not an adaptive response to the situation, considering who held the weapons and who had just won the war. One thing led to another, and the commander of the soldiers soon announced angrily that all the members of the caravan were going to be executed. Safeties started to click off on the guns of the 50 or so soldiers surrounding the vehicles. Like fish in a barrel, the vulture-trapping party had itself been trapped and faced imminent annihilation.

For Noel, the most disturbing aspect of the ordeal was not so much the prospect of oblivion, which was discouraging enough, but the discovery that his own reactions to "certain death" were so completely passive and uninspired. Mesmerized by the seemingly hopeless situation, he simply found himself staring apathetically at the dusty road and the rag-tag bunch of soldiers that were about to murder them all. There were no heroic impulses to make a run for it, and no profound last thoughts about the meaning of life. Things were not supposed to end in such a hum drum way.

Fortunately they didn't. At this dramatic moment of confrontation, Peter Mundy stepped calmly out of the second vehicle, maneuvered the sputtering park official aside, and began a soothing campaign of reconciliation, agreeing with everything the commander had to say, and skillfully defusing the situation to the point that the barricade was finally dropped and the caravan was allowed to proceed on down the road. Peter's superb performance snatched victory from the talons of certain defeat and, needless to say, earned our lifelong gratitude – tempered slightly by a recognition that his permit problems had led to the mess in the first place.

Unfortunately, the ordeal was not yet over. The end of the road, where the trapping party camped, was not much farther on, and two days later the sounds of heavy weaponry became audible from the campsite, detonating back toward the barricade. The soldiers had not been paid in some time and had begun their own private civil war! Sleeping was fitful enough because of the continuous grunts and howls of leopards and lions just beyond vision from the campfire (the campsite turned out to be directly under a leopard roost tree), but there was also no way to forget recent events at the barricade or to ignore the explosions in the distance. No one could predict what might happen next.

With the main exit from the park cut off by the violence erupting back up the entrance road, the trapping party was now isolated except for a primitive road running southeast to the Mozambique border then back out to civilization to the southwest. This road was thought to have been cleared of land mines from the war, but this was not entirely certain. Fortunately, a two-way radio was available with which to communicate back to park headquarters, and it proved possible to make arrangements for helicopter evacuation of most personnel. Noel and John, however, ended up in a party nervously returning by the Mozambique border road in a V-bottomed vehicle designed to survive land mines.

Vulture trapping in Zimbabwe: **above**, Peter Mundy (left) and Angus Anthony (right) prepare impala bait for cannon-netting operation; **below**, head of Lappet-faced Vulture trapped with cannon net. The Lappet-faced Vulture is the closest counterpart species to the California Condor among the Old World vultures.

Before the departure, however, Peter Mundy (who never allowed a bead of sweat to form on his forehead through the entire trip) supervised the set-up of two carcass trapsites. At each site Noel and John had a chance to watch vulture feeding frenzies and become familiar with the details of cannon-netting operations. For these efforts the research van was camouflaged with burlap to look like a giant termite mound and served as an effective blind. The trapsites attracted large numbers of vultures, which gave a tremendous show in demolishing the carcasses. Trapping efforts were successful and allowed close examination of individuals of several species. No birds were injured in the trapping operations, although many exhibited small cuts and bruises on their heads, evidently acquired during the tumultuous competition for food at the carcasses.

The success and relatively low risks of the cannon net convinced us that this was the best available method to use with California Condors. The Vulture Study Group agreed to manufacture the custom-made cannon nets for the California efforts, and these nets became the primary means for trapping California Condors throughout the period of our studies.

Observations of Lappet-faced Vultures were another of the main goals of the African expedition. In Zimbabwe Noel and John had a chance to see this species both at carcass sites and nests during the short stay in the country. Despite being the largest vultures in southern Zimbabwe, the lappets were far from being in overall control of the carcasses watched. Their reluctance to challenge actively-feeding griffon vultures offered an instructive introduction to the complexities of interactions among scavengers at carcasses that we would later find paralleled in the deference normally shown by California Condors to Golden Eagles at carcasses. Clearly, carcass scenes provide all species involved with a variety of tough decisions relating to the risks involved in attempting to dominate one another to gain access to food.

From Angus Anthony, Noel and John learned that studies of the Lappet-faced Vulture in Zimbabwe had revealed that this species, like the California Condor, was basically territorial in nesting distributions, although birds from a number of nesting territories would often feed together at single carcasses. The lappets nested mainly in the tops of isolated, but not very tall, thorny trees, and their nests contained the bones of many of their food species. Many of the bones found were those of small mammals, and this reinforced the assessment of the Vulture Study Group that the Lappet-faced Vulture was to some extent an active predator as well as a scavenger at large vertebrate carcasses. In their emphasis on carrion, the Old World Vultures represent only one extreme in the variety of feeding habits found in the family Accipitridae. Other accipitrids, such as many eagles, also take considerable amounts of carrion, so it is not surprising that accipitrid vultures might sometimes dabble in live prey.

The taking of live prey is also known to occur occasionally in the New World Vultures, especially in the Black Vulture, and there are reports of it occurring regularly in Andean Condors, especially at guano-producing seabird colonies on islands off the coast of Peru. There, before colony guards largely wiped them out, Andean Condors historically assembled in large numbers to feast on the eggs and nestlings of cormorants, causing tremendous mortality (Murphy 1925). The taking of live prey has not yet been documented in wild California Condors, and this appears to be one of the more significant ecological differences between this species and the Lappet-faced Vulture.

Lappet-faced Vultures were also present in strong populations in Namibia, another of the African countries visited by Noel and John. Here Charles Clinning had been studying lappets for a number of years. He reported that pairs often spaced successful breeding efforts about 14 months apart, an interval that apparently accommodated the very long dependency period of their fledglings. However, because of apparent constraints from the dry season, the lappets laid eggs only during one period of the year (May to July), and when their greater-than-annual cycling in reproduction brought them past the end of the favorable period for egglaying, they apparently skipped breeding entirely until the start of the next favorable period. In this manner, successful pairs were sometimes able to fledge young in successive years, but then would miss a year before breeding again. Similarly, the most successful lappets studied by Angus Anthony in Zimbabwe had managed four successful breedings in six years. We would later learn that this schedule of events was very similar to that of the California Condor.

Aside from the Lappet-faced Vulture, the species Noel and John had the most opportunity to observe in Africa was the Cape Griffon Vulture, another species comparable to the California Condor in size, but very different in its tendency to nest in large cliff colonies. A number of Cape Griffon colonies were under intensive study by the Vulture Study Group, and with Joannie Dobbs from California and Peter Mundy, Noel and John visited the colony on Roberts' Farm in the Magaliesberg Range of South Africa. After exchanging pleasantries with Hugh Roberts and an impromptu seminar on Ronald Reagan and the state of American politics, the assembled party hiked up to the colony, climbing to several nests on accessible ledges and inspecting a number of half-grown chicks closely. Meanwhile, dozens of adults circled and sailed around the cliffs, sometimes landing only a few meters distant.

The Roberts' Farm colony was one of the colonies most severely stressed by calcium deficiencies resulting from a dearth of bones in nestling diets. Many of its chicks (about one quarter) exhibited wings that had been repeatedly broken and re-healed in grotesquely deformed patterns. These chicks had no chance of fledging successfully, although their parents continued to tend them faithfullly. In the nests and on the ground at the base of the nest cliff there were numerous pieces of glass, china, and bottlecaps that adults had evidently collected in an effort to provide substitutes for the bone fragments they were evidently having great difficulty in finding.

In returning down the slopes, Peter described the program being initiated by the Vulture Study Group to remedy the calcium deficiency problem by providing bone fragments at feeding stations for the colony. In the years that followed, these efforts proved highly successful in reducing the incidence of nestling wing-breakage nearly to zero (Richardson et al. 1986, Mundy et al. 1992).

At Russel Friedman's home near Johannesburg, Noel and John had a chance to closely examine several more of the calcium-deprived chicks from the Roberts' Farm colony. These chicks were undergoing epileptic-like seizures that may also have resulted from their unbalanced diets, although precise causes were unknown. In the midst of their seizures, the chicks whirled around in a frantic, uncontrolled fashion, and it was easy to imagine them

Cape Griffon Vultures of South Africa: ***above***, adult pair with nestling at the Roberts' Farm colony in the Magaliesberg in 1980. Unlike New World vultures, Old World species construct nests of twigs and other vegetation; ***right***, nestling Cape Griffon Vulture from the Roberts' Farm colony exhibits broken wings caused by calcium deficiency. Wing problems of this colony have now been corrected by supplemental provision of bone fragments at carcass restaurants.

falling from their cliff nest sites had they still been in the colony in the wild. In part, these seizures provided a plausible explanation for the substantial numbers of young being found dead at the base of the nest cliff.

Seeing these extreme problems first-hand in Africa, was an extraordinarily impressive experience. Although no one has ever documented such problems in the California Condor or any other New World vulture species, we were later to obtain abundant evidence that the California Condor was indeed another species that faced some significant difficulties in finding enough calcium to fuel bone-growth of its nestlings.

Aside from evaluating cannon-netting operations, observing Lappet-faced Vultures, and directly witnessing the effects of calcium deficiencies on nestling Cape Vultures, Noel and John were also greatly impressed by the amount of evidence that the Vulture Study Group was assembling on the widespread extent to which poisoning, especially with strychnine, was threatening many of the African vulture species. The major purpose of the poisoning campaigns was efforts of ranchers to reduce depredations on livestock by jackals and other carnivores, but there were also a disturbing number of poisoning incidents that were attributable to efforts of traditional witch doctors to obtain vulture organs for their allegedly magical properties. The extent of poisoning (especially well documented in Mundy et al. 1992), led us to develop a very different assessment of the potential impacts of historical mammal-poisoning campaigns on the California Condor than that offered by Dawson (1923), Harris (1941), Koford (1953), and Wilbur (1978b). As in Africa, strychnine was used extensively for predator control in California in earlier times. There can be little reasonable doubt that its impacts on the California Condor may have been similar to the impacts suffered by African vultures, despite the lack of much scientific documentation of poisoning episodes in California.

Altogether, the various vulture projects in Africa and Peru were of tremendous value in giving a wider perspective to the problems faced by the California Condor and offering techniques for the study and conservation of this species. The condor program of the 1980s owed much to colleagues in Africa and Peru, and its progress was significantly speeded by these parallel programs.

Development and Testing of Research Techniques

In the preceding chapter we outlined the reasons for choosing cannon-netting as a primary method for trapping condors and discussed the early development of radio-telemetry technology. In this chapter, we focus on the further development and implementation of these and other important research techniques for the new program. Without these techniques the program would have been far less successful over the few years left for the wild population.

Trapping Methods

Effective capture methods were essential for comprehensive investigations into the causes of the condor's decline and for the establishment of a captive population. Most of the birds trapped were immediately released back into the wild after being fitted with radio transmitters so that their movements, breeding habits, and mortality problems could be studied in detail. All the birds trapped were also blood sampled to allow analyses for environmental contaminants, pathogen problems, sex determination, and genetic studies. Fortunately, after the loss of a single condor chick in a handling accident in 1980, no birds were injured or killed in subsequent trapping or handling efforts.

Cannon-netting

As related in the preceding chapter, we decided to adopt the cannon net, already in use in South Africa, as the primary trapping technique for California Condors. The cannon net had first been developed by Clive Minton in England to capture large numbers of wading birds, and was later adapted for African vultures by David Houston (1974a), becoming the standard capture method of the Vulture Study Group subsequently. However, before using the cannon net with condors, it was important to test the net's firing characteristics under a variety of environmental conditions and to determine how it performed in capturing Turkey Vultures.

The cannon net proved to be a very simple and reliable trap even in moderate wind, but it was not entirely free of risks, especially with respect to fire. The explosives used to propel the net projectiles were blasting caps, and during a firing, tiny pieces of red-hot metal from the cap casings followed the projectiles out of the cannon mouths for a short distance. We soon learned that these tiny metal fragments could quickly ignite any organic material directly in front of the cannons, so before firings, it was important to clear areas in front of the cannons of all visible organic material, such as dried leaf litter. The risks of fire were much lower with a cannon net than with a rocket net, but they were still serious enough to demand some substantial precautions.

Most unfortunately, at one of the first test firings of the net over Turkey Vultures at a bait in early 1981, our efforts to remove flammable material from in front of the cannons proved insufficient. The net-firing ignited residual dry material on the trapsite, and flames spread rapidly into the dry grass surrounding the site and from there swept up a nearby hill, endangering several high-priced homes overlooking Lake Casitas. After futile initial efforts to contain the spreading fire, we watched in horror as the blaze moved directly toward the hilltop mansions where not only valuable properties, but human lives could be at stake.

Thankfully, the fire department responded extremely rapidly and the fire was quickly extinguished. No homes, people, or vultures were harmed. Nevertheless, it was another major public relations disaster. The adverse publicity generated by the unfortunate chick-handling accident in June of 1980 had just begun to subside, and now we had another conspicuous catastrophe on our hands to renew public opposition to the program. Press headlines proclaimed the incompetence and stupidity of the condor conservation team, and just as there was no defense for the loss of the chick, there was none for the fire.

Morale in the program, which we had thought could hardly drop lower, plunged to new depths, as opponents found fertile new grounds for ridicule and attack. It was a tough time to endure, and once again we had no one to blame but ourselves.

If any Turkey Vultures had been harmed in the fire incident we might well have seen the permanent prohibition of cannon-nets for use with California Condors. Fortunately none was harmed and we were eventually able to begin trapping efforts for condors with the cannon net, redoubling our efforts to clear each trapsite prior to net-firing. Although the program later developed a second trapping method for condors that posed absolutely no risks of fire – pit trapping – this second method was not nearly as efficient a method of trapping condors. The main technique remained cannon netting through the duration of the wild population studies, fortunately with no additional fire catastrophes resulting.

Pit-trapping

Pit-trapping is one of the oldest known methods of capturing raptors, and has been used by native Americans for centuries, possibly millennia (e.g., Schaeffer 1951, McGahan 1971). It is a very simple method. A trapper hidden in a subterranean pit under camouflage (commonly a basket cover) grabs the legs of a bird attracted to land at a bait on the ground in front of the pit. The bird is then pulled down into the pit or immobilized in place by the trapper.

For predatory species, the bait can be a live pigeon or some other similar species. The bait we used for carrion-feeding species was most commonly a still-born calf carcass. It was advisable to use a fresh carcass, as the trapper often had to wait for many hours inside the pit for a trapping opportunity, breathing whatever fumes might be generated by the carcass and enduring whatever gatherings of flies might accumulate. The bait had to be positioned well within reach of the trapper so that the legs of the bird could be grabbed without alarming it prematurely, and the trapper had to remain impervious to all compulsions to sneeze, scratch, or swat at irritating insects, so as to make no sounds or movements that might frighten off the quarry.

The necessity for icy immobility in the trapper and the need for the bird to stand in exactly the right position to be trappable are two of the major limitations of the technique. Another significant drawback is that only a single condor can be trapped at a time. With cannon-netting, the position of birds around a carcass is not so critical and multiple birds can be trapped at the same time. Thus the cannon net is inherently more flexible and reliable in trapping the birds that approach a carcass. Where fire hazards are especially great, however, pit trapping becomes the method of choice.

For the condor program, pit-trapping became the specialty of Pete Bloom who tested it out with Golden Eagles before finally using it successfully on condors. No significant complications developed in any pit-trapping effort.

Blood-sampling and Other Handling Operations

Perhaps the most informative data that can be obtained from a trapped condor come from blood sampling. Even small amounts of blood can provide information on disease problems, levels of environmental contaminants, sex, and genetic constitution of the individual – a tremendous amount of information for extremely little risk. Once condor trapping efforts became fully operational, a 17 cc blood sample was taken by syringe from a wing or leg vein of each trapped bird and divided appropriately for analysis. Specifically, a 2.5 cc subsample was sent to Arlene Kumamoto at the San Diego Zoo for sexing the bird by leukocyte culture; 10 cc were sent to Patuxent for analysis for organochlorines and other contaminants; 4 cc were used in pathogen analysis at the National Wildlife Heath Lab in Madison, Wisconsin, and for DNA systematic studies by Charles Sibley at Yale University; and 0.5 cc was used for heterozygosity analyses by Kendall Corbin at the Bell Museum of Natural History in Minnesota.

Sexing of birds was done by culturing a sample of white blood cells and later karyotyping cells at metaphase by a method originally developed by Brian Biedermann (Biedermann and Lin 1982). Brian helped launch the condor sexing efforts in 1982, and his method proved practical and reliable in sexing of all condors in the early years of the program. The sex chomosome differences between males (ZZ) and females (ZW) are directly visible under a microscope when cells at the appropriate stage of development are suitably stained.

In more recent years, the chromosomal method of sexing condors has been replaced by a more efficient DNA technique using microsatellite fingerprint analysis (Longmire et al. 1993, Griffiths et al. 1996). This latter technique can be run more quickly and on even smaller blood or other tissue samples than the leukocyte-culturing technique.

Contaminant analyses at Patuxent included determinations of the levels of a variety of organochlorines, heavy metals, and other toxins such as sodium fluoroacetate (compound 1080), and in some cases cyanide (Wiemeyer et al. 1986a,b; 1988). Pathogen analyses at the Madison labs were run on blood sera and smears.

Ken Corbin examined the amount of genetic variation in the remnant population through determination of blood enzyme polymorphisms (Corbin and Nice 1988). Sibley's genetic studies were important in establishing the closest relative of the California Condor (the Andean Condor) and in helping resolve the taxonomic position of the Vulturidae relative to storks and Old World vultures (Sibley and Alquist 1990). Later genetic analyses by Geyer et al. (1993), using in part the samples that Corbin had examined, established the degrees of relationship among all birds in the remnant population.

Birds were not anaesthetized during handling and blood sampling, but were restrained and monitored continuously by an attending veterinarian for heart and inspiration rates. Other handling operations involved weighing the bird, limited photography (especially of flight feather patterns), removal of a small feather sample for contaminant analyses, and attachment of radio transmitters. In cases where birds had to be held until they were sexed, they were maintained in a sky kennel until sexing was complete (normally 2 days).

Radio-telemetry

To minimize the need for re-trapping birds to replace dead radio transmitters, and to maximize the effective ranges of transmitters, we were early attracted to the potentials of solar-powered transmitters. Solar transmitters can generate enough power to be detectable from many miles away and can function for multiple years, so long as their component parts do not deteriorate in the sun and weather. We had earlier used solar radios very successfully in tracking long-term, long-range movements of Everglade Kites (Snyder et al. 1989), and anticipated similar success with condors.

The principal problem in using solar-powered radios with the kites lay in developing an attachment method that allowed the transmitters full exposure to the sun. We soon learned that transmitters that became even partially covered by feathers did not function properly. To avoid such coverage, we developed a special body harness of teflon straps that positioned a transmitter on a small plastic platform on top of the back feathers. This harness worked very well for the kites and produced no obvious stress in the birds.

At the same time that we were developing the solar harness system for the kites, Mike Wallace was experimenting with radio transmitter attachments for Turkey Vultures. He soon learned that body harness attachments did not work well with this species because it could work its flexible head and neck under the attachment straps and become entangled with the harness. In discussing these attachment problems with Mike, we suggested he try mounting a light-weight radio on a patagial (wing) tag since he was also routinely attaching patagial markers to his birds. A patagial mount would avoid entanglement problems and allow continuous exposure of a radio transmitter to the sun, solving in a different way the same problem we had faced with the Everglade Kite.

The patagial mount proved to work well, and Mike later developed this attachment method further with his work on Andean Condors (Wallace et al. 1994). Fortunately, both Turkey Vultures and Andean Condors are relatively large species and fly almost exclusively with soaring flight, so there were good reasons to expect that patagial radios would not give them problems in flight. Andean Condors in the field proved highly tolerant of their radios, and when we began work with California Condors, we decided to use the same basic system. Each patagial radio mount also carried a numbered tag to allow visual identification of the bird from a distance.

As with trapping methods, radio-tracking methods in California were first tested out with Turkey Vultures, both fledglings and adults. The vultures exhibited no obvious problems with their patagial units. One fledgling was recovered dead shortly after being radioed, but the cause of death was evidently predation by a Golden Eagle, as several eagle contour feathers were found intermixed with the feathers and other remains of the vulture. This bird was recovered only about a kilometer from its nest site, high on a grassy knoll, and was relatively easy to find on the ground by its radio signal. There was no evidence that the radio itself might have contributed to the bird's death. Eagle predation in this locality was later to reinforce our suspicions that the nesting distributions of California Condors could be importantly influenced by eagle abundance.

Other radio-tracked Turkey Vultures were followed up and down the coast from Ventura to Santa Barbara to as far north as Paso Robles. Their movements provided valuable experience for the research team in learning how to triangulate bird positions from the ground as well as how to follow them from a small plane. One of the Turkey Vultures radioed in 1981, who based his movements near Paso Robles, continued to be seen for the next five years (Arnold 1986).

The positive results achieved in radio-tracking Turkey Vultures in California, and similar positive results obtained by Mike Wallace with Andean Condors in Peru, gave strong encouragement that the same methods would also work well for California Condors. This proved to be the case.

To achieve an optimal balance between low weight and power of the solar transmitters, Noel spent a week with Bill Cochran of the Illinois Natural History Suvey in 1981. Their work resulted in a solar transmitter that weighed only 45 grams and had virtually no wasted space or excess potting material, yet gave an effective range exceeding 100 miles line of sight. This became the first solar design used with the California Condor in the field. At approximately 0.5% of the body weight of a condor, the transmitter fell well under the usual maximum weight recommended in avian radio-telemetry (3–5% of body weight).

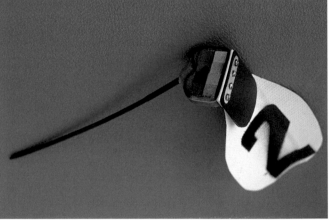

Radio-telemetry development: *top*, Bill Cochran (left) and Gene Bourassa (right) fabricate transmitter units in Ojai; ***bottom left***, inside view of long-lasting transmitter powered by a heart-pacemaker lithium battery; and ***bottom right***, solar-powered transmitter with associated tags designed for patagial attachment.

Solar transmitters have one inherent flaw that we considered to be very significant for condor studies. They will not function in darkness or in a situation where a bird might die upside down with its radios turned away from the sky. We felt it was essential to have a radio on each bird that might continue to function in darkness, as the locating and necropsying of dead condors was one of the most important goals of the condor program.

One solution to this problem would have been to couple solar cells with a rechargeable battery in the transmitter. The drawback of using this system was that rechargeable batteries only function for moderate lifetimes before giving out, and we were striving for units that might continue to function for multiple years. The solution we chose instead involved mounting a radio transmitter on each wing. One was solar-powered and the other, though of lesser range, was powered by a long-lasting lithium battery. The redundancy provided by having two transmitters on each bird proved important in locating birds for which one radio failed, including one of the birds that was recovered dead.

Radioed birds were all individually distinctive in their specific radio frequencies. To reduce the chances of confusing condor radio signals with signals from other sources we were able to arrange with authorities in the U.S. Department of Interior for use of a supposedly empty frequency band different from those used by other wildlife tracking projects. However, the frequency band chosen turned out not to be truly free of all extraneous signals, and we occasionally were faced with wasted efforts homing in on non-condor radio sources.

From late 1982 through 1986 radio-tracking of condors was under the primary supervision of first John Ogden and then Vicky Meretsky of the National Audubon Society. Most telemetry-tracking involved ground-based observers or observers in a small airplane, but efforts were also made to follow birds with an automated tracking system that analyzed signals picked up by fixed tower receivers at strategic locations. This system, designed by Bill Cochran, used antenna arrays on McKittrick Peak on the western slopes of the San Joaquin Valley, on Frazier Mountain at the south end of the condor range, and at a station farther north in the San Joaquin Valley itself. However, because of the distances involved, and because the uneven topography in the condor range did not permit detection of birds in many locations from the fixed towers, the accuracy and consistency of coverage provided by the automatic system was not nearly as good as could be obtained by intensive air and ground tracking. The most informative tracking information was obtained from airplane-tracking coordinated with ground-tracking.

For early airplane-tracking, the program was fortunate to have the use of a Cessna 180 on loan from the University of Wisconsin. Larry Riopelle, who had earlier flown us in Everglade Kite research in Florida, was the program's first pilot. Unfortunately, during an orientation flight when Larry was training Buck Woods to take over tracking duties in 1984, the Cessna was damaged beyond repair as the right front tire blew on landing and the plane flipped on the runway. Fortunately, neither Buck nor Larry was injured in the crash. Thereafter, airplane-tracking was conducted first with a rented Citabria and later with Buck's personal Citabria.

At best, tracking birds from the ground and airplane posed significant logistic problems, and we had the usual difficulty encountered in telemetry programs of radio transmitters occasionally malfunctioning or going off the air prematurely. A radio on one bird went instantly dead as the bird first took flight upon release. Other radios were sometimes intermittent in function or lost a large fraction of their power and range for part of their lifetimes.

The first California Condor trapped for radio-telemetry was a ring-necked juvenile captured at a cannon-net site in the Tehachapi Mountains in October of 1982. Phil Ensley, Pete Bloom, and Noel were the team that fired the net from a nearby blind when the bird came in to feed at a calf carcass after two Golden Eagles had finished feeding. Helen, one of the observers at a distance, had radioed the team in the blind of the approach of the condor. The distant observers arrived on the capture scene to aid handling efforts within minutes of the net firing, and all went smoothly.

Cannon-net trapping, radioing, and release of California Condors: **top left**, dawn preparation of trap-site in the Tehachapi Mountains; **middle left**, net-firing over an immature condor on Hudson Ranch; **bottom left**, left to right, Bruce Barbour, Jesse Grantham, Noel, and Pete Bloom attach radios to first telemetered condor in 1982; **top right**, Santa Barbara female (SBF) trapped in November 1982; **middle right**, John Ogden releasing radioed condor from sky kennel in 1984; and **bottom right**, REC in flight over Hopper National Wildlife Refuge in 1985, exhibiting patagial tags and transmitters.

At the time of trapping, we were operating under a state permit that allowed radio-telemetry of the condor only if it proved to be a male and would therefore not qualify as a "mate for Topa-topa", the single condor in captivity at the Los Angeles Zoo. Thus, the bird was immediately blood-sampled and held in a sky kennel while the blood sample was rushed to Arlene Kumamoto at the San Diego Zoo for a sex determination.

Two days later we learned the bird was definitely a male, so he could be radio-tagged and released. Attachment of patagial tag radios proceeded without complications, and the bird was christened IC1 (for first immature condor). His patagial tags each bore a large black 1 visible against a white background on the underside of the wing. The largely white patagial tags matched the white underwing triangles of the bird against which they rested.

On his release to the wild near the capture site after receiving radio tags, IC1 immediately took to the air and circled up with two other condors, disappearing fairly quickly beyond a ridge to the north. In succeeding days he was tracked closely as he continued to move north into the Sierra foothills. His behavior appeared completely normal and he was soon observed taking a meal at a deer carcass.

With the success of the first trapping and radioing efforts, the program was allowed to radio a second bird in the fall of 1982. This bird proved to be the adult male (SBM) of the Santa Barbara breeding pair who was cannon-netted together with his mate (SBF) by a team led by John Ogden on Hudson Ranch on November 13. SBM received patagial tags bearing a number 2 and was given the alternative radio-tracking name of AC2 (for adult condor 2). SBF was released unradioed, as we did not have clearance to radio more than one bird additional to IC1. Like IC1, AC2 and his mate took to the air immediately on release and showed no obvious abnormal patterns of behavior in the weeks to follow. When they proceeded to breed normally in the spring of 1983, all residual fears that radio-tagging might cause such problems as mate desertions and failures to breed became worries of the past.

Once radio-tracking of California Condors was finally underway, primary emphasis was given to achieving radio contact with all birds on a frequent basis to assess not only where they were but also whether they were behaving normally. We were especially concerned to find quickly any birds that had died so that their causes of death could be determined reliably. Birds that did not change location during days of good weather were potentially in trouble, and efforts were made to achieve visual contact with such birds as fast as possible. The rapid detection of the death of IC1 a year and a half after he was radioed was a result of this strategy, and because his body was recovered before it was discovered by other scavengers, it was possible to conduct a comprehensive necropsy and achieve a clear determination of the cause of death.

Birds whose radio signals suddenly went silent were also a concern. When this occurred at a time when a bird had only one functional radio, it often proved to be nothing more than a failure of the second radio. But when both radios from a bird went off the air simultaneously, it was cause for major search efforts. Both radios of CVM (AC7) went silent simultaneously during the winter of 1984–1985, and this led to mobilization of nearly the full field team in an effort to find the bird. Although the search was unsuccessful, a brief review of this episode serves to illuminate some of the practical difficulties and limitations

Pete Bloom (left) and Phil Ensley (right) with IC1, the first condor trapped in the modern program.

involved in the radio-telemetry program.

CVM (AC7) was first detected to be missing in late January of 1985, and immediately an extensive systematic search of condor range was initiated. Ultimately a weak signal on one of CVM's radio frequencies was detected deep in the Sespe Sanctuary, but after an effort to move in on the bird was begun, it became clear that the weak signal was actually a side band of one of SSF's radio frequencies and not after all a signal from CVM.

Another signal, this time on CVM's solar radio frequency, was picked up by the tower system emanating from the vicinity of the city of Bakersfield in the Central Valley. This signal was suspect from the start because of its atypical frequency peaking and because it transmitted day and night, whereas CVM's solar radio transmitted only during daylight. Whatever the source may have been, it presumably was not CVM, although the exact source was not located and identified.

Shortly thereafter, observers at the Hopper Mountain Refuge reported a visual sighting of a bird wearing a patagial tag with a number 7, evidently CVM. However, when we drove to Hopper to confirm the sighting, the only bird we could find was REC, whose patagial number was 9. Subsequent close examination of photographs taken of the bird that had been identified visually as CVM revealed that this bird was also REC. From a distance, the 9 on its patagial tag looked like a 7, and wishful thinking had completed the transformation.

Thus despite several false leads and the redundancy of having two functioning radios and numbered patagial tags, CVM was never located after disappearing. The cause of his disappearance was never determined. CVM was the only radioed condor of the 1980s whose ultimate fate was unknown.

Altogether nine wild California Condors were radioed during the intensive research program of the 1980s, and no problems with trapping or radioing procedures were detected with any of these birds. Three of the radioed birds were juveniles or subadults when first captured, whereas the other six were adults. Survival rates of the radioed birds proved to be much higher than the survival rates of birds that were not radioed, as we will discuss in detail in the chapter on mortality. Although reasons for this surprising difference were obscure (it may only have been a result of chance), the difference at least did not suggest any major detrimental effects of the radios on the birds.

Similar radios have been used for following all condors released to the wild in the past decade. Although some of the released birds have disappeared without a trace, the radios have allowed relocation of nearly all birds that have died, greatly enhancing the understanding of mortality factors affecting the species. To date, there has been no evidence that the radio transmitters themselves might in any way have been responsible for mortality of any condors.

PART III
RESEARCH RESULTS
OF THE NEW
PROGRAM

CHAPTER SEVEN

Censusing

At the start of the condor program of the 1980s we believed that radio-telemetry would play a major role in improving estimates of the size of the remnant population. It seemed reasonable to expect that the more birds might be radioed, the closer we could come to a rigorous full count of the population, assuming that radioed birds would also lead us to unradioed birds with some regularity and that predictable patterns in movements of both radioed and unradioed individuals might start to emerge. Radio-telemetry could also be expected to greatly enhance our ability to quantify reproductive and mortality rates of the population. Such information would be crucial in determining which factors were controlling population trends.

Unfortunately, the loss in mid 1980 of a state permit to conduct radio-telemetry left the program with no immediately obvious alternative means to improve censusing methodology. In the absence of anything better, we continued to rely in the near term on the annual October Survey that had been run since the 1960s. The fundamental shortcomings of the Survey were to become especially clear in its last two repetitions in 1980 and 1981.

From previous Surveys, Sandy Wilbur's population projections, and apparent overall rates of decline, we had estimated 25 ± 5 condors left in the wild population in early 1980. The October Survey of that year yielded 19 individuals, a figure reasonably consistent with a central estimate of 25, considering that the Survey covered only known high-use areas of condors. However, whether the 19 birds counted meant that there were only 19 birds in existence or whether 5 or 10 or even more birds had been missed in areas not covered could not be established from the Survey itself. The Survey documented only minimum numbers of condors and gave no means for estimating maximum numbers. Although the 19-bird total was not as low as the most pessimistic estimates that had been offered, it was not much higher and we had no way to judge how close the real population might lie to our central estimate of 25 birds.

The Survey of 1981 was even more disappointing, yielding only 11 (possibly 12) individuals. However, by that time we had enough other information to know that this total probably accounted for only about half the condors still in existence (Johnson et al. 1983, Snyder 1983). There was no escaping the conclusion that the Survey was at best an extremely crude way to estimate the total population. Furthermore, there did not appear to be any practical way to improve it sufficiently that it could ever allow accurate demographic calculations or conclusions. The condor range was far too large and much of it was far too rugged for thorough coverage to be a feasible goal. In addition, much of the range was controlled by private parties unwilling to allow access for condor observers. After the Survey's dismal performance in 1981, we concluded that it was sufficiently flawed that it was not worth pursuing further. Tinkering with details about the amount and distribution of coverage could not correct its basic inadequacy.

Development of a New Censusing Method

Fortunately, at the same time that the October Survey was expiring, we were beginning to develop an alternative method for censusing condors that quickly proved to be far superior, and indeed had some substantial advantages over radio-telemetry. This method was based on the establishment of a flight-photograph file for each condor in the wild population and depended on identifying and tracking individual differences in feather characteristics through time. It demanded no more sophisticated technology than readily-available 35 mm cameras, telephoto lenses, and color film, plus rudimentary darkroom facilities. Yet it led to total population counts that were probably error-free, once initial shake-down efforts were completed.

Censusing based on comprehensive individual identifications has now been developed to assess populations of a great variety of threatened species, ranging from macaws and manatees to great white sharks and humpback whales. In the early 1980s, however, such methodology was not widely known or employed in endangered species programs. Sandy Wilbur had earlier rejected the possibility of using feather patterns to accurately identify individual condors (Wilbur 1975) on the belief that many condors would exhibit the same molt patterns simultaneously, but this conclusion proved too pessimistic. Condors, in fact, vary greatly in feather molt patterns, and the differences among individuals proved ample to allow comprehensive identification of individuals. Some success in using molt patterns to identify and census Cinereous Vultures (*Aegypius monachus*) had been achieved earlier by Richford et al. (1975) on the island of Mallorca.

Credit for initiation of the individual identification technique for condors belongs largely to Eric Johnson of California Polytechnic State University, San Luis Obispo. Eric was someone we had known as a fellow graduate student when we were attending Cornell University in the mid 1960s. At the time of our arrival in California, however, we had not known of Eric's whereabouts for years, and didn't know he was teaching in the area. When he contacted us early in 1980 and offered his assistance in condor studies, we were both delighted to see him again and receptive to his offer. The staff of the Condor Research

Condor censusing by photography: ***above***, the most reliable site to observe and photograph foraging California Condors during the early 1980s was a highway pullout known as The Sign. On one occasion 14 condors were seen simultaneously from this location in 1980, roughly half the total population; ***left***, photographers on the Tejón Ranch document IC1 and associates.

Center was heavily committed to locating nesting pairs, continuous monitoring of the nesting pairs found, and testing of trapping techniques for condors, so Eric's availability to carry on other studies of condors, including observations on the foraging grounds, filled a definite need. He and his students were to become crucial collaborators in condor research efforts of the years to follow.

A censusing collaboration with Eric had its start in the summer of 1981 when he supervised a Forest-Service sponsored project of his ornithology students to study condor activity from a roadside observation point he had located that later became known as "The Sign." The Sign was a broad pullout alongside a secondary road running from nowhere to nowhere in the hills between Maricopa and Frazier Park. Marked by Los Padres National Forest boundary sign, it overlooked a spacious region of grasslands in the foothills of the San Joaquin Valley, including parts of three major cattle ranches: the Santiago Ranch, the Hudson Ranch, and the San Emigdio Ranch. Observations in the years to follow made it clear that the region was a major hub of condor activity, especially in summer, with essentially all condors in the population showing up in the vicinity at one time or another. The attractiveness of the area to condors appeared to result largely from excellent food supplies, especially still-born calves dropped in the early fall, and aborted calves from chronic "foothill disease" (Epizootic Bovine Abortion) earlier in the summer. Additional food came from continuous coyote control efforts on the Santiago Ranch, and from widespread deer hunting in the general region during the fall.

The condors frequenting the vicinity could be observed with no more exertion than what it took to open a car door, step outside, and raise a pair of binoculars. The main view was downslope to the north so that the sun was usually to the rear, giving excellent lighting conditions for sightings and photography. The condors often circled up close overhead, presumably because of the orientation of the slopes and the prevailing northerly winds. It was a remarkably good place to see condors. The largest single gathering of the species documented in the 1980s – 14 individuals – was seen from this location. The Sign also proved to be a great place to observe Rough-legged Hawks (*Buteo lagopus*), Ferruginous Hawks (*Buteo regalis*), Prairie Falcons (*Falco mexicanus*), and once even a Parasitic Jaeger (*Stercorarius parasiticus*).

No effort was made to keep the condor concentrations at The Sign a secret, and in any event the location was fully accessible to the public. With the high level of condor activity being found by Eric's team, word travelled quickly on local and national hotlines, and The Sign soon became a favored destination for birders, eventually displacing the top of Mt. Pinos as the best known and most reliable place to see the species. In fact, the annual Condor Watch and Tequila Bust ultimately shifted in part to this site from Mt. Pinos in the very last years of the wild population.

The crowds that developed at The Sign, especially on weekends, came well equipped with optical equipment and picnic coolers, but the location along a nearly deserted country road was not a place where passing motorists might expect to encounter anything more than deer and rattlesnakes. For those not stopping to find out what was going on, the intent throngs staring out over the valley with scopes and binoculars might have suggested a group of sports fanatics tracking a distant balloon race, or perhaps UFO enthusiasts awaiting the arrival of interplanetary spacecraft. Those who stopped to inquire were sometimes informed that participants were watching crustal movements along the San Andreas fault, which actually did run right down the canyon below. Probably very few guessed that the crowds were looking for condors, and even for those who had heard that condors were indeed the main attraction, there were hard-to-shake suspicions that condor watching just might be a cover for some other activity, probably subversive in character.

As the reigning master of ceremonies for The Sign, Eric presided over a gathering that grew to become a major social phenomenon persisting for a full five years before finally winding down. It was far from the strangest phenomenon ever to develop in a state that once hosted the Manson family, but it never involved nearby county residents to any significant extent, and was generally regarded by locals with a mixture of amusement and bewilderment. Alice Reyes, the elderly proprietress of the nearest gas station, complete with a dusty museum of pickled octopi and other marine invertebrates, seemed especially perplexed with the "environmentalists" invading her domain. At least no one got shot or stabbed, and the crowds surely enhanced local business. And as far as anyone knows, no spaceships ever landed nearby, and no participants were ever abducted to orbiting alien labs for weird breeding experiments or microchip implantations.

In the summer of 1981 Eric's team worked mainly on documenting seasonal occurrence, daily activity periods, and age ratios of condors foraging near The Sign (Johnson et al. 1983). But in an attempt to identify individuals, he and his students also began recording patterns of missing or broken flight feathers, especially secondary flight feathers (secondary flight feathers form the trailing edges of the wings, whereas primary feathers form the wing tips). With identifications of birds based tentatively on gaps in secondaries, Eric soon began to notice that although some birds repeatedly frequented the area from day to day, a continuing stream of new individuals also showed up over time. It began to appear that The Sign was a location used by most, if not all, of the remaining condors. Eric soon contacted us with these results and we sat down to discuss their implications.

Eric and his students had been making drawings of condor flight feather patterns. However, birds often did not get close enough or stay long enough to allow accurate detailed drawings. Furthermore, people sometimes transposed left and right wings in the recording process, "inventing" new birds that did not actually exist. In our observations at nests, we too had been attempting to use secondary feather gaps to identify breeding adults, and we likewise had run into the same difficulties.

Nevertheless, it was becoming clear from Eric's efforts that feather pattern characteristics might be truly distinctive for all individuals in the condor population, and might serve as a reliable means for censusing the population, if only the recording problems could be conquered. We began serious discussions of the possibility of abandoning visual recordings and adopting more rigorous photographic techniques. Photographs would prevent any transposition of left and right wings and could give a much more accurate record of feather damage and molt patterns, allowing more reliable individual identifications, so long as dates and locations of photographs were comprehensively documented.

At the outset we did not know whether primary or secondary flight feather patterns might be more useful for individual identifications, and we lacked information on how long

Analyzing flight photographs to identify individuals: ***right***, characteristic broken-off tips of primary 7 on the right wing and primary 8 on the left wing allowed easy recognition of an immature condor as "Broken Feather (BFE)" on September 22, 1982. Broken Feather was also distinctive on this date in having primaries 6 and 10 short and still growing on the right wing and primaries 7 and 10 short and still growing on the left wing (note primaries are numbered 10, 9, 8, etc., starting from the leading edges of the wing tips); ***below***, Noel (left) and Eric Johnson (right) sort flight photographs for the first full condor census in late1982.

it took the birds to replace molted flight feathers. Thus we had to feel our way along in interpreting photographs until these matters could be resolved. Only after a number of months were we able to develop a final methodology that proved to be relatively simple and unambiguous in identifying individuals.

Our first photographs in the fall of 1981 soon revealed that gaps in secondary feathers posed some interpretation problems. Long, slit-like gaps would form and disappear within a few seconds on a bird soaring overhead, so use of these gaps to identify birds could clearly lead to misidentifications. Thus, even though secondary patterns were relatively conspicuous, primary feather patterns (especially patterns in the fingerlike primaries numbered 3 through 10) proved to be much more consistent and reliable for identifications, so long as the photographic angle caught the wings with their flat surfaces exposed, not edge on. With practice, participants learned to time photographs for the moments when flat wings surfaces of a bird were best visible, and we began the accumulation of the sort of photographs that would allow long-term identifications of individuals and accurate censusing of the population.

To interpret primary feather patterns we had to determine how long it took a new feather to grow and replace one that was shed. Fortunately, condor primaries are sufficiently long that even though they grow in length at the rate of about 5–6 mm per day when emerging, it took nearly four months for a replacement feather to reach full extension. Furthermore, molt of a given primary normally occurred only once in two years. Once we had determined these rates with birds of known identity (mainly nesting birds) we could decide with a photograph of an unknown condor whether the bird might or might not be the same individual as another condor already photographed on another relatively recent date, so long as the birds had some feathers in molt. Because condors were highly variable in molt sequence and timing, and differed in their molt on left and right wings, we were ultimately able to confirm with the small population left that all individuals were distinctive in their molt patterns. Condors tended to be in primary molt from late winter to late fall, leaving only late fall through late winter as a period when all primary feathers were commonly full grown. Even during the winter period, when birds were mostly not in molt, we found we were generally able to track individual identities by individually distinctive patterns of feather damage.

Once we could see the method was working well, we expanded efforts to involve cooperators not only in the Condor Research Center and Eric's crew, but also in the Forest Service, the Bureau of Land Management, the Department of Fish and Game, and the general public. Eventually, everyone on the staff of the Condor Research Center carried suitable camera equipment wherever they went in the range of the species. Eric's crew continued to cover the sign area through 1985, contributing about 25% of all photographs. When the program got in full swing, we were obtaining photographs from all nesting areas, as well as all major portions of the foraging range, and several of the important roosting areas.

The photographs were taken on color slide film with 35 mm cameras equipped with strong telephoto lenses, but for permanent records, black and white negatives were made of the best quality photos of each bird for each date and location. Prints of these black and white negatives were enlarged to fill a 4" by 5" format and became the means by which birds were synonymized or differentiated and catalogued.

To classify individuals, we developed a 3-letter code name for each bird, based on its nesting location (if it was a known breeder) and sex. Thus, for example, SSF was the female of the pair nesting in the Sespe Sanctuary, and her mate through 1984 was SSM. Nonbreeders were also named with 3-letter codes, but these were not generally derived from geographic locations and did not end in the letters M or F, as sexes were generally unknown for nonbreeders at the times they were named. Examples of nonbreeder code names were BFE (a bird with several broken primary feathers) and HIW (a bird with a conspicuous hole in its wing feathers). Once birds of unknown sex were code-named, their names did not change, even though their sex often became known and they sometimes became attached to known nesting locations.

The First Comprehensive Condor Censuses

The first thorough photo census was run in 1982 and yielded a minimum total of 20 birds from 403 bird-location-dates by late summer of that year. However, expanded work in 1983 revealed that a single adult had been missed in the photo census work of 1982, so the adjusted late summer total for 1982 had to become a minimum of 21 individuals. No other undocumented birds ever turned up after the single extra bird of 1983, so we believe that after that point we were very likely documenting the total population exactly. Of the 21 birds accounted for in 1982, seven were immatures and 14 were adults (assuming the adult first documented in 1983 was also adult in 1982). This ratio strongly suggested a relatively healthy amount of recent reproduction in the population, and was similar to age ratios observed in large flocks by Koford and Miller et al. in earlier decades.

Unfortunately, total population counts declined steadily in the years that followed, and increasingly steeply. The total count for late summer of 1983 was 19 individuals, and by 1984 the count had dropped to 15 birds. Six more birds were lost over the winter of 1984–1985, leaving a total of just nine birds. Three of the nine were trapped into captivity in the summer of 1985, and of the six birds left, one more perished in early January of 1986. All the remaining birds were trapped into captivity by early 1987.

These data, coupled with information being simultaneously assembled on reproductive rates, indicated that mortality rates in the wild population were frighteningly high, averaging 26.8% per year for adults and 22.2% per year for juveniles for the period between early 1982 and early 1986. It quickly became clear that the major cause of decline was excessive mortality and not low reproduction. What was causing the mortality we leave for a later chapter.

So whereas we had originally believed that accurate censusing of the wild population might only become possible after a number of years of radio-telemetry, this did not prove to be the case. Photo-censusing provided accurate population counts within a year of its inception, and allowed continuous close monitoring of population trends thereafter. Through photo-censusing we were also able to establish the period of the year when most mortality occurred (fall through early spring), and to establish the ranges of individual birds over time.

Like censusing, these were research goals that we had originally believed would necessitate radio-telemetry. In fact, the only major goal that radio-telemetry was to fulfill, that was not also at least partially fulfilled by photo-census work, was the finding of birds that had died in the wild, allowing comprehensive necropsy and determination of causes of death. However, this one goal alone was more than important enough to justify full-scale implementation of radio-telemetry. Our only major regret in using the technique was that it was not started soon enough to allow collection of more abundant data on causes of mortality.

Comparison of Photo-censusing and Radio-telemetry

As a censusing technique, photo-documentation offered a number of substantial advantages over radio-telemetry. It was first of all a non-invasive technique that did not pose any of the risks involved in trapping and handling of birds. It was, secondly, a relatively inexpensive technique. Equipment costs were modest, and much of the manpower involved was voluntary. Further, it did not represent a full-time effort for any personnel, as photos were mostly taken incidentally to other activities. Radio-telemetry, in contrast, entailed considerable costs in trapping efforts, radio transmitters and receivers, and airplane-tracking time, and was a full-time effort for a number of people. Thirdly, photo-censusing yielded almost immediate accurate population counts, whereas radio-telemetry could not do so until nearly all birds in the population had been trapped and radio-tagged, a period of several years. Finally, photo-censusing yielded a number of spin-off benefits not offered by radio-telemetry, including the data for detailed molt studies and the direct involvement of the public in condor research and conservation.

In looking back on the photo work of the early 1980s, it's clear that it did not provide nearly as many bird-location-dates or nearly as thorough an accounting of the movements of some condors as radio-telemetry ultimately yielded (Meretsky and Snyder 1992). However, by the time radio-telemetry was fully functional in the mid 1980s, much of the census information needed for a good understanding of the species' decline was no longer obtainable, except that it had fortunately already been obtained by photo-documentation means. Thus, both techniques ultimately proved to be crucial elements in gaining an understanding of condor biology, and we wish to emphasize that they served to complement each other in various ways, rather than to imply that one might have fully replaced the other.

General Implications of Censusing Results

Overall, the census results obtained by the photo technique proved to be of tremendous value in a scientific sense, and were of incalculable value in the political sphere. Once it became clear in late 1982 that the condor population included only 20 or so individuals, there was no more denying that a crisis existed. The photo-census results were crucial in moving the condor program back into an intensive mode, including both captive breeding and radio-telemetry, a shift that began in late 1982 and has continued to the present.

If the condor program had instead proceeded as originally planned by relying on radio-telemetry to census the population, it seems almost inescapable that accurate census results might not have been obtained as quickly as they were, and a strong impetus toward captive breeding might have been delayed even further. From this perspective, it is not entirely clear if the handling loss of a chick in 1980 really delayed the program as much as it might first seem. The loss of clearance to conduct radio-telemetry in 1980 was a major stimulus to develop the photo-census methodology as an alternative. It proved to be an alternative that was superior in many respects, especially in the speed of obtaining needed census results.

Miscellaneous Considerations

In evaluating the photo census activities with condors, it is important to keep in mind several features that made the technique especially applicable for the species. First, the enormous size of the condor meant that useful identification photos could be taken from long distances, often hundreds of meters. Second, the soaring flight characteristic of the species meant that photos were rarely marred by wing flapping. Third, the relatively ponderous process of molt in the condor meant that feather patterns did not change so fast that it became difficult to take enough photographs to keep pace. Fourth, the highly irregular molt of the species and its extended seasonal duration maximized the number of feather pattern differences that existed among individuals and the fraction of the year that major differences could be detected. Fifth, the size of the population was small enough that the program was not faced with major logistic problems in processing, analyzing, and cataloging photos. In many other bird species for which one might envision similar techniques, one or more of the above features do not apply, presumably making the technique either much harder to implement or less conclusive in interpretation.

Although it is difficult to estimate just how many condors we might have been able to track successfully by the photo technique, we suspect that 50 or 60 birds might have been feasible. Conceivably, even larger numbers could have been managed with a major investment of time and energy. In principle, the technique could probably have been used successfully as far back as the 1960s, if only it had been thought of at that time. But what seems obvious to us now in hindsight was surely not obvious earlier, and our retrospective "what-if" comments should not be taken as criticisms of those who were faced with the truly daunting problem of censusing much larger numbers of condors with no known good techniques available.

The photo-censusing efforts used dark-room facilities provided by the Santa Barbara Natural History Museum and camera equipment bought, borrowed, and scrounged from many sources. We managed to clean out most major photo shops in the Los Angeles area of their used 400 and 500 mm telephoto lenses, and we found ourselves faced with making numerous wooden gunstock mounts to facilitate the flight photography. The original photos obtained were kept by the photographers participating, while we periodically made the black and white copies needed for analysis. Only once during the five years of photo work were we given misdated photographs, and in this instance we were able to track down the error and reconstruct the correct dates in a conclusive fashion that did not add any bogus birds to the population.

Once we became fully familiar with molt characteristics of the species, we realized that they provided many internal checks on bird identities, so we can be confident that all photos of sufficient quality to see primary patterns were clearly classified correctly. Although there was a residue of poor quality photos in which primary patterns were obscure, these photos were not used in analyses and should not be viewed as implying the existence of any birds additional to the known total.

Geographic coverage and the numbers of photographs increased steadily over the years, and by the end of 1985, the chances that we might be missing any birds in the known range seemed vanishingly small, especially considering the wide-ranging movements documented in all the known birds. Although we would have been delighted to discover any additional birds, possibly wandering in from some peripheral unknown population, no undocumented birds appeared after 1983, and all we ever obtained were endless photographs of the same known birds after that point.

However, toward the end of the existence of the wild population in 1986, well-publicized rumors arose that birds additional to the known birds might exist, based on a visual sighting of two condors of unknown identity in the northern part of the range by John Roser, a former member of the research team. We have no doubt that John saw condors, but the birds were not photographed and John had no receiver in hand to check if they were radioed. Although there were some people anxious to interpret John's sighting as proof of additional birds, there was never any strong evidence that the birds seen were not already known birds, and there was never any confirmation of any new birds to follow.

Photo-documentation continued through 1985, but by early 1986 the wild population was down to just five known individuals, all of them radioed, so it had become fully redundant with radio-telemetry. Photo-censusing was largely discontinued at this point, as the focus of the program turned to a final trapping campaign for the last few birds. Although there were still two final breeding attempts in the wild to be closely followed in early 1986, the days of intensive research on the wild population were nearly over.

For greater detail on photo analysis results and procedures, we refer the reader to Snyder and Johnson (1985a,b), Johnson (1985), Snyder et al. (1987a), and Meretsky and Snyder (1992).

CHAPTER EIGHT

Movements and Food

Studies of California Condor movements and use of range were most intensive from 1982 to 1986, when both photo-documentation and radio-telemetry were in use (Meretsky and Snyder 1992). Both of these techniques yielded the same overall picture of movements. However, the coverage provided by the two techniques differed, and together the two techniques provided a more complete assessment of movements than would have been possible with either technique alone.

The numbers of bird-location-dates accumulated were much fewer with photo-documentation than with radio-telemetry, but photo-documentation covered a longer period of time and sampled all individuals, giving a more inclusive assessment than telemetry of the behavior of the entire population. Radio-telemetry's strength lay in giving a very detailed documentation of the movements of certain individuals. Most condors, however, were never radioed and most radioed birds were only followed for relatively short periods before they were trapped into captivity during 1985 and 1986. Only two birds (SBM and IC1) were radioed between 1982 and 1984, and the additional birds that were followed by telemetry (SBF, HIW, SMM, SSF, CVM, PCA, and REC) were all radioed in late 1984. As discussed in Chapter 4, the primary reason for the delay in radioing birds was strong political opposition to intensive research activities, exacerbated by the loss of a chick in a 1980 handling accident. Poor luck in trapping efforts also played a role, especially during 1983 and early 1984.

Photo-documentation was described in some detail in the preceding chapter, and basic radio-telemetry in Chapter 6.

Condor Range

Almost without exception, large carnivorous birds maintain large home ranges because of the dispersed nature of their food supplies. As reviewed by Newton (1979), home ranges generally average in the vicinity of 30 to 190 square kilometers in size for various eagles, whereas smaller raptors more commonly have home ranges in the vicinity of 1 to 10 square kilometers in size. Home ranges for large scavenging species, which are dependent on food supplies that are especially rare and unpredictable in availability, are often much larger. For example, Coleman and Fraser (1989b) found that the relatively small Black and Turkey Vultures maintained overall individual ranges averaging about 150 and 370 square kilometers, respectively, in southern Pennsylvania and northern Maryland. Breeding pairs of Bearded Vultures in France used areas of roughly 300 square kilometers (Terrasse et al. 1961). Pairs of this same species in South Africa had overall (breeding and nonbreeding) home ranges of about 4,000 square kilometers (Brown 1991). Nonbreeding Andean Condors covered areas as large as 1,300 square kilometers during a year, while adults foraged as far as 200 km from their nests (Wallace and Temple 1987b).

As one of the largest of scavenging birds, the California Condor might also be expected to need relatively large foraging areas. Studies of the wild population in the 1980s confirmed this to be true. In fact, the data accumulated both by photo-documentation and by

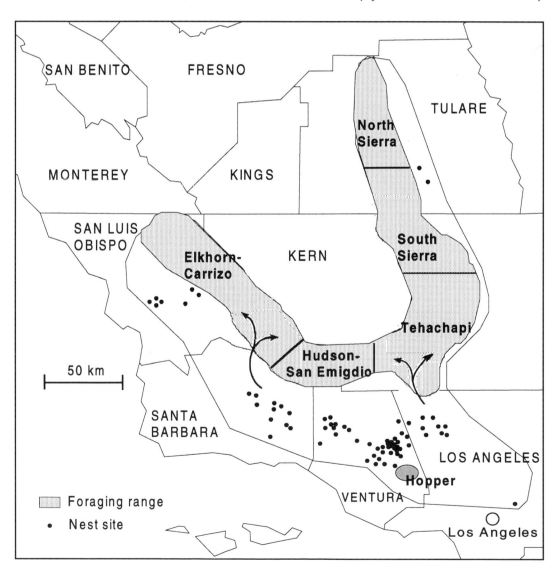

Range map of the California Condor population in the 1980s, illustrating distribution of recent nests (black points), major foraging areas, and typical routes of travel of two pairs from nesting areas to the foraging grounds.

radio-telemetry indicated that the overall foraging range used by each individual was virtu-ally the same as that of the entire population and included roughly 7,000 square kilometers of grassland in a large J-shaped region of the southern San Joaquin Valley foothills illustrated on page 140. Core foraging areas for breeding pairs were smaller, but still huge, as will be discussed below. Whether the near equivalence in overall foraging range of individuals and the population was also true in earlier times, when range of the species was considerably larger, is unknown. No means for recognizing individuals and studying their movements were available for earlier studies.

The condor's overall range included both foraging areas and mountainous nesting regions, and was roughly 20,000 square kilometers in extent in the 1980s (see map in Chapter 1). This range was similar to the range documented by Koford (1953), except that birds were no longer to be found using the coastal mountains and associated grasslands stretching north from San Luis Obispo County to Santa Clara County. Some use of this northwest region continued until the early 1970s, and there was still one known nesting pair in northern San Luis Obispo County until 1970, but thereafter no regular use of the northwest region was documented (see Wilbur 1978b). Wilbur called special attention to the apparently sudden disappearance after 1963 of a group of 15–20 condors roosting in San Benito County.

In foraging, breeding pairs of the 1980s usually flew directly from their nesting areas in the mountains surrounding the San Joaquin Valley to the nearest portions of the foothills of the valley, then wandered up and down the foothills from these points of access. Breeding birds were most often found in foothill regions closest to their nesting areas, but they were also detected with declining frequency in more distant foraging locations. The great major-ity of foraging records of breeding birds were within 50–70 km of their nesting areas, although they occasionally ranged as far as 150–180 km from active nests. The core foraging areas used by actively breeding pairs (defined as the areas represented by 95% of foraging range observations for various pairs) averaged about 2,500–2,800 square kilometers.

Brown (1991) found comparable differences between the overall ranges of South African Bearded Vultures and those used during breeding. Pairs had overall range sizes of about 4,000 square kilometers, but breeding ranges were smaller – about 600 square kilo-meters in the early breeding season and 1,300 square kilometers later in the cycle.

By further comparison, Houston (1976) found that Rüppell's Griffon Vultures in Africa ranged as far as 150 km from their nests while breeding, and were forced to do so with some regularity by the migratory habits of their primary food species. However, with regular for-aging at such distances, adult Rüppells Griffons characteristically lost weight and energy reserves during the breeding season.

Nonbreeding California Condors, both adults and immatures, were not obliged to return frequently to single home locations and ranged more freely, basing their activities mainly at traditional roosts scattered throughout the range. Evidence suggested that birds learned the full extent of the range as immatures and at least in part through association with other more experienced birds. This process apparently took place mainly while the birds were mid- and late-stage juveniles and subadults. For example, IC1 was documented visiting nearly all known nesting territories for the population during his fourth year of life (for details see Meretsky and Snyder 1992).

In an intriguing instance of nest visitation observed visually from a helicopter in 1984, we watched three condors flush from the branches around the sequoia nest hole studied by Koford (1953). This site was not known to have been active since 1950 (but was not monitored in many of the intervening years). The birds involved were believed to have been PPF, whose active nest was only 5 km away, and SSM and SSF, the Sespe Sanctuary pair who were not breeding at the time. (Note that apparent bird identities for this incident were earlier reported incorrectly in Meretsky and Snyder 1992, due to a transcription error.) Clearly the Koford sequoia nest, a very inconspicuous site tucked under a screen of live branches, was still known to the condor population in 1984, although it may have been unused for as long as 34 years. Knowledge of its location may have been transmitted simply by associations of birds through the generations.

Although their movements became relatively more constrained once they established nesting territories, condors still occasionally visited distant parts of the range, especially when they were not actually breeding. For example, although the SB pair limited their foraging movements largely to the southwest portion of the San Joaquin Valley foothills close to their nest site, we once photo-documented them, when they were not breeding, at the Blue Ridge roost of the Sierras in the far northeast portion of the range.

The last range of the condor wrapped around the southern end of the San Joaquin Valley proper, and condors confined their foraging almost completely to the hills overlooking the valley. Only once did we document an individual crossing over the valley bottom in moving from one side of the valley to the other. Normally birds simply went around the curve of foothills that formed the valley's southern limits. In contrast, the Turkey Vultures of the region often foraged over the flat valley bottom itself and rarely foraged in the southern fringing foothills, although they nested and roosted in these foothills. No good records exist of condors nesting in these same foothills, although they sometimes roosted in these foothills. Possible reasons for the condors avoiding this region for nesting are discussed in Chapters 10 and 11.

The near total avoidance of the San Joaquin Valley bottom by condors in recent times may have been due largely to the fact that the valley bottom was by these times nearly 100% crop lands, with relatively poor availability of large vertebrate carcasses. In part, it was also likely due to the near absence of any topographic relief in the valley bottom. Condors, unlike Turkey Vultures, have relatively heavy wing-loading (mass per wing area) and have much more difficulty becoming and remaining airborne over flat terrain (see wing-loading figures of Mundy et al. 1992). Over such landscapes condors are dependent almost exclusively on the uplift provided by thermal cells, a less consistent motive force than is produced by breezes blowing over hilly terrain.

As an illustration of the difficulties involved in foraging over terrain that offers generally poor flying conditions, Miller et al. (1965) described their observations of a condor on the Navajo Ranch in 1963 that could not get into soaring flight in still air after feeding on a sheep carcass. This bird had to remain overnight on the top of an oak tree near the carcass, awaiting better wind conditions. Similarly, we once watched an Andean Condor in Peru that was unable to get into soaring flight under windless conditions and had to land and walk far up a ridgeline to take off successfully. The vulnerability of condors to large mammalian predators is presumably substantial when they are grounded in flat terrain under poor flying conditions, and it is reasonable for them to prefer to feed in areas that do not pose such risks. Nevertheless, we emphasize that at least to some extent condors did utilize the bottom of the Central Valley (including the Sacramento and San Joaquin Valleys) for foraging in early historical times when much of the valley was still populated by large native or domestic ungulates (Wilbur 1978b).

Daily Movement Patterns

Daily travel distances and speeds varied greatly. The longest journey recorded for a single day was a 225 km move of IC1 from the northeast corner of the range south through the Sierras and Tehachapis and across to a roost just north of the Santa Barbara nesting territory. This journey demonstrated not only that this individual was familiar with virtually the entire range of the species, but that he was capable of flying nearly the full extent of the range within a single day. Another long single-day journey was made by the male of the Santa Barbara pair (SBM) several months after he lost his mate to lead poisoning. This journey involved a flight from his nest area through the Hudson and San Emigdio ranches to the Tejón Ranch in the Tehachapis and then back to his nesting area, a distance of approximately 200 km.

At the other extreme, birds sometimes did not leave their roosting locations during entire days, especially during periods of inclement weather. In good weather, however, it was common for birds to commute from roosts in the mountains to foraging grounds in the San Joaquin foothills and return within a day's time, a journey of perhaps some 100 km.

Ground travel speeds sometimes exceeded 70 kph for long distances when winds were favorable and condors could cruise along long ridge lines, taking advantage of topographic uplifts. However, travel more typically involved alternate periods of circling for altitude and periods of gliding during which altitude was steadily lost. Net ground speed of travel during such movements was much slower, at around 50 kph (see Spaar 1997 for comparative data on other large soaring birds).

Mated pairs commonly travelled together in foraging movements, at least when breeding activities did not demand attendance of one adult at the nest. It was also common to see more opportunistic and ephemeral associations of unpaired birds. Condors were clearly attracted to one another, but associations of unpaired individuals generally remained loose and frequently broke apart as time passed. The largest associations tended to form in favored foraging areas, but we also documented some relatively large associations near favored roosts. Koford (1953) similarly documented his largest assemblages in foraging and roosting areas.

In spite of frequent communal roosting, we obtained no rigorous data that condor roosts might function as "information centers" for food finding, as has been documented for roosts of Black Vultures by Rabenold (1983, 1987), and Buckley (1994). Condors at roosts commonly left for the foraging grounds and other destinations in a relatively independent manner, although there were also occasions when birds headed off together in at least initial headings toward the foraging grounds.

Intermittently social in movements, California Condors often travel in loose groups that break apart or coalesce through time. **Above**, four condors of a group of seven leave a common roost along Piru Creek to head north toward the foraging grounds in March of 1980. **Below**, pair members commonly forage together, as in this photograph of the CV pair over the Santiago Ranch near The Sign.

Use of Nesting Regions

Breeding adults were almost never detected in nesting areas other than their own, and the few exceptions were almost exclusively birds detected in immediately adjacent nesting areas or birds that had to overfly other nesting areas to commute to and from the foraging grounds. As will be discussed in the chapter on breeding behavior, visits of nonbreeding adults and immatures to nest areas were relatively infrequent, but when they did occur the visiting birds were often tolerated without overt aggression.

Movements of birds between the Sespe and Sisquoc nesting regions were highly unusual, and were limited almost entirely to nonbreeding birds. Consequently, the high counts of condors in the Sespe Sanctuary region (42 individuals) and Sisquoc region (32 individuals) during the late 1930s and early 1940s strongly suggested a total population much greater than Koford's estimate of 60, especially because the Sespe and Sisquoc regions account for only a modest fraction of the nesting territories known active in recent historical times.

The infrequency of condors moving along the interior mountains parallel to the boundary of the San Joaquin Valley was recognized, even without individually identifiable birds, by Wilbur (1978b). As discussed in Chapter 3, this led him to conclude that the condor population was divided into a Coast Range subpopulation and a Sespe-Sierra subpopulation, which he believed rarely if ever mixed. However, although it is true that birds rarely crossed the boundary line between his hypothetical subpopulations in the interior mountainous regions, radio-telemetry and photo-documentation revealed that they frequently did so in the foothills region of the San Joaquin Valley. There was in fact no functional division of the species into two subpopulations.

The quite thorough mixing of the condor population on the foraging grounds made it probable that all individuals in the population of the 1980s had intermittent interactions with all other individuals. Thus, despite the relatively large range of the species and the low numbers of condors, all individuals presumably had ample opportunities to assess all other individuals as potential mates. We do not believe that a failure of birds to find mates was a significant factor in the decline of the species.

Seasonal Changes in use of Foraging Zones

The main foraging grounds used in the 1980s can be divided into six reasonably distinct zones. Five of these were portions of the San Joaquin Valley foothills: the Northern Sierra, Southern Sierra, Tehachapi, Hudson-San Emigdio, and Elkhorn-Carrizo zones. The sixth was the Hopper National Wildlife Refuge, a relatively small grassland immediately south of the Sespe Sanctuary near Fillmore.

The seasonal usage patterns of these foraging grounds in the 1980s were similar to patterns reported historically for the same zones. Thus, we noted that the principal use of the Sierra zones occurred during the summer, matching historical reports (Koford 1953, Miller et al. 1965, and Wilbur 1978a). The Tehachapi foraging grounds were used most heavily in the mid fall, while use of the Hudson-San Emigdio zone peaked in late summer and early fall, matching the historical patterns reported by Wilbur (1978b) and Johnson et al. (1983). The strong spring peak in use of the Elkhorn-Carrizo zone during our study may also have matched historical patterns, judging from sightings listed in Koford (1953), Miller et al. (1965), and Wilbur (1978b), although this correspondence is less certain. Finally, our observations of winter and spring condor activity in the Hopper National Wildlife Refuge area match earlier reports of Koford (1953), Miller et al. (1965), and Wilbur (1978a).

For the most part, seasonal shifts in foraging appeared to coincide with local changes in food availability, although condor traditions may also have played a role. The fall peak in condor use of the Tehachapi zone appeared to be correlated with heavy use of this zone for deer-hunting, with many records of birds feeding on deer gut piles and on deer killed but not recovered by hunters. The late summer peak in the Hudson-San Emigdio zone appeared to be tied to the availability of aborted calves of cattle (Johnson et al. 1983). The main food supply in the Hopper zone was also calving mortality, which historically had peaked in winter and spring (Koford 1953). In 1985, when condors were again discovered using this zone, they were feeding on a naturally-occurring calf carcass. Reasons for the spring peak in the use of the Elkhorn-Carrizo zone and the broad summer peaks in the Sierra zones were less clear.

Although there was a generally good correlation between seasonal use of various foraging zones and food supplies, the shifts from one zone to another sometimes seemed to occur regardless of food availability. The Condor Research Center provided a steady supply of food in the Hopper zone in late spring and summer of 1985, but the birds abandoned the zone by summer in accordance with historical patterns. Wilbur (1978a) similarly found strong seasonality in the use of artificially-provided carcasses in the Hopper zone in spite of steady availability of food. Also in 1985, condors made their traditional shift from the Hudson-San Emigdio zone in late summer and early fall to the Tehachapis in midfall, despite the continued provision of food on Hudson-San Emigdio. Since there continued to be natural foods available in unprovisioned zones (in addition to the carcasses provided at artificial feeding sites) this persistence of seasonal shifts in foraging is not really surprising. As Wilbur et al. (1974) and Wilbur (1978a) found in earlier years, feeding programs were only partly successful in controlling foraging activities of the wild population.

The overall stability of seasonal foraging patterns in the face of artificial provisioning appears to reflect the fact that most birds continue to travel quite widely among feeding zones throughout the year and have continuous opportunities to compare food supplies among zones. Maintaining familiarity with food supplies through much of the foraging grounds may be adaptive for several reasons. Even relatively reliable food sources are not completely predictable. Timing and abundance of carcasses may vary substantially from year to year within a zone, and mammalian scavengers or Golden Eagles may often prevent condors from feeding at some sites. In addition, unpredictable carcasses can be found throughout the foraging range at any time during the year. And in exceptional cases, unexpected local abundances of food occur, such as are created by disease outbreaks (Miller et al. 1965). These food supplies can only be discovered with a foraging strategy that emphasizes monitoring of large areas. Birds accustomed to a food supply that is spatially and temporally unpredictable can be expected to retain wide-ranging prospecting behavior and to be slow to abandon such behavior even if a constant food supply develops at a fixed location.

However, evidence from Andean Condor studies of Mike Wallace and Eurasian Griffon Vulture studies of Michel Terrasse indicates that under some circumstances the wide-ranging behavior of large scavenging birds can be modified to very confined foraging patterns. On the north-west coast of Peru, a region with a remarkably constant food supply of washed-up seabirds and marine mammals, Wallace found several pairs of Andean Condors that limited their foraging activities to stretches of beach only several kilometers long. Terrasse found that it was difficult to expand the foraging range of released adult Eurasian Griffons in southern France beyond subsidy sites immediately adjacent to the release areas.

Strategies in Carcass Exploitation

Being first at a carcass is not necessarily the best strategy for a large vulture, as the first bird to arrive faces special risks in evaluating the safety of beginning to feed. These risks appear to be especially significant in the complex predator-scavenger environment of central Africa, where the first birds to find a carcass commonly sit in nearby trees for hours before descending to feed, apparently inspecting the surroundings for potential threats from concealed predatory mammals and perhaps making sure that the intended meal is truly dead and not just asleep (see also Heinrich 1988). In Africa, the first birds to actually land at a carcass are often the smaller vultures, such as Hooded Vultures and White-headed Vultures, which commonly approach with trepidation and which may only be able to gain food directly from carcasses at the earliest stages of carcass exploitation. Once the first birds have started to feed, however, they advertise by their very presence that the carcass is safe to approach. Large vultures can now move in, displacing the smaller species without major risk. Advantages in safety may outweigh those of being first in many circumstances, especially for species that can compete well for access to carcasses.

Nevertheless, where competitor mammalian scavengers occur in large numbers and where the numbers of avian scavengers assembling at a carcass are large enough to consume more than the amount of food represented by the carcass, it is important for large vultures not to wait too long in starting to feed (see discussion in Mundy et al. 1992). In this context it is relevant to describe one of the carcass scenes centered around dead impalas that Noel and John Ogden had a chance to observe from a blind in Zimbabwe in 1980, courtesy of Peter Mundy and Angus Anthony. Here hordes of White-backed Vultures (*Pseudogyps africanus*), together with lesser numbers of Hooded Vultures, Marabou Storks (*Leptoptiles crumeniferus*), White-headed Vultures, and Lappet-faced Vultures, delayed in descending to the carcass through most of an afternoon, then finally rushed in to strip it bare just a few minutes before dark. It was tempting to conclude that they could wait no longer without risk of losing the carcass to hyenas and other mammals overnight. Up until that point they were extraordinarily cautious in approaching the carcass any closer than nearby trees.

Surprisingly, the first species to approach and feed on the carcass in this case was the Marabou Stork (a revenant if there ever was one). That this species of stork is in part a carrion-feeder and exhibits a partially naked head as an apparent adaptation to that role, is an interesting commentary in itself on the potential relationship of storks to New World

Impala carcass exploitation by scavenging birds in Zimbabwe: **top**, first arrivals were Marabou Storks, who managed to exclude several vulture species in initial stages but whose bills were poorly adapted to tearing off meat; **middle**, the main feeding frenzy was dominated by White-backed Griffon Vultures who sometimes stood on top of one another in their eagerness to feed. One Lappet-faced Vulture on the edge awaited more peaceful times; **bottom**, once the White-backed Griffons had largely finished and mostly stood in the vicinity with their heads raised, Lappet-faced Vultures were able to take over the carcass, now largely reduced to skin and bones.

Vultures. This species also possesses conspicuous inflatable air sacs in the throat region, another apparent link of the storks with the New World vultures (Rea 1983).

California Condors do not presently have to deal with a diverse and abundant array of scavenger mamals as competitors or predators at carcasses. Still they are normally cautious in coming to carcasses and are quite wary of human approach when feeding. This wariness may well be a reflection of much more intense interactions with mammalian scavengers in the past. In historic times, there were wolves, and grizzly bears to contend with, and during the Pleistocene there were lions, dire wolves, and sabre-toothed cats. Today the only mammalian threats left in the region are coyotes and foxes (and more rarely mountain lions and black bears).

The most abundant and capable food competitor faced today by the California Condor is the Golden Eagle, a predator-scavenger that is widely distributed in the last foraging range of the condor. Condors have a complex relationship with Golden Eagles at carcasses, and do not often challenge this species for access to food, even though they weigh close to twice as much as the eagles. Very likely, the formidable talons of the eagles pose a threat that is not worth taking under most circumstances, and condors usually wait for eagles to finish eating before they approach a carcass. However, evidence suggests that one of the fledgling condors in the recent release program was a victim of Golden Eagle predation at a carcass (Meretsky et al. in press).

Golden Eagles themselves do not normally challenge each other for food and normally feed one at a time on a carcass, though an eagle may often chase another eagle off a carcass when the latter is reaching satiation. Eagles waiting for a chance at a carcass often rest patiently on the ground in the vicinity with condors, sometimes in substantial numbers. One carcasss put out for condors in the 1980s attracted 17 eagles. Under such circumstances, condors sometimes give up without ever getting access to a carcass and fly off to resume foraging elsewhere.

However, adult condors do challenge eagles and succeed in displacing them from food on some occasions. Whether these have been cases of especially hungry condors is not known, but the existence of such instances is an indication of the presumably complex decision-making that condors are faced with in dealing with competitors. We have not observed juvenile condors having any success in displacing eagles, and it may well be that age, size, and experience are all crucial factors for gaining access to food (Wallace and Temple 1987a).

Unambiguous dominance relationships at carcasses may reduce risks for all concerned, and various features of coloration of different-aged condors may be important in establishing some stability in dominance relationships. Immature condors lack the clear white underwing triangles of adults that appear to be used in exerting dominance, just as white underwing triangles appear to function in carcass takeovers by Lappet-faced Vultures in Africa (König 1983). Changes in head color with age may similarly function in allowing quick age recognition and efficient development of dominance relationships.

Once condors gain access to carcasses, they commonly feed in groups, and such group feeding may facilitate the penetration of carcasses with tough hides. Historic movie footage taken by J.R. Pemberton of a large group of condors feeding on a sheep carcass in the Cuyama Valley closely resembles the tumultuous mounds of griffon vultures that one can still see today on carcasses in central-southern Africa (pileups appropriately termed the "American football team" by African vulture researchers).

Condors rarely are the first species to arrive at a carcass, and commonly key in on the activities of other scavengers. In southern California, Common Ravens (**above**) are often the first to arrive, often followed by Golden Eagles (**below**). Golden Eagles are typically highly aggressive at carcasses, viciously chasing off other members of their own and other species and normally feeding only one at a time.

Above, condors do not generally challenge Golden Eagles for access to food but usually wait patiently in line for pre-arriving eagles to sate themselves. **Below**, attempts of an immature condor (PAX) to gain access to a calf carcass in 1982 are met by aggressive defense by an eagle.

Diet

One of the weakest aspects of condor studies in the 1980s was a failure to gain truly comprehensive data on the diet of the species. Many food items were documented during the 1980s, but strong biases in the way observations were made preclude using these data, or earlier diet data, to make rigorous conclusions as to the relative importance of various food items to the species. As a result, it is not presently possible to specify which sources of lead contamination have been most significant in the decline of the species, a matter of some importance in attempting to reduce this contamination. Although we are reasonably confident that a substantial proportion of the species' diet in the fall was hunter-shot deer, we have little information on the extent to which the birds fed upon Animal Damage Control (ADC)-killed coyotes (with potentials for both lead and cyanide poisoning). We likewise have little information on the extent to which they took ground squirrels killed by plinkers (recreational shooters) and large mammals dispatched by fur-trappers, all generally killed with lead ammunition.

Many of the carrion foods documented in the 1980s were carcasses of still-born calves that were deliberately provided by the program. But since condor feedings were especially likely to be documented for such carcasses (because the carcasses were generally monitored by observers), these feedings gave no quantitative indication of the natural extent to which condors fed upon calf carcasses.

Potentially, a comprehensive effort to document feedings of radioed birds by tightly coordinated aerial- and ground-tracking might have yielded much less biased diet information. Plans to initiate such an effort were discussed once a good sample of birds was radioed at the end of 1984. Unfortunately, the effort never took place, due largely to other priorities that enveloped the program during the crisis year of 1985.

What we are left with is a number of biased sources of information that together give at least some qualitative indication of diet characteristics of the species, but do not allow many quantitative conclusions. The following generalizations are about as far as we can go in characterizing condor diet:

1. Condors have been reported historically to feed on carcasses of a wide variety of vertebrate species, including cattle (especially calves), horses, burros, mules, pigs, sheep, goats, domestic dogs, domestic cats, deer, elk, coyotes, bobcats, jackrabbits, mountain lions, grizzly bears, skunks, ground squirrels, kangaroo rats, whales, sea lions, and salmon (Koford 1953, Miller et al. 1965, Wilbur 1978b). The list is long and diverse, but is perhaps most notable for an absence of birds and reptiles. We suspect the apparent absence of these latter groups may be in part an observational artifact (see below), but it at least seems clear that the major dietary emphasis has been on mammalian carrion. Koford (1953) claimed that more than 95% of the species' diet was made up of carrion of cattle, sheep, ground squirrels, deer, and horses, but this claim, although potentially true, was evidently not based on any rigorous quantitative diet determinations.

2. Studies of condor diet in the Pleistocene, based on bones found in nests in the

Condor diet strongly emphasizes mammalian carrion: ***above***, in early times, condors were sometimes known to feed on dead whales, such as this blue whale photographed in 1986 along the Big Sur, although no records of condors feeding along the seacoast are known for the historic population of the 20th century; ***below***, in modern times the most frequently documented food for the species has been cattle, especially calves, as in this 1982 photograph of the Santa Barbara (SB) pair at a baitsite. Members of this pair were easy to differentiate as the male (right) lacked the typical vertical line of short dark feathers in front of the eyes.

Grand Canyon, Arizona, similarly suggest an emphasis on mammalian carrion (Emslie 1987). However, the species taken differed strikingly from species fed upon in recent times, undoubtedly because of massive extinctions of large vertebrates at the end of the Pleistocene and the introductions of many species of domestic livestock. Emslie's list of condor foods from the Pleistocene includes mammoths, bison, horses, camels, and mountain goats, and he attributed the disappearance of the condor from the inland West largely to extinction of most of these creatures.

3. Studies of bone and pellet materials found in condor nests during the 1980s suggest substantial usage of small vertebrates, although the possibility that some bone materials in nests were not brought in by the condors must be acknowledged (Collins et al. 2000). Excluding condor nests that had also clearly been used as nests by other species (e.g. Turkey Vulture, Red-tailed Hawk, Common Raven), we found evidence for the ingestion of a number of previously unrecorded taxa, mostly mammalian, but also including some reptiles and birds. The newly recorded mammalian species included gray fox, longtail weasel, and pocket gophers. Reptile materials included a coachwhip snake; bird remains included feathers of a grebe. The diversity of materials found also included many bone fragments of cattle, coyotes, ground squirrels, kangaroo rats, and sheep, a considerable variety of mollusc shells, and remains of one barnacle. We do not know how long these materials may have been in the nests, but some nests had been used by condors for centuries, so some of the bone materials might be equally old.

4. No cases of wild condors taking live prey have been documented. This may be in part an observational artifact, but it seems reasonably safe to conclude that live prey are at most very uncommon in the diet. There are no recorded historical instances of California Condors taking eggs and young of seabirds on islands off the California coast, although such behavior has been well documented for Andean Condors in Peru (Murphy 1925). Nevertheless, the discovery of Pleistocene California Condor bones in association with bones of seabirds and other scavengers in a variety of sites on San Miguel and Santa Rosa Islands off southern California (Orr 1968; Guthrie 1992, 1993, 1998) strongly suggests that condors may have fed on seabirds in these locations in the distant past, either as carrion or living prey. In observations of captive California Condors, Mike Clark of the Los Angeles Zoo has video-taped instances of them killing rats with their bills when the latter entered nesting/roosting chambers. It is not known if these rats were eaten. Such predation may have represented primarily the defense of nesting-roosting space from intruders.

5. California Condors have often been seen feeding on medium-sized or relatively small vertebrate carcasses, but have generally been seen to pass up carcasses of full-grown cattle and horses (although they do feed on them on some occasions). It is highly likely that this apparent bias reflects the great difficulty the birds have in penetrating the tough hides of full-grown steers and horses, as suggested by Koford (1953), but it may also reflect the relative rarity of bones small enough to swallow in carcasses of full-grown ungulates. A preference for small carcasses seems likely from the overall observations of Koford (1953) and Miller et al. (1965).

6. California Condors actively collect bone materials as part of their diet, and not just from carcasses. Observations indicate that they deliberately ingest small light-colored hard objects wherever they find them, and this tendency accounts for the small pieces of bone, mollusc shells, plastic, metal, and bottlecaps found in nests. Collins et al. (2000) reported that 12% of the bone-like materials in contemporary condor nests were human artifacts. By comparison, Plug (1978) found that approximately 45% of bone-like objects in nests were human artifacts in populations of Cape Vultures that were stressed by low calcium supplies, whereas only 8% of bone-like objects were human artifacts in populations that were free of calcium deficiencies. Virtually all bones and bone-like objects found in contemporary condor nests have been less than 10 cm in length, similar to Cape Vulture colonies free of calcium stress (Plug 1978). In calcium-stressed Cape Vulture colonies, longer bone fragments have been more frequent, apparently because the birds had difficulty finding small fragments. These comparisons are consistent with a conclusion that the recent condor population has not been under severe stress from calcium deficiencies, although it may have suffered some mild problems in procuring adequate calcium supplies.

7. California Condors generally avoid consuming large quantities of skin and fur in working on carcasses and concentrate instead on soft tissues. This bias is reflected in the infrequency of pellet-casting seen in the species and in the modest amount of pellet material found in nests.

8. Data from the 1980s, Finley (1910), Koford (1953), and Miller et al. (1965) generally suggest that California Condors prefer relatively fresh carcasses to ones that have undergone major putrefaction (although they will feed on the latter on occasion, possibly when fresh carcasses are unavailable). A preference for fresh carrion has been demonstrated in field experiments on Turkey Vultures by Houston (1986).

9. There is almost no evidence of California Condors feeding on road-killed vertebrates, unlike Turkey Vultures, Black Vultures, and even Golden Eagles. To our knowledge, the only record of such behavior in California Condors was a sighting of a single condor feeding on a jackrabbit on a remote country road in the Cuyama Valley (Miller et al. 1965). Reasons for the apparent avoidance of road-killed foods are unknown, but may relate to the general wariness of humans shown by feeding condors.

10. There are a number of historical records of California Condors feeding on fish and marine mammals, but the birds evidently abandoned such foods in recent decades in spite of the fact that the remnant population lived within easy commuting distance of the Pacific Ocean. Marine carrion appears still to be an important food resource for certain Andean Condor populations in South America. The failure of remnant 20th century California Condors to exploit the substantial carrion resources that still exist along the coast of California requires explanation. Perhaps it reflects especially heavy human predation on beach-feeding condors or the substantial human disturbance characterizing beach habitats in California. Significantly, Kelly Sorenson very recently documented released California Condors feeding on a dead sea lion along the Big Sur, a development that must be viewed with some con-

cern in view of recent high levels of contaminants, including PCBs, in marine mammals along the California coast.

11. On average, California Condors must ingest one full meal every two to three days to maintain body weight, judging from food consumption rates and crop-storage capacities of captives measured by Bill Toone, Cathleen Cox, and Mike Wallace at the Los Angeles and San Diego Zoos. These calculations closely parallel those for the similar-sized Cape Vulture (Mundy et al. 1992). Nevertheless, California Condors are well adapted to withstand substantial periods of food deprivation, and adults in good condition evidently take more than a month to lose enough weight to die of starvation.

History of Changes in Food Supplies

Because food supplies are a major controlling force in the biology of most avian species, many researchers have examined the potential importance to the California Condor of mammalian carrion supplies. In particular, Koford (1953), Miller et al. (1965), Wilbur (1978b), Studer (1983), and Emslie (1987) have all presented information on the changes in availability of potential condor foods through time and have attempted to evaluate the likely impact of these changes.

During the Pleistocene, when condors ranged over much of North America, the species had access to a great diversity of large vertebrates for food. This diversity may well have been the most important factor allowing the species' wide distribution (Emslie 1987). At the very close of the Pleistocene, however, many of the large mammals disappeared. Causes for their disappearance are still debated, but they include predation by humans, who evidently arrived in the New World at about the same time (Martin 1967). Whatever the reason for their disappearance, we can assume that the extinction of these species represented a massive loss of food resources for the California Condor. The restriction of the condor to the West Coast region appears to date from the same time. The mammal species that disappeared included mammoths and mastodonts, lions, dire wolves, sabre-toothed cats, ground sloths, and various species of bears, horses, and camels. Their extinction represented a fundamental revolution in the mammalian fauna of the continent.

Nevertheless, the post-Pleistocene mammalian fauna of the West Coast still included large herds of elk, bighorn sheep, and pronghorn, as well as thriving populations of wolves, grizzly bears, mule deer, and beaver. These food supplies were evidently adequate to sustain California Condor populations, especially in conjunction with marine carrion available in coastal areas.

Settlement of the West Coast by Europeans, first by Spaniards and later by other nationalities brought another massive change to food supplies. Herds of native ungulates dwindled drastically from unregulated hunting and were largely replaced by herds of domestic cattle. Southern California in the early 19th century became a vast cattle ranch supplying leather for the East Coast shoe industry, as described in detail by W.H. Dana (1840) in his engrossing Two Years before the Mast. It seems likely that food supplies for condors remained strong through this period, especially because most cattle were raised for their hides alone, with their meat often unutilized and left for scavengers.

During the latter part of the 19th century, the floor of California's Central Valley was converted progressively to cropland. The grazing of livestock, mainly cattle and sheep, became limited largely to the foothills that were too steep for planting crops. Koford (1953) described various changes in livestock numbers and land use in the condor range that together caused a considerable decrease in foraging habitat and potential food supplies before 1940. He documented a major decline in numbers of sheep in Ventura and Kern Counties in the early 1900s and again in the 1930s. Although cattle numbers increased during that time, Koford concluded that the increase did not make up for the loss of sheep.

Wilbur (1978b) argued for a continuing deterioration of food supplies for condors from 1940 through the 1970s. Much of this was due to conversion of ranchlands to urban developments, especially in regions near the Sespe Sanctuary. For the period from 1950 through 1969 he presented data indicating that range cattle declined by about a third and sheep by about a quarter in Ventura County. Wilbur believed that food supplies during this period may still have been adequate for the condor population from fall through spring, but he was concerned that summer food supplies might be deficient, as he was aware of little cattle mortality during this season.

Declines in acreage devoted to cattle grazing continued through the early 1980s, as documented by Studer (1983), and continue to this day, as ranchlands continue to be converted to other uses. Nevertheless, Miller et al. (1965) presented data indicating that despite losses of acreage devoted to grazing, overall populations of both cattle and sheep increased significantly during the decades following Koford's study and that native mule deer experienced even greater increases. By calculating the numbers of carcasses available to condors in each area, these authors suggested that overall food supplies greatly exceeded the needs of the condor population and that there were no seasons of the year when food was scarce. Miller et al. (1965) further documented very low percentages of utilization of carcasses by condors in major grassland foraging areas, strongly suggesting that the species was not troubled by food scarcity.

Thus, critical evidence is lacking that the undeniable losses of foraging habitat have been a major factor in the historic problems of the condor. Miller and the McMillans were emphatic in their assessment that condors did not face significant food limitations. Although Wilbur was much less optimistic on this score, his supplementary feeding program near the Sespe Sanctuary provided no clear evidence of food limitations, and he documented no clear population or reproductive effects that might be attributable to food scarcity. Miller and the McMillans were impressed that if food were limiting, one would expect to see evidence for reproductive problems in the species. We share this expectation. As we consider in some detail in Chapter 11, no good evidence for such problems has ever been assembled for any era.

Our basic belief regarding potential food problems is that even though foraging habitat has clearly been diminishing for many decades, the condor population has been sufficiently depressed by non-food stresses that it has not approached the limits of available food in recent times. In a potentially comparable situation, Donázar and Fernández (1990) and

Fernández et al. (1998) discuss the interactions of a recovering population of *Gyps fulvus* in Spain with its food supply. Their data suggest that for much of recent history the population has been too low (relative to food supplies) for food availability to exert any reproductive effects on the population. Only in very recent years has the population grown large enough for the average productivity of pairs to begin to show a decline that is likely traceable to food limitations.

The following chapters on condor reproduction and mortality suggest reasonably healthy levels of breeding effort and success in the remnant population of the 1980s, with none of recent nest failures attributable to food scarcity. In fact, considering the basically erratic nature of carrion food supplies, it is remarkable that feeding rates at nests have been as consistent as they have. Further, there have been extremely few documented cases of starving condors, and most of these can be attributed to the effects of poisons such as lead which can seriously affect the abilities of individuals to find or digest food. We are not suggesting that present-day food supplies might necessarily be adequate for a much larger condor population than that of the 1980s, but that food limitations do not provide a compelling basic explanation for the historical decline of the species.

CHAPTER NINE

Nest Sites

In this chapter, as elsewhere in this book, we use the term nesting territory to indicate the area encompassing the various nest sites used or investigated by a pair over a multi-year period, whether or not much active defense of the area against other condors occurred. The alternative nest sites of a pair were normally spread out over a number of adjacent canyons and were commonly not visible from one another. Territories were non-overlapping in the remnant population, although, as will be discussed in the next chapter, there were occasional instances of pairs alternately inspecting sites in separate and distant territories. These instances occurred when the pairs were evidently newly formed from birds that had formerly occupied the separate territories but had lost former mates.

Only 2 of the 25 nest sites used for egg laying in the 1980s were sites that had been documented historically. Instead most active sites were newly discovered by a process of following adults. This was an effective method, but was often highly labor intensive because of the infrequent visits of birds to their nests, the long distances between alternative nest sites, and the rugged terrain of the nesting regions. The process normally began with several-day watches of potential nesting regions from exposed hilltops that gave good coverage of large areas. The best lookouts were often hilltops near the bottoms of basins, as the birds are most visible when silhouetted against the sky, and thus when they are viewed from relatively low locations.

Under optimal conditions condors could be spotted from as far away as 20 km with a telescope, and although mere specks at such distances, they could usually be recognized by their behavior. In particular, if they were circling in the sky, the length of time it took them to make complete circles usually averaged about 16 seconds, a distinctly longer period than the 12–14 seconds typical of Bald or Golden Eagles. The only other common soaring raptor in the nesting regions was the Red-tailed Hawk (*Buteo jamaicensis*), which usually circles in about 8 seconds.

Adult condors that were obviously commuting into the mountains from the major foraging grounds in the foothills of the San Joaquin Valley were of major interest. Athough they often could not be followed from a single observation point to their destinations, their paths indicated where the next observation point along the way should be sited, and over a period of days or weeks, they could be traced to nest sites by such means. The use of this same methodology was described by Ian McMillan (1968) for the early egg collector, Kelly Truesdale, who nearly obliterated the egg production of one condor pair in San Luis Obispo County during the first decades of the present century.

Success in nest-finding depended on concentrated scanning over long periods and a feeling for when one observation point should be abandoned for another. The process was inherently slow, as visits to nests by adults sometimes occurred only at several-day intervals. In fact, during incubation, adults sometimes did not relieve their mates for more than a week (the maximum documented interval was 10 days), making it especially difficult to find nests at this stage. Before egg laying and immediately after hatching of young, visits were much more frequent, and nest-finding was much easier.

Thus the process of finding nesting territories and nests was largely old-fashioned non-technological field biology. Although we had originally anticipated that radio-telemetry would be crucial in this process, not a single active nesting territory was originally located by this means. This was largely because radio-telemetry came relatively late in the program, and by the time it was implemented, essentially all nesting territories had already been located. Nevertheless, radio-telemetry was valuable in pinning down some individual nest sites in the last years of the field program.

Searching for nest sites in the 1980s normally involved long vigils observing condors from strategic lookouts. Here Jack Ingram monitors activities of the pair active in the Sespe Sanctuary from "Jack's OP," a lookout with coverage of several, but not all, of the nest sites used by the pair.

Access and Logistic Problems

Finding condor nests was surely one of the most strenuous, yet enjoyable, aspects of the program, as it entailed exploration of some of the wildest and most beautiful terrain left in southern California. The regions occupied by nesting condors were mostly dominated by low brush or chaparral, but they contained many fantastic areas of sandstone cliffs, spires, and arches varied with spectacular waterfalls, grassy *potreros* (meadow-like openings in the brush), and flower-choked slopes during the spring months. Some of the nest sites were in densely forested regions – riparian forests of oak at low elevations and high-elevation zones of coniferous forest. Others were in more open locations. Most of the terrain was steep, and much of it was broken by geologic features exhibiting evidence of recent tectonic activity. The San Andreas fault passes along the north boundary of the most concentrated region of nests, making it a region of frequent and sometimes severe earthquakes. At least two of the historic cliff nest sites were known to have collapsed during the 1970s.

Yet despite the spectacular terrain and proximity of the condor range to human population centers along the coast, we found that relatively few hikers penetrated into the back country, presumably mainly because of the difficulties in moving through unyielding chaparral vegetation. There were few trails and only a few old overgrown fire roads. In fact, access to the back country was much more difficult than it had been in Koford's day, when many more roads were kept open for fire control. We were faced at times with vegetation so dense that we could not wriggle through it, crawl under it, or struggle over it. Gaining access to condor use areas was often a painstaking process of trying a variety of potential routes until a way through could be discovered. This was particularly true of the Sespe Sanctuary region, which had not burned in decades and was a labyrinth of scrubby trunks and thorny branches. In many regions the only feasible routes of access were following stream courses, but these were often difficult to negotiate because of boulder-fields and impassable waterfalls. For some nest sites the only way we were able to gain access to observation points was by slowly cutting trails through the brush.

One of the most difficult sites of all to approach was the historic nest site studied by Finley and Bohlman in 1906, despite its location in Eaton Canyon immediately adjacent to Los Angeles, and despite the fact that it is a site that can be reached (barely) without ropes. The precise location of this site was lost for many decades, partly because Finley had published a photograph in 1908 giving an erroneous position for its location. This was presumably done deliberately to reduce the chances of egg collectors finding and depredating the site. The site was refound with some remarkable detective work by Fred Sibley in 1968. After exhaustive searching of the canyon, Fred recognized a fallen pine snag on the slopes as the very snag in which Finley and Bohlman had photographed the condor pair in their most famous photograph. Once the snag was located, it was a fairly simple matter to find the nearby site, which was nothing more than a hollow behind a slab of rock leaning against a near-vertical rock wall.

When we revisited the Finley–Bohlman site in 1983 to collect old condor eggshells we found that reaching it entailed a precarious scramble up near-vertical slopes, and we wondered how Finley and Bohlman had ever managed to get there packing heavy plate cameras

Three historic condor nest cliffs from the early 20th century (arrows indicate nest cave locations): **above**, the Truesdale nest in San Luis Obispo County yielded several eggs to early collectors and was visited by William Leon Dawson in 1911; **bottom left**, the Whitaker nest along Piru Creek yielded a young condor for the National Zoo in 1904, and was visited by Frank Chapman in 1906. The surroundings were the basis for the condor diorama still on exhibit at the American Museum of Natural History; and **bottom right**, the Finley–Bohlman nest of 1906 lies in Eaton Canyon overlooking the Los Angeles basin, and is one of the most difficult sites to approach.

One of only two nest sites known in burn-out cavities of giant sequoias, the sequoia nest of 1984 gave evidence of numerous previous condor nestings. Approximately 100 feet (30 m) from the ground, the nest site was less than halfway up the tree from its base.

and other gear. We found it was wiser to make a final approach to the site with ropes than to clamber up the treacherous slopes without protection, and we later found ourselves obliged to use ropes to exit from the canyon itself when we tried a route out that proved much worse than our entry route. The Finley–Bohlman site is sufficiently inaccessible that the chances someone might stumble upon it accidentally are virtually nil.

Another extremely difficult nest to access was a site 100 feet (30 m) up in a giant sequoia tree that was active in 1984. Reaching the base of the nest tree presented no problems, but the ascent to the nest site to remove a late stage nestling for the captive flock took several days of planning and some painstaking aid-climbing, more akin to scaling a sheer rock face than normal tree climbing. Rob Ramey, John Yablonski, Victor Apanius, and Phil Ensley found their endurance and skills sorely tested in the process. As the veterinarian attending the chick removal, Phil trained for weeks prior to the climb by roping up and down eucalyptus trees in San Diego.

Human disturbance was not a major general threat to condor nests simply because it was so difficult to get close to most nests. Whether or not they were in official sanctuaries, most nests were in places that were as immune to human invasion as if they had been patrolled by armies of armed guards. In all the years of nest-watching we very rarely had to deal with unauthorized intruders. Of the very few instances, one involved a lost troop of boy scouts. Another involved several deer poachers. In both of these cases the intruders gave no sign that they were aware there were condors in the vicinity and there were no indications that they caused any significant disturbance to the birds. Both these sites were supposedly protected by sanctuary status, whereas the great majority of nest sites we observed were not.

Nevertheless, in sifting one of the nest sites that Koford studied in 1940 (Koford #4), we found a spent rifle bullet in the nest litter. Vincent Vitale of the Ventura County Sheriff's Crime Laboratory examined the bullet and concluded that it probably had been fired into the nest site, as red sandstone grains embedded in the head of the slug matched those of the nest walls. It seems reasonable to hypothesize that it may have been fired at a condor standing in the site. Moreover, there was hair packed into the center hollow of the slug, suggesting that it had later been ingested by a condor. Because objects on the nest chamber floor may be repeatedly ingested and regurgitated by nestling condors, this one slug could conceivably have been responsible for the poisoning of generations of condor nestlings (although we note that no condor bones were found in the site). The nest from which this bullet was recovered was located within 0.5 km of an oil-well pad, making it one of the most vulnerable sites to human depredations. The great majority of sites were far from commonly traveled trails and roads.

Difficulties with access and logistics were not the only problems we faced in nest-finding activities. There were occasional encounters with black bears and mountain lions, chronic worries relating to the quality of stream water available for drinking, a few sprained ankles, and occasional instances of observers getting thoroughly lost. Nevertheless, through the duration of studies, there were no major personnel calamities. In view of the number of person-years of back-country investigations that were involved, we counted ourselves very lucky in this respect. Perhaps the closest brush with disaster was when Louis Andaloro fell asleep at the wheel along a precipitous mountain highway as he was commuting to the field. He awoke hanging upside down from his seat belt in the wrecked vehicle, fortunately on the uphill side of the highway.

To reduce chances of back-country disasters, field observers normally carried two-way radios on the Forest Service frequency. The network of repeaters on the Forest Service system allowed observers to communicate with home base from almost all locations. Noel in particular will always be thankful for this communication system, as he suffered an incapacitating kidney stone attack while observing one of the more remote nests in 1980. Help was soon on its way.

Nesting Dispersions

Once nesting territories of pairs were located, the process of finding specific nests became progressively easier as observers became familiar with routes of access and the locations of alternative nest sites used by the pairs. The pairs proved to be faithful to their territories over the years and were moderately repetitive in the various sites they prospected and used for nesting. The conservative occupancy of nesting territories greatly aided efforts to multiple-clutch wild pairs during the mid 1980s.

The maps below show the geographical placement of various nest sites of the 1980s (1) in the territory used by SSF with her two successive mates and (2) in the territory used by SBF and SBM. These maps are representative of the nesting patterns shown by all pairs studied. For each pair, the sites actually used for nesting were only a subset of the sites investigated.

Maps illustrating the spacing of successive nests of the SS (top) and SB (bottom) pairs in the 1980s. Condors typically changed nest sites in successive attempts regardless of whether or not the attempts were successful.

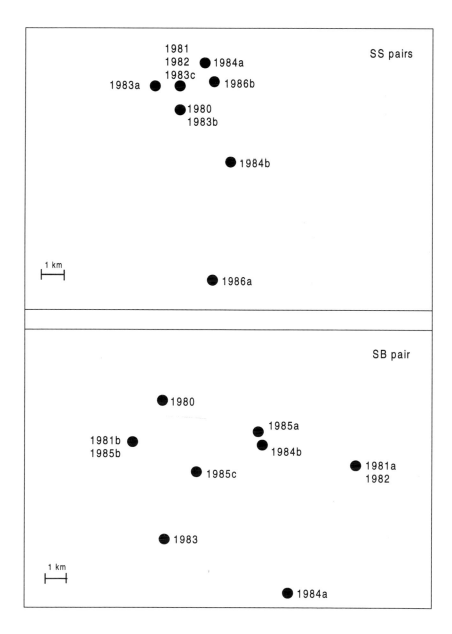

Table 1. Patterns of use and re-use of nest sites by condor pairs of the 1980s.

Pair	Year	Site	Distance (km) from previous site	Outcome of nesting
CCF×CCM	1980	A	—	Successful fledging
	1982	B	0.1	Failure (egg rolls out of site)
		A	0.1	Failure (raven destroys egg)
	1983	A	0.0	Egg to artificial incubation
		C	2.9	Egg to artificial incubation
	1984	D	2.4	Egg to artificial incubation
		E	0.8	Egg to artificial incubation
		F	0.4	Egg to artificial incubation
SSF×SSM	1980	A	—	Failure to unknown cause
	1981	B	0.9	Successful fledging
	1982	B	0.0	Chick taken captive
	1983	C	1.0	Egg to artificial incubation
		A	1.1	Failure (apparent loss to raven)
		B	0.9	Chick taken captive
	1984	D	1.5	Egg to artificial incubation
		E	3.7	Egg to artificial incubation
SSF×REC	1986	F	4.9	Failure (egg crushed, raven?)
		G	8.0	Egg to artificial incubation
SBF×SBM	1980	A	—	Failure (chick dies in handling)
	1981	B	10.2	Failure (egg lost to unknown)
		C	11.5	Failure (chick dies at hatching)
	1982	B	11.5	Successful fledging
	1983	D	11.0	Egg to artificial incubation
	1984	E	6.9	Egg to artificial incubation
		F	8.1	Egg to artificial incubation
	1985	G	0.4	Egg to artificial incubation
		C	7.6	Egg to artificial incubation
		H	3.7	Egg to artificial incubation
CVF×CVM	1981	—	—	Successful fledging, nest site not located
	1983	A	—	Chick taken captive
	1984	B	4.0	Egg to artificial incubation
PPF×SMM	1984	A	—	Chick taken captive
TP pair	1980	A	—	Successful fledging

The distances between successive nest sites of given pairs varied greatly, with an average move of 3.8 km between nesting attempts (Table 1). The greatest distance documented between alternate nests actually used for egg laying by a single pair was 12.6 km, although we observed pairs investigating sites that were even farther apart. The pair that nested in a sequoia tree in 1984 was observed and photographed investigating another site that was about 95 miles (150 km) distant only three days before the calculated day of egg laying. This second site was a former nest site of the male of the pair.

It is possible that with the reduced size of the condor population in the 1980s and the relatively large number of potential nest sites to choose from, the remaining pairs were able to expand the sizes of their nesting territories to include more sites than would have been normal in earlier years. Unfortunately, no comprehensive information is available on sizes of nesting ranges of historical pairs, although it is known that they often nested much closer together than was seen in the 1980s. In the 1940s Koford documented one case of two pairs nesting only 1.3 km from each other and another case in which active nests were only 1.5 km apart. In the 1980s, the closest simultaneous condor nestings were 13 km apart, although two potentially homosexual pairs that did not lay eggs were associated with sites only 2.6 km apart in 1981–82.

Of three recent pairs successfully fledging young, two moved to different nest sites for their next nesting attempts, while the third renested in the same site (Table 1). Similarly, most pairs have switched nest sites after nesting failures, although one recent pair failed twice in succession in the same site. Thus the usual pattern, at least in recent years, has been for pairs to change nest sites in successive nesting attempts, regardless of the outcome of the attempts. The adaptive significance of frequent nest switches is unknown, but they might serve to reduce the threats of parasite infestations. Routine changing of nest sites in successive breeding efforts is also known for the cliff-nesting Bearded Vulture (*Gypaetus barbatus*), although it is generally uncommon in other vulture species (Mundy et al. 1992).

Despite the strong tendency for pairs to change nest sites, they usually adopted previously-used sites. A large majority of nests found to date (47 of 72 sites in the survey to be discussed below) had clearly been used for multiple condor nestings, judging from eggshell evidence, excrement layers on cave walls, and other data.

As discussed in the previous chapter, most birds in the population may have known of the location of a large fraction of the recently active nest sites. Visiting individuals, especially juveniles, were seen on occasion in the vicinity of most active nests. IC1 in particular was documented visiting essentially all recently active territories during his fourth year of life.

Roosts and Water Sources

Most active condor nests were serviced by nearby roosts. These were most commonly cliff potholes or branches near the tops of tall trees, often bigcone Douglas firs. Cliff potholes used for roosting were typically shallow and developed conspicuous tongues of condor whitewash dripping from their entrances. In contrast, most whitewash buildup in condor nests was internal. At nests serviced by pothole roosts, the male and female adults typically roosted in separate potholes. Individual roost trees commonly accommodated both adults simultaneously.

Nearby roosts, however, were not an essential feature for nests. The second nest site used by the CC pair in 1983 had no nearby roost sites. Instead the adults normally flew 3 km from the nest to roost in trees that were situated close to other nests that they had previously used.

Similarly, most nests had immediately adjacent water sources for drinking, but some did not. Condors drank from a variety of water sources, including the tops of waterfalls and catchments in potholes. The pair nesting in a sequoia tree in 1984 commonly drank from a natural cavity high in the nest tree itself. Since water sources sometimes went dry seasonally, the birds were faced with retaining some flexibility in their use of specific sources. A water-

High exposed waterfalls are attractive to condors as sites for drinking and bathing: ***above***, Sisquoc Falls in Santa Barbara County was a concentration point for the species in the 1930s, with as many as 32 individuals seen here simultaneously; ***below***, the pool above the falls in the Hole-in-the-wall cliffs of the Sespe Sanctuary was likewise once used heavily by condors, with several high counts of over 30 individuals in the vicinity during the 1940s. Condors nested in cliffs adjacent to both falls.

fall spilling over "hole-in-the-wall" in the Sespe Sanctuary was a famous gathering place for condors in the 1940s and was used for both drinking and bathing (see Koford 1953). Condors also commonly used Sisquoc Falls in Santa Barbara County for both drinking and bathing. Still another important drinking and bathing site was a waterfall high on the south slopes of Pine Mountain.

Overall Distribution of Nests

As illustrated in the preceding chapter, the distribution of nests found during the modern program, and back through the 1940s formed an arc through the mountains surrounding the southern San Joaquin Valley. In earlier times nests were reported from as far south as in the mountains of Baja California south and east of Ensenada (Swann 1924, Lumé 1938) and as far north as the mountains not far south of San Francisco in Santa Cruz County (Koford 1953). However, condors may also have nested north of San Francisco, perhaps even as far north as the Columbia River between Oregon and Washington. No concerted efforts to find nests appear ever to have been made in this portion of the historic range. Although the validity of nesting records in Baja California has been questioned by some authors (e.g. Kiff 1977) we see no compelling reasons to reject them. The apparently consistent presence of condors in the Sierra San Pedro Martir early in this century leaves little doubt that a breeding population was resident there.

Recent nests were all distant from the main foraging areas in the foothills of the San Joaquin Valley, even though some apparently suitable cliff areas with caves exist in the foraging areas. Moreover, there are no historical data to suggest that these cliffs have ever been used for nesting. We will consider potential reasons for this absence of nesting activity in the foraging grounds in Chapter 11.

Because pairs under close study all used multiple sites and because all territories contained numerous sites of apparently good quality, it does not appear likely that the species has been limited in recent times by nest-site availability. Nevertheless, on several occasions we documented condors using substandard nest sites whose characteristics predisposed the sites to failure (e.g. the first nest site of the CC pair in 1982). Because the birds used these sites in spite of the presence of better quality sites nearby, it appeared that either we were missing factors making these better sites unavailable or the birds had some deficiencies in their abilities to select optimal sites.

Nest Site Characteristics and Their Relationship to Nesting Success

To understand more fully the factors affecting nest-site choice and their influences on nesting success, we conducted a survey of 72 nest sites used historically and during the modern program. In addition to our own site information we used data collected by Fred Sibley, who had found a substantial number of nests in the 1960s, and data from Carl Koford's (1953) study of 15 condor nests. In the following paragraphs we summarize the survey results. More detail is given in Snyder et al. (1986).

The 72 nests studied were all protected sites at least partially shielded from the weather and can be classified into several major categories: 37 pothole sites in cliffs, 21 cave sites in cliff crevices or cracks, 6 sites in crevices among boulder piles on cliffs or steep slopes, 6 sites that were best described as overhung ledges on cliffs, and 2 sites in burn-out holes in trunks of giant sequoia trees. As is typical for New World vultures in general, condors used a wide diversity of nest-site types. Although we found no nests in dense thickets in flat terrain, as has been seen in other vulturids, it is possible that California Condors have used such sites, perhaps in other regions of their former range.

Pothole nests were characteristically found in sandstone formations and were usually smoothly rounded, relatively shallow caves in vertical or nearly vertical cliffs. They appeared to have been formed by internal weathering of depressions forming in the cliff faces and were not generally associated with fractures in cliffs. Crevice or crack sites were much more irregular in shape and followed fracture lines, often for many meters. Overhung ledge sites,

Many of the recent nest sites were in sandstone formations: *above*, the Santa Barbara female (SBF) incubates her 1983 egg in a pothole nest that was first found by Dick Smith in 1973. The egg from the 1983 nesting produced Almiyi in captivity, a female who has since produced many of her own progeny. Note characteristic "bathtub ring" of excrement on the cave walls resulting from earlier nestings; *below*, the West Gorge nest site of the Sespe Sanctuary (SS1) pair was used for three different nestings in the 1980s, producing three chicks: WGI, Xolxol, and Cachuma. Two of the three still survive in captivity and have produced numerous offspring.

like crevice nests, were found in a variety of cliff types and were highly variable in shape. Sites in boulder piles were also highly variable in shape and size. The two sites in sequoia trees most closely resembled pothole sites in dimensions and size.

In elevation above sea level, all sites fell below 2,000 m (6,500 ft), and the great majority lay between 600 m and 1800 m (2,000 ft and 5,900 ft), with a fairly even distribution within this range. This distribution indicated considerably more nesting at moderately high elevations than was recorded by Koford (1953), but the difference was probably due to our more intensive nest-searching activities at all elevations and was not likely an indication of any real shift in nesting elevations over time. The highest nest found was a site in a giant sequoia tree at 1,830 m (6,000 ft). Sites above about 1,500 m were subject to snows during the incubation period in late winter and spring, whereas lower elevation sites, depending on specific location, were sometimes subject to summer temperatures as high as 43 °C (110 °F). Nevertheless, we found no significant correlation between nesting elevation and laying date in the 29 cases for which accurate egg-laying dates were available.

The overall distribution of compass directions faced by nest entrances was random. However, when the nests were divided into sites at elevations above 945 m (the median elevation) and sites below 945 m, an interesting pattern emerged. Low nests showed a tendency (not quite statistically significant) to face north, while high nests showed a highly significant tendency to face south (with high nests differing highly significantly from low nests in orientation). These results suggest that condors may tend to choose warmer sites at high elevations and cooler sites at low elevations, much as Mosher and White (1976) reported for Golden Eagles.

However, without knowing the exact availability distributions of potential nest caves at high and low elevations (prohibitively difficult distributions to determine), one could argue that the distributions of nest orientations might be more a reflection of cavity availability than of condor directional preferences. Our rough and nonquantitative assessment of this possibility is that we strongly suspect that there is indeed a biased tendency of potential nest cliffs to face south at high elevations in the main condor nesting region, whereas we find it hard to discern if there might be any directional bias in potential nest cliffs at low elevations. Thus we are inclined to be fairly skeptical that condors might have any true directional preferences in nest orientations relative to elevation.

Entrance sizes of nest sites tended to be highly variable. There was no obvious upper size limit, and at the lower limit condors appeared willing to use any entrance they could squeeze through. The lowest entrance height recorded was 30 cm (12 in), and it is doubtful if condors could enter anything with a much lower ceiling. The narrowest entrance was only 20 cm (8 in) wide and this likewise was probably about as narrow as the birds could negotiate.

Nest depths were also highly variable, but there was a preponderance of sites with rear walls about 1.5 to 2.0 m from the entrances, probably reflecting the prevalent use of potholes, which are not usually more than about 2 m deep. In general, the birds placed their eggs as far back in the caves as there was suitable level substrate and an adequately high ceiling. This generally meant that eggs were laid in relatively dark portions of the sites. However, ambient light levels at the egg positions of all sites were at least strong enough that we could discern the basic internal structure of the sites without a flashlight. One site that a condor pair investigated and defended (but did not use for egg laying) in 1983 was, nevertheless, effectively completely dark at the only possible nesting location at the end of a long curving tunnel.

Unlike Koford (1953), we did not find any consistent tendency for condors to lay their eggs between confining walls. In a number of sites the egg was simply placed close to a wide rear wall. Egg positions were not always level. Six nests were located with bottoms sloping more than 5 degrees at the egg position. From one of these, an egg accidentally rolled out of the entrance and over the cliff edge in 1982. From another, an Andean Condor nestling rolled out of the entrance and over the cliff edge during an unsuccessful cross-fostering experiment in 1983 (miraculously, the nestling recovered in captivity). Evidently, the degree of slope at the egg position is an important characteristic not always fully appreciated by the condors.

Ceiling heights at the egg position varied from 38 to 229 cm, with a distribution peaking strongly between 50 and 75 cm (20–30 in). One 1984 condor pair (CV) was observed investigating a site with a ceiling only 30 cm high, but the birds could not stand up in this cave. They soon apparently lost interest in it, and eventually laid elsewhere. Thirty-eight centimeters (16 in) may represent an approximate lower limit for an acceptable ceiling height. The relatively low variance seen in ceiling heights at the egg position suggests strongly that condors are sensitive to this parameter in their choice of egg locations.

Nest substrates averaged about 8 cm in depth and ranged from about 1 to 20 cm deep. In several instances the levels of condor excrement on the cavity walls indicated that the substrate depth had changed significantly over the years. Excrement in active condor nests normally rises to a height of about 35–40 cm above floor level. Cases of bands of excrement high on walls and separated from the floor by bands of clean wall clearly indicated loss of substrate subsequent to nesting. Conversely, deeply buried eggshell fragments and partially buried bands of excrement indicated recent rises in substrate levels.

At least at the time of inspection, almost all nest substrates were dry, although one heavily used historical site showed signs of recent entry of water to the nest bottom and watermarks on the cave walls indicated susceptibility of another site to flooding. The classic nest site studied by Finley and Bohlman in 1906 has only a partial ceiling. Eggshell fragments found in this site in 1983, presumably dating from early in the century, were noticeably crumbly from apparent exposure to water.

Nest substrates were often conspicuously surfaced with small chunks of rock and debris in the egg position, and it was clear from direct observations that adult condors deliberately reach out to gather these chunks in their bills from the vicinity of the egg position. Thus condors do modify their nest sites to a limited extent and appear to prefer to rest their eggs on pads of coarse gravel and other loose material. In some sites, however, eggs have rested on substrates of nearly pure sand or silt, apparently because little gravel and debris was available for pad construction.

Besides small chunks of rock, nest substrates commonly included woodrat (*Neotoma*) droppings, twigs, leaves, acorns, bone fragments, trampled pellet material, tiny eggshell fragments, and sometimes sea shells. The bones included small skeletal fragments of a variety of large mammalian species that had probably been fed upon by the adult condors (Collins et al. 2000). Many sites also contained abundant bones of woodrats that probably entered the sites with no assistance from the condors. Only two nests contained condor bones (a humerus, and a humerus and tibiotarsus, respectively, all from nestlings). By comparison, one late Pleistocene condor nest in the Grand Canyon of Arizona contained the skeletal remains of at least five different condor individuals (Emslie 1988c).

Occasionally man-made artifacts were found in sifting nest substrates (see photograph in Chapter 1). These included bottle caps (two recent sites), a pull-tab from an aluminum can (one recent site), fragments of a white comb (one recent site), jagged fragments of glass (two recent sites and one historical site), fragments of an aluminum can (one recent site), fragments of hard plastic (three recent and one historical site), archaic flashbulbs presumably left by photographers in a site active during Koford's study in 1941, and a spent lead bullet (one historical site discussed earlier). Although it is not certain what agents brought in these artifacts, we strongly suspect that most were brought in by the adult condors as a result of their swallowing bone- or shell-like objects in an effort to satisfy calcium needs of their nestlings, much as has been reported for Cape Vultures (*Gyps coprotheres*) by Mundy (1982). The sites where the artifacts were found were sufficiently remote from past human activities (with the exception of the site with the bullet and the site with the flashbulbs) that it is unlikely that the objects were brought in by man or by woodrats. Nevertheless, it is possible that some objects in some sites may have been brought in by Common Ravens.

Condor nests were also used to some extent by other species, including Turkey Vultures, Common Ravens, and Red-tailed Hawks. Six nests, including the primary site (Koford #1) studied by Koford (1953), contained eggshell material from Turkey Vultures, indicating probable former use of the cavities by this species and considerable overlap in nest-site preferences between the two species. The sites used by the Turkey Vultures ranged from one of the shallowest condor nests (1.5 m in depth) to one of the deepest (10.0 m deep). Very likely, Turkey Vulture eggshells were not found in more sites because this species nests only in certain local portions of the nesting range used by the recent condor population.

Common Ravens in southern California characteristically nest in very small-entranced holes, generally far too small for use by condors. However, one former condor nest cave, a relatively shallow (1.1 m deep) and narrow-entranced (64 × 71 cm) hole, contained an old raven nest in 1982 and a new raven nest in 1984. The attractiveness of this site to ravens provides a possible explanation for a case of condor egg breakage documented here by Koford in 1946.

Another condor site had stick remains of a Red-tailed Hawk nest and contained red-tail eggshells and feathers as well as the many remains of snakes, small mammals, and small birds. Like the site used by ravens, this site was a small pothole, only 0.8 m deep.

Arthropods were also cohabitants of many nests. Clouds of gnats (*Dasyhelea* sp.) were found in four of the deepest, darkest sites (all deeper than 4.9 m). In one of these we were able to observe interactions of the condors and gnats from a distant blind, as the entrance to the site was large and the floor ran straight into the hillside. The gnats caused nearly constant irritation and head-shaking in the birds. Late in the incubation period the male adult moved the egg from its original position to a position 3 m closer to the entrance in apparent response.

Koford (1953) noted three condor nests with blood-sucking Mexican chicken bug (*Haematosiphon inodora*) infestations. In two of the sites there were hundreds of these bugs at the time the young condors fledged. We found no *Haematosiphon* infestations in any of the nests investigated during our study. However, it should be emphasized that we entered only six nests of the 1980s at times when they contained nestlings and did not closely inspect the sites during these visits. Koford also reported many ticks of the species *Argas reflexus* in one nest cave. We found no tick infestations during our study.

At one small active site of 1985, several dozen bumblebees (*Bombus* sp.) were found on the cavity ceiling shortly after the start of incubation. Furthermore, honeybee (*Apis mellifera*) hives were found in or immediately adjacent to six nests, including one of the sites studied by Koford (1953). For three of these sites it is unknown if condors and honeybees were ever present at the same time, but in two recent nests and one historical site both species were definitely present simultaneously. In one of these, an active site of 1984, the entrance to the honeybee hive was only 56 cm from the condor egg. Nevertheless, there was no evidence that the close proximity of this hive caused the birds any difficulty. Whether there might be any preferential tendency for condors to nest near hymenopteran colonies for the protection this might provide against terrestrial predators is unknown. In fact, whether occupancy by bees preceded or followed occupancy by condors is not known for any of the above sites.

Sadly, as described in Chapter 3, the honeybee infestation of one of the historical sites we checked, a site documented active in 1904 by Frank Chapman (1908), was not known to us at the time Bay Roberts roped into the site from the top of the cliff. Bay's travails in escaping an angry swarm of site defenders convincingly revealed the potential benefits to condors of nesting near bee hives, but sacrificing Bay to prove the case was hardly our intent.

All nest sites were rated as to their accessibility to large terrestrial predators such as black bears (*Ursus americanus*) and coyotes (*Canis latrans*). Sites were classified as walk-in sites (accessible), scramble-in sites (questionably accessible), and rope-in sites (completely inaccessible). Of the 72 sites, 16 (22%) were walk-ins, 8 (11%) were scramble-ins, and 48 (67%) were rope-ins. In spite of the relatively frequent use of accessible sites, no clear cases have as yet been documented of predation on eggs or young by terrestrial predators (Koford 1953, Snyder 1983). However, an instance was observed by Jan Hamber in 1983 of a black bear obviously attempting to climb to the CV condor nest, a rope-in site containing a nestling. The bear failed to reach the nest, although it got to within a few meters by climbing a tree in front of the nest cliff; its motives seemed clear. In another instance, a pair of condors were seen closely "escorting" a black bear away from a walk-in SB nest site with a nestling only about 100 m distant. The bear did not discover the site. Black bears are presently abundant in the main condor nesting region in Ventura and Santa Barbara Counties, but it is important to note that this species was not present in the region until the 1930s when individuals were introduced from Yosemite (Schoenherr 1992). Before then, the main condor nesting region was occupied instead by grizzly bears, with unknown but probably substantial appetites for succulent young condors.

One questionable case of mammalian predation on a condor nestling was recorded by Bleitz (1946) who found chewed remains of a nearly full-grown condor and tracks of bobcat (*Lynx rufus*) and raccoon (*Procyon lotor*) in a walk-in nest cave. Apparently these animals had eaten the breast and one wing of the bird, but it was unclear if they were the cause of the nestling's death or only scavengers of a carcass already dead for other reasons.

The relatively frequent use of walk-in sites vulnerable to terrestrial predators is noteworthy, because condors are not compelled to occupy such sites. All recent nesting territories have had numerous good quality rope-in sites available to the birds. However, risks from terrestrial predators are not the only risks to consider in evaluating nest site quality. In certain respects walk-in sites are sometimes superior to rope-in sites. In particular, they are often less risky with respect to accidental falls of nestlings.

Falls from nest sites appear to be especially frequent from rope-in sites that lack external porches or slopes where nestlings can exercise their wings. At one such site observed closely in 1983, the nestling was seen repeatedly attempting to perch on the steeply sloping entrance, losing its balance, and nearly falling out of the site. At another such site discovered by Fred Sibley in 1968, the nestling was first found on a slope about 30 m under the site, apparently having survived a fall from the entrance. At still another such site found by Fred Sibley in 1966, a late-stage nestling was discovered dead at the base of the cliff, apparently having fallen some weeks earlier. Evidently the use of small potholes lacking external porches poses risks to chick survival, especially if the sites are located high above the bases of nest cliffs. The frequent use of relatively low cliffs by condors may in part be a reflection of such dangers, and the frequent use of walk-in sites by condors may in part reflect a balancing of risks of chick losses from falls against the risks of easy entry by terrestrial predators.

Forty of the 72 nests studied had well-developed external porches. Another 11 sites lacked external porches but at least had enough space inside to allow full wing exercise. However, 21 sites lacked both the internal or external space for unimpeded wing-flapping, and chicks were faced with fledging from these sites without the benefit of full wing exercise during development.

We also assessed most sites for their vulnerability to Common Ravens. For 55 (87%) of the sites checked, untended eggs could have been seen by ravens flying past the entrance. Eggs would not have been visible in only eight sites, primarily very deep and dark sites. Thus, the vulnerability of most condor nests to ravens has been quite high.

Direct observations indicated that once ravens did see a condor egg, they often made persistent attempts to steal it. Their potential for success was high, considering the length of the condor incubation period and the fact that condors commonly leave their eggs untended during nest exchanges. Ravens were sometimes remarkably brazen in their attempts to take eggs. In one instance (CC territory in 1983) Rob Ramey observed an individual entering a nest cave and directly jabbing under the abdomen of an incubating condor. The condor made only clumsy efforts to fend off its assailant, although the raven did not succeed in destroying the egg. In other cases we have seen ravens following condor pairs in and out of caves as the latter have prospected nest sites prior to egglaying. As we will discuss further in Chapter 11 ravens represented the most pressing reproductive difficulty faced by the recent condor population.

Breeding Behavior

California Condors conduct their lives at a slower pace than many smaller birds. Still, their behavior is complicated and difficult to follow at times, especially during breeding activities. Gaining a good understanding of condor reproductive biology and behavior demanded continuous observations of nests for periods of many months. Only through such coverage could we make accurate estimates of the rates of various activities and obtain data on rare, but important events, such as encounters with predators.

We watched nests from distant brush blinds or even more distant lookouts. Most blinds were positioned on the opposite sides of canyons from the nest caves to allow as direct a view as possible into the cave interiors. Depending on local topography, the blinds were usually a third to a half mile (0.5 to 0.8 km) away from nests, although the well-concealed blind for the sequoia nest was closer (circa 100 m) because the dense surrounding forest did not allow a more distant view.

Campsites for observers were established out of view from nests and farther away from nests than blinds. Shelters took the form of caves, tents, or A-frame wooden huts, the latter generally pitched near sources of drinking water. With steady use and improvements, most camps became comfortable refuges from the elements. However, none could match the elegance of the campsite that Carl Koford constructed for his nesting studies of 1939. Koford's camp included a spacious cave for sleeping, truly comfortable and ingenious stone chairs, and a raised stone hearth that still can be seen intact today, silently commemorating his historic research.

It took endurance and concentration to keep track of nesting events for even a single day of full dawn to dark coverage. Yet the effort it took to get to some nesting areas often made it most efficient for individual observers to maintain watches over many consecutive days and sometimes longer. The record in observing persistence was held by John Schmitt, who once sustained a watch of a nest in Santa Barbara County for five straight weeks. In the latter years of the program the most usual schedule for nest watchers was five days on, alternating with five days off. Two people were generally needed to keep each nest continuously monitored.

Because male and female condors look alike in size and coloration, one of the most basic challenges of studying breeding pairs was determining the roles of the two sexes in various activities. Observers learned to distinguish individuals of pairs through subtle differences in facial and feather patterns, although which was the male and which the female often did not become clear until copulations or egg-laying activities were observed or individuals were trapped and sexed through blood samples. For over a year the super-dominant bird of the CC pair was believed to be the female, and was only later confirmed to be the male. Males were dominant in most productive pairs, although the female of the SB pair was often aggressive to her mate, chasing him around the nesting territory and supplanting him from perches. Females of other pairs also occasionally showed aggression to their mates.

Events at nests were often unpredictable and ranged from nervous encounters between condors and bears to sudden arrivals of military jet aircraft screaming low overhead in daring maneuvers. Winter storms sometimes buried high-elevation nest sites, condors, and observers in snow. At other sites oven-hot summer temperatures left observers wishing they were so buried. Periods of dense fog were especially frustrating, as the birds' activities continued, but were very difficult to follow as nest caves faded in and out of view. An egg of the SS2 pair was destroyed during one foggy stretch in 1986, but because of poor visibility, observers were unable to determine whether the loss was caused by the ravens around the site or some other factor.

Fortunately, biting insects were generally few in condor range, although the blind overlooking the Sequoia nest site of 1984 became notorious for its noxious flies. At some sites observers had to be continuously vigilant against attacks from giant pajaroello ticks. These speedy terrestrial blood suckers left ugly wounds that took weeks to heal and seemed especially fond of human ankles. Not known as carriers of human diseases, they were nevertheless the vectors for "foothill disease" of cattle, which led to numerous aborted calf carcasses fed upon by the condors.

Near one nest site we once watched in amazement as a helicopter crew from Los Angeles, evidently unaware of the condors in the vicinity, released pest raccoons that had been trapped from urban neighborhoods. Raccoons are accomplished egg and nestling predators, and unfortunately they were already loose by the time we got to the chopper. Near another site, Helen was alarmed to discover the remains of a home-made incendiary balloon flapping in a patch of chaparral, an unsolicited contribution of some aspiring, but fortunately incompetent, arsonist. Near still another nest site John Schmitt watched an errant (and thankfully unarmed) cruise missile come crashing to the earth far from its programmed destination in Nevada. John radioed in the news and wound up directing military aircraft to the impact site when they failed to find the missile on their own. Other surprises included occasional encounters along trails with unidentified camouflage-clad paramilitary groups. Certain portions of the Sespe drainage were used for illegal marijuana cultivation, and observers had to be careful not to blunder into such operations. The dead body of Ronald Hughes – one of Charles Manson's attorneys – had turned up on the edge of the

Sespe Sanctuary just a few years before we arrived in California, perhaps intended as a helpful contribution to the condor feeding program.

Late in the afternoon of July 4, 1984, a lightning strike ignited a fir snag and surrounding forest just 150 meters from the active sequoia nest. Forest Service crews battled the blaze through the night as the female condor, her chick "Sporktron", and Dave Ledig watched the progress of operations from their observation points in the vicinity. Conceivably, this event, like many others, might have caused all sorts of inner turmoil in the condors, but the female never budged from her perch during the crisis.

Altogether, condor pairs proved remarkably tolerant of occasional catastrophes around their nests, and there were no cases of nest desertion following disturbance, despite the dire warnings of Koford and the McMillans. From this standpoint the precautions we followed in limiting observations to distant blinds and lookouts may have been largely unnecessary. However, we were as concerned about habituating condors to human presence as disturbing them, so in hindsight our general avoidance of close approach to the birds was probably very beneficial. Carl Koford found that "Oscar," the nestling at his most intensively studied nest, which was observed from a relatively near distance, became fully accustomed to his frequent close presence, and as a fledgling exhibited almost no fear of humans. In earlier studies of Cooper's Hawks, we had found that human-accustomed nestlings subsequently suffered especially high mortality from shooting and other human influences (Snyder and Snyder 1974). Habituation to humans has proved one of the main hurdles in releasing captive California Condors to the wild (see Chapter 17).

Prior to the 1980s, only a single pair of breeding California Condors had been closely studied through most of the reproductive cycle. This was a pair watched by Carl Koford in a region of Ventura County that later became the Sespe Condor Sanctuary. In 107 days of observation between March 23, 1939 and March 24, 1940, Koford meticulously recorded the activities of this pair through much of the incubation, nestling, and fledgling dependency periods. He also made much more fragmentary observations of the behavior of other pairs at their nests. Koford's observations revealed many of the basic patterns of condor breeding behavior and provided a baseline for the interpretation of reproductive activities of more recent pairs.

No observations of condor breeding behavior were made during the Miller–McMillan study of the early 1960s, and only incidental observations were made during the studies of Sibley and Wilbur in the late 1960s and 1970s. Dick Smith and Jan Hamber observed a pair in Santa Barbara County during the mid–late 1970s, but it was not until the early 1980s, with the advent of the intensive research and conservation program, that the reproductive behavior of the species again became a focus of major observational studies.

Observations of the 1980s were concentrated on pairs with eggs and nestlings to determine such features as feeding rates and rates of changeovers between males and females in attending nests, as well as to closely document the interactions between adults, their specific behavior patterns at different stages, development of behavior patterns of nestlings, the interactions of adults with nonresident condors, and the interactions of the birds with potential nest predators. However, not all pairs were located soon enough in the breeding season to allow the study of the early stages of breeding cycles, and many nestings were subject to egg and chick removals, precluding studies of the latter stages. Certain pairs that were discovered after they had fledged young and certain pairs that never laid eggs were covered less intensively than the pairs that were available for study in the egg and nestling stages.

Specifically, six different egg-laying pairs were studied through all or parts of the incubation and/or nestling periods during one or more years. Observations were also made of the nest investigations and courtship activities of two pairs that never laid eggs and were suspected to be homosexual. In addition, we studied two pairs that were tending fledged young, and another pair that was known to be heterosexual but lost the male adult just prior to the point when egglaying was anticipated. Table 2 details the number of days of observation and the stages of nesting represented for all nests. Altogether, nearly 3000 days of obser-

Table 2. Summary of observations of nesting territories 1980–1986.

Pair	Nesting year	Range of observation dates	No. days observation	Nesting stages during observation period
PC1	1979–80	Feb 27 to Dec 31,1980	48	fledgling
CC	1980–81	Mar 4,1980 to Oct 15,1981	299	pre-egg, egg, nestling, fledgling
SB	1980	Jan 2 to Dec 31, 1980	144	pre-egg, egg, nestling
SS1	1980	Feb 26 to Dec 31, 1980	51	pre-egg, egg, nestling(?)
TP	1980-81	Mar 22 to Dec 23,1981	10	fledgling
SB	1981	Jan 9 to Dec 7, 1981	222	pre-egg, egg, nestling
SS1	1981–82	Jan 14,1981 to Feb 21,1982	134	pre-egg, egg, nestling, fledgling
SM	1981	Nov 14,1980 to Dec 23,1981	60	pre-egg (homosexual?)
CV	1981–82	May 11 to Dec 26,1982	10	fledgling
CC	1982	Jan 8 to June 19	112	pre-egg, egg
SB	1982–83	Jan 10,1982 to Feb 22,1983	261	egg, nestling, fledgling
SS1	1982	Apr 20 to Aug 19, 1982	115	pre-egg, egg, nestling
PC2	1982	Dec 6,1981 to Dec 30, 1982	82	pre-egg (homosexual?)
SM	1982	Jan 3 to Dec 30, 1982	77	pre-egg (homosexual?)
CC	1983	Feb 1 to Jun 6, 1983	120	pre-egg, egg
SB	1983	Mar 4 to Dec 31,1983	76	pre-egg, egg
SS1	1983	Feb 1 to Nov 6, 1983	277	pre-egg, egg, nestling
CV	1983	Feb 14 to Aug 4, 1983	110	pre-egg, egg, nestling
PC2	1983	Jan 4 to Jul 15, 1983	59	pre-egg (homosexual?)
CC	1984	Jan 16 to Nov 12, 1984	64	pre-egg, egg
SB	1984	Jan 13 to Sep 4, 1984	82	pre-egg, egg
SS1	1984	Jan 16 to May 23, 1984	90	pre-egg, egg
CV	1984	Jan 17 to May 9, 1984	81	pre-egg, egg
PP	1984	Mar 20 to Sep 15, 1984	180	egg, nestling
SB	1985	Jan 22 to Jun 17, 1985	111	pre-egg, egg
HP	1985	Jan 21 to May 13, 1985	67	pre-egg
SS2	1986	Jan 10 to Apr 20, 1986	83	pre-egg, egg

Note: Eggs taken for artificial incubation from nearly all nestings from 1983 onward; pair member identifications for various pairs were: CC (CCF/CCM), SB (SBF/SBM), SS1 (SSF/SSM), SS2 (SSF/REC), TP (birds unnamed), PC1 (birds unnamed), PC2 (PCA/PCB), SM (SMA/SMM), CV (CVF/CVM), PP (PPF/SMM), HP (UN1/BFE).

vation of nesting pairs were made during seven years.

In this chapter we summarize the main discoveries made during the nesting observations of the 1980s. We compare our data, where relevant, with the earlier data of Koford and with data obtained subsequently on breeding behavior of captives at the Los Angeles and San Diego Zoos.

Mate and Territory Fidelity

California Condors characteristically showed strong loyalty to their mates and nesting territories over the years. No cases of divorce between pair members were observed, and cases of birds accepting new mates were limited to instances in which former mates had died. Established pairs did not change nest territories, so long as the pairs remained intact. When their mates died, however, birds sometimes changed territories in the process of forming new pair bonds. In other cases of mate loss, birds retained their original territories as new mates adopted their territories. As a general result, territories tended to exhibit long histories of use, although the specific birds occupying the territories changed occasionally over the years.

The extent of territorial defense was variable. In 1982 we saw recurrent bouts of active defense of the territorial boundary between the PC2 and SM pairs. These bouts generally involved aerial chases, but in some cases actual physical contact occurred as birds knocked one another off perches. Also on a number of occasions we saw vigorous territorial aggression of adults toward their own progeny. This occurred when the adults initiated new breeding attempts at times previous progeny were still in transition to independence.

However, in most other cases we saw few or no signs of territorial defense. Intruding condors usually entered territories freely, even to the extent of landing at the entrances of active nests, without any overt aggression being shown by the territory holders. In one case we even witnessed the CC pair courting and copulating unopposed in the near vicinity of the SM pair and its nest. In contrast, when two subadults visited the CC nest for two days in July of 1980, the female of the resident pair was obviously highly agitated and repeatedly interposed herself between the curious visitors and her chick. Although her aggression was not extreme, she remained in the nest vicinity for an exceptionally long period, apparently concerned about the situation.

Koford (1953) similarly reported a general absence of overt territorial defense in nesting condors, although Finley (1908b) reported nesting adults chasing away a subadult or adult that approached their nest. Whether the degree of tolerance for intruders may have been related to the degree of kinship between intruders and residents is not known. Kinship information was lacking for virtually all instances observed.

Although responses to other condors were inconsistent, nesting condors showed more regular tendencies to defend the immediate vicinity of nests against predators such as Golden Eagles and Common Ravens. Condors commonly chased off ravens, and almost invariably chased off eagles, although eagle intrusions were generally uncommon. With both ravens and Prairie Falcons (*Falco mexicanus*), condors often found themselves on the receiving end of aggression, and their success in driving off ravens was often limited, with the ravens returning almost immediately.

Condors were not generally aggressive towards approaching humans, and often seemed more curious than fearful. However, in one instance (July 4, 1983) a male condor flew in to "threaten" us when we climbed to inspect an inactive potential nest site in his territory. The bird (SSM) landed on a rock only about 10–15 m distant and was quite intimidating as he inflated his air sacs and performed three bouts of startling snorting, hissing noises in approximately 10 minutes (for a photograph of the same bird in aggressive posture on another occasion see Chapter 1). This bird had an active nest with a chick about a kilometer away at the time, and although we had earlier seen him investigate the site we were checking, it was not a former nest site and did not appear to be a viable potential nest site as it had no flat substrate to accommodate an egg in its rocky interior. Why he defended the site was not obvious.

Nesting pairs used their territories as a home base even when not actually nesting, although during nonbreeding periods it was common for territories to be empty of condors for several days. During such periods, the pairs often cruised to distant parts of the foraging range and roosted in cliffs or tall trees in or near the foraging range. Such trips, however, were typically interspersed with irregular visits back to home territory where the birds again roosted in habitual locations.

Except for the incubation and early nestling periods, when it was essential for one member of a pair to attend the nest, pair members tended to stay together in movements away from their nesting territories, as was clear from visual observations in nesting territories and photographic and radio-telemetric monitoring of the foraging grounds. However, these tendencies varied considerably from pair to pair. The SB pair showed the most consistent tendency to forage together, and likewise members of the CV pair were often seen foraging together. In contrast, members of the PP pair of 1984 (SMM and PPF) were never observed together on the foraging grounds or at associated roosts while they were breeding. For example, PPF was commonly documented using the Blue Ridge roost during the latter stages of breeding, but never together with SMM.

The PP pair was a new nesting pair in 1984 and appeared to be made up of the remnants of two other pairs that held very distant nesting territories in previous years. The male's former territory was known to be about 150 km from the nest site the pair occupied in 1984, and there is a good chance the latter was a former nest site of the female. Potentially, SMM and PPF were long accustomed to forage in largely different areas, and possibly the loyalty of these birds to habitual foraging areas was strong enough to override any tendencies for them to forage together. Despite their apparent general independence in movements, the pair did a creditable job of rearing their nestling during the 1984 breeding season and exhibited no problems with feeding rates or other aspects of nest attendance, as we will discuss in more detail below.

Pair Formation and Territory Adoption

The data available from the 1980s indicated that pair formation often involved a bird (experienced or inexperienced) that paired with and adopted the territory of an experienced and established breeding bird that had just lost its previous mate. Between 1981 and 1985 we witnessed the formation of five new pairs: UN1/BFE, SSF/REC, PCA/PCB, SMM/SMA, and SMM/PPF. Only two of these pairs (UN1/BFE and SMM/SMA) appeared to be *de novo* pairings in which birds settled on a territory without one of the two being previously associated with the territory (at least in the immediate past). The other three cases were apparent or potential cases of birds joining other birds in the established territories of the latter. Even in the cases of apparent *de novo* pairings, it is noteworthy that the territories and nest sites chosen were clearly historically active, as evidenced by old condor eggshell and whitewash in the sites.

In the two cases where we suspected that a new pair had formed from remnants of two previous pairs, both of which had held previous territories (PCA/PCB and SMM/PPF), the new pairs took some time to decide which of the former territories to adopt. In fact, the SMM/PPF pair was seen and photographed visiting the former nest site of SMM only days before laying an egg in what was likely a former nest site of PPF, some 150 km away. Similarly, the PCA/PCB pair of 1981–83 was documented commuting between the nest site and territory they eventually settled on (PC) and another territory (TP) some 30 km away. Various observations suggested that these may have been the former territories of the two birds.

During the winters of 1984–1985 and 1985–1986 several breeding pairs lost members in a period of high mortality. Subsequently, the surviving members of three of these pairs (SSF, SBM, and CCF) continued to base their activities in their habitual territories, evidently waiting for new mates to appear. However, two other widowed birds (UN1 and SMM) showed no obvious tendency to stick with their territories after loss of their mates. In both of these latter cases, the birds had been associated with their territories for relatively brief periods (less than a full year). In contrast, REC continued to frequent his nest area after his mate was trapped into captivity, even though he had been associated with this territory for less than a full year.

Courtship Behavior and Copulations

We have relatively little data on the normal seasonal timing of pair formation but in the case of SSF and REC, it was clear that a solid bond was forming in the November–December period of 1985. Formation of the SM and PC2 pairs also apparently took place in November and December. In general, courtship activities were mostly recorded in the late fall, winter and early spring, but sometimes occurred at other times of the year.

We recognize a number of behavioral components of pair formation and territory adoption that might loosely be termed courtship behavior: coordinated pair flights, mutual grooming, and sexual display. In coordinated pair flights condors circled and cruised through their territories, soaring closely side by side. Depending on an observer's position, the birds often appeared to fuse optically into a single flying object larger than either bird alone. This effect may be more than accidental as it may serve to advertise occupancy of the birds' territory more effectively and to a greater distance than if

Pair-bonding activities include mutual preening, especially of the head region, and characteristic synchronized pair flights in the nesting territory. **Above**, the SM condor pair, possibly a homosexual pair of males, mutual preens on a talus slope near their nest site in late 1981. **Below**, the PC2 pair cruises its nesting territory in typical pair flight in 1982.

they flew far apart.

Pair flights are one of the first signs of incipient pair formation. For example, during the spring of 1982 we watched a bird with very distinctive feather damage (UN2) appear successively in four different established territories where it engaged in pair flights with members of three of the resident pairs. None of these courtship attempts led to the bird's acceptance by any resident, and he (or she) soon gave up and left each territory.

The pair flights of condors seem to be similar to the "tandem flights" discussed for various griffon vultures by Mundy et al. (1992). However, these authors attributed a social hierarchy function to the flights, rather than a courtship function, because of the frequent signs of aggression seen in the higher bird in such pairs. Nevertheless, Mouze and Bagnolini (1995) present evidence for *Gyps fulvus* that tandem flights appear to function in pair maintenance, with the female normally taking a position above her mate in space. In condors, we have no information on the positioning of one sex relative to the other, but observations suggest that both territorial advertisement and courtship could be important functions of the flights. It would be hard to eliminate a potential courtship function in view of the above observations of UN2.

In condor pairs that progressed beyond initial courtship, we commonly observed mutual grooming activities. In these activities the birds perched side by side on a rock or limb of a tree and used their bills to nibble at each other's skin and feathers, especially in the head and neck regions. Grooming normally appeared gentle, but we occasionally saw instances where a bird grabbed loose folds of a partner's neck skin in its bill and did not let go even when its partner moved to a position where holding on was absurdly awkward. The bill of a condor is an extremely sharp tool for severing meat and skin, so mutual grooming may pose some risks if not pursued with restraint.

Sexual displays were normally performed only by males. As described by Koford (1953), Wilbur and Borneman (1972), and Wilbur (ms), a displaying bird extended its wings in partially drooped position, stretched its head and neck forward in drooped position, and slowly strutted its feet up and down in exaggerated fashion as it swayed back and forth and often circled its mate on foot. During display, the air sacs in the head and neck region were often, but not always, inflated, revealing brilliant orange and pink patches of skin.

In our observations sexual display commonly led to copulation. In mounting, the displaying bird stepped onto the back of his partner, where he stood awkwardly with his wings flapping and his bill grabbing his partner's neck skin apparently to aid in balance. Mounting episodes were relatively lengthy compared with those of other birds, and generally continued for about a minute. When successful they concluded with the male bending his tail under that of the female to achieve cloacal contact, while flapping his wings. A female seeking to reject a copulation attempt simply moved away or nipped at the male's head with her bill when he attempted mounting.

Koford (1953) noted sexual display on more than 30 occasions, but none of these led to copulation. The one copulation he observed was not preceded by display. These facts caused him to question the relationship of the two activities. Similarly, Wilbur and Borneman (1972) recorded display preceding copulation in only 3 of 8 copulations, and

Courtship display and mating of the captive pair UN1 and HIW: ***above***, the male in display characteristically extended his wings partially, drooped his head and neck, and strutted his legs up and down as he slowly circled his mate; ***below***, mounting often followed display and normally lasted on the order of minute, as the male flapped his wings slowly for balance and grabbed the neck of the female with his bill.

Wilbur (ms), like Koford, observed many instances of display not leading to copulation. In contrast, our more extensive data on pairs studied in the pre-egg stage (Table 3) show a very strong tendency for copulations to be preceded by display, while about half of the displays seen were followed by copulation attempts. These data clearly establish a strong, but not invariable linkage of the two activities.

Most commonly, sexual displays were performed as the birds perched near each other on the top of a cliff, boulder, or hillside. However, the displays were sometimes performed on tree limbs or inside nest caves. In the latter locations, physical contraints often prevented the full circling behavior of the female by the male.

Both Koford (1953) and Wilbur (ms) noted only single birds (presumably males) displaying, and these birds usually, but not always, directed their displays toward single birds (presumably females). Our observations corroborate those of Koford and Wilbur for most pairs, although in many cases we knew the identities and sexes of the birds and were confident that they were cases of males displaying to females. In only one instance did we have clear evidence for a full wing display being offered by a female in the wild (CCF in 1983).

Nevertheless, we observed two pairs in 1981, 1982, and 1983 in which both birds gave the characteristic displays simultaneously in most instances, and in which sexual display, though frequently observed, was never seen to lead to successful copulation. In both pairs (the SM and PC2 pairs) we saw attempted mountings by both pair members on different occasions, but none of these mountings lasted for more than a few seconds. Our suspicions were strong that both pairs might have been homosexual pairs of males, and indeed no eggs were laid by either pair. However, we were able to confirm the sex of only one bird in each pair. The two unsexed members of these pairs perished before a program to trap and sex wild birds through blood samples was finally implemented. The two members of these pairs

Table 3. Courtship displays and copulations in wild California Condor pairs

	Pair						
	SS1	CC	SB	CV	HP	SM	PC2
Years included in data analysis	83–84	80–84	84–85	84	85	81–82	82–83
No. courtship displays observed	78	58	50	15	9	17	66
% cases both birds display	0	0	0	0	0	88–100	79–82
% displays followed by mounting attempts	68	47	76	47	56	50	31
No. copulation mountings attempted	56	36	44	10	7	12	25
% mountings follow displays	96	83	90	70	100	67	83
Mean duration of displays in seconds	54	68	57	65	34	84	70
Mean duration of mounting attempts in seconds	54	66	51	46	60	5	7

Note: mean duration of mounting attempts for SM and PC2 pairs approximate as all mountings abortive and many were timed only roughly.

Courtship display of SMM to
PPF atop their giant sequoia
nest tree in 1984.

that were ultimately sexed were both males (one of whom, SMM, had been earlier christened "Lady of the Lake" in accord with his most usual position on the bottom in copulation attempts with SMA).

Homosexual pairs are not unknown in vulturids. Toone and Wallace (1994), for example, described a female/female pair of Black Vultures (*Coragyps atratus*) at the San Diego Wild Animal Park that copulated apparently normally and laid a normal two-egg clutch, sharing incubation in typical fashion. Homosexual pairs have also been described in many other avian species.

Still, we hasten to acknowledge that sexual displays have been seen given by female California Condors on an irregular to regular basis in the captive flock (Cox et al. 1993, Harvey et al. 1996), although male displays have been much more frequent. Accordingly, we cannot completely rule out the possibility of heterosexuality for the two wild pairs in which both members gave full sexual displays.

It is notable that another component of courtship behavior that is commonly observed in birds of prey, feeding of the female by the male, was never recorded in condor observations of the 1980s. Nor to our knowledge has it been recorded in condors or other vultures by others (e.g. Mundy et al. 1992). On very rare occasions adult female condors did approach their mates with the begging-flapping behavior typical of nestlings soliciting food, but these instances appeared to represent an appeasement strategy toward hyperaggressive mates and did not result in any clear transfers of food. Both male and female condors readily regurgitate food to feed their nestlings, so "courtship feeding" would certainly be physically feasible.

Perhaps males do not normally feed their mates because prior to egg laying, pair members normally forage together and feed from the same large food sources. Under such conditions, they are both usually in a similar state of food satiation, and feeding of the female by the male might offer little in the way of a valuable extra nutritional bonus in initiating reproduction.

In most birds of prey, where feeding of females by males is common, males characteristically shoulder the entire burden of foraging for the pair in the early stages of breeding (see Snyder and Wiley 1976, Newton 1979). In these species the contributions of males allow females to avoid energy-demanding foraging activities, help them to quickly produce large clutches (often representing a substantial fraction of female body weight), allow them to guard the clutch consistently during the egg-laying period, and allow them to shoulder the primary role in incubation. In condors, the single-egg clutch comprises only about 3% of a female's body weight and is presumably much more easily provided from the female's own foraging resources than in these other species. Further, since only a single egg is laid, the female has no need of additional food to complete her clutch. Incubation is shared about equally between males and females, allowing each sex to forage on its own, alternately, once the egg is laid. The relatively minor size difference between male and female condors equips both sexes about equally for incubation and brooding duties, as well as for nest-defense.

Nest Investigations and Preparations

New World vultures are not known to build obvious nest structures, and we have not seen them bring in nesting material from outside their nest caves. However, both sexes of condors do substantial amounts of preparation of nest substrates, gathering up beakfuls of sand and small pieces of rock, twigs, and other debris from within their caves to form coarse platforms of litter on which their eggs will rest. As observed by telescope at a distance, adults typically gathered these materials as they stood in the existing or future egg position and reached out to grab them off the nest floor with the bill. Such activities commonly resulted in the egg resting on a crude disc of litter (see for example Plate 22 in Koford 1953). In caves with little debris, however, the egg sometimes ended up resting on little more than a substrate of sand.

Away from their nests we occasionally saw condors carry objects in their bills but never saw them fly with objects in their feet. At the time he was tending a nestling in 1983, the male of the CV pair was several times seen biting off a green sprig of bigcone Douglas fir and flying off with it in his bill in a direction away from the nest site and out of sight. The purpose of this behavior was unknown, and it was never seen in any other condor. Birds feeding at carcasses sometimes moved short distances with food held in the bill.

Over a period of weeks to a month or more before egg laying, condor pairs typically investigated a variety of potential nests within their territories. During investigations the birds entered the sites, moved substrate around with their bills, and perched, copulated, preened, and sometimes roosted in the vicinity. In some cases pairs quickly focused their attentions on single sites, so that it was apparent that these sites would likely become the sites used for egg laying. In most cases, however, pairs continued to investigate a variety of sites up almost to the point of egg laying. During early and mid stages of the nest investigation period it was usually very difficult to predict which site would actually receive the egg. Keeping track of pairs at this stage was often a scramble, as alternative sites were often miles apart and out of view from one another in different canyons.

In a typical nest investigation, a pair spent up to several hours in and around a site before flying off to forage or to investigate a different site. So long as they stayed together in movements, it was safe to assume that egg laying was not imminent. However, in the final day or two before egg laying, the male typically went off to forage alone, leaving his mate in the nesting territory. At this stage the female typically went to fill her crop at a nearby water source. Just before egg laying she also typically remained in her prospective nest site overnight for the first time. Though she commonly remained attached to a single nest site in the last few days, she sometimes continued to check a variety of sites. When her mate eventually returned from the foraging grounds, he sometimes had to check all the various nest sites they had been investigating to relocate his mate. This suggested that he, like ourselves, was largely in the dark in predicting which site the female might chose for egg laying.

The behavior of taking on a crop-full of water just prior to egg laying has also been seen by Don Sterner in captive California Condors at the San Diego Wild Animal Park and provides a valuable clue to the approximate timing to be expected for egg laying. Why drinking often occurs just before egg laying is unclear. Perhaps it functions in part in maintaining physiological water balance in the final stages of egg formation.

Don Sterner at San Diego and Mike Clark at Los Angeles have also often observed captive females searching for and ingesting bone fragments in their cages in the last days before egg laying. Bone ingestion at this stage may provide supplementary calcium for eggshell formation. Although such bone ingestion has not been observed in wild females, this could easily be an observational artifact. It may normally occur on the foraging grounds out of view of nest observers.

Egg-laying Behavior

Few naturalists ever have an opportunity to witness egg laying in a wild bird species, even though they may have studied birds all their lives. In many species, of course, the process takes place within a cuplike or concealed nest structure so it is difficult to observe directly. In the condor, there is no substantial nest structure to conceal matters, but the process is often hidden from view by the depth of the nest cave or by obstructions in the cave entrance. Fortunately, Noel once was able to see the entire process clearly in a shallow cave. From a hidden location on a ridge about a third of a mile away, he had a direct view of the cave's interior through a telescope and no intervening vegetation or rocks obscured the details of what happened.

The date was February 14, 1982, and overcast skies allowed exceptionally high resolution viewing through the telescope. We had been expecting egg laying from this bird (CCF), as she had been spending increasing amounts of time in the site, patiently shaping the floor with her bill. Still, we did not know exactly how it would happen and found the actual process quite surprising.

Several minutes before laying – which took place at 14:06 in the afternoon – the bird rose from a sitting position and faced into the cave from just inside the entrance. Now tremors began to shake her body every 9 to 10 seconds, and her tail and wing feathers were slightly spread. Noel knew instantly that something important was about to happen and that he should not even blink for fear of missing the events to follow. Suddenly, the egg simply came shooting out of the female's cloaca to land in full view on the floor of the cave entrance. Amazingly, she laid it from a standing position, and the egg fell to the ground with apparent force, though it did not roll across the floor and was evidently unharmed. Perhaps the cushion of loose litter she had earlier gathered at the laying position was important in softening the impact and preventing rolling.

Once the egg had been expelled, the female slowly pivoted to look at it intently, bending down with her bill almost touching it a minute after laying, then again raising her head. During the next five minutes she bent down from a standing hunched position to touch the egg briefly with her bill three times. Then finally, six minutes after laying, she settled down on the egg in steady incubation after tucking it on top of her feet in the usual incubation position adopted by vulturids.

Unfortunately, the egg laid in the above instance was fated to a relatively short lifetime. The floor of the nest cave sloped significantly to the outside and the egg ultimately rolled out of the cave and over the cliff edge on February 26. Nevertheless, the pair followed with a replacement egg 40 days later and again chose a site that was relatively shallow and observable from a distance. However, laying of this second egg took place behind a small projection of rock that partly obscured the view. As observed by Joe Russin, the bird evidently again faced into the cave at the time of laying and laid the egg from a standing position. Although the exact moment of laying could not be exactly determined, it appeared to take place at approximately 10:52 in the morning, and the female began steady incubation a few minutes later.

Still a third case of egg laying by the same female in a different nest cave was witnessed by John Roser at 13:23 on March 12, 1984. Again the female faced into the cave and laid from a standing position with her wings slightly spread, and again John was able to see the female shudder several times over about a three minute period prior to laying. John could not see the actual emergence of the egg as the bird's drooped tail blocked the view, but he saw the egg immediately thereafter. In this laying, the female stood hunched over with her bill near the egg for eleven minutes before settling down to incubate.

The major features of egglaying witnessed in the wild have also been observed in captivity by Don Sterner and Mike Clark. These include laying from a standing position, the tendency to face into a nest chamber while laying, and the relatively quick initiation of incubation after laying.

All three cases of egglaying witnessed in CCF in the wild took place near midday, but this timing may not be usual for the species. Most captive females observed by Don Sterner and Mike Clark have laid eggs overnight or in early morning. However, CCF in captivity has continued to exhibit a strong tendency to lay eggs during midday, just as she did in the wild.

Don Sterner and Mike Clark have also observed that captive females characteristically utter a wheezing-squealing noise at the moment of egg expulsion. In the wild, the distances from blinds to nests have been far too great for such sounds to be audible.

Incubation Period

Both sexes participated alternately in incubation, with shifts averaging several days in length. Mean lengths of incubation shifts are given in Table 4 for the pairs followed most intensively through the incubation period. These data show some possible general tendencies of females to incubate for longer stints than males, although in all pairs male and female incubation lengths did not differ statistically. In one case (the CC pair) the male generally surpassed his

Table 4. Lengths of incubation shifts at intensively studied California Condor nests.

Pair and year	Egg number	Number of male shifts	Mean male shift (days)	Number of female shifts	Mean female shift (days)	Mean overall shift (days)
PP 1984	1	9	1.88	10	2.60	2.26
SB 1985	3	9	1.98	8	3.25	2.58
SS1 1983	3	7	3.43	7	4.31	3.87
CC 1983	2	6	6.24	5	5.48	5.89

mate in incubation attentiveness. Among the various pairs, the CC pair showed by far the longest average incubation shifts (close to 6 days per shift). The PP pair showed the briefest (only 2.26 days per shift). Statistically, pairs all differed significantly from one another in lengths of incubation shifts except the PP and SB pairs.

When relieved of incubation duties, the off-duty adult normally left the nesting territory to forage on its own. However, in nestings of the CC pair in 1982 and 1983, the male (CCM) was extremely reluctant to give up incubation duties when his mate (CCF) returned from foraging, and he repeatedly drove her off from the immediate nest vicinity. As a result, incubation was frequently disrupted, and the egg was often left unwarmed for periods of a half hour and longer. His longest documented shifts were approximately 9 and 10 days in length in 1983 and 1982, respectively. These were the longest incubation shifts documented in any condor during our studies. Similar cases of aggressive male dominance of incubation have also been seen in captivity, both in California and Andean Condors. But in certain captive pairs studied by Don Sterner, Mike Clark and Cathleen Cox it has been females that have aggressively dominated incubation.

Incubation shifts tended to be relatively short at the condor nest studied by Carl Koford in 1939 and averaged only 26.7 hours per shift in five full shifts documented. However, these data were likely biased low because of his relatively short observation periods. Many of his observed incubation shifts were incomplete, and what the true average shift may have been is unknown.

In many incubation exchanges, the incubating bird left the nest to circle in the air with its returning mate before the next shift started. Such circling behavior was sometimes restricted to the nest canyon, but sometimes extended into adjacent canyons. Periods of such circling sometimes exceeded a half hour, and eggs were thus often left unguarded for significant intervals. On some occasions, the circling behavior of the pair was followed not by a nest exchange, but by the previously incubating bird returning to resume incubation. In other exchanges, the incoming bird landed directly at the nest entrance before the incubating bird left the egg, so the egg was never left unattended in the exchange process.

During their turns at the nests, birds occasionally stood up to stretch and preen, to gather sand or debris within reach to place around the egg, to come to the nest entrance to look outside, or occasionally to fly off to drink water from a nearby waterfall or other water source. The birds nesting in a sequoia tree cavity in 1984 sometimes drank from a water-filled cavity higher up in the dead top of the nest tree. In settling back on the egg after a break, a bird commonly rolled the egg with its bill in re-positioning it on its feet.

Breaks from incubation averaged about once every 1.7 hours during a sample of 15 days of observation of the CC pair in 1980. However, at another nesting of the same pair in 1983, incubating birds were pestered by dense clouds of gnats at the egg position and exhibited much more frequent incubation breaks as an apparent result. Also possibly because of the gnats, the male adult moved the egg several meters from its original position deep in the nest cave to a position much closer to the entrance during one shift. Although this move resulted in an apparent reduction in gnat harassment, it did not completely solve the problem. The egg of this pair was taken for artificial incubation and was replaced with a dummy telemetered egg to study incubation temperatures. During a week-long period of monitoring, breaks from incubation were clearly indicated by sudden drops in the egg temperature records. These breaks occurred every 59.8 min on average, and were more frequent at night than during daylight (1.2 vs 0.8 breaks per hour, respectively). Core egg temperature of this dummy egg fluctuated continuously and never reached a stable plateau.

This was the same pair of condors that habitually fought over incubation rights, so the frequent breaks in incubation apparently caused by the gnats may have exacerbated the stress to the egg caused by aggression. The detrimental deterioration of the embryo documented by candling when the egg was taken for artificial incubation would likely have resulted in death of the embryo if it had remained in the wild (see Risser 1983). Nevertheless, the egg did recover under artificial incubation and produced a surviving chick (Sespe) who is still a productive member of the captive flock.

Hatching of Eggs

We were fortunate to see the hatching process of CCF and CCM in 1980. We did not know then how long incubation lasted in the species, though we assumed it might be close to sixty days, judging from information on Andean Condors breeding in zoos. By May 11, 1980 we had been watching the incubation activities of the pair for approximately fifty-four days, and we were lucky to be observing a site in which the egg was fully exposed to view from a distance. Unfortunately, it was a site whose interior could be seen only indistinctly on sunny days because of heat shimmer across the canyon. Our clearest views of the egg were in the early morning and evening when the atmosphere was most stable.

The egg, in any event, was rarely in view, except for brief periods when the tending adult rose to change position or to turn the egg before settling down again with ponderous restraint. We also glimpsed the egg every few days when the adults exchanged incubation duties at the nest.

Pipping of the egg was first visible on May 11 as an irregular raised area of shell about the size of a dime. By May 12 and May 13, the pip hole had enlarged to a dark perforation in the shell closer to the size of a quarter. At times when the adult stood up off the egg and atmospheric conditions were stable, we were able to see the hatching process in great detail. With the Questar telescope we could even see the egg tooth of the chick wavering across the opening in the shell. But most surprisingly, we could see clearly that the adult sometimes nibbled around the pip hole with her bill, breaking off bits of shell with her lower mandible and thus directly assisting the youngster in the hatching process. Parentally-assisted hatching of eggs is not often documented in birds, and we were not anticipating such observations.

From first pipping of a condor egg to actual hatching takes close to three days. Unfortunately we did not get to see the final moment with this egg, as it happened in the dark between the evening of May 13 and the morning of May 14. Nevertheless it was clear that with these condors, unlike many other birds, the process was a cooperative one between adult and chick and perhaps allowed the chick to conserve energy during its entry into the world. Close observations of the hatching of naturally-incubated eggs of California Condors and Andean Condors at the San Diego Wild Animal Park by Don Sterner have since confirmed that such parental participation in hatching is a common occurrence.

A somewhat different form of cooperation between adult and hatching chick occurred at the third nest of the SS1 pair in 1983. Here the final emergence of the chick was witnessed directly on July 2 by Leon Hecht, and took place as a result of the adult condor briefly standing on the egg! This caused the broad end of the shell to separate from the rest of the shell. In the following minutes the adult again stood on the chick, still mostly in its shell, several more times. Whether this behavior was anything other than accidental, we do not know, but it seemed likely that it may have been mainly clumsiness on the part of the adult. On other occasions we often witnessed adults kicking their eggs across the nest floor in inept attempts to settle down on them. In any event, the chick (Cachuma) appeared healthy and vigorous from the start, despite her apparently unusual entry into the world.

In a third case of hatching witnessed in the wild, at the sequoia nest of 1984, the raised lip of the nest cavity unfortunately obscured a clear view of the egg. John Schmitt was able to determine the timing of hatching reasonably accurately from the behavior of the tending adult, but the chick was only finally glimpsed several hours after the event.

Nestling Period

Brooding of a chick was nearly continuous for the first two weeks of the nestling phase, except during breaks for feedings. The steadiness of brooding, however, declined greatly in the third and especially fourth weeks, and brooding during the day ceased at about one month. Consistent brooding overnight ceased at about the same time, but overnight nest attendance by adults sometimes continued erratically for another two to three weeks. The last recorded overnight attendance by an adult at a nest was on the night of the 55th day of the nestling period at the CC nest of 1980.

For the first month, when one or the other adult was normally in continuous attendance at or near the nest, adults relieved each other on a near daily basis. This rate of changeovers was much greater than the rate seen during incubation. For example, although incubation shifts at the SS1 1983 nest averaged 3.9 days in length, attentive shifts at the same nest averaged only 1.2 days for the first four weeks of the nestling period. Similarly, attentive shifts at the PP nest of 1984 dropped from 2.3 days during incubation to only 0.8 days during the first four weeks of the nestling period. The immediate dramatic increases in changeover rates seen after hatching suggested that the more relaxed changeovers during incubation and the great variability in changeover rates among nests during incubation were not dictated by such factors as food availability.

As brooding declined late in the first month of the nestling period, the overall attendance of adults at nests showed a rapid decline and then stabilized at a lower level from about the start of the third month through the rest of the nestling period. Details can be seen in the graph below and in Table 5. During the latter stages, nest caves were normally attended by adults less than 5% of the daylight hours and adults were present in the nest vicinity only about 25% of the daylight hours.

Numbers of feedings per unit time dropped steeply during the first few weeks and then

Average tendencies of five intensively studied condor pairs to attend their nests during the nestling period (see Table 5). Bottom curve gives average percent of daylight hours at least one adult was at the nest. Top curve gives average percent of daylight hours at least one adult was in the nest vicinity (within view from the observation blind).

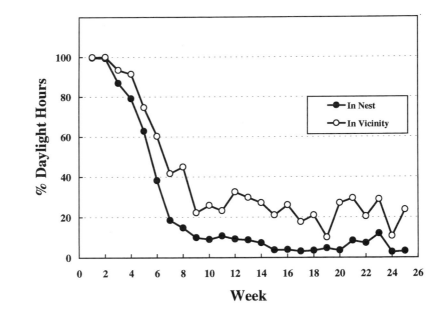

Table 5. Percent of daylight hours at least one adult attends nest or remains in nest vicinity.

Week of nestling period	CC 1980		SB 1982		SS1 1983		CV 1983		PP 1984	
	nest	nest vic	nest	nest vic	nest	nest vic	nest	nest vic	nest	nest vic
1	99.6	99.6			99.2	100			99.9	100
2	99.6	100			98.6	100			99.6	100
3	94.0	98.8	80.3	98.2	75.0	76.6			97.8	100
4	87.7	89.9	63.3	96.6	86.5	91.7			78.9	87.2
5	51.5	52.5	65.5	85.9	69.6	78.0			64.7	81.9
6	43.9	49.9	45.7	72.9	32.7	48.3			30.3	69.7
7	27.0	29.3	23.9	39.2	16.6	37.4	6.2	66.4	18.1	35.7
8	22.2	23.3	16.0	61.6	11.5	41.2	6.7	48.2	17.0	50.2
9	5.6	6.2	24.8	41.2	2.9	6.1	7.9	39.4	7.7	17.6
10	10.1	11.5	21.1	56.1	1.3	16.7	4.3	26.8	7.8	18.0
11	4.6	5.6	32.8	56.2	7.3	17.3	1.8	21.6	7.0	14.7
12	14.5	22.2	10.1	45.5	4.7	15.3	4.0	53.4	12.2	25.6
13	4.3	6.0	18.5	39.9	14.7	32.2	2.8	54.3	3.1	15.9
14	3.3	6.4	17.5	27.7	7.5	29.6	3.0	43.9	4.7	28.0
15	1.6	5.7	4.7	16.3	4.0	19.9	1.8	27.7	5.8	35.2
16	1.1	1.9	5.0	34.9	3.8	31.7	1.3	21.4	7.8	40.1
17	3.6	6.5	2.0	17.4	4.8	31.3			1.4	15.1
18	2.5	2.5	4.8	15.9	1.8	22.8			4.5	42.3
19	6.4	10.1	0.8	6.6	6.6	13.1				
20	3.9	35.7	3.1	18.3						
21	2.6	23.3	14.0	35.3						
22	3.1	21.7	10.8	18.8						
23	8.8	20.9	14.8	36.7						
24	2.6	10.6								
25	3.1	23.6								

stabilized at a lower level during the last months of the nestling period, as indicated in the accompanying graphs and Table 6. Specifically, adults fed their chicks about once every two hours in the first week, but by the latter stages of the cycle, chicks received an average of only about one feeding every 10 hours, and were given no feedings at all on about one quarter to one third of the days. Occasionally, chicks even went without food for two consecutive days, although this occurred only 13 times in 605 days of observation during the

Table 6. Numbers of observed feedings at intensively studied California Condor nests through the nestling stage.

Week of nestling period	Nesting pair and year														
	CC 1980			SB 1982			SS1 1983			CV 1983			PP 1984		
	m	f	tot	m	f	tot	m	f	tot	m	f	tot	m	f	tot
1	19	12	31				11	42	53						
2	11	26	37				13	24	37						
3	18	9	27				26	12	38						
4	15	8	23	5	8	21	19	15	34						
5	12	9	21	7	13	20	5	12	17				14	10	24
6	10	8	18	3	11	15	7	7	14				10	9	19
7	6	8	14	5	7	13	3	6	9	6	1	7	4	9	13
8	7	2	9	2	6	10	5	9	14	11	4	15	6	7	13
9	2	8	10	7	5	14	3	1	4	9	7	16	6	6	12
10	5	5	10	4	5	9	2	4	6	2	5	7	3	4	7
11	5	3	8	3	4	8	7	8	15	6	3	9	4	7	11
12	5	4	9	7	3	10	7	4	11	6	7	13	5	5	10
13	5	4	9	3	7	10	3	3	6	7	2	9	5	4	9
14	3	6	9	6	4	10	8	5	13	5	4	9	6	4	10
15	4	4	8	2	4	6	6	6	12	5	3	8	7	3	10
16	2	3	5	4	3	8	5	3	8	3	4	7	7	3	10
17	7	2	10	3	3	6	6	2	8				4	3	7
18	5	2	7	7	1	9	5	3	8				1	2	3
19	6	5	12	4	1	7									
20	4	4	8	5	2	7									
21	5	5	10	2	2	4									
22	3	4	7	4	5	9									
23	5	3	8	5	3	8									
24	4	4	8												
25	2	3	6												

Note: Timing of egglaying and hatching of chicks was unknown for CV 1983 nesting and SB 1982 nesting. These nests were arbitrarily assigned the median egg laying date for the wild population – February 14. Timing of hatching known exactly for other nests. For the first few weeks of the nestling phase, feedings could not be tracked accurately at the SB 1982 and PP 1984 sites because chicks often out of sight behind obstructions so data for these weeks are omitted. Total observed feedings during a week not always a sum of male and female feedings as sex of feeding adult occasionally not determined. Chicks from CC 1980 and SB 1982 nests fledge naturally in wild. Chicks from the SS1 1983, CV 1983, and PP 1984 nests taken into captivity in mid-late nestling stages.

Average feedings per hour at five intensively studied condor nests through the nestling period (see Table 6)

Average percent of observation days that chicks received no feedings for the five intensively studied condor nests in Table 6.

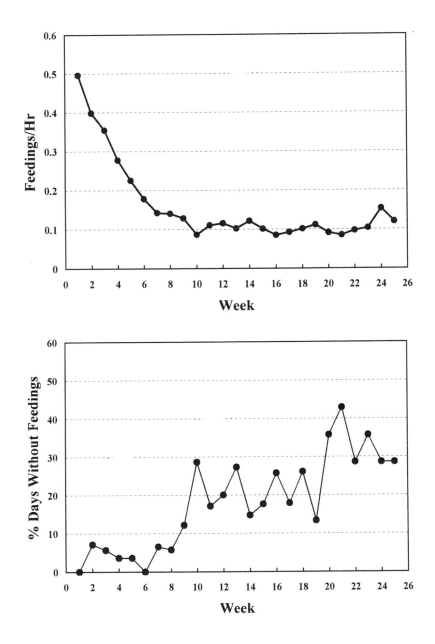

nestling periods of the five most intensively studied nests. Only one instance was recorded of a chick receiving no food for three straight days. Days without food were highly unusual in the early stages. In general, each parent made about 3–5 feeding visits to the nest and fed the chick about 5 times during each week in the latter stages.

The relative uniformity in overall feeding rates seen at various nests did not in itself suggest any major problems in finding food for breeding. Nevertheless, either because of differences in pair quality or perhaps foraging range quality, there were some minor differences in consistency of feeding among the pairs (Table 7). The most consistent of the closely studied pairs was the SS1 1983 pair, which showed the highest rate of feedings per hour, failed to feed its chick on only 15% of the days in weeks 10 through 25, and had no consecutive no-feeding days. The most inconsistent pair was the SB 1982 pair, which exhibited a relatively low rate of feedings per hour, failed to feed its chick on 30% of the days in weeks 10

Table 7. Comparisons in feeding characteristics among intensively studied pairs during nestling period.

Pair and year	Total days observed	No. days no feedings	No. cases of consecutive no-feeding days	% days no feeding, weeks 10–25 of nestling period	Mean feedings per hour, weeks 10–25 of nestling period
CC 1980	174	39	5	29	0.104
SB 1982	143	30	7	30	0.095
SS1 1983	121	11	0	15	0.122
CV 1983	67	11	1	23	0.089
PP 1984	100	9	0	14	0.100

through 25, and had 7 pairs of consecutive no-feeding days. Nevertheless, the female chick of this pair (BOS) fledged successfully, and when she died a year later of cyanide poisoning from a coyote trap, her weight (8.4 kg) was excellent for a female.

The chicks from all other pairs included in Table 7 still survive as productive breeders in captivity. Only one, the chick of the CV pair (Cuyama), was underweight when he was taken captive (5.8 kg at an estimated 17 weeks of age). However, this chick had a heavy load of ectoparasites when he was taken captive, and it is unclear whether his low weight may have been due primarily to the parasites or to a deficiency in the amount of food provided by his parents. Feeding frequency (feedings per hour) at this nest was indeed the lowest rate of the five pairs studied intensively, but this does not necessarily mean that the chick was receiving less food than the other chicks. The regularity of feedings at this nest (% of days with feedings) was average.

We emphasize that the numbers of feedings per unit time clearly do not give a tight indication of quantity of food given chicks at various stages. When chicks are tiny, their crops hold very small quantities of food compared with later on, so that the quantity of food provided to chicks presumably increases greatly even as numbers of feedings decline during the cycle. But since chicks were fed by regurgitation, we were unable to determine the quantity of food being transferred in the field except by very rough evaluation of the distention of a chick's crop after a feeding. In raising the first chicks in captivity, Bill Toone at the San Diego Zoo was able to establish that actual food consumption averaged about 47 g per day at 2 days of age, 111 g per day at 7 days, 267 g per day at 14 days, and 440 g per day at 21 days.

Males and females fed their chicks with roughly equal frequency overall (Table 8), although there was a statistically significant preponderance of male feedings at the CV nest of 1983. As during incubation, the sexes exhibited approximate equality in investments in nestling care.

During early stages, an adult typically sat close to the chick when not actually brooding. At such times, the adult often watched the chick closely, occasionally preened the chick's down, and sometimes snapped at insects in the vicinity. The chick sometimes picked up such objects as leaves and molted feathers and attempted to manipulate them. Adults occasionally

Table 8. Numbers of feedings of chicks by adult males and females at five intensively studied California Condor nests during the nestling period..

Nest and year	No. male feedings	No. female feedings	No. unknown sex feedings	Total feedings
CC 1980	170	151	3	324
SB 1982	88	97	19	204
SS1 1983	142	167	0	309
CV 1983	60	40	0	100
PP 1984	82	76	0	158
Totals	542	531	22	1095

took these objects from the young and discarded them out of reach by the young.

In a feeding, the adult faced the chick and the chick put its head most of the way into the adult's mouth, swallowing food rapidly from the adult's gullet. With a newly hatched chick, the feeding process apparently was initiated by the adult, which lowered its bill to the young's level and either presented the side of its beak or opened it and took the chick's head in its bill. The chick often did not start begging until a feeding was underway, when it began beating its tiny wings stiffly during breaks in the meal. Older chicks begged before and during feedings by loosely flapping their opened wings, which were held out horizontally with tips dragging on the ground. Their whole bodies shook with the effort.

Although most feedings took place bill to bill, an adult occasionally regurgitated food which fell to the ground and was then picked up and ingested by the chick or the adult. Regurgitating food onto the ground is also a common response of chicks disturbed by intruders at nests.

In the latter part of the nestling period when chicks often began to wander on foot away from the nest entrance onto adjacent slopes and ledges, begging flaps were probably especially important in helping parents locate their chicks. A band of white down on the upper wing surfaces of older chicks contrasts with the black contour feathers and makes begging movements conspicuous even from a distance.

In the mid to late nestling period, a visit to the nest by an adult usually began with a feeding consisting of several bouts of contact interspersed with breaks. To standardize analyses we considered a single feeding to have ended once there were no more bouts within a 15-minute period. During breaks between bouts an adult sometimes temporarily restrained a frantically begging youngster by placing a foot on its neck and clamping it to the substrate. Foot-clamping of a chick's neck also appeared to be a common way for an adult to remove a nestling's bill from its throat at the end of a feeding.

During breaks between bouts, the adults often appeared to be bringing food up to their mouths, with visible reverse peristaltic movements in the breast and crop area. Adults also sometimes tossed their heads up and down in what appeared to be a pumping motion before initiating feeding bouts. Feedings ended with the parent raising its head or beginning some other activity, such as cleaning the beak and head by rubbing on the substrate. Generally a period of social interaction followed, during which the adult and chick sat

4 Aug – 18 Aug, 19 Sep – 13 Oct 1981
West Gorge creek, Sespe Condor Sanct.
Ventura Co. Calif.
Schmitt
32

Sketches by John Schmitt of
the Sespe Sanctuary condor
nestling (WGI) prior to and
after fledging in 1981.
Behaviors illustrated include
self-preening, sunning,
capturing vegetation,
sleeping, feeding of the chick
by a parent, and mutual
preening of chick and
parent.

down in contact and preened each other, twining necks together and rubbing heads and necks over each other's bodies in a process we generally termed "neck-wrestling". Sometimes, however, the adults became aggressive, directing nips or blows to the chick and preening it with roughness.

During periods when adults were absent, chicks mainly divided their time between periods of sitting alert, preening their feathers, and sleeping. Older chicks also spent lesser amounts of time picking up and manipulating objects such as sticks, feathers, stones, bones, and leaves. They sometimes dug into the substrate with their bills and ingested light-colored objects selectively when they encountered them, probably as a means of obtaining calcium. Older chicks also exhibited periods of exercise – flapping their wings, leaping about, rapidly turning while jumping, capturing objects in the beak and then whirling around and carrying them away, and so on. They also exhibited mock prey-capture behavior with their feet, stabbing out to clamp objects to the substrate without gripping them. As mentioned in Chapter 1, the presence of this behavior in chicks (but not adults) suggests that the ancestors of condors may have had at least partially predatory habits.

If the structure of the nest cave and its surroundings permitted, chicks began to wander outside the entrance to explore their surroundings as early as 6 weeks old. During early ventures outside, they appeared clumsy and suffered frequent slips and falls. Their activities included mock battles with vegetation, bursts of wing-flapping and the curious inspection of all manner of objects in the vicinity. A nestling at the CV nest of 1983 (which had no external porch to permit outside perambulations) often narrowly avoided falling out of the site in his apparent eagerness to experience something additional to the interior of his nest cave. Overall, older condor chicks appeared to be highly inquisitive and at times very active creatures, daily learning how best to interact with their environment in a manner that showed far more experimentation and apparent intelligence than are exhibited by most raptor nestlings.

Fledging Behavior and the Post Fledging Period

Defining the point of fledging in condors is a somewhat arbitrary endeavor. Chicks commonly roamed freely on foot outside their nest caves from an early age and did progressively increasing amounts of wing exercise that sometimes lofted them into the air for short distances, though they remained within easy walking distance of the nest entrances. For convenience, we define fledging here as the first flight that took a nestling beyond a walking commute to the nest entrance. Thus, the fledging flight was the first flight that took the youngster into territory that it had not yet experienced on foot.

Fledging flights were observed at three different nests of the 1980s and took place when chicks were five to six months of age (specifically 178 days, approximately 163 days, and an unknown age, respectively), covering distances ranging from about 20 m to 300 m. The fledglings were exceedingly clumsy in flight at first and only gradually acquired the finesse needed for graceful soaring and alighting. First flights typically involved desperate flapping with the feet dangling. Early attempts at landing appeared to be almost completely uncontrolled, with the birds often coming in at entirely inappropriate altitudes relative to potential perches. Such poorly controlled landings were still observed in the fledgling of the PC1 pair in March of 1980, likely at least 4 months after its first flights.

Fledglings sometimes terminated their first flight attempts by plunging deeply into clumps of chaparral and disappearing from sight for days. In time they moved progressively greater distances from their nests to land on exposed ledges and slopes with increasing reliability.

The chick at Koford's intensively studied nest of 1939 fledged sometime between 142 and 147 days of age, although fledging was not witnessed. This relatively early departure from the nest cave apparently did not represent a typical fledging, as the chick remained almost stationary in brush below the nest cave for the next month where he was visited periodically by his parents. At 174 days of age, this bird finally flew back up to the nest cliff itself, and we suggest that this age might more properly be considered the age of fledging. Koford's intensively studied nest was a pothole in a vertical cliff that did not allow the chick to move on foot outside the cave itself. It is possible that well before the chick was ready to fly, it simply fell accidentally from the nest cave entrance during wing exercise and was unable to return. As mentioned above, we commonly witnessed near falls of the CV chick of 1983 (Cuyama) out of a similarly structured nest cave during periods of wing exercise.

The three chicks observed in their first flights in the 1980s (REC 1980, WGI 1981, and BOS 1982) were not seen to attempt major flights again for several days, but instead moved around on foot. First flights of all three occurred in the absence of adults. In one case (WGI), the fledgling first flew and landed on a rocky knob about 160 m distant. When an adult returned, the fledgling begged strongly and the adult alighted next to it, but the fledgling refused feeding and continued to do so for four more days. Eventually it made a short flight back to near its nest cave, alighted on the ground, and ran toward the cave. As an adult alighted nearby, it begged and finally fed.

Fledging flights were seen as early as mid September and as late as early November in the 1980s, and young remained completely dependent on their parents for about another half year. One youngster that flew relatively early on September 22, 1982 (BOS) was first seen following its parents to the foraging grounds on February 1, 1983. During March of 1983 its parents became increasingly aggressive towards it and drove it from the breeding area, finally beginning a new cycle by laying an egg about March 31. Similarly, the fledging of the WGI chick from the SS1 nest of 1981 on September 14, was followed by a nesting of his parents in 1982, starting with egg laying at an estimated date of April 1. In contrast, the 1980 fledgling of the CC pair (REC) remained closely associated with his parents through the spring and into the summer of 1981 after his relatively late fledging on November 7, 1980. His parents showed no signs of reinitiating breeding in 1981. Similarly, Koford saw no signs of reinitiation of breeding in his intensively studied pair whose chick was produced on a seasonal schedule similar to the CC chick of 1980 (hatching dates of May 4 and May 13–14, respectively)

Whether adults ever initiate breeding attempts in years following late attainment of flight of their young (November or December) is undocumented. We suspect that this may occur only if the young do not survive long into the next year. As adults have been seen feeding fledglings on the foraging grounds in summer and fall (see Koford 1953), it appears that partial dependency on adults may sometimes continue for as long as about a year after first flights. Topatopa, the long-standing captive at the Los Angeles Zoo who was taken from the wild as a recent fledgling, still exhibited begging behavior as a subadult in his fifth spring after hatching (Todd 1974), although this may well have been an artifact of captivity. We have not observed begging behavior in ring-necked juveniles or subadults in the wild.

Summary of Timing and Duration of Reproductive Stages

Dates of egg laying in wild California Condors have ranged from late January to early May, with the latest dates all being cases of replacement eggs after losing first or second eggs (see Table 18 in Chapter 16). Incubation periods, which have been documented primarily in captivity, have averaged about 57 days, with a range from 53 to 60 days. This is a slightly shorter incubation period than that known for the slightly larger Andean Condor (mean of 58.6 days in data provided by Don Sterner), but a period virtually identical to that of the Cape Vulture, a species almost identical to the California Condor in size and weight (see Mundy et al. 1992).

As the majority of eggs and chicks in the 1980s were taken into captivity, few accurate data exist for the length of the nestling period, and as discussed above, there is room for some debate as to how fledging might best be defined in the species. Nevertheless, it appears that the first true venture flights away from the nest cave may normally occur in chicks roughly 160–180 days old, a month later than they occur in the Cape Vulture (Mundy et al. 1992). With the spread of laying dates known for the species, fledging can sometimes be predicted to occur as early as the beginning of September and as late as early December. Although no actual December fledgings have been documented in the wild, we suspected that PAX, a progeny from an undiscovered nest of the CV pair in 1981, might have represented such a fledging because his documented flight feather molt in 1982 was significantly retarded relative to that of all other first-year wild chicks studied in the 1980s (Snyder et al. 1987a).

Very few data exist for the length of full and partial dependency of chicks on adults after fledging, although it appears likely that full dependency normally lasts about 5–6 months and partial dependency may continue for as long as about a year after fledging.

Overall, the timing and duration of reproductive events that can be summarized from data to the present show a very close correspondence to the timing and duration of reproductive events summarized by Koford (1953) in his Figure 10. Present data show a somewhat wider range of egg-laying dates than that given by Koford, but differences are not great.

The timing and duration of breeding events show a number of differences between condors and similar-sized griffon vultures. Most notably, the lengths of the nestling periods and fledgling dependency periods appear to be considerably briefer in griffon vultures (see Mundy et al. 1992, Robertson 1985). Why these differences exist is not obvious.

Interactions Between Pair Members

For the most part, the interactions between pair members were gentle and seemingly affectionate throughout the breeding cycle, although bouts of aggression occasionally broke out in most pairs, usually with males aggressive to females. Aggressive postures in perched birds included (1) a head-forward threat in which a bird stretched out its neck and head toward its opponent, sometimes with the bill opened, (2) partial wing extension revealing the white underwing triangles, and (3) inflation of the air sacs in the head and neck regions. Submissive postures included (1) a hunched-over stance with head directed away from an opponent, and (2) deflated air sacs in the head and throat region. In the air, aggressive interactions generally involved one bird pursuing another, occasionally lunging at its opponent with opened bill or biting it.

The most extreme examples of intrapair aggression, as noted above, were those observed in the CC pair, especially in 1982 and 1983. The male of this pair (CCM) was extremely reluctant to allow the female (CCF) to take over in incubation, and repeatedly drove her off as she sought to take her turns on the egg. This sometimes occurred even after the male had been incubating as long as nine or ten consecutive days without food. It sometimes took the female several days of repeated approaches to her incubating mate before she was finally able to resume incubation. In the process of driving off the female, the male frequently left the egg unattended for many hours of the day, risking severe damage to the embryo through cooling stress.

In 1983, when the program finally began taking eggs into artificial incubation to create a captive flock, we were at last in a position to rescue eggs of the CC pair that came under severe risk. Vigorous conflict broke out over their second egg of the year when the female attempted to take over incubation from the male at the end of his first incubation shift. Even though this egg was not originally scheduled for artificial incubation, it quickly became apparent that it would likely suffer embryonic death from cooling neglect if we were not to intervene. Consultation with Cyndi Kuehler of the San Diego Zoo led to a decision authorized by both the state and federal authorities that the egg should be taken into artificial incubation if it was left unattended for as many as 3 hours in a day.

The day after this decision (April 7) Sandy Pletschet documented the egg suffering incubation neglect for over 4 hours. The male had been incubating for 6 days at that point, but seemed resolutely opposed to allowing his mate access to the egg. We immediately began preparations for a potential egg pickup the following day. Sandy's narrative notes for April 8 are given in Appendix 1 (at the end of this chapter) and provide an excellent account of the events that transpired. We hope the reader may take the trouble to read this chronicle, as it will not take long and will provide a good appreciation of the senseless hysteria with which this pair battled over access to their egg. It also provides insight into how exhausting it sometimes was to keep track of events at nests and indicates just how active and mobile the birds could be under stress. The squabbles between the male and female continued without respite until the egg was finally taken in early afternoon.

Sandy's narrative notes provide a vivid example of the frenetic behavior of this pair during nest exchanges in the incubation period of both nesting attempts of 1982, the second nesting attempt of 1983 (above), and the first nesting attempt of 1984, as well as during the early nestling period of 1980. The female, although submissive to the male, was tenacious in her attempts and always succeeded in the end, apparently simply wearing her mate down to the point where he finally ceased opposition.

However, the relationship between the male and female was finally seen to change decisively with the above pair on April 29, 1983, when Dave Clendenen observed another attempt by the female to take over incubation from the male. She at last became physically aggressive toward him, biting him at the base of his bill and causing him to recoil as he guarded the egg (now a dummy replacement). After half a dozen of these biting episodes, the male meekly yielded control of the egg to the female. All nest exchanges between members of this pair for the rest of 1983 were peaceful, with the male quickly accepting the female without overt aggression. Nevertheless, battles over incubation again developed with the laying of the first egg of 1984.

Significantly, this female eventually came into captivity after the death of her mate in the wild, but exhibited vigorous aggression to all male condors initially caged with her as potential new mates. So strong was her aggression, she was ultimately re-sexed by blood-testing to confirm that she was really female. It is tempting to attribute the aggressiveness of this bird to her history of coping with her hyper-aggressive former mate in the wild.

Bouts of aggression were also seen at times in other pairs, but none led to the excessive egg neglect seen in the CC pair. In the SS1 and PP pairs, like the CC pair, most aggression was limited to males. But in the SB pair we saw aggressive episodes in both sexes and often the female was more aggressive than the male. The only productive pair that seemed quite consistently non aggressive to each other was the CV pair. However, our observations of this pair were limited. It seems possible we might have seen aggression in them as well had we had a chance to study them for a longer period.

Interactions with Potential Predators and Protectors

As a cliff-nesting species, the California Condor is faced with interactions with other cliff-nesting species during reproduction. Within condor range in California, the cliff-nesters include various wrens, swallows, swifts, and phoebes, as well as larger species such as Common Ravens, Prairie Falcons, Red-tailed Hawks, and Golden Eagles. Of these, the main ones of concern during the 1980s were Golden Eagles, Common Ravens, and Prairie Falcons. Peregrine Falcon (*Falco peregrinus*) populations were still greatly depressed in condor range during this period, and we witnessed no close nestings of this species to condors during our studies. Carl Koford's field notes from the 1930s and 1940s indicated much more substantial Peregrine populations. We suspect that interactions of this species with condors may have been frequent at that time, perhaps paralleling the sorts of interactions we witnessed with Prairie Falcons in the 1980s. We watched such interactions between Peregrine Falcons and Andean Condors in Peru in 1980.

Encounters with Golden Eagles were generally uncommon in most condor nesting territories, but when eagles appeared the condors usually drove them far away with vigorous flapping chases. As will be detailed in the following chapter, Golden Eagles were twice seen making serious attempts to capture condor chicks near their nest entrances (once in the SS1 territory and once in the SB territory), and it appears that eagles can represent a very serious threat to condor nesting success. However, the only condor nesting territory in which Golden Eagle sightings were at all frequent was the CC territory in which eagles apparently nested on several occasions in the cliffs high above the condors. Here, however, the condors often received protection from the eagles by the aggressive behavior of abundant Prairie Falcons nesting nearby. Direct encounters of the CC condors with eagles were highly unusual. None occurred in the immediate vicinity of the successive condor nests and no predation attempts of eagles on condor chicks were witnessed in this territory.

In general, it was clear that the condors were nesting almost entirely in regions of eagle scarcity, and we are inclined to view this fact as an important feature of the species' nesting habits. Perhaps the tendency to nest in eagle-free areas has been produced by the persistence of long-term condor nesting traditions only in regions where nesting success has generally been high enough to ensure production of enough birds to replace birds being lost by normal mortality factors.

Common Ravens were sufficiently abundant and widespread in condor range that it is questionable that the condors had any spatial ways to avoid them. In fact nearly all active condor territories and nest sites of the 1980s were also Common Raven territories. Responses of the condors to ravens were frequently highly aggressive, involving vigorous lunging chases both on foot and in the air, but sometimes the condors responded to ravens with relative passivity. The ravens, in turn, were often aggressive to the condors, dive-bombing them in the air and harassing them on the ground. Ravens clearly represented a major threat to condor eggs and often boldly entered condor nest caves and closely approached incubating birds. On one occasion Helen directly witnessed a raven destroying an unattended condor egg, and we obtained strong circumstantial evidence of several other similar occurrences. Nevertheless, we also observed several cases of ravens failing to damage condor eggs when they entered nests at times condors were absent.

When condors attended their eggs they were generally competent in defending them from ravens. But as discussed above, they sometimes left their eggs unattended and completely vulnerable to raven attack during nest exchanges. This failure to guard eggs consistently during exchanges contrasts dramatically with the behavior of Rüppell's Griffon Vultures (*Gyps rueppellii*) in Africa, another species that suffers significant threats of egg and chick predation from various ravens and eagles (Houston 1976). Rüppell's Griffons essentially never leave their eggs or young chicks unattended. Similarly, Cape Vultures (*Gyps coprotheres*), which face predation threats to their eggs and chicks from Black Eagles (*Aquila verreauxii*), essentially never leave their eggs and young unattended during exchanges (Mundy et al. 1992).

In view of the evident magnitude of the raven threat, there does not appear to be any obvious reason why condors do not employ the same strategy as Rüppell's and Cape

Vultures. Clearly some condor nest exchanges proceed without leaving the egg unguarded. The puzzle is why all condor nest exchanges do not follow this pattern. As discussed in the preceding chapter, it is also puzzling why condors have not consistently chosen nest sites with structural characteristics protecting them from ravens.

In our studies of the Puerto Rican Parrot in the 1970s (Snyder et al. 1987b) we found a comparable situation of poor nest-guarding against predation threats by Pearly-eyed

Condors defend their nesting territories against avian predators posing threats to their eggs and young. **Top left**, the SS1 pair vigorously chases a Golden Eagle from the vicinity of their active nest in late October 1981. Their progeny of the year was already on the wing for a month, but was still tied to the nest vicinity. **Top right**, the SM pair of condors chasing off a Common Raven from their nest vicinity. **Bottom**, the threats posed by abundant eagles may underlie the absence of condor nesting records from otherwise suitable cliffs in the foraging grounds. Eagle Rest Peak on the Wind Wolves Preserve.

Thrashers. The most reasonable explanation for the failure of the parrots to guard their nests more effectively was that the thrasher appeared to be a very recent invader of the parrot range. There might not have been enough time for the evolution of effective defensive behavior in the parrots. Could a similar explanation apply to the condors' difficulties in evading ravens?

Unfortunately, there is no definitive documentation about how abundant ravens may have been in the condor range in past decades. Fossil remains at sites such as Rancho La Brea in Los Angeles clearly indicate the presence of at least some Common Ravens in the region back into Pleistocene times. In Carl Koford's field notes ravens were a reasonably common species in the condor range in the 1940s. However, there appears to be general agreement in field workers whose memories extend back to those times (e.g. Ed Harrison) that ravens are much more abundant now than they were formerly. In the nearby Mojave Desert region there is documentation for increases of Common Ravens as high as 1500% in recent decades (Knight et al. 1993). Similarly, Derek Ratcliffe (1997) has documented a significant increase in the raven populations of Britain during the present century. As a species that has benefitted greatly from the activities of man, for example through road-killed food supplies, the Common Raven may have become a far greater menace to condors in recent years than in former times. If so, there simply may not have been enough time for the development of reliably effective condor defenses.

We found no evidence to suggest that Prairie Falcons might represent a direct threat to condor nesting success, in spite of many opportunities for them to attack fully exposed eggs or chicks. We also failed to see any cases of condors aggressively challenging Prairie Falcons. Instead, the encounters observed between the two species were entirely cases of the falcons aggressively diving on adult condors as the latter came into the vicinity of falcon nests. The falcons challenged all large avian species coming into their nesting areas.

Despite the annoyance that condors face in nesting close to the falcons, it appears that when this occurs the condors can receive substantial benefits. The falcons in effect serve as guards of the condor nests by excluding eagles and ravens from the vicinity. This is not to suggest that we have any evidence that condors deliberately choose to nest close to the falcons. In fact it is difficult to see how they could commonly achieve this, as they generally lay eggs before the time the falcons arrive on territory, and the exact sites chosen for nesting by the falcons vary from year to year.

It is also doubtful that they might volunteer to nest in proximity to the falcons, in view of the harassment they have to endure when they do. Observations of the CC pair in 1980 suggested that condors may deliberately avoid such situations. Here the condor pair was a bit delayed in egglaying (possibly they were relaying after an early failure), but appeared to be settling on a towering cliff with a number of excellent potential nest caves in early March. However, a pair of Prairie Falcons moved into the same cliff and soon began diving aggressively on the condors. In apparent response to these attacks, the condors moved immediately to another site about two kilometers distant where they laid their egg. Nevertheless, another pair of Prairie Falcons moved into this second cliff almost immediately thereafter and chose a pothole site just 70 m from the condor cave, directly facing it from across a narrow ravine. The condors had no choice but to persevere, and did ultimately succeed in fledging a chick, but they had a difficult time as they struggled to approach and leave their nest without being torn apart by the falcons.

On many occasions, a condor approaching the above nest never even got close before it was forced by the falcons to turn aside and flee down canyon. In an apparent attempt to lighten its load as it fled, the condor sometimes regurgitated mouthfuls of slimy food that cascaded to the ground. Nevertheless, the condors always managed to get to their nest in the end, often by retreating to a safe distance, then sailing in very high over the nesting canyon and descending to the shelf in front of the nest in long powerful stoops that the falcons could not deflect. Once on the ground, the condors ducked their heads and rushed into the nest, usually unharmed. However, on one occasion Helen saw the male neglect to hunch over and the falcon dealt a blow to his head with her talons that sent him into a 360 degree somersault down the slope!

Two years later, when we were again studying the same condor pair nesting in the same canyon, the closest Prairie Falcons were nesting in a different and more distant site in the canyon. This site was not close enough to allow the falcons to function as effective guards of the condor nest against ravens although they may still have provided some significant benefits against eagles. Ravens were able to settle in to nest immediately adjacent to the condors and were involved in two successive nesting failures of the condors.

In this same year it also became clear that the Prairie Falcons risked their own safety in defending their nest cliffs. On March 29, David Clendenen observed an immature Golden Eagle passing close by the falcon aerie. It responded to one of the falcons in the midst of an attack by reaching out with one foot, snatching its tormentor in midair, and killing it instantly.

Prairie Falcons were extremely abundant in certain condor nesting regions. For example, in 1984 we documented the existence of no fewer than five nesting pairs of this species within a 2.4 km radius of the territory center of the CC pair. Over the long haul, the abundance of falcons in this territory may have been a major factor in allowing the long-term persistence and success of nesting condors, despite the regular occurrence of both eagles and ravens in the region.

The complexity of behavioral interactions of condors with natural enemies proved to be one of the most fascinating aspects of our breeding behavior studies. Although we were left with many questions incompletely answered as to why condors behaved the way they did, we developed an enormous respect for the flexibility and diversity of the species in dealing with the challenges of its environment. California Condors are far from automatons with monotonously predictable behavior. Instead, they are clearly a species with enormous individual plasticity, a plasticity perhaps most comparable to that of primates elsewhere in the animal world. Each condor under close study proved to have its own distinct personality, yet each was capable of repeatedly surprising us with the new and unexpected.

Appendix 1.

Narrative notes of Sandra Pletschet (edited slightly) for April 8,1983 at the second nest of the year for the CC condor pair. Egg neglect caused by aggression of the male to the female led to an egg pickup in early afternoon.

05:55 – I arrive at the forward blind to begin observations but can see only about 2 m into the nest. I assume the male is still there incubating. Weather clear and calm, about 55 degrees F, good visibility.

09:08 – female flies in low along the nest canyon from the south.

09:09 – female lands on nest cave perch.

09:10 – male walks to the nest entrance and looks out at the female, female is facing the sun about 1 m from the male.

09:12 – female flies, male flies, male chases female.

09:13 – male lands on top of nest rock above nest, female lands on top of same rock system about 20 m to south.

09:14 – male flies from perch to female, lunges at her, she flies and he chases her, following her every move south along nest canyon.

09:15 – male chases female out of sight south along nest canyon.

09:23 – male chases female from west behind nest canyon ridge.

09:24 – male is regularly lunging at female: he folds his wings and dives down at her, male follows female closely.

09:29 – male chases female up north part of nest canyon, they circle back.

09:30 – male flies to female and lunges at her, she flees and he chases her.

09:31 – male lands on ledge perch, male chases female.

09:32 – male lands on top of nest rock, male chases female.

09:33 – male chases female up north nest canyon, they circle back to nest area, seeming momentarily peaceful (i.e., looks like normal pair flight).

09:34 – female attempts to land at nest cave perch, male lunges at her, she flushes.

09:35 – male lands on top of nest rock, soon flies.

09:36 – female attempts to land at nest cave perch, male supplants her momentarily, male chases female, raven dive bombs male.

09:37 – female attempts to land at nest cave perch, male lunges at her, they circle the nest cliff.

09:38 – male is chasing female and a raven is chasing both. They are circling close to the nest cave.

09:39 – male lands on ledge perch (about 10 m from nest cave), female lands on nest cave perch, they are looking at each other.

09:42 – male supplants female, both birds fly, female lands back on nest cave perch and male again supplants her, this time taking the perch, female flies.

09:44 – female lands on lower nest cave perch, male chases her off and then into the air. Male chases female, female again tries to land on lower nest cave perch and male lunges at her.

09:45 – male lands on nest cave perch, female is circling nest cliff, then lands on top of south nest rock.

09:46 – male moves into mouth of nest cave, looking out.

09:47 – he walks back into nest cave, but soon walks back to entrance, looking out, female lands on ledge perch.

09:50 – female lands on lower nest cave perch.

09:51 – male moves into cave out of my sight, female has her side to me and the sun, her ruff is midway up.

09:55 – female moves to in between lower nest cave perch and nest cave perch.

09:56 – male moves to nest cave entrance looking at female – they are about 2 m apart

09:57 – male is looking into nest cave.

09:58 – male walks back into nest cave out of sight, female moves to nest cave perch, she is looking into the cave.

10:00 – female has her beak to the ground – looks like she may be sifting sand – her ruff is up.

10:10 – female turns sideways, moves a few steps closer to male.

10:12 – female moves to main entrance of nest cave

10:13 – female walks back into nest cave.

10:22 – for about the past 10 minutes female has been inching her way back into the nest cave, taking one or two steps at a time.

10:25 – female continues to move into cave out of my sight, she soon reemerges to mouth of cave, looking out.

10:27 – male lunges at female, chases her out of cave into air to north part of nest canyon.

10:29 – male chases female, they fly behind a ridge about ½ mile north along nest canyon.

10:31 – pair flies over nest canyon ridge (they have gained altitude) from the NW.

10:33 – they circle down to in front of the nest cliff, the male is following the female exactly, patterning her every move.

10:35 – male lands on top of the south nest rock, female on the cliff face below.

10:36 – male chases female.

10:37 – male chases female south along nest canyon.

10:38 – female attempts to land on nest cave perch, male lunges at her, she flushes, he follows in chase.

10:39 – female lands at nest cave perch and then walks to mouth of cave, male lands on ledge perch (see drawings).

10:40 – male flies to nest cave perch, enters cave and lunges at female, she flushes and male chases female circling nest cliff.

10:42 – male lands on nest cave perch, female on ledge perch.

10:44 – male walks into nest cave out of sight, female looking toward entrance, ruff up, crop about 50% full.

10:47 – female flies to lower nest cave perch.

10:48 – female moves to nest cave perch and looks into nest cave.

10:51 – female moves to mouth of cave, looking in.

10:53 – female walks perhaps 1 m into cave, facing into nest cave.

10:55 – female bows head facing male with her beak to ground.

10:58 – female takes a few more steps back into nest cave.

11:02 – female is barely visible in back of nest cave.

11:04 – female takes 2 or 3 steps toward male.

11:05 – female turns toward entrance, facing out.

11:07 – male lunges at female then chases her out of cave into air, male chases female toward me, they fly overhead and circle back to the nest cliff.

11:09 – female attempts to land on north perch, male supplants her, taking perch, female flushes, landing on top of south nest rock.

11:10 – female circles nest cliff then lands on ledge perch, male and female looking at each other.

11:14 – male moves to mouth of nest cave, female to lower nest cave perch.

11:15 – female to nest cave perch, male lunges at female and chases her, and they circle the nest cliff area.

11:17 – male lands on nest cave perch, female attempts to land next to him, he chases her and they circle the nest cliff area.

11:20 – male continues to chase female back and forth along nest canyon.

11:22 – male regularly dive bombs female from above, folding his wings and diving toward her. When he is not doing this, he follows her every move.

11:25 – male lands, female lands at nest cave perch.

11:26 – male lunges at female, she flees.

11:27 – male chasing female, male lands on nest cave perch, female lands on lower nest cave perch, they are looking at each other.

11:29 – male moves into nest cave, then to rear out of sight, female moves to nest cave perch.

11:30 – female moves to cave entrance.

11:31 – female takes a few steps into cave.

11:34 – female to rear of cave nearly out of sight.

11:39 – male lunges at female, chases her out of nest cave, she flushes and flies to a nearby perch that is out of sight (she flew behind the nest rock – north side and appeared to be landing). Male is at mouth of cave looking out.

11:48 – female lands on nest cave perch, she is looking up at male who is perhaps 1–2 m away, looks back at her

11:49 – male moves to back of cave out of sight, female moves to mouth of cave looking in.

11:55 – male chases female out of cave.

11:56 – birds circling area

11:57 – female lands momentarily on top of nest rock, male lunges at her, she flies, he chases her.

11:58 – male is patterning female's every move.

12:00 – male chases female close overhead, they fly toward the southeast and circle gaining altitude, back overhead, male is lunging at female.

12:02 – They return to nest area and circle (now I miss 4 minutes of notes) trying to calculate time on and off nest today.

12:06 – female at nest cave perch, male supplants her taking perch.

12:07 – female attempts to land on ledge perch, male supplants her, taking perch.

12:08 – female attempts to land on nest cave perch, male supplants her taking perch, female lands below cliffs on far south side in brush about 150 m away.

12:09 – male moves into cave out of sight.

12:10 – female flies to nest cave perch.

12:11 – female moves to nest cave entrance, I talk with Noel on radio, miss 2–3 minutes.

12:16 – male chases female out of nest cave and into air, male chases female to NW where I lose sight of them behind a ridge.

12:22 – pair flies in from behind nest canyon ridge, they circle down to nest cliff area.

12:23 – male lands on nest cave perch, male flies north along nest canyon, circles back.

12:24 – female lands on ledge perch, male and female are looking at each other.

12:25 – male moves to mouth of nest cave.

12:26 – male moves to rear of cave out of sight.

12:27 – female flies to nest cave perch, facing into nest cave, moves to entrance.

12:29 – female walks back into nest cave nearly out of sight.

12:33 – I see wings flapping, birds lunging – generally quite a commotion between the male and female in the hole, dirt flying, female runs out of the hole with male chasing her, she flushes and lands on top of nest rock. Male is at mouth of the nest cave looking out.

12:35 – female flies to north part of nest canyon, circles back, lands on lower nest cave perch, male still looks out of cave entrance, now at female.

12:37 – male moves back into cave.

12:42 – female hop jumps to nest cave perch

12:45 – female to mouth of nest cave.

12:46 – female walks toward rear of cave.

12:48 – female out of sight in rear of cave.

12:54 – female is sitting in cave, barely in sight.

13:01 – female stands up, faces out of cave, then faces in bowing (I assume) to male.

13:06 – female has moved to a meter into cave, facing out

13:08 – male is standing behind female.

13:10 – male lunges at female, she flies and circles nest cliff.

13:12 – male chases female.

13:15 – female attempts to land on nest cave perch, male supplants female, she flies to perch on top of south nest rock, but only momentarily, then circles nest cliff

13:16 – female lands on ledge perch which is about 10 m from male on nest cave perch.

13:19 – male walks into cave, female flies to lower nest cave perch

13:20 – male moves back into nest cave out of sight.

13:21 – female hop jumps to nest cave perch, she looks into cave, lowering her head with her beak to the ground.

13:22 – female to nest cave entrance, she walks back into cave where she is barely visible. Note: glare from sun is causing visibility to diminish.

13:26 – male lunges at female causing her to run out of cave, he follows close behind and into the air. I get a radio call from Noel in position below nest – "We're going for it."

13:28 – Noel and Victor Apanius climb into nest cave, pair is circling in front of nest.

13:30 – They have got the egg in the case and are climbing down, leaving a dummy egg in the nest, pair still circling.

13:33 – Noel and Victor are out of sight in brush below nest, pair circling nest cliff area.

13:35 – male lands on top of south nest rock

13:36 – female lands on top of nest rock perhaps 20 m from male.

13:40 – male flies south in nest canyon out of sight. Female flies and lands on ledge perch where she stands for the next 13 minutes.

13:54 – female flies out above nest canyon, circles back to same ledge perch.

13:57 – female flies to nest cave perch

13:58 – female moves to nest cave entrance, looks around the inside of the cave, then back to the entrance looking out, then moves back into cave.

13:59 – female out of sight. Again she walks to the nest entrances, looks out, then back out of sight again.

14:00 – female moves from back of cave to mouth again, looking out.

14:01 – female back into nest cave out of sight.

14:03 – female to entrance, looking out.

14:05 – moves back into rear of nest cave.

14:14 – helicopter for egg pickup flies over nest canyon in front of nest cliff and lands on ridge to northeast, female comes quickly to mouth of cave, looks startled, facing out of cave.

14:16 – helicopter leaves, flying to south with the egg.

14:17 – female walks back into nest cave, presumably to incubate dummy egg.

Summary: Today's fights were even fiercer than yesterday's. From the time the female arrived until taking of the egg, the male was apparently at the egg only 124 minutes and off 132 minutes. Actual incubation time probably much less than 124 minutes.

CHAPTER ELEVEN

Breeding Effort and Success

In his monograph on the California Condor, Sandy Wilbur (1978b) proposed that recent reproduction of the species was greatly depressed, not by low breeding success but by failure of many birds to initiate reproduction. He believed that progressive reductions in food supplies, especially in the vicinity of the Sespe Sanctuary, could be one of the main factors underlying a failure to breed, and he attempted to remedy this situation by providing carcasses, mainly of deer and goats, at a feeding station on Hopper Refuge adjacent to the sanctuary. There was no clear evidence, however, that the feeding program produced improved breeding in the sanctuary or elsewhere (see Wilbur et al. 1974, Wilbur 1978a).

Partly because of Wilbur's concerns, we began a detailed study of quantitative aspects of condor reproduction at the very start of the modern program in 1980. We were especially anxious to gather additional data on how much reproduction was going on in the population, first to learn whether the reproductive effort situation was truly as grim as Wilbur believed, and second to determine causes of any breeding difficulties that might exist so that effective corrective measures could be devised. Locating and observing nests from a distance did not require any special permit clearance, so this phase of the program did not depend upon obtaining a state permit for intensive activities and was not affected by loss of the first state permit in mid-1980. Detailed distant nesting observations began in February 1980 and continued for as long as wild breeding pairs existed.

Analyzing Reproductive Effort

From previous studies of Wilbur and his colleagues, we initially knew of only two pairs recently active in the wild population. One (SS1) was in the Sespe Sanctuary and the other

(SB) was in central Santa Barbara County. Both these pairs were still active in 1980 and continued to be active in subsequent years. They were ultimately the two pairs from which we learned the most about condor reproduction.

Aside from studying these two pairs, a major fraction of our initial work was devoted to attempts to locate additional pairs by checking other nesting areas that had been known active historically and by following condors seen in the back country in hopes they might lead us to nests. Success was almost immediate, as we found and made close observations of two additional pairs in the spring of 1980. Both pairs were located outside of the Sespe Sanctuary, and both were active in areas that had not been previously recognized as nesting areas. Nevertheless, we were able to obtain evidence that both nesting areas had been active for at least several years, successfully fledging young in a number of instances.

One of the two newly found pairs (PC1) was tending a dependent young from the previous year and did not lay during 1980. There had been sightings of another apparent fledgling at the same cliffs in 1977. The other pair (CC) was watched on a daily basis from the laying of an egg in March to the successful fledging of a youngster in October. Interviews with mineral prospectors who had been working the nesting canyon and an unpublished report of Steve Hoddy, a raptor enthusiast familiar with the area, indicated probable earlier fledgings of young condors in the immediate vicinity in 1972, 1975, and 1978.

We also identified still another successful pair (TP) early in 1981. This pair continued to tend a dependent fledgling into the late summer of 1981, although we were never able to locate its exact nest site. The nesting area of this pair was exceedingly rugged and difficult to reach and was characterized by a labyrinth of cliffs and sub-cliffs that were difficult to check more than partially for the nest cave or caves that presumably were there. Another apparent fledgling had been sighted in this area in 1968, and there could easily have been additional fledglings through the 1970s, as the area was not checked comprehensively by condor biologists during this period.

Thus data from the very start of the new program indicated a substantial amount of breeding still going on in the population – a minimum of five active pairs, with four of them laying eggs in 1980. This was considerably more than the roughly two active pairs per year claimed for the 1970s in Wilbur's (1978b) studies, despite a presumed continuing decline in population size since the time of Wilbur's assessment.

However, there was no reason to suspect that the increase in number of active pairs known represented a real increase in breeding. More likely, it was only a reflection of better, but still not yet complete, documentation of what reproduction was taking place. In large measure, the better documentation was a result of a tremendous increase in manpower – roughly a four-fold increase – now devoted to the task (see Snyder 1983 for details). Further, our searches for nesting activity covered many regions that had not been checked in recent years. Wilbur's observations had been limited largely to the vicinity of the Sespe Sanctuary, where he had been joined only by John Borneman and sometimes Dean Carrier in searching for nesting pairs. The only other concerted efforts to find condor nests during the 1970s were those of Dick Smith and Jan Hamber, who concentrated on the single SB pair in Santa Barbara County (Smith 1978).

Table 9 presents the basic statistics on the reproductive activities of wild condor pairs

Table 9. Wild California Condor pairs with identified nest territories (1980–1986).

Pair	Years known active in 1980s	Egg-laying pair?	Documented previous nesting activity in territory
CC	1980–81,1982,1983,1984	yes	fledglings in 1972,1975,1978
SS1	1980,1981,1982,1983,1984	yes	fledgling in 1940, egg in 1941, eggs in 1964,1966,1967, 1969 fledglings in 1975,1976,1977
SS2	1986	yes	yes, same territory as preceding
CV	1981–82,1983,1984	yes	probable nestling in 1976
SB	1980,1981,1982,1983,1984,1985	yes	fledglings in 1972,1976,1977
TP	1980–81	yes	fledgling in 1968
PC1	1979–80	yes	fledgling in 1976
PC2	1981,1982,1983	no	yes, same territory as preceding
SM	1981,1982	no	yes, unknown date
PP	1984	yes	fledgling in 1969
HP	1985	no	yes, unknown date

Note: The HP pair in 1985 would likely have laid an egg but the male (BFE) was lost before egglaying; the PC2 and SM pairs of 1981-1983 were potentially homosexual as they were not observed performing successful copulations; nest sites in territories noted as "yes, unknown date" showed evidence of previous use, but years of use were unknown. Sources of documentation for fledglings in CC, CV, TP, PC, and PP territories in late 1960s and 1970s were USFS personnel and various private parties.

Table 10. Breeding status of wild California Condors in the early breeding season (adapted from Snyder and Snyder 1989).

Bird category	1982	1983	1984	1985	1986
Total condors	23	19	15	10	5
Breeding pairs	4	4	5	2	1
Nonbreeding pairs	2	1	0	0	0
Unknown status pairs	1	1	0	0	0
Unpaired male adults	0	0	2	2	3
Unpaired female adults	1	1	1	2	0
Unsexed unpaired adults	2	1	0	0	0
Immatures	6	5	2	2	0
Percent adults paired	82	86	77	50	40
Percent adults breed	47–59	57–71	77	50	40

Note: from 1983 onward, all eggs and nestlings were removed for captive breeding program; mortality of five adults over the winter of 1984–85 disrupted four breeding pairs; the male of a new pair in 1985 was lost early in the breeding season and although no egg was laid the pair was ranked as a breeding pair because it was known to be heterosexual and copulations were proficient; two pairs in 1982 and one pair in 1983 did not perform proficient copulations and may have been homosexual.

found during the modern program. Our skill in finding and studying pairs steadily improved over the years. Prior to 1982 we could well have missed a few nestings. In 1982 and 1983 there were still single pairs for which we were unable to find nesting territories, and we do not know if these pairs attempted breeding. From 1984 on we are reasonably confident that we located all nesting pairs, and by 1982 we were able to maintain nearly continuous distant coverage on all active pairs that were located during the breeding season.

Table 10 presents summary data on the reproductive status of adults in the population from 1982 onward. Our data on population size and numbers of pairs were not thorough enough to allow inclusion of 1980 and 1981 in this table. Not all pairs documented in the 1980s were egg-laying pairs. In fact, two pairs studied closely in 1981–1983 demonstrated an inability to perform successful copulations, although they investigated nest sites and went through other reproductive behavior patterns in an apparently normal fashion. As discussed in the preceding chapter, we suspected that these pairs might in fact be homosexual pairs of males because the identity of individuals on top in copulation attempts was not consistent and because both members of both pairs gave the courtship displays normally seen only in males.

Homosexual pairings could have been largely a result of an excess of males and limited opportunities for heterosexual pairings developing by chance in the remnant population. Sex ratios deviating noticeably from 1:1 are a common chance result when populations dwindle drastically, but do not in themselves suggest chronic or pervasive sex ratio problems for a species. In the case of the condor we know of no good evidence for an overall sex ratio bias. Although Wilbur (1978b) tabulated 64 males and 42 females in historical records of the species (mostly museum specimens), the sex ratio of 161 condors hatched in captivity between 1983 and 1998 (72 males and 89 females) was slanted in the opposite direction (data from Kuehler 1996 and Mike Mace). Together these figures total 136 males and 131 females, a ratio very close to and not significantly different from 1:1.

Although the sex of a number of individuals alive in 1982 and 1983 was never determined, if we assume that the two known nonlaying pairs were comprised of males, there could have been as few as 6 females in 17 adults in early 1982 and 6 females in 14 adults in early 1983. One of the survivors of the two potentially homosexual pairs of 1981–1983 (SMM), re-paired heterosexually in 1984 and produced a viable offspring in the wild in that year. The other (PCA) eventually re-paired heterosexually in captivity and began breeding successfully in 1991.

Despite the existence of two nonlaying pairs in the early 1980s, the data in Table 10, in conjunction with data and extrapolations presented in Snyder (1983), do not suggest any major difficulties with reproductive effort, at least back to the late 1970s. Of special importance was our documentation of 8 apparently different dark-headed condors (1–3 year olds) in early 1981. In tracing back how many pairs it would have taken to produce these juveniles, given what is known about condor reproductive rates and reproductive success, it is possible to calculate that the eight juveniles implied the existence of at least six, and more likely seven or eight breeding pairs in just preceding years. This many breeding pairs accounted for almost all adults presumably alive during the period, as we were also accounting for at least two subadults and the eight dark-headed juveniles in 1981 (see Snyder 1983; Johnson et al. 1983).

From 1982 through 1984, for which we have nearly complete data, most adults were clearly paired and attempted breeding, and as discussed above, the two known pairs that clearly did not lay eggs may have been homosexual – possibly in part or *in toto* because of sex ratio fluctuations in the remnant population. Egg-laying pairs accounted for 47–59% of adults in 1982, 57–71% of adults in 1983, and 77% of adults in 1984, figures that average only slightly less than the percent of known pairs laying eggs in four species of vultures in Africa (Mundy 1982): Lappet-faced Vulture (76%), White-headed Vulture (82%), Hooded Vulture (79%), and White-backed Vulture (86%). However, since these African figures, unlike the condor figures, were not based on complete population assessments and did not account for unpaired adults and pairs without nests, the percentages of all adults that were members of egg-laying pairs in these species would probably have been less. If we limit ourselves in the condor data to percent of known pairs laying eggs to make the figures more directly comparable to the African species data, the percentage figures for 1982 through 1984 rise to 57-71, 67-83, and 100. These figures average 80%, which is almost identical to the average for the four African species, 81%.

Massive mortality greatly disrupted the make-up of condor pairs over the winter of 1984–1985, so the lower percentage of adult birds paired and breeding in 1985 and 1986 was not surprising. By 1986, there was only one female left in the wild, and this bird did breed. Another female (CCF) still present in the wild in 1985 showed no interest in any of the remaining males, and later demonstrated a continuing reluctance to form compatible pair-bonds in captivity, only finally starting to produce eggs again in 1995. CCF also had great difficulty in coordinating incubation activities with her mate CCM from 1982 to 1984.

In overview, Wilbur's conclusion that a main cause of the recent population decline was a breakdown in reproductive effort was surely incorrect for the late 1970s and 1980s. Further, we know of no good reasons to suspect it was correct for earlier years. An overall failure of condor pairs to attempt breeding is difficult to prove unless all potential nesting areas are carefully monitored in the early breeding season, an enormous task that was far beyond the available manpower of the 1970s. Although Wilbur found very few active pairs, he did not actually document any nonbreeding pairs, and in examining his field records we believe that his conclusion that most adults were not breeding may have been primarily a consequence of the fact that his research was concentrated so heavily in the Sespe Sanctuary region. He found little reproductive activity in this region (as did we in the 1980s), but he simply did not determine what breeding activity may have been going on elsewhere.

Condor reproduction in the 1980s was taking place mainly in non-Sespe locations, and there is good evidence to suggest that most and possibly all of the nesting territories we found active during the 1980s in regions outside the sanctuary (SB, CC, PC, TP, SM, HP, CV, and PP) were also active and producing young, at least intermittently, during the 1960s or 1970s (see Table 9). The young produced from these territories, with the exception of young from the SB territory, are not included in Wilbur's (1978b) production summaries, and we emphasize that the young documented in Table 9 probably represent only a fraction of the young produced in these territories in the late 1960s and 1970s. Further, there could well have been additional active territories in those years that received no documentation at all. The non-Sespe territories that Wilbur and his colleagues did visit were checked so briefly, infrequently, and incompletely that much condor breeding activity could easily have been missed.

The incomplete monitoring of historically and recently active territories that characterized the late 1960s and 1970s provided only a minimal basis for estimating total production in the population. Just from the fragmentary evidence that does exist, it appears likely that there were at least seven fledglings that went unacknowledged in Wilbur's summaries for this period. Actual production for these years could easily have been several times as great as Wilbur presented, despite his belief that his totals were likely near complete.

However, in potential support of Wilbur's conclusion that the condor population was suffering from low reproductive effort, it is important to note that the percentages of condors that were reported as immature on the October Surveys in the late 1960s and early 1970s were exceptionally low. Whereas the percent of ageable condors that were immature on the Surveys from 1965 through 1967 were 29, 30, and 21, respectively; from 1968 through 1974 the percentages were 11, 13, 9, 12, 12, 6, and 12 (averaging 10.7) – an apparent major drop. After 1974 the percentages again rose above 20 (see Verner 1978). One explanation for the changes in percentages could have been a drop in reproductive effort through the late 1960s and early 1970s, and it is clear that these low percentages constituted one of the major factors leading some observers to suspect a collapse in breeding effort.

Before proceeding further, however, it is well to consider the extent to which observer errors and biases might have contributed to these percentages and to examine what other causes could have produced the percentage changes (assuming their validity). An independent estimate of percentage immatures can be constructed for these same years from figures given by Wilbur (1978b, 1980). For the same period (1968–1974), Wilbur reported composite probable totals of immatures of 10, 10, 13, 8, 8, 6, and 4 birds, respectively, while his estimated total population declined from about 55 individuals to 40 individuals (by interpolation, based on a uniform rate of decline). These figures yield estimated immature percentages that average much higher (17.4) than those from the October Survey – i.e., 18, 19, 26, 17, 18, 14, and 10. These percentages and those from the October Survey are highly significantly different from each other statistically, and the considerable discrepancy between the two sets of values suggests major sampling and observation errors, perhaps in both sets of values.

We have earlier suggested that Wilbur's (1978b) composite probable totals of immatures could easily be underestimates of the true numbers simply because of the relatively few person-hours of observations on which these totals were based (Snyder 1983). Immature percentage estimates could also have been low for some of the October Surveys for a variety of reasons. For one thing, distinguishing among age classes is often extremely difficult under field conditions, especially when birds are relatively distant. With continuously changing personnel involved in the surveys, judgments as to ages of birds may not have been made consistently over the years. Especially difficult are discriminations between subadults and adults, for which the potential for error is great even with experienced personnel. Two or three subadults misreported as adults in any one year could have resulted in a major underestimate of the true immature percentage.

Further, it is important to emphasize that the percentage of Wilbur's personal condor sightings that included immatures, and the average number of immatures seen per sighting day by all observers, showed no clearcut depression during the late 1960s and early 1970s (Wilbur 1980). Both these findings, although also subject to errors, are hard to reconcile with a major depression in immature percentages during the same period. Especially because of these results, we view the possibility that there was a true depression in percent immatures in the late 1960s and early 1970s as resting on a very uncertain foundation.

But even if we assume there was a real depression in immature percentages, a leap to a conclusion that the population had largely stopped breeding would be unwarranted because there were other potential factors that could have caused the depression. Changes in immature percentages, if valid, could result as well from changes in rates of nesting success or from age-specific variations in mortality. Especially heavy mortality of juveniles in just one year could result in depressed immature percentages for a number of years, as birds do not reach adult plumage for 6 years. With small populations, heavy mortality of juveniles could be nothing more than a chance effect.

Another possibility is that the apparent drop in immature percentages from 1968 through 1974 might have reflected increased nesting failure at the height of the DDT era. However, the nesting success data available from the DDT era do not confirm this possibility (Snyder 1983). We will consider potential impacts of DDT much more closely later in this chapter. Here, we report only that the evidence for important DDT impacts on condor reproduction is very weak.

To sum up, concerns that the condor population may have been suffering from low reproductive effort do not rest on a convincing foundation. For the 1960s and early 1970s the sorts of data needed to substantiate such a possibility do not exist. For the late 1970s and 1980s all evidence points strongly to the opposite conclusion. The overall pattern of decline in known use of nesting areas over the years does not suggest any anomalous drop in reproduction in the late 1960s and early 1970s, but only a steady decline paralleling the population decline (Snyder 1983). Overall food supplies for the condor population were apparently declining through the 1960s and 1970s (Wilbur 1978b), but we never obtained any evidence that these food supplies were low enough to cause problems either with nesting effort or nesting success.

Quantitative Assessment of Condor Nesting Success

In calculating nesting success, ornithologists normally assess the percentage of the pairs starting nesting that succeed in fledging young. To make such an assessment accurately it is important to find active pairs very early in the breeding season. Success will be overestimated if pairs that fail early are not detected. For consistency, we assume here that egg laying defines the start of a nesting attempt and that success is achieved once a youngster takes its first flight. Other definitions could be used, such as considering a nesting attempt to start at the time a pair first begins to investigate nest cavities and considering it successful only when a youngster reaches full independence from its parents. Nesting success defined in this latter way is normally less than success defined in the first way, although it better assesses the full level of nesting success in a population. However, so that our computations might be comparable to calculations that have been made with other vulture species and so that the sample sizes of analyzable nests would not decline to zero for historical nests, the first definition of nesting success is a more appropriate one to use.

Unfortunately, even using the first definition of success, virtually none of the nests found prior to 1939 provide useful information on natural nesting success. The great majority of these nests were robbed of their eggs or young, and virtually all nests that were not robbed were not followed to a known outcome. Consequently, we have limited our analyses of historical nests to unrobbed nests found after 1938, which include essentially all historical nests ever studied intensively. Historical nests were divided into those found during the pre-DDT (1939–1946) era and those found during the DDT era (1947–1972) to allow comparison of potential differences in nesting success in the two periods. Most analyzable nests from the pre-DDT era were those studied by Koford; the great majority for the DDT era were those found by Sibley.

In attempting to evaluate levels of historical nest success, we earlier (Snyder 1983) calculated results for only (1) those nesting attempts that were found at the egg stage and (2) nesting attempts that were found later but whose outcomes would probably have been determined even if they had failed early. The latter were primarily nests that researchers were checking regularly and where they either found nestlings or evidence of early failures from eggshells, feathers, etc. These restrictions greatly reduced the numbers of nests qualifying for analysis. The resulting small sample sizes in themselves argue for some caution in interpreting the results.

During the pre-DDT years 22 condor nestings were documented, but 13 of these must be excluded from analysis because they were nests that failed because of egg collectors or were nests found at the nestling or fledgling stage that probably would not have been detected if they had failed at the egg stage. Of the remaining nine nests, six were followed to a known conclusion, whereas three had unknown outcomes. Minimum nest success (assuming all nests of unknown outcome failed) was two nests out of nine successful in fledging young (22%). Maximum nest success (assuming all nests of unknown outcome succeeded) was five nests out of nine successful (56%). Since two of the three nests of unknown outcome made it at least to the nestling stage, actual nest success was probably closer to 56% than to 22%, as the great majority of undisturbed condor nests observed at the nestling stage have resulted in fledged young.

For the DDT years, 30 condor nestings were documented, but 18 of these must be excluded from analysis because they were found at the nestling or fledgling stage and probably would not have been found if they had failed at the egg stage. Of the remaining 12 nests, 10 were followed to a known conclusion, whereas two had unknown outcomes. A majority of the analyzable nests were found relatively late in the breeding season but were located in sites being checked regularly for nesting activity so that there is a good chance that early failures would have been detected. Minimum nest success for the DDT years was four nests out of 12 successful (33%). Maximum success was six nests out of 12 successful (50%). These figures do not suggest any appreciable change in nesting success from the pre-DDT years.

Using a slightly smaller sample of nests, Sibley (1968) similarly calculated a 45% success rate for nests of the 1960s and likewise concluded that this success rate did not differ appreciably from the rate characterizing the nests found by Koford in the 1930s and 1940s.

Calculations of nesting success for years covered by the modern program (1980s) are complicated by extensive manipulations of nests after 1982. In the following analysis, we have included (1) nesting efforts observed at the egg stage that were allowed to proceed at least to the late nestling stage or to failure, and (2) nesting efforts observed at the egg stage which we planned to follow through to fledging but from which we had to remove eggs to captivity to avert threats which would almost certainly have caused failure of the nests. These latter nests were ranked as failures, although surviving young were produced in captivity in all cases. Since known natural failures have been very rare past the mid-nestling stage (Snyder 1983), we have also included as successes three nests from which we took late-stage nestlings into captivity and one nest from which we lost a chick in a handling accident in 1980. However, we have ranked one nest as uncertain in outcome. We took a chick from this nest into captivity in 1982, because feeding rates dropped substantially after one parent disappeared (the bird returned several weeks later). We made the foregoing decisions in an effort to come as close as possible to a realistic estimate of natural nesting success of egg-laying pairs for the 1980s.

The data so treated yield either seven or eight nests successful out of 17 between 1980 and 1986, or 41 to 47% nest success, a value very similar to the historical rates (Snyder 1983) and to that of other New World and Old World vultures. Jackson (1983) found nest success rates for egg-laying pairs to average 37.6% for Black Vultures, and 53.3% for Turkey Vultures. The data of Mundy (1982) and Mundy et al. (1992) indicate that success of egg-laying pairs ranged from about 40 to 60% for the solitary-nesting Hooded, Lappet-faced, and White-headed Vultures, although it generally exceeded 60% for the colonial-nesting griffon vultures.

Thus, we have been unable to find any clear indications from either reproductive effort or success that the remnant California Condor population was having any major difficulties in breeding. The percentage of adults documented in egg-laying pairs was reasonably high up until 1985 and was comparable with what has been documented in other large vulture species. Similarly, although the nest success figures for the condor are approximations based on small sample sizes that have posed some problems in interpretation in all eras, they lie within the normal range documented for other solitary-nesting vulture species. In any event, the exact values of nest success for the condor are of far less importance to the demography of the species than are mortality rates, as we shall see in analyses in the next chapter.

Factors Affecting Nesting Success

In Table 11 we present the apparent causes of failure in the nesting attempts rated as failures in the 1980s. In six, possibly seven, of the 17 nesting attempts of this era, the nesting failed during the incubation period and egg breakage was involved. There were 5 actual or probable cases of breakage and 1 additional case where the egg destruction was imminent due to ravens but the egg was taken captive in time. There was still another case where nest failure may have been due to egg breakage or alternatively to loss of a chick shortly after hatching, but the precise stage of failure was unknown. Ravens could have been involved in all the cases of egg breakage, and were surely involved in at least five cases, at least as a contributing factor. The only other major factor associated with nesting failures in the 1980s was known or potential behavioral upsets in breeding pairs (a total of 5 cases). Four of the five cases involved the CC pair which suffered from intense aggression between the male and female adult leading to repeated episodes of egg neglect and high vulnerability of their eggs to embryonic death by chilling or to loss to ravens. The fifth case involved the apparent disappearance of the male of the SS1 pair for a period of 25 days during the middle of the nestling period of 1982. This disappearance might have had a behavioral cause or might have been caused by a temporary poisoning incident or disease episode. Another contributing cause to

Table 11. Actual and projected causes of failure in 1980s condor nests considered failures.

Pair and year	Failure actual (A) or projected (P)	Main cause	Contributing causes, comments
CC–1982	A	egg rolls over cliff	intra-pair conflicts, conflicts with ravens, sloping floor of nest cave
CC–1982	A	raven smashes egg	intra-pair conflicts leading to egg neglect
CC–1983	P	death of embryo due to egg neglect, cooling (egg actually revived in captivity)	intra-pair conflicts leading to egg neglect, gnats affecting incubation constancy, embryo badly damaged by cooling
CC–1984	P	raven predation on egg (egg actually saved in captivity)	potential intra-pair conflicts leading to egg neglect, raven threat extreme
SB–1981	A	apparent egg breakage	cause unknown
SB–1981	A	chick dies immediately after hatching	cause unknown – disease?, genetic?
SS1–1980	A	egg breakage or early chick death	possible raven involvement
SS1–1982	A	egg breakage	probable raven involvement
SS1–1982	P	low feeding rates (chick actually survives in captivity)	chick captured because of disappearance of male adult, nest could alternatively be considered successful as male adult reappears later
SS2–1986	A	egg breakage	raven involvement, relatively thin eggshell

failure was a sloped nest floor in one nest that predisposed the egg to roll out of the cave and over the cliff edge. Finally, one and possibly two nests failed when chicks died from unknown causes at about the point of hatching.

Egg breakage was as frequent in historical nests as it was in the 1980s. Three (possibly four) of nine analyzable nests suffered breakage in the pre-DDT years as compared with five (possibly six) of 12 analyzable nests during the DDT years and five (possibly seven) of 17 analyzable nests of the 1980s. None of the cases of egg breakage in either historical period was directly witnessed by observers, so the potential role of ravens in causing the breakage is speculative. Nevertheless, Koford in his field notes recognized the potential role of ravens in causing at least some of the breakage, and in the 1980s we found condor eggshell in an ancient raven nest adjacent to one of Koford's nests that failed because of egg breakage in the 1940s. Also in the 1980s there was an active raven nest within 5 m of one of the sites where multiple cases of egg breakage had occurred in the 1960s. Finally, we found successive raven nests in the 1980s in another of the sites in which Koford documented egg breakage in the 1940s. Thus, it is plausible that ravens could have been involved in many of the historical cases of egg breakage, just as they were directly seen to be involved in most cases of breakage during the 1980s. The alternative possibility that eggshell thinning could have been a major factor leading to egg breakage, just as it was involved in egg breakage in many other species during the DDT era, is a topic we will consider in detail at the end of this chapter. All evidence suggests that shell thinning was not a major factor in egg breakage for the condor.

Evidence thus suggests that ravens were the most important threat to condor nesting success in the 1980s and possibly also in earlier years, and there is no necessity to invoke other major factors to explain the high rate of egg breakage known for the species. In one case in the 1980s (CC 1982) Helen directly observed a raven pounding its bill into a condor egg. In another, the egg was lost over the cliff edge during a tussle between the incubating condor and a raven (see Chapter 14). In two other cases we found condor eggshell in raven nests adjacent to condor nests that were known to have suffered egg breakage. Although breakage was not witnessed directly, ravens had been observed harassing these pairs intensively. We recognize that the presence of condor eggshell in raven nests does not prove the ravens were the primary cause of egg destruction, but it certainly is powerfully consistent with this possibility.

In addition, we observed intense raven harassment of still another pair that lost its egg right at laying, but fog prevented observers from seeing the precise role of the ravens as breakage occurred. Essentially all nesting pairs of condors during the 1980s were harassed by ravens, at least during some nesting seasons, and we also observed numerous instances of condors successfully thwarting ravens attempting to take their eggs.

Yet despite the evidently important threat represented by ravens, several condor pairs of the 1980s chose to nest in exposed sites within 100 m of active raven nests when they could have chosen more distant and safer sites. An extreme example was the CC pair of 1984 that nested on an overhung ledge just 3 m from a pair of nestbuilding ravens. Battles between the ravens and condors at this site were intense, and dust boiling out of the nest cave as the two species repeatedly challenged each other. The condor egg in this instance was perched precariously on a ledge just inches from the cliff edge. It had essentially no chances for survival in the wild, especially because of the history of egg neglect in this particular pair, and we took it into captivity shortly after laying. As in other cases, a number of alternative sites were available to this pair which would surely have been much safer from ravens.

A natural enemy that does not show up in the above statistics on causes of nesting failure, but may nevertheless be an important factor affecting both nesting success and nesting distributions, is the Golden Eagle. Through the 1980s we recorded a number of instances of Golden Eagles coming into condor nesting areas only to be met by vigorous aggressive chases from adult condors, sometimes involving flapping flights of more than a kilometer. Twice, once in the SB territory and once in the SS1 territory, John Schmitt directly witnessed eagles in stoops aimed at condor nestlings at the entrances of their nest caves. Fortunately in both cases, adult condors were present nearby and were able to intervene, preventing almost certain loss of their chicks. These were among the most dramatic occurrences seen during the intensive nest-observing years, and clearly indicated that the eagles represent a major threat to nesting success, especially considering the fact that (1) chicks past the age of 6 weeks spend large portions of the day outside their nest caves (when nest structure allows this), and (2) during the bulk of the nestling period adult condors are normally not in their nesting areas for about 75% of the day (see Table 5 in preceding chapter), leaving their chicks unguarded and fully vulnerable. The witnessed cases of condors saving their chicks from eagle stoops were highly fortuitous in that the adult condors just happened to be present nearby at the times of attacks.

The major defense that condors appear to have from predation of eagles on their chicks is where they choose to nest. The central mountainous areas where we found the condors nesting, and where Sibley, Koford, and everyone else found them nesting earlier, are exactly the areas where Golden Eagles are least abundant in the general region. This is presumably because the general habitat in these areas is too densely vegetated to allow optimal foraging for eagles. Instead the eagles congregate much more heavily in more open potrero or grassland habitats, especially in the foothills of the southern San Joaquin Valley where condors have also traditionally foraged. But despite the existence of cliffs with caves that appear structurally adequate as nesting sites in the foothills region (for example in Santiago Canyon and on Eagle Rest Peak), and despite the fact that nesting in these cliffs would have relieved the condors of much of their investments in commuting between nests and foraging areas, we are not aware of any documented nestings of condors in these locations. Judging from the intensity of their occasional interactions with eagles in the mountainous regions, condors would find it difficult to nest successfully in the foraging regions simply because of their dense eagle populations.

Wilbur (1978b) believed that condor reproduction might be enhanced by providing the population with artificial nest sites on the foraging grounds in the foothills of the San Joaquin Valley. We believe it is highly questionable that condors would have accepted such sites or that they would have been able to breed successfully in such sites. We do not believe that reproduction of the remnant population was in any way limited by availability of nest sites or that the long distances between most available sites and the foraging grounds were any deterrent to breeding, despite Wilbur's fears that they might be. No program of nest-site creation in the foraging areas was ever mounted.

Potential Effects of DDT on Condor Reproduction

Besides occasional nest-failures due to structurally suboptimal nest sites and more frequent failures due to natural enemies, condors have also faced potential reproductive losses to environmental contaminants. Of special concern have been the potential effects of DDT, a chlorinated hydrocarbon pesticide known to have caused widespread reproductive failure among many birds of prey during the period starting right after the end of World War II and lasting until the early 1970s, when most uses of this chemical were finally curtailed in the U.S. (Ratcliffe 1970, Hickey 1988). As was documented repeatedly in a great many species of carnivorous birds, DDE (the primary form of DDT in birds) caused major thinning of eggshells and greatly increased egg breakage rates that were associated with major population declines. In addition, direct mortality of birds caused by cyclodiene pesticides such as dieldrin was simultaneously stressing the same populations and was probably even more important in the declines (Newton 1988; Snyder 1990).

The possibility that DDE might have been involved in the decline of the California Condor was first raised by Kiff et al. (1979) in a paper that described massive eggshell thinning in the species in the 1960s. In a small sampling of shell fragments collected mainly by Fred Sibley, these authors found (1) that shell thickness of the 1960s averaged about 30% lower than historical shell thickness, (2) a highly significant correlation of DDE concentrations in shell membranes with the degree of shell thinning, and (3) apparent structural changes in thin shells that correlated with DDE contamination. They concluded, quite reasonably, that the condor appeared to be one of the most sensitive species known to DDE contamination, and that DDE contamination could have been an important factor in the decline of the species.

However, sample sizes leading to these conclusions were small and we were puzzled by documentation in the Condor Research Center files suggesting normal or near normal condor nest success rates and egg breakage rates through the 1960s. At the start of the modern program in 1980, we immediately began follow-up efforts to investigate the potential effects of DDE more thoroughly, in collaboration with Kiff and others. This research involved the analysis of much more diverse samples of eggshell fragments and attempts to replicate the DDE-shell thinning correlation that had been found earlier. In the process we made a number of surprising discoveries that were inconsistent with the earlier plausible inferences of Kiff et al. (1979). In fact, the overall evidence strongly suggested that DDE probably had had no major effect on condor reproduction through the 1960s and probably was not having any significant effect on reproduction in the 1980s, despite a major depression in eggshell thickness in the 1960s and residual thinning seen in eggshells of the 1980s (Snyder et al. ms).

Our primary findings were (1) a failure to replicate the highly significant negative correlation of DDE concentrations in eggshell membranes with eggshell thickness found by Kiff et al. (1979), although there was a marginally significant correlation between these variables, (2) a demonstration instead that eggshell thickness in the condor was mainly related to

To gather evidence on potential effects of DDT on the thickness of condor eggshells, shell materials were collected from numerous condor nests and directly analyzed for concentrations of DDE (the primary metabolite of DDT). **Above**, Pete Bloom sifts eggshell fragments from a condor nest overlooking Alder Creek, a nest potentially active during the mid 1960s, the era of most intensive DDT use. **Below**, the DDE content of these and other eggshell fragments analyzed yielded no strong relationship with eggshell thickness.

egg size, (3) a demonstration for all time periods that shells that broke in nests were no thinner than shells that hatched, suggesting strongly that shell thinning was not likely a major cause of breakage, and (4) a confirmation that condor eggshells were uniformly very thin in the 1960s (averaging 28–29 % thinner than historical eggs), but no confirmation that this phenomenon had any clear impacts on reproduction of the species.

The failure to replicate a highly significant correlation of DDE concentrations with eggshell thickness presumably traced in part to a discovery that DDE was not stable in eggshell membranes and tended strongly to decline in time, possibly due to evaporation. Thus because many shell fragments were not analyzed until long after eggs were hatched or broken, the DDE concentrations measured were presumably not an accurate reflection of original DDE concentrations in eggs, and this fact alone might obscure any possible correlation of shell thickness with DDE concentrations.

But even more importantly, once we began to take whole eggs into captivity for artificial incubation in 1983, we immediately discovered that eggshell thickness showed a very strong correlation with egg size (see graph below), allowing an alternative explanation for the strong shell thinning of the 1960s – small eggs. The percentage variation in shell thickness that was explained by egg size was sufficiently great (81% in the 1980s) that at best DDE might explain only a minor part of the variation, unless DDE itself was a factor causing small eggs in the species (an effect we could not verify, although it remains a possibility). One female of the 1980s, SSF, was laying particularly small and thin-shelled eggs (averaging 25.6% thin), yet her eggs were hatching normally and she was the most productive female of this period. Furthermore, the frequent sightings of condors in her territory back through the 1970s and into the 1960s suggested that she herself may have produced a number of the thin-shelled eggs collected from her territory in the 1960s. Nevertheless, because egg size was not known for any of the eggs of the 1960s (samples were limited to fragments collect-

Relationship between equatorial eggshell thickness and egg weight in California Condor eggs of the 1980s. Egg weight explained 81% of the variation in shell thickness during this period

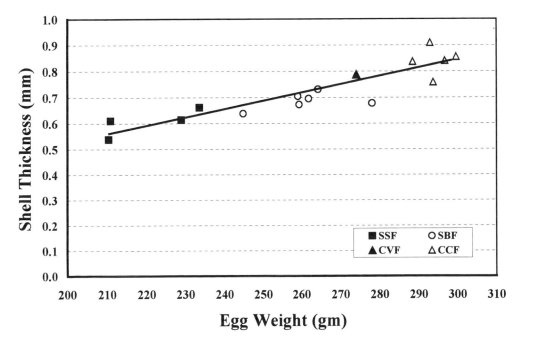

ed from nests), it was not possible to directly confirm that eggs of the 1960s might have been relatively small, although this appears to be the most likely explanation for the thin shells.

Because eggshell thickness shows an overall strong relationship to egg size across all birds in general, it follows that thin-shelled eggs may not be especially susceptible to breakage, so long as the eggs are relatively small. Perhaps the best evidence that condor eggs of the 1960s might have been relatively small was the fact that shells of eggs that broke in nests in the 1960s were no thinner than the shells of the eggs that hatched (the same was true for the 1980s and pre-DDT years). Moreover, overall egg breakage rates were no higher in the 1960s than in earlier and later periods. These results are not consistent with shell-thinning being a major factor leading to breakage, and strongly suggest the thin-shelled eggs of the 1960s may have been of normal strength, something that would be improbable if they were not also small.

However, the lack of any thickness correlations with breakage is completely consistent with ravens being a major cause of breakage because shell thickness is surely not an important factor in whether a raven can destroy a condor egg. Ravens can easily penetrate condor eggshells of any thickness, as was apparent in our observation of a raven hammering open an egg of the CC pair in 1982. This was one of the thickest-shelled eggs known for the species in the 1980s.

Why condor eggs may have been especially small in the 1960s is a presently unresolved question. But since egg size is in general a relatively stable and heritable trait in birds, and since a highly significant correlation exists in the present captive flock between eggs sizes of parent female condors and egg sizes of their daughters, it is possible that some genetic event or sampling bias may have been involved. The potential importance of sampling bias should not be excluded because the 13 eggshell samples of the 1960s can be reduced to the production of only 4 females, judging from egg dates and locations of nest sites.

Regardless of whether eggs may truly have been generally small in the 1960s, there is no good evidence from the reproductive data for the species that small or thin-shelled eggs seriously affected productivity, either in the 1960s or the 1980s. No matter how one may interpret the nesting success data for the 1960s, there were many fledgling condors produced in this period, a situation entirely unlike the near zero production of young known for populations of U.S. Peregrine Falcons, Brown Pelicans, and Bald Eagles in the same time period. Specifically, 30 condor nestings were found at various stages in this period and 24 apparently produced nestlings or fledglings (Snyder 1983).

The egg that most suggested potential negative effects of DDE on nesting success in the 1980s was an egg laid in 1986 by SSF. This was by far the thinnest-shelled egg we ever documented (44% thinner than the historic mean), was grossly abnormal in structure with a massively disrupted surface crystalline layer, and was heavily contaminated with DDE (130–180 parts per million in lipid). This egg broke shortly after laying.

However, despite the circumstantial evidence that the breakage of this egg might have been due to shell weakness and DDE contamination (Kiff 1989), it is unclear whether the breakage was caused by shell weakness or by ravens. The nest site was under continuous observation by project personnel, and ravens were intensely harassing the pair around the

One of the eggs laid by the Sespe Sanctuary female (SSF) in the wild in 1986 was extremely thin-shelled and abnormal in structure. This egg broke shortly after laying, but whether breakage was due to shell weakness or to predation by Common Ravens was unclear. The abnormal structure of this egg may have been due to a long period of fasting by the female prior to egg laying and was not clearly caused by DDE contamination.

site at egg laying and could plausibly have destroyed the egg. Unfortunately, it was not possible to see directly into the site because of dense obscuring fog at the time of breakage, and the actual destruction of the egg was not witnessed.

Furthermore, there is another plausible explanation for the extreme shell thinning and abnormal structure of this egg that does not involve DDE. Continuous direct observations of SSF indicated that she did not feed for more than 12 days prior to egg laying, and it is reasonable to conclude that this may have placed her under considerable nutritional stress. Nutritional stress alone has been documented as a cause of thin eggshells and abnormal shell structure (including disrupted surface crystalline layers) in birds (Narbaitz et al 1987; Cooke 1973). It seems very possible that this effect, rather than DDE, might have caused the extreme properties of this egg.

Supporting evidence for this conclusion comes from other eggs laid by SSF. After loss of the above egg to breakage in early 1986, SSF recycled with a second egg about a month later. This egg had almost identical levels of DDE but was fully normal in thickness and structure for this female. If DDE caused the problems in the first egg of the year, why not the second egg? Interestingly, SSF was observed returning from the foraging grounds with a bulging crop just 3 days before laying of her second egg of 1986, so it appears unlikely that she was under major nutritional stress for this egg.

Additionally, it is important to emphasize that over the years SSF laid one other egg that was exceptionally thin and surface-disrupted (32% thinner than normal), although it was not quite as thin as the first egg of 1986. This egg was produced in 1984, and significantly it too followed a long period of fasting (at least 8 and possibly as many as 11 days). This egg was not under threat of raven predation, did not break while it was still in the wild, and hatched normally under artificial incubation.

Thus even if SSF's first egg of 1986 broke because of shell weakness, it is not at all clear that this weakness was caused by DDE, and evidence suggests that it might have been due to nutritional stress. We have no explanation for why SSF might have fasted for the periods that she did before laying her exceptionally thin eggs of 1986 and 1984.

In sum, although we are hardly contesting the widespread detrimental effects of DDE on wildlife, which have been amply documented in many raptor species (see for example, Snyder et al. 1973), the evidence that we were able to gather simply does not support a conclusion that DDE contamination was a major cause of the condor population decline through the era of DDT use. Although condors did show some general contamination with this pesticide in the 1960s and 1980s, and laid many thin-shelled eggs during these decades, the thin-shelled eggs exhibited no demonstrably enhanced probability of breakage and reproductive rates of the species appeared normal. The shell thinning documented was associated mainly with small egg size (at least in the 1980s), although certain especially thin-shelled eggs may have resulted in part from nutritional stress. Thus, even though many authors (e.g. Risebrough 1986, Caughley 1994) have accepted the conclusion of Kiff et al. (1979) that DDE contamination was likely a major cause of the condor decline, a close look at available evidence fails to support this claim.

Potential Genetic Effects on Condor Reproduction

As a last topic of discussion in this chapter, we believe it is important to consider potentially detrimental genetic effects that may have been affecting condor reproduction. The condor population of the 1980s was of severely reduced size and had been relatively low in size for decades. Under such conditions the amount of genetic diversity left in a population is likely to decline and inbreeding problems may appear. DNA fingerprinting studies of the founder population for captive breeding strongly suggested that the California Condor was relatively low in genetic diversity (Geyer et al. 1993). Were there any indications of genetic problems, such as fertility or hatchability problems, in the remnant wild population?

On the surface, at least, fertility and hatchability of wild-laid condor eggs of the 1980s were excellent. Of 24 eggs for which fertility could be assessed, all 24 were fertile (100%). Only 4 failed to hatch successfully or died immediately after hatching, for a hatchability rate of 83%. In themselves, these data give no evidence for genetic difficulties, as these figures are comparable to or exceed fertility and hatchability data for most other avian species in the wild. However, since 16 of the 24 eggs were incubated in captivity, it is possible that overall hatchability of the condors might have been biased a bit high. Arguing against this possibility is the fact that only 1 of 8 eggs incubated in the wild failed to hatch successfully whereas 3 of 16 eggs incubated artificially did not produce surviving young.

Despite excellent fertility and hatchability, there were other data to suggest that all might not be perfectly well with the wild population from a genetic standpoint. Specifically, of the five reproducing pairs watched most intensively through the 1980s (CC, SS1, SB, CV, and PP) only one (PP) appeared to be relatively normal in reproductive characteristics. It is possible that some of the abnormalities noted had a genetic basis. Although the abnormalities observed did not result for the most part in reproductive failures, they were of concern and need to be presented here.

Specifically, the CC pair exhibited chronic problems in coordination of incubation duties between the male and female adults, with chronic egg neglect and some nest failures as a result. Whether these behavioral problems had any genetic base is unknown. The SS female laid the smallest eggs ever documented for the California Condor, yet these eggs hatched normally in almost every case. Egg size in general has a strong genetic component. The SB pair exhibited some difficulties in hatchability of eggs, producing two chicks that died right at hatching and a third egg that experienced early embryonic death. A yolk infection was found in one of two chicks dying at hatching, and this could be interpreted to suggest that pathogen problems might have been more likely than genetic problems with this pair. Finally, the CV pair consistently produced chicks with behavioral or morphological abnormalities. One of their progeny, PAX, exhibited a chronic tendency to gape (hold its bill open) in the field. Another (Cuyama) exhibited a wing-droop tendency. Still a third exhibited abnormal skull and limb development and failed to hatch successfully in 1984. These last problems were perhaps the most suggestive of genetic difficulties of any of the problems documented in the 1980s population. Other potential genetic difficulties will be discussed in the chapter on captive breeding.

In conclusion, although we believe it is important to consider all plausible threats to condor reproductive success in some detail, to focus too intently on potential or real genetic, nest-site, contamination, and natural enemy problems with the California Condor is to miss the major point that overall reproduction in the species appeared to be reasonably successful through all eras. This is not to suggest that efforts to increase reproductive success would not be beneficial for the species (and we will consider some of the actions that have been taken in this regard in Chapter 13). It is to suggest, however, that the major causes of the species' decline must have lain in the mortality sphere, rather than the reproductive sphere.

CHAPTER TWELVE

Mortality

By 1982 and 1983, it was becoming increasingly clear that the remnant condor population was still reproducing quite well, with reasonably good levels of both reproductive effort and success. Evidence as to how well the population was faring with mortality was a little slower to accumulate. An accurate determination of mortality rates depended on the development of accurate censusing methods and the ability to identify individuals through time. These capacities were only first achieved in 1982, and it was only by early 1985 that it became clear that mortality rates were truly excessive, averaging roughly 25% per year for both adults and immatures. Only by late 1983 and early 1984 did the first documentation of specific causes of recent mortality begin to emerge. By that time it was already very late to try to correct the most important threats.

Mortality Rates

With a presumed minimum age of first breeding of 6 years in the wild, a clutch size of only one egg, and a breeding success rate of 40–50%, the California Condor is not a species that can withstand high annual mortality rates. Taking the reproductive information accumulated for the species in the early 1980s as a given, Meretsky et al. (in press) calculated what survival rates would be needed for the population to remain stable. For these calculations the following reproductive parameters were assumed to accurately characterize the population:

1. 50–80% of adult condors are members of breeding pairs in any year.
2. Adult pairs breed in two out of three years if successful in fledging young.
3. Adult pairs breed annually if unsuccessful.

4. Adult pairs lay replacement second eggs after 25–75% of failures of first eggs.

5. The nesting success rate is 40–50% per egg-laying attempt.

6. First breeding occurs at age 6 to 8.

7. Clutch size is invariably one egg.

The derivation of these parameters is discussed in detail in the preceding chapter and Chapters 14 and 16.

Perhaps the most speculative of the above figures are those giving the frequency with which pairs might lay replacement eggs after nesting failure. Deliberate egg removals in the early 1980s indicated that most and possibly all pairs were capable of replacement laying when eggs were taken early in the breeding season. But we have little information on natural occurrence of replacement laying, and its frequency presumably depends on when in the breeding season nesting failures occur. Historical data suggest that the great majority of nesting failures occur during the egg stage (Snyder 1983), but there have been relatively few data on exactly when during the egg stage most failures occur. From the nests we did not manipulate in the 1980s we calculate that 57% of seven documented natural nesting failures were apparently followed by replacement eggs within the same breeding season. But this sample size is too small to allow much confidence about overall replacement-laying rates, especially with respect to the probability of triple-clutching. Accordingly, Meretsky et al. modeled very wide probability bounds for the laying of second eggs after failure of first eggs (from 25 to 75%) to hopefully encompass the actual overall rate. The incidence of natural triple-clutching is probably so low as to be negligible in its impacts on overall productivity, so triple-clutching potentials were not included in the model.

With the above figures as a basis, the maximum permissible mortality rates ranged between 6.7 and 13.4 % annually when mortality rates of immatures were assumed to be the same as those of adults (see Table 12). Under pessimistic assumptions as to reproductive performance for the population (age of first breeding of 8 years, 50% of adults breeding, replacement eggs after 25% of nesting failures, and 40% nesting success), the population could tolerate no more than 6.7 % overall annual mortality to remain stable. Under optimistic assumptions (age of first breeding of 6 years, 80% of adults breeding, replacement eggs in 75% of cases, and 50% nesting success), the population could tolerate an overall annual mortality rate of 13.4%. Splitting the difference between minimum and maximum reproductive assumptions leads to a "most likely" conclusion that the population needs to maintain an overall annual mortality rate of approximately 10% or less to allow stability or population increase.

Meretsky et al. also calculated mortality rates for theoretical populations in which immature mortality rates exceeded adult mortality rates – the situation generally found in most vertebrate species. Specifically, they calculated permissible mortality rates when immature mortality rates were twice as high as adult mortality rates. To obtain stable populations under pessimistic assumptions as to reproductive performance, immature mortality rates had to be less than 10.6%, while adult mortality rates had to be less than 5.3%. Under assumptions of maximal reproductive performance, immature mortality rates had to be less than 19.0%, while adult mortality rates had to be less than 9.5%. These figures come out very

Table 12. Results of deterministic modeling of stable California Condor populations (adapted from Meretsky et al. in press). Breeding success acounts for mortality in the first year of life. Probability of renesting indicates chance a pair will lay a second egg after a failed first egg in a single breeding season. Mortality by age shows the relationship between immature (I) and adult (A) mortality. Sex ratio assumed 1:1.

			Modeling assumptions				Calculated mortality	
% Ads. breed	% Breed success	Prob. of renest	Chicks/ ad F/ year	Age first breed	Age last breed	Mortality by age	Adult mortality	Juvenile mortality
Pessimistic								
50	40	0.25	0.2300	8	50	I = A	0.067	0.067
50	40	0.25	0.2300	8	50	I = 2A	0.053	0.106
Most likely								
65	45	0.50	0.3729	7	75	I = A	0.099	0.099
65	45	0.50	0.3729	7	75	I = 2A	0.075	0.150
Optimistic								
80	50	0.75	0.5500	6	100	I = A	0.134	0.134
80	50	0.75	0.5500	6	100	I = 2A	0.095	0.190
Maximum conceivable								
67	100	0.0	0.6700	6	100	I = A	0.149	0.149
67	100	0.0	0.6700	6	100	I = 2A	0.104	0.208

similar to those given by Verner (1978), even though he based his projections on very different reproductive assumptions. The similarity in results stems largely from fortuitous compensating effects of various reproductive assumptions.

Actual mortality rates for the wild population were determinable only in the years for which we had detailed and complete information on population size, age ratios, and removal rates for the captive population – the period from 1982 to 1986. If March 1 to February 28 is taken as the annual period for calculation of mortality losses, the overall mortality rate for the population from early 1982 through early 1986 was 26.6% per year, as calculated on a deaths per bird-year exposure basis, or 18.9, 16.7, 43.2, and 27.5% for the four years respectively. Although the deaths per bird-year method of calculating mortality rates differs from the method used by Snyder and Snyder (1989) for the same period of time, the results are quite similar for the two methods (26.6% vs 23.8%).

Notably, the average mortality rate for adults (26.8%) calculated by Meretsky et al. was not lower than the average rate for immatures (22.2%), but virtually the same, if not slightly higher. This fact suggests that the specific mortality factors involved may not have been ones that were markedly age dependent. The calculations of Snyder and Snyder (1989) gave similar results (24.0% mortality for adults and 23.1% for immatures). In contrast, studies of mortality conducted with other bird species, including other vulture species (e.g. Houston 1974b), have normally yielded mortality rates of immatures that have been considerably higher than those of adults.

Thus, actual overall condor mortality rates exceeded the calculated maximum rates permissible for population stability during each of the four years of accurate data. In fact, they averaged two to four times as high as permissible, and implied an average life span for individuals (4 years) that was shorter than the time it took individuals to reach an age of first breeding (6 years). These data and calculations showed clearly that the main cause of decline of the species lay in excessive mortality. Even if nest success were to improve to a highly improbable 100% (see "maximum conceivable" assumptions in Table 12), mortality was still too high to sustain a stable population, as 100% nest success, even coupled with maximal breeding effort, would imply a maximum permissible overall annual mortality rate of no more than 14.9% for the population to remain stable, assuming equal mortality of adults and immatures.

The inescapable conclusion to be drawn from these calculations is that the only realistic hope for reversing the decline of the wild condor population would have to be found in a major improvement in survival of birds. Although it was possible to envision some modest to substantial increases in nesting success through intensive management (e.g., through effective counter-raven measures), these increases could not be expected to neutralize more than a small percentage of the excess mortality characteristic of the population. However, achieving a major reduction in mortality in the wild would depend crucially on an accurate determination of the major causes of mortality and the development of specific means to counter these threats.

Causes of Mortality

Prior to 1980, a great variety of mortality factors had been documented for free-flying condors. These included capture and ritual sacrifice of birds by prehistoric and historic Indian tribes, shooting of birds for curiosity, quills, and museum collections, as well as miring of birds in oil seeps and collisions of birds with overhead wires (see Koford 1953; Miller et al. 1965; Wilbur 1978b). Unfortunately, because of major biases in the way data were accumulated, the historical record could not be viewed as a thorough and comprehensive assessment of which sources of mortality had been most important in the decline.

For example, at face value historical evidence suggested that both museum collecting (often involving shooting) and shooting for other reasons had been major causes of condor mortality. In fact, in the thorough tabulation of documented condor losses throughout history by Wilbur (1978b), museum and other purposeful collecting accounted for 177 of 301 losses overall. In addition, shooting accounted for 41 of the 64 losses where a cause was identified and where the cause was not museum or other purposeful collecting. Nevertheless, the fraction of total condor mortalities that these 301 records represented during the period under consideration was both unknown and probably very tiny. Further, it is virtually certain that the mortalities documented were an extremely nonrepresentative sample of mortalities occurring in the population as a whole.

By its very nature, museum collecting was a form of mortality that was thoroughly documented in the historical record, regardless of what fraction of overall mortality it may have represented. Similarly, other shooting mortality was likely relatively well documented because (1) shot birds are often kept and displayed, (2) birds abandoned by shooters are likely to be found by others because most shooting occurs near roads and trails, and (3) shooting is a cause of death that is relatively easy to diagnose because of obvious wounds and broken bones. By contrast, birds dying of disease or slow-acting poisons would be unlikely either to be found or to be correctly diagnosed (at least historically). They could easily be completely missed in a historic tabulation, even though such mortality factors might conceivably be much more important overall than shooting or museum collecting.

Clearly, Wilbur's tabulation could not be relied upon to reveal all or necessarily even the most important sources of mortality faced by the species, either historically or in more recent times, and Wilbur made no claims that it did. And although we do not wish to ignore the impacts of shooting and museum collecting, we believe that the historical record falls far short of proving that these were major causes of the decline. In any event, purposeful collecting of condors for museum specimens reached a peak around the turn of the century and subsided greatly after that period. There was no evidence to suggest that it still represented a threat to the wild population in the 1980s. Indiscriminate shooting, on the other hand, was still a plausible threat.

To gain a good understanding of what mortality factors were most important for the remnant population of the 1980s, the conservation program badly needed an efficient and unbiased way to find dead condors for necropsy. Fortuitous discovery of dead birds would never meet these needs. Radio-telemetry, however, offered strong potentials for increasing efficiency and reducing bias, and for this reason we fought hard for implementation of this technique with as many condors as possible. Unfortunately, radio-telemetry came sufficiently late in the program that relatively few dead condors were discovered before it became advisable to bring all birds into captivity.

In fact, the mortality rate of radioed condors, for some unknown reason, proved to be highly significantly less than that of nonradioed condors (Snyder and Snyder 1989), a most unfortunate result with respect to mortality information not gained. Specifically, from 1982 onward, only 3 of 9 radioed birds died (one of which was not recovered), whereas 12 of 15 nonradioed birds apparently died (10 of which were not recovered). Although the exposure times of radioed and nonradioed birds were not strictly comparable, the proportions dying in the two groups were highly significantly different, a result suggesting that the radios in some obscure way might have protected the birds from mortality. This difference was especially striking over the winter of 1984–1985, when only 1 of 8 radioed birds perished whereas 5 of 7 nonradioed birds died. For this latter comparison exposure times were equivalent in the two groups. We are reluctant to conclude that the radios in any way protected condors and are inclined to attribute the high degree of statistical significance here to a bizarre stroke of chance, but these data at least suggest that the radios themselves were not a significant source of mortality.

Despite the relatively small sample size of condors found dead, the causes of mortality documented in the 1980s forced a complete reassessment of what the main mortality threats to the species might be.

Case History No. 1 – IC1

Lead poisoning was the most prominent mortality factor documented in the 1980s. **Left**, John Schmitt examines corpse of IC1 found in March 1984 underneath an apparent roost snag. **Right**, x-rays revealed a bullet fragment in the bird's digestive tract, and chemical tests revealed lethal levels of lead in its liver and blood.

IC1, a male of unknown parentage, was actually the second free-flying condor recovered dead in the 1980s, but we consider his death first to facilitate a meaningful discussion of causes of mortality. IC1 was the very first bird we had radio tagged (in October of 1982). He was subadult at the time he was found dead in the vicinity of the Blue Ridge roosting area, near Springerville in the Sierras. On the day he was discovered dead (March 22, 1984) we were watching the condor nest in a sequoia tree in the southern Sierras. Over the radio network we heard Larry Riopelle, the program's radio-tracking pilot, report ominously that IC1's radio signal had not budged from the roost area throughout the day. Larry persuaded Jesse Grantham, who was on the ground not many miles distant, to drive to Blue Ridge to see if the bird might be in trouble. We too began the drive to Blue Ridge. Jesse got to the bird just at dusk and found that he was dead on a grassy slope underneath an apparent roost snag. We arrived at the scene shortly thereafter, but after dark. To permit a thorough examination of the bird and its surroundings in daylight without disrupting any potential evidence as to the cause of death, we left the bird in place overnight. John Schmitt volunteered to spend the night nearby to protect the bird's carcass from depredations of nocturnal scavengers.

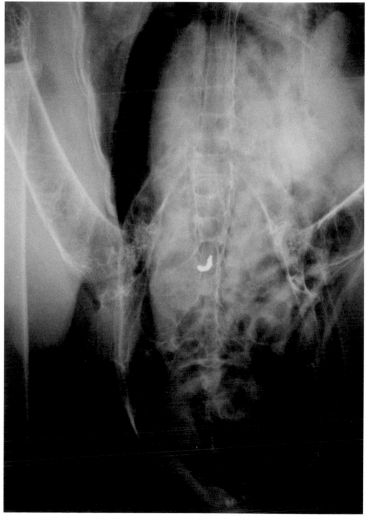

Early the next morning we began a detailed examination of the bird when he was still covered with overnight frost. He had lost one radio, but he retained the other, a solar unit. Fortunately this faced the sky, and continued functioning, allowing efficient location of the bird. A careful search of the area around the dead bird yielded no obvious clues as to the cause of death, although it appeared from position of the carcass that the bird may have fallen from the roost snag or collided with it. There were no obvious bullet holes to suggest the bird might have been shot, and no tracks or traces of any other potential predators in the vicinity.

In mid morning Noel drove the bird to the Springerville airport, where he met Larry Riopelle for a direct flight to San Diego. Necropsy by Marilyn Anderson at the San Diego Zoo in the afternoon revealed considerable non-lethal tissue damage and fractured ribs on one side of the breast. This injury could have been caused by the bird colliding with a branch in falling to the ground, or perhaps by a collision in making an uncoordinated landing attempt. Regardless of the exact scenario, a potential cause of death was immediately apparent in X-rays, which revealed a small sliver of copper-coated lead in the bird's digestive tract, evidently a bullet fragment.

Lou Locke, a USFWS researcher who had once confirmed lead-poisoning as a cause of death of an Andean Condor, arrived in San Diego late on the day of necropsy. Lou took one look at the X-rays, gave a sigh of dismay, and warned that we might face some tight censorship by the USFWS if the bird proved to be lead-poisoned. At the time, the controversy over lead vs steel shot was a major issue, and USFWS researchers dealing with lead toxicity were routinely muzzled in reporting such instances. Nevertheless, when subsequent analyses of the bird's tissues revealed that lead concentrations (35 parts per million wet weight in liver) were well within the lethal range (see Janssen et al. 1986), the Service fortunately made no attempt to suppress the results. Possibly because the cause of death was clearly a lead bullet fragment, not lead shot, and because personnel outside the USFWS were involved in the necropsy and would be difficult to censor, there was nothing to be gained by such a step. No potential cause of death other than lead was found.

IC1 was the first confirmed California Condor dying of lead poisoning, although there had been an earlier lead-poisoning mortality of an Andean Condor at Patuxent (Locke et al. 1969), and two earlier lead-poisoning mortalities of King Vultures at an unidentified municipal zoo (Decker et al 1979). It is extremely doubtful that IC1 would ever have been found without radio-telemetry, and we at last had confirmation of a cause of death that we had suspected might be a major mortality factor in the wild, despite its complete absence from historical condor mortality records.

Case History No. 2 – BFE

Another condor mortality to lead poisoning was confirmed a year later with BFE, a 7-year old male who was initiating his first breeding attempt. We had been observing BFE making repeated nest inspections with his mate UN1 in the HP nesting territory of Ventura County throughout mid February 1985. Copulation success and frequency suggested an egg was imminent. However, the pair, neither of which was radio-tagged, left for the foraging grounds on February 25, and only UN1 returned to the nesting area on February 27. BFE was not seen again until 9 April when he was found emaciated and near death by a Tulare County rancher on cattle patrol. A rescue team including Ben Gonzalez, a veterinarian from the Los Angeles Zoo, was immediately dispatched to the site, but the bird died minutes after he was located by the team.

At the time of death BFE weighed only 5.47 kg, approximately 60% of normal male body weight. It is possible that he had been losing weight for as much as six weeks, as he no longer continued associating with his mate after about February 26 and it seems likely that the pair breakup may have been caused by the same toxic event as led ultimately to the bird's death. At the time of death, lead concentrations in the bird's liver were well into the toxic range at 23 ppm (parts per million), and although no metallic fragment was found in the bird's digestive system, the cause of death was assumed to be lead poisoning, with a possible contributing role of zinc toxicity (see Janssen et al. 1986, Wiemeyer et al. 1988). One of the common effects of lead poisoning is paralysis of the digestive system, leading to eventual starvation and death (Eisler 1988). This seemed the likely progression of events for this bird.

BFE was not a radio-tagged bird, and his discovery in a remote area was an extremely fortuitous event.

Case History No. 3 – SBF

A third case of lead-poisoning began to unfold in the fall of 1985 with SBF, a bird being closely tracked by radio-telemetry. On November 23, SBF was trapped to replace a defective radio transmitter. A routine blood sample was also taken and the bird was then immediately released. On analysis, the blood proved to contain an alarmingly elevated level of lead (1.8 ppm) and the veterinarians advising the program recommended she be immediately recaptured for chelation treatment. Unfortunately she proved difficult to recapture and was not taken until January 3, 1986, by which time she was sufficiently weakened that it was possible to run her down and capture her by hand on Hudson Ranch.

At the point of capture, her body weight was still strong at 8.11 kg, but this weight included a substantial amount of rotten food (likely more than a kilogram) in her crop. She was obviously failing to pass food through her digestive system, presumably a result of crop paralysis. Her blood lead level at the point of capture was 4.2 ppm, and X-rays revealed not only a metallic fragment in her ventriculus, but also eight spherical pellets of lead shot imbedded in her soft tissues. The metallic fragment in her ventriculus had an irregular shape that did not suggest a derivation from lead shot. The veterinarians involved concluded that the shot pellets in her tissues were not the source of the high lead levels in blood and represented an unrelated nonlethal shooting event in the history of the bird.

The bird responded quickly to chelation therapy with EDTA and blood lead levels dropped below 1 ppm within 6 days. Unfortunately, the crop-paralysis did not go into remission, and the bird continued to lose ground nutritionally. Though she continued to eat eagerly, food did not pass through her digestive tract and had to be periodically removed as it was putrefying in her crop. The bird was given fluids and nutrients intravenously, but continued to lose weight. Her digestive functions never did recover and she ultimately died on January 18 at a weight of 6.5 kg (including the weight of attached tubing and catheters).

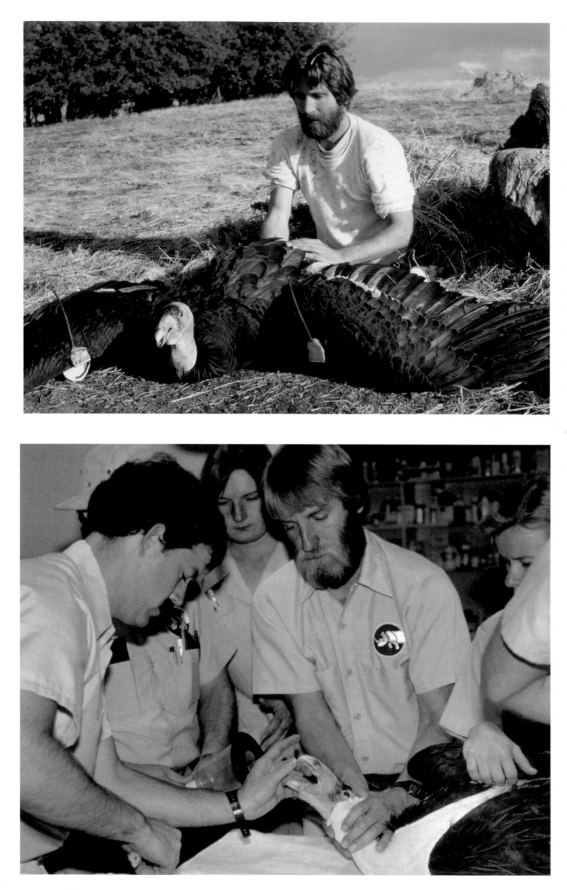

Another victim of lead poisoning was the Santa Barbara female (SBF) who succumbed in early 1986. **Above**, Pete Bloom with SBF pit-trapped in late November 1985 to replace her radio transmitters. A blood sample taken before she was released proved to be high in lead, but it was not possible to recapture the bird until early January 1986. **Below**, at the time of recapture SBF was no longer digesting food and continued to lose weight until death, despite chelation therapy and intravenous feeding at the Zoological Society of San Diego. Don Janssen (left) and Don Sterner (right) adjust feeding tubes for the stricken bird.

Thus the lead poisoning of SBF apparently followed a course similar to that experienced by BFE (but different from that of IC1), in that SBF was slowly starving to death after several weeks (perhaps more than a month) of being unable to process food. Mundy et al. (1992) suggested that a rough threshold for starvation death of large vultures lies at about two thirds of normal body weight. Although SBF was evidently still above this value in weight, she was not far above. In contrast, IC1 was in quite good weight at the time of death (8.08 kg with a nearly empty crop), and it seems likely that the proximate cause of his death might instead have been an acute nervous system disorder resulting from the lead contamination. The level of blood lead in IC1 at the time of death was 24.0 ppm, by far the highest level yet recorded in any condor and considerably higher than the highest blood lead level detected in SBF (4.2 ppm).

Case History No. 4 – BOS

The first condor recovered dead in the 1980s was not found by radio-telemetry, but through a strange sequence of events that only gradually became clarified. Early in the evening of November 23, 1983 we received a phone call from Eric Johnson. He had just been called by the foreman of the Santiago Ranch who had discovered a dead condor. The bird had been found on National Forest lands a short distance beyond the ranch boundaries only an hour or two earlier. Eric was on his way to pick up the bird, and Noel immediately headed across the mountains to meet him and take the bird down to San Diego for necropsy at the zoo.

Feather molt patterns quickly revealed that the bird involved was BOS, a yearling female that had been fledged by the SB pair in 1982 and was frequently seen foraging on Hudson and Santiago Ranches. The body of the bird was quite fresh, indicating a recent death, but the contorted posture of the carcass, with wings partly extended and head under one wing, suggested a violent sort of death. There was considerable mud on the bill and face of the bird, and the fact that a clod of muddy earth interlaced with mammalian fur (later identified as coyote) was gripped by one of the bird's muddy feet was remarkable. Condors do not normally grip objects in their feet, and we were immediately suspicious that the bird might have tangled with an M-44 cyanide coyote trap. We knew that the Animal Damage Control branch of the U.S. Fish and Wildlife Service (the ADC) was conducting routine cyanide poisoning of coyotes on the Santiago Ranch and that animals dying of cyanide poisoning commonly died very quickly and violently.

The drive to San Diego took about 6 hours overnight, and Marilyn Anderson, pathologist at the zoo, was waiting to begin necropsy early in the next morning. The bird was in excellent weight for a female (8.4 kg), and thorough necropsy revealed no gross abnormalities to suggest a specific cause of death. Marilyn concluded that the mortality of the bird appeared to be a "metabolic death," such as could be caused by poisoning. Tissue samples were sent to the Patuxent Wildlife Research Center for analysis for a variety of poisons, including cyanide.

The following day we returned with Eric Johnson and others to inspect the site where the bird had been found. Noel also began a dialogue with U.S. Fish and Wildlife and California Fish and Game officials as to the best way to proceed in investigating the incident. These discussions led to a carefully neutral phone call that Noel placed with the local

Cyanide poisoning from an M-44 coyote trap was the presumed cause of death of a condor in 1983. **Above**, BOS was found dead by the ranch foreman of the Santiago Ranch with mud on her face and one foot clutching a clod of mud and coyote fur. **Below**, x-rays at the San Diego Zoo by Marilyn Anderson (left) and Art Risser (right) revealed no foreign bodies or other abnormalities. Although chemical tests were inconclusive, the bird's mouth was laced with the "tracerite" dye that is mixed with cyanide powder in coyote traps.

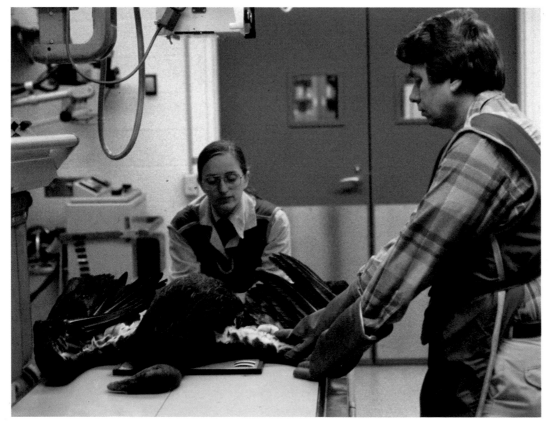

chief of the ADC to suggest a meeting to consider the possibility that there might have been an inadvertent poisoning of the bird by cyanide trapping efforts on Santiago Ranch. Despite the matter-of-fact tone of Noel's request, the first remark uttered by the ADC official was an explosive "witch-hunt," that suggested he was not favorably inclined toward investigation of the poisoning possibility.

By the following morning, ranchers all over southern California had been alerted by parties unknown that the condor program stood poised to take coyote trapping away from them. Because of the potential involvement of cyanide poisoning in the death of the bird, we were facing war not only with ranchers but with a sister agency in the Fish and Wildlife Service. Emotions were running high.

Regardless, the meeting proposed by Noel did take place six days after discovery of the bird and involved both state and federal officials, the trapper who was poisoning coyotes on Santiago Ranch, and his immediate superior. The trapper took us on a tour to see all the coyote traps on the ranch, and we also revisited the site where the bird had been found dead. None of the trap sites was muddy, but we could not be sure if we were actually being shown all trap sites. The site where the bird had been found by the ranch foreman was perhaps half a mile from the nearest trap we were shown, but as we had already seen on the day after necropsy, the recovery site was a gravelly slope with a substrate entirely unlike the mud in the feet or on the face of the bird, and there likewise was no dead coyote to be seen in the vicinity.

M-44 coyote traps are tiny inconspicuous objects that look much like spools of thread. The outer surface of the "spool" is smeared with a scent concoction, not food, and the hollow inner cyllinder is spring-loaded to fire a charge of cyanide into the mouth of a coyote attracted by the scent to pull on the external spool. The coyote trapper was setting the M-44s out in double arrays, and this suggested a mechanism for how a condor could get into direct trouble with an M-44, despite the fact that condors were not known to respond to odor in foraging. If an M-44 in a double array were to fire and kill a coyote, this coyote could then become a carcass bait for condors, which could then be attracted into close proximity to the second M-44 which was still live. We had previously watched condors messing around and tugging on nearby objects in the vicinity of carcasses that were dominated by eagles, as they awaited a chance to get on the carcasses. Under such circumstances a condor might plausibly pull on an M-44 and trip it off. There was also a possibility that a condor might directly ingest cyanide poison by eating or attempting to eat the tongue of an M-44-slain coyote. In addition, a condor might be poisoned secondarily from eating flesh from other parts of a poisoned coyote carcass.

Results from direct testing of the condor's tissues for contaminants were not clearcut. Tests for lethal levels of contaminants other than cyanide (especially lead, strychnine, and compound 1080) were negative. Those for cyanide were hard to interpret. Patuxent had not previously done significant experimentation with this toxicant, and although detectable and somewhat elevated concentrations of cyanide were found in blood from the bird's heart region, the concentrations appeared to be below those that were known to be lethal (Wiemeyer et al. 1986a, 1988).

However, just what tissue levels of cyanide might be expected in a bird that may have

M-44 cyanide traps (**above**) look much like spools of thread and are covered with a scent concoction to induce coyotes to tug on them and cause cyanide powder to be fired into their mouths. That BOS might have directly triggered the firing of an M-44 gains plausibility from the fact that the coyote trapper in the area was using double M-44 sets, one of which might have killed a coyote, providing a carcass bait for the condor. The second nearby set could have been triggered by the condor if it was denied access to the carcass by an eagle and engaged in the typical tugging behavior on nearby objects photographed in PAX (**below**) under similar circumstances.

succumbed to a brief but massive exposure to cyanide in the oral cavity was unknown. Death of animals from M-44s is commonly so rapid (a matter of seconds) that it seemed likely there could be uneven distribution of this toxicant through a bird's body at the time the circulatory system shut down. Coyotes hit by the M-44s rarely get more than a few feet away from the traps, and Smith (1995) demonstrated nearly an order of magnitude difference in cyanide concentrations in right and left ventricles of the heart in coyotes killed by coyote "getters." Depending on just exactly where the blood sample from BOS originated (it was known only that it came from somewhere in the heart region), the wrong conclusion could be reached.

Furthermore, it was also known that at least under some circumstances cyanide levels in tissues declined progressively postmortem (Ballantyne et al. 1974). Since the Patuxent analyses were not run until January 1984, and the condor carcass was not frozen until a day or two after the presumed time of death, there was some question as to whether the measured cyanide levels were representative of levels at the time of death.

Fortunately, despite the unclear results from the direct determinations of tissue cyanide levels, there was another way to detect if the condor had been exposed to cyanide from an M-44. Six days after the death of the bird, the Fish and Wildlife Service informed the San Diego Zoo that all cyanide poisons used by the ADC were mixed with cadmium sulphide fluorescent particles ("tracerite") that would be visible under the UV illumination of a black-light. These fluorescent particles were added to the cyanide to allow a rapid and conclusive determination of whether a dead animal (usually someone's pet dog) had been exposed to an M-44. San Diego Zoo personnel quickly obtained a black-light and looked for fluorescence inside the mouth of the bird. No fluorescence was observed.

A month later, San Diego personnel again made an effort to look for fluorescence in the condor's mouth. This time they also looked for fluorescence in the mouths of several coyotes killed by M-44s. They again used the same black-light as in late November, but an additional black-light from another source was also used as a safeguard against potential black-light malfunctions. Once again no fluorescence was noted in the mouth of the condor. But significantly, no fluorescence was seen either in the mouths of the coyotes killed by M-44s. This latter finding was inexplicable, and suggested that either both black-lights were malfunctioning or that something else was wrong with procedures.

An explanation for these results came several weeks later. On January 19, 1984, all parties concerned, including state and federal officials from a number of agencies, the ADC, and the Condor Research Center attended a meeting in San Diego convened by Peter Savarie, a Fish and Wildlife Service research pharmacologist from the Denver Wildlife Research Center. There was considerable tension in the air, as a reason for the meeting had not been clearly articulated, though all assumed it had something to do with the dead condor. Noel attended for the Condor Research Center and found himself at a gathering so extraordinary, it could have been a scene from a cold-war spy movie.

Peter Savarie was the master of ceremonies and he immediately instructed all attendees that there was to be absolutely no talking or other communication among people present. He then explained that the fluorescent material in cyanide powder could not be seen under a black-light unless it was viewed under a dissecting microscope. This information had not previously been transmitted to San Diego Zoo personnel, so their earlier searches for fluorescence in the mouth of the condor and in the mouths of M-44-killed coyotes could not have been successful even if the fluorescence had been present. Thus, we were all now gathered together to have yet another look for fluorescence in the mouth of the condor, this time under the requisite conditions.

Savarie first prepared slides of known tracerite and cyanide-tracerite powder used in M-44s, dimmed the room lights, and invited each of us in turn to look through a dissecting scope at the slides. The field of view in the scope sparkled like yellow diamonds from the fluorescent material on these slides.

Next, Savarie prepared a slide of scrapings from the mouth of a coyote that died of unknown causes, and again we took our turns viewing the slides. All could see that there was no fluorescence on these slides.

Then Savarie prepared slides of scrapings from the mouth of an M-44-killed coyote. Once again the field of view in the scope sparkled like yellow diamonds.

Now Marilyn Anderson removed the dead condor from the freezer and wheeled the bird on a cart out in front of everyone. Savarie took scrapings from inside the mouth of the bird and transferred them to a fresh clean slide. The slide was placed under the scope and black-light, and the room lights were again dimmed. One by one we inspected the slide. There was no ambiguity. The slide lit up like a field of yellow diamonds indistinguishable from the slides from the M-44-slain coyote and the known tracerite samples – as classic a "smoking gun" as one might ever expect to see.

Still no one spoke a word. However, in the eerie silence it is safe to say that no one present questioned any longer whether the bird had been exposed to cyanide poison. The "witch-hunt" was over, but not with an outcome favorable to the ADC.

Further scrapings revealed that there was no fluorescence farther down the condor's digestive tract than its mouth. Earlier necropsy had shown that the bird's crop was empty. These findings seemed to suggest that the exposure of the bird to the cyanide was a primary exposure to an M-44 itself and not a secondary exposure through eating coyote flesh. However, it also seemed possible that a condor attempting to eat the tongue of an M-44-slain coyote might get a lethal dose of cyanide in its mouth before ingesting any flesh or might immediately regurgitate any flesh ingested (although in the latter case one would expect some flourescence farther down the digestive tract than the mouth). The meeting was adjourned with no further comment from Savarie or anyone else. All parties soon emerged into the sunlight outside to go their separate ways.

Cyanide now stood strongly implicated as the probable cause of the bird's death despite lack of evidence for clearly lethal tissue cyanide levels. Marilyn Anderson's final report concluded that cyanide was the presumed cause of death, and mentioned that in addition to the above evidence, there were signs of kidney and brain damage visible in microscopic histological examination that appeared consistent with cyanide poisoning. Also consistent with cyanide poisoning was the fact that cyanide residues later detected in necropsy of both IC1 and BFE were much lower than in BOS.

Unfortunately, followup cyanide toxicity studies with a variety of birds, including vultures, at Patuxent (Wiemeyer et al. 1986a) failed to achieve a satisfactory clarification of tissue residue matters, perhaps in large part because the birds in these studies were dosed with cyanide delivered to the proventriculus via a gel capsule (a mode of exposure very different from that received from M-44 traps). As discussed by Ballantyne and Marrs (1987), lethal levels of cyanide in blood tend to be much lower in animals inhaling cyanide in than in animals ingesting this toxin. Thus, the cyanide residues found in BOS are still difficult to interpret but surely do not rule out cyanide as the cause of the bird's death because of (1) a potential decline in cyanide levels post-mortem until the time of analysis, (2) a potentially major inhalation component of exposure of the bird to cyanide, and (3) a potentially major bias resulting from just exactly where in the bird's body the blood sample originated.

On the assumption that BOS had indeed been the victim of cyanide poisoning (a conclusion we accept as the only reasonable diagnosis), we find it hard to avoid an inference that someone had moved her carcass prior to its discovery by the ranch foreman. Assuming BOS had received a substantial dose of cyanide (and the amount of fluorescence in her mouth suggested this), we would not expect her to have gone very far from the trap on her own power after poisoning. This seems especially unlikely because she was found dead in a contorted posture with mud on her bill and face, and was still clutching a clod of mud and coyote fur in her foot, which would seem to indicate she was already under extreme duress at the site of poisoning. It is highly improbable that she might subsequently have taken off on a coordinated flight still clutching the clod of earth in one foot, as condors normally run to take off from the ground and would be hard pressed to do so clutching anything in one foot. They are simply not known to carry objects in their feet in any event. Similarly, that BOS might have walked any substantial distance from the trapsite still clutching a clod of mud and coyote fur in one foot seems highly unlikely. The clod-clutching posture of the bird's foot only seemed reasonable as a terminal violent event at the site of poisoning.

It is also worth noting that M-44-poisoned coyotes characteristically paw at their mouths, rub their snouts on the ground, and die quickly in the immediate vicinity of the traps. The mud on the bill and face of BOS could well have resulted from similar desperate "snout-rubbing" behavior near the trap, as could a short weed stalk jammed in the socket of her left eye. Notably, most of the fluorescence found in her mouth was concentrated on the left side.

Why the carcass might have been moved is of course speculative. But assuming it had been, it seems possible that someone may have been motivated to dump a cyanide-poisoned condor where it would not likely be discovered by anyone else. If indeed this was the motivation, the site where the bird was found represented a reasonable destination and was presumably a much more discreet means of disposal than taking the bird off the ranch via the main road entrance where someone else might be encountered en route. Evidently, it was only the greatest of coincidences that the ranch foreman chose to try out a new gun beyond ranch boundaries on the day in question and stumbled on the carcass.

The Santiago Ranch is closed to public access, and trespassers are unusual. It would be a stretch to envision some trespasser happening upon the dead bird at a trapsite on the ranch, and even more of a stretch to imagine the trespasser dragging the carcass off the ranch and then abandoning it a quarter mile onto National Forest property. The portion of the

National Forest where the bird was found was only infrequently hiked by the general public, especially at the season when the bird was killed. Reasonable candidates for moving the bird's carcass were extremely few.

The upshot of all these events was that the Fish and Wildlife Service temporarily (as of January 1984) prohibited use of M-44s within the range of the condor, and initiated a biological evaluation of the risks associated with these devices. These consultations resulted in a reauthorization of M-44s in condor range, but with the restriction that they would henceforth be allowed only in single, rather than multiple sets. Specifically, in a memorandum of September 9, 1985, ADC was instructed by the U.S. Fish and Wildlife Service to conform to the following guidelines within condor range:

> M-44 sodium cyanide devices may now be used in the condor range as long as the wrapped capsule holder is placed below the surface of the ground and covered with a protective cover, such as a cow chip, flat rock, tree bark, etc., so they are not visible to condors. According to current use restrictions M-44's cannot be placed closer than 30 feet to any livestock carcass.
>
> M-44's must "NOT" be set in pairs or groups. M-44's shall be placed as a single set, no closer than 1,000 feet from another M-44.

This strategy was evidently based on an assumption that the threat of cyanide poisoning to condors was a threat of primary poisoning from the M-44s themselves rather than secondary (or primary) poisoning resulting from the birds eating or attempting to eat parts of M-44-poisoned coyotes.

However, the risks of the latter sorts of poisoning were never adequately clarified. Wiemeyer et al. (1986a) determined that a lethal dose of sodium cyanide for vultures was about 5.0 mg per kg body weight, when administered in a gel capsule. For a condor weighing 8–9 kg, this would be about 40–45 mg of cyanide. Since the amount of sodium cyanide in one M-44 charge is about 890 mg, it would appear that a condor would have to ingest only about 5% of this amount to receive a lethal dose. Thus, a condor attempting to eat the tongue of a cyanide-poisoned coyote might be at considerable risk of exposure to a lethal amount simply as a residue on the tongue of the coyote. These quantitative considerations do not allow much confidence that shifting from exposed double to covered single sets of M-44s would represent an adequate response to the cyanide threat. Condors are well known to relish the tongues of vertebrate carcasses.

The above memorandum of the Fish and Wildlife Service to the ADC dismissed the potential threat of cyanide poisoning of condors through contact with coyote carcasses with the following statement:

> Cyanide gas is so volatile it is highly unlikely that a residue would remain that was toxic enough to poison secondarily (e.g., poison a condor feeding on a coyote killed by cyanide). Once the cyanide capsulte ejects, most cyanide is either dispersed into the air or is metabolized to the less toxic thiocyanate.

However, these assertions were not backed up with any experimental testing of potential toxicity of cyanide-poisoned coyote carcasses to scavengers, and contrary to what is implied in the memorandum, the cyanide in an M-44 is not cyanide gas (HCN), but NaCN, which is not volatile. NaCN can be expected to remain as such in the environment unless dissolved in an aqueous medium (see Eisler 1991), and the need for full solution of the NaCN on the tongue of a coyote to convert it to HCN was not addressed in the memorandum. The willingness of the Fish and Wildlife Service to exonerate M-44s for use with coyotes in condor range without directly testing the toxicity of tongues of M-44-killed coyotes to nontarget wildlife species as a function of time after firing of an M-44 device remains an unexplained and unsettling puzzle.

In addition to the cyanide threats represented by ADC coyote-control efforts, we learned on our tour of the ADC trapline that the trapper was also using leg-hold traps for coyotes and then dispatching trapped coyotes with lead bullets, leaving the carcasses as potential food for condors and other scavengers. Thus it was also important to consider modifications of carcass-disposal procedures so as to prevent lead poisoning of condors. With respect to this question the Fish and Wildlife Service decreed in the same memorandum cited above that:

> Aerial shooting, shooting from the ground, denning, snaring, and leghold traps are allowable control methods as long as *steel shot is used* (aerial shooting) and/or *animals killed by lead shot are buried or removed from the condor range.*

Although these procedural changes seemed to represent an effective way to address the threat of lead poisoning by the ADC, they still left unresolved the question of potential cyanide threats to condors. If coyotes killed by cyanide were in fact a threat to condors it was not obvious how M-44s could be used without significant risks for condors. There was no apparent way to conduct operations that would ensure a trapper preceding condors to cyanide-killed coyotes. In contrast, a trapper could reliably precede condors to lead-contaminated coyote carcasses, since the lead contamination was caused by the trapper in person.

How much of an overall threat might have been represented by M-44 cyanide poisoning of coyotes remains murky. The apparent moving of the above cyanide-poisoned condor from a trapsite gives us little confidence that other cases of condor deaths to M-44s might ever be reported. However, we do note that the overall ADC Program Final Environmental Impact Statement of 1979 acknowledged that "In fiscal year 1977, three vultures were killed by M-44 devices used in the ADC program out of a total of 8,424 animals killed." What species of vultures were involved and whether these vulture deaths resulted from primary or secondary exposure were not detailed.

Conceivably the cyanide threat may have been a major one. Although we earlier (Snyder and Snyder 1989) questioned the degree of threat posed by cyanide poisoning on the assumption that the main cyanide risk might be limited to direct contact with M-44s, we have since become increasingly concerned that contact of condors with cyanide-poisoned coyote carcasses alone might represent a substantial risk, not so much from secondary poisoning as from a direct primary contact of the birds with sodium cyanide residues left on the tongues of poisoned coyotes. With the present incomplete state of knowledge concerning risks, we see no practical way to employ M-44 traps that might offer a reasonable margin of safety to condors. Only complete prohibition of these devices in condor range would suffice. Fortunately, M-44s were finally banned in California in late 1998 by a voter initiative (not by action of the federal or state governments).

In overview, it is conceivable that the U.S. Fish and Wildlife Service itself was unintentionally one of the major threats to survival of the remnant condor population. The Service faced a clear conflict of interest in being charged simultaneously with administering the endangered species program and coyote control programs, the latter through the ADC. Coyote control efforts, as practiced in the early 1980s, entailed both cyanide and lead poisoning threats to condors. And although McMillan (1968) made a case that coyote control efforts may have increased deer populations in portions of condor range, it is not at all clear that any food benefits of the control practices could have balanced their risks, especially when food seems unlikely to have been a major limiting factor for the recent condor population.

In more recent years, the administration of the ADC has been transferred out of the US FWS to the U.S. Department of Agriculture and the agency has been renamed Wildlife Services. Unfortunately, this still leaves the federal government as a whole with an unresolved conflict of interest regarding condor conservation and coyote control. We are unsure that moving ADC out of the USFWS represents a positive advance in achieving optimal regulation of potentially dangerous poisoning activities.

General Evaluation of Lead and Cyanide Threats

The four diagnosed condor mortalities represented only 27% of the deaths occurring between 1982 and 1986. They cannot be considered a sufficient basis from which to generalize conclusively about overall mortality threats to the species. Although these mortalities may have been a less biased representation of the mortality actually occurring than the historical records of fortuitously found dead condors, they may still have incorporated some significant biases. Nevertheless, it is striking that (1) three of the four mortalities were attributable to the same cause – lead poisoning, (2) all four cases appeared from their timing to be independent events, and (3) all four were due to poisoning of sorts that had not been well documented earlier for the species. No matter how one might view the data, lead poisoning now loomed as enough of a threat that it was plausible to consider it potentially the most important mortality problem faced by the species.

How much of a threat might be represented by cyanide poisoning was much harder to evaluate, especially because additional cases might be unlikely to surface, regardless of their frequency. We presently consider it to have been a potentially important threat, especially because Mundy et al. (1992) also reported the death of Bearded Vultures in Africa as a result of cyanide "getter" devices in two separate incidents in the 1980s. Details as to whether the poisoning of these vultures might have been "primary" or "secondary" were not provided.

The probable importance of lead-poisoning has been reinforced by several additional lines of evidence:

1. Ten of 16 Turkey Vultures examined in a 1981 study in southern California contained elevated lead levels in their bones (Wiemeyer et al. 1986b).

2. Five of 14 living wild California Condors sampled for blood lead concentrations between 1982 and 1986 had elevated lead levels (Wiemeyer et al. 1988). Two of the five (IC1 and SBF) subsequently died to lead poisoning, and a third (CVM) subsequently disappeared without being recovered.

3. Thirty-nine percent of the blood samples from 66 Golden Eagles in the range of the condor in 1985–1986 had elevated lead levels (Pattee et al. 1990).

4. A condor found shot in 1976 had elevated lead levels in bone similar to the bone lead levels of IC1 after death from lead poisoning (Wiemeyer et al. 1988).

5. Mortality rates for juvenile condors from 1982 through 1986 were virtually identical to those for adults, a plausible result if lead poisoning was a major cause of mortality, but not a result consistent with many other sources of mortality (see lack of age differences in lead contamination of Golden Eagles found by Pattee et al, 1990).

6. Almost all documented mortality of condors between 1982 and 1986 occurred during the fall to spring period (see Table 13), a result consistent with lead toxicity, assuming lead exposure results mainly from hunting (see also Pattee et al. 1990), but not as consistent with other potential sources of mortality (e.g. 1080 poisoning). However, the observed seasonal timing of mortality is also consistent with cyanide poisoning, as M-44s were not normally deployed during the summer months.

7. In 1997 three condors in the release program in California suffered lead poisoning as a result of feeding on a single hunter-shot deer carcass (Hendron 1998). Fortunately, this poisoning was detected early enough that the birds were brought into captivity and successfully detoxified, although the outcome could easily have been otherwise. Although birds in the release program have fed primarily on provided clean carcasses, increasing numbers of incidents of them feeding on other carcasses have been documented, resulting in increasing chances of exposure to the lead threat still in existence in the condor range.

8. In 1998 three additional condors in the release program suffered lead poisoning and had to be given chelation therapy, although the specific sources of contamination were not identified (Hendron 1998). Again all three birds survived, but one of the three nearly died from the contamination prior to capture.

These additional lines of evidence clearly document a substantial level of exposure to lead in California's carrion-feeding birds in recent times and strongly support lead-poisoning as a major mortality factor. Moreover, they strongly suggest that the documented cases of condor mortality to lead poisoning in the 1980s were much more than simply bizarre chance

Table 13. Timing of disappearance of photodocumented wild California Condors (adapted from Snyder and Snyder 1989).

Bird	Date last observed
WGI	August 10, 1982
UN3	September 11, 1983
CCM	October 27, 1984
PPF	October 27, 1984
CVF	November 6, 1984
PCB	November 15, 1983
SSM	November 17, 1984
BOS	November 23, 1983 (victim of cyanide poisoning on this date)
SBF	January 18, 1986 (dies of lead poisoning on this date but poisoned by late November 1985)
CVM	January 22, 1985
SMA	March 15, 1982
IC1	March 21, 1984 (dies of lead poisoning on this date, presumably poisoned earlier)
BFE	April 10, 1985 (dies of lead poisoning on this date but apparently poisoned by late February 1985)
UN2	April 15, 1982

Note: one additional adult (not photo-documented), a mate of PPF, disappeared after May 31, 1982.

events that might be unlikely to recur. On the contrary, they appeared to be a reflection of a chronic underlying pattern of contamination that had presumably been present since the first western settlers arrived on the West Coast.

Where exactly was the lead contamination coming from? Blood lead levels of captive condors held in urban zoo environments proved to be relatively low, strongly suggesting that atmospheric lead from automobile exhaust was not the primary source (Wiemeyer et al. 1986b). Instead the likely source was ingested lead from carrion foods that had been shot and still contained lead ammunition fragments or shot pellets. The principal candidate sources appeared to be various game species shot by hunters (especially deer), and pest species, such as coyotes and ground squirrels, shot by ranchers, plinkers, and the ADC. In addition, foxes, bobcats and other fur-bearing mammals trapped in the range for their pelts were commonly dispatched with lead ammunition after being caught in leghold traps. Their skinned carcasses were then left for scavengers.

Historically, most wildlife losses to lead poisoning have traced to ingested lead shot, not bullets, although Alan Harmata and his associates have recently documented poisoning mortalities of Bald Eagles to bullet fragments in the northern Rockies. The metallic fragments causing the death of IC1 and SBF also appeared to be bullet fragments. What sort of ammunition may have poisoned BFE is unknown.

That the major poisoning threat to condors might come from bullets, rather than shot, is also suggested by the fact that the large majority of hunted animals known eaten by condors, such as deer, coyotes, and ground squirrels, are species typically killed with bullets in California. Records are infrequent of condors eating species hunted with shotguns, such as rabbits, waterfowl, and quail. And although large mammals shot for trophies and meat are normally removed from the field by hunters, they are typically gutted in the field to reduce spoilage and facilitate transport. Gut piles, many of which presumably contain lead bullet fragments, are well known as favored foods for condors. In addition, some hunter-shot game species are never recovered by the hunters, as in the incident described above of released condors poisoned at a deer carcass. Coyotes and other pest species shot with bullets by ranchers and plinkers have traditionally been left where they have been encountered, fully available to condors.

In particular, the coyotes shot by the ADC in leg-hold traps up until the time practices were changed in 1984 and 1985 could have been a significant part of the lead-threat to condors. In addition, the U.S. Fish and Wildlife Service could also have been inadvertently responsible for some lead poisoning of condors through the supplementary feeding program carried on during the 1970s, as some of the carcasses provided to wild condors at that time were animals that had been shot.

The tiny size of the lead fragments found in the digestive tracts of the poisoned condors suggested a high sensitivity to this contaminant. Toxicological data suggested that the equivalent of a single lead shot pellet might be enough to kill a condor, providing it was continuously exposed to an acidic environment in the bird's gut. In addition there are several other factors that might predispose the species to especially high vulnerability to lead. First, condors are deficient in one mechanism for removing lead fragments from their digestive tracts that is available to raptorial birds in general – pellet casting. Most birds of prey daily regurgitate indigestible portion of their diet (mostly commonly fur, feathers, and lizard scales) in the form of pellets, and this can also rid them of lead fragments. Condors only rarely cast pellets, almost surely because they feed primarily on soft tissues of their prey and rarely ingest fur and feathers. Thus lead fragments ingested by condors may be much more likely to remain in the digestive system than lead ingested by other diurnal raptors.

Second, condors may have a propensity to ingest small hard objects (normally bone) in their food as a result of their apparent difficulty in obtaining enough calcium in their diet (see discussion in Chapters 1, 5 and 8). We think it is possible that condors might preferentially ingest any lead pellets or bullet fragments they might encounter in the soft tissues of their prey, mistaking them for pieces of bone.

Third, there is some preliminary evidence that New World vultures might metabolize lead differently than do some accipitrid birds of prey. In dosing experiments with Red-tailed Hawks and a Turkey Vulture, Reiser and Temple (1981) found that the vulture absorbed lead more rapidly and was much less efficient in excreting lead than the hawks. Under equivalent dosing regimes the vulture soon acquired much higher blood lead levels than the hawks. This apparent metabolic difference could be another reflection of chronic calcium deficiencies in the diet of vultures, as lead is very similar to calcium chemically (both are deposited in bone, for example). Vultures may be programmed to "hang on" to calcium in their metabolic pathways because it is usually a nutrient in short supply, and this tendency could lead to a retention of lead as well, as an inadvertent byproduct.

Taken together, the above metabolic and behavioral factors could result in condors having a high vulnerability to lead contamination, relative to accipitrid raptorial birds. Nevertheless, Turkey Vultures, which presumably have many of the same traits as condors, have not suffered anything like the population declines suffered by the condor (Pattee and Wilbur 1989). Perhaps the comparative success of Turkey Vultures traces in part to their much greater reproductive potentials. Turkey Vulture pairs commonly fledge two young per year and normally breed on an annual basis. Turkey Vultures may also have fewer problems in obtaining enough calcium in their diet, as they fairly commonly feed on very small prey species with bones that are small enough to ingest easily (e.g. Paterson 1984). Their biochemical tendencies to conserve calcium (and lead) may differ from those of condors as a result.

Other Threats

Lead and cyanide poisoning were surely not the only mortality threats faced by condors in the 1980s. Although it is possible that these were the most important threats, the lead shot pellets found in the soft tissues of SBF in 1985 also clearly indicated a continuing threat of direct shooting mortality, as did the apparent shooting of a condor in 1976 (Wiemeyer et al. 1983). Miller et al. (1965) made a persuasive case for widespread risks from shooting in the condor range, and two recent incidents (1998, 1999) of released condors being shot make clear that this problem is still with us. To some extent, mortality from shooting may be underrepresented in birds recovered through radio-telemetry, as some gunners may destroy radios on birds they have shot, making it difficult for researchers to recover such birds. However, only one radioed bird of the 1980s (CVM) disappeared without being recovered, and other circumstances than shooting might have produced this result. Of four recent released birds that have disappeared without being recovered, only two had functioning radios when they disappeared.

We were also concerned about continuing threats of condor collisions with overhead utility wires. Koford (1953) reported two cases of collision deaths (one case with a surveyor's stake and one with a fence wire) and a condor was directly observed colliding with phone wires in 1965 and dying as a result (Brunetti 1965). Collisions with overhead wires have been shown to be a major source of mortality for various raptors, cranes, and waterfowl (Olendorff and Lehman 1986, Brown et al. 1987, Brown 1993, Brown and Drewien 1995), and the steadily increasing numbers of powerlines and phone lines crisscrossing the condor range seemed likely to be taking an increasing toll on the species.

Further evidence of this threat has come more recently through the losses of seven juvenile condors to overhead wires in condor releases conducted since 1990 (Meretsky et al. in press). In fact, collisions and/or electrocutions have been the major source of mortality in early releases. However, this result has undoubtedly been due in part to the tendency of early-released, captive-reared condors to be attracted to human structures, a tendency that was not known for the historic wild population. Collisions and electrocutions by power lines have been a substantial problem for large vultures in Africa, as discussed in detail by Mundy et al. (1992).

Another type of collision threat arose with the development of numerous "wind farms" in the 1980s. These massive arrays of windmills have been deliberately encouraged by the California state goverment as a source of clean electrical energy, but have turned out as well to be a significant new source of mortality for large flying birds. No condors have as yet been documented colliding with the windmills, but studies are showing substantial numbers of collision deaths of other large vultures and eagles attributable to these mechanical contraptions (Hunt 1997, Acha 1998).

In addition, there were other kinds of poisoning still practiced in the condor range in the 1980s to which the condor might have been susceptible. Miller et al. (1965) reported a case of 3 condors apparently poisoned by strychnine at a carcass put out to kill coyotes in 1950. One of the three birds died, while the other two recovered, bolstered by food and water provided on their behalf. Another apparent strychnine-poisoned condor was found at a coyote bait in 1966 (Borneman 1966). This bird recovered from the poisoning at the Los Angeles Zoo and was returned to the wild. By the 1980s the role of strychnine in coyote control had been largely replaced by cyanide M-44s and leg-hold traps, but this poison was still used to a limited extent in ground squirrel control, along with zinc phosphide, and especially compound 1080 (sodium fluoroacetate). Strychnine has also been implicated as a major cause of death of African Vultures in recent years (Mundy et al. 1992).

Another toxicant posing a substantial threat to the condor historically was thallium sulfate, widely used in ground squirrel control programs. As discussed by Koford (1953), this poison came into major use in southern California in 1926 but by the late 1940s was replaced pretty much completely by compound 1080. Thallium poisoning campaigns killed various raptorial birds and Turkey Vultures (Linsdale 1931), so it is likely that they also killed some condors during the second quarter of the century.

Because of the very widespread use of 1080 since its introduction in 1945, its potential for poisoning condors has been debated for decades. In condor range this poison has been used primarily for control of ground squirrels and kangaroo rats. But although both Koford (1953) and Miller et al. (1965) reported many instances of condors feeding on the 1080-poisoned squirrels and rats, no certain evidence of negative effects of this toxicant on condors has been obtained to this day.

Experiments on the toxicity of 1080 by Ward and Spencer (1947) and Fry et al. (1986) revealed a high degree of resistance in Turkey Vultures, as compared to a high sensitivity in many mammalian species. Specifically, a toxic dose of 1080 to Turkey Vultures ranged between 20 and 100 mg per kg of body weight, depending on ambient temperature, as compared with 0.06 mg per kg in canids and 0.5 mg per kg in ground squirrels. In accord with this major difference, Hegdahl et al. (1986), in a field study of the effects of 1080 squirrel poisoning on nontarget species in Tulare County, California, found that aerially-distributed 1080 grain baits caused no mortalities in radio-tagged raptors and vultures, but did result in considerable mortalities of coyotes, rabbits, and other mammals.

Fry et al. (1986) found that Turkey Vultures commonly regurgitated 1080-laced foods. This behavioral response presumably helps reduce exposure to the toxicant, and is a mechanism that may be present in condors as well. At the same time, these researchers expressed concerns that sublethal effects (lethargy and unresponsiveness) that were apparent at half the

Other potential mortality threats faced by the wild condor population have included collisions with wind-powered generators and miring in oil ponds. Wind farms, such as this array in the Tehachapi Mountains (**above**), have been promoted as an environmentally friendly source of "clean" electric energy. Yet recent studies have revealed high rates of mortality of large raptors and vultures due to collisions with such structures. **Below**, oil ponds associated with drilling operations are required by law to be screened to prevent access by wildlife. Yet uncovered oil ponds, such as this one on the San Emigdio Ranch, still could be found within condor range in the 1980s, with unknown effects on condors.

short-term lethal dose might lead ultimately to death of some individuals in a field context. Fry et al. also expressed concerns about cumulative effects of 1080 on the nervous system following repeated exposures.

Although no direct studies have been conducted of 1080 toxicity to California Condors (for obvious reasons), no 1080 was found in any of the condors that were necropsied in the 1980s. If results with Turkey Vultures might generalize to its larger close relative, a California Condor would probably have to ingest many times its own body weight in poisoned ground squirrels to obtain a lethal dose. This assumes it might only ingest the squirrels themselves (secondary poisoning) and not ingest the poisoned grain in their cheek pouches that caused their death (primary poisoning). However, it is uncertainties over this ingestion question that have fueled continuing debates, as it is still not known whether the condors commonly ingest the poisoned grain in squirrel cheek pouches. If they do, the chances that they might ingest enough 1080 for toxic or debilitating effects would be much greater.

In observations of Koford (1953), condors did not swallow ground squirrel carcasses whole, but dismembered the carcasses in feeding on them and did not necessarily ingest all parts. Although Koford found one whole squirrel skull in a condor nest site, it is not clear to what extent the contents of cheek pouches might be ingested. We had no observations of condors feeding on ground squirrels during the 1980s, but in our own sifting of some 72 condor nest sites (Collins et al. 2000) we found bones of ground squirrels with some frequency, including jaws but no skulls. As Miller et al. (1965) pointed out, however, the risks of ingesting cheek pouches containing poisoned grain could be more significant with kangaroo rats, because condors often swallow these animals whole.

Giving some further insight into these questions was an unpublished study of A.I. Roest of California Polytechnic University, San Luis Obispo conducted in 1969. In this study a captive Turkey Vulture was maintained on an exclusive diet of 1080-poisoned ground squirrels for a period of over a month. There were no effects seen in the vulture, which was ultimately returned to the wild. But perhaps the most interesting aspect of the study was that in feeding, the vulture never consumed the heads of the squirrels and also avoided eating viscera:

> "The vulture seemed to feed almost exclusively on muscle tissue, which was carefully removed from the bone, and also ate the heart, liver, kidneys, etc. The head, stomach, and intestinal tract were never eaten."

Should such selective feeding behavior generalize to other Turkey Vultures and condors, the risks of 1080-squirrel campaigns to these birds would presumably be minimal.

In view of the widespread 1080 poisoning of ground squirrels and kangaroo rats in the condor range, and in view of the known widespread feeding of condors on the mammals killed in 1080 poisoning campaigns, it would be surprising that any condors might still have been left in the 1980s if these campaigns were a substantial threat. Also arguing against a major role of 1080 poisoning in the condor decline of the 1980s is the fact that most all condor losses documented in this period occurred during the fall to spring period (Table 13), whereas 1080 poisoning of rodents occurs almost exclusively in the late spring and summer period. Because of these arguments, we suspect that the threat to condors from

1080 rodent control efforts has been relatively minor. However, we believe it is still an open question whether any condors were killed by these campaigns, especially in view of the sublethal effects documented in Turkey Vultures by Fry et al. (1986). The issue may always remain unresolved, as 1080 was outlawed for use in ground-squirrel control in 1985.

In addition, it is important to recognize that in the early years of 1080 use, this toxicant was also placed in meat baits to poison coyotes, which it did very efficiently. But because many other nontarget species were also killed by such poisoning, use of 1080 in coyote control was outlawed in 1972. No condor deaths to 1080-laced meat baits were documented, and raptor deaths due to consumption of these baits were evidently rare (Eisler 1995). Nevertheless, it is difficult to completely rule out some contribution of these poisoning operations to the decline of the condor in the 1950s and 1960s.

Another toxicant that has been used illegally in carcasses to poison coyotes in some regions is antifreeze (ethylene glycol). The death of one released condor in 1992 was traced to this material, although it is unknown if it ingested the anti-freeze in a carcass or perhaps through drinking at a puddle where someone had drained his car radiator.

Still Additional Threats

Two recent deaths of released condors were caused by drowning in a slippery-sided pothole. The birds had evidently entered the site to drink or bathe but were unable to escape (Meretsky et al. ms). Houston (1996) and Piper (1993) reported similar drowning incidents with other vulture species, especially in cattle watering troughs. Koford (1953) also mentioned a report of a condor found dead in a water tank in 1941. In addition, Robinson (1939) reported that several condors were evidently killed about 1927 by wading into pools of oil near Maricopa, possibly mistaking them for water. Exposure to oil or tar pools may also have killed the many Pleistocene condors documented in the Rancho La Brea deposits of Los Angeles. The attractions of condors to water sources places them at chronic risk of such mortality incidents. Although documented recent cases of drownings or mirings are few, the extent of continuing risk is largely unknown.

No mortalities of condors documented in the 1980s or other recent years were attributable to catastrophic weather events, habitat perturbations, or earthquakes, although such occurrences should not be forgotten as having occasional importance for the species. Hurricanes and tornados are exceeding rare in southern California, and in fact the weather is generally exceedingly benign, rarely even rising to the intensity of a thunderstorm. Although rain fronts are of regular occurrence in the winter months, and rain is sometimes heavy, accompanying winds are usually modest and fronts rarely last more than a day or two. Such weather is generally unlikely to cause direct mortality of either adults or nestlings. Nevertheless, two condors recovered dead in Santa Barbara County in 1936 were believed to have died from battering in a violent hailstorm (Rett 1938).

Southern California is far more famous for another sort of violent catastrophe – earthquakes. The San Andreas fault runs directly through condor range in a roughly northwest–southeast orientation and has served as a focus for many severe quakes throughout history. Major earthquakes have the potential for collapsing condor nest sites and causing mortality of chicks and adults within. Although the probability of such events is no doubt exceedingly low, we note that two nest sites studied by Carl Koford in the 1940s had collapsed by the time of our studies in the 1980s. Whether collapse in these cases was due to earthquakes, we do not know, and there is no evidence that collapse caused any condor mortality in either case.

Perhaps the most frequent habitat perturbation that can directly threaten condor survival and nesting success has been fire. Chaparral habitat is well adapted to tolerate periodic fire, but fires occurring during the condor nesting season can pose major risks to the survival of chicks in nests that lie in their paths. We witnessed a number of major fires during the 1980s, including the horrendous Wheeler Fire of 1985, which nearly forced us to evacuate our home, and scorched some 47,750 ha of back country habitat, including some major areas used by condors. The heat generated by this fire was enough to melt metal highway signs, and had there been any active condor nests in its path, such heat alone would no doubt have incinerated their contents. Adults presumably have little difficulty in avoiding such fires, however, and no mortality of adults or chicks occurred in the Wheeler Fire.

The Sespe Sanctuary region remained virtually fire-free from the time of Koford's studies through the 1980s, and the resulting brush-buildup made it exceedingly difficult to traverse the area. Thus none of the decline of nesting condors in this region through this period could have been caused by fire. An intense fire finally ignited a substantial portion (approximately 3500 ha) of the sanctuary in 1997, but chaparral recovers so quickly after fire, the traces of this fire are already disappearing rapidly, just as there is virtually no trace to be seen now of the Wheeler Fire of 1985. When we first began studies in 1980, we could still detect traces of the Liebre fire that swept through the CC territory in the late 1960s, but this fire evidently was not enough to cause any long-lasting abandonment of the territory by condors.

Summary of Major Threats to the Species

The historical record, together with more recent data and a measure of reasonable inference, leaves no reasonable doubt that the decline of the condor has been driven primarily by a variety of mortality factors. We doubt that reproductive malfunctions have ever been a major difficulty for the species, although we grant that the taking of nestlings for ritual sacrifice could be considered a reproductive stress rather than a mortality stress. However, for the sake of discussion here we consider losses to ritual sacrifice to be a mortality factor and at one time possibly the most important mortality factor faced by the species, conceivably sufficient in magnitude to have caused significant local population declines long before the arrival of Europeans.

The arrival of European settlers brought several new mortality threats. Unrestrained shooting (in part for quill collecting) and poisoning (mainly with strychnine) directed at mammalian predators such as wolves and grizzly bears likely increased the pressures on the species greatly. Shooting activities also posed indirect threats of lead-poisoning, which may well have been even more damaging than the direct threats of shooting. Unlike many previous authors, we do not minimize the potential impacts on the species of strychnine poisoning and shooting for quills, but consider these stresses to have been of substantial importance, especially in the latter half of the nineteenth century and early part of the twentieth century, when overall stresses on the condor population may have been especially great.

Museum collecting of free-flying birds became a significant stress only around the turn of the 20th century. Its importance has often been overemphasized, largely because it has been so well documented compared with other threats. Even at its height, we consider it a stress of much less real importance than poisoning with strychnine and lead and even perhaps shooting for quill collection. Collecting of condor eggs has never been plausible as a major threat, especially in view of the capacities of the species for replacement-clutching and the fact that only on the order of 60 condor eggs were ever collected historically (see Wilbur 1978b). Museum collecting of free-flying birds and eggs and shooting for quills declined greatly by early in the present century, leaving various forms of poisoning and wanton shooting as likely the predominant threats through most of the rest of the century.

Collisions with overhead wires have surely been an increasing threat through the present century, but we suspect they have been a threat of only moderate importance overall. Other more miscellaneous causes of mortality, such as drownings and losses to fire and hailstorms have probably affected the species throughout its history but have never threatened its existence. The threats of real significance have been those posed by our own species. We doubt strongly that there has ever been a period of population increase or stability for the condor since it was first described by western scientists over two hundred years ago, despite claims of Koford (1953) and Miller et al. (1965) to the contrary. That the species lasted as long as it did in the wild is probably much more an indication that its early numbers were greatly underestimated than a reflection of any periods of population recovery. The most important threats to the species have been relentless.

Although the overall data available on causes of condor mortalities are still insufficient to allow a thoroughly comprehensive assessment, the picture has been becoming steadily clearer as mortalities of released condors continue to occur and be studied. Despite many biases and uncertainties in the historical data, we rate various forms of poisoning as likely the most important threats throughout the historical decline of the species. Recent data suggest strongly that lead poisoning has been the single most important threat and very likely sufficient in itself to have produced a continuously declining historic condor population, especially in view of the very high levels of wildlife shooting and consistent use of lead ammunition that have characterized the condor range in the past two centuries (see McMillan 1968). The numerous cases of lead poisoning in recent condor releases make it highly probable that the risks from lead poisoning remain severe enough that it is unlikely that condors can be successfully reestablished in regions where this threat remains effectively unaddressed.

For recent decades, we recognize two specific sources of lead poisoning that might account for a large fraction of condor losses: (1) use of lead ammunition in deer hunting, and (2) use of lead ammunition to dispatch leg-hold-trapped coyotes by the ADC (a threat presumably no longer in operation). During our studies in the early 1980s and during earlier studies of Wilbur (1978b), condors obviously concentrated in the Tehachapi Mountains during the fall hunting season and fed heavily on the remains of deer. Large numbers of deer were shot in this region each year. For example, the Tejón Ranch alone sometimes recorded in excess of 200 deer shot by hunters in a season. It is entirely plausible that inadvertent lead poisoning resulting from deer hunting could have been the most important single cause of the condor's extirpation.

Further, the acute lead poisoning of three released condors from a single deer carcass in 1997 raises concerns that the massive losses of condors over the winter of 1984–1985 might have had a similar cause. The social nature of feeding in this species predisposes it to multiple mortality events from single contaminated carcasses, and available data on timing of losses in the winter of 1984–1985 allow the possibility that most of the birds lost in this period could have been stricken in a single incident, though there is no direct evidence of this. The pivotal significance of the excessive mortality of 1984–1985 is a subject to which we will return in Chapter 14.

In broad view, however, it would be a major mistake to focus all attention on lead poisoning and the above two sources of lead poisoning. Although these may have been especially significant threats, all sources of mortality are contributive in a demographic sense, and the mortalities stemming from other sources of lead poisoning and other mortality factors cannot be safely ignored. Collision deaths and shooting still remain significant threats, though we suspect they may be lesser threats than lead poisoning. Cyanide poisoning from coyote trapping efforts may also have been a significant threat, although the magnitude of this threat has been very difficult to evaluate. Other threats, such as drownings, can also be expected to continue to take a toll of the species. As much as possible, all mortality threats need to be minimized if there is to be hope of reestablishing viable wild populations. Mortality threats that have developed in the release program will be considered in more detail in Chapter 17.

PART IV
CONSERVATION
IN THE 1980s

CHAPTER THIRTEEN

Field Conservation and Habitat Preservation

A principal goal of condor research in the 1980s was the identification of major factors limiting survival and reproduction (Snyder 1986). As we discovered specific problems, we attempted both to determine their severity and to devise appropriate remedies, where possible. Part of this process was an effort to determine and correct habitat-related limitations for the species. This entailed identifying important use areas and evaluating anticipated future stresses on these areas that might be countered by appropriate habitat management measures. The hope was that by attacking a variety of problems simultaneously, we could reduce the stresses on the species enough to allow the population to increase.

However, we recognized at the outset that this strategy might fail for several reasons: (1) there might not be enough time to identify the most important stress factors, (2) there might not be enough time to develop effective corrective actions for stresses that could be countered, and (3) some of the most important stress factors might turn out to be uncorrectable even if unlimited time were available. With the wild population as low and declining as rapidly as it was, and with the substantial uncertainties regarding success, it seemed absolutely essential that a captive population of condors be established simultaneous with efforts to aid the wild population. A captive flock could serve both as a back-up measure in the event of failure of field conservation measures and as a source of birds to bolster the wild population. Surrogate studies with the Andean Condor and other vulturids had given substantial encouragement that the California Condor would respond well to captive husbandry and would be reintroduceable to the wild from captivity.

In this chapter we consider the field efforts to aid the wild population in the 1980s. In the following chapter we look at the efforts made to establish a captive population.

Reduction of Reproductive Stresses

As detailed in Chapter 11, overall productivity of the wild population was reasonably strong in the 1980s. However, during nesting observations we identified a number of problems whose correction could significantly benefit the species. Unfortunately, some of these problems (e.g., behavioral incompatability between pair members and production of abnormal chicks) were apparently outside the realm of management efforts. Others, particularly nest-site deficiencies and depredations of ravens, did offer opportunities for development of effective corrective measures. In seeking solutions to these problems, however, we faced both legal restrictions and constraints related to potential disturbance of the condors. Thus, although we observed extreme threats to egg safety resulting from choices of deficient nest sites in several cases, we were not always free to respond immediately to these deficiencies, and there were risks in responding that had to be weighed against potential benefits.

Correction of structural nest-site deficiencies

To minimize disturbance to actively nesting pairs, we delayed efforts to correct structural flaws of nests until after breeding attempts were finished. Unfortunately, in most cases the specific sites involved were not used again during the early 1980s so we had no opportunity to evaluate the effects of the improvements. Because condors almost always change nest sites in successive breeding attempts, the benefits of post-breeding nest improvements can only be evaluated over long periods during which the birds eventually reuse the sites.

Rough substrates

When we began nesting studies in 1980 we were aware that Fred Sibley had noted in 1967 that one condor nest in particular (Koford's Nest #5) seemed to have a very rough and rocky bottom and that this site had suffered several known cases of egg breakage. Because the rough bottom might have contributed to the breakage, Fred had cleared out some of the more jagged rocks. We likewise considered it plausible that rough substrates might lead to egg damage (Snyder 1983), so we also made efforts to reduce the amount of jagged gravel and rocks on the floors of a few nests early in our studies.

However, our evaluation of the risks of such substrates was to change completely as we made further observations of nesting pairs. At sites where we could directly observe the behavior of adults, we often watched them deliberately collecting rough rocky materials and depositing these in the egg position with their bills. It seemed highly unlikely that they would do this if it were to increase risks of egg damage. We also became aware that most of the egg damage occurring in the wild was a result of raven predation, not rough substrates. In addition, even though some eggs were scored superficially by contact with rough substrates, we began to realize that loose raised substrates could help curtail uncontrolled movements of eggs, provide protection of eggs against flooding of nest bottoms, reduce contact of eggs with soil pathogens, and perhaps absorb some of the shock eggs experience in hitting the substrate in the laying process. Condors are relatively clumsy in incubation and normally rest an egg on their feet as they warm it. When they stand up, as they do periodically, the egg tends to roll off their feet and across the nest floor. Depending on the speed of standing up and the nature of

Many nests, such as the nest cave of the CC pair in 1983 (*above*), had exceedingly rough substrates, and concern that these substrates might damage eggs stimulated early efforts to provide softer substrates as replacements. Nevertheless, direct observations revealed that parent birds deliberately gathered the rough gravel materials and no significant damage attributable to rough substrates was documented. *Below*, risks of raven predation were much more certain, and a variety of control measures, including shooting, were attempted for nests under immediate threats from this species. Bruce Barbour holds a raven that had been attempting to steal the egg of the CC pair in 1982. Despite removal of this bird, the egg was later lost to raven predation.

the floor, such rolling can result in an egg smashing into a hard wall, or even lofting out of the cave itself and off into space. This latter outcome was once observed by the early egg collector, Kelly Truesdale, much to his dismay, when he flushed a condor off its nest (McMillan 1968). To the extent that irregular substrates can dampen rolling, they may actually be an important advantage to condors rather than a disadvantage.

With this improved perspective on the significance of rough substrates, we ended our initial efforts to smooth out nest bottoms. Overall, none of the egg breakage occurring during our studies was clearly linked to substrate roughness or smoothness, so our early efforts to improve nest substrates were probably of little consequence. Only one of the nests where we smoothed the substrate was used again subsequently. Although this second nesting failed, the failure was clearly due to a raven, not to quality of the substrate.

Sloped bottoms

A much more certain threat to nesting success was posed by the sloped bottoms of several nest sites. In one of these sites in 1982, the egg ultimately did roll out of the nest cave to its destruction, and in another in 1983, an Andean Condor chick rolled out and over the cliff edge during a failed attempt to foster the chick under California Condor parents. In a third site in 1984, the egg was perched precariously on a sandy ledge that sloped increasingly steeply down to the outside without any barriers in between. In this latter case the egg was taken for artifical incubation before a catastrophe ensued. With sites such as these we made routine efforts to correct faulty slopes by levelling the substrates and providing raised boundary barriers to confine eggs to nest chambers. None of the sites modified, however, was reused by condors, so efficacy of these measures must be rated as unconfirmed.

Lack of external porches

Another sort of basic structural flaw that we attempted to correct at one site was the lack of an external porchlike area where the nestling could stretch and flap its wings. At the nest involved (the CV territory of 1983), we repeatedly observed the nestling almost falling out of the site as it attempted to balance on the nest lip to exercise its wings. We were concerned that we might easily lose this chick to a fall, as Fred Sibley had documented several apparent falls of chicks from nest sites in the 1960s. Because of this threat and a narrowly failed attempt of a black bear to get to this nestling, we took it into captivity much earlier than originally planned. We then constructed a platform-like stone porch for the nest site using rocks and mortar. However, the pair used a different site for its nesting of 1984 and then perished over the winter of 1984–1985, so there was no opportunity to determine if the nest modifications might have been beneficial.

Exposed nest substrates

As noted in Chapter 9, observations of nesting condor pairs indicated that the risks of raven predation on eggs were in part dependent on how visible nest bottoms were from the outside. Once ravens detected a condor egg as they flew by a nest cliff, they usually made persistent attempts to enter the site, presumably seeking a potential meal. The sites that evidently were safest from ravens had structures that placed the incubating condors and their eggs out of sight from the entrances.

Other efforts of various sorts were employed to increase chances of condor nesting success. ***Above***, at the CV site of 1983, from which a nestling narrowly missed falling to the cliff base on numerous occasions, an external porch was constructed of masonry to allow safe nestling wing exercise in future nesting attempts. Other sites, such as the CC site of 1982 (***below***) were provided with masonry baffles to obscure eggs from the view of passing ravens.

To address the apparent risks of exposed nest bottoms, we provided two raven-troubled sites with rock baffles to obscure the view of the nest contents from the entrances. Not all sites under threat from ravens had structures that would allow construction of baffles, but this approach seemed advisable, where possible. A number of condor nests had natural structures that achieved the same end, so we presumed that condors might readily accept such modifications. However, as in the other modifications described above, neither of the sites that was modified was used subsequently by condors, so the effectiveness of these modifications was unconfirmed.

Reduction of raven threats by other means

With evidence accumulating that ravens represented the most pressing threat to nesting success of condors, and with the structure of most condor nest sites not allowing the sorts of modifications described above, we also tried other methods of countering ravens.

At two condor sites under severe threats from ravens, we resorted to the brute force method of shooting the ravens. One of these was the second nest in the CC territory of 1982, where Bruce Barbour finally managed to shoot one member of the resident raven pair when it was distant from the condor nest. However, continued observations revealed that the remaining member of the pair gained a new mate almost immediately so the control effort had little or no beneficial effect. In fact, we failed to eliminate either member of the reconstituted raven pair, and it was at this very condor nest that Helen later directly observed a raven destroying the condors' egg.

The other nest where we tried to eliminate ravens was the nest in a giant sequoia tree in 1984 where one or more ravens were repeatedly landing right on the lip of the condor nest less than a meter from the incubating bird. These ravens were apparently nesting in an immediately adjacent sequoia. Their persistence in checking the condor nest suggested that sooner or later they might very well make an approach at a time when both condors were off the nest simultaneously and then have an open opportunity to destroy the egg.

To counter the threat at this nest, a bait station for ravens was quickly set up on a nearby lumber road that was out of sight from the condor nest. Here Jim Crew of the California Department of Fish and Game shot eight ravens in the following days. Evidently, at least one of the ravens eliminated was from the pair harassing the condors, as raven harassment of the condor nest ceased immediately, although there continued to be a pair of ravens (probably reconstituted) active in the adjacent sequoia tree. Thus the control efforts in this case appeared to be successful, and the condor egg hatched successfully, producing a surviving chick.

Another method tried unsuccessfully at another active condor nest of 1984 was an attempt to cause selective desertion of an immediately adjacent raven nest. Victor Apanius took a position near, but out of sight of the condor nest, where he could aim a mirror to silently flash reflections of the sun into the eyes of the ravens as they approached their own nest. Although Victor was highly proficient in giving the ravens repeated blasts of pseudo-lightning, as evidenced by their sudden evasive behavior, they did not abandon the site. We ultimately took the condor egg at this site into captivity, as the repeated assaults of the ravens on the incubating condors left little hope that the latter might succeed in hatching a chick.

All of the above methods of countering ravens were cumbersome, and none was reliably effective. During late 1984 we began a collaboration with Debra Quick of the Los Angeles Zoo to develop an alternative method that might offer major advantages in effectiveness, selectivity, and permanence of effects. The method envisioned was aversive conditioning of local ravens to reject condor eggs. Aversive conditioning had been used successfully to counter egg predation by a variety of predators in a variety of contexts, including raven predation on eggs of Sandhill Cranes in Oregon (Nicolaus 1987; Nicolaus et al. 1983). There did not appear to be any reason it could not work as well to counter raven predation on condor eggs.

In brief, the conditioning would involve inducing resident local ravens to sample condor-like eggs (for example swan eggs) that had been laced with an emetic substance, such as landrin (Quick and Hill 1988). This material is tasteless but rapidly induces a violent vomiting response. Usually with only a single experience, predators such as ravens develop a strong tendency to avoid repeat sampling of eggs of the same appearance. A major advantage of the method is that the ravens subjected to the conditioning are not killed and normally remain on the scene. This minimizes the risks of inexperienced ravens, with no strong convictions as to how noxious condors eggs might be, taking their place.

Unfortunately, hopes to test this methodology in the field in 1985 did not come to fruition, in part because of bureaucratic delays in project approval by the Patuxent Wildlife Research Center and in part because essentially all condor nesting pairs disappeared to mortality factors over the winter of 1984–85. In the crisis atmosphere of the spring of 1985, the research program turned its attention to other emergency issues. Ultimately, however, such methodology may prove to be of great importance in efforts to reestablish self-sustaining condor populations in the wild. Potentially the method could substantially enhance the nesting success of reintroduced condors for only a minimal investment of time and materials.

Reduction of Mortality Threats

As discussed in Chapter 12, the major stress factors faced by the wild condor population were very clearly mortality factors. Although the wild population was lost before the relative importance of various mortality factors could be rigorously evaluated, the most important factor documented in the 1980s was lead poisoning, apparently resulting from ammunition fragments in carcasses of hunted animals. Other known mortality factors of apparent, but perhaps lesser, importance were shooting, collisions with overhead wires, and poisoning from M-44 cyanide traps set for coyotes. Mortality rates were sufficiently high in the 1980s that the only way to revitalize the condor population was through major reductions in these factors. All, unfortunately, posed substantial management difficulties.

Lead poisoning

Three principal ways to counter the lead poisoning threat in the near term were considered: (1) conversion of the condor range into a no-hunting zone (2) adoption of alternative nontoxic ammunition for the condor range, and (3) subsidizing the population with clean food supplies. None of these alternatives proved a practical solution in the time frame left for the wild condor population. The first alternative would have removed long-standing privileges from the hunting community and would certainly have been opposed by some factions. Because personnel of the California Department of Fish and Game indicated that possibly over half the deer shot in California were taken illegally, it also posed major, probably insurmountable, problems in enforcement. The condor would stand alone as the only species causing the loss of hunting privileges, and this threatened to make it a very visible and vulnerable target for retaliation. It would take only one or two vengeful hunters with some knowledge of condor habits to wipe out the species. Such backlash could easily overwhelm any benefits of a hunting moratorium. So, apart from the political difficulties that would be involved in achieving a hunting ban, there were good reasons to fear it would not help the condor and in fact might rapidly accelerate its decline. No one within the recovery effort saw any real promise in the no-hunting solution, and it was never proposed to the California Fish and Game Commission.

The second alternative suffered from that fact that at the time, no good alternatives to lead bullets had been developed. Although steel shot was then being promoted as an alternative to lead to solve toxicity problems for waterfowl, the problems for the condor apparently did not stem primarily from shot in carcasses, but from bullet fragments. Steel bullets, although they existed and were used by the military, were not a viable alternative to lead bullets from a hunting perspective because they were designed mainly to cripple, rather than kill. Unlike lead, steel does not normally fragment on contact with a target animal but normally passes on through the animal's body, causing much less tissue damage and much lower killing rates. Steel bullets had no potential to gain acceptance by the hunting community. Further, in the time frame left for the wild condor population, there was no hope of developing other alternatives that might be both non-toxic and good ammunition from a hunting perspective. Although such alternatives are now under development over a decade later and offer strong hopes for aiding future releases of condors to the wild, the non-toxic ammunition solution was simply not available in time to help the historic wild population. Even when good non-toxic alternatives become available, there remains the political problem of ensuring that these alternatives become the only ammunition types used in areas of concern.

The third alternative – providing clean carcasses for the wild population – was the one actually tried when the lead poisoning threat became clear in the mid 1980s. However, from the start we believed this solution was likely to fail because of the poor results that Sandy Wilbur had had in getting consistent use of carcasses by wild condors in the 1970s. Nevertheless, we supported the feeding program for whatever benefits it might provide. Concerted efforts to feed wild condors with clean carcasses began on Hudson Ranch in the spring of 1985. However, as will be described in Chapter 14, these efforts did not result in a strong dependency on the clean food provided. Although carcasses were made continuously available on this ranch and were used to some extent by condors, the wild population largely shifted, as was traditional, to feeding on hunter-shot deer in the Tehachapis during the fall of 1985. Efforts were then started to offer clean carcasses in the Tehachapis, but these attracted very few condors. Moreover, in the late fall one of the very birds that was most frequent at the clean carcasses on Hudson (SBF) came down with a fatal exposure to lead, very likely from deer remains in the Tehachapis. Clearly the feeding program was not an adequate answer to the threat.

Collisions

Collisions with overhead wires and turbines are another mortality factor susceptible to control. In fact recent research indicates that bird strikes can be greatly reduced by conspicuous markers that can be attached to powerlines (Beaulaurier 1981; Koops and de Jong 1981; Brown and Drewien 1995). However, the expense of attaching such markers to lines is substantial, and local power companies in California indicated their reluctance to bear these costs, in part because marker installation would constitute a recognition of their liability for collision deaths of condors.

Since powerlines stretched across many areas of the historic condor range, and since essentially no information was available on which particular lines might pose the most significant threats to the species, it would have been difficult to design an effective and economical line-marking program. Powerline collisions have proved to be the major known source of mortality in releases of captive-reared condors to the wild, but this result may stem in large part from behavioral tendencies of the first birds released to gravitate toward human structures. This problem may be substantially reduced in the future without recourse to line markers, especially by releases of parent-reared birds and aversive conditioning of birds with hot-wired poles and buildings, as will be discussed in Chapter 17.

In the context of the 1980s there was no good information on the frequency of collisions in the wild population, although we suspected from studies of other large birds, that this could have been a significant factor. Some studies on the effects of markers on lines had been run by that time, but markers were not a solution that could be proposed with any credibility without some information on which specific lines posed significant threats. Alternative suggestions, such as putting powerlines underground, would have been prohibitively expensive and beyond any practicality. We take the threat of powerline collisions very seriously and consider it to be one of the principal threats that needs to be addressed in release efforts, but there was not much that could be done about it during the period the original wild population still existed. In the long term, what strategies may be necessary to keep collisions at an acceptably low level may vary from release area to release area.

Cyanide poisoning

After the death of a condor from cyanide poisoning in late 1983, the U.S. Fish and Wildlife Service placed a temporary ban on use of cyanide traps for coyote control in condor range. This ban was lifted in 1985 on the assumption that risks might be reduced to acceptable levels by requiring that cyanide traps be set in single arrays only. In Chapter 12 we discussed our dissatisfaction with the logical basis for this ruling, and our fears that such trapping may still represent a significant threat to condors where it is permitted. Fortunately, M-44 cyanide traps were banned in the state of California in late 1998 by a voter initiative, although this does not affect use of these devices elsewhere.

Shooting

So long as guns are legal and widespread in use there will be risks of condors being shot. Most previous researchers have focused on this threat as likely the most important threat to the condor, and although we believe it may not be as important as lead poisoning and may be substantially overrepresented as a mortality source in historical records, we also consider it still to be a significant threat. In practical terms, the solution to this threat may lie mainly in establishing no-hunting reserves and in better education of hunters, although we cannot expect even massive education to reduce the threat to zero. A tremendous amount of education of hunters has already taken place, much of it nonspecific in the form of endless wildlife films on TV. The hunters of today are generally more discriminating than the hunters of several decades ago (for a graphic account of hunters of that era see McMillan 1968). The condor program of the 1980s received extensive media publicity that undoubtedly led to better abilities of hunters to recognize the species and much better understanding and sympathy of hunters for the plight of the species.

We had no direct evidence of condor shootings in the 1980s, although SBF was carrying shot in her tissues when she died in 1986. Nevertheless, there may have been some losses to shooting during that period. Unfortunately, the practicality of blanket shooting bans was very low, as discussed above. The condor program never recommended such an approach in any era.

Whether viable condor populations can be sustained in regions where hunting is legal and where it is limited to non-toxic ammunition, is a question that cannot be answered with presently available data. Although we suspect this may be possible if hunting can be closely coupled with intensive hunter education efforts, it remains an open question.

Habitat Preservation

No species can exist without adequate amounts of the habitat to which it is adapted, and it is a fundamental truism of conservation that the great majority of endangered species are threatened mainly by habitat loss or modification. That habitat limitations were a major problem for the California Condor was a basic premise of conservation efforts for many years, reflected in a major emphasis on sanctuary establishment and efforts to create multiple wilderness areas within the range of the species. As a "creature of wilderness," the condor was perceived to be threatened primarily by the loss of wilderness. The solution to its woes seemingly had to include actions to prevent degradation of undisturbed habitat important to the species and to prevent human access to secure sanctuary areas. In particular, habitat preservation was assumed to be the most pressing conservation need of the condor by Koford, Miller, the McMillans, and the FOE alliance. Most other individuals and organizations have likewise considered habitat conservation to be an essential element of condor conservation, although not always to the extent advocated by the foregoing parties.

Major habitat preservation actions in condor range through the early 1990s are listed below, as tabulated in part by Wilbur (1978b) and Jurek (1983):

1937 – Establishment of 485 ha Sisquoc Condor Sanctuary in Los Padres National Forest.

1947 – Sespe Condor Sanctuary of 14,000 ha established in Los Padres National Forest.

1951 – Sespe Condor Sanctuary enlarged to 21,450 ha, including a prohibition on surface entry in most critical condor areas.

1964 – Creation of 60,370 ha San Rafael Wilderness Area in Los Padres National Forest.

1969 – Acquisition of 31 ha San Cayetano inholdings for Sespe Condor Sanctuary by U.S. Forest Service.

1970 – Secretary of the Interior places a moratorium on all oil and gas leasing in the Sespe Sanctuary.

1970 – Secretary of the Interior takes a stand against Sespe Water Project, because of anticipated impacts on condors.

1970 – U.S. Bureau of Land Management places a moratorium on all mineral leasing activities within areas delineated as especially important to condor survival.

1971 – U.S. Forest Service prepares a habitat management plan for the condor setting guidelines for management of condor habitat on National Forest lands.

1971 – Acquisition of 65 ha Huff's Hole condor area in San Luis Obispo County by the Nature Conservancy and the U.S. Forest Service.

1972 – Firearms closure of Sespe Sanctuary and adjacent condor habitat instituted by Los Padres National Forest supervisor.

1973 – California State Legislature prohibits low aircraft flights over Sespe Sanctuary.

1973 – Acquisition of 130 ha Green Cabins inholding in Sespe Sanctuary by the National Audubon Society.

1975 – Acquisition of Coldwater Canyon tract inholding in Sespe Sanctuary by the California Department of Fish and Game.

1975 – Acquisition of the 728 ha Hopper Mountain National Wildlife Refuge adjacent to Sespe Sanctuary by the U.S. Fish and Wildlife Service as condor feeding habitat.

1976 – Designation of California Condor Critical Habitats by Secretary of the Interior.

1976 – Acquisition of 63 ha Squaw Flat inholding of Sespe Sanctuary by the Forest Service.

1978 – Creation of 67,715 ha Ventana Wilderness Area and 8,775 ha Santa Lucia Wilderness Area, in Los Padres National Forest.

1981 – Nature Conservancy and U.S. Forest Service complete purchases of 126 ha of private parcels of condor nesting habitat.

1981 – Acquisition by Wildlife Conservation Board of a 235 ha private parcel in the Blue Ridge condor roosting area for the Department of Fish and Game.

1983 – Acquisition of 45 ha Cottrell Flat and Willett Hot Springs inholdings in the Los Padres National Forest by the U.S. Forest Service.

1983 – Acquisition of 354 ha in the Blue Ridge condor roosting area by the U.S. Fish and Wildlife Service.

1983   Acquisition of 65 ha of the Elkhorn Plain by the Department of Fish and Game.

1984 – Acquisition of 133 ha Oak Flat and Ten Sycamore Flat properties for the Los Padres National Forest by the U.S. Forest Service.

1984 – Acquisition of 356 ha Peck Ranch for Blue Ridge condor area by the Department of Fish and Game

1984 – Creation of 28,790 ha Dick Smith Wilderness Area in Los Padres National Forest.

1985 – Acquisition of 194 ha Indian Creek parcel for the Los Padres National Forest by the U.S. Forest Service.

1985–87 – Acquisition of 5478 ha Hudson Ranch and adjacent properties to become Bitter Creek National Wildlife Refuge by the U.S. Fish and Wildlife Service.

1992 – Creation of 88,910 ha Sespe Wilderness Area, 15,440 ha Chumash Wilderness Area, 11,980 ha Matilija Wilderness Area, 5,706 ha Garcia Wilderness Area, and 5,868 ha Silver Peak Wilderness Area within the Los Padres National Forest; also expansion of the San Rafael Wilderness Area by 18,780 ha and Ventana Wilderness Area by 15,380 ha.

1992 – Adoption of Wild and Scenic River designation for 50.7 km of Sespe Creek, 53 km of the Sisquoc River, and 31.4 km of the Big Sur River.

Despite these considerable efforts, the condor population continued to decline. As studies progressed in the 1980s, we obtained no clear evidence that the remnant population was suffering from habitat limitations per se. There were no signs that birds were having difficulty finding enough food and no signs that there was any shortage of adequate nest sites, roost sites, or other habitat features. Had there been significant problems in these spheres we would have expected to see problems such as low breeding effort or low breeding success. No such problems were materializing. Instead the main problems were turning out to be mortality factors that evidently were keeping the population depressed below a level where habitat limitations could exercise any significant effects.

The species was clearly not a habitat specialist and there appeared still to be ample supplies of the basic habitat resources needed by the relatively few birds left. Furthermore, many of the habitat resources being utilized by the species – in particular, foraging habitats – were not wilderness habitats in the first place. They were highly modified grassland habitats under intensive human management for grazing purposes. Nesting habitat was largely unchanged from early times and was not under any significant threat of being lost, as it was almost entirely under U.S. Forest Service jurisdiction and much of it was protected by sanctuary status. Foraging habitat, however, was almost entirely privately owned ranchlands that were being progressively converted into development projects. If problems with insufficient habitat were to develop for the species, they would most likely be problems of insufficient grassland foraging habitat.

Studer's habitat trend study

Although there appeared to be ample foraging habitat still in existence for the remnant population in the 1980s, ranching was not a land use that could long survive in regions of expanding urbanization. Some foraging regions, for example the Simi Valley–Moorpark region, had been converted almost completely to residential developments. Even if food supplies were not currently limiting for the species, they could be expected to become so at some point in the future if ranching continued to decline, especially if condor numbers were ever to increase. Thus there was a clear need to study factors affecting ranching to design means for ensuring adequate amounts of high-quality foraging habitat into the future.

To examine trends in ranching practices in detail, the Audubon Society sponsored an interview study by Cynthia Studer in the early 1980s. This study was focused on Kern County cattle ranches in particular, and considered a variety of factors potentially important to condors. These included trends in stocking rates, proportions of ranches that practiced cow-calf vs stocker (non-breeding herd) operations, trends in cattle mortality, proportions of ranches that allowed hunting activities, and proportions practicing various forms of predator or pest control.

The picture emerging from Studer's (1983) study was that a progressive loss of ranchlands to other land uses was continuing, but that reasonably stable food supplies for condors existed on ranches that continued to graze cattle. Kern County ranchers were not seeing dramatic changes in mortality rates of their cattle and made few efforts to remove carcasses of dead livestock from the range. Most, however, did report chronic problems with illegal hunting on their lands and most felt driven to practice various forms of predator and pest control, especially directed at ground squirrels. There was no trend toward stocker operations (which offer relatively little food for condors) from cow-calf operations, and the major potential threat to condors, apart from risks of shooting and poisoning, appeared to be the basic economic difficulties that ranchers were experiencing in staying in business. The Williamson Act, giving significant tax benefits to ranchers keeping their land in cattle operations, was clearly a major factor in delaying the loss of ranchlands to other uses.

The Hudson Ranch issue

The principal specific habitat issue that was to surface in the 1980s concerned the potential loss of the Hudson Ranch, a roughly 50 square kilometer area of grassland in the southwestern San Joaquin Valley foothills. In late 1982, just as we began to accumulate data indicating that this ranch was being used with frequency by condors, plans were announced by the owners for its development into a residential-agricultural complex. Efforts to spare this ranch from development were immediately spearheaded by the National Audubon Society, which lobbied Congress to appropriate monies for its purchase. At that point, the principal problems of the condor were still largely speculative and there was no reason to consider Hudson Ranch as anything other than an important and positive component of the foraging range. We fully supported the original Audubon Society initiative on purchase of Hudson Ranch, although we would later come to see the acquisition of this ranch more as a diversion from immediate crucial conservation actions for the species than as a fundamental near-term benefit.

Once the campaign to acquire Hudson Ranch was underway, there was no turning back. The image of the ranch ultimately became unrecognizable as more and more arguments of less and less merit were used to justify the purchase. In the view of its main supporters, the ranch became not just one of a number of heavily used foraging areas, but an ideal and finally "the only" place where it made any sense to release captive condors to the wild (Anonymous 1985). As the ranch was nearly 30 km from the nearest known condor nest site and was surrounded by other ranches on which a variety of activities dangerous to condors were practiced, this claim was more than a little excessive. The ranch also came to be touted as the ideal place to subsidize the wild population with clean food, thus effectively countering lead poisoning problems. Claims were made that condors were getting *most* of their food from Hudson during intensive carcass provisioning efforts of 1985.

As we gained specific knowledge of the threats faced by the species, however, we came to realize that Hudson Ranch was in fact one of the poorest places to release captives. Careful analysis of condor feeding records on Hudson in 1985 further revealed that the condor population was gaining only a minor portion of its food resources from the ranch (see following chapter). Nevertheless, the ranch was ultimately acquired as the Bitter Creek National Wildlife Refuge.

Elements of the campaign to acquire Hudson Ranch were reminiscent of earlier campaigns to establish the Sespe Sanctuary and a Sespe-Frazier Wilderness Area. The biology of the species once again became subverted to the goal of habitat acquisition, and dogma replaced good data as supporters proclaimed the critical nature of the acquisition to survival of the species. In practical terms this may be the only way to acquire large sanctuaries, but in the case of Hudson Ranch, the disparity between reality and propaganda became especially great.

Possibly the most detrimental aspect of the ranch-acquisition campaign was not so much the inaccurate perceptions of the condor used to promote the acquisition, as the fact that the campaign proved to be a major force working against the establishment of an adequate captive population of condors. In the fiscally conservative atmosphere of the mid 1980s, the U.S. Fish and Wildlife Service put off the actual purchase of Hudson Ranch even after monies had been appropriated by Congress for this purpose, and even into late 1985 there were doubts that the purchase would take place. At the same time many of us were urging that it was essential that the last few condors be captured to ensure the viability of a captive population. The National Audubon Society clearly feared that bringing the last birds into captivity would be a death knell for efforts to acquire Hudson Ranch. This fear was a major factor driving its efforts to prevent capture of the last birds (see Chapter 15).

In effect, the last few birds were being "held hostage" in the wild in part to ensure completion of the purchase. Although the last birds were ultimately captured, and Hudson Ranch was also ultimately acquired, the events of this period provide another condor example of how preserve creation can sometimes be at odds with other aspects of species conservation.

Only the future will reveal whether the purchase of Hudson Ranch was a major positive step for condor conservation. Presumably the outcome will depend on many factors, especially trends in management of adjacent ranches and success in conquering the lead-poisoning problem. Two very important developments in addition to the habitat acquisitions listed above that could lead to a major positive role of Hudson Ranch in the future have been the recent acquisition of the adjacent San Emigdio Ranch for conservation purposes by the Wildlands Conservancy, and the creation of a Carrizo Plains Natural Area on the opposite side of Hudson Ranch. However, hunting is presently an accepted activity for the Carrizo Plains Natural Area and ultimately will have to be phased out or restricted to nontoxic ammunition if the region is to become viable condor habitat. Efforts to restrict hunting to nontoxic ammunitions on the Carrizo Plains Natural Area are currently underway, although the matter is not yet fully resolved. On the minus side, plans for development of the Tejón Ranch (on the east side of the San Emigdio Ranch) may lead to eventual loss of that huge ranch as condor habitat. In the long run, the condor will clearly need foraging habitat somewhere if it is to exist in viable wild populations, although it is not yet clear that the last range of the species will be an area that can sustain the species in the future. The following chapter will provide more detail on the intense controversies surrounding the Hudson Ranch issue and on how they affected the establishment of a viable captive population.

Summary

Taken together, the various efforts made in the 1980s to help the wild condor population were clearly not enough to reverse the decline. In fact the decline of the wild population not only continued unabated, but actually accelerated during this period. By 1985 it had become clear that there was no possibility of salvaging the wild population by any means, and the only hope left for the species was captive breeding in the short term. As we will detail in the next chapter, the process of establishing a captive population, although it did subtract some individuals from the wild, was not the major cause of the continuing decline up to 1985. After that point, however, it was the major factor in the final loss of the wild population, consciously and deliberately.

CHAPTER FOURTEEN

Formation of a Captive Flock

Of all field observations of condors ever made, possibly the most significant and positive were those of the CC nesting pair dating from February 1982, although at the start, the events involved seemed only the greatest of tragedies. Fortunately, the events were fully documented by the research team, or their positive aspects would never have been realized. Our perennial opponents, the Friends of the Earth (FOE) alliance, took delight in announcing that the best thing that could ever happen to a condor nest would be that it would never be found or observed by the condor program. But if this nesting pair had not been watched closely, it is entirely possible that there might be no viable population of condors left today.

On duty observing the condor pair in question was Jack Ingram, a British expatriate sound engineer who split his time between condors and overseeing the acoustics of concerts at the Universal Amphitheater in Los Angeles. Jack had joined the condor research program after we came across him independently observing the same condor pair in a remote location in April 1981. We concluded his skills in having found the pair on his own and his obvious fascination with the species might be major assets to the program. Bringing him in as a collaborator proved extremely beneficial. Jack's incredibly sharp eyes, wilderness savvy, and gourmet field cooking were to become famous in the years to follow.

On the morning of February 26, Jack had been crouched since dawn in a well-hidden blind some 600 m from the pair's nest cave where he had been watching the events of the morning with increasing gloom. The pair had been incubating their egg of the year for nearly two weeks, but things were not going smoothly. The male was a devoted father, but alas he carried his parental commitments to the extreme of repeatedly excluding his mate from taking her normal turns in incubation. He acted as if he believed his mate's only role was to produce the egg, and after that he was in total charge. He chased her off again and again, treating her as some sort of threat rather than as a partner in breeding efforts. Only when he was presumably driven by thirst and hunger to make trips to the foraging grounds, sometimes after more than a week of incubation, did he relinquish the egg to her care. His mate was as determined as he, however, and persisted steadily in her approaches, waiting for a chance to gain control of the egg.

In 1980 the same pair had nested without any arguments over incubation rights and successfully fledged a youngster that by late 1986 was to become the last condor left in the wild. Now they were nesting again, but everything seemed to be going wrong. In addition to the behavioral conflicts, the nest site they had chosen, unlike their spacious nest cave of 1980, was a cramped, shallow cave with a floor slanting to the outside and a rough rocky apron in front dropping steeply over a precipitous cliff about a meter from the entrance. A more miserable nest site would be hard to imagine. It gave little protection from the elements, none from the sharp eyes of local ravens, and none from the inexorable force of gravity.

Early on this fateful February 26, the female, after being repeatedly rebuffed, had finally managed to inch close enough to her incubating mate that she was able to pull the egg out from under him with her bill. But in the process, the egg rolled uncertainly out of the cave and out onto the apron in front. Fortunately, it stopped rolling before plunging over the edge, apparently blocked by some irregularity on the ledge. The male, possibly worn out from conflicts with his mate, remained where he was, and his mate settled down to warm the egg on the cliff edge. Would he try to regain the egg or would he now leave? Would she be able to roll it back uphill into the cave when he left, if he ever did, or would she not even try? Could she possibly control the egg well enough not to lose it over the edge of the cliff? The situation seemed excessively risky, and things quickly got worse.

The local pair of ravens spotted the egg and began to move in closer and closer, at first landing nearby, then walking right in amongst the condors in insolent confidence. The female condor rose to lunge at a raven, the male lunged at the female, and the egg began rolling again, down the steeper slope toward the edge.

Jack's notes recorded the inevitable: "It just seemed to wobble to the edge, bounced twice in the first meter or so, then smashed about two meters down the brown cliff on a prominence in a sheet of yellow yolk" In a moment, the pair's reproductive attempt was over, and one of the few hopes for an increase in the condor population for the year had been lost. It was a bitter outcome, but at that time we lacked all state clearance to intervene in such situations. The condors seemed like their own worst enemies, both in their choice of a terrible nest site and in their inability to share nesting duties smoothly.

After breakage of the egg, both the condors and the ravens descended to feed on the remains, through the rest of the morning. This was indeed a melancholy aftermath, but at least the condors salvaged some nutritional benefits from the disaster.

The loss of the egg raised additional concerns. Would this pair's bickering behavior prove to be a curse in all future breeding attempts? In 1980, similar aggressive behavior of the male toward the female had developed only after their egg had hatched and did not threaten survival of their chick. Now, with vigorous aggression breaking out immediately after egg-laying, we were worried that the pair might never again be able to incubate an egg successfully to hatching.

Risky nest caves helped stimulate formation of a captive condor flock. **Above**, the floor of the cave chosen for nesting by the CC pair in early 1982 sloped dangerously to the outside, and the egg rolled over the edge 12 days after laying. Fortunately this event led to proof of replacement-clutching in the species and to the deliberate use of replacement-clutching to form a captive flock at minimal cost of individuals to the wild population. **Below**, another site with similar risks of egg loss was the third nest cave used by the CC pair in 1984. Positioned dangerously close to the cliff edge, the egg at this site was also under severe threat from ravens nesting only 10 feet (3 m) distant. It was taken into captivity shortly after laying and produced Pismo, one of the most productive breeders in the captive flock.

Continued observations in the days that followed, however, brought a new and more optimistic perspective to the situation. The pair did not immediately leave their nesting canyon, but remained to resume pre-nesting activities. The very next day, the male was observed making courtship displays to the female, extending his drooped neck and wings and strutting his legs up and down. It was still relatively early in the breeding season, and the situation offered perhaps the best opportunity we might ever have of determining whether the species might be able to relay after egg loss.

Most species of birds will relay after nest failure if it happens early enough in the breeding season. Although this had never been conclusively documented in the California Condor, several potential cases had been noted (Harrison and Kiff 1980, Snyder and Hamber 1985). We strongly suspected that the absence of conclusive evidence was simply due to the fact that the species had never been watched closely enough. If replacement laying could be rigorously documented, it would offer a potential for establishing a captive flock in a way that would stress the wild population the least, and could be the means to break the political impasse over establishing a captive flock. With this in mind, we continued to maintain steady distant coverage of the CC pair, despite our limited manpower.

Fortunately, the pair did not move far, so we did not have any difficulty in keeping track of events. In fact, much to our relief, they soon returned to the site they had used successfully in 1980, although they also investigated a number of other caves in the same cliff system. Copulations resumed over the weeks that followed, and we became steadily more hopeful that the pair would indeed relay. They did, and as we had hoped, the site for their second egg proved to be the 1980 nest site. The egg appeared on April 7, almost exactly 40 days after the loss of the first egg.

Unfortunately, the aggressive behavior of the male resumed immediately after the second egg appeared. We again watched him making endless chases of the female away from the nest site, sometimes continuing for a kilometer down the canyon, followed by his return to the nest site with the female not far behind.

We were not alone in observing these senseless chases. The local ravens watched as well, perhaps as puzzled as we were by the aberrant behavior, but nonetheless appreciative of the easy opportunity it gave them for a meal. On April 29, as the male was again chasing his mate down the canyon, one of the ravens entered the condor nest and quickly drove its bill into the egg. This act finished off the condors' second breeding effort of the year in a definitive way, but there is a good chance the egg was no longer viable at that point in any event. Periods as long as several hours were going by with the egg not being warmed. In most species of birds, such fitful incubation would result in the death of the embryos in their eggs.

The loss of the second egg of the CC pair in 1982, like the loss of their first egg, was an undeniably tragic development. But with full publicity given to these events, it became very clear to all interested parties that not only would condors lay replacement eggs, but that their eggs had a very significant chance of being lost naturally in the wild. These two considerations were actually very positive political ingredients in the development of a strategy for establishing a captive flock through deliberate replacement-clutching of wild pairs.

Gaining Authorization for Replacement-Clutching and Other Intensive Measures

The development of permit clearance to begin deliberate replacement-clutching did not just happen automatically following the events just described. These events certainly provided a compelling argument for the comparative advantages of taking eggs to establish a captive flock and dramatized the risks of not intervening with troubled pairs. But it took some additional events, some of which were quite unrelated to permit questions, for the program finally to gain permission to take first eggs from the wild population the following year. These events are worth recounting, as they well illustrate how both chance and logic can sometimes collaborate to produce important progress.

We have already discussed the importance of the first accurate census figures for the wild population that were also being obtained during 1982. These figures clearly indicated that the species was in desperate shape and that continued reliance on traditional conservation strategies held no hope of success.

In addition, during late summer of 1982 the program gained permission on an emergency basis to capture a nestling condor whose father (SSM) had disappeared unaccountably during the mid-nestling period. The chick's feeding rates had dropped significantly and its chances for survival were questionable with only a single adult left to care for it. The capture of this chick, once it was cleared by state and federal authorities, took place without complications even though it became ominously scheduled for Friday, August 13. Had we been superstitious we might have decided to report in sick that day, recalling our last experience in chick-handling in 1980. But this time, the chick was handled only briefly in the process of getting it into a sky kennel, and a veterinarian was on hand to aid against any unforeseen difficulties. All aspects of the operation proceeded smoothly, with Phil Ensley of San Diego Zoo doing most of the handling. Here at last was a concrete demonstration that not all intensive activities might be lethal for the species.

Surprisingly, the male parent of the chick, SSM, proved not to have perished after all and reappeared after having disappeared for several weeks. We have always wondered if he had not been the victim of some temporarily debilitating accident, sickness, or poisoning event to have abandoned nesting activities in mid breeding season. In any event, his mysterious disappearance proved fortunate in allowing the program its first opportunity to move back toward intensive activities.

Thus there were three major positive developments that set the stage for resumption of full-scale intensive activities by the program: accurate censusing results, proof of natural replacement-clutching, and success in the emergency taking of a chick into captivity. In spite of these developments, we were still handcuffed by a state permit that allowed essentially nothing of an intensive nature to occur.

All through the last half of 1980, all of 1981, and most of 1982, the staff of the Condor Research Center had worked hard to reverse the denial of state permission to conduct intensive conservation and research activities with the condor. Trapping and radio-tracking methods were evaluated closely and tested with surrogate species, including the Andean Condor in Peru and Turkey Vultures in California. In addition, Mike Wallace was getting excellent results with releases of captive-reared Andean Condors to the wild in Peru. Meanwhile both the Zoological Society of San Diego and the Los Angeles Zoo were busy constructing state-of-the art facilities to house captive condors. Yet permit application after permit application to the California Fish and Game Commission fell victim to contrary recommendations of the Department of Fish and Game. It was not that all intensive activities were totally forbidden, but that the restrictions were so severe that nothing more than token activities would be possible at best.

The permit granted in 1982, for example, was still focused on capture of a mate for Topatopa as a gesture toward captive breeding. Radio-telemetry could be initiated only if a candidate bird trapped as a potential mate turned out to be the wrong sex (i.e., male). These minimal steps would not be of any substantial benefit for the species relative to the actual needs for captive breeding and radio-telemetry. Topatopa, as a human-oriented, long-term captive, was probably the worst possible candidate male that one could propose for captive breeding in the first place. Relegating the initiation of radio-telemetry to a roll-of-the-dice sex outcome meant that there might be only a roughly 50% chance that even one bird might be radioed during the year. Although these tough restrictions might have seemed a viable middle-ground political move to the Fish and Game Department, they were a continuing programmatic disaster from any rational biological perspective.

Most staff of the Condor Research Center were ready to give up in despair. The species was surely fast losing ground, and again for another year there was virtually no clearance to do the things that obviously needed to be done. Further, it would be the Condor Research Center, not the California Department of Fish and Game, that would take full blame when the species went under. The Department was proving to be little more than a roadblock standing in the way of an effective program, despite its early agreement to be a partner.

With such dismal prospects in view, the National Audubon Society announced in the summer of 1982 that it was about to withdraw from the program if a reasonable state permit was not forthcoming. The president of the society, Russell Peterson, contacted Charles Fullerton, the head of the Department of Fish and Game, to persuade him of the seriousness of the Audubon Society's concerns. Despite some assurances from Fullerton, there was no clear indication that Peterson's efforts had been enough to yield a satisfactory permit.

Instead Fullerton announced that the emphasis of the program should be moving toward habitat preservation concerns, and that he was going ahead with plans for the development of a public conference in Santa Barbara to discuss such matters. But by the time this conference actually took place in November of 1982, much had changed on the political front, and visions of movement of the program toward habitat concerns had largely evaporated. Despite being attended by essentially all living opponents of the condor program, the conference ended up confirming the need for intensive efforts. The only question left unresolved was just how fast radio-telemetry and captive-breeding operations would be implemented.

Perhaps one of the most crucial developments mobilizing this evolution was an apparently unrelated chain of events that brought new political allies into the fray, including members of the California Fish and Game Commission. As leader of the Fish and Wildlife Service's condor program in California, Noel was asked to make an official inspection of the Los Angeles Zoo's prospective facilities for housing captive California Condors. Though there were by then increasing doubts that the birds for these facilities might ever materialize, Noel made a first inspection on February 1, 1982. Unfortunately, he found that the cages, although of an excellent design, still contained numerous scrap metal fragments in their nest-box substrates and outdoor flight areas. He informed the keeper involved that these metal fragments would all have to be removed before the facility could be cleared for occupancy by condors. Ingestion of foreign objects was a common cause of death in zoo animals. In fact, William Finley's captive condor of 1906, General, was ultimately a victim of ingestion of a foreign object. Sharp metallic objects, such as nails and bits of cage screening, had the potential for lethal perforation of a bird's digestive system, and what is more, condors were known to have a propensity for ingesting shiny objects.

In early April, Noel was again asked to inspect the zoo's cages. This time he brought a substrate sifter to make sure that no metallic objects might still be present. Unfortunately, he still found a few nails and other pieces of metal on this second inspection, and he again informed the keeper involved that a completely thorough search must be made to remove all such objects before use of the cages could be approved. This whole sequence of events was repeated still a third time on August 30. At this point Noel wrote a report to his superiors at Patuxent questioning the commitment of the zoo to the sort of operational standards that would be necessary for condor maintenance.

Evidently, the reasons why Noel was continuing to refuse to OK the cages were not transmitted up the line in the Los Angeles Zoo hierarchy, and in early October 1982 he found himself invited to a session with officials of the zoo to explain and discuss the situation. This meeting proved to be of tremendous importance, not only in solving the cage-safety problem, but also in solving many other problems faced by the overall program. Attending the meeting were Marcia Hobbs, the zoo's chief fund-raiser, and Ed Harrison, a board member who had once been a field companion of Carl Koford. Both held a consuming passion for condors and a strong desire to see the condor program become a success, and as a result of the meeting both became thoroughly involved in finding ways to restore sanity to the program. Together with Warren Thomas, the director of the zoo, they proved to be an awesome force. Thus, in leading to the mobilization of some powerful political allies, the offending pieces of cage metal can be plausibly credited as producing major progress in the program.

Marcia Hobbs, as it turned out, was both the goddaughter of Ronald Reagan and a close friend of one of the Fish and Game Commissioners, William Burke. And although we were still acting under the restriction that we were not to make approaches to commissioners, such restrictions did not apply to Marcia. She took it upon herself to discuss matters with Mr. Burke, and within hours of the meeting to discuss cage problems at the Los Angeles zoo, Noel found himself invited to Burke's home. At this meeting, Burke expressed amazement when he learned that personnel of the Condor Research Center had been forbidden by Washington officials to contact him and other commissioners. He indicated that this lack of interaction had handicapped the Commission in making the best possible decisions with respect to condors. Noel had a chance to outline the progress being made in the program and the permit concerns of the Research Center, including the pressing needs to conduct an adequate radio-telemetry program and to launch an adequate captive breeding operation, primarily through replacement-clutching of wild pairs. It was clear from the meeting that Burke was sympathetic to the arguments and concerns expressed, and he promised immediate efforts to correct the deficiencies of the existing permit.

Several days later, Brian Kahn, another of the Commissioners, put in a phone call to the Condor Research Center, and Noel and John Ogden had an opportunity to present the same case. Then, shortly thereafter, Charles Fullerton suddenly announced his support for a broad new condor permit which would initiate a real captive breeding program through replacement clutching of all wild pairs in 1983 and a radio-telemetry program that would involve significant numbers of birds. A new and more liberal permit became a reality at the November meeting of the Commission, initiating a new and extraordinarily productive era in relationships with the state of California. Equally important, the condor program had now gained the very active participation of officials of the Los Angeles Zoo in solving political problems. This proved to be of crucial positive importance in many other issues in the years ahead, both at the state and federal levels. Although the Los Angeles Zoo certainly had its own interests at stake in many of these issues, it also became an extraordinarily effective political force in aiding many other aspects of the program. Likewise, the contributions of the Zoological Society of San Diego to the program were far from limited to issues affecting its own domain. Without the efforts of both these institutions, the prospects for ultimate success of the program would have been minimal.

Replacement-clutching of Wild Pairs

The first year of egg pickups, 1983, brought many challenges from the weather. It was a severe El Niño year with almost continuous late winter and spring rains, broken only by ephemeral periods of clearing. As the pickups demanded conditions benign enough to allow safe helicopter access to the back country, we found ourselves wrestling with major logistic problems in coordinating the efforts. For one egg laid in Santa Barbara County we even had problems getting a pickup crew to the site on the ground because of flood waters of the Santa Ynez River, and were eventually obliged to evacuate the crew by boat.

Fortunately, we had the skilled assistance of Rob Ramey in coordinating logistics and the able collaboration of Aspen Helicopters of Oxnard in conducting the pickups. In every instance, Aspen responded quickly and surely to our radioed requests despite cramped landing conditions in some cases and marginal weather in others. Aspen was centrally located to most nesting areas and was able to maneuver a chopper to most pickup sites well within an hour of an alert. From there it flew the eggs directly to the San Diego Zoo for artificial incubation. Aspen Helicopters had evolved from a previous firm named Condor Helicopters, and they took a special interest in the program, donating half the costs of transport to the cause. In effect, Aspen's Charlie McLaughlin, Jim Dalton, and Rick Throckmorton became full functioning members of the condor recovery effort.

The very first egg pickup was by far the most worrisome. We could scarcely afford any slip-ups, considering the length of time it had taken to get to this point. But we had no choice but to move ahead, not really knowing how the birds would respond to egg-taking operations, how well the incubator suitcase would function, and how well we would be able to coordinate helicopter operations. Bill Toone from the San Diego Zoo joined us for the first attempt and suffered through all its agonies.

The first site involved was a nest of the CC pair that was tucked in a narrow gorge, necessitating a substantial ascent from the nest cave to the nearest possible helipad site. The route to the site did not entail any rope work, but the only approach was along a ledge to the rear of the site from which we could learn of activities of the birds only through radio contact with observers on an opposing ridge.

For the actual process of removing the egg we faced a dilemma in that a condor normally incubates an egg by resting it on its feet. If abruptly startled, an incubating bird can

Egg-taking operations entailed construction of helipads and finding a safe way to access each nest. It also demanded close coordination of events with personnel of Aspen Helicopters. **Above**, during the first egg pickup in 1983, Bill Toone (left) and Noel (right) arrive at the helipad with the egg in an incubator suitcase that was earlier used for pickups of Whooping Crane eggs in Canada. Egg temperature in the suitcase was regulated by hot water bottles. **Below**, for pickup of the second egg of the SS1 pair in 1984, the helicopter is met by a field crew including Fred Sibley, who had discovered the nest location and later gave the resulting chick its name – Squapuni.

spill the egg across the nest floor as it quickly rises to a standing position. As mentioned in the preceding chapter, Kelly Truesdale once even witnessed an egg come sailing out of a nest cave when he flushed a bird too abruptly (McMillan 1968). At all costs, we wanted to avoid such an outcome, so our first strategy was to wait for a natural incubation exchange between adults when the egg would be unattended.

Unfortunately, incubation exchanges between adults often come only at several-day intervals, and with the El Niño conditions of 1983, we could not count on exchanges taking place under weather conditions that would allow helicopter access. After waiting fruitlessly for several days for a natural exchange, through weather conditions that varied from bad to worse, we finally came to the conclusion that we were being overly cautious. Once the weather finally cleared, we decided to try a different technique by which we could control the timing of a pickup. The alternative tried, and used successfully on this and all succeeding pickups, was to move in slowly toward the nest site from the rear, talking just loud enough to catch the attention of the incubating bird, but not so loud as to cause it to panic. As watched by observers in radio contact on the opposing ridge, the bird responded exactly as we had hoped by rising slowly from the egg then standing curiously near the cave entrance, with no evident risk of egg damage. We then were able to move quickly to the cave, flushing the bird in the process.

By the time of our last egg pickups several years later, the process of encouraging a condor to leave its egg nonviolently had evolved into a ceremony that we all agreed should be retained intact. Steve Kimple, our state representative on the field team and a master of story telling, was the designated condor flusher and would slowly approach the nests, gently intoning the same sleazy joke to each sitting bird. It was surely the best of all his tales, and Steve always insisted that the only reason the birds would ever get up off their eggs was to hear the punch-line better. While some may question the dignity of these procedures, it was well that the inherent tensions of this stage of a pickup could be relaxed by some means. The instant the incubating bird finally left the nest cave with the egg still safely in place was always a moment of enormous relief.

The final approach to most nest sites involved rope work, usually by Rob Ramey, Dave Clendenen, and Victor Apanius, and ropes were set in place only after incubating birds had left their nest caves. Eggs were handled only with sterile gloves and were quickly placed in a foam-insulated incubator suitcase for transport to the zoo. The suitcase used was the same suitcase from Patuxent that had been used successfully for early Whooping Crane egg pickups and was heated by hot water bottles prepared just before the pickups. Although such paraphernalia now seems quaint and primitive, it worked effectively, and no egg failures can be attributed to apparatus failure.

Still there were many uncertainties and unpredictable developments to contend with. Once an active nest with an egg was confirmed, a suitable nearby level location for constructing a helipad had to be found. Clearing the pad sometimes involved labor through the night to remove the rocks and dense chaparral. An egg pickup crew had to be assembled on short notice, and sometimes trails had to be constructed to allow access to the nest cave. On one pickup in the Sespe Sanctuary, we and the rest of the crew got lost in fog and drizzle trying to get to the site overnight. We wound up tracing a long hard circle through the

Rob Ramey places a condor egg in a transfer case at the CV nest cave of 1984. Eggs were handled only with sterile gloves and usually arrived at the San Diego Zoo within 3 hours of being taken. The chick from this egg proved deformed and inviable, a recurrent problem with chicks of the CV family line.

dense trackless chaparral that ground to a halt when we at last noticed that we were back at a point that we had passed hours earlier. Giving up, we camped in nearby caves and started in anew at dawn.

Perhaps the closest we came to disaster was at a nest site in Santa Barbara County in 1985, where the wind rose to a howling intensity shortly after we had completed removal of an egg but before the helicopter arrived. Jim Dalton was only barely able to land the chopper, and Noel and Jim took off down canyon just moments before conditions became totally impossible for flight. Unfortunately in the haste to leave the area Noel had not fastened his seat belt. Only a half mile from the nest the chopper hit one last turbulent downdraft that "lifted" him and the egg transport case in his hands right to the ceiling, breaking one egg case thermometer in the process. Thankfully, the descent back to seat level was not violent, the egg was unharmed, and it ultimately hatched successfully.

At another pickup in Santa Barbara County in 1985, the high elevation and tight access to the helipad in a narrow gorge made maneuvering extremely nerve-racking. Although Charlie McLaughlin was able to land the chopper without incident, takeoff, with the weight of Noel, Dave Ledig, and a condor egg suitcase added to the payload did not go well – the air was just too thin. As the chopper rose unsteadily from the pad, it suddenly dipped to one side with the blades narrowly missing a huge boulder by only a few feet. The pickup crew in the vicinity dove for what cover they could find, while Charlie managed a desperate reversal of the chopper's orientation, guiding it over some low chapparal on the other side of the pad and down the gorge to safer altitudes, grazing brush in the process. Helicopters were the only feasible way to conduct egg pickups in remote locations, but there were times we would gladly have exchanged them for other alternatives, had there been any.

During the first year of egg pickups, birds were allowed to incubate their eggs naturally for a minimum of three weeks before they were removed for artificial incubation. This gave the eggs a substantial period of natural incubation and avoided the critical period from about day 5 to day 21 of incubation during which embryos would be relatively sensitive to mechanical shaking and vulnerable to damage during transport. However, when hatching success proved 100% under artificial conditions in 1983 and the birds proved to have good potentials for replacement laying in the wild, we changed strategies in subsequent years to take eggs within the first five days of laying to maximize the chances of repeat layings.

This change put a considerable burden on the nest-monitoring team. Condors often inspect many potential nest sites in the weeks before laying, and the sites are often scattered among a number of different canyons, sometimes five or more miles apart. There were no infallible clues indicating which cave would be used for laying, and we were often surprised by the site chosen. The race to confirm the actual nest site and prepare it with a nearby helipad often took several days and left us with little time to spare in pulling off egg pickups within the 5-day deadline.

Despite the difficulties in locating condor nests within a few days of laying, we were nearly always successful, and the strategy of proceeding as fast as possible in taking eggs led to a total of three pairs of condors demonstrating a capacity for triple-clutching within a single breeding season. So under optimal conditions, a single pair subjected to egg removals was theoretically capable of producing nine young in a three-year period, a production similar to that of many songbirds, and an enormous increase over the apparent normal maximum of two young in three years for unmanipulated pairs. Fortunately, it was possible to gain the benefits from a major stimulation of these capacities in both 1983 and 1984, before the catastrophic mortality of the winter of 1984–1985 destroyed nearly every breeding pair in the population.

Details on the results of multiple-clutching wild pairs are given in Table 14, and are reported in part in Snyder and Hamber (1985). Between 1983 and 1986, 16 eggs were taken for artificial incubation from a total of five different pairs (the female was the same bird in two of the five). Thirteen of the eggs produced surviving chicks for a success rate of 81%,

Table 14. Replacement eggs laid by wild California Condor pairs (adapted from Snyder and Hamber 1985).

Pair and year	Egg #	Laying date	Date egg lost or taken	Days until egg lost or taken	Days until replacement	Distance (km) to replacement site
CC (CCF and CCM)						
1982	1	14 Feb	26 Feb	12	40	0.1
	2	7 Apr	29 Apr	22	none laid	—
1983	1	2 Feb	23 Feb	21	35	2.9
	2	30 Mar	8 Apr	—	—	—
1984	1	12 Feb	13 Feb	1	28	0.8
	2	12 Mar	13 Mar	1	31	0.4
	3	13 Apr	16 Apr	3	none laid	—
SS1 (SSF and SSM)						
1983	1	10 Feb	8 Mar	28	(31)	1.1
	2	(6 Apr)	(7 Apr)	(1)	(30)	0.9
	3	7 May	—	—	—	—
1984	1	7 Mar	8 Mar	1	31	3.5
	2	8 Apr	10 Apr	2	none laid	—
SS2 (SSF and REC)						
1986	1	(6 Mar)	(7 Mar)	(1)	(37)	8.0
	2	13 Apr	15 Apr	2	none laid	—
SB (SBF and SBM)						
1981	1	late Feb	late Mar	unknown	approx 1 month	11.5
	2	27 Apr	—	—	—	—
1983	1	31 Mar	26 Apr	26	none laid	—
1984	1	15 Feb	20 Feb	5	27	8.2
	2	18 Mar	20 Mar	2	none laid	—
1985	1	14 Feb	17 Feb	3	26	7.6
	2	15 Mar	19 Mar	4	27	3.5
	3	15 Apr	23 Apr	8	none laid	—
CV (CVF and CVM)						
1984	1	12 Mar	15 Mar	3	none laid	—

Note: values in parenthesis are approximate; CC egg 2 of 1983 taken on Apr 9 was replaced with dummy telemetered egg which was incubated until June 4; CC eggs 1 and 2 of 1982, SS1 egg 2 of 1983, SS2 egg 1 of 1986, and SB egg 1 of 1981 were all lost naturally in the wild; other eggs in column 4 were all placed in artificial incubation; SS egg 3 in 1983 and SB egg 2 in 1981 hatched naturally in the wild.

far exceeding the natural fledging success rate of 40–50% for eggs incubated in the wild. Further, four of the five pairs exhibited a capacity to lay replacement eggs. The single female (CVF) that did not demonstrate replacement-clutching was alive for only one egg-pulling attempt. This attempt took place relatively late in the breeding season, so whether she too might have been capable of replacement-laying was not thoroughly tested. We suspect that she was, as she had earlier produced a chick (PAX) that evidently had fledged very late in 1981, implying it was likely from a replacement egg.

Of the three eggs that did not produce surviving young in captivity, one was apparently a very early embryonic death, another hatched a chick that died shortly afterwards of a yolk-sac infection, and the third produced a physically abnormal and inviable chick with only a partial skull and deformed limbs. None of these failures had any clear relationship with the egg removal and artificial incubation procedures, and it seems likely that all three eggs would also have failed if left in the wild. Fortunately, none of the egg failures occurred during the first year of egg taking, which might have raised political resistance to further replacement-clutching efforts.

The total production of young in 1983, including young hatched in the wild, was six individuals, a massive increase over the average of two young per year that had been produced by the population in the previous three years. Results were even better in 1984, when seven young were produced. But by 1985, the number of egg-laying pairs in the wild had crashed to a single pair. Although this pair was successfully triple-clutched, producing two surviving young, the brief era of massive increases in production by the wild population was over, not because of any failures in replacement-clutching techniques, but because of a simple dearth of breeding birds. The single egg-laying pair of 1985 lost its female to lead-poisoning at the end of the year, but in 1986 a new pair formed among the five surviving birds in the wild and laid two eggs, one of which produced a fledgling in captivity (the female of this pair had lost her former mate over the winter of 1984–1985).

As detailed in Table 14, the interval between losing or taking eggs and laying replacement eggs ranged from about 26 to 40 days (mean of 31 days). Egg-laying dates ranged from February 2 to March 31 for first eggs and from February 2 to May 7 for all eggs including replacements. The latest date for egg loss that was followed by a replacement egg was April 7, although there were several cases of earlier egg loss that were not followed by replacements. Overall, time between losses and replacements showed no significant relationship to the length of incubation before egg loss, although such a relationship appeared to exist in the data through 1984 (see Snyder and Hamber 1985).

In all cases observed, the birds changed nest sites to lay replacements. The distances between successive nest sites varied from about 100 m to 11.5 km, with a mean of 4.0 km. In only one case (the first case conclusively documented with the CC pair in 1982) were successive nests in the same canyon. Presumably it was mainly this tendency to move long distances to lay replacements that prevented Koford and the early egg collectors from discovering the capacity of the species to lay replacement eggs. Nevertheless, with the high market value of condor eggs, it is surprising that none of the early collectors evidently discovered this capacity. In part, this "failure" could have represented a recognition on the part of any collectors who may have witnessed replacement clutching that giving any publicity to their discovery would only result in dropping the price of eggs in the market, as other collectors would surely increase their take as a result. Eben McMillan once told us that he strongly suspected that his old friend Kelly Truesdale knew of replacement clutching in condors but adaptively kept his mouth shut on the issue.

Debates over the Speed of Forming a Captive Flock

The process of replacement-clutching, successful as it was, nevertheless raised some contentious issues within the program. In particular, debates were vigorous as to whether any young should be allowed to fledge in the wild in the near term and whether both first and second eggs should be taken for artificial incubation. These issues stemmed from different perceptions as to the relative weight that should be given to establishing a captive flock versus sustaining the wild population. In 1983 and 1984, no one was arguing that the wild population was beyond hope, but there were major difficulties in achieving a consensus on just how fast a captive population should be established. Although the taking of eggs was clearly the method with the least impact, there was no way a captive flock could be established without some impact on the wild population. What level of impact should be considered tolerable was unclear.

A major problem in allowing chicks to fledge in the wild was the fact that wild chicks remained dependent on their parents and generally inhibited egg laying in their parents in the next year. This was especially true for chicks produced relatively late in the year, as for example from second or third eggs. In fact, the only cases we had documented of pairs laying eggs concurrent with survival of their chicks from the previous year were cases in which chicks fledged very early in the first year and parents did not lay until late in the next breeding season. Thus, although one could greatly increase reproduction in one year by pulling first eggs for artificial incubation, if chicks were allowed to fledge in the wild from subsequent eggs, it would be highly unlikely that their parents would lay in the next year. Maximal production of young over a several year period could only be achieved by preventing fledging of chicks in the wild.

In the early stages of forming a captive flock, when genetic representation of wild pairs was still a major concern, we argued that taking of captives should take precedence over wild fledgings, even though this did penalize the wild population to some extent. Others were more concerned that production of young in the wild should not be totally lost in any year. This conflict came to a head over the fate of a youngster hatched in the wild from a third egg of the SS1 pair in 1983. We, along with a number of other participating parties, urged that this youngster be taken captive to ensure that its parents would lay in 1984, as by that time we still had only two young in captivity to represent the pair genetically. Others, especially within the National Audubon Society and Fish and Wildlife Service, argued that the chick should be radioed and allowed to fledge in the wild, even though this would probably decrease production of chicks in the following year. In particular, Patuxent Fish and Wildlife Service administrators asserted that the program was becoming seriously unbalanced toward captive breeding and that the research benefits to be gained from a radioed chick should take precedence. Further, Charles Fullerton was on public record as recommending that at least one condor should fledge in the wild in any year. Consensus was not in sight on the fate of this chick.

Aside from debates over impacts on the wild population, we were still concerned about the risks of handling a chick for the length of time it would take to attach radios. We remembered all too well how quickly a chick had expired in 1980 on handling, and we had yet to radio any bird in less time than it took that chick to perish. Furthermore, radioing of a chick could only be done in the late nestling stage. All our data at that point on comparative handling characteristics of chicks and adults (both in the wild and captivity and both California and Andean Condors) suggested that late-stage chicks were especially susceptible to stress. Early-stage chicks and adults took handling much more safely. Veterinarians at the San Diego Zoo had just had a late-stage Andean chick collapse from stress during very brief handling, and they were especially concerned that we avoid taking such a risk with wild California Condor chicks. Loss of another chick in handling could still be lethal to the program, which was just finally getting into gear, and we believed strongly that this risk was not worth taking. The California Fish and Game Commissioners were also highly concerned over how another handling death of a chick might affect the program, whereas Fish and Wildlife Service and Audubon Society administrators argued the risk was exaggerated. Regardless of the comparative merits of the opposing positions, permission to radio a chick at this time was dependent on clearance from the Commission and this did not appear at all likely.

Final resolution of the conflict over the speed of establishing a captive flock was achieved only through a consensus Recovery Team plan that Noel worked hard to facilitate. This plan called for near maximal replacement-clutching of wild pairs to be coupled with an early release program of captives to the wild to start once any pair was represented by five captive progeny. Thus pairs would be encouraged to breed at a near maximal extent by pulling eggs and by preventing nearly all wild fledgings in the short term. But the short-term reproductive deficits of the wild population would soon be more than made up by deliberately releasing some of the young produced from the continued taking of wild eggs into captivity. This strategy was put forth by the Recovery Team and accepted by all parties in the program in 1984. In accord with the basic strategies of the plan, enough support developed for capture of the controversial SS1 chick that it was taken captive just before fledging in 1983.

As predicted, the SS1 pair did lay again in 1984, producing two more surviving young in captivity. These breedings proved to be their last, however, as the male was lost to unknown causes over the winter of 1984–85. Thus, if their 1983 chick had not been taken captive, there would presumably still be only two progeny of the pair in captivity (unless the 1983 fledgling had been taken captive subsequently). As it actually turned out, the pair became represented by five progeny, the goal set for each pair by the Recovery Team. The female adult of the pair also became a captive in 1986 after a decision was later made to bring all the last wild birds into captivity.

Subsequent genetic analysis of the captive flock by DNA fingerprinting techniques (Geyer et al. 1993) was to reveal that the SS family line (especially SSM) was relatively distinctive, and thus was of special importance in maximizing the genetic diversity of the flock. In retrospect, it appears that gaining good representation from this family line may have been an especially valuable achievement.

We also took another chick into captivity in 1983. This one came from the CV pair whose

Several of the birds for the captive flock were taken as nestlings: ***above***, the most controversial was Cachuma, a progeny of the SS1 pair who was captured by Victor Apanius (left) and Phil Ensley (right) about a month before fledging; ***below left***, Cachuma was transported by sky kennel to the helipad by, front to rear, Phil, Steve Kimple, Maeton Freel, and Victor; ***below right***, the taking of the sequoia chick involved arduous rope work, again by Phil Ensley (right) and Victor Apanius (left), aided by Rob Ramey and John Yablonski (out of view).

nest we first found in the summer, long after hatching of its egg. Like the SS1 pair, this pair laid again in 1984, although the chick produced was inviable. Both adults of this pair disappeared over the winter of 1984–85, so in the end the total representation from this pair in captivity was just two individuals (the 1983 nestling, Cuyama, and a juvenile presumed produced in late 1981, PAX).

The totals taken into captivity in 1983 thus included two nestlings and 4 eggs from four pairs. Two of the eggs came from the CC pair, which as discussed earlier, had chronic problems in coordinating incubation duties. Their second egg was not originally cleared for artificial incubation, but was taken under emergency conditions when it became apparent that it was not being incubated adequately (see Chapter 10). Despite severe degeneration of blood vessels presumably caused by the long periods of cooling during parental disputes, this egg recovered under artificial incubation and produced a viable fledgling (Risser 1983).

In 1984, a total of one nestling and eight eggs from five different pairs were taken into captivity. Six of the eggs produced surviving fledglings, and again one pair (CC) triple-clutched. The third egg of the CC pair was originally scheduled to hatch and fledge in the wild, but had to be taken under emergency conditions when it came under severe threat from ravens. The one nestling taken in 1984 came from a newly formed pair in the Sierra Nevadas nesting 100 feet (30 m) up in a giant sequoia. Although the nest was found early enough to have allowed an egg pickup, the risks involved with scaling the tree were sufficiently great that we followed a more conservative strategy of taking the chick close to fledging.

Only one pair (SB) laid eggs in 1985. It produced 3 eggs, all of which were artificially incubated, but only two of which hatched. In 1986, again only one pair laid eggs. This was a new pair in the Sespe Sanctuary. Their first egg was lost naturally shortly after hatching, apparently either to raven predation or to damage from other causes (it was extremely thin-shelled). Their second egg produced a normal chick under artificial incubation.

Hatching of the First Chick

The first chick to hatch in captivity was Sisquoc, an offspring of the behaviorally disturbed CC pair, and the publicity that attended this event was phenomenal. Press coverage was both national and international and was all positive. Nevertheless, we immediately ran into difficulty with the release of sensitive information on the nest location from which Sisquoc had originated.

We had previously agreed with other participants in the program that captive-produced chicks were to be code named by the nesting areas from which they originated. But this naming was for internal recognition purposes, not for public consumption, as we did not want to publicize exact locations of condor nesting pairs. We were not even thinking about what the birds might be called for public purposes, and unfortunately, no one anticipated the need for a public-consumption name for the jammed press conference attending the hatching of the first chick. When the subject of a name for the bird came up, one zoo official mentioned the confidential in-house nest-area name, a major disaster.

Immediately after the press conference, but before news went out, we got together with Art Risser, then curator of birds at San Diego, to see how we could salvage something from the blunder. We came up with the idea that the captive-reared chicks should all receive native Indian names that would not reflect current nesting areas. Thus "Sisquoc" came into instant existence, Art quickly notified reporters, and the in-house nesting-area name never hit most papers. In fact, the in-house name also died internally, as we decided to use the Indian names for all purposes.

We were totally unprepared for the extent of media interest in the captive-hatched condors. Yet it now seems clear that the political problems for the program posed by the FOE alliance all but vanished as a result of the positive public interest that developed. Once an ungainly, but cute and apparently happy condor chick became featured on magazine covers and newspaper front pages across the country, the public simply did not relate any longer to stark anti-captivity rhetoric. The FOE alliance persisted for a while in their opposition to the taking of captives and other intensive activities, but they had suddenly become a lonely voice without media support, ignored by virtually everyone. They had been vanquished by a smiling condor chick named Sisquoc, not by the force of any arguments that we had ever advanced, and no one was more pleasantly surprised than we were.

Relationships between Zoos

One of the potential problems with captive breeding that never did develop was destructive competition between the zoos involved. This outcome was largely avoided by major efforts by both zoos to subordinate such motives to the greater goal of success in the entire program in which both could share. Although Los Angeles had a long term identification with condors in housing Topatopa since the late 1960s, San Diego started initially with greater expertise in artificial incubation, and was given the responsibility of artificial incubation of the first condor eggs taken from the wild. This initial asymmetry, however, was countered by San Diego itself early in the program, in an act that must be considered, at least in part, a major triumph of "preventative political wisdom" well illustrating the skills of the people involved.

As described above, the first bird to come into captivity in the modern program was not an egg but a chick, Xolxol, taken on an emergency basis in late 1982. By decision of the state, it was taken to the San Diego Wild Animal Park. However, not long after its arrival in San Diego, Art Risser took the initiative to have Xolxol transferred to Los Angeles where he could grow up in the company of Topatopa, the only other California Condor in captivity at the time. In purely biological terms, this move was important to reduce the chances of malimprinting of the chick, but in political terms, it was also extraordinarily important in demonstrating San Diego's willingness to pass on publicity benefits to Los Angeles. It set the stage for a general and productive willingness of the two zoos to work together that has lasted to the present and has been of incalculable benefit to condor conservation efforts. We are not suggesting that there has been no competition between these two institutions, but that to a remarkable degree the competition has been beneficial, rather than deleterious.

Capture of Free-flying Birds

In addition to the birds taken as eggs and nestlings, the original captive flock also included a number of birds trapped as free-flying individuals (Table 15). Aside from Topatopa, who was taken in 1967, only one such bird (PAX) was taken before 1985. PAX was trapped in late 1982 as a potential mate for Topatopa. He turned out to be a male, however, and under terms of the state permit would have to be released back to the wild. But because PAX also exhibited worrisome health characteristics, relatively low weight and a chronic gaping problem, the veterinarians at the zoos appealed to the Fish and Game Commission that he be made part of the

Table 15. Makeup of the original captive flock of California Condors in 1987 (adapted from Snyder and Snyder 1989).

Bird	Sex	Age (yrs) in 1987	Age (yrs) in 1999	Year taken captive	Family line (parentage)
CCF	F	13 (min)	25 (min)	1985	CC (parents unknown)
REC	M	7	19	1987	CC (son of CCF and CCM)
Sisquoc	M	4	16	1983	CC (son of CCF and CCM)
Sespe	F	4	16	1983	CC (daughter of CCF and CCM)
Piru	F	3	15	1984	CC (daughter of CCF and CCM)
Inaja	F	3	15	1984	CC (daughter of CCF and CCM)
Pismo	F	3	15	1984	CC (daughter of CCF and CCM)
SSF	F	13 (min)	25 (min)	1986	SS (parents unknown)
Xolxol	M	5	17	1982	SS (son of SSF and SSM)
Tecuya	F	4	16	1983	SS (daughter of SSF and SSM)
Cachuma	F	4	16	1983	SS (daughter of SSF and SSM)
Anapa	F	3	15	1984	SS (daughter of SSF and SSM)
Squapuni	F	3	15	1984	SS (daughter of SSF and SSM)
Nojoqui	M	1	13	1986	SS/CC (son of SSF and REC)
SBM	M	13 (min)	25 (min)	1986	SB (parents unknown)
Almiyi	F	4	16	1983	SB (daughter of SBF and SBM)
Ojai	F	3	15	1984	SB (daughter of SBF and SBM)
Kaweah	M	2	14	1985	SB (son of SBF and SBM)
Malibu	F	2	14	1985	SB (daughter of SBF and SBM)
PAX	M	6	18	1982	CV (son of CVF and CVM)
Cuyama	M	4	16	1983	CV (son of CVF and CVM)
SMM	M	11 (min)	23 (min)	1986	SM (parents unknown)
Sequoia	M	3	15	1984	SM/PP (son of SMM and PPF)
HIW	M	7	19	1985	HW (parents unknown)
UN1	F	11 (min)	23 (min)	1985	UN (parents unknown)
PCA	M	11 (min)	23 (min)	1986	PC (parents unknown)
Topatopa	M	21	33	1967	MC (parents unknown)

Note: parentage of REC and PAX assigned from field behavioral data.

captive flock rather than be released again to the wild. Although retention of this bird was opposed by Charles Fullerton, the Fish and Game Commission gave its blessing, noting that this bird appeared to fit the description of an immature of unspecified sex being requested for captivity quite independently by the US Fish and Wildlife Service at the same time.

The other eight birds to be taken captive as free-flying birds were all trapped between 1985 and 1987 when it became clear that the remnant wild population could not be maintained by any reasonable means. The capture of these birds represented an abandonment of hopes for sustaining the wild population through early releases. The circumstances surrounding this shift in strategies deserve detailed consideration, as this was clearly the most contentious issue ever to envelop the program.

The Crisis of 1985

By the end of 1984, two family lines of condors were represented by five progeny apiece in the captive flock. In line with the early release plan developed by the Recovery Team and approved by all participating agencies in 1984, it appeared that releases of some young from these family lines might be feasible in 1985 if both pairs could be multiple-clutched in that year.

Unfortunately, the winter of 1984–1985 proved catastrophic for condor survival in the wild. Neither of the pairs with five progeny in captivity endured to the breeding season of 1985 (both lost male adults). Two other pairs active in 1984 were also lost (one lost the female adult and the other lost both adults), and an additional new pair that formed early in 1985 similarly lost one member before egg laying. Altogether there was only a single breeding pair left in the population by the middle of the 1985 breeding season. A full 40% of the population had perished in the space of a few months, and the reproductive potential of the population was nearly destroyed in the process.

The plans for early release of captive progeny produced by continued multiple-clutching of wild pairs had been based implicitly on reasonably good survival of breeding pairs in the population. Events revealed this assumption to have been much too optimistic. Many participants, including ourselves, concluded that the early-release plan was already inviable before it had a chance to be implemented, even though we had worked hard to gain approval for this plan. Others hung on to former hopes, despite the fact that the basic conditions of the approved plan for early releases (five permanent captives from each family line) could not be met by any pair. A year-long battle over the wisdom of attempting to sustain the wild population with releases versus bringing all the last birds into captivity was soon underway.

First indications of the catastrophic mortality of the winter of 1984–1985 came when we began watches of the known nesting territories in January of 1985. We immediately discovered that most of the territories were now occupied by only single birds. We then expanded our photo-censusing activities greatly, but none of the missing birds turned up anywhere in the range of the species during the weeks that followed. By March, we were convinced that they had perished. We sounded the alarm that six birds from the population had apparently been lost and that mortality had unfortunately hit the breeding pairs especially hard.

It was clear that on the basis of the approved plans of the Recovery Team, minimum requirements for an early release program could not be met. Together with some other participants in the program, we suggested that the situation was now so serious that it seemed essential that the remaining wild birds should be taken captive. The wild population appeared clearly to be inviable, while the captive population was still much too small and too low in genetic diversity to be considered adequate. It was, in fact, far below the level of adequacy that had been defined by the Recovery Team in 1984. Everything now seemed to depend on establishing a viable captive population, as there was no way an early release program could hope to overwhelm the grim mathematics of the sort of mortality just seen in the wild population. Among other difficulties, the producing pairs for a release program no longer existed.

The responses to our suggestions varied from angry antagonism and disbelief to acceptance. Some observers, including administrators in the Fish and Wildlife Service and Audubon Society, argued that it was much too soon to conclude that the six birds were truly missing and that we would have to wait until late summer to be sure. In their view, the birds might have just moved somewhere else, abandoning their mates and territories (a most improbable scenario). Others who accepted our censusing conclusions were convinced that bringing in the last birds was politically impossible. Moreover, they believed that this would doom habitat preservation efforts, even though the Forest Service pledged publicly at the time to maintain the sanctuaries so long as there were reasonable chances for future reintroductions. The Audubon Society was particularly concerned that bringing in the last wild birds might affect their efforts to make a federal preserve out of Hudson Ranch, a campaign not yet completed, although federal monies had been committed to it. We had difficulty understanding how habitat preservation efforts might take precedence over the critical need for establishing a viable captive population without which habitat for the species would be irrelevant. Still, the argument that the last birds had to be left in the wild to save habitat attracted many supporters.

In addition, Audubon Society researchers and supporters argued that the birds had to be left in the wild to preserve foraging and nesting traditions. Regardless of whether these traditions were worth saving, we doubted they could be better preserved by leaving birds in the wild to die at the horrendous rate we were witnessing than by taking them into "protective custody," with options left open for later return to the wild.

In April 1985 the Recovery Team met to consider the crisis and voted unanimously that there should be no releases of captive condors to the wild in 1985. The team also decided to ask a broad sampling of the nation's most experienced population geneticists to evaluate the genetic adequacy of the existing captive flock before formulating any formal recommendations as to how many additional birds might be taken captive. Recommendations from these geneticists were received rapidly. Their unanimous conclusion was that because of the limited numbers of family lines represented, the existing flock did not possess a sufficiently safe level of genetic diversity to guarantee long-term survival of the species. Every geneticist consulted urged that even to approach a genetically adequate situation, all the remaining wild birds should be added to the captive flock. The possibility that some of the captives might never become breeders made this recommendation even more urgent.

Shortly after these recommendations were received, Kendall Corbin provided preliminary results on the extent of blood enzyme polymorphism in most of the remaining condors. Results indicated relatively low heterozygosity in comparison with levels found in other bird species, suggesting that the remnant population might already be seriously deficient in genetic diversity.

Although these results and recommendations were received promptly after the April meeting of the Recovery Team and were circulated widely, no meeting of the Team followed to discuss their implications and to develop additional recommendations. Recovery Team members anxiously sought such a meeting, but the Fish and Wildlife Service would not allow it. Instead, urged on by the Audubon Society, the Service came out with its own recommendations in May 1985 without any consultation with the Recovery Team or its own field biologists in California. These recommendations were that three birds in the wild flock should be taken captive and replaced with three birds released from captivity to the wild. These recommendations were not based on a clear concept of demographic or genetic imperatives, and they did not recognize the evident serious inviability of the wild population and the futility of releasing captives into such a population. Releases could not be expected to prolong the existence of the wild population for long, if at all, but they would surely diminish the chances of establishing a viable captive population.

Shortly thereafter, the California Fish and Game Commission came out with its own recommendations. Aware of the previous deliberations of the Recovery Team and the recommendations of the population geneticists, the Commission authorized the trapping of all wild birds and agreed with the Recovery Team that no birds should be released to the wild in the near term. The only point in common between the Fish and Wildlife Service and the Commission was that three wild birds could be trapped into captivity, and this was accomplished during the summer of 1985. The fate of the other six wild condors was debated vigorously through the summer and fall of 1985, with the Fish and Wildlife Service initially advocating leaving all these birds in the wild, while the Commission continued to press for their immediate capture.

By advocating the release of three captives, the Fish and Wildlife Service had effectively reversed its earlier backing of the Recovery Team plan, specifying that releases to the wild should not involve captives having fewer than five captive siblings. This reversal was evidently based in part on an assumption that mortality risks for birds in the wild could be greatly reduced by an intensive feeding program with lead-free carcasses that had been initiated on Hudson Ranch in the spring of 1985. Hopes for success in this approach were strong among many Audubon Society and Fish and Wildlife Service personnel, even though evidence from the earlier feeding program of Wilbur indicated that one could not reasonably get the wild population to abandon well-established feeding traditions, so long as food continued to be available in many other parts of the foraging range. Claims were even made that the wild birds were getting most of their food from the feeding program on Hudson. We asked to see the evidence that this was indeed so, but none was forthcoming.

Since, however, there was a considerable amount of data available on how much food captive condors need to maintain body weight, on their crop storage capacities, and on how long it takes a wild condor at a carcass to fill its crop, it appeared that data adequate for an analysis of what fraction of wild condor diet was being supplied by carcasses on Hudson must exist in the detailed records of the Condor Research Center carcass observers. Data from July 1985 were far more detailed and comprehensive than data for other months, and July is normally a peak month for condor activity on Hudson, so we analyzed these data for food consumption, taking care to err on the high side when there was any uncertainty about how much a particular condor had consumed at the baits.

Results were not encouraging. A very generous interpretation of the overall records indicated that the wild population was getting only about 20% of its food needs from the provided carcasses. If this percent could be converted into the percent of mortality reduction to be expected from the feeding program (an optimistic conversion, because at least some mortality was coming from non-food sources, and because condor use of carcasses on Hudson was much less in most months than in July), it was evidently inadequate to protect the wild population from more than a small fraction of the threats it faced. Although we circulated this analysis on an informal basis in late summer of 1985, it had no detectable impact on proponents of the feeding program. Faith in the feeding program remained high until December of 1985, when lead poisoning of a bird known to feed with some frequency on Hudson effectively ended the debate.

One problem with the late-spring proposal of the Fish and Wildlife Service to go ahead with condor releases was that there were no longer any birds behaviorally suitable for release. The five birds that had been held at the Los Angeles Zoo for potential release under the original Recovery Team plan of 1984 had already been taken out of pre-release isolation. This had occurred in response to a request of the USFWS to make cage space available to house the by then almost mythological "mate for Topatopa" that the USFWS expected to trap in the near future. Considering the cage space then available, the most logical way to house Topa's prospective mate was to put her in the adjacent cage in which the "pre-release" birds were being held, moving them elsewhere. Further, in accordance with the accepted 1984 plan of the Recovery Team, the birds that were being isolated in this cage clearly no longer met the criteria for release because of death of parental birds and thus were to be used instead for captive breeding. Following the unanimous reaffirmation of this policy at the Recovery Team meeting of April 1985, there was no reason to continue pre-release isolation of these birds. They were taken out of isolation and now exposed to normal captive-breeding conditions under which they did see keepers and were allowed to associate them with food (a situation to be avoided in birds destined for release).

When the Audubon-supported Fish and Wildlife Service proposal to go ahead with releases anyway materialized several weeks later, it came as a total surprise to nearly everyone involved with the program in California (including ourselves). Furthermore, neither the Fish and Wildlife Service nor the Audubon Society admitted that they were now turning their backs on the 1984 plans they had just agreed to. Instead they publicly accused the Los Angeles Zoo of having unilaterally sabotaged the release program by taking pre-release birds out of isolation, an accusation that continued to be circulated for many months despite its inaccuracy. Removal of the birds from isolation presumably would not have occurred if the Fish and Wildlife Service had sought Recovery Team advice in developing strategies or given some indications of its intentions to the team.

The Recovery Team was allowed only one more meeting during the crisis, a session closely supervised by Washington Fish and Wildlife Service officials in August 1985. At this meeting the Team continued to be unanimous that there should be no near-term releases of captives to the wild. But whereas the team had been split on the issue of bringing in additional birds in its April meeting, by the time of the August meeting there was a consensus that at least three of the controversial six birds left should be captured. By November an informal poll of team members indicated a consensus favoring the capture of all remaining wild birds, but all further meetings of the Recovery Team were prohibited by the Fish and Wildlife Service after the August meeting.

The American Ornithologists' Union (AOU) Condor Committee, which met to consider the crisis in May 1985, took a stance similar to the initial position of the Recovery Team. They recommended no near-term releases of captives to the wild and were ambivalent on disposition of the last wild birds, stating that all should be taken captive on biological grounds, but that to preserve the existence of the research program and to aid in habitat preservation efforts, several should be left in the wild.

One of the unfortunate aspects of leaving any birds in the wild was the fact that most of the remaining wild birds were males while the captive flock had an excess of females. Thus, each male left in the wild deprived the captive flock of a potential pair, and as was recognized by the AOU committee, the demographic potentials of the captive flock were as important as, if not more important than, the genetic potentials. The number of potential heterosexual pairs in captivity by late summer of 1985 was eight. Bringing in all the last remaining birds would have added 50% to this potential, a substantial increase in the short term, both genetically and demographically.

In late August, a compromise was reached between the Fish and Wildlife Service and the California Fish and Game Commission entailing the capture of three more wild birds for captive breeding. Both agencies also agreed to pursue an "aggressive policy" of releases of captives to the wild. Exactly what an "aggressive policy" of releases implied was not specified. An important component of the compromise was an agreement that all wild condors would be brought into captivity if one more wild bird perished.

But although the Fish and Wildlife Service had agreed to fully authorize the trapping of three more birds by mid-September, it did not do so, primarily because of Audubon Society opposition to the compromise (which included the threat of a lawsuit). Authorization by the Fish and Wildlife Service for the capture of three additional condors did not occur until late October, when to break the impasse, the California Fish and Game Commission specifically agreed to consider release of three condors in the spring of 1986 if birds suitable for release were available at that time and if agreement could be reached as to where a release might take place. In its October statement to the California Fish and Game Commission, the Fish and Wildlife Service failed to reaffirm its earlier support for taking the rest of the wild population captive in the event of any more mortality of wild condors, although this option was left open in the Environmental Assessment written to cover the situation. Although the Fish and Game Commission still favored all birds coming into captivity and no near-term releases of captives to the wild, it took the position that it was better to get at least three more of the wild birds into captivity in the short term than to risk getting none of them into captivity in a continued stalemate. The Commission was still left in a position where it could veto releases because of the conditions attached.

In early November 1985, strategies for the California Condor were discussed at length at the Third International Vulture Symposium held in conjunction with the Raptor Research Foundation meetings in Sacramento. The condor session attracted a near capacity audience of international experts, many of whom were astounded by the politics of ongoing controversies. Many fine commentaries were offered, however, and we will never forget the compelling presentations for bringing in the last birds that were put forth by Ian Newton and David Houston of the United Kingdom. The condor symposium led to a resolution that was adopted on a nearly unanimous basis by the meeting participants that (1) all the remaining wild condors should be taken captive as soon as possible, (2) no releases of captives should be attempted until a healthy, self-sustaining captive population was achieved, and (3) releases of California Condors to the wild, once they became advisable, should be limited to regions that offered effective protection from detrimental human influences.

These recommendations ring as true today as they did in 1985. But even though they represented a strong consensus of a large fraction of the biologists directly involved in raptor and vulture conservation worldwide, there was no response from the Fish and Wildlife Service or the Audubon Society. The basic conflict in strategies between the California Fish and Game Commission and the Fish and Wildlife Service/National Audubon Society axis still remained unresolved.

This continued to be the situation until an event occurred that a number of us were privately predicting might have to happen before the politics of the situation could be resolved – the death of still another condor. Although absolutely no one was eager to see the loss of another individual, the particular condor involved (SBF) turned out to be a relatively fortunate one from a couple of standpoints: (1) she was already represented in captivity by four progeny, and (2) she settled the issue of whether the feeding program could effectively protect the remaining birds. She was another victim of lead poisoning, the very mortality threat the feeding program was supposed to counter, and she was a member of the very pair that the Audubon Society had proclaimed were the birds safest from this threat because of their strong tendency to take food from the feeding program on Hudson. If the feeding program could not protect this bird, it could hardly be expected to protect others.

In fact, SBF had spent much of the fall of 1985 feeding on the Tejón Ranch, not on Hudson. She may well have received her lethal contamination from feeding on remains of hunter-shot deer in spite of belated efforts to provide clean calf carcasses on Tejón as well as on Hudson. SBF's evident lack of commitment to the feeding program and her lethal contamination were a political disaster for the Audubon Society. There was now no escaping the conclusion that the feeding program was not adequately successful and that the wild population could not be protected from further losses. This was the same conclusion we had put forth months earlier on the basis of feeding records at Hudson.

The poisoning of SBF and the political developments caused by this poisoning proceeded as follows. On November 23 SBF had been captured to replace her defective radio transmitters. A blood sample taken at this time, but not analyzed until after the bird was released, proved to be heavily contaminated with lead. This finding led program veterinarians and toxicologists to recommend that the bird be recaptured immediately for treatment. Further, the detection of high lead levels in this condor (she had low lead levels when tested earlier) proved to be a crucial development in convincing top Fish and Wildlife Service officials that the remaining wild condors were still at high risk.

In mid-December 1985, the Fish and Wildlife Service announced that it now concurred with the longstanding position of the California Fish and Game Commission that all the remaining wild condors should be taken captive and that there should be no near-term releases of captives to the wild. The reversal was attributed primarily to the high lead levels in the November-trapped condor, but also to an absence of captive birds behaviorally suitable for release in 1986, and to the fact that a new pair bond was forming in the wild between one of the birds slated for capture and one of the birds to be left in the wild in the October decision. The Fish and Wildlife Service at the time of its announced policy-shift still had not yet acquired Hudson Ranch, a purchase strongly advocated by the Audubon Society, although monies for the purchase had been allocated by Congress.

However, before trapping of the last birds could begin, the Audubon Society filed suit to obtain an injunction against capture of the last wild birds. The suit alleged that the Fish and Wildlife Service's decision was arbitrary and capricious and that taking the last birds captive would doom habitat preservation efforts, especially the purchase of Hudson Ranch. Audubon won the first round in the courts, but was ultimately defeated on appeal, an episode we will discuss in more detail in the next chapter.

Meanwhile, SBF was finally recaptured on an emergency basis and brought into intensive care at the San Diego Wild Animal Park in early January. Seemingly, the entire staff at the park was brought into action on her behalf, and when we travelled south to witness these efforts, we found the hospital jammed with vets and keepers working non-stop to revive the bird. Without a doubt, this was the most profoundly stirring scene of commitment toward saving the species we were ever to experience. Alas it was too late. Despite round-the-clock efforts to bolster and detoxify the stricken bird, SBF died on January 18, 1986. For all those involved in the campaign to save her, this was a moment of intense grief, exhaustion, and anger.

The death of SBF must have been an important factor in the ultimate defeat on appeal of Audubon's legal case to prevent the trapping of the last birds. With all legal restrictions finally removed in the spring of 1986, the way stood clear for capture of the remaining five wild condors. In mid 1986, however, another challenge against trapping the last birds arose from an activist group of native Americans, in part Chumash and in part Mexican American. Two of the remaining five condors were trapped by June 1986, but a letter of July 1, 1986 from the lawyer for the native Americans advised the USFWS that "If there is to be a capture of all Condors, the religious practices and Chumash religion will be irreparably harmed." The Chumash group also demanded that "if there is to be any future trapping that all such trapped condors should be released onto the Santa Barbara Channel Islands and not imprisoned into Zoo settings." On July 10, 1986, the Native American Heritage Commission passed a resolution requesting the USFWS to cease and desist from further condor captures and to abide by their responsibilities related to Indian religious rights (U.S. Constitution; Treaty of Guadalupe Hidalgo; American Indian Religious Freedom Act, P.L. 93–641, USC 1996).

A series of nervous meetings between this group and USFWS and CDFG representatives were held during the summer of 1986. These led to an agreement by the USFWS that

Chumash representatives could be present for the trapping of the last three birds so that appropriate ceremonies could be performed. The USFWS did not agree that the remaining birds would stay in the wild or that the trapped birds would be released on the Channel Islands. As it turned out, a Chumash representative did attend the first day of resumed trapping efforts in September of 1986, but thereafter Chumash personnel declined to appear. All the last condors were captured by the spring of 1987.

The Dust Settles

Thus the full process of forming a captive flock of California Condors was an involved and quarrelsome affair. Delayed for decades by the effective opposition of Carl Koford, Alden Miller and their followers, the process was delayed again at the outset of the modern program in 1980 by the political ramifications of our handling loss of a wild nestling. The process was at last initiated in late 1982 with the emergency taking of a chick into captivity, and accelerated rapidly in 1983 and 1984, mainly through the multiple-clutching of wild pairs and artificial incubation of their eggs. With the loss of nearly all breeding pairs over the winter of 1984–1985, however, the multiple-clutching approach lost most of its potential, and there were substantial concerns that the captive flock was still genetically and demographically deficient. The wild population was clearly inviable by this time, and there was no easy method to reverse this situation. After a tremendous battle culminating in a failed lawsuit of the Audubon Society against the Fish and Wildlife Service in early 1986, and following the resolution of differences with the Chumash Indians, the last wild birds were all taken captive by early 1987.

As finally assembled at the Los Angeles Zoo and San Diego Wild Animal Park in 1987, the original founding captive population of California Condors included 27 individuals (Table 15). Fourteen of these birds were female, and 13 were male, a close to even sex ratio, although the flock had been strongly biased toward females at earlier stages. In fact, of the first 10 condors hatched in captivity during the multiple-clutching years nine were female (a result differing significantly from chance, assuming a 1:1 sex ratio to be normal for the species). The bias toward females was not brought back to near equilibrium until the last wild male was captured in 1987.

Ten of the 27 captives (seven males and three females) were trapped as birds with experience as free-flying birds in the wild, although Topatopa and PAX had only limited free-flying experience. Seventeen birds were reared in captivity (13 from the egg stage and four from the nestling stage).

The family line information given in Table 15 is necessarily incomplete, as a number of the birds were from unknown parents and because the relationships of various family lines to one another were all unknown. Subsequent DNA analyses of the founding birds by Geyer et al. (1993) have indicated that the birds cluster in three different lineages, although all may be relatively closely related. Even Topatopa, the captive taken in 1967 seems to be relatively closely related to others in the captive flock. Thus genetic diversity appeared to be quite limited in the founding flock, and concerns still remain today as to whether enough diversity is present to allow long-term persistence of the species.

Ages of captive-hatched and captive-reared birds are all known accurately, but ages for most of the birds trapped from the wild as adults are highly speculative. Some may be far older than the minimum figures given in the table. So although Topatopa, at 33 years of age in 1999, appears in the table to be the oldest bird in the flock, he may in fact be considerably younger than some of the other birds. Only one of the original founding birds of 1987 has as yet died in captivity (UN1 in March 1999), so maximum longevities of these birds may prove to be substantial.

One final point we believe should be addressed here is whether the establishment of the captive flock was a major cause of the simultaneous decline of the remnant wild population. With the exception of Topatopa, a starving wild fledgling of 1967, no captives were taken before 1982, so the decline of the species prior to that time can hardly be attributed to this cause. After early 1985, on the other hand, the decline was nearly 100% attributable to this process, consciously and deliberately, as the consensus became strong that the remnant wild flock was inviable. The period of most interest was from early 1982 to early 1985, during which there were still sincere hopes that the decline of the wild population might be reversible. During this period, only one condor was allowed to fledge naturally in the wild, while the wild population declined from 23 to 9 individuals.

How many wild condors would there have been in early 1985 if captives had not been taken? We can estimate this number by assuming that the wild population would have naturally produced young at the same rate in 1983 and 1984 that it did in 1980, 1981, and 1982 (actually a generous assumption as the wild population was shrinking through this period). Under this assumption there would have been five additional birds fledged in the wild, one in 1982, two in 1983, and two in 1984. In addition, since we trapped one yearling for the captive flock in 1982 (PAX), he must be added to the total. The total of six additional birds, however, has to be adjusted by natural mortality that presumably would have occurred during the period from 1982 to 1985. When this is done, the total of six drops to four. Thus, in the absence of multiple-clutching and the taking of captives, the expected total wild population by the spring of 1985 would have been only 13 individuals, still representing a massive decline from the 23 birds of early 1982. The taking of captives during this period accounts for less than one third of the population decline and cannot be considered the major cause of the decline (Johnson 1985).

That 15 captives were simultaneously gained between 1982 and early 1985, mainly by deliberate multiple-clutching of wild pairs, indicates that benefits to the captive population were nearly four times as great as the losses to the wild population that can be attributed to the acquisition process. Had these 15 captives instead been trapped as free-flying birds, and had the mortality and reproductive rates of the wild population continued unchanged, the impacts on the wild population would have been considerably worse, ranging from an estimated 5–6 birds left in the wild in early 1985 if all 15 captives had been taken in 1982, to zero birds left in the wild if all 15 had been taken as late as late 1984 or early 1985. Evidently the trapping of free-flying birds would have been far more stressful for the wild population than was the multiple-clutching process actually pursued.

The Audubon Lawsuit and the Valentine's Day Docufesto

If anyone had suggested early in 1980 that within a few years' time the two major cooperators in the condor program, the U.S. Fish and Wildlife Service and the National Audubon Society, would be opposing each other in a major lawsuit over the fate of the species, we would not have believed them. Both organizations initially shared very similar views on the major issues of condor conservation and stood shoulder to shoulder in fighting for the new program. Nevertheless, they eventually came to differ fundamentally over the relative importance of establishing a viable captive flock versus habitat acquisition, and it took a court battle to settle this difference. When matters were resolved, Audubon was no longer a participant in the conservation program.

The rift between Audubon and the Fish and Wildlife Service, although an extreme case, was just one of many examples of how the alliances among organizations and individuals shifted dramatically over the years. As different issues came to dominate condor conservation efforts, former enemies became partners and former allies became opponents with astonishing frequency. Perhaps because so many issues were involved, the program remained in almost perpetual flux during the years of our participation and never settled down into a predictable pattern for more than brief periods.

The Audubon suit against the Fish and Wildlife Service's decision to take the last wild condors into captivity was filed in January 1986. Noel immediately phoned the lawyers for the Fish and Wildlife Service and offered to assist in any particulars in their preparation of a defense. His offer was received cordially, but we never heard back from the lawyers. Instead, we first learned of the details of the suit after the Fish and Wildlife Service had lost its defense in the District Court in Washington D.C. Full copies of the suit proceedings then became available as a matter of public record.

The Audubon suit (National Audubon Society versus F. Eugene Hester et al., U.S. District Court for the District of Columbia, Civil Action No. 86-0053) alleged that the Service had acted improperly in several legalistic respects in making its December 23, 1985 decision that the last remaining wild birds should be taken captive. Perhaps the most surprising and important of these allegations was an argument that the Fish and Wildlife Service had no "new" information on which to base a change in its former position that some birds should remain in the wild. In particular, the Audubon Society claimed that on November 26, 1985 when the Fish and Wildlife Service publicly reaffirmed its earlier position that some birds should stay in the wild, it already knew (1) about the lead poisoning of SBF, (2) that a new pair bond was forming between two birds that had been designated to remain in the wild and to be taken captive, respectively, and (3) that no behaviorally suitable captive birds were available for release. Thus, all three of the reasons given by the Fish and Wildlife Service for its policy-shift decision of December 23, were not cause for any new decision and the decision must be considered "arbitrary and capricious" because it differed from the position of the Service on November 26.

However, as we were all well aware, the primary event causing the Fish and Wildlife Service to change its position was surely the detection of high lead levels in the blood of SBF at the very end of November 1985. Audubon had proclaimed this bird and her mate to be the very safest birds from such poisoning because of their frequent presence at the clean carcasses being provided on Hudson Ranch, so the poisoning of this bird was a clear demonstration that the feeding program was not proving successful in protecting the birds. Virtually no one in California, and apparently few in Washington, missed the significance of lead poisoning of this particular bird. Clearly the rest of the birds remaining in the wild were still at high risk and could not be expected to survive for too much longer.

The truly bizarre aspect of the legal case was the fact that in the lawsuit documents U.S. Fish and Wildlife Service personnel agreed with the Audubon Society that information about lead poisoning of SBF was already available prior to the Service's November 26 statement (see affidavit of J. M. Scott which states that analysis results were available on November 24). We knew this simply was not so, and checked on the specifics with the San Diego Zoo veterinarians who had taken the blood sample and sent it off for lead analysis. Their records showed unambiguously that the blood sample was taken on November 23, was received by the analysis laboratory on November 26, and was analyzed on November 29, with results reported back to San Diego on November 30. The Zoo then notified the U.S. Fish and Wildlife Service of the alarming results. No one in the Fish and Wildlife Service could possibly have known of the lead poisoning of SBF on November 26.

We also checked with the San Diego Zoo veterinarians as to whether anyone in the Fish and Wildlife Service, including their lawyers, had asked them for the documentation on the dates of the lead analysis, either before or after agreeing with Audubon Society in the lawsuit that information on lead poisoning of SBF was available before November 26. The answer was negative. As the "no new information" allegation was one of the major points raised by the Audubon Society in its suit, and was one of the major arguments used by the court in siding with the Audubon Society, it seemed inconceivable that the U.S. Fish and Wildlife Service would not have sought out these documents in its own defense and made them part of its response, let alone that the Service would have agreed to Audubon's version of the timing of events. The Fish and Wildlife Service could have disposed of the "no new information" argument in a completely conclusive fashion had it consulted properly with cooperators and its own personnel in California in preparing its case. Whether or not this failure to consult may have represented anything more than simple incompetence, it appeared to be a key factor in Audubon's victory at the District Court level.

Fortunately, since top U.S. Fish and Wildlife Service officials decided to appeal the injunction granted to the Audubon Society, the opportunity now existed for other parties to become involved in the case to help clarify issues. At this point several California organizations – the Los Angeles and San Diego Zoos and the California Fish and Game and Commission – became committed to writing *Amicus Curiae* [friend of the court] briefs supporting the U.S. Fish and Wildlife Service position. The Los Angeles Zoo also petitioned to become an official "intervenor" in the appeal, but was turned down because this necessitated consent from the parties involved in the suit, which was not forthcoming. We assisted in the preparation of the *Amicus Curiae* brief from the two zoos, and although this was far from field biology, it was one of the most instructive and memorable periods in our years in the condor program. We are convinced that in many respects, the brief submitted was far more persuasive than the appeal generated by the Fish and Wildlife Service, and may have been a significant factor in the reversal of the District Court's decision on appeal.

As acrimonious as the suit between the Audubon Society and Fish and Wildlife Service proved to be, it at least served to illuminate certain matters that had been very difficult for those of us in the field in California to comprehend. Surprising high-level Fish and Wildlife Service memos that we had never seen earlier became part of the official suit documentation, and once these documents became public, they provided a much better understanding of what factors were most important in motivating certain major parties and the lengths they were willing to go to achieve their ends.

The legal case made it clear that a major motivating factor for the Audubon Society was a fear that bringing all birds into captivity would be the end of its campaign to persuade the government to acquire Hudson Ranch. Although this fear in part represented an understandable reaction to delays in acquisition of the ranch that had been seen until then, it also apparently reflected the fact that Audubon personnel had staked their credibility before Congress in advocating the importance of the Hudson Ranch acquisition. To us, it appeared that the acquisition of Hudson Ranch had become a "monument" that Audubon hoped to build for its role in the condor program, and it was venturing everything on achieving this goal. The campaign had seemingly lost all sense of proportion. Whether or not there might be a viable condor population still in existence to occupy this ranch in the future was evidently a lesser consideration.

In any event, the fears of the Audubon Society eventually proved to be groundless, as even though the remaining wild birds were all taken captive, Hudson Ranch was ultimately acquired and made into a National Wildlife Refuge. The ranch, however, has remained virtually empty of condors since its acquisition, and it still remains uncertain that it will ever become habitat for a viable wild condor population.

Besides the negative effect that capturing all birds was perceived to have on acquisition of Hudson Ranch, this action also threatened other sacred cows. In particular, certain parties within both Audubon and the Fish and Wildlife Service feared that taking all the last birds captive might jeopardize the continuation of the field condor program and its associated funding. In their judgement, with all birds in captivity there would be no reason for the government to fund a continuing condor program, and in effect, birds had to remain in the wild (at serious risk) to save the program. We heard this fear expressed by mid-level administrators in both organizations, and we believe it was an even more important consideration for some administrators than the Hudson Ranch issue. Although some believed that ultimate conservation of the species itself would be jeopardized if the field program were even temporarily lost, the essence of the position was that conservation of the program was more important than conservation of the species, at least in the near term. To a certain extent, this argument was even accepted by the AOU condor committee in mid 1985.

The strong motivation to save the condor program needs to be considered not just in the context of operations in California, but also in the context of operations on the East Coast that were being supported by condor monies. In fact, much of the money that was being appropriated for condors was not going to California, but was supporting a variety of East-Coast activities, especially at the Patuxent Wildlife Research Center in Maryland.

Ironically, taking the last condors captive did not represent the threat to the program that some administrators feared. Early in 1985 a number of us in the program proposed a viable alternative that would allow taking the last California Condors captive without loss of the program. This proposal, based on a suggestion of Cathleen Cox of the Los Angeles Zoo, was to conduct experimental temporary releases of Andean Condors to the wild in California during the period all California Condors would be in captivity. Such releases would be valuable for testing techniques to be later used with California Condors, but we were well aware they would also solve problems of program continuity for administrators in Audubon and the Fish and Wildlife Service.

Unfortunately, this proposal was greeted with a high level of skepticism by many administrators, at least in part because they believed it would be difficult to get public support for even temporary experimental releases of an alien condor species in California. The proposal was not viewed as a viable alternative to leaving the last California Condors in the wild, and did not solve the conflicts during 1985, even though it did ultimately gain full acceptance by both the public and the Fish and Wildlife Service and did, in fact, ultimately "save" the program. Even as late as the spring of 1986 mid-level administrators in both Audubon and the Fish and Wildlife Service were still urging that some California Condors be left in the wild and that near-term releases of captive California Condors to the wild go forward – by then, strategies that were recognized as bankrupt by virtually all field personnel.

In retrospect, much of the agony of 1985 resulted from a basic betrayal of recovery team function that took place both in Audubon and the Fish and Wildlife Service. Recovery teams, to be sure, are only advisory bodies with no administrative authority, but when they are properly constituted and functioning well, they represent an expertise in designing conservation strategies that administrators are normally well advised to heed. If the Condor

Recovery Team of the mid 1980s had not been ignored and side-stepped by administrators who were far less qualified than the team, either in a biological or political sense, much of the conflict of the period could have been more quickly and amicably resolved. Indeed by the end of 1985 the team had reached a consensus that the last birds should be taken captive, and it had long been in agreement that there should be no near-term releases of captives to the wild and that the purchase of Hudson Ranch should go forward (all of which recommendations eventually did prevail).

Fortunately, the California Fish and Game Commission was far more respectful of the expertise of the Recovery Team, and based its decisions largely on team recommendations, defying pressures from the Fish and Wildlife Service and Audubon Society, and working actively to gain implementation of the strategies that ultimately came to be accepted.

Many East Coast administrators, in contrast, did not appear to value the Recovery Team recommendations, and had no apparent hesitancy in ignoring these recommendations or misrepresenting them to high level officials in both organizations. For example, one of the Fish and Wildlife Service memos that surfaced in the legal suit revealed that the head of the Patuxent Wildlife Research Center had completely misrepresented the position of the Recovery Team in the spring of 1985 to the Chief of the Division of Wildlife Research. The official Recovery Team position at that time was that releases to the wild should be limited to birds with five siblings in the permanent captive flock. No such birds existed, yet this memo claimed that near-term releases were consistent with Recovery Team policies. During this period we also had phone calls from board members of the Audubon Society seeking information on Recovery Team recommendations. These individuals were disturbed to learn that the real Recovery Team position bore little resemblance to what they had been told was the Recovery Team position by Audubon administrators.

Ultimately, most of the administrators involved in these misrepresentations suffered a major loss of credibility and influence within their organizations, but for a long period during 1985 they managed to control the situation. Fortunately, there were enough other organizations involved in the program, and enough of an open forum existed for discussion of opposing views, that strategies based mainly on short-term expediency and contrary to good biology and good politics finally collapsed.

Surely much of the convergence in strategies among mid-level Audubon and Fish and Wildlife Service administrators through this period depended on the fact that the Fish and Wildlife Service budget for the condor program was largely a result of Audubon annually lobbying an add-on condor appropriation through Congress. Mid-level administrators within the Service (whose own domains depended in part on this funding) were well acquainted with this connection, and it should not be especially surprising that they came to favor goals espoused by Audubon, regardless of whether or not these goals might have differed from goals recommended by the Recovery Team or by Service biologists in California.

However, the commonality in purpose among these Service administrators and Audubon administrators did not extend to the highest and lowest levels of the Fish and Wildlife Service, where any perceived funding dependency on Audubon was of much less importance. Throughout the crisis period of 1985 and 1986, there was actually much more commonality in purpose between the highest and lowest levels of the Fish and Wildlife

Service than there was between either of these and the middle levels of the Service. Unfortunately, communications between the lowest and highest levels were frequently distorted by the middle levels of the Service. The lowest levels, limited by military-style chain of command restrictions, had no way to know whether their recommendations were being transmitted accurately to the highest levels, except during the occasional instances when the highest levels made efforts to contact the lowest levels directly.

An Alternative Plan

The events of 1985, especially those making it clear that a viable wild condor population no longer existed, revealed that the existing official Recovery Plan for the California Condor was no longer relevant to the realities of condor conservation. Over the winter of 1985–1986 we participated in the development of an overall plan for condor conservation that could serve as an interim replacement for the existing Recovery Plan, even though there was no functioning Recovery Team left at that point (the Fish and Wildlife Service refused to allow the existing team to meet and offer formal recommendations). Efforts to develop an alternative plan resulted in the circulation of a document entitled "The California Condor Program, a proposal for the next essential steps." This document evolved from discussions among some 13 individuals, including Noel, from the San Diego and Los Angeles Zoos, the U.S. Forest Service, the U.S. Fish and Wildlife Service, the Western Foundation of Vertebrate Zoology and California Polytechnic University, San Luis Obispo. Although not official policy of any organization, it represented a consensus recommendation from a large fraction of the people working actively with condor conservation at the time. Commemorating its release on February 14, 1986, the proposal also became known locally as the "Valentine's Day Docufesto."

Principal recommendations of the document were (1) capture of all the remaining wild California Condors for the captive breeding program, and thus full reliance on captive breeding as a near-term tool for preserving the species, (2) implementation of temporary surrogate releases of Andean Condors in California to test release techniques, study mortality factors, and evaluate the feasibility of establishing wild populations dependent on artificially-provided clean food in confined ranges of relatively safe habitat, and (3) potential implementation of releases of California Condors in the same areas once the captive population of California Condors had increased to a safe demographic and genetic level and pending successful results with the Andean Condor releases.

The feeding program for the wild California Condor population in 1985, like that in the 1970s, had demonstrated that it was not feasible to get experienced wild birds to feed exclusively on carcasses at a feeding station. However, prospects for achieving such a goal with released captive-reared birds appeared much more favorable. In fact, Mike Wallace found in his work in the early 1980s that it took considerable effort to get released captive-reared Andean Condors in Peru to abandon a reliance on provided food. It was reasonable to suggest that released captive-reared California Condors would be ignorant of wide-ranging foraging patterns, and would have no inducement to learn such patterns if food might be offered consistently in one location. Thus, it might be possible to keep them fully dependent on clean food indefinitely so long as they were not mixed with experienced birds that might lead them to feed on "unauthorized" food and so long as the releases were limited to areas where competing natural food supplies were very low. Specifically, the Sespe and Sisquoc Sanctuary regions were suggested as areas with low natural food supplies and high nest-site abundances that appeared favorable for successful reintroductions.

If populations loyal to provided food could be achieved, birds could be reestablished in the wild without exposure to the lead-poisoning problem that appeared to be the main cause of extirpation of the historic wild population. Such a strategy would be much easier in the short term than strategies of creating large no-hunting reserves or developing non-toxic ammunitions that could replace lead.

However, such a strategy could only be successful if releases were limited to captive-reared condors. If any of the last wild-caught adults were returned to the wild, they could not be expected to remain dependent on a clean food subsidy. They would almost surely return to wide-ranging foraging habits, and would potentially serve as role-models that could encourage any captive-reared birds also released to adopt the same risky foraging patterns. Release of any of the wild-caught adults only made sense if the lead-poisoning threat could be fully addressed in the wild environment.

The Valentine's Day Docufesto filled a vacuum in planning efforts. Once the Audubon lawsuit was settled in the spring of 1986, it provided a basis for action of a new Condor Recovery Team that was formed as efforts were made to trap the last wild condors into captivity. It did not represent an ultimate strategy for the conservation of the species, but an interim plan, and it was not certain that its basic assumptions about controllability of released populations by subsidy would be fulfilled. As we shall see in the chapter on the release program, the actual releases of Andean Condors and California Condors have not proceeded exactly as predicted in the document. In part, this appears to be because releases have not been conducted in a manner likely to maximize chances of keeping birds dependent on provided food. It has become advisable once again to reevaluate and redesign strategies.

With the final decision made to capture the last wild condors in 1986 and with general support gathering for experimental releases of Andean Condors in California, we made a personal decision to leave both the condor program and the USFWS. We were greatly relieved that many of the policies and strategies we had fought for were at last being accepted. It was also a great relief that no more of the remaining wild birds died before they were all captured. We were exhausted by the continuous conflicts, Noel had developed stress-related health problems, and our relationships with administrators on the East Coast had become sufficiently strained during the battles of 1985 that we simply wanted to retreat to a much less confrontational existence, and for a time, at least, to think about something other than condors. The Service indicated its intent to transfer Noel out of the field condor program to conduct other activities at Patuxent, but these held no attractions. Noel resigned his position in the late spring of 1986, and in the summer we began experimental reintroduction studies of Thick-billed Parrots in Arizona for the Arizona Game and Fish Department.

PART V
RESTORATION

CHAPTER SIXTEEN

Captive Breeding

Although captive breeding was originally envisioned as a supportive, rather than a central conservation technique for the California Condor, it proved to be absolutely crucial for the salvation of the species. First proposed by the San Diego Zoo in 1950, then re-proposed by the California Condor Recovery Team in 1976, by the American Ornithologists Union-Audubon Advisory Committee on Condors in 1978, and by the newly reconstituted condor program of 1980, the deliberate taking of birds to form a captive flock was not actually launched until late 1982 when the wild population had declined to just 21 individuals. Because of genetic considerations and the uncertainties involved in achieving quantitatively adequate captive production, this last-minute start for the process was not a conservative strategy. Had it been politically feasible, it would have been wiser to have started considerably earlier, perhaps when there were still twice or three times as many individuals in existence.

At the time deliberate assembly of a captive flock was started, there was only a single male, Topatopa, already in captivity. The species had never been bred in confinement, although extremely few condors had ever been held in captivity, and it is not clear that a heterosexual pair had ever been placed together in the same cage. A number of eggs had been laid by captives at the National Zoo early in the century, but none of these resulted in chicks. All were presumably infertile.

Thus, at the time captive breeding efforts were launched, there were substantial uncertainties as to whether the efforts had been initiated in time and might succeed. Good results had by then been achieved by a number of institutions in captive breeding of a variety of vulturids, including the Andean Condor, but we were well aware from our experience with captive Puerto Rican Parrots that endangered forms were sometimes considerably more difficult to breed than their closest relatives. If this also proved true for the California Condor, the numbers of individuals still alive might not be enough to allow formation of a viable captive breeding population. In contrast to many mammals – for which successful breeding is a result of chance encounters or promiscuity, rather than pair formation – most bird species, including condors, are dependent on successful pair bonding to achieve reproduction. Yet many have great difficulty forming compatible pairs in captivity. For many, one is fortunate indeed to get even a quarter of the individuals in captivity into production of young.

Despite these early concerns, captive breeding has proved highly successful with the California Condor. All individuals originally taken into captivity have become productive breeders, and the captive population has increased rapidly in size. The level of reproduction in captivity has far exceeded even the most optimistic early projections, and is a great credit to the concerted efforts and capacities of the Los Angeles Zoo, the Zoological Society of San Diego, and the Peregrine Fund, building on earlier efforts of the Patuxent Wildlife Research Center with Andean Condors. In anticipation of an eventual need for captive breeding of California Condors, Ray Erickson at Patuxent had wisely implemented a program to develop husbandry techniques for this close relative at the very start of the endangered wildlife research program of the Fish and Wildlife Service in 1966 (Erickson and Carpenter 1983). Even earlier, the Zoological Society of San Diego had achieved renown for successful captive breeding and double clutching of Andean Condors (Lint 1943, 1951). This latter institution reinitiated extensive husbandry research with Andean Condors in 1979.

Even Topatopa, the human-oriented bird brought into captivity as a fledgling in 1967, finally fathered his first progeny in 1993, although finding a compatible mate for him was difficult and took a number of tries (Cox et al. 1993). As we had feared during the early 1980s, when the State of California limited taking of captives to finding a mate for Topatopa, he proved to be one of the most recalcitrant birds to breed, and probably would not have paired with any of the wild adult females that might have been captured at that time. Possibly because of his long history in captivity, Topatopa was subordinate to all wild-caught females he was placed with in the late 1980s. Pairing success was only finally achieved by caging him for several years with Malibu, a captive-reared juvenile female he could dominate.

In this chapter we review the main aspects of captive propagation of California Condors through 1998. Our primary basic sources of information on this subject have been the successive California Condor Studbooks (Kuehler 1989, 1993, 1996), Kuehler and Witman (1988), Kuehler et al. (1991), and additional data kindly provided by Mike Mace, Don Sterner, and Bill Toone of the Zoological Society of San Diego, and Mike Clark and Cathleen Cox of the Los Angeles Zoo.

Description of Breeding Facilities

The first captive breeding facilities for the California Condor were constructed at the San Diego Wild Animal Park and the Los Angeles Zoo, based on design features that had been developed for Andean Condors at the Patuxent Wildlife Research Center. In the original facilities, pairs were housed in spacious flights, each at least 80 feet (24.4 m) long, 40 feet (12.2 m) wide and 20 feet (6.1 m) high, and each provided with a large cavelike wooden nest chamber elevated above the substrate. Flights were arranged in parallel, with a service corridor behind a visual barrier running along the ends of successive cages. Observation blinds were provided for each flight, and later video cameras were installed to allow continuous non-intrusive monitoring of breeding pair activities from remote locations.

The first breeding facility at the San Diego Wild Animal Park, the condorminium, was finished by the end of 1981, whereas the first facility at the Los Angeles Zoo became operational at the end of 1982. Additional facilities were constructed at both the Los Angeles Zoo and at the San Diego Wild Animal Park by the end of 1989 to accommodate the space needs of the growing captive population. Yet another facility was built at the Peregrine Fund in Boise, Idaho by the end of 1993. Some of the more recent cages for condors have been somewhat smaller than the original ones at Los Angeles and San Diego, but have still been a minimum of 40 feet (12.2 m) x 20 feet (6.1 m) x 20 feet (6.1 m) in dimensions.

Pairing and Caging Strategies

A principal concern in initiating captive breeding was avoiding pairings between close relatives because this could lead to genetic problems. It was reasonable to assume that the remnant population was already somewhat inbred and that further inbreeding might substantially harm the vigor of the population. Also, with a wild population that had been at relatively low numbers for several decades, there were concerns about the extent of genetic diversity that doubtless had already been lost by the species and about preserving as fully as possible the diversity that was still present. To this end, it was important to get as many individuals into production as possible and to equalize genetic contributions of family lines to succeeding generations as much as possible.

Although the degree of genetic relationship among the original captives was mostly unknown at the time captive breeding was initiated, it was at least possible to avoid pairings between known siblings and between parents and known offspring. Birds were originally placed with potential mates that were at least not known to be close relatives. Later, when DNA analyses were completed (Geyer et al. 1993), it became possible to pair and re-pair birds on a more certain genetic basis to more effectively maximize outbreeding.

Efforts were made to achieve roughly equal numbers of condors among institutions and as complete as possible a genetic representation of family lines at each institution. This provided security against a loss of significant parts of the gene pool that could otherwise result from a catastrophic accident at one institution. That such catastrophes are a threat to be taken seriously was vividly illustrated by a wild brush fire that jeopardized the main condor breeding facility at the San Diego Wild Animal Park in 1993. Fortunately a contingency plan for such an occurrence was in place and sufficient kennels for transporting all birds out of the facility were continuously available at the facility. The birds were all successfully evacuated to another location at the Park as the fire approached, then had to be evacuated again as the fire shifted to threaten this second location. No birds were harmed or lost in the emergency, and the original condor pens fortunately withstood the fire with no significant damage.

The condor facility at the Los Angeles Zoo also successfully weathered a fire emergency in 1988. Although the fire was contained before sweeping through the condor facility, condors were all kenneled and poised for movement to safer quarters at the height of the emergency, and had the fire continued they doubtless would all have been moved successfully.

To date, the captives have not generally been allowed choices in pair formation, but have each been placed together with single preselected mates (Toone and Risser 1988, Cox et al. 1993, Hartt et al. 1994). Nevertheless, pairing success has been relatively good, although problems have arisen in certain instances where the normal dominance of males over females was not obtained, as in the example of Topatopa mentioned above. Another individual showing such problems was CCF, a female who proved to be dominant over most males, and was only finally successfully paired in 1995. In addition, Hartt et al. (1994) found that condors reared together in their early years tended to make relatively poor "mates" when they reached maturity. This apparent "rejection" of early associates as later mates is presumably not a mechanism to prevent pairings of siblings, as condors in the wild are always raised as singletons. Instead, it may be an adaptation of the species to avoid subsequent pairings of birds with their own parents. Rejection of early associates as later mates is a widespread phenomenon among mammals and birds (Harvey and Ralls 1986), and was first recognized over a century ago in humans by Westermarck (1891). In itself, it provides support for efforts to achieve deliberate outbreeding in the captive condor population.

It would be possible to avoid the problem of mate rejections resulting from early associations by raising birds in isolation from other condors in captivity, but this practice would pose general risks of abnormal behavioral development that potentially might be even more detrimental. Instead, in recent years hand-reared birds, at least in San Diego, have often been raised in same-sex groups so that their future mates could be chosen from a maximal pool of birds they would not recognize from early associations. Further, to the extent that parent birds in captivity are now allowed to rear some of their own offspring, the chances both of abnormal behavioral development and categorical rejection of early unrelated associates that might actually be good potential mates on genetic grounds can be expected to be problems of the past.

Production Summary

Production statistics through 1998 have been detailed in the California Condor Studbooks (Kuehler 1996) and in additional information provided by Don Sterner and Mike Mace. The first successful breeding in captivity was achieved in 1988 at the San Diego Wild Animal Park, only a year after the last wild bird was taken captive. By the following year the Los Angeles Zoo was also breeding condors successfully. The breeding records, as summarized in Table 16, reveal a trend of rapidly increasing numbers of fledglings until 1993, then a plateau of production at 15 birds per year for three years, followed by a resumed increase. The plateau in production in the mid 1990s represented a stage when essentially all original captives had been brought into production, but before individuals from the first generation produced in captivity had reached maturity and could provide additional production to the total. The current increase is resulting largely from production of young by second generation breeders in captivity adding to the totals from first generation breeders.

Table 16. Total captive production of California Condors (1988–1998).

Year	Institution	Number of egg-laying pairs	Number of fertile pairs	Total eggs	Percent eggs fertile	Total fledglings
1988	ZSSD	1	1	1	100	1
1989	ZSSD	3	2	4	75	3
	LAZ	2	1	3	33	1
	total	5	3	7	57	4
1990	ZSSD	5	3	8	63	4
	LAZ	4	4	7	86	4
	total	9	7	15	73	8
1991	ZSSD	5	3	10	60	4
	LAZ	6	5	12	83	8
	total	11	8	22	73	12
1992	ZSSD	6	5	10	60	4
	LAZ	5	4	11	82	8
	total	11	9	21	71	12
1993	ZSSD	7	6	10	90	9
	LAZ	5	5	9	100	6
	total	12	11	19	95	15
1994	ZSSD	6	6	12	92	10
	LAZ	5	5	9	100	5
	total	11	11	21	95	15
1995	ZSSD	6	6	11	91	8
	LAZ	5	5	7	100	7
	PF	2	0	4	0	0
	total	13	11	22	77	15
1996	ZSSD	4	3	6	83	3
	LAZ	7	7	17	100	14
	PF	5	1	8	13	1
	total	16	11	31	74	18
1997	ZSSD	7	5	11	82	8
	LAZ	6	6	12	100	10
	PF	8	1	9	22	1
	total	21	15	32	72	19
1998	ZSSD	7	5	10	70	6
	LAZ	6	6	13	92	8
	PF	9	4	14	43	6
	total	22	15	37	68	20

Meanwhile, only a single bird of the individuals originally taken captive has died (UN1 in March 1999), so the total population has been increasing rapidly, subject to some losses in the initial release efforts of second generation birds. As detailed in Table 17, all 27 of the birds originally taken captive from the wild have become members of egg-laying pairs. By 1998, 26 of the 27 had produced fertile eggs, and by 1999 the very last of the original group finally fathered a fertile egg. The rapid increase in numbers swelled the overall count of individuals alive to more than 150 as of summer 1998. This matches our estimate of numbers of condors alive around 1950. It seems almost certain that this total will continue to grow at a rapid rate. Clearly the captive population is proving demographically vigorous, and early fears that the species might not breed readily in confinement have been replaced with chronic concerns about finding enough space to house the swelling captive population.

Genetic Analyses

Blood samples taken from many of the individuals in the remnant wild population and from the founding population for captive breeding were analyzed by Corbin and Nice (1988) for blood enzyme polymorphisms and by Geyer et al. (1993) for DNA fingerprint relationships. Although final results of the Corbin and Nice study did not reveal any clear genetic problems in the species (contrary to preliminary conclusions reported in Snyder and Snyder 1989), the Geyer et al. (1993) study, based on a much more thorough genetic sampling of the species, suggested that genetic diversity in the remnant population was somewhat depressed from what might be expected, based on studies of other species. For example, Geyer et al. compared the extent of genetic similarity found among individuals in the captive California Condor population with that in a small sampling of captive Andean Condors from various zoos. They found that the California Condors were clearly more closely related to one another than were the Andean Condors to one another.

The analyses of Geyer et al. also indicated that the original captive population of California Condors was made up of three relatively homogeneous genetic associations or clans, as follows:

> Group A – SSF and her offspring Xolxol Tecuya, Cachuma, Anapa, Squapuni, and Nojoqui.
> Group B – UN1; HIW; and SBM and his offspring Almiyi, Ojai, Kaweah, and Malibu.
> Group C – CCF and her known offspring REC, Sisquoc, Sespe, Piru, Inaja, and Pismo; PCA; SMM and his offspring Sequoia; Topatopa; and PAX and Cuyama (the offspring of CVF and CVM).

Of considerable interest was the fact that Topatopa did not prove to be a particularly distinctive individual in spite of his origin at a time when the wild population still included on the order of 60 individuals. There had been hopes that he might prove an especially valuable bird genetically.

The first captive taken by the modern program was Xolxol (**top**), shown here on his introduction into a large cage at the Los Angeles Zoo by Mike Cunningham (far left) , Bill Toone (center), and Art Risser (right) in 1983. The first pair of condors to breed in captivity were UN1 and HIW (**middle**), who produced a chick at the San Diego Wild Animal Park in 1988. At all breeding facilities, activities of captives are continuously monitored by remote video (**bottom**). Here Bill Toone and (left) Helen (right) discuss operations at the San Diego facility.

Also of considerable interest was the fact that SSM (deceased since 1985) was evidently the most genetically distinctive individual in the remnant wild flock. Although he was not sampled directly, his progeny were and exhibited a substantial genetic distance from other birds, whereas his mate was closer genetically to others in the flock. Thus Geyer et al. suggested that the progeny of SSM and SSF might prove to be especially valuable to the genetic diversity of the captive population.

The immediate strategy that evolved as a result of the Geyer et al. study was an effort to adjust the pairings in the captive flock to conform to a goal of pairings between rather than within clans. In this effort UN1 and HIW, the first pair to breed in captivity, but a pair that turned out to be formed of individuals from the same clan (see above), were separated and re-paired with new non-clan mates in 1992. Similarly, a pair made up of Sequoia and Sespe was broken up and re-paired with new mates in 1993. However, the very productive pairing of PCA and Pismo was left intact, despite their common membership in the same clan. PCA was a bird exhibiting some questionable characteristics in the wild (e.g., unusual flight feather molt, see Snyder et al. 1987a). He appeared to be potentially homosexually paired in the early 1980s, so we questioned how productive and valuable a breeder he might prove to be in captivity. Nevertheless, he has proved to be an extremely productive bird in his pairing with Pismo, producing consistently fertile eggs that have hatched without complications and usually two vigorous surviving fledglings per year.

Potential Genetic Problems

Results of the first 11 years of captive production also allow an evaluation of the extent to which the population might be suffering from genetic difficulties. In particular, it is important to examine the possibility that the population might be experiencing abnormally low fertility rates or abnormally high rates of embryonic death of eggs. Problems in these spheres are commonly associated with severe inbreeding, presumably reflecting an increased incidence of homozygous exposure of lethal or deleterious genes (see Romanoff and Romanoff 1972, Lacy et al. 1993, Westemeier et al. 1998).

Overall fertility of eggs in the captive flock, at 75.9%, has not been as high as desirable, but most of the infertile eggs observed have not clearly been a result of genetic problems. Instead, available evidence suggests that most infertile eggs can be attributed to inexperience or behavioral incompatibilites within some pairs – especially reflected in failures to perform adequate copulations (Harvey et al. 1996). As can be appreciated from the graph below, fertility within pairs has shown a marked tendency to increase with successive eggs, and once pairs have begun to produce fertile eggs they have rarely laid any infertile ones. Furthermore, fertility of first eggs has been much higher (75%) in pairs with at least one member with egg-laying experience, than in pairs with no known egg-laying experience (26%). These features suggest behavioral factors, rather than genetic difficulties, as the major cause of the infertility seen.

Fertility has been strong enough that there has been no compelling need for the development of intensive fertility-enhancing efforts such as artificial insemination. The most effi-

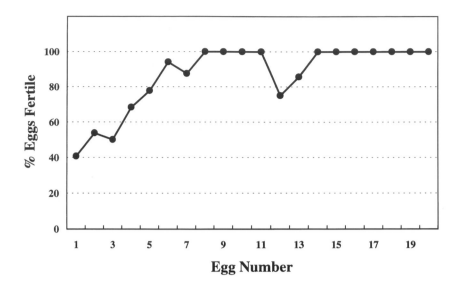

Average fertility of captive-produced eggs as a function of career egg number for all pairs. Fertility showed a strong tendency to improve with experience.

cient remedy for pairs producing chronically infertile eggs appears to be re-pairing the birds involved with new and hopefully more compatible mates, an approach that has already proved successful in certain cases (Table 17).

By comparison, fertility seen in the remnant wild condor population of the 1980s and in the surrogate captive population of Andean Condors at the San Diego Zoo was considerably higher. In a sample of 16 eggs from the wild California Condor population between 1983 and 1986, fertility was actually 100%, an exceedingly high rate for any population. Significantly, these eggs all came from naturally established wild pairs of mostly older, experienced, birds. Fertility of 42 Andean Condor eggs at the San Diego Zoo (mostly from two well-established pairs) averaged 95% between 1981 and 1998, also a comparatively high rate compared to other bird species (e.g., Westemeier et al. 1998).

Survival of eggs through to fledging has also been reasonably good. The rate of fledgling production for captive-produced fertile eggs from 1988 through 1998 was 81%, with no obvious systematic trends up or down through the years. Survival of wild-produced captive-reared fertile eggs through to fledging in the early 1980s was also 81% (13 of 16 eggs). Like the data on fertility rates, the data on survival rates do not suggest major genetic problems with the captive population, as the rates documented compare favorably with rates documented in wild populations of many other bird species.

One feature that does suggest potential genetic problems in the captive population has been the apparently high frequency of malpositioned embryos observed (see further discussion below under problems in hatching). Seventeen of 154 late-dead or hatching fertile eggs of the California Condor that have been examined closely have shown malpositioning problems (11.0%). Although surviving chicks have been salvaged from roughly half of these eggs by intensive remedial measures, and thus malpositioning problems do not show up consistently in the survival statistics of captive-reared eggs, this rate of malpositioning appears high compared to what limited data are available for other species. In the Andean Condors used as surrogates in the breeding program at San Diego, for example, malpositioning has been seen in only one instance, representing only 5% of late-dead or hatching fertile eggs examined closely. Hutt (1929) in a study of various domestic chicken strains found malposition rates

Table 17. Captive reproduction (1988–1998) of California Condors taken from wild.

Bird	Sex	Mate	Age (yr) at first egg	Total eggs	Known fertile eggs	Percent eggs known fertile	Number of fledglings
CCF	F	Mandan	unk	9	9	100	9
REC	M	Squapuni	6	16	16	100	8
Sisquoc	M	Tecuya	7	6	0	0	0
		Shatash		2	0	0	0
Sespe	F	Sequoia	7	2	2	100	0
		HIW		10	10	100	8
Piru	F	Tumusai	11	6	3	50	2
Inaja	F	SBM	8	10	9	90	7
Pismo	F	PCA	7	12	12	100	12
SSF	F	SMM	unk	13	12	92	9
Xolxol	M	Ojai	8	13	10	77	9
Tecuya	F	Sisquoc	7	6	0	0	0
		Shasta		7	4	57	4
Cachuma	F	Cuyama	6	19	19	100	14
Anapa	F	Kaweah	5	18	17	94	13
Squapuni	F	REC	6	16	16	100	8
Nojoqui	M	Molloko	7	8	8	100	8
SBM	M	Inaja	unk	10	9	90	7
Almiyi	F	PAX	6	21	15	71	12
Ojai	F	Xolxol	6	13	10	77	9
Kaweah	M	Anapa	4	18	17	94	13
Malibu	F	Topatopa	6	13	8	62	6
PAX	M	Almiyi	8	21	15	71	12
Cuyama	M	Cachuma	6	19	19	100	14
SMM	M	SSF	unk	13	12	92	9
Sequoia	M	Sespe	6	2	2	100	0
		UN1		9	9	100	7
HIW	M	UN1	8	8	8	100	7
		Sespe		10	10	100	8
UN1	F	HIW	unk	8	8	100	7
		Sequoia		9	9	100	7
PCA	M	Pismo	unk	12	12	100	12
Topatopa	M	Malibu	25	13	8	62	6

averaging about 8.6% of late-dead or hatching fertile eggs at various institutions. The extent of inbreeding in these strains was not specified, but all were inbred strains.

The cases of malpositioning in California Condors do not appear to be clearly limited to any particular family lines although a suspiciously high number of cases (7) have turned up in eggs of SSF and progeny of SSF, and a slightly lesser number (6) in eggs of SBF and her progeny, potentially indicating some genetic associations. Although no malpositioning problems were ever documented for the original wild population of California Condors until eggs were brought into captivity, such problems would not have been detectable by the research methods in use, so it is not possible to compare the recent incidence of malpositionings in captivity with pre-1983 wild data. Two of 16 eggs brought into captivity from the wild between 1983 and 1986 suffered from malpositioning, essentially the same rate as has been seen in captive-produced eggs.

Another problem that has turned up three times with Squapuni has been "bubble eggs" (eggs with abnormal air cell formation), leading to a failure to hatch successfully in two of the three instances. Causes of this abnormality are unknown but could well be genetic as they have only appeared with this one bird.

Also of some concern have been the several cases of apparent congenital abnormalities cropping up in the CV family line. Such abnormalities were seen most dramatically in 1984 in a deformed and inviable chick produced from an egg laid by CVF and CVM in the wild, but may also have been reflected in a chronic gaping problem in PAX (a wild-produced progeny of CVF and CVM), and in a wing-droop problem in Cuyama (a partially captive-reared progeny of the same pair). In more recent years in captivity, several additional chicks with deformities (chondrodystrophy) have turned up among the progeny of Cuyama and Cachuma. Ralls et al. (ms) suggest that this trait may be due to homozygous expression of an autosomal recessive gene present heterozygously in both these birds. If so, both the SS and CV family lines may host the gene, and it may be present in many other carriers in the captive flock. Although chondrodystrophy has not yet appeared in progeny of any other captive pair, this would not be expected except where both parents are carriers of the gene. Cuyama and Cachuma have recently been split up and re-paired with other mates in an attempt to eliminate overt expression of the trait in their future progeny.

Thus, although overall fertility and survival statistics do not suggest major genetic problems in the captive population, there are some indications of genetic difficulties, especially in what appears to be a high malpositioning frequency (particularly in the SS and SB family lines?) in bubble eggs of Squapuni, and in physical abnormalities in the CV and potentially SS family lines. Shablina et al. (1997) and Bryant and Reed (1999), present evidence that an accumulation of deleterious genes can be expected in endangered species held in benign (relaxed selection) environments in captivity and can be expected to make it progressively more difficult for captive populations to readapt to the wild.

Breeding Seasons in Captivity versus the Wild

The seasonal distribution of egg laying in captives shows a breadth somewhat greater than that documented in the wild, perhaps mainly a result of much larger sample size in captivity (Table 18). Although there have been many more January layings of first eggs in captivity than in the wild (and now even a December laying in captivity in late 1998), the median dates of first eggs are very similar between the wild and captivity, and the distributions of first-egg dates are not significantly different for the wild and captivity. For second and third eggs, however, wild eggs have tended to come later, perhaps mainly a result of prompter taking of eggs for artificial incubation in captivity than in the wild.

Table 18. Seasonal timing of California Condors eggs in the wild and captivity (through 1998).

Week		First eggs		Second eggs		Third eggs	
		Captive	Wild	Captive	Wild	Captive	Wild
Jan	4–10	1					
	11–17	4					
	18–24	11					
	25–31	14	1				
Feb	1–7	18	1	1			
	8–14	23	5	2			
	15–21	20	1	5			
	22–28	11		11			
Mar	1–7	10	2	8			
	8–14	6	1	14	1		
	15–21	6		9	2	5	
	22–28	2		11		1	
	29–Apr 4	3	1	12	1	3	
Apr	5–11	1		11	3	1	
	12–18	1			1		2
	19–25			1			
	26–May 2				1		
May	3–9					1	1
Median dates		Feb 12	Feb 14	Mar 15	Apr 6	Mar 22.5	Apr 13

Multiple-clutching

Instances of multiple-clutching have been frequent in captivity, as in the wild, with many pairs producing two eggs and some pairs producing three eggs in some years. Through 1998, seventeen captive females had demonstrated a capacity for double-clutching, and six had demonstrated a capacity for triple-clutching. Only five egg-laying females had laid no more than one egg in a season, and all five were birds that had just come into production, so had had few opportunities for multiple-clutching. Thus multiple-clutching appears to be a nearly uniform capacity for the species in captivity as it was in the wild.

Essentially all captive eggs laid through 1994 were taken into artificial incubation, a policy that encouraged re-laying and maximal egg production but led to consistent hand (puppet)-rearing of chicks. From 1995 on, some pairs have been allowed to incubate their own (usually second) eggs and rear their own chicks to produce fledglings of maximum value for reintroduction. The reduced numbers of pairs exhibiting triple-clutching in the most recent years traces to this policy shift.

The intervals between eggs and replacement eggs in captivity have resembled those documented in the wild population (Snyder and Hamber 1985), with a pronounced peak for the

Table 19. Egg recycling intervals in wild and captive California Condors (1980–1998).

Recycling interval (days)	No. cases in captivity	No. cases in the wild	No. cases total
25	2	0	2
26	8	1	9
27	18	2	20
28	10	1	11
29	11	0	11
30	7	1	8
31	4	3	7
32	3	0	3
33	5	0	5
34	2	0	2
35	0	1	1
36	1	0	1
37	2	1	3
38	1	0	1
39	1	0	1
40	3	1	4
41	1	0	1
44	1	0	1
45	3	0	3
46	2	0	2
47	1	0	1
48	1	0	1
49	1	0	1
50	1	0	1
53	1	0	1
56	1	0	1
57	1	0	1
58	1	0	1
63	1	0	1
70	1	0	1

combined distribution coming at 27 days after egg loss or removal for artificial incubation, and a long skewed spread of records at longer intervals (Table 19). The earliest re-laying interval to date has been 25 days, whereas the most retarded interval was 70 days. The mean for the combined distribution is 33.2 days, similar to the intervals reported earlier for the wild population by Snyder and Hamber (1985) and the captive population by Harvey et al. (1996).

Age of First Breeding and Reproductive Senescence

With the large number of known-age birds in captivity, it has been possible to document the ages of first breeding (egg laying) for many individuals, as summarized in Table 20. In the wild, the earliest known age of breeding was six years, documented for REC in 1986, and the absence of records of condors breeding in less than full adult plumage suggested that breeding any earlier was unusual at best. In captivity through 1998, there were likewise many instances of birds laying eggs for the first time at six years of age. However, there were also seven instances of birds egg laying at five years of age and one instance of a four-year old in an egg-laying pair (long before full adult plumage had developed). Breeding at a relatively young age is often found in captive populations and may relate to a number of permissive features of captivity such as reliable and nutritious food supplies and provision of exclusive nesting areas inaccessible to competitors. However, only one of the eggs laid by condors younger than six years has so far proved fertile. Thus the data from captivity are in general accord with six years as an age of first breeding and indeed many individuals have not produced fertile eggs until seven or eight years of age.

Age of first breeding in Table 20 did not show a marked difference between sexes, and although males averaged slightly younger at first breeding than females, both for eggs in general and for first fertile eggs, the sex differences were not statistically significant. In wild populations of *Gyps fulvus*, Blanco and Martinez (1996) found a substantial fraction of breeding pairs to include immature-plumaged females but none to include immature-plumaged males. Causes of this bias were uncertain, although it did suggest a younger age of first breeding for females than for males.

Only one bird, SSF, has shown indications of senescence in breeding, a bird whose reproductive history may extend back for many decades (see discussion in Chapter 11). SSF

Table 20. Ages at first breeding for captive California Condors (1988–1998).

Age (yrs)	First eggs		First fertile eggs	
	No. of males	No. of females	No. of males	No. of females
4	1			
5	4	3	1	
6	7	6	3	3
7	4	9	5	5
8	3	2	1	4
9			1	
10			1	
11		1		
12				
13				2

has not laid eggs in any of the past four years, despite regular production in the wild with SSM and REC from 1980 to 1986 and consistent production with SMM between 1989 and 1995 in captivity. During the past four years SSF has continued to be caged with SMM and has undergone preliminary breeding activities each year, so her recent failure to lay eggs may possibly represent true reproductive senescence. Also suggesting this possibility is the fact that two of her last three eggs (in 1994 and 1995) were extraordinarily small (less than 200 g in weight) and remain the smallest eggs ever recorded for the species. SSF's age, although unknown, could conceivably be more than a half century. Available data suggest that her territory in the wild may have been occupied continuously back to the 1930s, although shell thickness from one egg collected by Koford in this territory in 1941 was much greater than typical shell thickness of SSF, suggesting a different female occupying at least part of this territory at that time. One Andean Condor at the National Zoo, hatched originally in San Diego, was known to father fertile eggs until an age of 55.

Incubation and Hatching Procedures

Artificial incubation of the first condor eggs taken into captivity at the San Diego Zoo was under the direction of Cyndi Kuehler. Cyndi also directed the incubation efforts of the first captive-produced eggs at the San Diego Wild Animal Park, whereas Susan Kasielke was in charge of parallel efforts at the Los Angeles Zoo. Early artificial incubation procedures benefitted greatly from previously accumulated data on artificial incubation of Andean Condor eggs at Patuxent and other institutions, especially with respect to temperature and humidity regimes.

Because eggs under artificial incubation experience different environmental conditions than eggs under natural incubation (especially because temperature and humidity conditions fluctuate much more greatly under natural incubation), there were concerns that artificially incubated eggs might be somewhat weaker than naturally incubated eggs and might have more difficulty completing the relatively stressful hatching process. Presumably chicks assisted in the hatching process might be able to hatch with enhanced energy reserves for the first hours post hatching. For this reason, the incubation team at San Diego practiced procedures for helping chicks out of eggs with chicken eggs, before working with their first condor eggs. All the first California Condor chicks hatched in captivity were also helped out of their shells. This process was not entirely unnatural, as our observations at the 1980 nesting of the CC pair in the wild indicated that parent birds may also give some assistance to their chicks in hatching by nibbling away pieces of shell around the pip hole. Close observations of eggs allowed natural parent hatching in captivity also indicate that adults often assist in breakout of their chicks by nibbling at the progressing shell opening, both in Andean and California Condors.

Assisted hatching is not without risks, because even after pipping, an embryo retains some blood circulation in membranes lying just underneath the shell. If pieces of shell are broken away prematurely, blood vessels that are still functioning can hemorrhage and lead to the death of the chick. The process of assisting in hatching must not proceed too quickly.

Artificial incubation of condor eggs involved candling to determine fertility and the progress of air cell formation, and flexible control of humidity to ensure a proper rate of weight loss through development. **Above**, candling involves shining a bright light through the shell and can reveal presence of an embryo at about 4–5 days after laying. **Middle**, to ensure successful hatching, many of the first chicks were carefully helped out of their shells. **Bottom**, Cyndi Kuehler assists the hatching of Sespe, a chick that barely survived excessive incubation neglect from the CC pair while still in the wild.

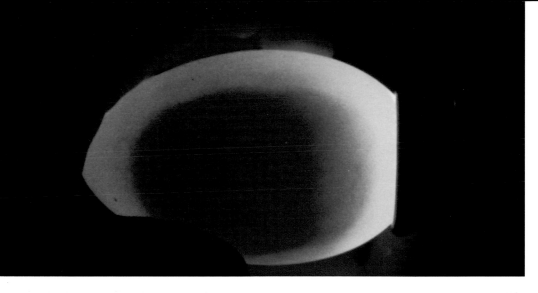

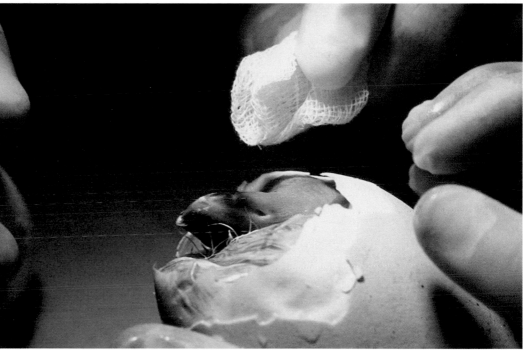

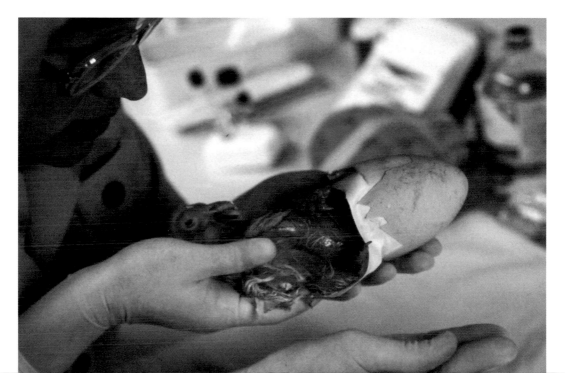

No problems were encountered in the assisted hatching of California Condor eggs, as the risks were well recognized in advance and guarded against. In recent years eggs at both San Diego and Los Angeles have usually been allowed unassisted hatching unless problems have developed during the hatching process.

The principal environmental factors under control in artificial incubation are temperature, humidity, and turning rates of eggs. The conditions used for most condor eggs have been a temperature (dry bulb) of 97.5 to 98.0°F (36.4–36.7°C) and a humidity regime that results in a weight loss (much of this being water loss) of about 12–14% through development. At San Diego, the original turning regime implemented was an automatic machine turn every two hours coupled with an additional half turn by hand every 12 hours. In more recent years the regime has been changed to a machine turn every hour coupled with a quarter turn by hand every 12 hours.

Relative humidities in the incubators have been varied widely, as calculated continuously by computer program, to achieve a desired rate of egg weight loss as a steady progression. However, with certain eggs, weight loss through evaporation of water content of the eggs has been so slow that it has not been possible to drop the humidity low enough to produce the desired rate. During incubation of eggs in the first years, when an overall weight loss of 10–12% was the goal (based on experience with other species) a number of cases of edematous (fluid-bloated) chicks were encountered, especially with eggs losing only about 10% of weight during development. This led to a conclusion that lower humidities and faster rates of weight loss in general might be beneficial. Most eggs in recent years have achieved a weight loss of 12–14% by the time of hatching and the incidence of edematous chicks has dropped.

At San Diego there have been some preliminary indications that natural parental incubation through the first week or so seems to result in eggs that lose weight more easily, so in recent years several pairs with a history of edematous chicks have been allowed natural incubation for the first part of the incubation period. Nevertheless, most eggs taken into artificial incubation have continued to be pulled on the day of laying or the day after.

To gather data on incubation temperatures and constancy in the wild, we placed a telemetered dummy egg made from a swan egg (courtesy of Jerry Stewart) in a nest site of the CC pair in 1983 at the time their second egg was taken into captivity. This egg was readily accepted by the pair and incubated for 10 days. The telemetry results obtained revealed very frequent breaks in incubation constancy and a highly fluctuating temperature environment for the egg totally different from the nearly constant temperatures experienced by eggs in artificial incubation. Core egg temperature never reached the temperature being used in artificial incubation, although it did closely approach this temperature. However, direct observations were also possible of the incubating birds at this nest, and these revealed that they were harassed incessantly by clouds of gnats, which were the apparent cause of highly agitated incubation behavior. The data obtained were evidently not typical of wild pairs.

Fertility of eggs is normally first detectable at four days by candling (shining a bright light through the egg). At this stage the embryo first becomes visible as a dark spot lying on the surface of the yolk. In succeeding days blood vessels proliferate from the embryo into the egg and fertility becomes steadily more obvious. From about day 5 through day 21, the embryo establishes membrane connections with egg components and is especially vulnerable to mechanical shaking disrupting these connections. Eggs must be handled with great care during this period to avoid complications.

Pipping of an egg (the first breakage of the shell in the hatching process) normally occurs at just under three days before actual hatching (mean of approximately 68 hours, both for self-hatched eggs and eggs assisted in hatching), and the full incubation period for successfully hatched eggs has ranged from 53 to 60 days. Earlier, Snyder (1988) reported an incubation period of 54 to 58 days, based on eggs that had been hatched in captivity through 1986. However, the much larger sample of eggs incubated through 1998 has expanded the known range and given a better indication of the distribution of incubation periods (Table 21). There is a significant overall relationship of incubation period to egg weight (size) in the species, with larger eggs taking longer to hatch than smaller eggs. The most common incubation periods, 56 through 58 days, represent over 80% of the periods measured to date, and the overall mean incubation period was approximately 57 days, both for self-hatched eggs and eggs assisted in the hatching process. Incubation periods of eggs naturally incubated by adult condors in captivity have been very similar to incubation periods of eggs that have been artificially incubated, both averaging about 57 days.

By comparison, the length of incubation in the slightly larger Andean Condor has ranged from 54 to 63 days (mean of 58.6 days) for the Zoological Society of San Diego. No significant correlation between egg weight and incubation period was found in the Andean Condor.

Table 21. Incubation periods of captive California and Andean Condors (1988–1998).

Incubation period (days)	Number of eggs	
	California Condors	Andean Condors
53	1	0
54	2	1
55	6	1
56	23	3
57	38	3
58	35	6
59	11	10
60	3	7
61	0	2
62	0	0
63	0	1
Total incubation periods	119	34
Mean length of incubation	57.2 days	58.6 days

Note: incubation periods for California Condors averaged 57.4 days for eggs hatching without assistance and 56.9 days for eggs assisted in hatching.

Problems in Hatching: Edematous Chicks, Malpositions, Pathogens

Although overall hatching success has been quite favorable, many of the eggs failing to produce surviving chicks have succumbed at about the time of hatching, both in the wild and in captivity. A few of these failures have been traceable to yolk sac infections, but the most frequent causes of hatching difficulties have been edematous chicks and malpositions of embryos within the eggshells.

The occurrence of edematous chicks has been one of the most important factors necessitating assisted hatching in many eggs, as such chicks often have difficulty in rotating properly within the shell in the hatching process, apparently getting stuck in place. Because edematous chicks have also been relatively frequent in Andean Condor eggs under artificial incubation, it seems likely that the causes of the problem may be primarily related to differences between artificial and natural incubation, rather than to potential genetic difficulties.

Malpositioned embryos are ones in which the relative orientations of appendages and the head have been abnormal or in which the entire embryo has been abnormally oriented relative to the shell. Sometimes malpositioning has involved embryos that have developed in reversed orientation with respect to the narrow and broad ends of the egg. In these, the head end of the embryo has been aimed at the narrow end of the egg and the chick's head has not had an opportunity to pierce the air cell at the broad end prior to hatching. Malpositioned embryos often fail to pip the eggshell. In some cases it has been possible to remedy this problem and achieve successful hatchings by effecting a "windowing" of the shell with a manually created pip to allow the chick access to air, but in 10 out of 17 cases malpositioned chicks have not survived the hatching process despite artificial breakout of the chicks from their shells.

Although the overall incidence of malpositioned chicks (11.0 % of fertile eggs) has been relatively high in the California Condor, it is unclear at present whether the causes of malpositioning are to be sought mainly in faulty incubation conditions or in genetic difficulties. In studies of other bird species, malpositioning has been related to both genetic and environmental factors (Landauer 1967, Romanoff and Romanoff 1972). The lesser frequency of malpositions in Andean Condor eggs incubated artificially (under similar conditions) suggests that for the California Condor the problem may have a substantial genetic component, although genetics may not account for the entire problem. In an effort to reduce malpositions, the frequency of turning eggs under artificial incubation has been increased in recent years, but malpositions have continued to occur with some frequency.

Pathogen problems have been rare in the captive flock and limited almost entirely to occasional bacterial yolk sac infections in hatchlings (*Pseudomonas* and *Escherichia coli*). Older birds have been almost completely free of infections, and mortality of adults due to accidents or any other causes has been close to zero. One of the eggs produced in the wild by the SB pair in 1984 yielded an inviable chick with a yolk sac infection on hatching in captivity. Whether the contamination might have originated with the female parent or through some subsequent breach of the egg's defenses was unclear. However, it is worth noting that an egg of this same female (SBF) from three years earlier similarly resulted in a chick that apparently died at or shortly after hatching in the wild. It is conceivable that this female may have had some pathogen problem in her reproductive tract, though this conclusion is obviously highly speculative.

The threats posed by pathogens in captivity have been addressed primarily by rigorous prophylactic health measures in handling of eggs and in preventing exposure of adults and juveniles to exotic diseases. The condor rearing facilities at both the San Diego Wild Animal Park and Los Angeles Zoo have been physically separated from holding and rearing facilities for other species, and the staff servicing the condor facilities have been limited to individuals who do not have contact with other species at these institutions. Although the California Condor, by virtue of its normal diet, is a species that must be relatively capable of withstanding assault by the pathogens often present in rotten meat, these isolation precautions have been designed to reduce the potential exposure to other pathogens, especially exotic pathogens, that can be expected to invade any zoo facility housing animals from around the world. No effort has been made to raise young condors in sterile environments, as this could negatively affect the development of their immune systems. To the contrary, young condors under artificial rearing have often been deliberately fed regurgitant from adult condors to establish normal gut flora and fauna.

Diet and Rearing Procedures

The rearing of the first nestling condors by the Zoological Society of San Diego was coordinated by Bill Toone. Newly hatched condors were fed a diet of newborn ("pinky") mice supplemented by extra calcium. During the second, third, and fourth weeks the chicks were shifted to older stages of mice (containing more calcium and fur roughage), and after a month they were given a varied diet of beef spleens, rabbits, rats, and trout, a fare that is sometimes varied with basic feline diet. Diet at the Los Angeles Zoo has been similar, with a reliance on pinky mice in early stages, switching to rats, horsemeat, and commercial feline diet at later stages.

Weight gains of eight captive-reared chicks reared by the Zoological Society of San Diego through the nestling period (Piru, Sisquoc, Almiyi, Tecuya, Ojai, Sespe, Inaja, and Anapa) are graphed below (data courtesy D. Sterner). By comparison with the typical S-shaped weight-gain curve of other avian species, the captive condor curves, although still S-shaped, are quite flat in shape and usually lack the pronounced overshoot of adult weight in the late nestling stage that is found in many species. Whether weight-gain curves of wild condors may exhibit a similar shape is unknown, as no studies of weight gains of wild chicks were pursued after the early loss of a condor chick in a handling accident in 1980. However, the weight gain curves of the captive condors are extremely similar in shape to those of wild Turkey and Black Vulture chicks studied by Coleman and Fraser (1989a), which likewise show no general overshoot of adult weights late in development. As pointed out by these workers, growth rates of vulturids tend to be relatively slow compared with growth rates of similar-sized species in the family Accipitridae, although they closely resemble growth rates of similar-sized storks.

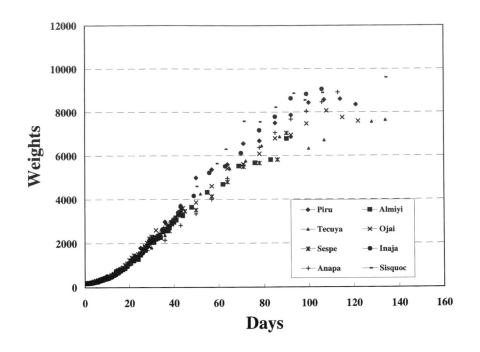

Weight in grams of eight captive-reared condor chicks through the nestling period (data courtesy Don Sterner of San Diego Wild Animal Park). Normal adult weight averages about 8100 grams in females and 8800 grams in males. Of the captives illustrated only Sisquoc is a male.

In the wild, condor chicks are fed exclusively by regurgitation, presumably mainly on the soft tissues of vertebrate carrion, but including some bone material. Mundy et al. (1992) have noted that breeding adult Old World vultures commonly take on bone as the last items ingested during a meal at a carcass. Presumably, this normally results in chicks receiving pieces of bone among the first items offered during a feeding by their parents.

Efforts have been made to minimize as much as possible the opportunities for chicks to see humans during development to reduce chances of malimprinting of the birds on humans. Hatchling condors that have not been allowed parent rearing have been fed and groomed by condor-head puppets in controlled-environment isolettes during early stages. Although it has been valuable to weigh chicks on a daily basis through the first few weeks to be sure that they are gaining proper nutrition, this has normally been done with the head of the bird covered so it has not been able to see people during the process. Similarly when birds have been given routine annual health examinations their heads have normally been covered during the process.

Considerable publicity has been given to the use of condor puppets in feeding and preening chicks to minimize chances of imprinting of nestlings on humans. However, it is not clear the nestlings are truly "deceived" by the puppets or deceived for very long. As realistic as the puppets seem, there is no way for them to be perfect mimics of adult condors in behavior.

Once they reach an age of several weeks chicks have become adept at picking up food on their own from a feeding pan. At this stage condor chicks have normally been grouped together, and while puppet feeding has continued, the associations with others of their own species have also presumably helped minimize chances of imprinting on humans. Under such procedures, the condor chicks have shown no signs of becoming fully imprinted on humans and have readily paired and reproduced with their own kind. However, they have

To minimize the chances of improper imprinting of chicks on humans, chicks that have not been parent-reared have been raised by condor puppets during early stages of growth. At later stages, puppet-reared chicks are allowed to socialize with one another in common cages.

not become fearful of humans. Their behavioral tolerance of humans has presumably been an advantage with respect to their careers as captive breeders, but has not been advantageous with respect to releases to the wild, as will be discussed in the next chapter.

Value of Andean Condors as Surrogates in Captive Breeding

The Endangered Wildlife Research Program of the USFWS has generally followed a policy of establishing captive populations of close relatives of endangered species to aid not only in captive breeding efforts for endangered forms but to facilitate research into other aspects of recovery efforts. Thus the program for the endangered Whooping Crane has been aided by parallel efforts with closely related, but nonendangered Sandhill Cranes, just as nonendangered captive Hispaniolan Parrots have proved a valuable complement to direct efforts with the endangered Puerto Rican Parrot. The Andean Condor, although itself an endangered species, is far less endangered than the California Condor and has been an extremely valuable surrogate for work with the California Condor, both in developing and refining husbandry techniques, and in numerous other aspects of the program, such as developing release techniques to the wild for the California birds (Carpenter 1982, Erickson and Carpenter 1983). Andean Condors also served beneficially in developing a radio-telemetry program for the California Condor, by allowing evaluation of alternative transmitter attachment methods both in captivity and in the wild. They served as an ideal surrogate with which to test trapping techniques before they were tried out on California Condors.

In captivity, the Andean Condors have provided a baseline against which to compare various features of California Condor performance (e.g., fertility rates, malposition rates), and have more directly served in such roles as providing a source of fertile eggs to give experience in chick rearing to inexperienced California Condor pairs without risks to valuable California eggs. For the first California Condor chicks raised in captivity, they provided regurgitant to establish presumably favorable gut microflora and fauna. In addition, basic artificial incubation regimes that have proved successful for the California Condor were first developed with the Andean Condor.

Few endangered species have as similar a close relative as the Andean Condor is to the California Condor, and this has aided the program immensely in developing crucial techniques with minimal risks to California Condors. Without such a surrogate species, the program would necessarily have had to proceed more slowly in many respects and with a significantly higher degree of risk.

CHAPTER SEVENTEEN

Releases to the Wild

Reestablishment of any species that has been lost from the wild depends on correcting the major limiting factors responsible for the species' disappearance. Biological studies of the California Condor in the 1980s established beyond any reasonable doubt that the principal causes of decline were mortality factors, rather than reproductive factors. And by the time all California Condors were in captivity, considerable evidence had accumulated to suggest that inadvertent lead poisoning might be the most important, although surely not the only, mortality threat to the species. It seemed unlikely that reestablishment of the species in the wild could be achieved without effective countermeasures to at least this threat, although success might also depend on effective reduction of other mortality threats as well.

In Chapter 12 we considered historic sources of lead contamination that might be affecting condors, especially remains of hunter-shot deer and carcasses of pest species such as coyotes and ground squirrels shot by ranchers, recreational shooters, and Animal Damage Control (ADC) agents. Most of these sources are still present and widespread today. Yet releases of captive condors to the wild were initiated soon after first breeding of the species in captivity. It is important to consider how these releases were justified, in view of their apparent contradiction of the basic principle that reestablishment efforts should not precede correction of major limiting factors.

Justification for Early Releases

Despite the continued presence of the main sources of lead contamination in the environment, several factors supported rapid initiation of releases. These were (1) a perceived

The first releases of condors to the wild in California were temporary experimental releases of Andean Condors. The very first release site (***above***) was a rock outcrop on the Hopper Mountain National Wildlife Refuge adjacent to the Sespe Condor Sanctuary, where Andean Condors were released in December of 1988. The Andean Condors performed reasonably well on release (***below***) although one bird was lost to a collision with an overhead wire.

potential for countering the lead poisoning threat in the near term by keeping released birds dependent on a subsidy of clean carcasses, (2) the expectation that documentation of mortalities of released birds would significantly expand knowledge of other mortality factors important to the species and speed their reduction, and (3) a perceived value in sustaining the program and program personnel through a transition period between wild population studies and a full-scale reestablishment program. Because of these considerations we supported a rapid development of release efforts. Early releases were in potential conflict with a goal of achieving a genetically and demographically vigorous captive population, but this conflict could be side-stepped by conducting first efforts with surrogate Andean Condors, rather than California Condors. Until surplus California Condors were safely available, releases of Andean Condors could give the program a significant head start in improving release techniques and reducing mortality factors.

Food subsidy was not originally viewed as the ultimate solution to the lead problem, but as an interim solution that could be phased out when better solutions became available, solutions that would involve true removal of lead-contaminated food from condor range and would not demand endless investments of funding and manpower. The hope that released birds could be maintained for long periods on food subsidy was based on the experience of Mike Wallace in releasing Andean Condors to the wild in Peru (Wallace and Temple 1987b) and the experience of Michel Terrasse in releasing Eurasian Griffon Vultures to the wild in France (Terrasse 1985, 1988). Wallace found that released captive-bred Andean Condors exhibited a strong tendency to remain dependent on subsidy and that getting the birds to search for natural carcasses was a long, involved training process, accustoming the birds to seeking food at multiple sites. Terrasse similarly found that it was very difficult to get released griffon vultures to accept naturally available carcasses or even new subsidy stations while steady subsidy was available at his original subsidy station.

But although the goal of both the Peru and French efforts was to achieve a transition of released birds to natural carcasses, the goal envisioned in early planning discussions for California Condors was to prevent such a transition so long as lead contamination threats still existed in the range. Because of the continued presence of lead threats, it was important to keep released birds dependent on single subsidy stations. Providing them with multiple subsidy stations would encourage them to develop normal food-searching behavior and ultimately would run the risk of exposing them to lead contamination. In addition, release of any of the experienced wild-trapped birds to the wild was to be avoided, as they could be expected to return quickly to foraging widely on naturally-occurring lead-contaminated carcasses and could attract naive captive-reared birds into doing the same. To increase the chances of keeping birds dependent on clean subsidy it was also wise to conduct releases in areas with low natural food supplies. The abundant nest sites and low natural food supplies to be found in the Sespe and Sisquoc Sanctuary regions made them favored initial areas for release attempts.

The long-term feasibility of keeping released captive-bred condors dependent on subsidy had not been tested at the time releases were initiated. It represented only an extrapolation based on the results of studies in Peru and France. Should the feasibility of maintaining released birds on subsidy actually prove to be quite low in the context of California releases, the whole basis for early reestablishment efforts would come into question. Birds losing dependence on subsidy would presumably be exposed to all the same mortality factors as made the historical wild population inviable.

But given an assumption that captive-bred released birds could indeed be held dependent on subsidy (in spite of the failure of previous attempts to get wild-experienced condors to become dependent on subsidy), the early release program appeared to be consistent with the axiom that reestablishment efforts should be attempted only upon correction of primary limiting factors in the wild. Although lead-contaminated foods still remained in the wild, poisoning would be avoided by extended food subsidy.

The First Releases

The first release of captive California Condors to the wild followed several previous releases of Andean Condors and took place in the Sespe Condor Sanctuary on January 14, 1992. The event was a culmination of hopes for all who had labored over the years toward the preservation of the species. Many who were no longer direct participants in the program, including ourselves, travelled long distances to be present. For us, it was also a wonderfully nostalgic opportunity to return to wilderness terrain that we had once trod in much more anxious times and a chance to renew contacts with others who had fought through the intense battles of a decade earlier. It was a profoundly happy celebration. It was also a clear reply to those who had long questioned the commitment of the conservation program to return condors to the wild.

Although the 1992 release was only an initial symbolic step toward reestablishing viable wild populations and involved only two California Condors together with two Andean Condors, it was a milestone in the long process of restoring the species. Significantly, it came less than five years after the last bird of the original wild population had been taken into captivity. By this time, reproduction of the captive population was accelerating rapidly, and the immediate genetic goals of the breeding program were being rapidly achieved. Trial releases with Andean Condors in the same region had gone moderately well. These birds had stayed dependent on food subsidy and stayed free of lead poisoning, although they had exhibited an undersirable degree of tameness and a tendency to seek out developed areas, necessitating their eventual retrapping. One bird was also lost to a powerline collision.

First releases of both Andean and California Condors were under the overall supervision of Mike Wallace of the Los Angeles Zoo, who had conducted previous successful release programs with Andean Condors in Peru and Black and Turkey Vultures in Florida. The techniques used were basically an extension of those used in these earlier programs, although both previous release programs differed from the California Condor releases in that they involved integration of captive-reared birds into existing wild populations of the species involved. The California Condor releases were all into habitat empty of established wild populations, and the relative difficulty experienced so far in these releases may be due largely to this difference.

A summary of all 18 releases of condors to the wild conducted by early 1999 is presented in Table 22. These releases included two temporary experimental releases of Andean

One of the first two California Condors released to the wild in January 1992 (**above**) contemplates a first flight in front of its release cave atop the Arundell cliffs of the Sespe Condor Sanctuary. Six more California Condors were installed at the same release structure in October 1992 (**middle**) and were released in December of 1992. After release (**below**) the birds continued to be fed in front of the release cave. Scale at center provided a convenient non-invasive way of tracking bird weights before and after release.

Table 22. Summary of Condor releases December 1988 to June 1999 (adapted from Meretsky et al. in press).

Release date	Release location	Number, species released	Aversive condit?	Parent rear?	Elapsed bird-months	Deaths	Interventions	Annual mortality rate	Adj. mort. rate	Status
Dec 88–Feb 89	Sespe	7An	N	N	61.25	1	0	0.20		Birds retrapped for behav. prob.
Jan–Feb 90	Sespe	6An	N	N	89.0	0	1	0.0	0.15	Birds retrapped for behav. prob.
Jan 92	Sespe	2An 2Ca	N	N	51.75	1	0	0.23		Ans retrapped, Ca relocated to Lion Cyn11/93, retrapped 3/94 for behav. prob.
Dec 92	Sespe	6Ca	N	N	67.5	3	0	0.53		Birds relocated Lion Cyn 11/93 retrapped 3/94 for behav. prob.
Dec 93	Lion Cyn	5Ca	N	N	57.5	2	0	0.42		Birds retrapped 3/95 for behav. prob.
Mar 95	Lion Cyn	6CA	Y	N	228.0	1	2(3)	0.05	0.18	Ongoing
Aug 95	Lion Cyn	8Ca	Y	N	335.25	1	3	0.04	0.17	Ongoing
Mar 96	Castle Cgs	4Ca	Y	Y	103.5	2	1	0.23	0.35	Ongoing
Nov 96	Lion Cyn	4Ca	Y	N	49.0	2	0	0.49		3 birds moved to Castle Cgs 1/97 2 still in wild
Jan 97	Ventana	4Ca	Y	N	12.5	0	0	0.00		Birds retrapped for behav. prob.
Nov 97	Ventana	5Ca	Y	Y	92.5	0	0	0.00		Ongoing
Nov 97	Lion Cyn	4Ca	Y	N	53.5	2	0	0.45		Ongoing
Jan 99	Ventana	7Ca	Y	Y/N	27.0	0	0	0.00		3 puppet-reared birds returned to captivity for behavior probl.
Mar 99	Lion Cyn	6Ca	Y	N	12.0	1	0	1.00		Ongoing
Dec 96	Vermillion	6Ca	Y	Y	127.75	2	0	0.19		Ongoing
May 97	Vermillion	9Ca	Y	N	176.0	2	1	0.14	0.15	Ongoing, 3 birds behav prob. 8/98 but not retrapped

Release date	Release location	Number, species released	Aversive condit?	Parent rear?	Elapsed bird-months	Deaths	Inter ven-tions	Annual mortality rate	Adj. mort. rate	Status
Nov 97	Vermillion	4Ca	Y	N	68.0	1	0	0.18		Ongoing
Nov 98	Hurricane	9Ca	Y	Y/N	58.75	1	0	0.20		Ongoing

Note: Last four releases in Arizona, rest in California; interventions in parentheses account for multiple interventions on a single bird; release of Dec 88-Feb 89 done in three groups – 17 December 1988, 21 January 1989, 14 February 1989; release of Jan–Feb 90 done in two groups – 3 January 1990, 20 February 1990; release of May 97 done in two groups – 14 and 27 May 1997.

Condors alone between 1988 and 1990, a combined release of Andean and California Condors in 1992, and 15 subsequent releases of California Condors. All releases have been conducted within historical condor range in California and Arizona. The specific sites chosen have been the Sespe and Sisquoc (Lion Canyon) regions in the heart of the recent range, the Castle Crags and Ventana Wilderness regions farther north in California, and the Vermillion and Hurricane cliffs regions in the upper Grand Canyon of Arizona. These sites have been chosen on a variety of grounds, including proximity to former condor concentration areas, extent of surrounding undisturbed habitat, remoteness from urban developments, and existence of feasible access for release crews. In addition to the US Fish and Wildlife Service, other agencies taking major roles in the releases have been the Los Angeles Zoo, the Zoological Society of San Diego, the Ventana Wilderness Society, and the Peregrine Fund.

All releases have been conducted with captive-reared fledglings, rather than adults. Birds for the first releases were all reared and given pre-release training at the Los Angeles Zoo, although many were hatched in San Diego (some Andeans also came from other zoos). The early California Condor releases all involved puppet-reared birds, rather than parent-reared birds. Priority at that stage was still being given to achieving a maximum rate of growth of the captive California Condor population through maximal multiple-clutching. Maximal multiple-clutching precluded much in the way of parent-rearing by captive pairs.

To reduce chances of condor chicks imprinting on humans and to promote their socialization with other members of their own species, the birds reared for the first releases were first fed and preened by hand puppets resembling adult condors, as described in the preceding chapter. Limited socialization of chicks with other chicks was allowed at about two weeks of age, and full contact with other similar-aged chicks was provided at about two months of age through the rest of the pre-release period. In the latter stages when chicks were capable of ripping apart food for themselves, food was either provided in the dark or through visually occluded chutes. Chicks were generally moved from the zoo environment to release cages in the field at about 4–7 months of age.

Release cages in the field consisted of cave-like roost boxes connected to large outside screened areas allowing extensive wing and ambulatory exercise and a full view of the surroundings. For actual releases several weeks to months later, birds were confined in the roost structures with sliding door panels blocking the entrances while outside screened areas were

Problems of released birds have included excessive tameness of puppet-reared individuals and mortalities to various causes. Three individuals from one of the Lion Canyon releases (**above**) invaded the Pine Mountain Club near Frazier Park in 1994 where they received handouts of hot dogs from bystanders. Birds from this release, together with birds from subsequent releases, returned to vandalize Pine Mountain Club in 1999. One individual from the first release in 1992 (**below**), as examined here by Dave Ledig, succumbed to anti-freeze poisoning, possibly from drinking at a puddle where someone had drained his car radiator.

torn down. Releases followed gentle opening of the door panels by remote control. Following release, the birds were fed at subsidy sites near the release cages.

During the entire pre-release period major efforts were made to prevent chicks from seeing humans so that they would not associate humans with food or become habituated to their presence. However, there were several sorts of exceptions to this rule. Newly-hatched chicks were generally handled without concealment or puppets during the first days of post-hatching life when they showed only very limited signs of reacting to visual stimuli. In addition, birds sometimes viewed humans when they were being handled for weighing. It was important to track weight gains of chicks to be sure of their proper development, and although efforts were made to keep their heads covered during weighing, there were occasional instances when head coverings were accidentally shed. There were also occasions when nestlings poked their heads back through the puppet entry ports into their rearing chambers and had an opportunity to view human puppeteers directly. Finally, just prior to release, birds were provided with radio-transmitters and they were sometimes able to view humans during the attachment process. In addition, it is important to note that the pre-release birds were generally held in standard rectangular cage structures and were not fully shielded from the sounds of civilization, such as human voices, vehicle noises, generator noises, etc., although efforts were made in later releases to mask such noises with white-noise generators and recordings of natural sounds.

Despite the considerable efforts to isolate pre-release birds from human contact, condors in the first releases showed excessive tendencies to come into civilized areas and to approach humans without fear, sometimes accepting food offered to them by bystanders. We emphasize that fledglings in the wild have also tended to be quite approachable by humans (also sometimes accepting food from hikers), but there have been virtually no historical instances of either young or adult wild condors coming into towns to land on

Table 23. Causes of mortalities and near mortalities of released condors December 1988 to June 1999.

Cause	Early (1988–1993)		Recent (1994–1999)		Totals	
	Actual mortalities	Near mortalities	Actual mortalities	Near mortalities	Actual mortalities	Near mortalities
Collisions	4	0	3	0	7	0
Lead poisoning	0	0	0	6	0	6
Disappearances	0	0	4	1	4	1
Drownings	0	0	2	0	2	0
Starvation	0	0	2	2	2	2
Shooting	0	1	1+(1)	0	1+(1)	1
Antifreeze	1	0	0	0	1	0
Cancer	0	0	1	0	1	0
Golden Eagle	0	0	1	0	1	0
Coyote(?)	0	0	(1)	0	(1)	0
Unknown injury	0	1	0	0	0	1
Found dead	0	0	1	0	1	0

Collision mortalities (including electrocutions) were frequent in early releases, possibly in part because of familiarity of the birds with pole structures prior to release. Released Andean Condors (**above**), like California Condors, commonly landed on utility poles, but unlike California Condors, were not observed roosting on poles. Aversive conditioning to utility poles by means of hot-wired poles in release cages, seen here at the Ventana release site (**below**), has apparently reduced tendencies of birds to land on utility poles, and collision rates have dropped substantially.

buildings or phone poles. The latter behaviors were frequent in the early releases and continue to be seen in many released birds today. The excessive interactions with civilization exhibited by the first released birds were clearly not an indication of normal wild behavior and strongly suggested that existing pre-release conditioning procedures needed significant improvement.

However, we call attention here to an apparent difference between Andean and California Condors in the early releases. Both Andean and California Condors frequently landed on phone poles, but the tendency for California Condors to do so was clearly much stronger than that of Andean Condors. California Condors, in fact, commonly roosted on these structures, whereas the Andeans very rarely did so. Reasons for this difference are unknown, but might reflect innate differences between the species in perch preferences.

The frequent interactions of post-release birds with humans and human structures in the early releases appeared to have been one of the main factors producing a high mortality rate from collisions with overhead wires. In Table 23 we present the data on all cases of mortalities and near mortalities (mortalities averted by emergency action) of released birds documented through mid 1999, and it can be seen that collisions have outranked all other causes of actual mortalities in frequency.

The 1994 Workshop on Release Methods

The obvious behavioral problems seen in the first several releases were discouraging for the release crew who had worked hard to achieve minimum contact of condors with humans. In response to these problems, the Fish and Wildlife Service convened a workshop in September of 1994 (Anonymous 1994) to review the problems and search for solutions. Noel was one of the outside personnel invited to participate in this workshop. During the discussions he presented some findings from releases of Thick-billed Parrots to the wild in Arizona that had relevance to the condor releases, especially data indicating severe survival problems with hand-reared birds and the advisability of limiting releases to birds of only the highest behavioral quality (Snyder et al. 1994).

Several sorts of solutions to the behavioral problems being seen in releases were discussed. Of principal interest were (1) solutions that involved aversive conditioning of pre-release puppet-reared birds to humans and human structures and (2) solutions that removed pre-release birds from all contact with humans and typical human structures by switching to parent-rearing of pre-release birds and by moving breeding pairs into remote naturalistic field enclosures. Noel was a strong advocate for the latter sorts of solutions, although he also supported experimentation with aversive conditioning.

The specific sorts of aversive conditioning discussed included the hot-wiring of dummy utility poles placed in pre-release cages and the aggressive capture of birds in the cages with nets. The problems anticipated with aversive conditioning included the possibility that birds might habituate to humans handling them with nets rather than increase their wariness of humans. In general, it was known that negative conditioning of animals tends to produce more temporary results than positive conditioning.

Also discussed at the workshop was the slow rate of progress of the program in achieving a removal of lead threats to condors in the wild, either by creating large no-hunting preserves or by promoting a switch from lead ammunition to nontoxic alternatives. This was an issue that troubled us greatly, and although the Recovery Team had been proposing for several years the screening of potentially nontoxic alternatives made of copper and other materials, no action had yet been taken by the USFWS on these proposals, purportedly because of a lack of funding. Yet at the workshop, it became clear that testing of these alternatives on Turkey Vultures would cost only on the order of $30,000, a tiny fraction of the monies ($1 million plus) being spent annually on releases and captive breeding at the time. In response to pressures exerted at the workshop, the USFWS finally made a commitment to find funding for these experiments (although it took 3 more years before the experiments actually took place and results have still not been published).

With respect to the other major alternative for removing lead threats from the wild (creation of large no-hunting preserves) workshop participants learned of the recent creation of a Carrizo Plains Natural Area by the Bureau of Land Management and other cooperating agencies, justified in part by its potential future values as a feeding area for condors. Unfortunately, as soon as the preserve was created, it was opened by the California Fish and Game Commission to hunting activities. Thus, its values in reducing lead contamination for the condor were nullified, unless alternative nontoxic ammunitions might someday become mandatory in the reserve. Efforts to restrict hunting to nontoxic ammunitions in the Carrizo Plains Natural Area have been initiated in recent months.

Subsequent Releases

Releases since the 1994 workshop have implemented some, but not all, of the recommendations developed at the workshop. Aversive conditioning, including hot-wired poles in cages and aggressive capture of birds with nets, has become standard training procedure for puppet-reared birds in California, and there have now also been several releases of parent-reared fledglings (also given hot-wire conditioning). Aversive conditioning has also been practiced post-release, for example by chasing off birds that come into developed areas. However, as yet there have been no efforts to implement parent-rearing in isolation from man by moving breeding pairs out of the humanized environments of zoos into field environments (an approach urged both at the workshop and by Verner 1978).

The incorporation of aversive conditioning has had only questionable beneficial effects, as cases of condors coming into civilized areas still continue to occur in puppet-reared birds, despite the aversive conditioning. For just one example, recent newspaper headlines detailed the entry of three such birds from the Arizona releases into a visitor center in Colorado (Lofholm 1998), an incident that was also publicized on national news radio. Other recent incidents have involved birds entering campgrounds and wrecking camping equipment, walking up to stopped motorists along highways, and landing on buildings in developed areas.

Clearly, the aversive conditioning of puppet-reared birds has not produced birds that avoid humans and human structures as much as the original wild population once did.

Nevertheless, at least the tendency of birds to land on utility poles has apparently been greatly reduced, most likely by the training with hot-wired poles. Simultaneously, overall mortality rates of released California Condors to collisions have dropped greatly on a per bird basis, and overall survival rates have improved noticeably from the first releases (Tables 22 and 23). However, in most releases mortality rates have still remained higher than the10% rate needed for long-term population stability or increase, assuming normal reproduction (see Chapter 12 and Meretsky et al., in press).

The most encouraging of the releases to date has been the November 1997 release of parent-reared birds in the Ventana Wilderness Area. No mortalities of birds have as yet occurred in this release, and the birds have shown virtually no inclination to come into set-tled areas and interact with humans or human structures. The exemplary performance of this group stands in sharp contrast to the behavior of a group of puppet-reared birds released at the same site in January 1997. Despite aversive conditioning of both groups, the birds in the earlier release came repeatedly into settled areas to interact with humans and were soon retrapped because of their dismal performance.

In January 1999, three additional puppet-reared, aversively-conditioned birds were released into the Ventana group, in part to see if their behavior might fall in line with the experienced parent-reared birds already released, but all three soon had to be retrapped because of excessive human-oriented behavior. Meanwhile, additional parent-reared birds released into the group at the same time have performed in a manner similar to the original group of parent-reared birds, exhibiting no appreciable tendencies to approach humans or civilized landscapes.

Thus, the results of the recent Ventana release efforts strongly suggest a major behavioral superiority of parent-reared birds over puppet-reared birds, even those that have been aver-sively conditioned. As reported both by David Clendenen and Kelly Sorenson, parent-reared birds have simply been much wilder from the start, commonly hissing and striking the insides of their sky kennels during transport, and showing none of the calm acceptance of such operations that is shown by puppet-reared birds. Further, since the parent-reared birds in the Ventana releases were still reared in zoo environments, the results suggest that parent-rearing itself may be the most crucial factor in minimizing attractions of birds to humans and civilized landscapes, rather than zoo versus non-zoo environments for rearing. However, as none of the birds released to date have been reared in non-zoo environments, it remains to be seen how much additional benefit might be gained by combining parent-rearing with non-zoo environments.

Other releases of parent-reared birds have not given as clearcut results as the recent Ventana releases, but the parent-reared birds in these other cases were early mixed with hand-reared birds (in one case pre-release and in two cases shortly after release) which may have detrimentally affected their behavior. Nevertheless, it is worth noting that 76% of the 21 parent-reared birds released overall are still alive in the wild, while only 49% of 67 pup-pet-reared birds released overall remain in the wild, again suggesting general advantages of parent-rearing.

Finally, it is important to keep in mind that as promising as the Ventana releases of parent-reared birds have been in yielding birds with behavioral avoidance of structures and humans, the birds in these releases have not yet been out long enough to lose strong dependency on subsidy. If and when that occurs, they can be expected to develop problems with lead poisoning, as we discuss in the next section.

Resurgence of Lead Poisoning and a General Evaluation of Mortality Threats

Although tameness and collision problems have shown some improvement in recent releases, especially in the Ventana releases of parent-reared birds, other aspects of releases have worsened. The most ominous development has been a resurgence in cases of lead poisoning in the last two years. Birds that have been out in the wild more than a year or two have begun to feed on naturally-available carcasses outside of the subsidy program, once again exposing the species to lead contamination. In 1997 three of ten birds that were observed feeding on an abandoned hunter-shot deer carcass developed lead poisoning. Fortunately, the problem was detected immediately, and the birds were successfully captured and detoxified by chelation therapy in captivity (Hendron 1998). In addition to these three birds, five additional condors of 1997 developed high enough blood lead concentrations to indicate exposure to lead contamination, although concentrations were not high enough to warrant chelation therapy and the birds recovered unaided.

Three more cases of lead poisoning necessitating chelation treatment occurred in 1998, including one bird that came very close to dying in the field before it too was captured and successfully detoxified. In addition two other birds of 1998 developed high enough blood lead concentrations to indicate exposure to lead contamination, but recovered without chelation therapy.

Only one released bird exhibited elevated blood lead levels in the years prior to 1997. This was a bird of 1992 with a measured blood lead level of 1.6 ppm. Although this bird was not recaptured to be chelated, its blood lead level dropped below the detection limit (< 0.1 ppm) only a little over a month later. This gives rise to some doubts as to the validity of the earlier lead determination, as this was a relatively rapid unaided detoxification judging from data on other species (see Eisler 1988).

None of the birds developing acute lead poisoning in the release program have died as a result, but in large measure this can be attributed to skill of the release crew in detecting lead-exposed birds promptly and the successful chelation therapy given to the poisoned birds. In the long term such emergency measures clearly do not represent a viable way to counter the lead-poisoning threat either from expense or efficacy standpoints. Thus for the purposes of analysis, it might be more defensible to consider the birds saved by chelation therapy as actual mortalities. If we do so (see adjusted mortality rates in Table 22), the releases in which these mortalities occurred (releases of March and August 95, March 96) would exhibit annual mortality rates of 18%, 17%, and 35%, respectively, instead of the unadjusted values of 5%, 4%, and 23%, respectively. The adjusted rates substantially exceed the maximum permissible for sustainability (10%), assuming normal reproduction.

The recent cases of lead poisoning have all emerged in the releases that have been ongoing for the longest time. Condors in other releases are now also beginning to abandon subsidy for natural carcasses, and it is reasonable to expect lead poisoning incidents in these other releases as well. A strong case can now be made that releases as they are currently practiced are inconsistent with the most fundamental axiom of reestablishment efforts — that they be conducted only when major causes of original extirpation have been effectively countered.

At least in part, the declining dependency on subsidy seen in recent years seems likely to have developed because releases have all used multiple, rather than single, feeding sites. This practice has likely caused, or at least speeded, a transition to wide-ranging foraging behavior. Indeed, multiple feeding sites represent the usual training procedure to encourage released scavenging birds to abandon subsidy. In the condor program multiple feeding sites have been employed deliberately to elicit "natural" foraging behavior in the birds, despite the fact that natural foraging behavior was the apparent cause of the high susceptibility of the historic wild population to lead poisoning. Without widespread discussion or acknowledgment, the original goal of self-sustaining, subsidy-dependent wild populations has been quietly abandoned for a goal of naturally-foraging wild populations presumably vulnerable to all the stresses that made the historic wild population inviable.

The resurgence in cases of lead poisoning and lead exposure and the high frequency of collision deaths seen in the releases to date (Table 23) give support to the emphasis given to lead poisoning and collisions by Snyder and Snyder (1989) with respect to the historical decline. Similarly, the low frequency of shooting incidents seen in releases to date supports their view that the direct risks of shooting have traditionally been overemphasized. Although shooting has long been the principal villain in speculations about the sources of condor mortality (see Dawson 1923; Koford 1953; Miller et al. 1965; Wilbur 1978b), only two instances of apparently shot birds and one instance of a bird shot at unsuccessfully had emerged during releases through mid 1999. Collisions (7 cases) and lead poisoning (6 cases necessitating chelation and 7–8 other cases of exposure) have been the main problems.

Despite the numerical dominance of collisions (including electrocutions) as a cause of actual mortalities of released birds, we are inclined to rate lead poisoning as a more important factor for the historical population and for future released populations for the following reasons:

1. The virtual equality of mortality rates in adults and immatures of the original wild population, as documented in Chapter 12 and by Snyder and Snyder (1989), seems much better explained by lead poisoning than by collisions (or electrocutions). Ingestion of lead in carcasses can reasonably be expected to be equally likely in adults and immatures, whereas collisions (and electrocutions) tend to be considerably more frequent in immatures than in adults in large birds (e.g., Leshem 1985; Brown and Drewien 1995; Hunt 1997);

2. The documented lead poisoning frequency in the releases would presumably have been much higher in the absence of food subsidy, even though food subsidy is proving to be a less than fully effective means of reducing lead poisoning threats

under current strategies; and

3. The high collision frequency in early releases has dropped noticeably in more recent releases, possibly due mainly to initiation of aversive conditioning with hot-wired poles (and buildings) and releases of parent-reared birds. The historic wild population exhibited no significant tendency to land on poles and buildings.

The other sources of mortality and near mortality in Table 23 were apparently less pervasive than the threats of collisions and lead poisoning. The two drownings occurred when condors apparently entered a pothole to drink or bathe and were unable to exit. This may have been largely a result of the fortuitous existence of a slippery-sided pothole near one of the release sites and probably does not indicate any special vulnerability of released birds to such difficulties. Drownings, especially in artificial cattle watering troughs, have also been noted as a significant source of mortality for wild populations of other vultures (see Houston 1996; Piper 1993). The instance of a cancer death probably had nothing to do with release procedures. The instance of antifreeze poisoning may have resulted from a bird drinking from a puddle in which someone had drained his car radiator. It occurred near a heavily used recreation area that the bird was frequenting. The instances of starvation and food-stressed birds were all cases of birds experiencing difficulty in competing with earlier-released birds at food subsidy sites shortly after release, or experiencing difficulty in orienting to food subsidy sites. The one bird dying of apparent Golden Eagle (*Aquila chrysaetos*) predation was attacked at a carcass food source. Most released juveniles have quickly learned to avoid eagles at food sources. The "coyote-killed" bird may have been only scavenged by a coyote and may have died of other causes. Of the four birds that simply disappeared, only two had functioning radio transmitters at the time of disappearance. Their causes of death are unknown.

Solutions to Mortality Threats

As discussed above, collision frequencies have been declining, perhaps in large part because of the training of birds with hot-wired utility poles and the use of parent-reared birds in some releases. But whether viable wild populations can be achieved in the absence of additional efforts to reduce collision/electrocution frequencies remains unclear. Recent research with waterfowl in Colorado (Brown and Drewien 1995) suggests that collision risks can be substantially reduced (> 60%) by modifying overhead wires with conspicuous markers to enhance their visibility. Presumably the same could be done to reduce collision risks within condor range. The costs of installing such markers are substantial, however, and without good knowledge as to which particular overhead wires might be especially threatening, considerable resources could be wasted in ineffective efforts to reduce this problem. Knowledge of the geographic pattern of collision risks is presently insufficient to allow efficient employment of markers as a means to reduce such risks.

Aside from hot-wire training and the potential use of line markers, the most cost effective and successful ways to minimize future collision/electrocution frequencies may be to limit releases to relatively remote locations and to parent-reared birds. Whether additional benefits could be obtained by rearing birds in field enclosures that do not resemble rectangular human structures and allow total isolation of birds from the sights and sounds of humans and civilization remains to be tested. The apparent failure of aversive conditioning alone to produce consistent avoidance of humans and human structures may have been a result of habituation of the pre-release birds to the negative conditioning procedures of the training process or a result of other positive reinforcement the birds have received from humans and structures during rearing procedures.

One solution that might be proposed to the lead threat would be to restrict food subsidization to single sites in future releases. Although it is still not certain that birds can be held indefinitely dependent on single subsidy sites, this solution has never been tested. Testing this strategy would presumably necessitate retrapping all birds that are already taking food from natural carcasses and starting over with naive birds. Unfortunately, this solution at best poses perpetual food subsidy obligations and expense and represents a permanent distortion of the natural foraging behavior of the species. It is also possible that it may not work, as birds may eventually drift off subsidy regardless.

In our view two more promising and potentially more permanent solutions involve (1) creating large no-hunting preserves and/or (2) effecting a switch from lead ammunitions to nontoxic alternatives in regions of condor releases. In view of the large size of individual condor ranges documented in the historical population (Meretsky and Snyder 1992) and the large size of condor ranges seen in release efforts to date, the creation of sufficiently large no-hunting preserves to provide effective protection from lead poisoning entails substantial financial investments and potential political difficulties. Nevertheless, a start toward such a goal has been made by federal acquisition of the Hopper National Wildlife Refuge (Percy Ranch) and the Bitter Creek National Wildlife Refuge (Hudson Ranch), by the establishment of a Carrizo Plains Natural Area (not presently a no-hunting reserve but likely soon to be limited to nontoxic ammunitions), and by recent acquisition of the Wind Wolves Preserve (San Emigdio Ranch) by the Wildlands Conservancy. These lands comprise a substantial fraction of the historic foraging range of the condor, but not yet a large enough fraction to offer a secure potential for reducing the lead poisoning threat to safe levels within this range. Other ranches within the historical range still earn substantial fees by selling hunting rights to deer, elk, and pronghorn hunters. In addition, the U.S. Forest Service, the B.L.M., and the state of California still allow and encourage hunting activities on many of their lands within historic condor range.

Meanwhile experimentation with alternatives to lead ammunition has resulted in the development of a new TTB ammunition material (a composite of tin, tungsten, and bismuth that is sometimes called TTC, an acronym for tin-tungsten composite). This material appears to be at least equal to, and potentially better than, lead in hunting characteristics, yet at the same time has proved non-toxic in ingestion tests conducted so far with Mallard Ducks and Turkey Vultures (data from R. Risebrough and V. Oltrogge; Ringleman et al. 1993). As this ammunition may soon be commercially available, at a cost not greatly exceeding that of lead ammunition, a regional switch to its use may not pose many of the political difficulties that were seen with the substitution of steel shot for lead shot in waterfowl hunting. The TTB material also appears to be a superior material for the kinds of hunting that require shot, and may provide a welcome alternative to both steel and lead shot.

In January of 1998 we had an opportunity to meet the creator of the new TTB ammunitions, Victor Oltrogge, and to see how his ammunitions compared to lead in firing and impact characteristics. Victor drove down from Colorado, and Dave Clendenen, a representative from the Recovery Team, joined us from California. Together we spent a day near our home firing Victor's new bullets and shot into targets made of long stacks of water-soaked phone directories. These targets simulated living tissue in density and allowed us to trace what happed to the bullets on impact. The lead and TTB bullets proved indistinguishable in their tendencies to expand and fragment in penetrating the phone directories, suggesting very similar potentials in killing game species, a crucial comparison.

In addition, we learned that the TTB ammunitions can be fabricated with densities exceeding that of lead, which provides a potential for significantly greater range than lead. They are also reasonably close to lead in softness, and do not pose the risks of damage to gun barrels that have been seen with steel shot. All these characteristics should make the TTB ammunitions highly desirable for hunters.

Following this demonstration, we were able to arrange through Ben Brown for hunters to field-test TTB ammunitions on the Gray Ranch in southwestern New Mexico, one of the sites that has been considered for future California Condor reintroductions. Results so far indicate high user satisfaction with the TTB materials with respect to their accuracy, range and killing power for game.

Another development that bodes well for an overall transition from lead to TTB ammunitions has been the development of plans of the U.S. military to switch from lead to TTB ammunition (their "green bullet program"). Once underway, such a switch may rapidly reduce the costs and enhance the competitive position of TTB ammunitions in the overall market, simply as a result of production scale and familiarity of consumers with the product.

TTB ammunitions are not the only nontoxic ammunitions under development. Pure copper bullets, which also have proved to be nontoxic when fed to Turkey Vultures (data of R. Risebrough), have been on the market for a number of years. However, although these other alternatives appear very promising from a toxicity standpoint, they have not generally matched lead and TTB in hunting characteristics. Copper, for example, is less dense, but harder than lead so it offers some disadvantages in range and killing power.

If new nontoxic ammunitions can replace lead ammunition in release regions for the condor, the need for no-hunting preserves may diminish. In fact, an argument can be made that if hunting can be truly limited to nontoxic ammunitions, the food benefit to condors resulting from unrecovered shot game and discarded viscera piles could make hunted areas better condor habitat than no-hunting areas. However, prospective food benefits may not balance the direct risks of condors being shot that are inherent in any strategy that encourages shooting activity in condor range. Which might be the greater effect is not obvious, though presumably the risks of illegal shooting can be significantly reduced by intensive education efforts.

We believe that the ultimate goal of condor conservation efforts should be the establishment of self-sustaining wild populations that are natural as possible and as free of intensive management investments as possible. Compared to the long-term commitments and potentially low success represented by perpetual food subsidy, and compared to the high costs of establishing adequately large no-hunting preserves, the low investments represented by limiting ammunitions to nontoxic types in release regions and the potential effectiveness of such a solution appear generally preferable. However, ammunition conversions may prove an inadequate solution if not coupled with intensive hunter education efforts to minimize the direct risks of condors being shot.

The use of nontoxic ammunitions could be mandated by governmental regulations in condor range, although effective enforcement of such regulations could be difficult so long as lead ammunition is freely available elsewhere. It is important to remember that estimates of California Fish and Game Department personnel have indicated that perhaps more than half of the deer shot in the state are shot illegally in the first place. Expecting illegal hunters to conform to nontoxic ammunition regulations seems unrealistic. Perhaps the best hopes for effecting significant change might be on large private ranches where hunting can be tightly controlled by landowners. If such landowners could be persuaded of the values of limiting hunting to nontoxic ammunitions, with or without regulations, perhaps a general shift to the new ammunitions might follow relatively easily. Ultimately, we have considerable hope that hunters might come to prefer the new TTB ammunitions simply because of their superior hunting potentials. Once such a preference might become obvious, a uniform mandated phase-out of lead ammunitions might pose relatively few political difficulties. The benefits would be substantial for a wide array of wildlife species currently exposed to lead contamination, not just condors.

Potential Future Problems with Reproduction

Achieving adequately low mortality rates in releases is only half of the challenge in establishing demographically viable populations. The other half is establishing adequately successful breeding traditions. None of the released birds are yet old enough to breed, and it is presently unknown how successfully they may breed. We are particularly concerned about Golden Eagle threats to nestlings. As discussed by Snyder and Snyder (1989) and in Chapter 11, the principal defense of the historic condor population against eagle threats appeared to be a strong tendency to nest in regions where eagles were scarce. That released condors will automatically develop such tendencies to nest in safe regions is as yet unknown.

It is possible that the historical tendencies of condors to nest in relatively safe areas depended importantly on traditions maintained largely by the imprinting of young birds on natal areas and by juveniles learning additional appropriate areas through associating with adults. If imprinting is an important process in later choices of nest sites, released birds may tend to nest in the near vicinity of release sites, as has been seen in releases of Eurasian Griffons in France (Sarrazin et al. 1996). Because of the presence of substantial numbers of Golden Eagles at some of the specific sites chosen for releases so far, it is possible that condors will encounter relatively high eagle predation threats to their nestlings if and when they begin their first reproductive efforts in these areas.

To achieve adequate reproductive success in reestablished condor populations it may prove necessary to limit releases to sites where eagle predation threats are low, either because of a scarcity of eagles or because of an abundance of protective species such as Prairie Falcons that can serve to exclude eagles from the near vicinity of condor nests. For example, future releases in the Grand Canyon region may have to be confined to the inner gorge of the canyon where the great majority of Pleistocene nests of condors have been found and Golden Eagles are absent, rather than the rim country where current releases are taking place and Golden Eagles are common.

Still another significant threat to nesting success yet to be faced by released birds is the threat of egg predation by Common Ravens. Ravens appeared to be the most important threat to nesting success of the historic wild condor population (Chapter 11) and still occur in abundance in all current release regions except the Ventana Wilderness Area. Effective means for controlling their depredations have not yet been devised or tested, although it is possible that taste-aversion conditioning (see Nicolaus 1987; Nicolaus et al. 1983; Quick and Hill 1988) could be successful. The absence of fully effective defenses of nesting condors to the threats posed by ravens was one of the more puzzling results obtained during intensive observations of the wild population in the 1980s. How well released condors may deal with raven threats to their eggs is not yet known, but they seem unlikely to be any better adapted than the historic population, and may be worse.

Future Release Areas

Assuming success can be achieved in adequately reducing the threats of lead contamination and other mortality factors, and that adequate reproductive success can be achieved by control of the threats posed by eagles and ravens, there is every reason to believe that the California Condor can be reestablished successfully in the wild, and not just within the recent historic range in California and in the Grand Canyon. Other potential release regions include the Sierra San Pedro Martir in Baja California, Mexico where the species persisted until the 1930s, and some of the extensive rangelands of New Mexico, for example, the Gray Ranch and the Ladder Ranch, regions where condors persisted at least until about ten thousand years ago. Interest is currently especially high in developing a program for releases in Baja California.

To what extent releases in these various areas can be based on naturally available food supplies, and to what extent effective controls can be achieved over the threats of lead poisoning are of course some of the principal concerns in designing future releases. Full evaluations must also include assessments of the risks from Common Ravens and Golden Eagles. The goal in all releases should be to establish self-sustaining populations that pose a minimum of long-term investments in life-support measures such as food subsidy and control of competitors and predators.

Unfortunately, expansion of the release program to include additional sites at the present time poses potential penalties in rearing methodologies. By far the best release results

Successful reestablishment of Eurasian Griffon Vultures in the Massif Central of France mostly involved releases of adults rather than fledglings. Holding cages at the release site (**top**) were located immediately adjacent to the main feeding site for the released population. Adults proved relatively sedentary on release and quickly began breeding successfully in nearby cliffs (**middle**). Mortality rates of released birds have remained exceedingly low (< 2% annually), and although there have been some losses to electrocutions, there have been none to lead poisoning. The griffon program has in large part been inspired by the efforts of Michel Terrasse (**below**), and success has been achieved with surprisingly little expense.

achieved to date have been with parent-reared birds. Yet in order to gain good numbers of parent-reared birds, the captive-breeding program cannot pursue maximal multiple-clutching and must settle for fewer progeny overall. Proliferation of release sites forces the captive-breeding program to continue to maximize production and to produce largely puppet-reared progeny. Until releases are truly successful at any site, we favor restraint in establishing new sites. Judging from release results to date, the near-term rearing goal should become maximal production of parent-reared birds for release as opposed to maximal multiple-clutching.

Comparisons with other Release Programs

Compared with recent California Condor releases, the releases to the wild of Eurasian Griffon Vultures in France, of Bearded Vultures to the European Alps, and of Andean Condors in Colombia have been less problematic (Frey and Walter 1989; Liebermann et al. 1991, 1993; Frey and Bijleveld 1993; Sarrazin et al. 1994, 1996; Bustamante 1996). The main mortality factor found in the griffon releases has been electrocutions by power lines, but the overall adult mortality rate has remained less than 2% annually and the wild population has been expanding rapidly with a high reproductive rate. No problems with lead contamination have threatened this population, presumably because its diet has been focused on domestic animals supplied largely as subsidy. Relative success in releases of Andean Condors in Colombia may have resulted in part from lower risks of lead poisoning and collisions in the environment and especially from the opportunity to integrate released birds into already-existing wild populations. The Bearded Vulture reintroduction program in the Alps, has succeeded to the point of reproduction in the wild and has been characterized by low mortality, even though releases have been limited to fledgling captive-reared birds introduced into a region lacking a wild population.

In 1986 we had a chance to visit the French Griffon Vulture release program as guests of Michel Terrasse, and we were amazed to see how rapidly his efforts were resulting in a reproductively active population in an area where a wild population of the species had been absent for many decades. Released birds had almost immediately begun to nest in the cliffs adjacent to the release cages, and were already becoming a major tourist attraction for the region. It was also remarkable to hear how little the releases were costing (roughly $30,000 per year) a tremendous credit to the efficiency and dedication of the staff involved and a humbling comparison to the monies that would soon be spent on condor releases.

Notably, the success in France has been achieved mainly by releases of breeding pairs, rather than immatures. Although environmental conditions may be significantly more benign for the griffon releases than for California Condor releases, and this might explain much of their relative success, the possibility of releasing adult condors deserves some consideration. Unfortunately, under present conditions, release of any of the wild-trapped adult California Condors presently in captivity would likely pose immediate threats of lead contamination for these birds regardless of any provision of food subsidy. These birds could be expected to return quickly to the foraging habits they exhibited before capture. Moreover, although some have argued that such birds might serve as beneficial behavioral role-models for captive-reared birds, if they encourage captive-reared birds to forage on naturally-available carcasses they could quickly put these other birds at risk as well. Release of the wild-trapped adults only appears to make sense once the sources of lead contamination are removed from the range. Then, however, their release might prove a very positive strategy, especially if releases are still troubled with behavioral problems of released individuals.

Like releases of wild-caught adults, releases of captive-born adults pose apparent trade-offs between captive productivity and potentials for successful establishment in the wild. Further, no captive-reared breeders have been held in the behavioral isolation from man that appears to be important in developing adaptive wild behavior. Whether captive-reared adults might be as behaviorally flexible as immatures in adjusting to a wild environment is another concern. Nevertheless, if success proves elusive with releases of fledglings, future releases of captive-reared adults remain a possibility that may be worth some experimental testing, especially in view of the very conservative movement patterns that have been seen in released adult griffon vultures.

Some Summary Remarks

The behavioral problems that have troubled the releases of California Condors to the wild are evidently due mainly to puppet-rearing, as opposed to parent-rearing. This is not a surprising result, as similar difficulties have been experienced in other release programs utilizing hand- or puppet-reared stocks. During the early period of releases, there were reasons to avoid parent-rearing, as it would have reduced the rate of expansion of the size of the captive flock and slowed the achievement of genetic goals. Parent-rearing simply cannot be carried out simultaneously with maximal removal of eggs to encourage relaying. However, now that the captive population has reached a substantial size and genetic goals have been largely attained, we believe it would be highly beneficial for the program to shift to a goal of maximizing parent-rearing of birds and to discontinue releases of puppet-reared condors.

Unfortunately, only 7 of 18 young condors are being parent-reared in captivity in the 1999 breeding season, and some of these may be simply dispersed among various releases involving puppet-reared birds, rather than being tightly integrated in releases that are aimed at yielding fully parent-reared wild populations. The captive population now consists of 15 pairs producing fertile eggs, and it should be possible to approach this number of parent-reared birds for release each year. Further, this total could be significantly increased if puppet-reared birds currently in the wild were retrapped and made part of the captive-breeding population. The impressive behavioral superiority of parent-reared birds in the Ventana releases conducted so far suggests strongly that all releases should be converted into releases of parent-reared birds, and that strong consideration should be given to return of all puppet-reared birds to captivity. If not withdrawn from the wild, these birds pose a significant risk of permanently contaminating reestablished population with detrimental human-oriented behaviors.

The lesson that has been learned by a number of other release programs is that at least with species that are characterized by a large component of learning in their behavior, chances for success are often far greater with behaviorally sophisticated release animals than by flooding the environment with behaviorally compromised individuals (e.g., Kleiman 1989, Snyder et al. 1994, Miller et al. 1996). Relying on the hope that detrimental behavior patterns will simply disappear over time seems misguided, especially if the behavior patterns (such as accepting food handouts from passersby) continue to get positive reinforcement. The puppet-reared birds that have been in the wild the longest (the Lion Canyon birds released in 1995) still continue to show maladaptive human-oriented behavior, with no clear signs of improvement after five years of presumed cogitation on their proper places in nature. In late summer of 1999, these birds, together with more recently released Lion Canyon birds (16 individuals in all), descended for several weeks on the community of Pine Mountain Club near Mt Pinos and proceeded to trash property ranging from satellite dishes and roof shingles to screen doors. Eight birds even wound up in the bedroom of Les Reid (one of the most vocal opponents of the condor program in the 1980s) where they took bites out of his foam mattress. These exploits were publicized in lurid detail by newspapers and TV across the country.

Aside from the fact that such incidents are creating increasingly bad public relations for the release program, we view as them as providing increasingly strong evidence that puppet-reared birds (even with aversive conditioning) are not conquering their behavioral problems. Furthermore, relying on the hope that the behavioral problems may eventually self-correct may ultimately prove dangerous if supertame condors cause injury to bystanders. As we can testify from personal experience, the bill of the species is razor sharp and capable of inflicting substantial wounds.

When superior parent-rearing methods exist that evidently do not pose such risks, it seems quixotic to continue releases with inferior puppet-reared birds, especially when the latter compromise full implementation of the superior methods. The lesser numbers of birds that can be produced by parent-rearing, as opposed to puppet-rearing, are a small price to pay for freedom from the seemingly endless behavioral problems that have been troubling the program. At best, experimentation with new methods of puppet rearing seems unlikely to ever produce birds that can match parent-reared birds in behavioral quality, and instead of investing time, energy and monies in following such a course, we believe it would be much wiser to focus research into various potential methods of increasing the rate of production of parent-reared birds.

Unfortunately, the debate over rearing methodologies for releases has often diverted attention away from efforts to counteract the basic limiting factors faced by California Condors in the wild. Clearly, if viable wild populations are to be achieved, something must be done to ensure a massive lessening of the mortality risks that were faced by the historic wild population. Hopes that clean-food subsidy might produce a sustainable lessening in mortality have all but disappeared, as birds have been rapidly increasing their tendencies to feed on carcasses outside of the subsidy program, and cases of lead poisoning have reappeared with frequency in 1997–98.

In most avian reestablishment programs, mortality rates can be expected to be relatively high at the start of releases and then to stabilize at a lower level as problem birds are eliminated and birds gain skills in the wild. But so long as the lead contamination of natural carcasses continues to exist there are reasons to fear that mortality rates in condor releases may not show progressive declines, but progressive increases as the birds abandon clean food subsidy. Ultimately, if no effective ways of countering the lead threat were to be implemented and current feeding trends were to continue, there would be no reason to expect the mortality rates of the released birds to differ from the unsustainably high rates seen in the historic wild population.

With the rash of lead poisoning incidents in the past two years, there can be little lingering doubt that lead poisoning was a major, and plausibly *the* major, but surely not the only, cause of extirpation of the historic wild population. Evidently, reestablishing self-sustaining wild populations at affordable long-term costs will necessitate true removal of this threat from regions of release. Nontoxic ammunitions appear to be the most feasible means to achieve this end, although no-hunting preserves may have an important role to play in some regions. The alternative of starting over with single-site subsidy programs is less desirable from the standpoints of long-term expense, permanent distortion of foraging patterns of the species, and more questionable prospects for success. Although this approach has never been tested, at best it does not represent an optimal long-term solution.

It would be tragic indeed if the California Condor conservation program were to fail to achieve a real solution to the lead poisoning threat and if the release efforts were to become an endless expensive and hollow pouring of behaviorally compromised birds into the wild without ever achieving self-sustaining populations. We believe firmly that truly viable and naturally-behaving wild populations are an achievable goal if the will to create them exists. Very recent progress of the USFWS in persuading some important Californian landowners to adopt nontoxic ammunitions is a very positive development. But a real solution to the lead issue will probably necessitate full removal of the lead threat from the entire condor range, something that probably cannot be accomplished without a full governmental ban on use of lead ammunition. This may take some time to achieve, but stopping short of a full solution would be a major mistake. Unfortunately, while the U.S. military and lower levels of the USFWS have shown commendable initiative toward achieving a full conversion to nontoxic TTB ammunitions, the upper levels of the USFWS have thus far avoided addressing the issue, unaccountably missing the opportunity to take the lead in a campaign with substantial overall benefits for hunters and wildlife alike.

PART VI
A GENERAL
EVALUATION

CHAPTER EIGHTEEN

Overview

Although the California Condor is still with us, and in fact its numbers are now increasing rapidly, we live in an age when overall global biodiversity is steadily diminishing. The earth of today, without mammoths, moas, and giant teratorns, has already lost much of its recent biological riches. The earth of the centuries ahead will doubtless host far fewer species. Sadly, the wonders of Jurassic Park are only fantasy. Technology offers us no valid escape from the extinction crisis, and in fact it is surely one of the major contributors to the crisis. The dreary future we are surely headed toward is a world so dominated by our own species that there will be little room left for creatures that in any way threaten us or compete with us for resources or space.

Despite increasing international concern as to the magnitude of projected extinctions, the overall campaign to preserve biodiversity is proceeding fitfully. For the most part, only bits and pieces are being conserved, and the areas and species protected in the short term enjoy no ironclad guarantees of survival in a longer time frame. As we draft this chapter during the summer of 1998, enormous areas of forest are burning around the planet, demonstrating how vulnerable even large regions of protected habitat can be. The buffer areas needed to serve as refuges for the endangered life forms stressed by such catastrophes have in many cases already disappeared.

Further, the habitat preserves established in many countries have lacked the financial resources necessary for their protection against the relentless pressures of expanding human populations. The failure of some preserves to survive such pressures has led some conservationists to conclude that the only salvation for many protected areas may be to encourage "sustainable" economic activites within their boundaries. Unfortunately, as analyzed by critics such as Hirt (1994), Rice (1998), Soulé (1998) and Struhsaker (1998), "sustainable use" can often be hard to distinguish in practice from organized over-exploitation and degradation, despite the theoretical allure of the concept.

The short-term successes achieved in efforts to ensure the survival of a few charismatic species are indeed positive developments and need to be publicized as an important demonstration that extinctions can be avoided if enough concern and effort are given to the task. But as positive as they may be, these successes should not be misunderstood as a sign of the world coming into a conservation balance. The number of species on the brink of extinction increases daily. Although resources to prop up remnant populations of some charismatic species through such desperate measures as captive breeding may continue to exist into the immediate future, these species are the lucky few. Meanwhile, far more species are inexorably slipping away as their natural habitats disappear at a steadily increasing rate. For the vast majority of endangered forms there are no champions within our own species; no one even to chronicle their existence, let alone their demise. Most will disappear before they have even been given formal scientific names.

From a purely selfish perspective, there is an overwhelming logic and wisdom in our species achieving a benign and sustainable relationship with the natural world in its entirety, as has been eloquently argued in many fine books and articles (e.g., Wilson 1992, Payne 1995). Nevertheless, it's hard to find any convincing signs that we are moving anywhere but in the opposite direction, despite increasing international recognition of the crisis and accords such as the recent Biodiversity Convention (yet to be ratified by our own government). The fundamental causes of the downward biodiversity spiral – rampant human population growth and rising resource consumption patterns – are still in operation, and indeed are still considered beneficial trends in many circles. Unless deliberate or fortuitous events lead soon to a reversal of these forces, the losses of biodiversity ahead promise to be of immense magnitude.

Yet, as discouraging as the overall future for wildlife conservation may seem from today's perspective, we believe there is no challenge that is more important than the preservation of our planet's biodiversity. Every charismatic large vertebrate given enough habitat to be truly preserved in the wild can be the salvation of thousands of additional species sharing its range. Thus, a focus on such species may represent one of the most effective ways to limit the biodiversity losses ahead. At stake are not just the aesthetic values represented by our fellow creatures but the very survival of our own species. If not arrested, the continued degradation of viable ecosystems may ultimately result in collapse of the support systems for a majority of species alive today.

Compared with many other endangered species, the California Condor appears to be well positioned for survival in the near term, at least as a zoo curiosity, and possibly as a resident in the wild, whatever that may mean in the future. It has many of the characteristics that favor such persistence: a capacity to breed readily in captivity; an inherent ability to deal with disease threats; an inherent behavioral tolerance of our own species; an apparent disinterest in preying on people's barnyard animals, children, and pets; and a capacity to inspire human interest and empathy because of its great size and majesty in flight.

Even so, we wonder how the species may fare if human affairs ever again degenerate into worldwide depression, or war. Should such calamities recur (and why should we assume that they will not?), we doubt seriously that wildlife conservation will command much priority in human affairs. Instead, it is easy to envision a widespread consensus developing that sparing any resources for condors would be frivolous at the least, and more likely unpatriotic, risky, and unreasonable. During the World War of a half century ago, the large zoo animals of Europe commonly ended up on the dinner tables of desperately hungry people. Condor stew may not be the most savory of potential human foods, but starvation is a powerful motivating factor. If the condor might still be heavily dependent on humanity for its survival at the time of a major social calamity, the species' prospects would not be good.

Although this is not a general book on the biodiversity crisis, it would be a mistake to consider condor conservation in isolation, divorced from other conservation efforts and from the overall social and economic forces that are rapidly changing the world. We feel this book would be strangely incomplete if we did not attempt a final chapter on the future of condor conservation in relation to ultimate goals and the significance of the condor for endangered species conservation efforts in general. In assembling this chapter, however, we have limited ourselves mainly to issues within the field of conservation, rather than speculating on wider issues that might relate condor conservation to other global human concerns. These latter issues may ultimately prove far more important in determining the fate of the condor than the issues we will address, but our crystal ball gets murky when aimed in these directions. Trends in global warming, environmental pollution, and atmospheric ozone, for example, could affect condors in nearly infinite and unpredictable ways, almost all of them surely negative, but these clearly lie far beyond the scope of this book.

What we will review here are a number of themes drawn from the condor program that have a conservation significance transcending condor concerns alone, but which are commonly neglected in discussions of efforts to preserve endangered species. We will also look at some general near-term problems still faced by the condor program and at potential solutions to these problems. Unlike our perspective in most of the rest of this book, our viewpoint on these matters is one of conservationists outside the condor program, wishing the program well but nevertheless concerned about its rate of progress toward ultimate goals.

Unfortunately, present and past realities do not provide an infallible guide to the future, and we are well aware that unforeseen developments may undermine the value of some of the assessments and predictions we can offer, especially as time proceeds into more distant realms. Nevertheless, because our generalizations rest not only on the experiences of numerous people working to conserve condors over many decades, but also on the experiences of conservationists working to save other species, we hope that they may provide some useful insights.

The Roles of Captive Breeding and Intensive Research in Endangered Species Recovery

Although we have been strong supporters of captive breeding of the California Condor, under most circumstances this technique is not an optimal recovery strategy for endangered species (Snyder et al. 1996). Captive breeding has many features which make it risky and expensive to implement properly. Further, reliance on the technique often leads to neglect of better conservation measures. Many endangered species do not breed well in captivity and many are very difficult to reintroduce to the wild. After a number of generations, all captive populations inexorably evolve into populations that are better adapted to confinement than to the wild, making readaptation to the wild progressively more difficult. These problems, and others, have led to a relatively poor success rate in reestablishment efforts of captive populations to the wild (Griffith et al. 1989, Beck et al. 1994). In fact, many of the so-called "successes" in reintroducing captive populations turn out to be cases of reintroductions into only semi-wild environments where predators are absent or rare and where the species involved no longer retain historical behavior patterns that once adapted them to fully natural environments.

At best, captive breeding represents only a partial and short-term solution to the conservation woes of endangered species. To be successful it must be coupled with comprehensive reintroduction efforts based on correcting limiting factors in the wild and conserving or restoring wild ecosystems. The latter efforts unfortunately often lose urgency once captive populations are established. The existence of a vigorous captive population allows participants to relax and scale back their endeavors, as the species is already perceived as largely "saved" and beyond any risk of immediate extinction.

Attempts to reintroduce species into environments in which limiting factors have not been corrected cannot be expected to succeed. Such attempts can squander scarce conservation resources and can often continue endlessly in spite of their failure to produce self-sustaining wild populations (witness the decades of failed reintroduction efforts with Nene Geese, Whooping Cranes, and Masked Bobwhites – e.g., Black 1998). Programs conducted without comprehensive reductions of limiting factors in effect become perpetual "put and take" operations. Their proponents often begin to sound like compulsive gamblers as they paint pictures of the success that lies "just ahead" with just a little more tinkering with rearing and release methods.

In addition, poorly conceived reintroduction efforts sometimes pose risks of the spread of exotic diseases into habitats and populations formerly free of such problems. Where establishments are attempted in regions outside the original range of the species, unexpected interactions with other species can sometimes occur, resulting in the creation of pest species and the loss of formerly healthy populations of other species. Even where such problems have not developed, the success rate of captive breeding and reintroduction in recovery efforts for endangered species has not been impressive. The technique has unfortunately been invoked for many species without a recognition of its many drawbacks and risks, and often without a careful study of alternatives.

Nevertheless, there are cases where captive breeding represents the only near-term chance left for a species' survival because effective alternative solutions are either unknown or cannot be implemented quickly enough to rescue a declining population. The California Condor of the 1980s was a species badly in need of captive breeding, largely because of its tiny population size and rapid rate of decline, because comprehensive determination of its major causes of endangerment had been delayed too long by excessive fears of harmful consequences of intensive research, and because the major limiting factors, once determined, turned out to be factors that could not be quickly remedied. If the proper sorts of research had been implemented much earlier, it might have been possible to avoid both the complete dependence on captive breeding that now exists and much of the great expense and difficulties that are now entailed in the conservation of the species. Unfortunately, as populations dwindle toward extinction, the opportunities both for determining causes of decline and for developing effective optimal conservation strategies, dwindle simultaneously.

Accordingly, one of the most important themes we would like to develop in this general discussion is the high priority need for early intensive research into factors limiting wild populations, a need shared by conservation programs for all critically endangered species. The condor represents an especially clear case of the folly of attempting to conserve species using guesswork assumptions rather than the sorts of research that might make possible a determination of true causes of decline. For decades, a central operating assumption for condor conservation was that the species was threatened importantly by habitat loss and human disturbance of nesting areas and that the key to its conservation lay in habitat preservation and isolating the species as much as possible from direct contact with humanity. However, habitat loss and disturbance of nesting areas turned out to be only minor factors in the condor's decline. The major factor was excessive mortality, especially from poisoning. This remained largely unaddressed, mainly because of ignorance of how high mortality rates were and what was causing the mortality. The major threat of lead poisoning was only confirmed as the wild population was about to disappear, and unfortunately it was not a threat that could be easily or quickly reversed.

Intensive research activities can pose some threats to species, especially if they are implemented without adequate attention to minimizing impacts. However, the risks of not undertaking these activities and attempting conservation efforts without good knowledge of limiting factors are often far greater (see Caughley 1994, Caughley and Gunn 1996). Stopping 1080 poisoning will not help a species threatened mostly by lead poisoning, and preserving nesting habitat will not save a species threatened mainly by mortality factors on its foraging grounds. As beneficial as efforts to preserve condor habitat have been for the conservation of entire ecosystems, these efforts alone had no chance of saving the condor.

We do not want to be misinterpreted as standing against habitat conservation efforts for the condor. We are as eager as anyone for the continuation of the preserves that have been set aside and for the creation of new condor preserves, both on the foraging and nesting grounds. But we stand emphatically against any overall conservation strategy for the species that fails to focus mainly on ameliorating the major stress factors that have caused its endangerment. Unfortunately, many of the efforts to create preserves for the condor, from the early efforts for a Sespe Sanctuary to more recent efforts for a Sespe–Frazier Wilderness and for acquisition of Hudson Ranch, have had side effects that have worked against other aspects of the species' conservation. In part, they have proved to be a detrimental diversion from the task of addressing more crucial conservation threats.

The process of conservation of any threatened or endangered species is indeed a process of risk reduction. Unfortunately, faulty assessments of the many factors involved often lead to an underestimation of the risks of inaction and ignorance, and an overestimation of the risks of research. In addition, faulty assessments frequently confuse the risks to species with the risks to involved personnel and programs. The major condor controversies of 1985, as a case in point, were in substantial measure a result of administrators confusing risks to the condor with perceived (but demonstrably nonexistent) risks to the overall condor program. Further, because program administrators are much more likely to face personal risk if anything goes wrong with activities they have sanctioned than if a species simply wastes away through inaction, there is a common tendency for administrators to avoid supporting intensive research initiatives or to support them only at token, ineffectual levels. Unfortunately, this problem has characterized the recovery programs for many species. Breaking out from such restrictions in the condor program took prodigious efforts in the early 1980s, primarily at the state level.

In retrospect, the political battles of the 1970s and 1980s over risks versus benefits of intensive activities such as radio-telemetry and captive breeding now seem almost incomprehensible. Mainly because of the unrelenting opposition of a few environmental groups, needed intensive activities were delayed almost until the very end of the wild population's existence. Yet their implementation in fact posed virtually none of the direct risks imagined by opponents. Condors did not abandon their mates because they carried radio transmitters, and their gonads did not shrivel up because nests were closely observed or because eggs were removed from nests for artificial incubation. In fact, the species proved almost oblivious to such activities, despite the mythology that had been created about its behavioral intolerance of humanity. Only a single bird was lost due to intensive operations, while these same operations yielded a massive increase in reproduction of the wild population and a massive increase in understanding of the species' difficulties. If intensive research and conservation activities for the condor had been initiated much earlier than they were, the species might now be in far better shape than it is.

The condor is not the only endangered species that has suffered from anti-research attitudes, faulty risk analysis, and faulty assumptions as to the causes of decline. For example, one could simply substitute the name black-footed ferret for condor and read a very similar history of lost opportunities and mismanagement (Miller et al. 1996). For a sober evaluation of the penalties of such attitudes and practices with a variety of endangered species, the reader may wish to consult the thought-provoking accounts in Endangered Species Recovery, edited by Clark et al. (1994). The advisability of intensive research with endangered species seems to be a lesson that has to be learned anew with each endangered species. And seemingly with each, there will be factions that will oppose all intensive activities on the grounds that the greatest threat to the species is research itself, not to mention evil researchers bent on torturing the species. One searches in despair for signs that the lessons learned in conservation efforts with one species might commonly be applied to the conservation efforts for any other species.

The Importance of Diversity of Input and Balance of Power in Programs

Another important lesson from the condor program concerns the value of diverse inputs and a balance of power with respect to design and implementation of recovery programs. No one organization or individual can be counted on to have an infallible appreciation of the best strategies to follow in the conservation of any species. Neither should any one organization or individual be given monopoly power in the implementation of a conservation program for a species. The safest policy to follow is to organize programs so that diverse interests are guaranteed a voice in the design and implementation of strategies. Further, the strategies developed must be subject to continuous informed criticism and reevaluation.

In broad view, the history of condor conservation has been characterized by an alternation of periods of consensus and vigorous debate about strategies and goals. Periods of vigorous debate have tended to be stressful in the extreme for involved parties, and there has always been a strong tendency for organizations and individuals to seek victory by exercising power (e.g., silencing opposition by the exclusion of opponents from the debate) rather than by exercising logic or rigorous examination of alternatives. Unfortunately, when particular parties have had the power to control events and strategies in the program without development of true informed consensus, progress has generally been slow. A strong case can be made that progress has been most rapid when debate has been the most vigorous and a "creative tension" has forced the evaluation of alternative strategies in the field, with resolution of conflicts based on data rather than on authority or impassioned argument.

We did not always recognize the value of a balance of power and diversity of viewpoints. In fact, when we first joined the condor program in 1980 we were greatly troubled by the power of the State of California to counterbalance the power of the Fish and Wildlife Service. As representatives of the Fish and Wildlife Service and its ally the National Audubon Society, we felt that the State was often working at cross purposes with other cooperators and was standing directly in the way of progress. Because the State had power equal to the Fish and Wildlife Service in vetoing decisions affecting the condor, it was capable of forcing debate on many issues that would otherwise not have been raised by the Fish and Wildlife Service and other parties (ourselves included). At the time we viewed the endless discussions as "fiddling while Rome was burning." We were fully willing to support action in the absence of broad consensus, as the latter seemed unattainable in any event.

However, only a few years later, as issues evolved, we found we agreed more with the strategies of the State of California than with those of the Fish and Wildlife Service and National Audubon Society, and were deeply thankful that the State of California stood firm in opposing the latter strategies. In retrospect, progress in the program was extremely rapid in those years despite the conflicts, and the strategies that finally emerged were reasonable and well grounded in science. Without the conflicts and a constructive balance of power, the program could easily have gone down a much less favorable path. Despite the urgency of moving the program ahead, there was indeed enough time for the debates, and they were in fact a beneficial part of the process, not just a cumbersome impediment.

In truth, it is rarely pleasant to be arguing over alternative conservation strategies. But if these conflicts lead to a recognition of key issues and a resolution of key issues by accumulation of appropriate data, they can actually facilitate progress. Otherwise, faulty assumptions can sometimes hold sway for long periods without even being recognized as assumptions, and programs can stagnate pursuing strategies that have no chance of long-term success.

The key elements for maintaining a productive diversity of inputs and balance of power in a program seem to be as follows:

1. Maintenance of an open forum for debate of issues by *all* qualified and interested parties.
2. A commitment by responsible agencies to efforts to achieve an informed consensus on strategies based on open debate and open access of all parties to relevant data.
3. A commitment by all involved agencies to employ the most skilled individuals available for work on the species (as opposed to individuals that can only be counted on to toe agency party lines). The input of skilled researchers is a crucial component for success and cannot be bypassed safely. Without such personnel even the best of recommendations from advisory groups are unlikely to produce success.

The Utility of Recovery Teams and Recovery Plans

A third theme emerging from the condor program, closely related to the preceding, is the overriding value of well-constructed recovery teams in aiding recovery processes. As originally conceived following passage of the Endangered Species Act of 1973, recovery teams were set up as advisory groups of experts appointed and funded by the Fish and Wildlife Service to provide recommendations to the USFWS on the conservation of particular endangered species. The goal was to include a wide diversity of legitimate "stake-holders" on teams and the best biological expertise available. USFWS and state resource agency personnel were appropriate members of teams when they were directly involved in research and conservation of the species, but they, like everyone else, were to "shed their institutional ties" and speak for the species when functioning as team members.

The concept was basically a good one, and in our experience well-constituted recovery teams have automatically provided a forum for a wide diversity of inputs and helped foster a constructive balance of power in programs. The Condor Recovery Team of the early 1980s was one of three different species recovery teams we have worked with over the years. Like the other teams it was an excellent example of how a team can and should function. Membership of the team included the best available expertise on the species and an informed diversity of viewpoints. But most of all, everyone on the team shared a sincere commitment to find the best conservation solutions for the species. Where differences existed, there was always a genuine effort to find common ground and move ahead by means of acceptable compromise. There was also a general and sincere respect for the overriding importance of using good biological data in resolving issues.

Because the team included members drawn from all involved agencies, when consensus was achieved, it had broad political clout and generally led to decisions by responsible agencies that were both biologically sensible and politically viable. Although, as discussed in Chapter 14, the primary role of the team in setting directions for condor conservation was usurped in mid 1985 when fears arose in Fish and Wildlife Service and Audubon Society administrators that team recommendations might threaten the existence of program funding and program viability, the policies of the team eventually came to prevail anyway, although after the team had been abolished by the USFWS.

Recovery teams are not required by law for all endangered species and, because of limited funds and personnel, tend to be formed mainly for species of high public profile. Nevertheless, there have been a number of critically endangered high-profile species that have gone without recovery teams for long periods (e.g., Puerto Rican Parrot, Red-cockaded Woodpecker) and whose conservation programs have clearly suffered in the absence of functioning quality teams.

At the same time, it is important to recognize that not all recovery teams have been as successful as the condor team we worked with in the 1980s. Some teams have been set up deliberately to exclude the people with the best expertise on the species in question, and have included only faithful disciples of preconceived agency policies related to the species. Such teams cannot be expected to provide insightful guidance for species conservation. Teams composed entirely of "safe" (i.e., obedient) researchers and administrators lacking personal experience with the species represent a perversion of the basic virtues of the recovery team concept. Such teams seem to be most frequent when the responsible administrators desire to maintain maximum control of endangered species programs while giving only the appearance of being responsive to expert input. Poorly constituted recovery teams can sometimes be worse than no teams at all, as they can give the public a false impression that progress is being made in the conservation of species.

To help ensure an optimal constitution and functioning of recovery teams, we believe a few modifications to existing practices would be beneficial. Most importantly, we believe teams should be given more independence from governmental agencies than they presently enjoy. There are several components of this independence:

1. The decisions as to whether or not recovery teams should be formed or terminated for particular endangered species and who should be on these teams, should not be made unilaterally by regional directors of the USFWS. This concentration of power in the hands of regional directors has led to many abuses (Miller et al. 1994). We believe a much better arrangement would be for such decisions to be made by advisory groups in which the FWS is only one voting member. Such groups should include representatives as well of professional organizations such as the National Academy of Sciences, the Society for Conservation Biology, and the American Ornithologists' Union (in the case of endangered birds). For example, determining whether a recovery team is needed for a particular bird species and who should be on the team could be decided by a panel composed of single representatives each of the FWS, the American Ornithologists' Union, and the Society for Conservation Biology.

2. Recovery teams should be encouraged to communicate directly with the public, not discouraged from doing so, as is currently the practice of the FWS. The public, since it is funding the efforts, has a basic right to know what the most knowledgeable experts recommend for a species and has a right to view that information uncensored by agency biases. This idea does not in any way threaten the final authority of the FWS and state agencies to make decisions regarding endangered species, but would signal when the agencies are implementing actions that are not recommended by recovery teams and are ignoring input from recovery teams. The notion that recovery teams exist only to provide regional directors with advice on endangered species needs to be broadened to recognize that teams should provide advice to any and all interested parties.

3. As a generality, recovery team chairpersons should not be affiliated with the FWS or state resource agencies because government employees face fundamental limits in how independently they can act. Yet a recent survey of recovery teams by Miller et al. (1994) revealed that approximately 89% of team chairpersons were either FWS or state government personnel. During much of the condor crisis of 1985 the Condor Recovery Team could not even meet because the chairperson was an employee of the FWS who was instructed by the Service not to allow the team to meet (obviously because the FWS intended to pursue actions it knew the Recovery Team would not endorse). Several months later, this incarnation of the Condor Recovery Team was unilaterally dissolved by the FWS. These were fundamental mistakes on the part of the FWS that blinded the agency to the very expertise it so desperately needed in the crisis. Fortunately, the FWS did ultimately adopt the recommendations of the defunct Recovery Team, when other courses of action proved inviable.

4. When possible, team membership should include a substantial number of non-governmental experts. Under current practices, recovery teams for the FWS are made up largely of government personnel (approximately 77 percent of team members in a recent survey of recovery teams in Miller et al. 1994). Many of these personnel are vulnerable to reprisals if their recommendations deviate significantly from their agencies' goals and objectives. We are not suggesting that governmental personnel should be excluded from teams (in some cases governmental personnel are the principal experts on the species in question), but that their overall numerical dominance in team memberships is one of the factors most strongly limiting the independence and value of teams. Teams should not include voting members whose only function is to represent agencies, although teams need to consult intensively with agency representatives. The primary qualification for team membership should be true expertise with the species in question or closely related species or expertise with small population demography and genetics or other fields appropriate to the species in question.

Without true expert membership, without independence shielded from reprisals, and without open access of the public to team recommendations, recovery teams are commonly fated to devising ineffective recovery strategies, being ignored, or evolving into little more than rubber stamps for preconceived agency policies. Such fates are a betrayal of the spirit of the Endangered Species Act.

We make a strong distinction between recovery teams and recovery plans. Although in our experience properly constituted recovery teams have proved to be a valuable component of recovery efforts, official recovery plans, as required under the Endangered Species Act, have generally been a disappointment. The fundamental assumption of traditional recovery plans is that detailed long-range planning is both feasible and worthwhile. With most endangered species work, however, there is insufficient knowledge to plan intelligently very far into the future. Recovery plans have had a discouraging tendency to become obsolete within months or even weeks of being finalized, and sometimes even before finalization. Meanwhile they have demanded a tremendous amount of time, energy, and resources to develop and review.

Research on endangered species has repeatedly demonstrated that one generally cannot predict what will be learned and that early notions about the factors affecting species are often in error. The day-to-day advances in understanding frequently overturn long-held assumptions on how best to conserve species. With only small populations available for study, efforts to identify principal limiting factors are often affected by large temporal fluctuations in the importance of these factors. Conservation strategies have to change rapidly with the intrinsic instability of the information base. The process is basically inductive rather than deductive. It cannot usually be encapsulated successfully in a traditional recovery plan format because commonly many of the elements important for recovery are unknown at the start. The recovery plan process is not designed to accommodate rapid changes in understanding, for it is a laborious and time-consuming task to continually redraft plans to keep them consistent with current information and then gain approval for these changes. Although recovery plans are supposed to be reviewed annually and continuously updated, this almost never happens (GAO 1988), because the task is so overwhelming. The energies needed would clearly be much better spent in a more flexible performance of recovery actions under a much less ambitious planning arrangement.

In general, recovery plans are much too detailed and are burdened with many recommendations that are based on too little information. Commonly a substantial fraction of recommended actions are never funded or implemented or even taken very seriously (GAO 1988). Often many actions are of questionable value from the start and are only included for the sake of "completeness." There is no appreciable value in tabulating these low priority actions and little value in general in planning ahead in a detailed manner on more than an annual basis. Things just change too rapidly.

Instead of drafting standard recovery plans we would prefer to see teams follow a less ambitious path, at least for species where there is still much to be learned about limiting factors and the design of conservation actions. This path would emphasize interim and ad hoc documents addressing specific parts of the recovery process and specific time periods such as the breeding season of a given year. This is the way the California Condor recovery program operated during much of the 1980s. The recovery team made almost no effort to keep the official recovery plan updated and instead focused its attention on preparing documents that were much smaller in size and much more timely and limited in scope. These documents, like the recovery plan, were directed primarily toward the federal and state agencies in charge of administering the program, but they had much more influence than did the recovery plan itself. There was neither the time nor the staff to be constantly revising the full plan in an attempt to keep it current. The official recovery plan was generally viewed as a mostly irrelevant "after the fact" document that would have to be fixed up some day, rather than as a "predictive" document.

Because recovery plans become outdated rapidly and include many recommendations of questionable value, they should not generally be trusted for guidance in the long term. Trust should instead be placed in continuously functioning quality recovery teams and their most current ad hoc recommendations. Unfortunately, the finalization of a recovery plan for a species has often been the pretext for dissolving the recovery team (e.g., the first Puerto Rican Parrot Recovery Team), as if once a plan is generated there is no further need for expert input to the Fish and Wildlife Service. Nothing could be more biologically short-sighted and politically counterproductive.

Recovery plans have had a distressing tendency to become surrogate endpoints of recovery efforts, perhaps because they are tangible results that agencies can point to as accomplishments, whereas actual progress toward recovery goals is often much harder to define and evaluate. Yet the existence of a recovery plan tells us virtually nothing about whether progress toward recovery is taking place. In reality, substantial progress often occurs in the absence of an approved plan and, conversely, can fail to occur even when an approved plan exists. Recovery plans are at best a minor component of the functioning of an effective recovery effort. They are not completely without value, but their merits often do not justify their costs. Unfortunately, they have gained an overall status far beyond their true worth.

Despite their many weaknesses, we would not recommend that recovery plans be abolished completely. Instead, we believe they should be scaled back to brief and general narrative accounts of the state of knowledge about the factors limiting species populations, broad research needs, and potential conservation strategies. More focused interim and ad hoc plans, including detailed budgets and assignments of responsibilities, should form annual appendices to the general plan. The highly complex step-down outlines and multiyear budgets that form the bulk of many traditional recovery plans are rarely useful and should be abandoned in most cases as a misallocation of scarce funds and other resources.

Integration of Research and Management Efforts

A fourth subject deserving comment is the cumbersome and puzzling way the U.S. Fish and Wildlife Service organized endangered species activities in the 1980s and earlier. The Service followed a policy of supposedly clear separation of research and management activities in different branches. Essentially all activities we pursued in working toward conservation of the condor had both research and management components and yet administratively we were part of the research branch, not the management branch. In theory we were not supposed to conduct activities that could be classified as management. The height of absurdity in such an organizational framework was the notion that when we observed immediate threats of predators to condor nests in the wild, we should do nothing to control the situation ourselves but should call in a team of management experts. Considering the lack of time commonly available between recognizing problems and acting on them in an appropriate manner, we could easily have suffered major losses in following official protocol.

However, it would be unfair not to recognize that the impracticality of following protocol in such situations was generally fully recognized by administrators, and in fact we did often perform "management" actions ourselves, without going through normal procedures and without anyone getting upset in the organization. We faced the same need to integrate research and management functions in work with other endangered species, most notably the Puerto Rican Parrot, and here again the USFWS was generally tolerant about mixing functions, despite its overall adherence to a philosophy of separating functions.

Nevertheless, to the extent that these functions are separated administratively, inefficiencies and difficulties arise that would not otherwise exist. At least for endangered species work, we argue strongly for full integration of research and management functions to achieve maximal progress.

Yet despite the efficiency of such an approach, the conservation program for California Condors has been deliberately organized without any identifiable field research component since 1990, as if there might be no need for continuing quality research into such things as how to achieve maximal success in release techniques and maximal reduction of limiting factors. Perhaps it is not surprising that releases have been proceeding without a clear concept of goals and mostly without the use of standard experimental methodologies designed to test the importance of various release options (Meretsky et al. in press).

Unfortunately, with the recent division of the old USFWS into a research group working within the U.S. Geological Survey and a management group remaining in USFWS (the current release program is administrated under refuges) the administrative division in functions has become even more polarized. Managers simply cannot be expected to make insightful decisions unless they base them on properly designed and implemented research programs. To separate research and management functions into separately funded and compartmentalized administrative units is to guarantee a breakdown in the productive coordination of functions.

Goal Displacement

A fifth theme emerging from the condor program that we believe deserves some discussion is the danger of goal substitution. Here we are concerned with the subversion of the goal of rapid species recovery to other goals that can greatly slow the recovery process and greatly increase its costs. Conservation organizations dealing with endangered species are human organizations, whether they be private or governmental, and they are just as susceptible to pervasive bureaucratic forces as are any other organizations. Although conservation organizations may act initially with a commendable commitment and urgency to the goal of preserving particular endangered species, this commitment often changes through time into an overriding emphasis on conserving the organizations themselves. If the goal of preserving a species then comes into conflict with goals of organizational self-preservation and growth, job security, career advancement, fund-raising, and the exercise of power, most organizations will demand priority employee loyalty to organizational, rather than species goals. Thus, species in effect can become the means for achieving organizational goals rather than the primary goals themselves. Anything that threatens continuation of the organization (or its budget) must be opposed, even if saving the organization or preserving the budget entails partial sacrifice of the conservation prospects of the species in question or of other species. Further, any employee who argues that species concerns should take precedence over organizational concerns may be subjected to attack on the grounds of disloyalty to the organization.

The condor program of the mid 1980s provided excellent illustrations of all of the above tendencies, as was discussed in part in earlier chapters, especially Chapters 14 and 15, and it continues to do so. However, it would be a mistake to conclude that these tendencies are in any way unique to the condor program. They are pervasive and powerful forces, and it takes constant vigilance and counteractive measures if they are not to assume dominance in any endangered species program.

Conservation organizations dealing with endangered species face a fundamental conflict between achieving true success in conserving a species and at the same time ensuring continuing financial support and job security. The latter goals argue, to be sure, that species should be prevented from going extinct. But they argue as well that full species recovery need not be achieved too quickly, or the budget and jobs will go extinct. So long as some progress can be shown from year to year, who in the outside world will be so aggressive as to assert that minimal progress is not enough? Commonly, no one on the outside even knows the right questions to ask in evaluating a program, and programs can often decline greatly in effectiveness without any alarms being sounded. This judgement may seem overly cynical and severe, but it conforms fully with our experience with a variety of endangered species conservation programs over the long haul, including the condor program.

Specifically with respect to the condor program, the extraordinarily slow progress seen so far in achieving a true solution to the lead contamination problem in the wild is a case in point (see preceding chapter). The existence of a major lead threat to the species has now been known for 15 years, yet the threat still continues full-blown without a comprehensive program to combat it yet in place. Only modest progress has been achieved toward solving this problem, most of it happening without official encouragement and happening outside the program. And now with the mostly independent development of very promising nontoxic ammunitions, it still remains to be seen if the program will seize the initiative and successfully ensure full replacement of lead with these ammunitions in release areas.

Another example provided by the condor program is the slow progress in solving the behavioral problems in released birds. Instead of quickly implementing rearing methods that on the basis of other release programs could be expected to maximize the quality of released birds (i.e., parent rearing in remote field enclosures that have no resemblance to rectangular human structures), the release program, now in operation for nearly 12 years, has remained stuck in the groove of mainly releasing puppet-reared birds and trying to improve their dismal performance with aversive conditioning techniques, but then not even properly testing the effects of aversive conditioning. Further, the mixing of parent-reared birds with hand-reared birds in several releases has allowed no clear interpretation of the potential benefits of parent-rearing in these releases. And now that properly run experiments comparing puppet-reared with parent-reared birds have finally been run in the Ventana Wilderness Area and yielded results indicating a major superiority of parent-reared birds, the program continues to sanction releases of puppet-reared birds and to debate whether it should shift over to maximizing production of parent-reared birds instead of puppet-reared birds. Although we still remain optimistic that obvious solutions to the behavioral and lead toxicity problems will be implemented, each year effective solutions are delayed represents more than another million dollars out of the budgets of other needy conservation programs.

It is true enough that the process of recovery of endangered species is often slow at best. But the record of achievement of many programs argues forcefully that if recovery cannot be achieved relatively quickly, there is a good chance that the programs will evolve into self-perpetuating bureaucracies content with an enduring state of endangerment of the species in question and endless expenditures of scarce conservation funds. In our experience, these tendencies are as great with private organizations as with governmental organizations, so privatizing programs offers no realistic hope of relief, despite frequently heard assertions that government bungling and incompetence are the main problems. At least with governmental organizations there are some mechanisms to achieve accountability and change when abuses become too obvious. Private organizations can often conceal the skeletons in their closets much more thoroughly, and in our experience they are just as capable of bungling and incompetence as government organizations.

The amounts of money attached to major endangered species programs, such as the condor program, are not huge by governmental standards, but they are large enough by wildlife conservation standards to represent an attractive target for those in a position to gain control of them, both within and outside of the government. When these monies are perceived primarily as a long-term means of support for personnel and operations, they become a powerful goal in themselves, and generally inspire a primary concern for budget maintenance in program administrators. In important respects this concern is at basic odds with the goal of rapid recovery of endangered species, and underlies many of the current problems faced by condor conservation efforts.

Beneath the rhetoric, virtually all conservation organizations, private and governmental alike, are closely watching their bottom lines. Idealistic neophyte participants in endangered species programs soon find that this reality is not always consistent with the goals they hold of aiding endangered species in the most effective ways possible. Those who fight this reality risk losing their jobs; those who adjust, soon learn the art of misleading the public as to what really motivates their organizations most strongly. We are not so cynical as to believe that most conservation organizations do not care about real success in conservation efforts, but the capacity of the human mind to simultaneously pursue basically incompatible goals should not be underestimated.

We recognize that the basic desires of most administrators to achieve program stability or growth, simultaneous with progress toward recovery goals are often motivated mainly by their sympathetic concerns for the well-being of their associates. We are not suggesting that such concerns are intrinsically evil or have no importance, but believe that they often achieve sufficient predominance in the functioning of organizations that original goals of achieving real success with maximal efficiency in species conservation can be all but forgotten.

Our remarks here are not directed at the personnel at the field level of the condor program who, in our experience, have been extraordinarily idealistic and motivated strongly toward producing maximal benefits for the species throughout the history of the program. The problems have lain mainly higher up in the administrative levels of the organizations involved, where nearly all major policy decisions get made.

Funding of the Condor Program Past and Present – Implications

To explore further the relationships between monetary questions and program function, we believe a brief review of how the condor program has been funded and some of the implications of monetary matters on conservation policy is warranted. It is often said that to understand decision-making in any organization, it is essential to "follow the money."

Historically, the major sources of support for condor studies and conservation were (1) the U.S. Forest Service, particularly with respect to the work of Cyril Robinson in the 1930s and partial support of a series of patrolmen for the Sespe Condor Sanctuary in the 1950s, (2) the National Audubon Society which provided the principal support for Carl Koford's studies in the 1930s and 1940s, partial support for Sespe Sanctuary patrolmen in the 1950s, and aided the Miller–McMillan study of the early 1960s, and (3) the National Geographic Society which provided partial support toward the Miller–McMillan study. Neither the U.S. Fish and Wildlife Service, nor the State of California devoted significant resources toward research and conservation of this species until after the passage of the federal Endangered Species Preservation Act of 1966, which specifically authorized such work with listed species.

Nevertheless, the level of investment in condor studies remained relatively modest through the late 1960s and 1970s. During most of this period, program personnel were limited to single field researchers provided by the U.S. Fish and Wildlife Service, the National Audubon Society, and more irregularly, the Forest Service and the Department of Fish and Game. The USFWS researcher for the species was not even limited to condor studies, but had responsibilities with other endangered species in the California region as well. With these funding/personnel limitations and the historical limitations on research with the species, there was no way for major progress to take place in identifying and countering principal limiting factors affecting the species. There was an underlying attitude discernible in upper levels of the USFWS that condor conservation was a hopeless cause, not worth more than token investments of manpower and money. Although this attitude may not have been shared uniformly at all levels of the service, the overall posture of the organization was simply to quietly document the demise of the species.

This situation was to change dramatically in 1977–78 primarily because of the concern of certain personnel within the National Audubon Society that the species was heading inexorably toward extinction unless a major program to conserve it could be developed. With the collaboration of the American Ornithologists' Union, Audubon spearheaded the formation of an expert committee to evaluate the status of the species. The report of this committee served as the basic document to pressure the Fish and Wildlife Service into action and to lobby Congress for the funding necessary to establish a new program. Without these actions, the species would surely have been effectively lost by today, and the Audubon Society deserves major credit for the initiatives that averted this outcome.

With the level of funding that came along with the new program in 1980, condor research and conservation efforts (with the exception of major habitat purchases) have not been significantly limited by financial constraints to this day (and those who blame slow progress in the condor release program on funding limitations may wish to examine the rapid success in vulture releases achieved by Michel Terrasse and his colleagues in France on an annual budget only roughly one fiftieth as great). As originally set up, the new program received funding support from the U.S. Fish and Wildlife Service, the Forest Service, the Bureau of Land Management, and the National Audubon Society. Additional funding support also soon developed from the Zoological Society of San Diego, the Los Angeles Zoo, and the California Department of Fish and Game (although part of the support provided by the California Department was in reality monies transferred from the U.S. Fish and Wildlife Service to the Department to fund a state condor researcher). The overall budget through the early 1980s exceeded a million dollars a year, most of which was Fish and Wildlife Service monies, making the condor program one of the most expensive of all the U.S. Fish and Wildlife Service endangered species programs.

Nevertheless, the sheer financial magnitude of the condor program created a number of problems with respect to keeping things on track. Audubon's major role in creating the program and ensuring continuing funding for the program, gave this organization far more power in policy decisions than was enjoyed by other program participants. On one level this may have seemed fair enough, considering the major efforts and accomplishments of this organization with condors. However, it proved in the mid 1980s to be a major curse, as the Fish and Wildlife Service became far more responsive to Audubon's wishes than to the recommendations of either the Recovery Team or its own field personnel working daily with the species. In our judgement, the basic reason for this degree of influence was in large part monetary, although threats of lawsuits also played a role. Audubon was a major force in creating the large amounts of money in the program through its abilities to influence Congress.

Audubon was also the recipient of much of the monies in the program, as the large majority of personnel working in the field, including Helen, were Audubon employees funded at federal expense by transfers of monies from the USFWS to Audubon. In part, we were fully supportive of such transfers, because they allowed far greater flexibility in the hiring of personnel than did the federal Civil Service System – a cumbersome system of restrictions that interfered greatly with finding the best people for the jobs and letting go people who did not work out well. On the other hand, we were to live to regret the vast power enjoyed by Audubon as a result of its financial role in the program. Audubon, like all other agencies in the program, did not enjoy a monopoly of wisdom and competence with the species, and when its influence in large measure led to the pursuit of a variety of ill-advised strategies and abolishing of the Recovery Team in 1985, the program had lost, albeit temporarily, one of its most precious assets – a balance of power and expertise in guiding responsible agencies through very difficult times.

However, the tide turned, and had to turn, when the Fish and Wildlife Service finally reversed itself and joined hands with the California Fish and Game Commission in advocating bringing all the last birds into captivity. When Audubon then sued the Fish and Wildlife Service, it declared war on the agency, and the agency had no choice but to defend itself, however weakly it may have done so in court. Nevertheless, the USFWS did win the legal case on appeal, with substantial help from the California Fish and Game Commission, the Los Angeles Zoo, and the Zoological Society of San Diego. In the aftermath of this victory, Audubon Society had no role left in the recovery program, and the program found that it was far less dependent on Audubon's financial clout than some had believed.

At the time these events were transpiring, it was a relief to witness Audubon's departure from the scene. Now, we would welcome seeing them return to participate in the program. Whatever we may feel about the negative aspects of Audubon's participation in the mid 1980s, the overall role of Audubon in condor conservation has been a very major, and in many respects a very positive, one. We believe Audubon's future participation in condor matters could be beneficial.

The Fish and Wildlife Service, for its own role with condors, has vacillated between moments of true wisdom and courage and unfortunate lapses in resolve and insight in the face of outside political pressures. Regardless, we still maintain that the USFWS must remain the central authority in condor conservation matters and believe that fully privatizing the program would represent a tragic error. Efforts to move the program in the direction of privatization have now proceeded far down the road and present one of the more difficult challenges for the future.

In large measure, the private agencies involved in the condor program over the years have paid their own ways, including the Zoological Society of San Diego and the Los Angeles Zoo. Aside from the original construction of the first captive-breeding facilities in San Diego at federal expense, both zoos have contributed all support monies toward running the captive breeding program for the species, which has normally amounted to about a quarter of a million dollars per year for each institution. These institutions have also remained respectfully neutral about exhibit of condors to the public at their facilities, and this has yet to take place (though we personally have had no problems with this and exhibit of condors is now anticipated in the near future).

Nevertheless, with the high level of success in captive breeding of condors at both institutions, both quickly began to run out of space to house condors, and a consensus developed in the early 1990s that a third institution should be brought into captive breeding efforts with the species. To facilitate the choice of a third institution, the Recovery Team drew up a set of policy recommendations for the U.S. Fish and Wildlife Service. Among the various recommendations, perhaps the most pivotal was that any new participant in the captive breeding efforts should likewise be prepared to come in with its own funding. This recommendation, along with the other recommendations in the overall policy proposal was accepted by the Regional Director of the USFWS in Portland and became official USFWS policy at that point.

Thus it came as a surprise in mid 1992 to be informed by sources in Washington that a bill (actually a rider to an appropriations bill) had just passed the House and Senate, authorizing payment of several hundred thousand dollars to the Peregrine Fund not only to breed California Condors, but to conduct releases of California Condors in the Grand Canyon of Arizona. We soon learned that this bill was also a surprise to a number of key USFWS personnel who had been involved with the condor program, several members of the Condor Recovery Team, and the head of the non-game branch of the Arizona Game and Fish Department. Although the bill contradicted Condor Recovery Team recommendations and official US Fish and Wildlife Service policy and although protests were lodged by a number of parties with the Congressional Committee overseeing resolution of House and Senate versions of the bill, it was too late to effectively counteract what Congress had already passed. The upshot was that the Peregrine Fund soon became a major player in the condor program at continuing federal expense. To our knowledge, the US Fish and Wildlife Service as an organization made no protests over these developments, although some individuals within the Service were greatly disturbed. Other captive-breeding institutions, most notably the National Zoo, that had expressed interest in participating in the condor propagation program with the understanding that federal funding would not be provided, were left out of consideration.

By having their consensus policies on condor conservation effectively overridden by Congress and an outside private organization, the USFWS and other participating agencies in the program lost a considerable proportion of the power they formerly held in influencing the direction of events in the program. In a rapid turn of events the program had regressed to a situation similar to the mid 1980s when an outside private organization, the Audubon Society, assumed dominance in influencing USFWS condor policy, subordinating the role of the recovery team and USFWS personnel. While the participation of the Peregrine Fund in condor captive breeding is something we had recommended and continue to recommend (just as we continue to recommend participation by the National Zoo), the terms of such participation are leading to continuing problems.

The Road Ahead

In many respects, the historic plight of the condor bears comparison to the plight of the Peregrine Falcon in North America in the years following World War II. Both species evidently were suffering most significantly from environmental poisons, and only the nature of the specific poisons differed. For the condor, lead poisoning was the apparent major threat, while organochlorine pesticide poisoning was the major problem for the Peregrine. Fortunately, the causes of the Peregrine's woes were recognized relatively quickly and were effectively reversed by governmental restrictions on use of the offending materials. The wild population of Peregrines in North America has since recovered strongly, aided in part by release efforts. No one ever suggested that the key to saving this species was habitat preservation.

In contrast, the main causes of the condor's extirpation were long misunderstood and still remain uncorrected. The historical emphasis on habitat preservation, although perhaps of considerable intrinsic merit, did not and could not lead to recovery of the species. Further, current reestablishment efforts cannot be expected to succeed until the true causes of decline are corrected. Progress toward correcting basic limiting factors for the condor has been modest, while essentially all programmatic attention has been focused on details of rearing and release procedures, as if correcting such details could result in viable populations, and as if correcting basic limiting factors for the species was someone else's responsibility. We contest both assumptions, and suggest that the thrust of the overall program needs to be refocused on the issues of highest priority.

At the outset, we would like to state that we believe that the ultimate goal of condor conservation should be the speedy achievement and maintenance of viable, self-sustaining wild populations that are as free as possible of human management activities and are members of ecosystems that are as close to "natural" as possible. Captive populations or wild populations maintained on subsidized food supplies should not be viewed as end points in the conservation process. Nor should endless reintroduction efforts that have no hope of resulting in self-sustaining wild populations be considered an acceptable goal. Releases of condors to the wild should be based on reasonable confidence that major limiting factors have been or are being effectively countered by one means or another.

Although different observers will disagree as to what may constitute a fully "natural" ecosystem for the species, and in fact it is possible to argue persuasively that condors have not been dependent on fully "natural" ecosystems for centuries, the critical issue for us is not exactly how one may define what is natural and wild but that condors regain a capacity to live free in the wild without a need for constant "nurse-maid" attention from our species into the indefinite future. A continuing need for such attention would represent a basic conservation failure, not to mention a continuing major expense that would rob other worthy wildlife species of the resources that might otherwise be available for their conservation. Although we are not arguing for near-term cuts in funding of the condor program, the current costs of condor reestablishment efforts project to a perfectly enormous total in the years ahead if basic limiting factors remain uncorrected. Further, the time may come when such subsidies may no longer be forthcoming because of human economic or political crisis.

Thus success in condor conservation should not be measured in terms of total numbers of individuals in existence, nor in total numbers living in wild or semi-wild circumstances. These measures, by themselves, tell us little about the future viability of the species. In our view, success should be measured by the much more meaningful standard of true self-sufficiency in the wild, that is by achievement of effectively unmanaged wild populations that exhibit true long-term demographic viability, with reproduction equaling or exceeding mortality. By this standard, the condor recovery program still has a long way to go.

The most recent Recovery Plan for the California Condor (US Fish and Wildlife Service 1996) describes recovery criteria for the condor that as far as they go, are largely consistent with the above goals, as follows:

Recovery Objective: Downlist [the condor from endangered] to threatened.
Recovery Criteria: The minimum criterion for reclassification to threatened is the maintenance of at least two non-captive populations and one captive population. These populations (1) must each number at least 150 individuals (2) must each contain at least 15 breeding pairs and (3) be reproductively self-sustaining and have a positive rate of population growth. In addition, the non-captive populations (4) must be spatially disjunct and non-interacting, and (5) must contain individuals descended from each of the 14 founders.

However, the plan does not make clear why a large captive population (presumably costing on the order of $1 million annually) might be needed following the establishment of two vigorous wild populations. Further, it does not state whether or not the noncaptive populations should be on perpetual subsidy, and does not provide a comprehensive strategy for counteracting the major mortality threats of lead poisoning, shooting, and collisions. Nor does it discuss the logic of conducting releases of California Condors before limiting factors are effectively countered. Thus, the Recovery Plan gives little guidance on the most important issues facing the species.

Current releases of condors were originally envisioned as countering certain major limiting factors in the wild (primarily lead poisoning) by a subsidy of clean food. But as the 1996 Recovery Plan recognizes, and as recent evidence supports, keeping released condors, even captive-reared individuals, fully dependent on a perpetual subsidy may not be feasible (at least so long as releases continue to be conducted with multiple subsidy sites). Without a realistic hope that food subsidy may effectively counter the lead poisoning threat in the long term, the Recovery Plan leaves unanswered how current releases can be expected to result in self-sustaining populations, except to indicate that mortality threats to the population will continue to be studied so that solutions to these threats may eventually be found. In our view, the solutions in fact are already largely known, and need to be implemented immediately, not at some indefinite time in the future by means that are not yet identified.

We remain optimistic that unmanaged and viable wild condor populations can be reestablished, but we are deeply concerned about the recent rate of progress toward this goal. We suggest that progress would be greatly enhanced by a number of programmatic changes:

1. Adopting a policy of peer review.
The program could benefit greatly from an in-depth outside review by a panel of

truly experienced and first-rank conservation biologists. Such a panel in 1977–78 earlier proved highly effective in motivating major beneficial changes in the program. All conservation programs need in-depth outside review periodically, and the condor program is no exception. The panel should include only people free of vested interests in the program, and the charge of the panel should be to develop specific recommendations for the US Fish and Wildlife Service and California Fish and Game Commission that would ensure the fastest possible real recovery of the species. In developing recommendations, the panel should consult intensively both with diverse participants in the program and with responsible critics of the program. Recommendations should not be limited to biological matters but should concern as well the political organization of efforts. In fact, all aspects of the program should be fair game for consideration. Potential sponsors for the panel could include respected, but not directly involved organizations such as the National Academy of Sciences, the American Ornithologists' Union, or the Society for Conservation Biology.

2. Revitalizing the Condor Recovery Team.

The program could also benefit significantly by revitalization of the Condor Recovery Team, especially with new membership offering expertise in release methodology and basic biology of California Condors. The fact that the USFWS felt it was necessary to convene a workshop to solve problems in condor release methodology in 1994 was a clear indication that the Service and the Recovery Team were not coping adequately in developing release strategies. Unfortunately, very few Recovery Team members attended this workshop, and some of the most important recommendations from the workshop have never been implemented. Although Recovery Team membership has changed somewhat since the 1994 workshop, the team has as yet failed to promote a crash effort to counter lead contamination threats and has been content with near stasis in development of optimal release technologies, in part due to a failure to insist on standard experimental methodologies in release efforts and in part due to a failure to respond appropriately to the dismal results achieved with puppet-reared birds. It is symptomatic of malaise that the team as of this writing still does not include representation from the Ventana Wilderness Society, which is currently supervising the most encouraging release efforts with the species. It is also symptomatic of dysfunction that the team is presently considering a major proliferation of release programs without having yet achieved real success in reestablishment in even one site. Proliferation of programs in itself can be expected to lock the release program into inferior puppet-rearing procedures for releases.

3. Adopting a goal of viable and unmanaged wild populations.

There should be clear recognition of a principal goal of achieving viable wild condor populations that are as free of management inputs as possible. Although food subsidy is a tool to aid in establishment of populations, wild populations free of subsidy should be the stated ultimate goal. Captive populations should not be a long-term goal.

4. Fully integrating research and management.

There is an overriding need for the reestablishment of a quality research effort in the program, recognized organizationally and maximally integrated with "management" functions. There should also be regular publication of release results in peer-reviewed journals to allow the general conservation community an opportunity to evaluate progress of the program.

5. Reorganizing program funding.

The present asymmetry with which federal monies are used to support nongovernmental organizations (NGOs) participating in the program is inequitable and bad for morale and should be corrected. The earlier policy of the Recovery Team and USFWS that all NGOs participating in captive breeding and releases should pay their own ways is the simplest and most beneficial way to achieve equity and should be reimplemented.

6. Addressing limiting factors in the wild.

Extremely high priority needs to be given to removal of the threat of lead contamination from regions of condor reestablishment. Encouragement of the introduction of nontoxic ammunition types and/or creation of additional no-hunting preserves in foraging habitat appear to offer the most practical solutions to this problem, and efforts need to be made at all levels of government and the private sector to achieve momentum in implementing these solutions. Until the problem is solved, releases cannot be expected to result in self-sustaining wild populations.

7. Producing optimal birds for release and improving release methodologies with rigorous experiments.

Although the Zoological Society of San Diego, the Los Angeles Zoo, and the Peregrine Fund have been enormously successful in captive breeding California Condors, the production of optimal birds for release has lagged. Avaliable evidence strongly suggests that aversive conditioning of puppet-reared birds has not in itself provided the program with adequate reductions in the tendencies of birds to orient positively to humans and human structures and that parent-reared birds provide a much better potential for release. Future releases should be limited to parent-reared birds, and the puppet-reared birds released to date should be returned to captivity where they can become captive breeders and add to the production of parent-reared birds. There is no evidence as yet that released puppet-reared California Condors are "outgrowing" their excessive orientation to humans and human structures and some have now been in the wild for five years. And while some proponents of puppet-rearing argue that released puppet-reared Andean Condors in South America have shown improvement in such behaviors over time, these are birds that have been integrated into existing wild populations and have had an opportunity to learn appropriate behavior from wild-reared birds. This is a very different situation from the California releases. Under present circumstances, releases of wild-caught California Condors can only be expected to result in their fairly rapid demise (see next recommendation).

With genetic goals of captive breeding now being rapidly achieved, maximal parent-rearing should become the priority goal superseding maximal reproduction as the most important goal for rearing and releases. To the extent feasible, experiments with appropriate controls should be initiated to assess the benefits of moving source breeding pairs for parent-reared release birds out of urban zoo environments and into more naturalistic field enclosures.

8. **Limiting releases of wild-trapped condors to proper circumstances.**

If, and only if, the lead poisoning threat can be fully removed from condor release areas, consideration should be given to release of California Condors that were trapped as free-flying birds in the 1980s, assuming they have been amply represented by progeny in the captive flock. Pressures to release such birds before the lead contamination threat is fully addressed can be expected to result only in mortality of these birds and the permanent loss of their extremely valuable behavioral repertoires. We believe strongly that these birds still remember what it is to be fully competent wild condors. Packed within their brains are skills that may prove to be impossible to duplicate in the captive-propagation context. The program would be very poorly advised to risk losing these values prematurely, but should plan actively for the day when it becomes prudent to utilize them in releases. The longer full solutions to the lead contamination are delayed, the more likely these birds will no longer be alive to aid reestablishment efforts productively.

9. **Addressing future threats from Golden Eagles and Common Ravens in a timely fashion.**

Minimization of the threats of Golden Eagles and Common Ravens to future nesting efforts of released condors needs to be considered on an ongoing basis in evaluating potential release sites. Experimentation with taste-aversion conditioning of Common Ravens with condor-like eggs should be initiated in the near future, rather than waiting for raven problems to develop in released populations and then starting to address them. The raven threats were clearly identified in the early 1980s and presumably still exist. Field taste-aversion research was first proposed in 1984–85, and could be accomplished at very low cost.

We believe all the above recommendations are important and have not presented them in any hard and fast priority order. However, we suggest that 1 and 2 are of special importance. In fact, if 1 and 2 might be successfully implemented, there is a reasonable chance that the rest of the recommendations, or similar recommendations, might follow as a direct result.

None of the foregoing recommendations, with the possible exception of creation of new no-hunting preserves, demands major new expenditures of taxpayer monies. In fact over the long haul they can be expected to greatly reduce expenditures, if only by significantly speeding the conservation process. As it stands now, the program is within reach of achieving real success, but this may not happen without some changes in direction and emphasis in current policies. It would be tragic if the program were to wind up as a "put and take" operation, with endless releases and a continuing failure to achieve self-sustaining wild populations. It would also be tragic if the process of achieving self-sustaining wild populations were to take any longer or consume any more resources than might be necessary.

We offer these recommendations in a spirit of hoping to aid the conservation process and not in a spirit of denigrating any of the efforts that have been or are being made. All parties that have participated in conservation efforts for the species deserve respect for their positive contributions and sympathetic understanding for their mistakes. All, including ourselves, have made mistakes. We submit that this ought to be expected in any conservation effort, as no one is blessed with perfect insight. The crucial point for all concerned is to maintain a willingness to profit from mistakes and a desire to evolve in directions that lead to ultimate success as rapidly as possible.

Epilogue

For more than a century the California Condor has been considered a species in terminal decline. James Cooper wrote in 1890, "I can testify myself that from my first observations of it in California in 1855, I have seen fewer every year when I have been in localities suitable for them. There can be little doubt that unless protected our great vulture is doomed to rapid extinction." These sentiments were echoed by C.W. Beebe who stated in 1906, "Its doom is near; within a few years at most, the last individual will have perished." William Finley (1908a) similarly remarked, "unless the needed protection is given, this bird will undoubtedly follow the Great Auk." In 1911 William Hornaday wrote, "beyond all doubt, the skin-collecting ornithologists will exterminate it within the next twenty years, or less." William Leon Dawson in 1923 was certain there were less than 100 individuals left and probably no more than 40. He suggested that if ever there were to be a careful study of the species it would have to be undertaken within a decade. Alexander Wetmore in 1933 reported an estimate of only 10 individuals left in California, and Loye Miller in 1937 wrote that the California Condor "has developed such a strong candidacy for the pluperfect status" it seems "likely to win in spite of all we can do to stem the tide." In 1942 Miller asked, "Is not the California Condor a senile species that is far past its prime? Is it not a species with one foot and even one wing in the grave?"

Yet despite the gloomy unanimity of these early authorities, the species is still extant today. Its historic wild population lasted far longer than any of the early naturalists predicted, probably because there were many more birds in the wild than they suspected. Over the past decade the numbers of condors have been increasing rapidly in captivity and releases of captives to the wild have been initiated. Although viable, self-sufficient wild populations have not yet been restored, and have probably not existed for at least two centuries, there is no reason to despair that they are beyond achievement. The remaining obstacles to reaching this goal are becoming increasingly obvious and their solutions are not obscure.

The California Condor is still with us and is still an incredibly magnificent species. The degree of threat to its survival has been greatly reduced from past decades, thanks to the diligent contributions of a multitude of committed people. Nevertheless, the degree of success achieved so far should not be any excuse to relax the intensity of efforts to achieve full recovery. Like all other creatures on the planet, the condor deserves to exist as a self-sustaining, free-living, wild spirit, not simply as a captive or domesticated population and not simply as an inviable wild presence maintained by endless releases. We see no fundamental barriers to achieving this goal other than our own imperfections as a species in carrying out recovery efforts. These can all be overcome if there is the will to do so. We hope that there is and that a near century of conservation efforts will not have been in vain.

Acknowledgments

The condor program has been an often tumultuous venture involving the contributions of many individuals and organizations. We would like to acknowledge the efforts of all who have participated, regardless of their specific philosophies and orientations toward conservation and research, as surely all parties have worked toward the same goal of preserving the species.

Unfortunately, the number of contributors is large, and includes many people we have not even met, especially in very recent years. It would be impractical to mention all who deserve recognition. Instead, we will limit ourselves mainly to major contributors to the program of the 1980s, as that period is the main focus of the book and the era we know best.

Primary institutional support for the condor program over the years has come from the U.S. Fish and Wildlife Service, the National Audubon Society, the U.S. Forest Service, the California Department of Fish and Game, and the Bureau of Land Management, but during the 1980s a variety of other organizations also came to play important roles. Of special note were the contributions of the Zoological Society of San Diego; the Los Angeles Zoo; the Condor Survival Fund; Hawk Mountain Sanctuary Association; the Biological Sciences Department of California Polytechnic State University at San Luis Obispo; the Santa Barbara Museum of Natural History; the Western Foundation of Vertebrate Zoology; the Illinois Natural History Survey; the Santa Cruz Predatory Bird Research Group; the Los Angeles, Morro Coast, Kern, Santa Barbara, and Tulare County Audubon Societies; the Hearst Foundation; and Van Nuys Charities. This book, however, should not be considered an official expression of the viewpoint of any particular organization. It is our own personal assessment of the natural history and conservation of the species.

For brevity and convenience we have used the pronoun "we" throughout the book, but the reader should recognize that especially regarding results of studies in the program of the 1980s, "we" generally reflects in large measure the efforts of a remarkable staff of assistants and cooperators. In particular, we wish to acknowledge the following field personnel who worked closely with us in the parts of the program that were our domain: Louis Andaloro, Victor Apanius, Lee Aulman, Brad Bush, Dave Clendenen, Jan and Hank Hamber, Leon Hecht, Jack Ingram, Tom Lecky, Dave Ledig, Cindy McConathy, Sandy Pletschet, Rob Ramey, John Roach, Bay Roberts, John Roser, Joe Russin, John Schmitt, Meg Stein, Russell Thorstrom, and Teresa Woods. These people worked exceptionally hard and were responsible for a major part of the achievements of the modern program. Of all these, the most durable participant was surely Dave Clendenen, whose exemplary field role extended from 1982 until 1997, who still continues as a member of the Recovery Team, and who has provided many of the photographs and observations presented in this book.

We have also drawn on some of the results of the condor radio-telemetry program of the 1980s, run primarily by John Ogden and his National Audubon Society staff consisting of Bruce Barbour, Pete Bloom, Jesse Grantham, Vicky Meretsky, Larry Riopelle, Greg Sanders, and Buck Woods. Gene Bourassa of the USFWS and Bill Cochran of the Illinois Natural History Survey deserve special mention for their roles in designing the telemetry hardware and software used in early radio-tracking efforts, while Vicky Meretsky deserves special commendation for undertaking the formidable task of analyzing telemetry records. Other staff members of the Condor Research Center who made important contributions are Gary Falxa, Steve Kimple, Bill Lehman, and Cindy Studer.

Special acknowledgment should be given to personnel of the Zoological Society of San Diego and the Los Angeles Zoo, who have aided the program in many ways transcending the captive breeding of condors. In particular, mention must be made of Jack Allen, Marilyn Anderson, Mike Clark, Cathleen Cox, Mike Cunningham, Phil Ensley, Ben Gonzalez, Marcia Hobbs, Don Janssen, Cyndi Kuehler, Gary Kuehn, Arlene Kumamoto, Don Lindburg, Mike Loomis, Jim Oosterhuis, Art Risser, Amy Shima, Don Sterner, Cynthia Stringfield, Warren Thomas, Bill Toone, Rebecca Usnik, Mike Wallace, and Pat Witman for their many accomplishments.

Eric Johnson and his students at California Polytechnic State University made crucial contributions to censusing the wild population. A tremendous debt is also owed to John Borneman, David Houston, Peter Mundy, Fred Sibley, Michel Terrasse, Sandy Wilbur, and Mike Wallace for the research they have conducted with condors and/or other vulture species. The discoveries made by Fred Sibley in the 1960s were especially valuable to our efforts of the 1980s. Fred kindly revisited the condor program in 1984 and provided crucial help during the frenzies of multiple-clutching efforts of that year. The Vulture Study Group had a major role in aiding the initiation of operations in the 1980s, as did Mike Wallace with his research on Andean Condors in Peru. Recovery team members of the 1980s we would like to mention for their many contributions include Dean Carrier, Dave Harlow, Ron Jurek, Lloyd Kiff, Butch Olendorff, and Jared Verner.

USFWS staff at the Patuxent Wildlife Research Center who aided significantly in various efforts included Jim Carpenter, Scott Derrickson, Barbara Nichols, Randy Perry, John Rogers, and Stan Wiemeyer. Harry Ohlendorf, arranged for the transfer and use of a boat to allow detailed study of two lakeside condor pairs in the early 1980s, while Barbara Nichols kept the home office functioning through some very difficult times.

For the many helicopter-aided egg pickups we give profound thanks to the staff of Aspen Helicopters, especially Charlie McGlaughlin, Rick Throckmorton, and Jim Dalton, who at times were faced with some embarrassingly marginal helipads constructed in outrageous places. They nevertheless kept us and numerous condor eggs alive during repeated dashes from the mountains to the San Diego Zoo where Cyndi Kuehler was faced with the even much more daunting challenge of keeping the eggs alive and healthy through hatching. Our helicopter trips south to San Diego often included spectacular views of migrating gray whales offshore, but it was hard to focus on such splendors in the midst of the worries over making it to the zoo safely and quickly.

Aiding enormously in solving various political problems over the years were Jim Brett, Sheldon Campbell, Ed Harrison, Marcia Hobbs, David Houston, Jeff Lincer, Ian Newton,

Art Risser, and Warren Thomas. Also deserving our most heartfelt thanks through the crisis of 1985 were Fish and Game Commissioners Brian Kahn, Bill Burke, and Abel Galletti. Two Dick Smiths had important positive roles in the history of condor affairs – one from Santa Barbara in the 1970s and one who finally resolved USFWS conflicts over condor strategies in Washington in late 1985. Mike Cunningham and Caroline Kressly provided crucial financial support to the program at times of crisis.

For years subsequent to our participation in the condor program, we wish to mention the contributions of Hank Patee, Robert Mesta, and Marc Weitzel in leading various aspects of the USFWS field program and of Mike Wallace, Jim Wiley, Dave Clendenen, Gregg Austin, Mike Barth, David Ledig, Kelly Sorenson, Mark Vekasy and Shawn Farry in leading initial release efforts of condors to the wild. Jane Hendron has been especially helpful in supplying detailed information on various releases. The Ventana Wilderness Society, with its currently encouraging release results along the Big Sur, deserves special mention, as does the Peregrine Fund which has supervised condor releases in the Grand Canyon region and has taken on a major role in captive breeding of the species in recent years.

Funding to make possible the preparation of this book was provided by the Borden Corporation through the Zoological Society of San Diego. For this generous and crucial support we are especially grateful. Preparation of this book has been aided greatly by general input and review of various chapters by Dave Clendenen, Scott Derrickson, Rod Drewein, Steve Emslie, Jan Hamber, Eric Johnson, Fred Sibley, Don Sterner, Bill Toone, Jim Wiley, and Teresa Woods. Vicky Meretsky and David Houston deserve special thanks for working through the entire manuscript in detail and offering numerous improvements. Vicky Meretsky was also extremely helpful in resolving statistical questions, while Jan Hamber aided the search for historical materials. Nevertheless, we emphasize that none of the above people should be assigned any blame for shortcomings of the book.

For use of historical photographs we are especially indebted to Robert Easton, Gladys McMillan, Craig Bates, Ed Harrison of the Western Foundation of Vertebrate Zoology, the Museum of Vertebrate Zoology at Berkeley, the National Geographic Society, the U.S. Forest Service, the Southwest Museum, the Paquimé Museum of Casas Grandes, Chihuahua, and the Zoological Society of San Diego. Ruth Shea and Susan Koenig gave valued assistance in preparation of maps and graphs. John Schmitt kindly provided artwork to illustrate aspects of nestling behavior and head coloration changes of condors with age.

Finally, we wish to acknowledge the inspirational leadership of Ray Erickson, former chief of the Endangered Wildlife Research Program of the USFWS. Ray's important role in development of federal endangered species legislation and in creating a major focus on endangered species within the USFWS are an enduring legacy, and his foresight in developing a surrogate Andean Condor research program at Patuxent set the stage for much of the progress in condor conservation to follow. As a kind and generous former supervisor, he also motivated many of us in various projects to stay with the program through some years we will never forget.

Bibliography

Acha, A. 1998. Negative impact of wind generators on the Eurasian Griffon *Gyps fulvus* in Tarifa, Spain. *Vulture News* 38:10–18.

American Ornithologists' Union. 1998. *Check-list of North American birds. 7th edition.* American Ornithologists' Union, Washington, D.C.

Anonymous, 1985. *Audubon action alert, August 1, 1985.* National Audubon Society, Washington, D.C.

Anonymous, 1994. Ad hoc meeting to address status of California Condor. *Conservation Biology* 8:942.

Anthony, A.W. 1893. Birds of San Pedro Martir, Lower California. *Zoe* 4:228–233.

Arnold, M.J. 1986. *A radio-telemetry study of Turkey Vultures (Cathartes aura) in south-central California.* M.S. thesis, California Polytechnic State University, San Luis Obispo, California.

Arredondo, O. 1971. Nuevo genero y especie de ave fosil (Accipitriformes: Vulturidae) del Pleistocene de Cuba. *Separata de la Memoria de la Sociedad de Ciencias Naturales La Salle* 31(90):309–323.

Ballantyne, B, Bright, J.E., and P. Williams. 1974. The post-mortem rate of transformation of cyanide. *Forensic Sci.* 3:71–76.

Ballantyne, B., and T.C. Marrs. 1987. Post-mortem features and criteria for the diagnosis of acute lethal cyanide poisoning. Pp 217–247 in *Clinical and experimental toxicology of cyanides* (B. Ballantyne and T.C. Marrs, eds.), John Wright, Bristol, England.

Bartlett, W.H. 1905. The Shalako dance. *Out West*: June, pp 389–402.

Bartram, W. 1791. *Travels through North and South Carolina, Georgia, East and West Florida.* James Johnson, Philadelphia.

Bates, C.D., Hamber, J.A., and M.J. Lee. 1993. The California Condor and California Indians. *American Indian Art Magazine*, winter 1993: 40–47.

Beaulaurier, D.L. 1981. *Mitigation of bird collisions with transmission lines.* Bonnevile Power Admin., Portland, Oreg, 82 pp.

Beck, B.B., Rapaport, L.G., Price, M.S., and A. Wilson. 1994. Reintroduction of captive-born animals. Pp 265–284 in *Creative conservation: interactive management of wild and captive animals* (P.J.S. Olney, G.M. Mace, and A.T.C. Feistner, eds.), Chapman and Hall, London.

Beebe, C.W. 1906. The California Condor. *Bull. Zool. Soc. New York*, No. 20:258–259.

Bidwell, J. 1966. *Life in California before the Gold Discovery.* Lewis Osborne, Palo Alto, California.

Biedermann, B.M., and C.C. Lin. 1982. A leukocyte culture and chromosome preparation technique for avian species. *In Vitro* 18:415–418.

Black, J.M. 1998. Threatened waterfowl: recovery priorities and reintroduction potential with special reference to the Hawaiian Goose. Pp 125–140 in *Avian conservation, research and management* (J.M. Marzluff and R. Sallabanks, eds.), Island Press, Washington, D.C.

Blanco, G., and F. Martinez. 1996. Sex differences in breeding age of Griffon Vultures (*Gyps fulvus*). *Auk* 113:247–248.

Bleitz, D. 1946. Climbing for condors. *Pac. Pathways* 1(10):37–41.

Borneman, J.C. 1966. Return of a condor. *Audubon Mag.* 68:154–157.

Brodkorb, P. 1964. Catalogue of fossil birds: Part 2 (Anseriformes through Galliformes). *Bulletin, Florida State Museum Biological Sciences* 8:195–335.

Brooke, R.K. 1979. Tool using by the Egyptian Vulture to the detriment of the Ostrich. *Ostrich* 50:119–120.

Brower, D. 1990. *For earth's sake, the life and times of David Brower.* Gibbs-Smith, Salt Lake City.

Brower, K. 1983. The naked vulture and the thinking ape. *Atlantic Monthly*, October 1983: 70–88.

Brown, C.J. 1989. Plumages and measurements of the Bearded Vulture in southern Africa. *Ostrich* 60:165–171.

Brown, C.J. 1990a. Breeding biology of the Bearded Vulture in southern Africa, Part II: The nestling period. *Ostrich* 61:33–42.

Brown, C.J. 1990b. Breeding biology of the Bearded Vulture in southern Africa, Part III, The post-nestling dependence period. *Ostrich* 61:43–49.

Brown, C.J. 1990c. Breeding biology of the Bearded Vulture in southern Africa, Part I. The pre-laying and incubation periods. *Ostrich* 61:24–32.

Brown, C.J. 1991. Bearded Vultures in southern Africa. *WWGBP Newsletter* 14:17.

Brown, C.J., and I. Plug. 1990. Food choice and diet of the Bearded Vulture *Gypaetus barbatus* in southern Africa. *S. Afr. J. Zool.* 25:169–177.

Brown, W.M. 1993. Avian collisions with utility structures: biological perspectives. Pp 12-1–12-13 in *Proc. int. workshop on avian interactions with utility structures* (E. Colson and J. Huckabee, eds.), Electr. Power Res. Comm. and Avian Power Line Interaction Comm., Palo Alto, Calif.

Brown, W.M., Drewien, R.C., and E.G. Bizeau. 1987. Mortality of cranes and waterfowl from powerline collisions in the San Luis Valley, Colorado. Pp 126–136 in *Proceedings of the 1985 Crane Workshop* (J.C. Lewis, ed.). Platte River Whooping Crane Habitat Maintenance Trust and U.S. Fish and Wildlife Service, Grand Island, Nebraska.

Brown, W.M. and R.C. Drewien. 1995. Evaluation of two power line markers to reduce crane and waterfowl collision mortality. *Wildlife Society Bull.* 23:217–227.

Brunetti, O. 1965. *Report on the cause of death of a California condor.* Unpublished report, California Department of Fish and Game, Sacramento, California.

Bryant, E.H., and D.H. Reed. 1999. Fitness decline under relaxed selection in captive populations. *Conservation Biology* 13:665–669.

Buckley, N.J. 1994. *Communal roosting in vultures and the role of information exchange in the evolution of avian coloniality.* Ph. D. thesis, University of Oklahoma, Norman.

Bunzel, R.L. 1932. *Zuni ceremonialism.* University of New Mexico Press, Albuquerque.

Bustamante, J. 1996. Population viability analysis of captive and released Bearded Vulture populations. *Conservation Biology* 10:822–831.

Campbell, K., Jr. 1979. The non-passerine Pleistocene avifauna of the Talara Tar Seeps, northwestern Peru. *Royal Ontario Museum, Life Sciences Contribution* 118:1–203.

Campbell, K.E., and L. Marcus. 1990. How big was it? Determining the size of ancient birds. *Terra* 28:32–43.

Campbell, K.E., Jr., and E. Tonni. 1980. A new genus of teratorn from the Huayquerian of Argentina (Aves: Teratornithidae).

Contributions in Science, Natural History Museum Los Angeles County 330:59–68.

Campbell, K.E., Jr., and E. Tonni. 1981. Preliminary observations on the paleobiology and evolution of teratorns (Aves: Teratornithidae). *J. of Vert. Paleo.* 1: 265–272.

Campbell, K.E., Jr., and E. Tonni 1983. Size and locomotion in teratorns (Aves: Teratornithidae). *Auk* 100:390–403.

Carpenter, J.W. 1982. Medical and husbandry aspects of captive Andean Condors: a model for the California Condor. Pp 13–19 in *Annual Proceedings of the American Association of Zoo Veterinarians*, 1982.

Carrier, W.D. 1971. *Habitat management plans for the California Condor.* U.S. Forest Service.

Caughley, G. 1994. Directions in conservation biology. *J. Animal Ecology* 63:215–244.

Caughley, G., and A. Gunn. 1996. *Conservation biology in theory and practice.* Blackwell.

Chapman, F.M. 1908. *Camps and cruises of an ornithologist.* Appleton and Co., New York.

Clark, R.G., and R.D. Ohmart. 1985. Spread-winged posture of Turkey Vultures: single or multiple function? *Condor* 87:350–355.

Clark, T.W., Reading. R.P., and A.L. Clarke (eds.). 1994. *Endangered species recovery.* Island Press, Washington, D.C.

Clinton-Eitniear, J., and S.M. McGehee. 1994. Cannibalism by cathartid vultures. *Vulture News* 31:16–19.

Coleman, J.S., and J.D. Fraser. 1987. Food habits of Black and Turkey Vultures in Pennsylvania and Maryland. *J. Wildl. Manage.* 51:733–739.

Coleman, J.S., and J.D. Fraser. 1989a. Age estimation and growth of Black and Turkey Vultures. *J. Field Ornithol.* 60(2): 197–208.

Coleman, J.S., and J.D. Fraser. 1989b. Habitat use and home ranges of Black and Turkey Vultures. *J. Wildl. Manage.* 53:782–792.

Collins, P.W., Snyder, N.F.R., and S.D. Emslie. 2000. Faunal remains in California Condor nest caves. *Condor* 102:222–227.

Cooke, A.S. 1973. Shell thinning in avian eggs by environmental pollutants. Environ. Pollut. 4:85–152.

Cooper, J.G. 1890. A doomed bird. *Zoe* 1:248–249.

Corbin, K. and C.C. Nice. 1988. Genetic variation of California Condors. *J. Minn. Acad. Sci.* 53:27.

Cox, C.R., Goldsmith, V.I., and H.R. Engelhardt. 1993. Pair formation in California Condors. *Amer. Zool.* 33:126–138.

Coze, P. 1954. Twenty-four hours of magic. Arizona Highways: November, pp 10–35.

Cramp, S., and K.E.L. Simmons (eds.). 1980. *Handbook of the birds of Europe, the Middle East, and North Africa, The birds of the Western Palearctic, Vol II: hawks to bustards.* Oxford University Press, Oxford.

Dana, R.H. 1840. *Two years before the mast.* Harper, New York.

Dawson, W.L. 1923. *The birds of California.* South Moulton Co., San Diego.

Decker, R.A., McDermid, A.M., and J.W. Prideaux. 1979. Lead poisoning in two captive King Vultures. *J. Am. Vet. Med. Assoc.* 175:1009.

Diamond, J. 1993. New Guineans and their natural world. Pp 251–271 in *The biophilia hypothesis* (S.R. Kellert and E.O. Wilson, eds.). Island Press, Washington D.C.

Di Peso, C.C. 1974. *Casas Grandes, a fallen trading center of the Gran Chichimeca, vol 2.* The Amerind Foundation, Inc, Dragoon Northland Press, Flagstaff

Di Peso, C.C., J.B. Rinaldo, and G.J. Fenner. 1974. *Casas Grandes, a fallen trading center of the Gran Chichimeca, vol. 7.* The Amerind Foundation, Dragoon Northland Press, Flagstaff.

Donázar, J.A., and C. Fernández. 1990. Population trends of the Griffon Vulture *Gyps fulvus* in northern Spain between 1969 and 1989 in relation to conservation measures. *Biological Conservation* 53:83–91.

Douglas, D. 1829. Observations on the *Vultur Californianus* of Shaw. *Vigor's Zool. J.* 4(1):328–330.

Douglas, D. 1914. *Journal kept by David Douglas during his travels in North America, 1823–1827.* William Wesley and Son, London.

Driver, H.E. 1937. Culture element distributions VI: southern Sierra Nevada. *University of California Anthropological Records* 1(2):53–154.

Du Pratz, M. L. P. 1758. *Histoire de la Louisiane: contenant la découverte de ce vaste pays; sa description géographique; un voyage dans les terres; l'histoire naturelle, les moeurs, coutumes & religion des naturels, avec leurs origines; deux voyages dans le nord du nouveau Mexique, dont un jusqu'à la mer du Sud.* De Bure, l'Aine, Paris.

Eisler, R. 1988. *Lead hazards to fish, wildlife, and invertebrates: a synoptic review.* U.S. Dept. of Interior, Fish and Wildlife Service, Contaminant Hazard Reviews, Report 14.

Eisler, R. 1991. *Cyanide hazards to fish, wildlife, and invertebrates: a synoptic review.* U.S. Dept. of Interior, Fish and Wildlife Service, Contaminant Hazard Reviews, Report 23.

Eisler, R. 1995. *Sodium monofluoroacetate (1080) hazards to fish, wildlife, and invertebrates: a synoptic review.* U.S. Dept. of Interior, Fish and Wildlife Service, Contaminant Hazard Reviews, Report 27.

Emslie, S.D. 1987. Age and diet of fossil California Condors in Grand Canyon, Arizona. *Science* 237:768–770.

Emslie, S.D. 1988a. An early condor-like vulture from North America. *Auk* 105:529–535.

Emslie, S.D. 1988b. The fossil history and phylogenetic relationships of condors (Ciconiiformes: Vulturidae) in the New World. *J. of Vert. Paleo.* 8:212–228.

Emslie, S.D. 1988c. Vertebrate paleontology and taphonomy of caves in Grand Canyon, Arizona. *National Geographic Research* 4.128–142.

Emslie, S.D. 1990. Additional 14C dates on Fossil California Condor. *National Geographic Research* 6:134–135.

Emslie, S.D. 1998. *Avian community, climate, and sea-level changes in the Plio-Pleistocene of the Florida Peninsula.* Ornithological Monographs No. 50.

Erickson, R.C., and J.W. Carpenter. 1983. Captive condor propagation and recommended release procedures. Pp 385–399 in *Vulture Biology and Management* (S.R. Wilbur and J.A. Jackson, eds.). University of California Press, Berkeley.

Fannin, J. 1897. The California Vulture in Alberta. *Auk* 14(1):89.

Fernández, C., Azkona, P., and J.A. Donázar. 1998. Density-dependent effects on productivity in the Griffon Vulture *Gyps fulvus*: the role of interference and habitat heterogeneity. *Ibis* 140:64–69.

Fewkes, J.W. 1893–94. Tusayan katchinas. *Fifteenth Annual Report of the Bureau of American Ethnology* pp 251–313.

Finley, W.L. 1906. Life history of the California Condor I. Finding a condor's nest. *Condor* 8:135–142.

Finley, W.L. 1908a. Life history of the California Condor II. Historical data and range of the condor. *Condor* 10:5–10.

Finley, W.L. 1908b. Life history of the California Condor III. Home life of the condor. *Condor* 10:59–65.

Finley, W.L. 1908c. Home life of the California Condor. *Century* 75:370–380.

Finley, W.L. 1908d. California Condor. *Sci. Am.* 99:7–8.

Finley, W.L. 1909. General, a pet California Condor. *Ctry Life* 16:35–38.

Finley, W.L. 1910. Life history of the California Condor IV. The young condor in captivity. *Condor* 12:5–11.

Finley, W.L. and I. Finley. 1915. Condor as a pet. *Bird-lore* 17:413–419.

Finley, W.L. and I. Finley. 1926. Passing of the California Condor. *Nat. Mag.* 8:95–99.

Fisher, H.I. 1944. The skulls of cathartid vultures. *Condor* 46:272–296.

Fisher, H.I. 1947. The skeletons of Recent and fossil *Gymnogyps*. *Pacific Science* 1:227–236.

Ford, R. 1986. Saving the condor: Robert E. Easton's fight to create the Sisquoc Condor Sanctuary. *Noticias* 32(4):75–83.

Frazier, J.G. 1935. *The golden bough, a study in magic and religion.* MacMillan, New York.

Freeland, L.S., and S.M. Broadbent. 1960. Central Sierra Miwok dictionary with texts. *University of California Publications in Linguistics* 23:1–171.

Frey, H., and M. Bijleveld. 1993. The reintroduction of the Bearded Vulture *Gypaetus barbatus* into the Alps. Pp 3–8 in *Bearded Vulture Annual Report 1993* (H.Frey and J. Kurzweil, eds.). Foundation for the Conservation of the Bearded Vulture, Melk, Austria.

Frey, H., and W. Walter. 1989. The reintroduction of the Bearded Vulture *Gypaetus barbatus* into the Alps. Pp 341–344 in *Raptors in the modern world* (B-U. Meyburgh and R.D. Chancellor, eds.). World Working Group on Birds of Prey and Owls, Berlin, Germany.

Fry, D.M., Santolo, G., and C.R. Grau. 1986. *Final report for interagency agreement: effects of compound 1080 poison on Turkey Vultures.* Department of Avian Sciences, University of California, Davis.

General Accounting Office (GAO), 1988. *Endangered species: management improvements could enhance recovery programs.* GAO/RCED-89-5. Washington, DC: Resources, Community, and Economic Development Division.

Gambel, W. 1846. Remarks on the birds observed in upper California. *Proc.Acad. Nat. Sci. Phila.* 3:44–48.

Geyer, C.J., Ryder, O.A., Chemnick, L.G., and E.A. Thompson. 1993. Analysis of relatedness in the California Condors from DNA fingerprints. *Mol. Biol. Evol.* 10:571–589.

Gifford, E.W. 1926. Miwok cults. *University of California Publications in American Archaelogy and Ethnology* 18(8):391–408.

Gomez, L.G., Houston, D.C., Cotton, P., and A. Tye. 1994. The role of Greater Yellow-headed Vultures *Cathartes melambrotus* as scavengers in neotropical forest. *Ibis* 136:193–196.

Gonzales, C. 1966. The Shalakos are coming. *El Palacio*: Autumn, pp 5–17.

Grant, C. 1965. *The rock paintings of the Chumash: a study of a California Indian culture.* University of California Press, Berkeley.

Graves, G.R. 1992. Greater Yellow-headed Vulture (*Cathartes melambrotus*) locates food by olfaction. *J. Raptor Res.* 26:38–39.

Grier, J.W. 1973. *Avian spread-winged sunbathing in thermoregulation and drying.* Ph.D. thesis, Cornell University, Ithaca, New York.

Griffith, B., Scott, J.M., Carpenter, J.W., and C. Reed. 1989. Translocation as a species conservation tool: status and strategy. *Science* 245:477–480.

Griffiths, C.S. 1994. Monophyly of the Falconiformes based on syringeal morphology. *Auk* 111:787–805.

Griffiths, R., Daan, S., and C. Dijkstra. 1996. Sex identification in birds using two CHD genes. *Proc. R. Soc. Lond.* B 263:1251–1256.

Grinnell, J. 1905. Old Fort Tejon. *Condor* 7:9–13.

Grinnell, J. 1932. Archibald Menzies, first collector of California birds. *Condor* 34:243–252.

Guthrie, D.A. 1992. A late Pleistocene avifauna from San Miguel Island, California. Pp 320–327 in *Papers on avian paleontology, Los Angeles, CA* (K.E. Campbell, ed.,). Science Series 36, Natural History Museum of Los Angeles County.

Guthrie, D.A. 1993. New information on the prehistoric fauna of San Miguel Island, California. Pp 405–416 in *Third California islands symposium: recent advances in research on the California islands* (R.G. Hochberg, ed.). Santa Barbara Museum of Natural History, Santa Barbara, California.

Guthrie, D.A. 1998. Fossil vertebrates from Pleistocene terrestrial deposits on the Northern Channel Islands, southern California. Pp 187–192 in *Contributions to the geology of the Northern Channel Islands, Southern California* (P.W. Wiegand, ed.). American Association of Petroleum Geologists, Pacific Section, MP 45.

Harris, H. 1941. The annals of *Gymnogyps* to 1900. *Condor* 43:3–55.

Harrison, E.N., and L.F. Kiff. 1980. Apparent replacement clutch laid by wild California Condor. *Condor* 82:351–352.

Hartt, E.W., Harvey, N.C., Leete, A.J., and K. Preston. 1994. Effects of age at pairing on reproduction in captive California Condors (*Gymnogyps californianus*). *Zoo Biology* 13:3–11.

Harvey, P.H., and K. Ralls. 1986. Do animals avoid incest? *Nature* 320:575–576.

Harvey, N.C., Preston, K.L., and A.J. Leete. 1996. Reproductive behavior in captive California Condors (*Gymnogyps californianus*). *Zoo Biology* 15:115–125.

Hegdahl, P.L., Gatz. T.A., Fagerston, K.A., Glahn, J.F., and G.H. Matschke. 1979. *Hazards to wildlife associated with 1080 baiting for California ground squirrels. Final report on interagency agreement EPA-IAG-07-0449,* U.S. Fish and Wildlife Service, Environmental Protection Agency, Washington, D.C.

Hegdahl, P.L., Fagerstone, K.A., Gatz, T.A., Glahn, J.F., and G.H. Matschke. 1986. Hazards to wildlife associated with 1080 baiting for California ground squirrels. *Wildlife Society Bull.* 14:11–21.

Heinrich, B. 1988. Why do ravens fear their food? *Condor* 90:950–952.

Hendron, J. 1998. *Lead exposure/poisoning incidents involving California Condors.* US Fish and Wildlife Service, Hopper Mountain NWR Complex, unpublished report.

Henshaw, H.W. 1876. Report on the ornithology of the portions of California visited during the field season of 1875. Pp 224–278 in *Annual report upon the geographical survey west of the 100th Meridian in California, Nevada, Utah, Colorado, Wyoming, New Mexico, Arizona and Montana* (G.M. Wheeler, ed.). U.S. Government Printing Office, Washington, D.C.

Hickey, J.J. 1988. Some recollections about eastern North America's Peregrine Falcon population crash. Pp 9–16 in *Peregrine Falcon populations, their management and recovery* (T.J. Cade, J.H. Enderson, C.G. Thelander, and C.M. White, eds.). The Peregrine Fund, Boise, Idaho.

Hirt, P.W. 1994. *A conspiracy of optimism, management of the national forests since World War Two.* University of Nebraska Press, Lincoln and London.

Hornaday, W.T. 1889. *The extermination of the American bison.* Annual report of the National Museum, 1887, Smithsonian Institution, Washington, D.C.

Hornaday, W.T. 1911. *Popular official guide to the New York Zoological Park.* New York: New York Zoological Society.

Hough, W. 1917. The Sio Shalako at the First Mesa, July 9, 1916. *American Anthropologist* 19(3):410–415.

Houston, D.C. 1974a. Food searching in griffon vultures. *E. Afr. Wildl. J.* 12:63–77.

Houston, D.C. 1974b. Mortality of the Cape Vulture. *Ostrich* 45:57–62.

Houston, D.C. 1974c. The role of griffon vultures *Gyps africanus* and *Gyps ruppellii* as scavengers. *J. Zool., Lond* 172:35–46.

Houston, D.C. 1975. Ecological isolation of African scavenging birds. *Ardea* 63:55–64.

Houston, D.C. 1976. Breeding of the White-backed and Rüppell's Griffon Vultures, *Gyps africanus* and *G. rueppellii. Ibis* 118:14–40.

Houston, D.C. 1978. The effect of food quality on breeding strategy in griffon vultures (*Gyps* spp.). *J. Zool., Lond* 186:175–184.

Houston, D.C. 1979. The adaptations of scavengers. Pp 263–286 in *Serengeti: dynamics of an ecosystem* (A.R.E. Sinclair and M. Norton Griffiths, eds.). University of Chicago Press, Chicago.

Houston, D.C. 1980a. A possible function of sunning behavior by griffon vultures, *Gyps* spp., and other large soaring birds. *Ibis*

122:366–369.

Houston, D.C. 1980b. Interrelations of African scavenging animals. *Proc. IV Pan-Afr. Orn. Congr.* 307–312.

Houston, D.C. 1984a. A comparison of the food supply of African and South American vultures. *Proc. V. Pan-Afr. Congr.* 249–262.

Houston, D.C. 1984b. Does the King Vulture *Sarcorhampus papa* use a sense of smell to locate food? *Ibis* 126:67–69.

Houston, D.C. 1985. Evolutionary ecology of Afrotropical and Neotropical vultures in forests. Pp 856–864 in *Neotropical Ornithology* (M. Foster, ed.). Ornithological Monographs No. 36.

Houston, D.C. 1986. Scavenging efficiency of Turkey Vultures in tropical forest. *Condor* 88:318–323.

Houston, D.C. 1987. The effect of reduced mammal numbers on *Cathartes* vultures in Neotropical forests. *Biol. Cons.* 41:91–98.

Houston, D.C. 1988a. Competition for food between Neotropical vultures in forest. *Ibis* 130:402–417.

Houston, D.C. 1988b. Digestic efficiency and hunting behaviour in cats, dogs, and vultures. *J. Zool., Lond* 216:603–605.

Houston, D.C. 1989. Factors influencing the timing of breeding in African vultures. Pp 203–209 in *Raptors in the modern world* (B.-U. Meyburg and R.D. Chancellor, eds.), World Working Group for Birds of Prey: Berlin, London, and Paris.

Houston, D.C. 1990. A change in the breeding season of Rüppell's Griffon Vultures *Gyps rueppellii* in the Serengeti in response to changes in ungulate populations. *Ibis* 132:36–41.

Houston, D.C. 1994. Observations on Greater Yellow-headed Vultures *Cathartes melambrotus* and other *Cathartes* species as scavengers in forest in Venezuela. Pp 265–268 in *Raptor conservation today* (B.-U. Meyburg and R.D. Chancellor, eds.), World Working Group for Birds of Prey, Pica Press.

Houston, D.C. 1996. The effect of altered environments on vultures. Pp 327–335 in *Raptors in human landscapes* (D. Bird, D. Varland, and J. Negro, eds.), Academic Press, London.

Houston, D.C., and J.A. Copsey. 1994. Bone digestion and intestinal morphology of the Bearded Vulture. *J. of Raptor Res.* 28:73–78.

Howard, H. 1952. The prehistoric avifauna of Smith Creek Cave, Nevada, with a description of a new gigantic raptor. *Bulletin So. Calif. Academy of Sciences* 51:50–54.

Howard, H. 1962. A comparison of avian assemblages from individual pits at Rancho La Brea, California. *Contributions in Science, Natural History Museum Los Angeles County* 58: 3–58.

Howard, H. 1974. Postcranial elements of the extinct condor *Breagyps clarki* (Miller). *Contributions in Science, Natural History Museum Los Angeles County* 256:1–24.

Howard, H., and A.H. Miller. 1939. The avifauna associated with human remains at Rancho La Brea, California. *Carnegie Inst. Publ.* 514:39–48.

Hudson, T., and T.C. Blackburn. 1982. *The material culture of the Chumash interaction sphere, vol 1. Food procurement and transportation.* Santa Barbara Museum of Natural History, Ballena Press.

Hudson, T., and T.C. Blackburn. 1986. *The material culture of the Chumash interaction sphere, vol. 4. Ceremonial paraphenalia, games, and amusements.* Santa Barbara Museum of Natural History, Ballena Press.

Hudson, T., and E. Underhay. 1978. *Crystals in the Sky: an intellectual odyssey involving Chumash astronomy, cosmology and rock art.* Ballena Press and the Santa Barbara Museum of Natural History Cooperative Publication, Santa Barbara, California.

Hunt, G. 1997. *A population study of Golden Eagles in the Altamont Pass Wind Resource Area, second-year progress report.* National Renewable Energy Laboratory.

Hutt, F.B. 1929. Studies in embryonic mortality in the fowl. I. The frequencies of various malpositions of the chick embryo and their significance. *Proc. Roy. Soc. Edinburgh* 49:118–130.

Jackson , J.A. 1983. Nesting phenology, nest site selection, and reproductive success of Black and Turkey Vultures. Pp 245–270 in *Vulture biology and management* (S.R. Wilbur and J.A. Jackson, eds.), University of California Press, Berkeley and Los Angeles.

Janssen, D.L., Oosterhuis, J.E., Allen, J.L., Anderson, M.P., Kelts, D.G., and S.N. Wiemeyer. 1986. Lead poisoning in free-ranging California Condors. *J. Am. Vet. Med. Assoc.* 155:1052–1056.

Johnson, E.V. 1985. Commentary, California Condor population estimates. *Condor* 87:446–447.

Johnson, E.V., Aulman, D.L., Clendenen, D.A., Guliasi, G., Morton, L.M., Principe, P.I., and G.M. Wegener. 1983. California Condor: activity patterns and age composition in a foraging area. *Am. Birds* 37:941–945.

Jollie, M. 1953. Are the Falconiformes a monophyletic group? *Ibis* 95:369–371.

Jurek, R. 1983. Chronology of significant events in California Condor history. *Outdoor California* 44:42.

Kalmbach, E.R. 1939. American vultures and the toxin of *Clostridium botulinum. J. Am. Vet. Med. Assoc.* 94:187–191.

Kiff, L. 1977. The elusive condors of Baja California. *Audubon Imprint* 2(3):1–3,5.

Kiff, L. 1983. An historical perspective on the condor. *Outdoor California* 44(5):5–6, 34–37.

Kiff, L.F. 1989. DDE and the California Condor *Gymnogyps californianus*; the end of a story? Pp 477–480 in *Raptors in the Modern World* (B.-U Meyburg and R.D. Chancellor, eds.). World Working Group for Birds of Prey, Berlin.

Kiff, L.F., Peakall, D.B., and S.R. Wilbur. 1979. Recent changes in California Condor eggshells. *Condor* 81:166–172.

Kleiman, D.G. 1989. Reintroduction of captive mammals for conservation. *BioScience* 39:152–160.

Knight, R.L., Knight, H.A.L., and R.J. Camp. 1993. Raven populations and land-use patterns in the Mojave Desert, California. *Wildl. Soc. Bull.* 21:469–471.

Kofoid, C.A. 1923. An early account of the California Condor. *Condor* 25(1):29–30.

Koford, C.B. 1950. *The natural history of the California Condor (Gymnogyps californianus).* Ph.D. thesis, University of California, Berkeley.

Koford, C.B. 1953. The California Condor. *Natl. Audubon Soc. Res. Report* No. 4:1–154.

Koford, C.B. 1979. California Condors, forever free? *Audubon Imprint* 3(9):1–3,6–7, Santa Monica Audubon Society.

König, C. 1983. Interspecific and intraspecific competition for food among Old World vultures. Pp 153–171 in *Vulture biology and management* (S.R. Wilbur and J.A. Jackson, eds.), University of California Press, Berkeley.

Koops, F.B.J., and J. de Jong. 1981. Vermindering van draadslachtoffers door markering van hoogspanningsleidingen in de omgeving van Herrenveen. *Overdruk uit: lektrotechnick* 60:641–646.

Kroeber, A.L. 1925. Handbook of the Indians of California. *Bur. Am. Ethnol. Bull.* 78:1–995.

Kruuk, H. 1967. Competition for food between vultures in East Africa. *Ardea* 55:171–193.

Kuehler, C. 1989. *California Condor (Gymnogyps californianus) studbook.* San Diego Wild Animal Park, Escondido, Calif.

Kuehler, C. 1993. *California Condor studbook 1993.* Zoological Society of San Diego.

Kuehler, C. 1996. *California Condor studbook 1996.* Zoological Society of San Diego.

Kuehler, C.M., Sterner, D.J., Jones, D.S., Usnik, R.L., and S. Kasielke. 1991. Report on captive hatches of California Condors (*Gymnogyps californianus*): 1983–1990. *Zoo Biology* 10:65–68.

Kuehler, C. and P.N. Witman. 1988. Artificial incubation of California Condor (*Gymnogyps californianus*) eggs removed from the wild. *Zoo Biology* 7:123–132.

Lacy, R.C., Petrick, A., and M. Warneke. 1993. Inbreeding and outbreeding in captive populations of wild animal species. Pp 352–374 in *The natural history of inbreeding and outbreeding* (N.W. Thornhill, ed.). Chicago University Press.

Lammertink, J.M., Rojas-Tome, J.A., Casillas-Orono, F.M., and R.L. Otto. 1996. *Status and conservation of old-growth forests and endemic birds in the pine-oak zone of the Sierra Madre Occidental, Mexico.* Technical report No. 69, Institute for Systematics and Population Biology, University of Amsterdam, the Netherlands.

Landauer, W. 1967. *The hatchability of chicken eggs as influenced by environment and heredity.* University of Connecticut Agricultural Experiment Station, Storrs. Monograph 1.

Latta, F.F. 1976. *The saga of Rancho el Tejón.* Bear State Books, Santa Cruz.

Lemon, W.C. 1991. Foraging behavior of a guild of Neotropical vultures. *Wilson Bull.* 103:698–702.

Leshem, Y. 1985. Vultures under high tension. *Israel: Land and Nature* 10:149–153.

Lewis, M., and W. Clark. 1905. *Original journals of the Lewis and Clark expedition 1804–1806* (R.G. Thwaites, ed.), vol. 3, part 2, vol 4, parts 1 and 2. Dodd and Mead and Co., New York.

Lieberman, A., Wiley, J.W., Rodriguez, J.V., and J.M. Paez. 1991. The first experimental reintroduction of captive-reared Andean Condors (*Vultur gryphus*) into Colombia, South America. *AAZPA 1991 Ann. Conf. Proc.*:129–136.

Lieberman, A., Rodriguez, J.V., Paez, J.M., and J. Wiley. 1993. The reintroduction of the Andean Condor into Colombia, South America: 1989–1991. *Oryx* 27:83–90.

Ligon, J.D. 1967. Relationships of the cathartid vultures. *Occasional Papers, Museum of Zoology, University of Michigan* 651:1–26.

Linsdale, J.M. 1931. Facts concerning the use of thallium in California to poison rodents. *Condor* 33:96–106.

Lint, K.C. 1943. Rearing an Andean Condor. *Zoonooz* 16(4): 3.

Lint, K.C. 1951. Condor egg hatched in incubator. *Condor* 53:102.

Locke, L.N., Bagley, G.E., Frickie, D.N., and L.T. Young. 1969. Lead poisoning and aspergillosis in an Andean Condor. *J. Am. Vet. Med. Assoc.* 155:1052–1056.

Loeb, E.M. 1926. Pomo folkways. *Univ. Calif. Publ. Am. Archaeol. Ethnol.* 19:149–405.

Lofholm, N. 1998. Condors cruise Colorado. *Denver Post*, August 29, 1998.

Longmire, J.L., Maltbie, M., Pavelka, R.W., Smith, L.M., Witte, S.M., Ryder, O.A., Ellsworth, D.L., and R.J. Baker. 1993. Gender identification in birds using microsatellite DNA fingerprint analysis. *Auk* 110:378–381.

Lumé, C.R. 1938. Stalking America's mightiest bird. *Travel Mag.* 70(3):30–31, 52–53.

Lyon, M.W., Jr. 1918. Occurrence of California Vulture in Idaho. *Journ. Wash. Acad. Sci.* 8:25–28.

Mallette, R.D. 1970. *Operational management plan for California Condor.* California Department of Fish and Game, Sacramento.

Mallette, R.D., and J.C. Borneman. 1966. First cooperative survey of the California Condor. *Calif. Fish Game* 52:185–203.

Martin, P.S. 1967. Pleistocene overkill. Pp 75–120 in *Pleistocene extinction, the search for a cause* (P.S. Martin and H.E. Wright, Jr., eds.). Yale University Press, New Haven and London.

Mathewson, W. 1986. *William L. Finley, Pioneer Wildlife Photographer.* Oregon State University Press, Corvallis.

McCusick, C.R. 1976. Avifauna in *The Hohokam, desert farmers and craftsmen* (E.W. Haury, Ed.), University of Arizona Press, Tucson.

McGahan, J. 1971. The condor, soaring spirit of the Andes. *National Geographic Magazine* 139:684–709.

McMillan, E. 1981. Interview, spring 1980. Pp 139–156 in *The condor question, captive or forever free?* (D. Phillips and H. Nash, eds.). Friends of the Earth, San Francisco.

McMillan, I. 1953. Condors, politics and game management. *Central Calif. Sportsman*, repr. from December issue 13(12):458–460.

McMillan, I. 1968. *Man and the California Condor.* Dutton, New York.

McMillan, I. 1970. Botching the condor program. *Defenders Wildl. News* 45:95–98.

McMillan, I. 1971. The 1971 condor survey – a return to soundness. *Defenders Wildl. News* 46:386.

McMillan, I. 1985. Commentary: California Condor population estimates. *Condor* 87:446.

McPhee, J. 1971. *Encounters with the archdruid.* Farrar, Straus and Giroux, New York.

Meretsky, V.J. 1995. *Foraging ecology of Egyptian Vultures in the Negev Desert.* Ph.D. thesis, University of Arizona, Tucson.

Meretsky, V.J., and R.W. Mannan. 1999. Supplemental feeding regimes for Egyptian Vultures in the Negev Desert, Israel. *J. Wildl. Manage.* 63:107–115.

Meretsky, V.J., and N.F.R. Snyder. 1992. Range use and movements of California Condors. *Condor* 94:313–335.

Meretsky, V.J., Snyder, N.F.R., Beissinger, S.R., Clendenen, D.A., and J.W. Wiley. Demography of the California Condor: implications for reestablishment. Manuscript in press with Conservation Biology.

Merriam, C.H. 1979. *Indian names for plants and animals among Californian and other western North American tribes* (assembled and annotated by R.F. Heizer). Ballena Press Publications in Archeology, Ethnology, and History No. 14.

Millard, R. 1958. Feathered giant of the skies. *Coronet* 43(5):144–146.

Miller, A.H. 1953. The case against trapping California Condors. *Audubon Mag.* 55:261–262.

Miller, A.H., McMillan, I., and E. McMillan. 1965. The current status and welfare of the California Condor. *Natl. Audubon Soc. Res. Report* No. 6:1–61.

Miller, B., Reading, R., Conway, C., Jackson, J.A., Hutchins, M., Snyder, N., Forrest, S., and J. Frazier. 1994. A model for improving endangered species recovery programs. *Environmental Management* 18:637–645.

Miller, B., Reading, R.P., and S. Forrest. 1996, *Prairie night, black-footed ferrets and the recovery of endangered species.* Smithsonian Institution Press, Washington, D.C.

Miller, L. H. 1909. *Teratornis, a new avian genus from Rancho La Brea. University of California Publications, Bulletin, Department of Geology* 5:3305–3317.

Miller, L. H. 1910. The condor-like vultures of Rancho La Brea. *University of California Publications, Bulletin, Department of Geology* 6:1–19.

Miller, L.H. 1911. Avifauna of the Pleistocene cave deposits of California. *University of California Publications, Bulletin, Department of Geology* 6:385–400.

Miller, L.H. 1937. Feather studies of the California Condor. *Condor* 39:160–162.

Miller, L.H. 1942. Succession in the Cathartine dynasty. *Condor* 44:212–213.

Miller, L.H. 1943. The Pleistocene birds of San Josecito Cavern, Mexico. *University of California Publications in Zoology* 47:143–168.

Miller, L.H. 1960. On the history of the Cathartidae in North America. *Novedades Colombianas* 1:232–235.

Miller, L.H., and H. Howard. 1938. The status of the extinct condor-like birds of the Rancho La Brea Pleistocene. *Publications, University of California Los Angeles Biological Science* 1:169–176.

Minnich, R.A. 1983. Fire mosaics in southern California and northern Baja California. *Science* 219:1287–1294.

Mosher, J.A., and C.M. White. 1976. Directional exposure of Golden Eagle nests. *Can. Field-Nat.* 90:356–359.

Mouze, M., and C. Bagnolini. 1995. Le vol en tandem chez le vautour fauve (*Gyps fulvus*). *Can. J. Zool* 73:2144–2153.

Mundy, P.J. 1982. *The comparative biology of southern African vultures.* Vulture Study Group, Johannesburg.

Mundy, P., Butchart, D., Ledger, J., and S. Piper. 1992. *The vultures of Africa.* Academic Press, London.

Mundy, P.J. and J.A. Ledger. 1976. Griffon vultures, carnivores and bones. *S. Afr. Journal of Science* 72:106–110.

Mundy, P.J., and J.A. Ledger. 1977. The plight of the Cape Vulture. *Endangered Wildl.* 1:2–3.

Murphy, R.C. 1925. *Bird islands of Peru.* G.P. Putnam's Sons, Knickerbocker Press, New York.

Narbaitz, R., Tsang, C.P.W., Grunder, A.A., and J.H. Soares, Jr. 1987. Scanning electron microscopy of thin and soft shells induced by feeding calcium-deficient or vitamin D-deficient diets to laying hens. *Poult. Sci.* 66:341–347.

Newton, I. 1979. *Population ecology of raptors.* Poyser, Berkhamsted.

Newton, I. 1988. Commentary – changes in the status of the Peregrine in Europe. Pp 227–234 in *Peregrine Falcon populations, their management and recovery* (T.J. Cade, J.H. Enderson, C.G. Thelander, and C.M. White, eds.). The Peregrine Fund, Boise, Idaho.

Nicolaus, L.K. 1987. Conditioned aversions in a guild of egg predators: implications for aposematism and prey-defense mimicry. *Am. Midl. Nat.* 117:405–419.

Nicolaus, L.K., Cassel, J.F., Carlson, R.B., and C.R. Gustavson. 1983. Taste aversion conditioning of crows to control predation on eggs. *Science* 220:212–214.

Olendorff, R.R., and R.N. Lehman. 1986. *Raptor collisions with utility lines: an analysis using subjective field observations.* Final report, U.S. Dept. of Interior to Pacific Gas and Electric Company, San Ramon, California.

Olson, S.L. 1978. A paleontological perspective of West Indian birds and mammals. Zoogeography in the Caribbean. *Academy Natural Sciences Philadelphia, Special Publication* 13:99–117.

Olson, S.L. 1985. The fossil record of birds. Pp 79–256 in *Avian Biology Vol. VIII* (D.S. Farner, J.R. King, and K.C. Parkes, eds.). Academic Press, New York.

Olson, S.L., and H.F. James. 1982. Fossil birds from the Hawaiian Islands: evidence for wholesale extinction by man before western contact. *Science* 217: 633–635.

Orr, P. 1968. *Prehistory of Santa Rosa Island, Santa Barbara, CA.* Santa Barbara Museum of Natural History.

Owre, O.T., and P.O. Northington. 1961. Indication of the sense of smell in the Turkey Vulture from feeding tests. *Am. Midl. Nat.* 66:200–205.

Paterson, R.L. 1984. High incidence of plant material and small mammals in the autumn diet of Turkey Vultures in Virginia. *Wilson Bull.* 96:467–469.

Pattee, O.H., Bloom, P.H., Scott, J.M., and M.R. Smith. 1990. Lead hazards within the range of the California Condor. *Condor* 92:931–937.

Pattee, O.H., and S.R. Wilbur. 1989. Turkey Vulture and California Condor. Pp. 61–65 in *Western Raptor Management Symposium and Workshop.* National Wildlife Federation Scientific and Technical Series No. 12.

Payne, R. 1995. *Among Whales.* Scribner, New York.

Pennycuick, C.J. 1969. The mechanics of bird migration. *Ibis* 111:525–556.

Phillips, A.R. 1968. The instability of the distribution of land birds in the Southwest. Pp 129–135 in *Collected papers in honor of Lyndon Lane Hargrave* (A. Schroeder, ed.). Papers of the Archeological Society of New Mexico.

Phillips, D., and H. Nash. 1981. *The condor question, captive or forever free?* Friends of the Earth, San Francisco.

Piper, S.E. 1993. *Mathematical demography of the Cape Vulture.* Ph.D. thesis, University of Cape Town, Cape Town, South Africa.

Plug, I. 1978. Collecting patterns of six species of vultures (Aves: Accipitridae). *Annals of the Transvaal Museum* 31:51–63.

Quick, D.L.F., and E.F. Hill. 1988. Sublethal landrin toxicity: behavioral and physiological effects on captive vultures. *J. Wildl. Manage.* 52:233–237.

Rabenold, P.P. 1983. The communal roost in eastern cathartid vultures: an information center?. Pp 303–321 in *Vulture biology and management* (S.R. Wilbur and J.A. Jackson, eds.). University of California Press, Berkeley, CA.

Rabenold, P.P. 1987. Recruitment to food in Black Vultures: evidence for following from communal roosts. *Anim. Behav.* 35:1775–1585.

Ratcliffe, D.A. 1970. Changes attributable to pesticides in egg breakage frequency and eggshell thickness in some British birds. *J. Appl. Ecol.* 7:67–115.

Ratcliffe, D.A. 1997. *The raven.* T and AD Poyser.

Rea, A.M. 1981. California Condor captive breeding: a recovery proposal. *Environ. SW* 484:8–12.

Rea, A.M. 1983. Cathartid affinities: a brief overview. Pp 26–54 in *Vulture biology and management* (S.R. Wilbur and J.A. Jackson, eds.). University of California Press, Berkeley.

Reiser, M.H., and S.A. Temple. 1981. Effects of chronic lead ingestion on birds of prey. Pp 21–25 in *Recent advances in the study of raptor diseases* (J.E. Cooper and A.G. Greenwood, eds.), Chiron Publ., Ltd., West Yorkshire, U.K.

Rett, E.Z. 1938. Hailstorm fatal to California Condors. *Condor* 40:225.

Rice, R. 1998. Can forestry be sustainable? *Environmental Review* 5(11):1–6.

Richardson, P.R.K., Mundy, P.J., and I. Plug. 1986. Bone-crushing carnivores and their significance to osteodystrophy in griffon vulture chicks. *J. Zool., Lond* 210:23–43.

Richford, A.S., Stewart, J.G., and D.C. Houston. 1975. Status of the Black Vulture in Mallorca. *Ardeola* 21:225–243.

Ricklefs, R.E. (ed.). 1978. Report of the advisory panel on the California Condor. *Natl. Audubon Soc. Conserv. Report* 6:1–27.

Ringleman, J.K., Miller, M.W., and W.F. Andelt. 1993. Effects of ingested tungsten-bismuth-tin shot on captive Mallards. *J. Wildl. Manage.* 57:725–732.

Risebrough, R.W. 1986. Pesticides and bird populations. *Current Ornithology* 3:397–427.

Risser, A.C., Jr. 1983. What about that third condor egg? *Zoonooz* 56:14–15.

Robertson, A.S. 1985. Observations on the post-fledging dependence period of Cape Vultures. *Ostrich* 56:58–66.

Robinson, C.S. 1936a. *A report on study of life habits of the California Condor.* U.S. Forest Service, Santa Barbara.

Robinson, C.S. 1936b. *Protection of the California Condor.* U.S. Forest Service, Santa Barbara.

Robinson, C.S. 1939. *Observations and notes on the California Condor from data collected on Los Padres National Forest.* U.S. Forest Service, Santa Barbara.

Robinson, C.S. 1940. *Notes on the California Condor, collected on Los Padres National Forest, California.* U.S. Forest Service, Santa Barbara.

Romanoff, A.L., and A.J. Romanoff. 1972. *Pathogenesis of the avian embryo.* Wiley-Interscience, New York.

Sarrazin, F., Bagnolini, C., Pinna, J.L., Danchin, E., and J. Clobert. 1994. High survival estimates of Griffon Vultures (*Gyps fulvus fulvus*) in a reintroduced population. *Auk* 111:853–862.

Sarrazin, F., Bagnolini, C., Pinna, J.L., and E. Danchin. 1996. Breeding biology during establishment of a reintroduced Griffon Vulture *Gyps fulvus* population. *Ibis* 138:315–325.

Saunders, C.F. 1924. *The southern sierras of California.* Hutchinson, London.

Schaeffer, C.E. 1951. Was the California Condor known to the Blackfoot Indians? *J. Wash. Acad. Sci.* 41(6):181–191.

Schoenherr, A.A. 1992. *A natural history of California.* University of California Press, Berkeley.

Scott, C.D. 1936a. Are condors extinct in Lower California? *Condor* 38:41–42.

Scott, C.D. 1936b. Who killed the condor? *Nat. Mag.* 28(6):368–370.

Seibold, I., and A.J. Helbig. 1995. Evolutionary history of New and Old World vultures inferred from nucleotide sequences of the mitochondrial cytochrome b gene. *Phil. Trans. R. Soc. Lond.* B 350:163–178.

Shablina, S.A., Yampolsky, L., and A.S. Kondrashov. 1997. Rapid decline of fitness in panmictic *Drosophila* populations under relaxed selection. *Proceedings of the National Academy of Sciences of the United States of America* 94:13034–13039.

Shaw, G., and F.P. Nodder. 1797. *Vivarium naturae or naturalist's miscellany.* Vol. 9 (London, printed for Nodder and Co.).

Sibley, C., and J. Alquist. 1990. *Phylogeny and classification of birds of the world.* Yale University Press, New Haven.

Sibley, F.C. 1968. *The life history, ecology and management of the California Condor (Gymnogyps californianus).* Annual Progress Report, Project No. B-22. U.S. Fish. and Wildl. Serv., Patuxent Wildl. Res. Cent. 34 pp.

Sibley, F.C. 1969. *Effects of the Sespe Creek Project on the California Condor.* U.S. Fish and Wildl. Serv., Laurel, Maryland.

Simons, D.D. 1983. Interactions between California Condors and humans in prehistoric far western North America. Pp 470–494 in *Vulture biology and management* (S.R. Wilbur and J.A. Jackson, eds.). University of California Press, Berkeley.

Smith, D. 1978. *Condor journal: the history, mythology and reality of the California Condor.* Capra Press and the Santa Barbara Museum of Natural History.

Smith, D., and R. Easton. 1964. California Condor: vanishing American. McNally and Loftin, Santa Barbara.

Smith, R.A. 1995. Rapid quantitative determination of cyanide in biological fluids from coyotes killed with a coyote getter. *Vet. Human Toxicol.* 37:580–581.

Snyder, H.A., and N.F.R. Snyder. 1974. Increased mortality of Cooper's Hawks accustomed to man. *Condor* 76:215–216.

Snyder, N.F.R. 1983. California Condor reproduction, past and present. *Bird Conserv.* 1:67–86.

Snyder, N.F.R. 1986. California Condor recovery program. Pp 56–71 in *Raptor Research Report No. 5: Raptor conservation in the next 50 years* (S.E. Senner, C.M. White and J.R. Parrish, eds.). Raptor Research Foundation, Provo, Utah.

Snyder, N.F.R. 1988. California Condor. Pp 43–66 in *Handbook of North American Birds, Vol. 4* (R.S. Palmer, ed.), Yale University Press, New Haven.

Snyder, N.F.R. 1990. Review of Peregrine Falcon populations, their management and recovery. *Auk* 107:803–806.

Snyder, N.F.R. and J.A. Hamber. 1985. Replacement-clutching and annual nesting of California Condors. *Condor* 87:374–378.

Snyder, N.F.R. and E.V. Johnson. 1985a. Photographic censusing of the 1982–1983 California Condor population. *Condor* 87:1–13.

Snyder, N.F.R. and E.V. Johnson. 1985b. Photos key to condor census. *Outdoor Calif.* 46:22–25.

Snyder, N.F.R., and A.M. Rea. 1998. California Condor. Pp. 32–36 in *The raptors of Arizona* (R.L. Glinski, ed.). University of Arizona Press, Tucson.

Snyder, N.F.R., and H.A. Snyder. 1989. Biology and Conservation of the California Condor. *Current Ornithology* 6:175–267.

Snyder, N.F.R., and H.A. Snyder. 1991. *Birds of prey.* Voyageur Press, Stillwater, Minnesota.

Snyder, N.F.R. and J.W. Wiley. 1976. *Sexual size dimorphism in hawks and owls of North America.* Ornithological Monographs No. 20.

Snyder, N.F.R., Beissinger, S.R., and R.E. Chandler. 1989. Reproduction and demography of the Florida Everglade (Snail) Kite. *Condor* 91:300–316.

Snyder, N.F.R., Beissinger, S.R., and M.R. Fuller. 1989. Solar radio-transmitters on Snail Kites in Florida. *J. Field Ornithol.* 60:171–177.

Snyder, N.F.R., Derrickson, S.R., Beissinger, S.R., Wiley, J.W., Smith, T.B., Toone, W.D., and B. Miller. 1996. Limitations of captive breeding in endangered species recovery. *Conservation Biology* 10:338–348.

Snyder, N.F.R., Johnson, E.V., and D.A. Clendenen. 1987a. Primary molt of California Condors. *Condor* 89:468–485.

Snyder, N.F.R., Koenig, S.E., Koschmann, J., Snyder, H.A., and T.B. Johnson. 1994. Thick-billed Parrot releases in Arizona. *Condor* 96:845–862.

Snyder, N.F.R., Ramey, R.R., and F.C. Sibley. 1986. Nest-site biology of the California Condor. *Condor* 88:228–241.

Snyder, N.F.R., Snyder, H.A., Lincer, J.L., and R.T. Reynolds. 1973. Organochlorines, heavy metals, and the biology of North American accipiters. *BioScience* 23:300–305.

Snyder, N.F.R., Wiley, J.W., and C.B. Kepler. 1987b. *The parrots of Luquillo: natural history and conservation of the Puerto Rican Parrot.* Western Foundation of Vertebrate Zoology, Los Angeles.

Soulé, M. 1998. Is sustainable development a myth? *Environmental Review* 5(9):1–6.

Spaar, R. 1997. Flight strategies of migrating raptors; a comparative study of interspecific variation in flight characteristics. *Ibis* 139:523–535.

Stager, K. 1964. The role of olfaction in food location by the Turkey Vulture (*Cathartes aura*). *Los Angeles County Mus. Contrib. Sci.* 81:1–63.

Steadman, D.W. 1995. Prehistoric extinction of Pacific Island birds – biodiversity meets zooarchaelogy. *Science* 267:1123–1131.

Steadman, D.W., and N.G. Miller. 1986. California Condor associated with spruce-jack pine woodland in the late Pleistocene of New York. *Quaternary Research* 28:415–426.

Stewart, P.A. 1978. Behavioral interactions and niche separation in Black and Turkey Vultures. *Living Bird* 17:79–84.

Strand, F.G. 1998. *An analysis of the Homol'ovi fauna with emphasis on ritual behavior.* Ph.D. thesis, University of Arizona, Tucson.

Streator, C.P. 1888. Notes on the California Condor. *Oologist* 13(2):30.

Struhsaker, T. 1998. A biologist's perspective on the role of sustainable harvest in conservation. *Conservation Biology* 12:930–932.

Studer, C.D. 1983. *Effects of Kern County cattle ranching on California Condor habitat.* Master's thesis, Michigan State University, East Lansing.

Swann, H.K. 1924. *Monograph of the birds of prey. Vol 1, Part 1.* Weldon and Wesley, London.

Swarth, H.S. 1914. A distributional list of the birds of Arizona. *Pac. Coast Avifauna* 10.

Taylor, A.S. 1859a. The egg and young of the California Condor. *Hutching's Calif. Mag.* 3(12):537–540.

Taylor, A.S. 1859b. The great condor of California. *Hutching's Calif. Mag.* 3(12):540–543, 4(1):17–22, 4(2):61–64.

Taylor, M. 1986. "Mr. Santa Barbara County". *Noticias* 32(4): 60–74.

Terrasse, J.F., Terrasse, M., and Y. Boudoint. 1961. Observation sur la réproduction du Vautour fauve, du Percnoptère et du Gypaète barbu dans les Basses-Pyrénées. *Alauda* 29:1–24.

Terrasse, M. 1985. *Réintroduction du Vautour fauve dans les Grands Causses (Cévennes).* Fonds d'Intervention pour les Rapaces., Saint Cloud, France.

Terrasse, M. 1988. *Réintroduction du Vautour fauve dans les Grands Causses et Renforcement de population du Vautour Percnoptère.* Colloque "Réintroductions d'Especes Animales," Saint-Jean du Gard, Décembre 1988, pp 1–6.

Thouless, C.R., J.H. Fanshawe, and B.C.R. Bertram. 1987. Egyptian Vultures *Neophron percnopterus* and Ostrich *Struthio camelus* eggs: the origins of stone-throwing behaviour. *Ibis* 131:9–15.

Timbrook, J., J.R. Johnson, and D.D. Earle. 1982. Vegetation burning by the Chumash. *Journal of California and Great Basin Anthropology* 4(2):163–186.

Todd, F.S. 1974. Maturation and behaviour of the California Condor. *Int. Zoo Yrbk.* 14:145–147.

Toone, W.D., and A.C. Risser. 1988. Captive management of the California Condor (*Gymnogyps californianus*). *Int. Zoo Yrbk.* 27:50–58.

Toone, W.D., and M.P. Wallace. 1994. The extinction in the wild and reintroduction of the California Condor (*Gymnogyps californianus*). Pp 411–419 in *Creative conservation: interactive management of wild and captive animals* (P.J.S. Olney, G.M. Mace, and A.T.C. Feistner, eds.). Chapman and Hall, London.

US Fish and Wildlife Service. 1975. *California Condor Recovery Plan,* Washington, D.C., approved April 9, 1975, 63 pp.

U.S. Fish and Wildlife Service. 1996. *California Condor recovery plan,* third revision. Portland, Oregon. 62 pp.

Van Lawick-Goodall, J., and H. Van Lawick. 1966. Use of tools by Egyptian Vultures. *Nature* 212:1468–1469.

Verner, J. 1978. *California Condors: status of the recovery effort.* Gen. Tech. Rep. PSW-28, U.S. Forest Serv., Washington, D.C.

Wallace, M.P., Fuller, M., and J. Wiley. 1994. Patagial transmitters for large vultures and condors. Pp 381–387 in *Raptor conservation today* (B.-U. Meyburg and R.D. Chancellor, eds.), World Working Group for Birds of Prey, Pica Press.

Wallace, M.P., and S.A. Temple. 1987a. Competitive interactions within and between species in a guild of avian scavengers. *Auk* 104:290–295.

Wallace, M.P. and S.A. Temple. 1987b. Releasing captive-reared Andean Condors to the wild. *J. Wildl. Manage.* 51:541–550.

Ward, J.C., and D.A. Spencer. 1947. Notes on the pharmacology of sodium fluoroacetate – compound 1080. *J. Amer. Phar. Assoc.* 36:59–62.

Westemeier, R.L., Brawn, J.D., Simpson, S.A., Esker, T.L., Jansen, R.W., Walk, J.W., Kershner, E.L., Bouzat, J.L., and K.N. Paige. 1998. Tracking the long-term decline and recovery of an isolated population. *Science* 282:1695–1698.

Westermarck, E.A. 1891. *The history of human marriage.* MacMillan, London.

Wetmore, A. 1931a. *The California Condor in New Mexico. Condor* 33:76–77.

Wetmore, A. 1931b. The avifauna of the Pleistocene in Florida. *Smithsonian Misc. Coll.* 85:1–41.

Wetmore, A. 1933. The eagle, king of birds, and his kin. *Natl. Geogr. Mag.* 64(1):43–95.

Whitaker, G.B. 1918. Capturing the great American condor. *Overland Monthly* 71(5):390–392.

White, L.T., Jr. 1940. Changes in the popular concept of "California." *Calif. Hist. Soc. Q.* 19(3):219–224.

Wiemeyer, S.N., Hill, E.F., Carpenter, J.W., and A.J. Krynitsky. 1986a. Acute oral toxicity of sodium cyanide in birds. *J. of Wildlife Diseases* 22:538–546.

Wiemeyer, S.N., Jurek, R.M., and J.R. Moore. 1986b. Environmental contaminants in surrogates, foods, and feathers of California Condors (*Gymnogyps californianus*). *Environ. Monit. Assess.* 6:91–111.

Wiemeyer, S.N., Krynitsky, A.J., and S.R. Wilbur. 1983. Environmental contaminants in tissues, foods, and feces of California Condors. Pp 427–439 in *Vulture biology and management* (S.R. Wilbur and J.A. Jackson, eds.). University of California Press, Berkeley and Los Angeles.

Wiemeyer, S.N., Scott, J.M., Anderson, M.P., Bloom, P.H., and C.J. Stafford. 1988. Environmental contaminants in California Condors. *J. Wildl. Manage.* 52:238–247.

Wilbur, S.R. 1972. *Food resources of the California Condor.* U.S. Fish and Wildl. Serv., Patuxent Wildlife Research Center Administrative Report.

Wilbur, S.R. 1973. The California Condor in the Pacific Northwest. *Auk* 90:196–198.

Wilbur, S.R. 1975. California Condor plumage and molt as field study aids. *Calif. Fish and Game* 61:144–148.

Wilbur, S.R. 1978a. Supplemental feeding of California Condors. Pp. 135–140 in *Endangered Birds, management techniques for preserving threatened species* (S.A. Temple, ed.). University of Wisconsin Press, Madison.

Wilbur , S.R. 1978b. The California Condor, 1966–76: a look at its past and future. U.S. Fish Wildl. Serv. *North Am. Fauna* 72:1–136.

Wilbur, S.R. 1980. Estimating the size and trend of the California Condor population, 1965–1978. *Calif. Fish Game* 66:40–48.

Wilbur, S.R. 1983. The condor and the native Americans. *Outdoor California* 44(5):7–8.

Wilbur, S.R., and J.C. Borneman. 1972. Copulation by California Condors. *Auk* 89:444–445.

Wilbur, S.R., Carrier, W.D., and J.C. Borneman. 1974. Supplemental feeding program for California Condors. *J. Wildl. Manage.* 38:343–346.

Wilbur, S.R., Carrier, W.D., Borneman, J.C., and R.W. Mallette. 1972. Distribution and numbers of the California Condor, 1966–1971. *Amer. Birds* 26:819–823.

Wilson, E.O. 1992. *The diversity of life.* W.W. Norton and Co., New York.

Wink, M. 1995. Phylogeny of Old and New World vultures (Aves: Accipitridae and Cathartidae) inferred from nucleotide sequences of the mitochondrial cytochrome b gene. *Z. Naturforsch.* 50c:868–882.

Index